2004
CHILDREN'S WRITER'S & ILLUSTRATOR'S MARKET

1000+ EDITORS, AGENTS AND ART DIRECTORS WHO WANT YOUR WORK

EDITOR
ALICE POPE

ASSISTANT EDITOR
MONA MICHAEL

WRITER'S DIGEST BOOKS
CINCINNATI, OH

Editorial Director, Writer's Digest Books: Barbara Kuroff
Writer's Digest Books websites: www.writersdigest.com, www.writersmarket.com

Children's Writer's & Illustrator's Market. Copyright © 2003 by Writer's Digest Books. Published by F&W Publications, 4700 East Galbraith Road, Cincinnati, Ohio 45236. Printed and bound in the United States of America. All rights reserved. No part of this book may be reproduced in any form or by any electronic or mechanical means including information storage and retrieval systems without written permission from the publisher, except by reviewers who may quote brief passages to be printed in a magazine or newspaper.

International Standard Serial Number 0897-9790
International Standard Book Number 1-58297-191-9

Cover illustration by Gwen Connelly

Attention Booksellers: This is an annual directory of F&W Publications.
Return deadline for this edition is January 15, 2005.

Contents

© Tomie dePaola

Page 107

© Vicky Ruben

MARKETS

© Loreen Leedy

Page 165

© Random House Books for Young Readers

Page 29

From the Editor

You must work and work and work some more—happiness is a finished chore. So says Floyd to his fellow sand ant Bart in Bonny Becker's wonderful picture book *An Ant's Day Off*. But Bart is tired of working, and, as the book's title suggests, he takes the day off, getting past the guard ant, and venturing out of his anthill to explore the world—taking what just may well be the first day off in the history of antdom. Bart is smart.

I heard a news story on the radio the other day that really shocked me (and made me think of Bart): 19.5 billion dollars' worth of paid vacation goes unused by American workers. I know some of these ant-like people, but I don't understand them. If someone wants to pay *me* to not work, I'm so there.

Everyone needs a day off once in a while, even those among us who are self-employed—like writers and illustrators. What about the heard-at-every-writers-conference golden rule "write everyday"? I say whatever it takes to keep you inspired, creative and motivated to work on your craft is a good plan. If that means spending the day walking in the park instead of parked at your keyboard, great.

Often getting away from a work-in-progress is a good thing. Distancing yourself from your creative endeavors frees up your mind and helps you recharge—that's why we get hit with fabulous ideas in the shower, in the car, at the gym.

I noticed a sort of journey-as-destination theme popping up here and there in *Children's Writer's & Illustrator's Market* articles this year. Literary agent Erin Murphy discusses writers approaching the quest for publication as an adventure. (See Can an Unagented, Unknown Writer Get Published? Editors Sound Off on page 24.) Jane Yolen, simply says, "Value the process, not the product. Take joy in your writing." (See Writing Through Rejection: Advice from Jane Yolen & Vivian Van Velde on page 42.)

Part of that process, that adventure, that enjoyable journey, should involve sharpening your saw once in a while. The beauty of self-employment is not only the option of working in your P.J.s and forgoing showers, but the ability to plan your own schedule, and venture outside your anthill whenever you need to. (For tips on handling self-employment, see Kathleen Duey's great piece The Employee Within: Getting in Touch with Your Inner Corporation on page 52.)

Bart the sand ant encountered hungry frogs, a busy buzzy bee and gigantic drops of rain on his day off. He was equally scared and exhilarated by his new experiences before deciding to head back to his anthill and get past the guard once again. "I took the day off," Bart admitted to the burley ant guard. "I'm not doing anything. I'm being totally and completely useless. I floated down a stream, I almost took a nap, and I flew on a bee."

The ant guard admitted that he, too, once took a day off. But, he wisely advised Bart, "Always bring back a bit of something."

Illustration © 2003 Nina Laden

Alice Pope
cwim@fwpubs.com

Just Getting Started? Some Quick Tips

If you're new to the world of children's publishing, buying *Children's Writer's & Illustrator's Market* may have been one of the first steps in your journey to publication. What follows is a list of suggestions and resources that can help make that journey a smooth and swift one:

1. Make the most of *Children's Writer's & Illustrator's Market*. Be sure to read How to Use This Book to Sell Your Work on page 4 for tips on reading the listings and using the indexes. Also be sure to take advantage of the articles and interviews in the book. The insights of the authors, illustrators, editors, and agents we've interviewed will inform and inspire you.

2. Join the Society of Children's Books Writers and Illustrators. SCBWI, more than 18,000 members strong, is an organization for both beginners and professionals interested in writing and illustrating for children. They offer members a slew of information and support through publications, a website, and a host of Regional Advisors overseeing chapters in almost every state in the U.S. and in a growing number of locations around the globe (including France, Canada, Japan, and Australia). SCBWI puts on a number of conferences, workshops, and events on the regional and national level (many listed in the Conferences & Workshops section of this book). For more information, contact SCBWI, 8271 Beverly Blvd., Los Angeles CA 90048, (323)782-1010, or visit their website: www.scbwi.org.

3. Read newsletters. Newsletters, such as *Children's Book Insider*, *Children's Writer*, and the SCBWI *Bulletin*, offer updates and new information about publishers on a timely basis and are relatively inexpensive. Many local chapters of SCBWI offer regional newsletters as well. (See Helpful Books & Publications on page 352 for contact information on the newsletters listed above and others. For information on regional SCBWI newsletters, visit www.scbwi.org and click on "Publications.")

4. Read trade and review publications. Magazines like *Publishers Weekly* (which offers two special issues each year devoted to children's publishing and is available on newsstands), *The Horn Book*, *Riverbank Review*, and *Booklinks* offer news, articles, reviews of newly-published titles, and ads featuring upcoming and current releases. Referring to them will help you get a feel for what's happening in children's publishing.

5. Read guidelines. Most publishers and magazines offer writer's and artist's guidelines that provide detailed information on needs and submission requirements, and some magazines offer theme lists for upcoming issues. Many publishers and magazines state the availability of guidelines within their listings. Send a self-addressed, stamped envelope (SASE) to publishers who offer guidelines. You'll often find submission information on publishers' and magazines' websites.

6. Look at publishers' catalogs. Perusing publishers' catalogs can give you a feel for their line of books and help you decide where your work might fit in. If catalogs are available (often stated within listings), send for them with a SASE. Visit publishers' websites, which often contain their full catalogs. You can also ask librarians to look at catalogs they have on hand. You can even search Amazon.com (www.amazon.com) by publisher and year. (Click on "book search" then "publisher, date" and plug in, for example, "Atheneum" under "publisher" and "2002" under year. You'll get a list of all the Atheneum titles published in 2002, which you can peruse.)

7. Visit bookstores. It's not only informative to spend time in bookstores—it's fun, too! Frequently visit the children's section of your local bookstore (whether a chain or an independent) to see the latest from a variety of publishers and the most current issues of children's magazines. Look for books in the genre you're writing or with illustrations similar in style to yours, and spend some time studying them. It's also wise to get to know your local booksellers; they can tell you what's new in the store and provide insight into what kids and adults are buying.

 8. Read, read, read! While you're at that bookstore, pick up a few things, or keep a list of the books that interest you and check them out of your library. Read and study the latest releases, the award winners, and the classics. You'll learn from other writers, get ideas, and get a feel for what's being published. Think about what works and doesn't work in a story. Pay attention to how plots are constructed and how characters are developed or the rhythm and pacing of picture book text. It's certainly enjoyable research!

 9. Take advantage of Internet resources. There are innumerable sources of information available on the Internet about writing for children (and anything else you could possibly think of). It's also a great resource for getting (and staying) in touch with other writers and illustrators through listservs and e-mail, and it can serve as a vehicle for self-promotion. (Visit some authors' and illustators' sites for ideas. Read Yellapalooza: Running a Successful Online Critique Group, on page 63 and What A Site! Creating Websites That Work on page 75. See Useful Online Resources on page 355 for a list of websites.)

10. Consider attending a conference. If time and finances allow, attending a conference is a great way to meet peers and network with professionals in the field of children's publishing. As mentioned above, SCBWI offers conferences in various locations year round. (See www.scbwi. org and click on "Events" for a full conference calendar.) General writers' conferences often offer specialized sessions just for those interested in children's writing. Many conferences offer optional manuscript and portfolio critiques as well, giving you a chance for feedback from seasoned professionals.

11. Network, network, network! Don't work in a vacuum. You can meet other writers and illustrators through a number of the things listed above—SCBWI, conferences, online. Attend local meetings for writers and illustrators whenever you can. Befriend other writers in your area (SCBWI offers members a roster broken down by state)—share guidelines, share subscriptions, be conference buddies and roommates, join a critique group or writing group, exchange information, and offer support. Get online—sign on to listservs, post on message boards, visit chatrooms. (America Online offers them. Also, visit author Verla Kay's website, www.verlakay.com, for information on weekly workshops. See Useful Online Resources on page 355 for more information.) Exchange addresses, phone numbers, and e-mail addresses with writers or illustrators you meet at events. And at conferences, don't be afraid to talk to people, ask strangers to join you for lunch, approach speakers and introduce yourself, or chat in elevators and hallways.

12. Perfect your craft and don't submit until your work is its best. It's often been said that a writer should try to write every day. Great manuscripts don't happen overnight; there's time, research, and revision involved. As you visit bookstores and study what others have written and illustrated, really step back and look at your own work and ask yourself—honestly—*How does my work measure up? Is it ready for editors or art directors to see?* If it's not, keep working. Join a critique group or get a professional manuscript or portfolio critique.

13. Be patient, learn from rejection, and don't give up! Thousands of manuscripts land on editors' desks; thousands of illustration samples line art directors' file drawers. There are so many factors that come into play when evaluating submissions. Keep in mind that you might not hear back from publishers promptly. Persistence and patience are important qualities in writers and illustrators working for publication. Keep at it—it will come. It can take a while, but when you get that first book contract or first assignment, you'll know it was worth the wait. (Read First Books: Illustrators & Author/Illustrators on page 112 for proof.)

How to Use This Book to Sell Your Work

As a writer, illustrator, or photographer first picking up *Children's Writer's & Illustrator's Market*, you may not know quite how to start using the book. Your impulse may be to flip through the book and quickly make a mailing list, then submit to everyone in hopes that someone will take interest in your work. Well, there's more to it. Finding the right market takes time and research. The more you know about a company that interests you, the better chance you have of getting work accepted.

We've made your job a little easier by putting a wealth of information at your fingertips. Besides providing listings, this directory includes a number of tools to help you determine which markets are the best ones for your work. By using these tools, as well as researching on your own, you raise your odds of being published.

USING THE INDEXES

This book lists hundreds of potential buyers of freelance material. To learn which companies want the type of material you're interested in submitting, start with the indexes.

The Age-Level Index

Age groups are broken down into these categories in the Age-Level Index:

- **Picture books** or **picture-oriented material** are written and illustrated for preschoolers to 8-year-olds.
- **Young readers** are for 5- to 8-year-olds.
- **Middle readers** are for 9- to 11-year-olds.
- **Young adults** are for ages 12 and up.

Age breakdowns may vary slightly from publisher to publisher, but using them as general guidelines will help you target appropriate markets. For example, if you've written an article about trends in teen fashion, check the Magazines Age-Level Index under the Young Adult subheading. Using this list, you'll quickly find the listings for young adult magazines.

The Subject Index

But let's narrow the search further. Take your list of young adult magazines, turn to the Subject Index, and find the Fashion subheading. Then highlight the names that appear on both lists (Young Adult and Fashion). Now you have a smaller list of all the magazines that would be interested in your teen fashion article. Read through those listings and decide which ones sound best for your work.

Illustrators and photographers can use the Subject Index as well. If you specialize in painting animals, for instance, consider sending samples to book and magazine publishers listed under Animals and, perhaps, Nature/Environment. Since illustrators can simply send general examples of their style to art directors to keep on file, the indexes may be more helpful to artists sending manuscripts/illustration packages who need to search for a specific subject. Always read the listings for the potential markets to see the type of work art directors prefer and what type of samples they'll keep on file, and send for art or photo guidelines if they're available.

The Poetry Index

This index lists book publishers and magazines interested in submissions from poets. Always send for writer's guidelines from publishers and magazines that interest you.

The Photography Index

You'll find lists of book and magazine publishers, as well as greeting card, puzzle and game manufacturers, that buy photos from freelancers in the Photography Index. Copy the lists and read the listings for specific needs. Send for photo guidelines if they're offered.

USING THE LISTINGS

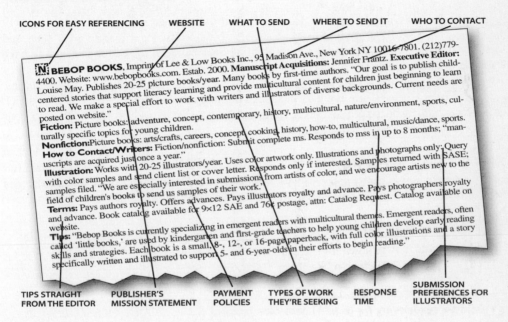

Many listings begin with one or more symbols. (Refer to the inside covers of the book for quick reference.) Here's what each icon stands for:

- N indicates a listing is new to this edition.
- indicates a listing is Canadian.
- indicates a listing is located in a country other than the U.S. or Canada.
- indicates a company publishes educational material.
- indicates an electronic publisher of publication.
- indicates a listing is a book packager or producer.
- ✓ indicates a change to a company's mailing address since last year's edition.
- A indicates a publisher only accepts submissions through agents.
- indicates a company's publications have received awards recently.

In the Book Publishers section, you'll find contact names after **Manuscript Acquisitions** and **Art Acquisitions**. Contact names in Magazines follow boldface titles such as **Fiction Editor**, **Articles Editor** or **Art Director**. Following the contact information in many of these listings are mission statements. Read these to get a general idea of the aim of certain publishers and magazines to help you decide whether to explore them further.

The subheadings under each listing contain more specific information about what a company needs. In Book Publishers and Magazines, for example, you'll find such things as age levels and subjects needed under the **Fiction** and **Nonfiction** subheads. Here's an example from a listing in the Book Publishers section:

Fiction: Picture books: adventure, animal, contemporary, fantasy, humor. Young readers: animal, contemporary, humor, sports, suspense/mystery. Middle readers: adventure, humor, sports. Young adults: humor, problem novels.

Also check the listings for information on how to submit your work and the response time. In Book Publishers and Magazines, writers will find this information under the How to Contact/ Writers subhead:

How to Contact/Writers: Query with outline/synopsis and 2 sample chapters. Responds to queries in 6 weeks.

For information on submission procedures and formats, turn to Before Your First Sale on page 8.

Also look for information regarding payment and rights purchased. Some markets pay on acceptance, others on publication. Some pay a flat rate for manuscripts and artwork, others pay advances and royalties. Knowing how a market operates will keep you from being shocked when you discover your paycheck won't arrive until your manuscript is published—a year after it was accepted. This information is found under **Terms** in Book Publishers, Magazines, and Play Publishers. Here's an example from the Magazines section:

Terms: Pays on acceptance. Buys first North American serial rights or reprint rights. Pays $50-100 for stories/articles. Pays illustrators $75-125 for b&w or color inside; $150-200 for color cover.

Under **Tips**, you'll find special advice straight from editors or art directors about what their companies want or don't want, or other helpful information:

Tips: "We are looking for picture books centered on a strong, fully-developed protaganist who grows or changes during the course of the story."

Additional information about specific markets in the form of comments from the editors of this book is set off by bullets (•) within listings:

• This publisher accepts only queries and manuscripts submitted by agents.

Many listings indicate whether submission guidelines are available. If a publisher in which you're interested offers guidelines, send for them and read them. The same is true with catalogs. Sending for catalogs and seeing and reading about the books a publisher produces gives you a better idea of whether your work would fit in. (You should also look at a few of the books in the catalog at a library or bookstore to get a feel for the publisher's material.) Note that a number of publishers offer guidelines and catalogs on their websites.

Especially for artists and photographers

Along with information for writers, listings provide information for photographers and illustrators. Illustrators will find numerous markets that maintain files of samples for possible future assignments. If you're both a writer and an illustrator, look for markets that accept manuscript/ illustration packages.

If you're a photographer, after consulting the Photography Index, read the information under the **Photography** subhead within listings to see what format buyers prefer. For example, some want 35mm color transparencies, others want black & white prints. Note the type of photos a buyer wants to purchase and the procedures for submitting. It's not uncommon for a market to want a résumé and promotional literature, as well as tearsheets from previous work. Listings also note whether model releases and/or captions are required.

Especially for young writers

If you're a parent, teacher, or student, you may be interested in Young Writer's & Illustrator's Markets. The listings in this section encourage submissions from young writers and artists. Some may require a written statement from a teacher or parent noting the work is original. Also watch for age limits.

Young people should also check Contests & Awards for contests that accept work by young writers and artists. Some of the contests listed are especially for students; others accept both student and adult work. These listings contain the phrase **open to students** in bold. Some listings in Clubs & Organizations and Conferences & Workshops may also be of interest to students. Organizations and conferences which are open to or are especially for students also include **open to students.**

COMMON ABBREVIATIONS

Throughout the listings, the following abbreviations are used:
- **ms** or **mss** stands for manuscript or manuscripts.
- **SASE** refers to a self-addressed, stamped envelope.
- **SAE** refers to a self-addressed envelope.
- **IRC** stands for International Reply Coupon. These are required with SAEs sent to markets in countries other than your own.

Before Your First Sale

If you're just beginning to pursue your career as a children's book writer or illustrator, it's important to learn the proper procedures, formats, and protocol for the publishing industry. This article outlines the basics you need to know before you head to the post office with your submissions.

FINDING THE BEST MARKETS FOR YOUR WORK

Researching publishers well is a basic element of submitting your work successfully. Editors and art directors hate to receive inappropriate submissions; handling them wastes a lot of their time, not to mention your time and money, and they are the main reason some publishers have chosen not to accept material over the transom. By randomly sending out material without knowing a company's needs, you're sure to meet with rejection.

If you're interested in submitting to a particular magazine, write to request a sample copy, or see if it's available in your local library or bookstore. For a book publisher, obtain a book catalog and check a library or bookstore for titles produced by that publisher. Most publishers and magazines have websites that include catalogs or sample articles (websites are given within the listings). Studying such materials carefully will better acquaint you with a publisher's or magazine's writing, illustration, and photography styles and formats.

Most of the book publishers and magazines listed in this book (as well as some greeting card and paper product producers) offer some sort of writer's, artist's, or photographer's guidelines for a self-addressed, stamped envelope (SASE). Guidelines are also often found on publishers' websites. It's important to read and study guidelines before submitting work. You'll get a better understanding of what a particular publisher wants. You may even decide, after reading the submission guidelines, that your work isn't right for a company you considered.

SUBMITTING YOUR WORK

Throughout the listings, you'll read requests for particular elements to include when contacting markets. Here are explanations of some of these important submission components.

Queries, cover letters, and proposals

A query letter is a no-more-than-one-page, well-written piece meant to arouse an editor's interest in your work. Many query letters start with leads similar to those of actual manuscripts. In the rest of the letter, briefly outline the work you're proposing and include facts, anecdotes, interviews, or other pertinent information that give the editor a feel for the manuscript's premise—entice her to want to know more. End your letter with a straightforward request to write (or submit) the work, and include information on its approximate length, date it could be completed and whether accompanying photos or artwork are available.

In a query letter, think about presenting your book as a publisher's catalog would present it. Read through a good catalog and examine how the publishers give enticing summaries of their books in a spare amount of words. It's also important that query letters give editors a taste of your writing style. For good advice and samples of queries, cover letters, and other correspondence, see Query Letter Clinic on page 20, and consult *How to Write Attention-Grabbing Query & Cover Letters*, by John Wood (Writer's Digest Books).

• **Query letters for nonfiction.** Queries are usually required when submitting nonfiction material to a publisher. The goal of a nonfiction query is to convince the editor your idea is perfect for her readership and that you're qualified to do the job. Note any previous writing experience and include published samples to prove your credentials, especially samples related to the subject matter you're querying about.

- **Query letters for fiction.** More and more, queries are being requested for fiction manuscripts. For a fiction query, explain the story's plot, main characters, conflict, and resolution. Just as in nonfiction queries, make the editor eager to see more.
- **Cover letters for writers.** Some editors prefer to review complete manuscripts, especially for fiction. In such cases, the cover letter (which should be no longer than one page) serves as your introduction, establishes your credentials as a writer, and gives the editor an overview of the manuscript. If the editor asked for the manuscript because of a query, note this in your cover letter.
- **Cover letters for illustrators and photographers.** For an illustrator or photographer, the cover letter serves as an introduction to the art director and establishes professional credentials when submitting samples. Explain what services you can provide as well as what type of follow-up contact you plan to make, if any.
- **Résumés.** Often writers, illustrators, and photographers are asked to submit résumés with cover letters and samples. They can be created in a variety of formats, from a single page listing information to color brochures featuring your work. Keep your résumé brief, and focus on your achievements, including your clients and the work you've done for them, as well as your educational background and any awards you've received. Do not use the same résumé you'd use for a typical job application.
- **Book proposals.** Throughout the listings in the Book Publishers section, publishers refer to submitting a synopsis, outline, and sample chapters. Depending on an editor's preference, some or all of these components, along with a cover letter, make up a book proposal.

A *synopsis* summarizes the book, covering the basic plot (including the ending). It should be easy to read and flow well. (See When Size Matters: The Synopsis, Short But Power-Packed on page 47.)

An *outline* covers your book chapter by chapter and provides highlights of each. If you're developing an outline for fiction, include major characters, plots and subplots, and book length.

Sample chapters give a more comprehensive idea of your writing skill. Some editors may request the first two or three chapters to determine if she's interested in seeing the whole book.

Manuscript formats

When submitting a complete manuscript, follow some basic guidelines. In the upper-left corner of your title page, type your legal name (not pseudonym), address, and phone number. In the upper-right corner, type the approximate word length. All material in the upper corners should be typed single-spaced. Then type the title (centered) almost halfway down that page, the word "by" two spaces under that, and your name or pseudonym two spaces under "by."

The first page should also include the title (centered) one-third of the way down. Two spaces under that type "by" and your name or pseudonym. To begin the body of your manuscript, drop down two double spaces and indent five spaces for each new paragraph. There should be one-inch margins around all sides of a full typewritten page. (Manuscripts with wide margins are more readable and easier to edit.)

Set your computer on double-space for the manuscript body. From page two to the end of the manuscript, include your last name followed by a comma and the title (or key words of the title) in the upper-left corner. The page number should go in the top right corner. Drop down two double spaces to begin the body of each page. If you're submitting a novel, type each chapter title one-third of the way down the page. For more information on manuscript formats, read *Formatting & Submitting Your Manuscript*, by Jack and Glenda Neff, Don Prues, and the editors of *Writer's Market*; or *Manuscript Submission*, by Scott Edelstein (both Writer's Digest Books).

Picture book formats

The majority of editors prefer to see complete manuscripts for picture books. When typing the text of a picture book, don't include page breaks and don't type each page of text on a new sheet of paper. And unless you are an illustrator, don't worry about supplying art. Editors will find their own illustrators for picture books. Most of the time, a writer and an illustrator who work on the same book never meet. The editor acts as a go-between and works with the writer and illustrator throughout the publishing process. *How to Write and Sell Children's Picture Books*, by Jean E. Karl (Writer's Digest Books), offers advice on preparing text and marketing your work.

If you're an illustrator who has written your own book, consider creating a dummy or story-board containing both art and text, and then submit it along with your complete manuscript and sample pieces of final art (color photocopies or computer printouts—never originals). Publishers interested in picture books specify in their listings what should be submitted. For tips on creating a dummy, refer to *How to Write and Illustrate Children's Books and Get Them Published*, edited by Treld Pelkey Bicknell and Felicity Trotman (North Light Books), or Frieda Gates's book, *How to Write, Illustrate, and Design Children's Books* (Lloyd-Simone Publishing Company).

Writers may also want to learn the art of dummy making to help them through their writing process with things like pacing, rhythm, and length. For a great explanation and helpful hints, see *You Can Write Children's Books*, by Tracey E. Dils (Writer's Digest Books).

Mailing submissions

Your main concern when packaging material is to be sure it arrives undamaged. If your manuscript is less than six pages, simply fold it in thirds and send it in a #10 (business-size) envelope. For a SASE, either fold another #10 envelope in thirds or insert a #9 (reply) envelope which fits in a #10 neatly without folding.

Another option is folding your manuscript in half in a 6×9 envelope, with a #9 or #10 SASE enclosed. For larger manuscripts, use a 9×12 envelope both for mailing the submission and as a SASE (which can be folded in half). Book manuscripts require sturdy packaging for mailing. Include a self-addressed mailing label and return postage.

If asked to send artwork and photographs, remember they require a bit more care in packaging to guarantee they arrive in good condition. Sandwich illustrations and photos between heavy cardboard that is slightly larger than the work. The cardboard can be secured by rubber bands or with tape. If you tape the cardboard together, check that the artwork doesn't stick to the tape. Be sure your name and address appear on the back of each piece of art or each photo in case the material becomes separated. For the packaging, use either a manila envelope, a foam-padded envelope, brown paper, or a mailer lined with plastic air bubbles. Bind non-joined edges with reinforced mailing tape and affix a typed mailing label or clearly write your address.

Mailing material first class ensures quick delivery. Also, first-class mail is forwarded for one year if the addressee has moved, and it can be returned if undeliverable. If you're concerned about your original material safely reaching its destination, consider other mailing options, such as UPS or certified mail. If material needs to reach your editor or art director quickly, use overnight delivery services.

Remember, companies outside your own country can't use your country's postage when returning a manuscript to you. When mailing a submission to another country, include a self-addressed envelope and International Reply Coupons, or IRCs. (You'll see this term in many Canadian listings.) Your postmaster can tell you, based on a package's weight, the correct number of IRCs to include to ensure its return.

If it's not necessary for an editor to return your work (such as with photocopies), don't include return postage. You may want to track the status of your submission by enclosing a postage-paid reply postcard with options for the editor to check, such as "Yes, I am interested," "I'll keep the material on file," or "No, the material is not appropriate for my needs at this time."

Some writers, illustrators, and photographers simply include a deadline date. If you don't hear from the editor or art director by the specified date, your manuscript, artwork, or photos are automatically withdrawn from consideration. Because many publishing houses and companies are overstocked with material, a minimum deadline should be at least three months.

Unless requested, it's never a good idea to use a company's fax number or e-mail address to send manuscript submissions. This can disrupt a company's internal business. Some publishers, however, are open to e-mail submissions. Simon & Schuster imprints set up an e-mail for submitting material, for example. Study the Book Publishers listings for specifics.

Keeping submission records

It's important to keep track of the material you submit. When recording each submission, include the date it was sent, the business and contact name, and any enclosures (such as samples of writing, artwork, or photography). You can create a record-keeping system of your own or look for record-keeping software in your area computer store.

Keep copies of articles or manuscripts you send together with related correspondence to make follow-up easier. When you sell rights to a manuscript, artwork, or photos, you can "close" your file on a particular submission by noting the date the material was accepted, what rights were purchased, the publication date, and payment.

Often writers, illustrators, and photographers fail to follow up on overdue responses. If you don't hear from a publisher within their stated response time, wait another month or so and follow up with a note asking about the status of your submission. Include the title or description, date sent, and a SASE for response. Ask the contact person when she anticipates making a decision. You may refresh the memory of a buyer who temporarily forgot about your submission. At the very least, you'll receive a definite "no" and free yourself to send the material to another publisher.

Simultaneous submissions

If you opt for simultaneous (also called "multiple") submissions—sending the same material to several publishers at the same time—be sure to inform each editor to whom you submit that your work is being considered elsewhere. Many editors are reluctant to receive simultaneous submissions but understand that for hopeful writers and illustrators, waiting several months for a response can be frustrating. In some cases, an editor may actually be more inclined to read your manuscript sooner if she knows it's being considered by another publisher. The Society of Children's Book Writers and Illustrators cautions writers against simultaneous submissions. The official recommendation of SCBWI is to submit to one publisher at a time, but wait only three months (note you'll do so in your cover letter). If no response is received, then send a note withdrawing your manuscript from consideration. SCBWI considers simultaneous submissions acceptable only if you have a manuscript dealing with a timely issue.

It's especially important to keep track of simultaneous submissions, so if you get an offer on a manuscript sent to more than one publisher, you can instruct other publishers to withdraw your work from consideration.

AGENTS & ART REPS

Most children's writers, illustrators, and photographers, especially those just beginning, are confused about whether to enlist the services of an agent or representative. The decision is strictly one that each writer, illustrator, or photographer must make for herself. Some are confident with their own negotiation skills and believe acquiring an agent or rep is not in their best interest. Others feel uncomfortable in the business arena or are not willing to sacrifice valuable creative time for marketing.

About half of children's publishers accept unagented work, so it's possible to break into children's publishing without an agent. Some agents avoid working with children's books because traditionally low advances and trickling royalty payments over long periods of time make children's books less lucrative. Writers targeting magazine markets don't need the services of an agent. In fact, it's practically impossible to find an agent interested in marketing articles and short stories—there simply isn't enough financial incentive.

One benefit of having an agent, though, is it may speed up the process of getting your work reviewed, especially by publishers who don't accept unagented submissions. If an agent has a good reputation and submits your manuscript to an editor, that manuscript will likely bypass the first-read stage (which is done by editorial assistants and junior editors) and end up on the editor's desk sooner.

When agreeing to have a reputable agent represent you, remember that she should be familiar with the needs of the current market and evaluate your manuscript/artwork/photos accordingly. She should also determine the quality of your piece and whether it is saleable. When your manuscript sells, your agent should negotiate a favorable contract and clear up any questions you have about payments.

Keep in mind that however reputable the agent or rep is, she has limitations. Representation does not guarantee sale of your work. It just means an agent or rep sees potential in your writing, art, or photos. Though an agent or rep may offer criticism or advice on how to improve your work, she cannot make you a better writer, artist, or photographer.

Literary agents typically charge a 15 percent commission from the sale of writing; art and photo representatives usually charge a 25 to 30 percent commission. Such fees are taken from advances and royalty earnings. If your agent sells foreign rights to your work, she will deduct a higher percentage because she will most likely be dealing with an overseas agent with whom she must split the fee.

Be advised that not every agent is open to representing a writer, artist, or photographer who lacks an established track record. Just as when approaching a publisher, the manuscript, artwork, or photos and query or cover letter you submit to a potential agent must be attractive and professional looking. Your first impression must be as an organized, articulate person.

For listings of agents and reps, turn to the Agents & Art Reps section. For additional listings of art reps, consult *Artist's & Graphic Designer's Market*; and for photo reps, see *Photographer's Market* (both Writer's Digest Books).

The Business of Writing & Illustrating

A career in children's publishing involves more than just writing skills or artistic talent. Successful authors and illustrators must be able to hold their own in negotiations, keep records, understand contract language, grasp copyright law, pay taxes, and take care of a number of other business concerns. Although agents and reps, accountants and lawyers, and writers' organizations offer help in sorting out such business issues, it's wise to have a basic understanding of them going in. This article offers just that—basic information. For a more in-depth look at the subjects covered here, check your library or bookstore for books and magazines to help you. We also tell you how to get information on issues like taxes and copyright from the federal government.

CONTRACTS & NEGOTIATION

Before you see your work in print or begin working with an editor or art director on a project, there is negotiation. And whether negotiating a book contract, a magazine article assignment, or an illustration or photo assignment, there are a few things to keep in mind. First, if you find any clauses vague or confusing in a contract, get legal advice. The time and money invested in counseling up front could protect you from problems later. If you have an agent or rep, she will review any contract.

A contract is an agreement between two or more parties that specifies the fees to be paid, services rendered, deadlines, rights purchased, and for artists and photographers, whether original work is returned. Most companies have standard contracts for writers, illustrators, and photographers. The specifics (such as royalty rates, advances, delivery dates, etc.) are typed in after negotiations.

Though it's okay to conduct negotiations over the phone, get a written contract once both parties have agreed on terms. Never depend on oral stipulations; written contracts protect both parties from misunderstandings. Watch for clauses that may not be in your best interest, such as "work-for-hire." When you do work-for-hire, you give up all rights to your creations.

Some reputable children's magazines, such as *Highlights for Children*, buy all rights, and many writers and illustrators believe it's worth the concession in order to break into the field. However, once you become more established in the field, it's in your best interest to keep rights

---

Contract Help from Organizations

Writers organizations offer a wealth of information to members, including contract advice:

Society of Children's Book Writers and Illustrators members can find information in the SCBWI publication Answers to Some Questions About Contracts. Contact SCBWI at 8271 Beverly Blvd., Los Angeles CA 90048, (323)782-1010, or visit their website: www.scbwi.org.

The Authors Guild also offers contract tips. Visit their website, www.authorsguild.org. (Members of the guild can receive a 75-point contract review from the guild's legal staff.) See the website for membership information and application form, or contact The Authors Guild at 31 E. 28th St., 10th Floor, New York NY 10016, (212)563-5904. Fax: (212)564-5363. E-mail: staff@authorsguild.org. Website: www.authorsguild.org.

to your work. (Note: Magazines such as *Highlights* may return rights after a specified time period, so ask about this possibility when negotiating.)

When negotiating a book deal, find out whether your contract contains an option clause. This clause requires the author to give the publisher a first look at her next work before offering it to other publishers. Though it's editorial etiquette to give the publisher the first chance at publishing your next work, be wary of statements in the contract that could trap you. Don't allow the publisher to consider the next project for more than 30 days and be specific about what type of work should actually be considered "next work." (For example, if the book under contract is a young adult novel, specify that the publisher will receive an exclusive look at only your next young adult novel.)

(For more information about SCBWI, The Authors Guild, and other organizations, turn to the Clubs & Organizations section.)

Book publishers' payment methods

Book publishers pay authors and artists in royalties, a percentage of either the wholesale or retail price of each book sold. From large publishing houses, the author usually receives an advance issued against future royalties before the book is published. Half of the advance amount is issued upon signing the book contract; the other half is issued when the book is finished. For illustrations, one-third of the advance should be collected upon signing the contract; one-third upon delivery of sketches; and one-third upon delivery of finished art.

After your book has sold enough copies to earn back your advance, you'll start to get royalty checks. Some publishers hold a reserve against returns, which means a percentage of royalties is held back in case books are returned from bookstores. If you have a reserve clause in your contract, find out the exact percentage of total sales that will be withheld and the time period the publisher will hold this money. You should be reimbursed this amount after a reasonable time period, such as a year. Royalty percentages vary with each publisher, but there are standard ranges.

Book publishers' rates

According to the latest figures from the Society of Children's Book Writers and Illustrators, first-time picture book authors can expect advances of $2,000-3,000; first-time picture book illustrators' advances range from $5,000-7,000; text and illustration packages for first-timers can score $6,000-8,000. Rates go up for subsequent books: $3,500-5,000 for picture book text; $7,000-10,000 for picture book illustration; $8,000-10,000 for text and illustration. Experienced authors can expect higher advances. Royalties for picture books are generally about five percent (split between the author and illustrator) but can go as high as ten percent. Those who both write and illustrate a book, of course, receive the full royalty.

Advances for hardcover novels and nonfiction can fetch authors advances of $4,000-6,000 and 10 percent royalties; paperbacks bring in slightly lower advances of $3,000-5,000 and royalties of 6-8 percent.

As you might expect, advance and royalty figures vary from house to house and are affected by the time of year, the state of the economy, and other factors. Some smaller houses may not even pay royalties, just flat fees. Educational houses may not offer advances or offer smaller amounts. Religious publishers tend to offer smaller advances than trade publishers. First-time writers and illustrators generally start on the low end of the scale, while established and high-profile writers are paid more.

Pay rates for magazines

For writers, fee structures for magazines are based on a per-word rate or range for a specific article length. Artists and photographers have a few more variables to contend with before contracting their services.

Payment for illustrations and photos can be set by such factors as whether the piece(s) will be black and white or four-color, how many are to be purchased, where the work appears (cover or inside), circulation, and the artist's or photographer's prior experience.

Remaindering

When a book goes out of print, a publisher will sell any existing copies to a wholesaler who, in turn, sells the copies to stores at a discount. When the books are "remaindered" to a wholesaler, they are usually sold at a price just above the cost of printing. When negotiating a contract with a publisher, you may want to discuss the possibility of purchasing the remaindered copies before they are sold to a wholesaler, then you can market the copies you purchased and still make a profit.

KNOW YOUR RIGHTS

A copyright is a form of protection provided to creators of original works, published or unpublished. In general, copyright protection ensures the writer, illustrator, or photographer the power to decide how her work is used and allows her to receive payment for each use.

Essentially, copyright also encourages the creation of new works by guaranteeing the creator power to sell rights to the work in the marketplace. The copyright holder can print, reprint, or copy her work; sell or distribute copies of her work; or prepare derivative works such as plays, collages, or recordings. The Copyright Law is designed to protect work (created on or after January 1, 1978) for her lifetime plus 50 years.

If you collaborate with someone else on a written or artistic project, the copyright will last for the lifetime of the last survivor plus 50 years. The creators' heirs may hold a copyright for an additional 50 years. After that, the work becomes public domain. Works created anonymously or under a pseudonym are protected for 100 years, or 75 years after publication. Under work-for-hire agreements, you relinquish your copyright to your "employer."

Copyright notice and registration

Some feel a copyright notice should be included on all work, registered or not. Others feel it is not necessary and a copyright notice will only confuse publishers about whether the material is registered (acquiring rights to previously registered material is a more complicated process).

Although it's not necessary to include a copyright notice on unregistered work, if you don't feel your work is safe without the notice, it is your right to include one. Including a copyright notice—© (year of work, your name)—should help safeguard against plagiarism.

Registration is a legal formality intended to make copyright public record, and it can help you win more money in a court case. By registering work within three months of publication or before an infringement occurs, you are eligible to collect statutory damages and attorney's fees. If you register later than three months after publication, you will qualify only for actual damages and profits.

Ideas and concepts are not copyrightable, only expressions of those ideas and concepts. A character type or basic plot outline, for example, is not subject to a copyright infringement lawsuit. Also, titles, names, short phrases or slogans, and lists of contents are not subject to copyright protection, though titles and names may be protected through the Trademark Office.

You can register a group of articles, illustrations, or photos if it meets these criteria:

- the group is assembled in order, such as in a notebook
- the works bear a single title, such as "Works by (your name)"
- it is the work of one writer, artist, or photographer
- the material is the subject of a single claim to copyright

It's a publisher's responsibility to register your book for copyright. If you've previously registered the same material, you must inform your editor and supply the previous copyright information, otherwise, the publisher can't register the book in its published form.

For more information about the proper way to register works and to order the correct forms, contact the U.S. Copyright Office, (202)707-3000. The forms available are TX for writing (books, articles, etc.); VA for pictures (photographs, illustrations); and PA for plays and music. For information about how to use the copyright forms, request a copy of Circular I on Copyright Basics. All of the forms and circulars are free. Send the completed registration form along with the stated fee and a copy of the work to the Copyright Office.

For specific answers to questions about copyright (but not legal advice), call the Copyright Public Information Office at (202)707-3000 weekdays between 8:30 a.m. and 5 p.m. EST. Forms can also be downloaded from the Library of Congress website: www.loc.gov/copyright. The site also includes a list of frequently asked questions, tips on filling out forms, general copyright information, and links to other sites related to copyright issues. For members of SCBWI, information about copyrights and the law is available in their publication: Copyright Facts for Writers.

The rights publishers buy

The copyright law specifies that a writer, illustrator, or photographer generally sells one-time rights to her work unless she and the buyer agree otherwise in writing. Many publications will want more exclusive rights to your work than just one-time usage; some will even require you to sell all rights. Be sure you are monetarily compensated for the additional rights you relinquish. If you must give up all rights to a work, carefully consider the price you're being offered to determine whether you'll be compensated for the loss of other potential sales.

Writers who only give up limited rights to their work can then sell reprint rights to other publications, foreign rights to international publications, or even movie rights, should the opportunity arise. Artists and photographers can sell their work to other markets such as paper product companies who may use an image on a calendar, greeting card, or mug. Illustrators and photographers may even sell original work after it has been published. And there are now galleries throughout the U.S. that display and sell the original work of children's illustrators.

Rights acquired through the sale of a book manuscript are explained in each publisher's contract. Take time to read relevant clauses to be sure you understand what rights each contract is specifying before signing. Be sure your contract contains a clause allowing all rights to revert back to you in the event the publisher goes out of business. (You may even want to have the contract reviewed by an agent or an attorney specializing in publishing law.)

The following are the rights you'll most often sell to publishers, periodicals, and producers in the marketplace:

First rights. The buyer purchases the rights to use the work for the first time in any medium. All other rights remain with the creator. When material is excerpted from a soon-to-be-published book for use in a newspaper or periodical, first serial rights are also purchased.

One-time rights. The buyer has no guarantee that she is the first to use a piece. One-time permission to run written work, illustrations, or photos is acquired, then the rights revert back to the creator.

First North American serial rights. This is similar to first rights, except that companies who distribute both in the U.S. and Canada will stipulate these rights to ensure that another North American company won't come out with simultaneous usage of the same work.

Second serial (reprint) rights. In this case, newspapers and magazines are granted the right to reproduce a work that has already appeared in another publication. These rights are also purchased by a newspaper or magazine editor who wants to publish part of a book after the book has been published. The proceeds from reprint rights for a book are often split evenly between the author and his publishing company.

Simultaneous rights. More than one publication buys one-time rights to the same work at the same time. Use of such rights occurs among magazines with circulations that don't overlap, such as many religious publications.

All rights. Just as it sounds, the writer, illustrator, or photographer relinquishes all rights to a piece—she no longer has any say in who acquires rights to use it. All rights are purchased by publishers who pay premium usage fees, have an exclusive format, or have other book or magazine interests from which the purchased work can generate more mileage. If a company insists on acquiring all rights to your work, see if you can negotiate for the rights to revert back to you after a reasonable period of time. If they agree to such a proposal, get it in writing.

Note: Writers, illustrators, and photographers should be wary of "work-for-hire" arrangements. If you sign an agreement stipulating that your work will be done as work-for-hire, you will not control the copyrights of the completed work—the company that hired you will be the copyright owner.

Foreign serial rights. Be sure before you market to foreign publications that you have sold only North American—not worldwide—serial rights to previous markets. If so, you are free to market to publications that may be interested in material that's appeared in a North American-based periodical.

Syndication rights. This is a division of serial rights. For example, if a syndicate prints portions of a book in installments in its newspapers, it would be syndicating second serial rights. The syndicate would receive a commission and leave the remainder to be split between the author and publisher.

Subsidiary rights. These include serial rights, dramatic rights, book club rights or translation rights. The contract should specify what percentage of profits from sales of these rights go to the author and publisher.

Dramatic, television, and motion picture rights. During a specified time, the interested party tries to sell a story to a producer or director. Many times options are renewed because the selling process can be lengthy.

Display rights or electronic publishing rights. They're also known as "Data, Storage and Retrieval." Usually listed under subsidiary rights, the marketing of electronic rights in this era of rapidly expanding capabilities and markets for electronic material can be tricky. Display rights can cover text or images to be used in a CD-ROM or online, or may cover use of material in formats not even fully developed yet. If a display rights clause is listed in your contract, try to negotiate its elimination. Otherwise, be sure to pin down which electronic rights are being purchased. Demand the clause be restricted to things designed to be read only. By doing this, you maintain your rights to use your work for things such as games and interactive software.

RUNNING YOUR BUSINESS

An important part of being a freelance writer, illustrator, or photographer is running your freelance business. It's imperative to maintain accurate business records to determine if you're making a profit as a freelancer. Keeping correct, organized records will also make your life easier as you approach tax time.

When setting up your system, begin by keeping a bank account and ledger for your business finances apart from your personal finances. Also, if writing, illustration, or photography is secondary to another freelance career, keep separate business records for each.

You will likely accumulate some business expenses before showing any profit when you start out as a freelancer. To substantiate your income and expenses to the IRS, keep all invoices, cash receipts, sales slips, bank statements, canceled checks, and receipts related to travel expenses and entertaining clients. For entertainment expenditures, record the date, place, and purpose of the business meeting, as well as gas mileage. Keep records for all purchases, big and small. Don't take the small purchases for granted; they can add up to a substantial amount. File all receipts in chronological order. Maintaining a separate file for each month simplifies retrieving records at the end of the year.

Record keeping

When setting up a single-entry bookkeeping system, record income and expenses separately. Use some of the subheads that appear on Schedule C (the form used for recording income from a business) of the 1040 tax form so you can easily transfer information onto the tax form when filing your return. In your ledger include a description of each transaction—the date, source of income (or debts from business purchases), description of what was purchased or sold, the amount of the transaction, and whether payment was by cash, check, or credit card.

Don't wait until January 1 to start keeping records. The moment you first make a business-related purchase or sell an article, book manuscript, illustration, or photo, begin tracking your profits and losses. If you keep records from January 1 to December 31, you're using a calendar-year accounting period. Any other accounting period is called a fiscal year.

There are two types of accounting methods you can choose from—the cash method and the accrual method. The cash method is used more often: You record income when it is received and expenses when they're disbursed.

Using the accrual method, you report income at the time you earn it rather than when it's actually received. Similarly, expenses are recorded at the time they're incurred rather than when you actually pay them. If you choose this method, keep separate records for "accounts receivable" and "accounts payable."

Satisfying the IRS

To successfully—and legally—work as a freelancer, you must know what income you should report and what deductions you can claim. But before you can do that, you must prove to the IRS you're in business to make a profit, that your writing, illustration, or photography is not merely a hobby.

The Tax Reform Act of 1986 says you should show a profit for three years out of a five-year period to attain professional status. The IRS considers these factors as proof of your professionalism:

- accurate financial records
- a business bank account separate from your personal account
- proven time devoted to your profession
- whether it's your main or secondary source of income
- your history of profits and losses
- the amount of training you have invested in your field
- your expertise

If your business is unincorporated, you'll fill out tax information on Schedule C of Form 1040. If you're unsure of what deductions you can take, request the IRS publication containing this information. Under the Tax Reform Act, only 30 percent of business meals, entertainment and related tips, and parking charges are deductible. Other deductible expenses allowed on Schedule C include: car expenses for business-related trips; professional courses and seminars; depreciation of office equipment, such as a computer; dues and publications; and miscellaneous expenses, such as postage used for business needs.

If you're working out of a home office, a portion of your mortgage interest (or rent), related utilities, property taxes, repair costs, and depreciation may he deducted as business expenses—under special circumstances. To learn more about the possibility of home office deductions, consult IRS Publication 587, Business Use of Your Home

The method of paying taxes on income not subject to withholding is called "estimated tax" for individuals. If you expect to owe more than $500 at year's end and if the total amount of income tax that will be withheld during the year will be less than 90% of the tax shown on the current year's return, you'll generally make estimated tax payments. Estimated tax payments are made in four equal installments due on April 15, June 15, September 15, and January 15 (assuming you're a calendar-year taxpayer). For more information, request Publication 533, Self-Employment Tax.

The Internal Revenue Service's website (www.irs.ustreas.gov) offers tips and instant access to IRS forms and publications.

Social Security tax

Depending on your net income as a freelancer, you may be liable for a Social Security tax. This is a tax designed for those who don't have Social Security withheld from their paychecks. You're liable if your net income is $400 or more per year. Net income is the difference between your income and allowable business deductions. Request Schedule SE, Computation of Social Security Self-Employment Tax, if you qualify.

If completing your income tax return proves to be too complex, consider hiring an accountant (the fee is a deductible business expense) or contact the IRS for assistance. (Look in the White Pages under U.S. Government—Internal Revenue Service or check their website, www.irs.ustrea s.gov.) In addition to offering numerous publications to instruct you in various facets of preparing a tax return, the IRS also has walk-in centers in some cities.

Insurance

As a self-employed professional, be aware of what health and business insurance coverage is available to you. Unless you're a Canadian who is covered by national health insurance or a full-time freelancer covered by your spouse's policy, health insurance will no doubt be one of your biggest expenses. Under the terms of a 1985 government act (COBRA), if you leave a job with health benefits, you're entitled to continue that coverage for up to 18 months—you pay 100 percent of the premium and sometimes a small administration fee. Eventually, you must search for your own health plan. You may also need disability and life insurance. Disability insurance is offered through many private insurance companies and state governments. This insurance pays a monthly fee that covers living and business expenses during periods of long-term recuperation from a health problem. The amount of money paid is based on the recipient's annual earnings.

Before contacting any insurance representative, talk to other writers, illustrators, or photographers to learn which insurance companies they recommend. If you belong to a writers' or artists' organization, ask the organization if it offers insurance coverage for professionals. (SCBWI has a plan available. Look through the Clubs & Organizations section for other groups that may offer coverage.) Group coverage may be more affordable and provide more comprehensive coverage than an individual policy.

Query Letter Clinic

An editor has a few spare minutes to peruse her slush pile. She's got 50-plus submissions on her shelf. She pulls out yours. You have about five seconds to make her want to read your manuscript. If your query doesn't grab her, there are plenty of others she can look at. Here, we'll take a look at a query and see how it can be improved.

The query for *Vinnie's Watering Hole* starts off weak. You won't make an editor interested in your manuscript by telling her your name. Get right into describing the story. Do that well and the editor *will* be interested.

When this query letter finally gets into the description of the story in the second paragraph, it's vague. What's a "flavorful" story? *Who* gathers at the watering hole? "Everyone" doesn't tell the editor enough. Do children gather there? Are the characters animals? Do they start as animals and turn into different versions of animals? What are the "amusing idiosyncrasies" each animal possesses after emerging from the watering hole. And—an important detail—who is Vinnie?

If the crux of a *Vinnie's Watering Hole* is simply that animals visit the watering whole and transform, that's too slight for a publishable picture book manuscript. Do the "idiosyncrasies" cause problems for the animals? Does chaos ensue? Is magic involved? Do the animals try to change back to their original forms? Something needs to happen beyond the transforming; there must be a plot. There must be a beginning, middle, and end, even for a story 537 words long. (See Lost in the Woods of Plot? Here's a Way Out on page 28.)

It's nice that the writer of this query is a mother and a grandmother, but that doesn't qualify her to be a children's writer. If you don't have special qualifications, it's not necessary to come up with something. However, your experience reading children's books over the years can be presented as publisher research. Favorite Dutton titles that lead the writer to believe her work

Key to Query Comments on page 21

❶ Your name is at the end of the letter—start off strong with an enticing description of your story.

❷ "Flavorful" is vague. Give details of the plot.

❸ Again, this description is vague. Who are the characters? Who is Vinnie? What are their idiosyncrasies?

❹ It's not necessary to give personal information that's not relevant to your story. Instead, tell what you know about the publisher and why your book is right for them.

❺ This sentence is unnecessary—it doesn't give the editor any information, just your opinion.

❻ Get to the point. No need to share your hopes. Wrap up with a simple, "I look forward to hearing from you."

❼ Don't worry about illustrations. This sentence identifies the writer as amateurish. If she had done some research, she would know how things work.

Original Query Letter

P.O. Box 999
Winchester CA 92596
909-555-1234
Author@aol.com

May 10, 2003

Meredith Mundy Wassinger, editor
Dutton Children's Books
Penguin Putnam Inc.
345 Hudson St.
New York NY 10014

Dear Ms. Wassinger,

Cut

1 My name is Meredyth Hiltz. I write you today about a children's picture book consisting of 537 words: *Vinnie's Watering Hole.*

The descriptions are too vague.

2 *Vinnie's Watering Hole* is a flavorful childlike tale. The story is set, where everyone gathers, at Vinnie's Watering Hole. The characters emerge as a variety of

3 unusual animals, each possessing amusing idiosyncrasies.

4 Having had three children of my own, and five grandchildren; children's books have been a large party of my life. I believe my story, *Vinnie's Watering Hole,*

5 will bring joy and laughter to any child's life. *Cut—the line doesn't provide any solid information.*

6 It is my sincerest hope that you will find my story worthy of your time and

7 publication. This picture book is accessible with or without illustration. I look forward to hearing from you in the near future.

Sincerely,

Keep your closing simple: "I look forward to hearing from you."

Don't mention illustrations in your query letter.

Meredyth Hiltz

Revised Query Letter

May 10, 2003

Meredith Mundy Wassinger
Dutton Children's Books
Penguin Putnam Inc.
345 Hudson St.
New York NY 10014

Dear Ms. Wassinger,

Imagine an elephant who can walk in the clouds; a lion who swims the back-stroke; a monkey who bounces higher than the trees on his spring of a tail.

When the jungle animals drink from their usual watering hole, they suddenly emerge with new-found talents like these in my 500-word humorous picture book for readers age 5-8 titled *Vinnie's Watering Hole*. Vinnie, a trickster jungle snake, has enchanted the animals' favorite watering hole. And while at first the animals have fun with their new skills, the jungle becomes chaotic, Vinnie is stealing their food, and they realize they must come up with a plan to foil the snake and bring things back to normal in the jungle.

As a mother of three and grandmother of five, I've read tons of picture books over the years, including Dutton titles like *Big Bad Bunny* by Alan Durant and *Sun Dance, Water Dance* by Jonathan London. I think *Vinnie's Watering Hole*, full of humor and adventure, would fit well into your line of picture books.

I look forward to hearing from you. I've enclosed a SASE for your reply.

Sincerely,

Meredyth Hiltz
P.O. Box 999
Winchester CA 92596
(909)555-1234
Author@aol.com

is right for this publisher would be effective. It's a good idea to give the editor a reason her publisher was chosen for this manuscript. Show her you're familiar with the books her company produces, and tell her why you think yours would fit in.

The third paragraph offers the writer's belief that her story "will bring joy and laughter into any child's life." How? Is it a humorous story? Say so in the beginning of the letter. Instead of mentioning "any child," how about giving a specific age-level for the story. This is useful information for an editor considering your query.

The final paragraph of the query states the picture book is "accessible with or without illustration." This seems to indicate that the writer is offering to submit the story with illustrations if requested. Stop right there: Unless the author is a professional illustrator, she should not try to provide illustrations. This is taken care of by the editor and art director after a manuscript is accepted for publication. Writers need not worry about this aspect of their picture book—just concentrate on the writing.

Can an Unagented, Unknown Writer Get Published? Editors Sound Off

BY ANNA OLSWANGER

Having an agent does not guarantee publication, one member of an online group wrote to her fellow children's book writers. *My suggestion is to start taking action and spend all your time reaching your writing goals.*

The response from another member of the same group was swift and unhappy:

Thanks for your optimistic letter. Unfortunately, like many of those on this list, what you say does not match my experience. I have a manuscript I started sending to publishers about five years ago. Although all publishers held onto it for 6-12 months and wrote to say they liked it, the book was eventually rejected. The reason given was that I did not have a known name.

Things are ten times worse today than when I started. All of the smaller publishing houses are being bought out by the bigger ones, and as soon as they are, they stop accepting unagented work from unfamiliar authors.

You say you don't need an agent to get published. Correct me if I'm wrong, but I would say that the number of publishing houses accepting work from unagented newbies is less than ten percent, and none of the writer's guides make it easy to discover which will actually look at a query and which will return it without a glance. Even calling the publishing house will get you the wrong information. The secretaries often don't know the difference between an agented query and an unagented query. The only way to get your foot in the door today is with connections.

If you can give us some real information—names of ten honest publishers who are truly open to new, unagented writers—then I will gladly admit you were right.

It's understandable that writers submitting work to ever-growing slush piles get frustrated—but is it really that difficult for an unpublished writer to get published? Is the picture that grim? To find out, we asked a number of editors and a few agents to respond to this online dialogue about the difficulties of breaking in. Read on for some straightforward—and often encouraging—comments from the trenches.

SUZANNE REINOEHL, Editor
Holiday House

At Holiday House, we accept unsolicited manuscripts and acquire approximately 5-10 unsolicited manuscripts each year. In our backlist, we have roughly the same number of unagented

---

ANNA OLSWANGER *lives in New Jersey where she writes for the Endowment Foundation of UJA Federation of Bergen County & North Hudson and teaches Jewish Children's Literature at Fairleigh Dickinson University. A frequent traveler on Amtrak, she also teaches business writing workshops for the Center for Training and Education at Johns Hopkins University and "Writing for Physicians" for the Stony Brook University Medical School. Anna's "Jewish Book Publishing News" column appears regularly in* the Association of Jewish Libraries Newsletter *and online. She's a long-time contributor to* Children's Writer's & Illustrator's Market. *Visit her website, www.olswanger.com.*

authors and illustrators as we do agented. We do look at every query letter and submission that enters our office, and there are other publishers who do as well. We believe that new, talented authors and illustrators can be vital contributors to the children's book world and are capable of bringing valued ideas and innovation to the industry in the long term.

The important thing to remember is Persistence with a capital P. Regardless of whether you decide to submit manuscripts to agents or to publishers directly, you must keep trying. It's hard to stomach repeated rejection, but it's an inevitable part of the submission process. What's right for one editor may not be right for another. It's a matter of making the right match. There are people in the industry who do take the time to review every manuscript carefully. A good manuscript with innovative ideas and characters will not be overlooked by everyone. Someone out there, be it an editor, publisher, or agent, will see the quality of the work and pursue it further.

STEPHANIE OWENS LURIE, President and Publisher
Dutton Children's Books

The one area of opportunity right now is in fiction. There are more children ages 11-14 than ever before, and the success of series like Harry Potter, The Princess Diaries, and A Series of Unfortunate Events and books like *The Sisterhood of the Traveling Pants* proves that they are avid readers. Dutton is responding by publishing more middle-grade and young-adult novels and fewer picture books. We seek commercial ideas and fresh, authentic narrative voices. We have several novels by first-time authors on our list, and not all of them were agented. In fact, last year we held our first Ann Durell Fiction contest, for best first middle-grade novel, and we found a winner and runner up. This year we are holding the contest again.

I acknowledge that the current market is challenging—perhaps the most challenging I've experienced in my twenty years in the business. It is not a good time for average or midlist books, and these days it may well take longer for writers to find the right editor. However, I've also seen that, with the right property, first-time authors can reach a bigger audience than ever before.

DIANNE HESS, Executive Editor
Scholastic Press

Whether or not we choose to publish an author has nothing to do with the author having an agent. Our publishing choices are made because we love a manuscript, have a vision for it, and feel it will make a significant contribution to children's literature. And we need to know that it's something we can sell. I personally get about 6,000 submissions per year. We cull through everything that comes in, and we can tell pretty quickly what isn't appropriate. We make a pile of things that look promising and quickly send back what we can't use. Coming through an agent doesn't guarantee us a better manuscript. However, reputable agents often work with the best authors with proven track records, and that makes a difference, particularly if it's an author whose previous work has won a major award, or was a best seller, or was distinct in some way. The author's track record is something I pay more attention to than the agent.

It is difficult to have something published for the first time. And even we are cutting back on what we read, as the submissions numbers have risen above what we can reasonably handle. With the proliferation of writers' conferences as a kind of industry, more writers are being encouraged than this constricting field can accommodate. But I think those who are serious, talented, and willing to hone their craft will find their way in—agent or not.

RUTH KATCHER, Executive Editor
HarperCollins Children's Books

I'm convinced that the children's book world is still one in which, with perseverance and luck, you can get published without an agent. That does not mean it is easy. The slush pile still gets read; individual editors still read the submissions addressed to them directly.

But I have gotten up at 5:30 a.m. on three days running to get a long novel ready for copyediting, writing the jacket copy in my head on the subway. I can see my personal slush pile from where I sit here in my office, along with a revision of a contracted novel, another manuscript under contract, and two proposals from authors I've been working with for some time.

My heart is with the unpublished authors, and I do try to give them some amount of personal attention, if not a personal response. But my first priority is to the books under contract and authors I'm working with already. My best advice to unpublished authors is to persevere, to make personal connections when possible but to have some faith in the system. And more than that, to spend their energy on their writing rather than on trying to beat the system. I can think of a number of unagented manuscripts we've signed in the last few years. Almost any agent and every editor I know, from assistant to editorial director, is eager to find new talent. It's why we got into the business! Keep writing, and have some faith that if you have the talent, you'll get noticed, even if it takes more time than we'd all wish.

ANN TOBIAS, Executive Editor, Handprint Books
Literary Agent, A Literary Agency

While I cannot speak for the entire children's book publishing industry, I have been at this business for a very long time. There are no words to express the thrilling, exciting, heart stopping wonder and exhilaration that comes from reading a manuscript by a newcomer who shows promise. If this writer's manuscript was truly promising, no editor would want to pass it by. She started sending her manuscript around five years ago, and it was held at each house from 6-12 months. By my reckoning, it had 5-10 readings by professionals. It is heartbreaking, but maybe she has to come to terms with the fact that her manuscript couldn't compete against other manuscripts.

ERIN MURPHY, Literary Agent, Erin Murphy Literary Agency
Former Editor-in-Chief, Northland Publishing

When I hear of writers thinking this way, I can plainly see all the work they have ahead of them. If a writer is not willing to approach marketing her work with curiosity, openness, and a willingness to learn, then she's likely approaching her writing the same way. If she can't find a way to promote herself to editors, she likely won't promote her book to booksellers, librarians, and children. If she looks with suspicion upon a fellow writer offering reasonable, enthusiastic, and optimistic advice, then she will look upon me the same way.

There are so many wonderful writers out there who look at the entire process of publishing as an adventure and a learning experience, who embrace the whole, and, when there's something that's particularly difficult for them, find a different angle to approach it from—why would I choose to work with someone who has such a poor attitude? She's lost the race before she's left the starting gate.

ALLYN JOHNSTON, Editorial Director
Harcourt Children's Book Division

I have never in my 18 years in publishing heard of anyone at any house turning down a project because the writer didn't have "a known name."

Of course, that author's experience of having to wait so long before being rejected is awful, and I wish I could say I've never heard of that happening either. But editors do get overwhelmed by the manuscript submissions, and it's usually the first thing we let slide when the pressure's on.

That said, I still believe that (beyond winning one of the big awards), there's not much in our jobs more exciting than discovering a fabulous new project in the mail. Yes, many houses do have "No Unagented Submissions" policies, but that's because we're all swamped by the zillions of submissions that aren't remotely publishable, and we have to do something to stem the tide. But there are still ways for creative, tenacious writers and illustrators without agents to get their work to editors and art directors.

Find out who edited the books you love. Look in acknowledgments for mention of an editor's name—perhaps the book was dedicated to the editor. Track down speeches from published authors whose books you admire and see if they mention their editor. Call houses and ask for the editorial department and politely—and briefly—ask who edited specific books. Then craft a great letter addressed to a specific person, mentioning a book or two of theirs that you admire and why. I can't imagine an editor who wouldn't feel the need to respond to that sort of attention to detail—even if the manuscript wasn't for her or him.

Remember, we really do want to find great new books to publish; we can't exist without them!

CLAUDIA SLOAN
Tallfellow Press and smallfellow press

Things have changed in the industry, but not just on the writer's side. We, the publishers, have a much harder time selling books (just to bookstores—I'm not even talking about to the consumer who may never even see the wonderful books we publish). But, there are still publishers that accept unsolicited, unagented manuscripts. We are one of them. Now, before anybody packs up that latest tome and sends it to me, please do your homework. Look at websites and find out specifically what publishers are looking for. Writers who skip this step are part of the reason for the slow response time. Here at smallfellow press we are only looking for funny, whimsical, clever, unique picture books and, unfortunately, because of the problems in the industry, we are not doing as many as we would like to. We do receive a lot of submissions and we may hold the ones we are interested in for a very long time, but we also return the ones we are not interested in a relatively short time. We do our best. If you have something wonderful and unique, it will find its way to the top. We are looking for those gems!

YOLANDA LeROY, Senior Editor
Charlesbridge Publishing

Let me throw out a scary statistic: Of the approximately 1,250 manuscripts Charlesbridge received in the first half of 2003, 13 were signed up. But although it's true that it's difficult to get published, and although it's also true that fewer and fewer publishers are accepting unagented manuscripts, it's not true that all the smaller publishing houses are being bought and enfolded into the corporate borg. Small independent publishing is alive and well, as I can attest to here at Charlesbridge, and we are proud of our reputation for nurturing emerging talent. Of the 24 traditional picture books on our 2004 lists, only three are agented. In our 2005 list, only one is.

DEBORAH BRODIE, Executive Editor
Roaring Brook Press

From the other side of the desk, in a small house, with a small staff, and always scrambling for time to get everything done, I am not one of the editors making it easier for unagented writers. We cannot accept queries or unsolicited manuscripts and still have the time and resources for the people we have already committed to. Yet we proudly publish many first-time people, more than most publishers, and not all have agents. It is one of my greatest joys to be able to work with new writers and illustrators right from the beginning. I am sad about not being able to do more, but it would also be great if writers spent some time thinking about what would help an overworked, underpaid editor notice their work.

Who got my attention? Authors and illustrators who attended classes I've taught, workshops I've led, or conferences where I've spoken; who have written for magazines or professional bulletins; or who were recommended by friends and colleagues. All of them, without exception, made the effort to learn about their craft, the process of revising, and the mechanics of the publishing business *before* they began networking.

I'm dancing as fast as I can, so my question to writers is: What can we do to be partners in this dance?

Lost in the Woods of Plot? Here's a Way Out

BY BONNY BECKER

So you're in the forest happily strolling along a faint, but unmistakable path, when suddenly your path disappears into a tangle of brush and you have no idea where to step next. Or maybe the path mysteriously sprouts into 20 paths and you can't decide which one to take. You stand there paralyzed for a day, a month . . .years.

Welcome to "plotting," one of the hardest parts of storytelling and the place where many—maybe most—stories and their authors get lost, at least for a while.

Is there a way out of the woods other than crashing desperately through the underbrush or mindlessly following path after path only to retrace your footsteps? Yes. It's called "classic story structure." It's the structure that underlies almost all stories from Tolstoy's *Anna Karenina* to *The Cat in the Hat*.

The idea that almost all stories have a common structure was expressed by Aristotle over two thousand years ago. And observers such as Joseph Campbell believe stories follow a mythic pattern as old as storytelling itself because that pattern is built into how humans perceive and respond to the world.

Story structure is not an exact map or a step-by-step route through the woods. You will still have to create your own unique path, your own unique story. As Robert McKee notes in his landmark book, *Story*, "Story is about eternal universal forms, not formulas."

But knowing something about story structure can help give you a vision of your final destination and landmarks along the way to help guide you there.

COMMON STORY ELEMENTS

These basic elements are common to almost all stories.
- You'll have a main character (hero) with a need or a want.
- In an effort to meet this need, your hero will leave the "ordinary" world and go in quest of the solution to his or her problem.
- The story will build through rising action—the stakes will get higher, the tension will mount, the tasks will become more difficult—until the story climaxes in an ultimate test for your character.
- Your hero will return to his ordinary world a changed person.

THE BEGINNING

Think of your story as a circle. In the beginning of the story, your hero is trapped in what writing instructors such as Chris Vogler in *The Writer's Journey* call the "ordinary world."

BONNY BECKER *is the published author of seven children's books ranging from the best selling picture book,* The Christmas Crocodile, *to the middle grade novel,* My Brother the Robot, *a Junior Literary Guild selection. Her latest picture book,* Just a Minute, *illustrated by Jack E. Davis, is a Fall 2003 Simon & Schuster release. She is also a frequent conference speaker with an expertise in story structure and a freelance editor, offering manuscript critiquing and editing for the children's market. You can learn more about her at www.bonnybecker.com*

Theodore Geisel's (a.k.a. Dr. Seuss) enduring genius shone through to the world when he met his editor's challenge of creating a children's book using only a specified set of 225 words. Children don't care how few words he had to choose from, or recognize the difficulty of meeting the challenge using perfect rhyme, rhythm, *and* adhering to classic story structure. The result, *The Cat in the Hat*, became a classic itself and induced generations of children to care about only one thing: "Read it again!"

Quite simply, your hero is in some current situation that isn't working for one reason or another.

For Harry Potter, it's living with a beastly aunt and uncle who treat him cruelly. For Dorothy in the *Wizard of Oz*, it's being stuck in Kansas—far away from a longed-for rainbow world. For the ant in my own picture book *An Ant's Day Off*, it's having to work every day underground never knowing sky or sun or rain.

Struggling with how to start your story? A good place is to simply start here in the "ordinary world."

In Linda Sue Park's Newbery-winning middle grade novel *A Single Shard*, chapter one deftly shows the reader that the main character, Tree-ear, is an orphan. He lives with Crane-man under a bridge. They are poor but honest. And we see Tree-ear's fascination with making pottery. The stage is set.

THE ESCAPE

The next step in the story cycle will be your hero's escape from this ordinary world. In screenwriting this is called the "inciting incident." In story structure based on mythology, it's known as "the call to adventure." The bottom line is something will happen to upset the balance in the hero's current life and bring about change.

For Harry Potter, the inciting incident is when he receives the letter inviting him to Hogwarts. For Dorothy, it's when Miss Gulch takes Toto. It's not necessarily the moment of change, but it's the event that "incites" change—the event that makes change seem inevitable. In *A Single Shard*, Tree-ear, caught sneaking a look at a master potter's work, accidentally breaks a pot lid. Clearly, life is going to change for this outcast orphan.

Your hero then leaves the ordinary world. Everyone gets in covered wagons and heads west. Heidi goes up the mountain. Dorothy gets whisked to Oz. Bart, the sand ant, climbs out of the nest.

Setting the stage may take several chapters or it might be virtually a single sentence as in the memorable first sentence of *Charlotte's Web*:

> "Where's Papa going with that ax?" said Fern to her mother as they were setting the table for breakfast.

Of course, this one sentence doesn't fully give us Fern's ordinary world. But we already know we're with a family and sense a rural setting in an older time. And we know that something is going to happen here. Whatever that ax is about, we know it's going to change things.

THE QUEST

So, your hero enters a new world. The world of the quest. In screenwriting, it's your second act. In a story or book—it's your middle. This is where the hero confronts obstacles and learns lessons. This is often where stories bog down. This is the middle of the forest. And it can be a dense, dark place full of dead ends and misleading paths.

Here you may find yourself writing scenes and events just because you have to get from Big Plot Point A to Big Plot Point B and *something* has to happen. But oddly, even though a lot is happening, for some reason, your story feels boring and arbitrary. Or this may be where you find yourself staring at a blank cliff side. And writer's block becomes more than an abstract term.

So what do you do when you realize you're just scribbling marks on paper? You can try to figure out why it matters. What are you *really* writing about? What is your theme?

Without theme, the obstacles and conflict you create in the middle will be just a series of "then this happened and then that happened" and, guess what, your hero is battling giant ants from space and nobody cares.

No matter how "big" and exciting you make your events, they won't have meaning unless

Bonny Becker's *An Ant's Day Off* proves that your characters don't have to be big to go through huge life changes and make tough decisions. Becker's main character, a worker ant who has never seen the sky, decides to step outside the anthill. The education he receives in the outside world and his subsequent decision to return to the anthill are turning points in the story.

they tie into a deeper story question. That deeper question isn't the plot. But it's the thing that gives meaning to the plot.

Premise vs. theme

Figuring out theme can be tricky. It's helpful to distinguish between "premise" and "theme." Premise is the basic plot—the "what happens" part.

In *Harry Potter*, for example, the premise (not the theme) driving the plot is how a boy learns to be a wizard. In *The Wizard of Oz*, the premise is Dorothy's quest to get home. In *An Ant's Day Off*, the premise is an ant daring to be the first ant ever to take a day off. But those describe plot, not theme.

Theme is the "why it matters that it happens" part.

In the *Wizard of Oz*, the theme seems to be something like: Maturity is achieved when a person internalizes various values (love, courage, thinking for one's self). It's a coming-of-age story.

Oz could have easily collapsed into just a series of events. And then Dorothy meets this funny character and then she meets that funny character. And, in truth, no matter how clever or interesting the characters were, you would have soon lost interest if the events didn't add up to something more. The reason this story holds our interest is it answers an unspoken, perhaps unconscious, question in story form. What does it take to be a whole person?

Theme can be a loaded word. Some writers prefer to think in terms of a story question. Or a unifying principle or controlling idea. Or they focus on character as Linda Sue Park does. She believes theme should grow out of the character and the story.

"If a writer begins with theme, the story is likely to be heavy-handed and messagey . . . the kind of book kids run away from," she notes.

Yet, in a meaningful story, theme is there. For example, to me, the theme underlying *A Single Shard* is the idea that craft—the mastering of a skill—can give life value and purpose.

It can be very hard to recognize your own theme. Our writing minds seem to like to play hide and seek with us. And many writers will say that only later did they realize what they were *really* writing about. Often our stories are driven by unconscious choices and decisions. But most writers will at some point take a stab at what they think their story is about and will make more conscious story decisions based on that.

THE ULTIMATE TEST

After your hero has faced various obstacles, developed various skills, observed various approaches to whatever his or her problem/issue/need/want is (it can be as passive as observing how others live—that's much of what Scout does in *To Kill a Mockingbird*—or as active as

---

Plot Problems? Ask Yourself the Right Questions

Most writers instinctively use classic story structure. After all, it's in our nature as humans. Check out your own story. Odds are you'll find you used many of these elements with no conscious intent on your part.

But you'll probably also find pieces missing or a middle that doesn't add up. Or an ending that isn't as powerful as you'd like. When that happens, you might think about these various points:

- What's my hero's cage/trap/problem? What's his or her "ordinary" world?
- What's going to upset the balance of forces in my hero's life? What's going to compel him or her to leave the ordinary world and search for an answer? What is the proverbial "last straw?"
- What do I think my hero is grappling with internally or thematically? And what could happen on his journey that would help illuminate that for him?

Try to be fair and thorough. The more deeply you explore your issue, the more interesting it will be to a reader. Don't shy away from the things you have no real answer for or seem contradictory or too difficult to figure out. Asking honest questions can make the difference between an interesting story and a didactic series of predictable encounters.

Theme is the question you're asking in story form. Your story will add up to an answer, but let your characters act with free will to arrive at that answer. Don't force your story to an already concluded answer.

- What will be my hero's ultimate test?
- What is the decision she will have to make and why does she make that decision?
- How will she be changed? What will be different in her "ordinary" world because of what she has experienced?

Frodo with his many battles in *Lord of the Rings*), the hero must be tested.

This has been variously described as "facing the dragon" or the "crisis" or the "ultimate test." It's what your story has been leading up to. It's where we see how and if the hero has grown from the quest.

In the *Wizard of Oz*, it might seem at first glance that it's when Dorothy faces the Witch, but actually it's when the wizard's balloon flies away. Dorothy realizes she has to turn to herself and all that she's learned to get home and she *decides* to trust the shoes.

In my own middle-grade, *My Brother the Robot*, it's when my boy hero, Chip, *decides* to race a robot he knows will almost undoubtedly win—but for a boy who's been avoiding challenging himself, it's an important choice.

In *A Single Shard*, it's when Tree-ear *decides* to continue his journey even though he has only a single shard from a ceramic pot to show the royal emissary the skill of his master. He puts his faith in the craft evident in a single piece of the whole work.

The key word here is *decide*. This is the point at which your hero makes his or her most important choice in the story. This is the peak moment of your story. Not the battle that follows, but the decision to battle or the way in which your hero chooses to battle.

What is the peak moment in *Star Wars*—a film in which George Lucas relied heavily on Joseph Campbell's ideas about mythic story structure? There's a huge emotional charge when Luke Skywalker blows up the Death Star, but the peak moment, the most important moment, is when Luke must choose between trusting in his instruments or in the Force. He decides to go with the Force and pushes away his navigational tool. Such a tiny gesture—he merely pushes away a piece of equipment. Such an emotional moment! The meaning isn't in the hero's actions, it is in the meaning of his action—his decision to act and why.

If you're trying to figure out where to take your story other than just the next random step down the road, McKee in *Story* suggests you look at your climax, your ultimate test, and backtrack from there. What value are you putting forward with this test and does the rest of your story add up to this moment and this choice?

HOME AGAIN

The final element to story structure is to bring your hero home a changed person. You come full circle. You'll need to take the reader back to that ordinary world and let the reader see how the world has changed for your hero because your hero has changed.

Dorothy goes back to the farm and sees it differently because of her experience in Oz. Tree-ear comes back to a world utterly changed from where he started. He's "adopted" by the potter and his wife and has earned the right to make pots himself; this poor orphan outcast has a home, a valuable skill, and a distinct place in his community.

My boy Chip comes back to a home where he's accepted for who he is, but he's also more willing to try new things than when he started.

PUTTING IT ALL TOGETHER

It's fun to see how all this works by taking a look at what may seem an unlikely candidate for classic story structure: Dr. Seuss' *A Cat in the Hat*. But it's all there.

The **ordinary world** and its problems are clearly established: It's a cold, cold wet day and the two kids in the story have nothing to do. They're bored and passive—unable to do anything but sit.

There's a distinct **inciting incident** with a BUMP that makes them jump and the entrance of the Cat. He changes everything about this boring rainy day.

In fact, he makes life **progressively more complicated**. More and more is at stake as he shows off his tricks. And when that's not enough, he introduces two characters even wilder than he—Thing One and Thing Two.

What's the **ultimate test**? It might seem it's the moment when the boy runs and gets the net

Linda Sue Park's Newbery Medal-winning mid-grade novel portrays a young orphan named Tree-ear in 12th century Korea who aches to become apprenticed to a Master Potter. Tree-ear's progression from hungry admirer to apprentice and then artist is just one journey for Park's multifaceted main character.

Illustration © 2001 Jean and Mou-sien Tseng. Reprinted with permission of Clarion Books.

to catch Thing One and Thing Two, but actually it comes earlier. It's that **moment of decision** when the boy finally decides that it's not okay for these creatures to be in his home. ("I do NOT like the way that they play.")

How about **theme**? For me, the theme is about the power of imagination or creativity. Sounds rather grand for this "simple" little kids' book, but look at the story. A boy is bored and passively sits waiting for his mother's return. An amazing (imaginative, creative) creature arrives on his doorstep. What follows is a demonstration that creativity is great fun, but unchecked creativity creates only chaos.

However, controlled creativity (the capture of Thing One and Thing Two) gives excitement and, oddly, responsibility to life. When did the boy act? When Thing One and Thing Two messed with his mother's things. Creativity is a messy business, but they had gone too far.

The Cat cleans up the mess—so isn't he the one solving the problem? Breaking that old, old rule about your main character solving the problem? No, the boy character remains the active, main character—because he's the character who made the necessary "ultimate test" choice. Remember it's that choice around which a story swings. And having taken control of his creativity, the boy can put it to work for himself.

By the end of that story, our boy is no longer bored and no longer passive. He even dares consider the possibility that he won't tell his mom what happened that day and this feels okay. Or at least it does to this Mom, because he acted responsibly when it was important.

The boy then invites readers to become more than passive observers themselves. He fires up the reader's own imagination with the ending question "What would you do?"

TO THINK OR NOT TO THINK

Did Theodore Geisel have this theme in mind when he wrote *The Cat in the Hat*? Probably not on a conscious level. He just wanted to tell a fun story having been challenged to create an early reader with a vocabulary list limited to 225 words. But he clearly struggled to make this story add up. In fact, he described the yearlong process of creating that book as something like "being lost with a witch in a tunnel of love."

Was Linda Sue Park thinking about the value of craft when she crafted A *Single Shard*? Probably not. But what she did have in mind was a character with a problem. "Actually two problems," she says. "An 'internal quest' and 'external quest.' Tree-ear's external quest is to find a way to make celadon pottery. His internal quest is to find a place where he truly belongs."

In writing the story, Park says there is a lot of instinct at play, but for her "all scenes must be tied directly to the quests—this is a completely conscious decision to which I adhere rigorously."

However, she notes with a smile, "I think Anne Lamont's 'shitty first draft' idea—just get the whole story down and fix it later—is better advice in general."

So if your writing is flowing, don't stop and think! Just get it down. If the path is clear, just keep walking!

But eventually you'll probably find you use both parts of your brain—instinct and conscious choices. And when it comes to the conscious choices part, take a look at classic story structure for some landmarks to guide you on your way.

Recommended Reading

There are a number of excellent books that can give you more ideas about story structure and how to use it in developing your story. Here are a few, including several screenwriting books. Screenplays have a distinct structure that has been analyzed extensively. Although the structure of a novel isn't exactly the same, the ideas from screenplay writing can be very helpful.

The Hero with a Thousand Faces, 2nd ed., by Joseph Campbell

The Writer's Journey, Mythic Structure for Storytellers & Screenwriters, by Christopher Vogler

Making a Good Script Great, 2nd ed., by Linda Seger

The Weekend Novelist, by Robert J. Ray

Story, by Robert McKee

The Writer's Guide to Crafting Stories for Children, by Nancy Lamb

Get Noticed: An Illustrator's Guide to Self-promotion

BY SUSAN KATHLEEN HARTUNG

Once upon a time, it was easy to get in to see an art director or editor. But as the children's book market grew, so did the number of individuals wanting to show their wares to the publishers. A glut of aspiring illustrators, coupled with tighter post-9/11 security, has made getting work onto the desk of an art director a real challenge. Personal meetings are becoming a thing of the past. And actual requests for a portfolio review seem to be going the way of the dinosaur. For a while it seemed the best way to get yourself noticed was a packet of color copies and a cover letter. Even those are rapidly turning into "Requested Materials Only," and of course you have to get noticed to receive the request.

So the big question is, how do you get noticed? There are three marketing tools every illustrator should utilize: a compact well-organized **portfolio**; a **website**, the new doorway into the art director's office; and **postcards**, a tried-and-true method that gives a lot of bang for the buck.

By combining these three marketing methods, your work will be easily accessible—and get noticed by the all-important art buyers.

Putting together an effective portfolio

Even though actual requests to see a portfolio are becoming less and less common, it's still a good idea to create a physical portfolio for conferences, drop-offs, and those rare one-on-one interviews. Your portfolio is still your ambassador, your representative. It reflects who you are, how you work, and of course, what you do. So it's important your portfolio stays up-to-date and looks clean, neat, and organized. Following are some do's and don'ts for portfolio presentations.

Do buy a presentation folder for 8½×11 sheets. These can be found at most major office supply stores for far less than you would pay through an art supply retailer. Select a folder that has a stiff cover and clear sleeves that turn easily. It does not have to look like the classic portfolio case. Try to find a folder with removable sleeves. If you can't find one, take a blade and ruler and cut out the extra pages once you're satisfied with the order and arrangement of your images. Look for a folder with a pocket for "leave behinds." If you can't find one, you can make one using a fairly heavyweight piece of clear acetate that you cut to size and attach with thin strips of double-stick tape. The clear pocket has the advantage of showing off your samples.

Don't spend a small fortune on your portfolio! They get lost, battered, and beaten on a regular basis.

Do spend enough money to get a relatively hardy folder, but make sure it's cheap enough that you won't feel ill if you need to replace it. By using color copies or color computer printouts

---

SUSAN KATHLEEN HARTUNG *grew up in Ann Arbor, Michigan, with her two older brothers and a beagle. She came to New York City where she earned her BFA from the School of Visual Arts. Susan is the acclaimed illustrator of the award-winning books* Dear Juno *by Soyung Pak and* One Leaf Rides the Wind *by Celeste Davidson Mannis (both Viking). She has forthcoming titles with HarperCollins and Lee & Low. When not illustrating, Susan can be found renovating her 140-year-old farmhouse. Susan lives with a small herd of dogs and cats in Brooklyn, Michigan.*

As soon as you pull up Susan Kathleen Hartung's website at www.susanhartung.com, you get a clear picture of what's available there. Simple icons and clear, to-the-point headings leave little guesswork and ensure users will find what they are looking for.

and a reasonably priced folder, it's no big deal if your portfolio is lost, stolen, or damaged. It will be relatively cheap and easy to replace.

Do show uniform size, quality color copies, or computer-printed samples in a presentation folder capable of holding standard $8\frac{1}{2} \times 11$ pages. The benefits here are that your portfolio is small and easy to handle, relatively cheap to replace, and it's easy and inexpensive to swap out images. Shrink oversized pieces to fit on an $8\frac{1}{2} \times 11$ page, but don't enlarge smaller images. By keeping your presentation size down to $8\frac{1}{2} \times 11$, you make it lightweight and easy to carry or mail out. Another advantage is that most picture books do not exceed 9×12—the $8\frac{1}{2} \times 11$ size can give a better feel for how your work would look in a picture book format.

Do label your portfolio on the cover or just inside the cover, with your name, address, and other contact information.

Don't show originals—ever! Treat your originals like gold. And quite frankly, they are. Original children's book art is becoming big business. In addition, your ownership of original sketches can be an important record should a conflict or legal issue arise. The only time a client should see an original is when you are submitting finished art for printing. Even sketches should be submitted as copies of the originals.

Don't show images of widely varied sizes in a huge portfolio. I can't tell you how many times I've gone to a portfolio review and seen these giant portfolios capable of holding a Volkswagen. It's just a bad idea.

Don't show more than one style. For a few limited illustration markets (such as greeting cards or in-house positions) multiple styles are often desirable. For the children's book market, it's inadvisable to show multiple styles in one portfolio. If you do have more than one style, pick the one you like best and focus on that. If you are unable to choose, limit yourself to no more than two styles and market them separately. The book market is all about showing consistency throughout a book—consistency of style, color, and character. When you show a wide range of styles, the art director or editor has no way of telling if you are capable of creating a consistent look.

Do show color and black & white work—as long as they are done in the same basic style. However, it is not necessary to show black & white work. Don't mix color and black & white work throughout your portfolio—arrange your work in sections of color and black & white. You may also want to order your images in each section by subject—for example, children, animals, series, realistic, fantasy, etc.

Do show one to two examples of a finished sketch. This will show editors and art directors what to expect for the sketch phase of a project. It is also an excellent opportunity to show off a piece that isn't finished.

Do make sure your images reflect subject matter appropriate for children. Your portfolio should contain any combination of the following: children, adults (parents or grandparents are good choices), animals (cats, dogs, bunnies, pigs, bears, and mice are most common), interior and exterior scenes. Show narrative scenes with good character interaction, rather than portraits; these suggest a visual story.

Do give each image it's own space. Do not put images on facing pages. The one exception is if you have images that are part of a series; those you may want to group together on facing pages.

Do include twelve to eighteen pieces in your portfolio. Fewer do not show enough. More can simply be too much to take in when doing a quick review of a portfolio. It's better to have ten pieces of "Wow!" than twenty pieces of "okay."

Creating an inviting website

Online portfolios have become the popular means to display samples. Getting those samples online is not as difficult as it may seem. There are many services that offer reasonably priced online portfolio pages, such as picture-book.com and theispot.com. These groups, among others,

The link to Susan Kathleen Hartung's online portfolio is just a click away from her home page. While it's still important to have a physical portfolio, the online portfolio is an essential ingredient to any artist's site. Many editors and art directors prefer to see something online before committing to an in-person interview.

offer detailed instructions and technical support to help you place your artwork online. For those who don't know the first thing about scanning artwork and creating digital files, places like Kinko's® offer the service for a small fee.

Gone are the days of having slides made of your work. These days, it is worth investing in a scanner or scanning services and copying your images into digital files. It makes them easy to catalog and access for all your needs.

An alternative to posting images with an online portfolio service is to learn how to do it yourself by creating your own website. It's no longer necessary to know how to write HTML code; creating your own basic website has been made easy. Most Internet service providers offer a free website, which also comes with easy-to-follow, step-by-step tutorials, templates, and readily available technical support. You can, of course, take it to the next step and contact your Internet provider about hosting a site with the domain name of your choice. This can usually be done very easily for an additional monthly charge plus the domain registration fee. And most service providers offer step-by-step guidance for the registration process.

You could also opt to invest in a Web design program. You will still need a website provided or hosted by your Internet service. However, you would be able to design a site with additional features not readily available through a guided template. The premiere program for do-it-yourself Web design is Adobe® GoLive™. It offers a wide variety of easy-to-use drag-and-drop features and excellent management tools. Adobe® also offers Classroom in a Book™ for GoLive™. It comes with an interactive CD and easy-to-understand tutorials and referencing.

Some illustrators choose to hire a professional designer. Although this can be an expensive choice, you will get a dynamic, professional-looking site.

Regardless of which option you choose, it is important to think about what you would like to have on your site. Showing off your work is of course the main goal, but it is nice to offer additional content. A brief biography and perhaps a current photo are a nice touch. It's also good to include links to organizations like the Children's Book Council (cbcbooks.org) and the Society of Children's Book Writers and Illustrators (scbwi.org) among others. Many of these sites will give you a reciprocal link. This sort of link exchange is an excellent way to gain free exposure for your site.

When creating your website, there are also things you should avoid. Do not put music on your site. What you may find a pleasant tune may grate on the nerves of the potential clients who view your site. Try to avoid an abundance of clip-art animations and flashing icons. Beyond distracting from your actual content, they slow down your site's loading time. Your best bet when designing a site is to keep it clean, simple, and easy to navigate. Just as your physical portfolio acts as your ambassador, so does your website. It's important your site gives the correct impression of who you are and what you do.

You don't have a computer? No problem. Many public libraries offer Internet access. There are also cyber cafes and places like Kinko's® where you can rent computer time.

Once you have created your online portfolio, how do you let art directors and editors know it's out there? Send out a postcard!

What makes a good promo postcard?

A well-designed postcard gives you a lot of bang for the buck. It is user friendly—no envelope to open, no pages to flip through, little-to-no reading involved. Postcards are relatively cheap to produce, cheap to mail, and skirt many security protocols. Postcards are also an inescapable form of advertising. Without even trying, the viewer will see either the image or your name, and in most cases both. The trick to getting work in this business (beyond talent) is name and style recognition, quickly followed by being in the right place at the right time. The best way to ensure this is to have a sample of your work pass over an art director's or editor's desk on a regular basis.

Part of a smart self-promotion strategy for illustrators includes sending postcard mailings to potential markets three or four times a year. But keep it simple. Just as on illustrator Susan Kathleen Hartung's postcard, include one strong image on the front and your clearly visible contact information, including your Web address and e-mail, on the back.

So how often is "a regular basis"? A minimum of three mailings a year is a good rule. That's a new mailing every four months. If possible, try doing a mailing every three months, especially in the beginning when you are trying to establish your name. This may seem a bit daunting, and a bit expensive, but there are ways of making it work without spending a fortune. There are many inexpensive postcard services available, including old standbys like ModernPostcard.com, and there are new companies popping up all the time. Do a little Internet surfing to find the best deal for your needs.

You can also generate postcards on your computer using a color printer. The only problem with this method is that most of the papers and card stocks available are still very flimsy. Before you take this approach, weigh the cost of paper, printer ink, and the time it will take against having it done professionally. You may find that the cost of having the cards printed is comparable. Remember—postcards are going to get you noticed. A professional-looking card can make a powerful statement.

One of the key things to keep in mind when designing a postcard is "less is more." In other words, keep it simple. Include a strong single image on the front and just the basics on the back. The basics are your name, phone number, and website and e-mail, if you have them. Include your street address to increase your chances of getting returns, which are very handy for updating your mailing list.

The most important information is your name and website, quickly followed by your phone number and e-mail. Size and placement of this information should reflect its importance. At the very least you want the viewers to see and register, at least on a subconscious level, the image and your name. You also don't want to make them work for the information by reading very small print or hunting for your web address and phone number out of a bunch of other extra bits of information. Small print can be good for identifying the piece on the front and a copyright notice, but larger type should be used for your name and contact information. Also try to keep your choice of typeface clear and easy to read. Some fonts may be wonderfully creative and fun looking but very difficult to read. And of course, be sure your layout complies with postal regulations.

Once you've created well-designed postcards, regular mailings to art buyers, along with a great website and a professional portfolio, are all the promotional tools you'll need to get your work noticed.

Writing Through Rejection: Advice from Jane Yolen & Vivian Van Velde

BY ALMA FULLERTON

One of the hardest obstacles writers have to overcome in their careers is the constant intake of rejection. If you let them, rejections can take a toll on your morale, and, for too many writers, that's enough to make them want to quit. Those who succeed in this business don't ever quit—no matter what.

Almost every writer gets rejections—even successful writers like Jane Yolen and Vivian Van Velde.

Jane Yolen has published more than 200 books. She's a poet, a teacher of writing and literature, and a reviewer of children's literature. Yolen's books and stories have won the Caldecott Medal, two Nebula Awards, two Christopher Medals, the World Fantasy Award, three Mythopoeic Fantasy Awards, the Golden Kite Award, the Jewish Book Award, and the Association of Jewish Libraries Award. (For a full list of Yolen's books visit her website www.janeyolen.com.)

Vivian Vande Velde has authored upwards of two dozen fantasy novels, including *Tales From the Brothers Grimm and the Sisters Weird* and *Smart Dog*. Many of her books have graced the accelerated reading programs for young adults in school systems. Van Velde's young adult novel *Never Trust a Dead Man* received an Edgar Award. Her novel *Companions of the Night* earned her an ALA Best Book for Young Adults.

Despite their many successes, Yolen and Van Velde still get their work rejected. Here they talk about the ups and downs of their careers and discuss how they keep their chins up when their work is sent back with a "No."

If you knew the writing profession came with so much rejection would you still have entered it?

Jane Yolen: I had 113 rejections on my poetry before I placed the first poem. So I knew.

Vivian Van Velde: Yes, I pretty much have to do it. Writing is like an addiction.

What made you keep pushing that first story/poem?

Yolen: Sheer cussedness.

Van Velde: I hesitate to say this, because it makes me sound as though I have an ego as big as a double-wide trailer, but even after 32 rejections—when I would have to retype the manuscript because it was beginning to look used (this was in the early '80s—before I wrote on a computer)—I would find myself still enjoying the story. Besides, the rejections I was getting didn't point to any one particular flaw, fixable or not. As long as there was no consensus as to why

---

ALMA FULLERTON *is a freelance writer based in Ontario, Canada. She's constantly juggling her daily schedule to make time for her two children, her husband, her writing, a full-time job, and training a therapy dog. Her work has appeared in various magazines, newspapers, and past editions of* Children's Writer's & Illustrator's Market.

the story was wrong, I decided that the publishers I was sending the manuscript to were wrong, and that it was just a matter of finding the right publisher.

Do you feel the joys of writing outweigh the downside of rejection? Can you tell me why?

Yolen: The two are separate. The joy I feel in writing has nothing to do with the hard and awful process of getting published.

Van Velde: Creating a story is hard work—but satisfying. Taking a passage (or a sentence, or a word) that's okay, but reworking, revising, finding a better way to say it—that's exhilarating. Having an editor validate my choices by paying for my words is lots of fun. And having kids tell me, "How did you look into my brain? How did you know how I think?" Wow!

Can you describe the most rewarding experience you've had in your career?

Yolen: I have had many wonderful moments—people who tell me their children have begun reading because of my books, or a woman whose mother recovered from a coma because of hearing my stories, etc. No one special moment.

Van Velde: I can't give one single answer here either. I loved winning the Edgar for *Never Trust a Dead Man*—very exciting. But a quieter moment was when I read a customer comment on Amazon about one of my short story collections. A reader said that at first she didn't like how the stories ended, but the more she thought about it, she realized that if they'd ended the way she originally wished, then they wouldn't have been as interesting or thought provoking.

Has there ever been a point in your career where you felt you could no longer believe in yourself as a writer?

Yolen: No. At the start of every new book (or when finishing a major project) there is always that tic: "Do I still have it? Will I ever write another book/story/poem?" But, of course, I recognize that as stupid and ignore it.

Van Velde: No. I sometimes get discouraged, but I don't lose all hope. When I read a really good book or hear a great author speaking, I sometimes think, "Who am I kidding with my stuff?" Or when I read a really bad book that has won a lot of acclaim for reasons that escape me, I get frustrated. But I get over it in both cases. In the long run, the good writer makes me want to be better. Even if I figure I'll never catch up.

What makes you continue to write?

Yolen: I write because the stories and poems and characters are in my head and have to come out.

Van Velde: I keep thinking of ideas I want to explore. When I read a story that makes me forget everything else (oops, sorry, no, dinner is not ready), I think, "That's what I want to do. I want to make people feel the way I felt when I was reading this."

Even now, do you still receive rejections for your writing?

Yolen: Got one just last week.

Van Velde: Absolutely. And I react to them the way I always have: If there's no comment, I send the manuscript out to the next publisher on my list. If there is a comment, I take some time to consider it. Sometimes I agree with what the editor is saying, and I make some changes; other times I figure, "Well, there's one editor who just didn't get it," and I send it out to that next publisher.

Do you ever take a break after a particularly hard rejection? Why or why not?
Yolen: Nope. That gives the rejection too much value and power in one's life.

Van Velde: Not that I hold a grudge or anything, but I do get mad more than depressed. I have been known to use the names of people who've ticked me off (including editors) as the villains, the oblivious blowhards, or the people who get killed in my stories.

How many times or for how long will you push a story receiving rejections because you think it's a winner?
Yolen: Twenty years? I just last year sold a book my agent and I had been attempting to place for twenty years. There are others.

Agents' Tips on Avoiding Rejection

Rejections are never totally unavoidable, but there are some things that will make agents/ editors instantly reject you. Here is a list of sure rejection triggers from agents Jennie Dunham and Barry Goldblatt.

Dunham's biggest submission turnoffs
- The letter comes addressed to "Dear Sir" (there are no men at her company), or to the agent before or after her name in an alphabetic listing. Also, people who address her by her first name when they don't know her.
- Handwritten notes.
- Explanations that friends, family, and students recommend the writing.
- "It's the next Harry Potter!" or comparisons to other well-recognized authors.
- Telling her that it will be a big seller and she'll be sorry if she turns it down.
- For picture books: "I'm hoping that you can help me find an illustrator since I don't know any. . . ."
- For novels: "I've written a fiction novel. . . ."

(Note: Do not send unsolicited manuscripts to Jennie Dunham. She accepts queries only.)

Goldblatt's pet peeves in submissions
- Not following submission guidelines.
- Misspelling his name.
- Sending multiple submissions or including any non-manuscript materials in the submission (dolls, food, etc.).
- Any submission with a cover letter that says any variation of the following: "My children/ grandchildren/fourth grade class/children at the local playground loved it!"
- An abundance of grammatical errors. (One or two small typos are passable, though writers really should make sure their manuscripts are perfect before submitting them.)
- Manuscripts with illustrations done by the author's young children or other unprofessional artwork.
- Single-spaced manuscripts and any other unprofessional behavior, which clearly indicates that, regardless of manuscript quality, he's never going to want to work with the writer.

Van Velde: There's no set time. I keep submitting as long as I'm excited by a project. *A Hidden Magic* was rejected 32 times. *The Conjurer Princess* didn't go out quite that often because there were fewer appropriate publishers to send it to, so it spent long periods of time in my file cabinet. Nine years after it was finished, it was accepted by Harper. (*Editor's note*: After the writer of this piece finished her article, she discovered that Yolen had edited five of Van Velde's books and desperately wanted to buy *The Conjurer Princess* but couldn't make it into a YA. Yolen was thrilled when it sold to Harper.)

But other projects have been out much less frequently. I'm satisfied enough to call it finished, to send it out; but after just a rejection or two, I think, "Well, no wonder it's being rejected." So I put the manuscript aside. Maybe, with time, I can settle for myself what's wrong. Or maybe, if I like the characters, I can eventually come up with a better plot for them. Or maybe the setting can be recycled into another story. I never throw anything out.

What makes you decide to drop a story?
Yolen: If I re-read it and see it has no value or I have written something else that supersedes it.

Van Velde: When, even if it's only been out a few times, I find it a burden to send out again, because I'm just not enthusiastic about it.

How important do you feel writing groups are for writers?
Yolen: Mine is invaluable. Others prefer to be alone in their work. Different strokes . . .

Van Velde: I'm a firm believer in writing groups. With a critique group, you can see what parts of your story make your group's eyes glaze over. They can tell you where they were confused, where they missed that your character was speaking sarcastically, where they guessed—too early—where the plot was headed. Writers understand each other as no one else can: the search for the perfect sensory detail; the procrastination when things aren't going well; the joy of that oxymoron—the "good rejection"; the frustration when a reviewer criticizes something that isn't pertinent. A supportive family is great, as is the support of non-writing friends, but the shared experience of writing makes support from other writers come at a whole different level.

Did your parents/teachers, and later your husband, always support your writing?
Yolen: My parents were both writers, so they were very supportive. I was the gold star kid in school for my writing. My husband has always been my first reader (and now my webmaster).

Van Velde: My parents always led me to believe that I could do whatever I wanted. My husband and daughter both still have a tendency to go to bookstores and rearrange my books to show them off to optimum advantage.

What would you say to someone who hasn't had that kind of support?
Yolen: Find someone to give you that support. Relative, friend, or in a workshop situation.

Van Velde: Writing is a hard life *with* the support of those close to you. You need quiet times to think and work details out; you need nurturing; you need tolerance for your mood swings those days the story is going well and those days it isn't. And it will probably take years—if ever—before you make as much money writing as you would at a regular job. It would be very hard to keep writing if your family didn't take you or your goals seriously, if they sabotaged you with interruptions, petty demands, lack of respect for what you do. Your question has depressed me because I bet a lot of wonderful writers have given up because they didn't have support.

Do you have any tips for writers to help keep up their morale?

Yolen: Look inward for validation, not outward. Take a hot shower after any rejection and tell off the stupid editor there, then dry off and move on.

Van Velde: Eat chocolate and read (not necessarily in that order). When you read a good book, one that whisks you away into another world, if you've got a writer's soul you've got to want to be able to do the same thing.

If you could give every new writer some piece of advice, what would it be?

Yolen: Value the process, not the product. Take joy in your writing.

Van Velde: Did I mention read, read, and read? Then try to analyze what it is that you liked about the story, and what you didn't like. How did that author suck you into caring so much about that character? What kind of foreshadowing would have made the too-coincidental twist work? If you thought a scene was boring, how could that have been fixed—fewer details, or more details that brought you into the story better? And remember, although selling a book to a publisher is wonderful, *that* isn't what makes you a writer. *Writing* is what makes you a writer. Actually writing. (As opposed to thinking about writing or talking about writing or making up mental reviews that would appear in *Publishers Weekly if* you wrote.) Finish what you write. Acceptance is just gravy.

Recommended Reading

Here are a few books to raise your writing morale when your work is rejected:

Take Joy: Essays on Writing, by Jane Yolen

The Right to Write, by Julia Cameron

The Courage to Write—How Writers Transcend Fear, by Ralph Keyes

Pushcart's Complete Rotten Reviews and Rejections, by Bill Henderson, Andre Bernard

The First Five Pages: A Writer's Guide to Staying Out of the Rejection Pile, by Noah T. Lukeman

When Size Matters: The Synopsis, Short but Power-packed

BY SUE BRADFORD EDWARDS

Page through your *Children's Writer's & Illustrator's Market* and note the numerous publishers who want a query letter and synopsis or a synopsis and sample chapters instead of a complete manuscript. Many writers pass over these publishers. Some don't know that a synopsis is simply a brief introduction that allows busy editors to judge whether they want to invest the time needed to read the entire manuscript.

Other writers know what a synopsis is—but not what it should include. As explained by author Kathleen Duey, "The trick is to communicate the character essence and event-logic of the book, the emotional arc of the protagonist, and a satisfying ending. Then stop. Anything that can be eliminated without weakening that purpose *should* be."

Still other writers don't understand why they should write a synopsis. Haven't they already crafted a complete manuscript? They need to realize how the process of writing a synopsis can diagnose potential problems within their manuscript.

The first step in solving all these problems is learning to write a strong synopsis.

And then it happened: plot without spoilers

When asked to describe their books, many writers launch into a blow-by-blow plot description. They recount every detail, no matter how minute, until their audience nods off. An overly detailed synopsis has the same effect. "A writer should explain the plot, but a blow-by-blow will bore the reader to tears—whoever it is," Random House Associate Editor Krista Marino says. "A general summary of the plot is needed, but I would suggest approaching the plot summary as one would approach writing flap copy for the jacket of the book. You want the reader to know what the book is about, but you don't want to tell them the entire story."

Avoid lengthy plot recitation with a narrow outlook. "A good synopsis will focus on overarching themes and character motivation," Candlewick Executive Editor Mary Lee Donovan says. Duey expands on this. "Follow the emotional arc of the protagonist," she says. "And include the plot events needed to make it vivid and easily understood." What does the main character want? Why? What must be done to get it? What stands in the way?

Author Gary Blackwood answers these questions in this excerpt from his *The Shakespeare Stealer* synopsis:

> Widge, the protagonist, is an orphan who's hired by a mysterious (and, yes, sinister) man named Falconer to copy down, in an early system of shorthand (which really existed), the whole text of Hamlet as it's being performed at the Globe Theatre. He's caught in the act, but his facility for lying saves him. He claims he's come there to be an actor and, to his dismay, the troupe takes him on as an apprentice. At first he sees this as just an

---

SUE BRADFORD EDWARDS *is perfecting her synopsis in St. Louis, Missouri. Her book reviews can be found in the* St. Louis Post-Dispatch. *Her articles for writers appear in* Children's Writer *newsletter, the Institute of Children's Literature yearbook and the SCBWI Bulletin. Visit her website at http://SueBradfordEdwards.8m.com.*

opportunity to copy the play more easily. But as he comes to know the members of the company, he begins to experience a feeling new to him—loyalty. For the first time in his life, he has made some friends. But he's also made a very dangerous enemy—Falconer. And as if his life weren't complicated enough, he finds himself having to play the role of Ophelia in a command performance before the Queen herself.

Blackwood doesn't tell how Widge meets Falconer, how he planned to hide long enough to record the play, or what lead to his capture. Still the reader knows enough of the plot and can identify the themes.

Highlighting Widge's emotional shift gives editors what they seek. "An editor will read and consider the synopsis in much the same way she would a complete manuscript," says Donovan. "In other words, she expects a taste of the emotional experience she'd get from reading the entire book." Pursue the character's goals, and emotions follow.

But how much detail is enough? "A synopsis should give the level of detail you'd tell someone over lunch, some friend, not completely close, who asked you what your new book was about. Enough of the plot should enter to get across the theme," says author Vicki Grove. Can you state your theme in one sentence? If not, you may need to give it some thought and rework your manuscript.

Test your plot summary by actually telling it to someone. "If you get halfway through," says Duey, "then hear yourself say something like, 'Wait, wait, I forgot to tell you that she follows her father to work one night in the first chapter and . . .' Whoa. Anything that makes you backtrack in your oral storytelling probably needs to be included in its proper sequence in the written synopsis." When you can relate the bare facts without backtracking, you've found the details you need.

Doing all of this with brevity takes practice and is incredibly difficult with your own story. "I'd advise writers to try to encapsulate the plot of a favorite book that is similar in scope and length to their story into one paragraph so as to get a better handle on how it can be done," Dial Senior Editor Cecile Goyette says. Practice this with several books and then try your synopsis again. Cut every plot element that isn't essential to give your reader the big picture.

If your synopsis feels choppy, fill in a few blanks. "A succinct and graceful listing of some

Enough Is Enough

Perhaps the most difficult part in writing a synopsis is achieving the necessary brevity. Simply stated, you want it to be as short as possible. When asked about length, the editors gave different answers. "Ideally, one page; two at most," Dial Senior Editor Cecile Goyette says. Hearing this, authors panic. How can this be enough to judge the merits of a manuscript? "We allow our longer submissions (such as chapter books or novels) to include a synopsis plus 10 pages of the text," Goyette says. "And that in concert is usually enough to determine whether or not the manuscript is something we may have an interest in." Many authors like Gary Blackwood successfully stick to a self-imposed one-page limit.

Other editors willingly read more—but not much more. "A synopsis for a middle-grade novel should be no more than a page, page and a half. Novels for older readers might require two to four pages," Candlewick Executive Editor Mary Lee Donovan says.

While editors vary on how much they'll read, keep it short. "I won't read through pages of summary," says Random House Associate Editor Krista Marino. "If I open a submission and find a lengthy explanation of what I'm about to read, I'll probably just give it a quick glance. If a writer decides to include a synopsis of her work outside of her cover letter, it should be brief and punchy."

of the plot events that fall between the pivotal scenes you must describe lets the editor know that the emotional arc is gradual, faceted, but keeps the focus clear," Duey says. "The character's emotional arc is the heart of the book." After all, character is central to the story.

Characters present the next hurdle in creating a brief synopsis.

Don't you forget about me: which characters to include

Just as the entire plot cannot be included, neither can every character. But who do you drop? Turn again to the main character's emotional arc for the answer. "The synopsis should touch upon characters that have primary influence in the main character's struggle," says Donovan. Duey agrees, "It makes sense to name as few characters as possible. Any character who is not key to the plot arc of the protagonist can be left out."

Look again at Blackwood's synopsis excerpt. He lists only three characters: Widge (the protagonist), Falconer (the antagonist), and the Queen. Though Widge certainly interacts with numerous actors at the Globe Theatre, none of them are named although their roles are understood. Look at your synopsis. Do you need to name each and every person in your protagonists sixth grade class? Cut anyone you can and generalize the rest.

Because of the synopsis' brief word count, scant information can be given about any character. "The reader of a synopsis needs a distillation of characters," says Donovan, "rather than a great many specific details about them." When asked how she condenses characters, Duey gave this example:

> *Shaken by the apparent suicide of the girl who had been her best friend since third grade, Trina is facing high school, her first real boyfriend, and her mother's growing attachment to a man she can't stand, in the worst possible way: alone.*

Much more than this comes out within the story. "The friend's name was Joey. She was brilliant and funny and beautiful and in despair over her father's mental illness," Duey says. "This might deserve a lot more ink in the book—but not in the synopsis."

Still unsure what to include? "I pretty much stick to the character trait or traits that are the basis of the story's conflict," Blackwood says. "For example, if the character is lost in the woods, the fact that he has no wilderness skills whatever is obviously important."

Because so many stories hinge on the characters' wants and fears, Grove's narrative focuses on these details:

> *Jess prefers the glow-in-the-dark stars on her bedroom ceiling to the scary, moving stars outside. And then she meets Lolly, who works the migrant stream and has never slept anywhere but under those scary, dancing stars—she loves them.*

What Jess fears has been shown, not told.

Examine your synopsis line by line. Is each character mentioned involved in the main character's emotional changes? Do you present only those details that drive the plot forward? Once you sort out the details, it is time to perfect your framework.

Open sesame!

While plot, theme, and character form the main body of every fiction synopsis, how to open the synopsis varies from project to project. "I like the unexpected and I love to see unconventional cover letters and synopses, so for me, normal openers and closers aren't really going to get my attention," says Marino. "Though it's different for everyone, I think most editors are hooked by things that are different so I would stress individuality, creativity, and confidence in your own written voice."

Duey's opening varies from synopsis to synopsis. "I always start with whatever propelled me into the project," she says, "usually the characters. It could be a conflictive plot event, or an unusual setting that begins the synopsis—once in a blue moon, some very clever, very short

Houston, We Have a Problem:
What Your Synopsis May Inadvertently Reveal

Even a well-written synopsis can be problematic, especially if you've chosen the wrong editor for your submission. "I can usually get a feel of a novel by the synopsis because generally it's written by the same person who wrote the book," says Random House Associate Editor Krista Marino. "Unfortunately, if I'm not intrigued or engaged by their writing style and talent, I'm sure I won't be by the manuscript itself."

An overlong synopsis hints at another potential problem. "If the author requires more than one to four pages to summarize their book, it may point to problems with a first draft," says Candlewick Executive Editor Mary Lee Donovan. "In other words, it may yet be finding its voice, its path, and its meaning. It might need trimming."

A story stripped to the basics is very revealing. "If you can tell by a synopsis that the author hasn't grounded the story and its main characters in a credible emotional reality, then the plot points are going to be less important," says Dial Senior Editor Cecile Goyette. "Also, I'm really hard-headed about logistics—a well-constructed fantasy has to be logical and convincing within its own construct. Since a synopsis has to take a more bare-bones approach and can't rely as much on style and other flourishes of language, any deficiencies in this regard are going to be more apparent."

statement of the theme that fascinates me." A strong hook is as essential in a synopsis as in a query letter or the manuscript itself.

The opening should also reveal some of what will come. "I start it out the same way I begin most books or stories or articles," says Blackwood, "by making a promise of some sort to the reader, letting him or her know what to expect." Here's the opening of his synopsis for *The Shakespeare Stealer*:

> *Deceit and disguise, sinister villains and swordplay . . .Sound like a classic adventure novel? I hope so, because that's the tradition I've tried to emulate in* The Shakespeare Stealer.
>
> *Widge, the protagonist, is an orphan who's hired by a mysterious (and, yes, sinister) man named Falconer to copy down, in an early system of shorthand (which really existed), the whole text of Hamlet as it's being performed at the Globe Theatre . . .*

The editor immediately knows this swashbuckling historic fiction focuses on adventure and mystery.

Don't just tell them. Give them a taste. "If this is a humorous piece, make the synopsis make the editor laugh a bit," explains Grove. "If it's high drama, make their hearts beat fast." Let the editor sample the romance, science fiction, or humor.

The opening must tell the editor more than what type of book it is. "A synopsis should open in a way that the editor knows immediately who the main character is, what the conflict or problem is, and a bit about the setting," says Donovan. Look at Blackwood's synopsis and the answers are obvious—Widge, stealing a play, Elizabethan London—all in three sentences.

A strong beginning must be followed by an equally well-crafted ending. "A synopsis should close with a clear explanation of how the main character has changed by the end of the book," says Donovan. Authors who fail at this should heed Goyette's warning: "Don't be cryptic, don't be cryptic, don't be cryptic," she says. "For me, the mission of a synopsis is not to tease but rather to provide straightforward information, conveying all major plot elements, especially the ending. It should avoid metaphor and instead favor clarity, simplicity, and precision. Too often authors try to tease by leaving out critical information, such as the ending." If you aren't being cryptic and your character's growth remains unclear, does your manuscript also fail in this regard?

Who, may I ask, is speaking?

As with the manuscript itself, voice in the synopsis is a vital part of grabbing and holding the editor's attention. And not only must it be gripping, it must mirror that of the novel. "I use basically the same sort of style I use in all my writing: I try to keep it clear, concise and conversational," Blackwood says. "As for tone, if it's a humorous novel, I try to reflect that in my prose; if there's mystery or adventure, I try to use lots of action verbs and atmospheric words." A quick glance at *The Shakespeare Stealer* synopsis reveals how he does this. *Disguise*, *swordplay*, and *apprentice* reflect suspense, danger, and a bit of history. What terms can you use to mirror your story's tone?

If you've tried to use specific mood-setting terms and the voice and tone still don't come through, do a little research. "A good warm-up to writing the synopsis is to read the jackets of favorite books," Donovan says. "Jacket copy is a selling tool, must tell a lot in little space, and must capture the tone, spirit, and style of the book. The synopsis, too, is a selling tool, and must tell the editor what she can expect if she were to request the entire manuscript." Note how the copy for a dark mystery differs from a light-hearted fantasy or a touching romance.

Then sit back, relax, and write. Yes, relax. "If the author has the talent to achieve a compelling and effective voice in her manuscript, she's not going to have much of a problem conveying this in a synopsis," says Goyette. Because once you know what to include, it's just a matter of practicing until you're happy with your synopsis.

So write synopsis after synopsis. Carefully select plot elements, characters, and character traits. When a brief, gripping synopsis flows from your fingertips, you'll know you have it right.

More Synopsis Tips

First and foremost, a synopsis is part of a package. "Synopses are sales tools that will be mailed to overworked people drowning in printed matter," Kathleen Duey reminds her fellow writers. "So make them easy to read and understand."

Clarity is key. "An editor will be looking at the writing in a synopsis," says Candlewick Executive Editor Mary Lee Donovan, "as a predictor of the author's skill and talent." Dazzle them with your best writing and don't forget the basics. "This is the first glimpse an editor has of a writer's work, so it should be error free," says Random House Associate Editor Krista Marino. A bad first impression does lasting damage while a good first impression encourages them to read on.

Also avoid over-writing. "I think it's hard for writers to step back from their stories and explain them in simple terms. I have problems with this myself when I'm writing catalog copy and flap copy," Marino says. "You love the story so much, and know all the subtleties so well, it's hard to separate the main idea from the details. Because of this, many writers don't know when to stop and they end up with a short version of the novel. Which is bad, bad, bad."

Belief in one's abilities is central to avoid over-writing. "Confidence in her story, her talent, and the value of what she has to say to young people is key to cracking the effective synopsis," says Donovan. "Only then can she relax and sell—not oversell—her work."

The Employee Within: Getting in Touch with Your Inner Corporation

BY KATHLEEN DUEY

Authors are self-employed. *Self employed.* Those words stir the heart, don't they? They imply risk, courage, self-reliance, self-determination, self respect—you can almost hear the soaring violins: *It'll be scary at first, but you'll run your own life. You'll be the boss! It'll be lunch time when you say it's lunchtime. You can work when the kids are at school.*

(two-beat dramatic pause) *You'll be able to work in your PAJAMAS!*

That's all true, of course. You will be your own employer. But you will also be your own employee—and you will have to play both roles well to succeed. When I ask writers in my SCBWI retreats and other workshops to identify their biggest roadblock—the thing that stands between them and writing success—the responses are overwhelmingly *not* about the writing itself. They are most often career/business concerns: how to find time to write; how to sell what is written; how to get family and others to recognize the importance of writing time; how to promote the books and run the career once they are published.

I have spent a lot of time trying to answer these questions for myself. I've come to think of my career as a group effort, except there is no group. No matter what kind of writing you do, whether or not you have an agent, you will still be self-employed, both Employer and Employee. So welcome to YouCorp. Let me give you the tour.

YouCorp's operations vary in size and scope from one writer to the next. Some write one book every other year; others write twelve in the same amount of time. Some write literary fiction, others focus on commercial success; some strive for both. The common denominator: At YouCorp, you are the Production Department, from senior executive to floor-sweeper—and every position in between. You will also oversee and staff four other major departments:

- Research & Development
- Sales
- Publicity, Promotion & Marketing
- Accounting

The whole operation, for most of us, is housed in one room, or on a desk in the corner of a living room or bedroom, or if you are just getting started, half the kitchen table, half the day. The departments overlap and executive focus will shift from one to another, but it is obvious that they all revolve around Production, so it seems best to start there.

PRODUCTION

Writing—creating books—is the center of your writing career. Obvious? At first, it sure is. Later on, that simple fact can get lost in the whirlwind. As needed, remind yourself of the center post of any writing career: The Work is everything. The Production Department—which is just

KATHLEEN DUEY *has published over 60 children's books. Her current projects include The Unicorn's Secret (eight titles for Aladdin); Hoofbeats (two quartets for Dutton/Puffin); The Academy of Magic (a trilogy for Atheneum); and The Faeries Promise (8 titles for Aladdin). She speaks at schools, bookstores, libraries, and writers' events nationwide. For more information, visit www.kathleenduey.com.*

another way of saying Your Artistic Output—is the heart of YouCorp and should be handled accordingly.

EMPLOYER: As boss, you want efficient, high-quality production. The more premium output, the more work to sell, which means more income, prestige, and growth. If production fails, you will see ominous signs: Dust on your keyboard; bank accounts shrinking; your mother-in-law describes your writing as a cute hobby. Or, as your career advances: Your editor expresses concern that too much time is going by between books. Within the bounds of solid art and craft, and without courting exhaustion, the more production the better.

People in my workshops often describe the writing process as beyond analysis, subject to the vagaries of the muse, beyond their control. The employer at MeCorp is appalled when her staff says anything like this. The employer at YouCorp might want you to rethink things, too. Hold a staff meeting. Here's what you can tell your employee:

Next time you have a great writing day, look for the reason(s) why. Did you work earlier than usual? Later? More hours at the keyboard? Fewer? Had you stopped in the middle of a scene the day before—and so had a "running start"? Did those character dossiers get you going? Was it meeting and interviewing the boy who has the same part-time job as your character? Did you sleep enough hours last night? Did you finally re-read *Bird by Bird* or *Writing Down the Bones* or *Art and Fear*?

Your formula for a great writing day will be different from anyone else's. Some need a steady supply of how-to-write books, enough sleep, silence while working, elaborate outlines. Others work best with rock music on the Bose™, food to pick at, and deadlines that force a daily page quota do or die. Some writers never discuss work in progress. Others need a critique group, two long-suffering friends, and a cousin to talk to daily.

Find out what makes YouCorp's Production staff more productive. Notice and attend fiercely to Production's needs—first, last, and always. Without it, YouCorp will collapse.

EMPLOYEE: You know the boss has a point. You could probably write more, and better. Make it an ongoing project to discover, honor, and support your process. Improve. Write deeper and better with every project you undertake. Write with a will, with every bit of intelligence and art you can muster. The boss will buy you books about writing, send you to seminars and conferences. Take notes, come home, and work hard. If you take your work very seriously, so will the Boss—and everyone else.

RESEARCH & DEVELOPMENT

EMPLOYER: For YouCorp to run smoothly over time, you need to have reasonably continuous creative output. If you finish each book, then sit quietly, absorbing life for months (or years) waiting for artistic inspiration, the slow pace will eventually undermine YouCorp's efforts. You should shorten downtime if you can—unless, of course, a long break between books is what Production needs in order to write better in the long run. (Check with staff on this.)

A lot of writers have more ideas than they can possibly write. I tend to. My problem—and I know a lot of writers share it—is remembering the brilliant ideas more than a day or two, especially if I am deeply involved in other projects.

Solution: Staff an R&D department. Make it clear to staff that all ideas are valued and viable until proven otherwise. Don't discourage what may often look like a waste of time. For many writers, development looks suspiciously like daydreaming.

EMPLOYEE: R&D is a very simple department at MeCorp. It used to be a box; now it's a file drawer. The file houses lots of sketches and notes on napkins; business cards with scribbled notes on the back; photos, newspaper and magazine clippings; printouts from the Internet world news sites with headlines like "5000-year-old Bronze Factory Discovered in Pompei," "Girl Admits Lie: Abduction Faked," "Meme Patterns Resemble Hydraulics," "Cat Sues Owner"; and whatever else catches my heart/humor/intellect. There is no attempt at organization.

Now and then, I paw through the stuff. It sifts itself. I put what most interests me into its own folder in my "idea and inspiration" file drawer. I add to the folders when something comes to mind.

You will find your own methodology. The point is to keep the backburners on simmer. For me, writing a page or two—the setting and a character's voice—will restart the flow months, even years, later.

Corporate Communication for the Self-employed: Nailing Down a Schedule

Employer: We have production problem. The novel hasn't moved an inch in two months.

Employee: Well, I have a day job, too, you know. And three days a week, I take Julie to soccer practice and Luke to T-ball after school. When we get home, there's dinner, homework, and I have to spend at least some time with my husband.

Employer: It sounds like you're a candidate for part-time, not full-time. We do flextime. But we need an accurate estimate. How much time can you give us?

Employee: I should work an hour or two every night at least. Three or four would be better. I just get so distracted and I'm tired by then and I really don't do my best work at night. But the mornings are tough because the kids are—

Employer: I apologize for interrupting, but I have to ask. Do you want this job?

Employee: Of course I do. I want to sell at least one novel a year and I have six picture books that are simmering and—

Employer: So when *can* you work?

Employee: (*long pause*) I can commit to an hour every evening and four hours on Sunday afternoons.

Employer: Great. We can work with that. Sunday can be for the novel and the shorter sessions for picture book development and whatever else.

Employee: That's a good idea. I can make novel idea notes all week on my day-job lunch hour.

Employer: Great. See you Sunday.

SALES

EMPLOYER: At first, let the Production Department have the spotlight. Let the staff learn to write well and get production rolling. Only then should marketing begin. Staff at YouCorp might excel at sales—if not, you might want to outsource ASAP. Because of exploding submission rates (and the too-often poor quality of manuscripts received) publishers rely on agents to winnow the piles; many accept manuscripts only from literary agents.

If the staff at YouCorp produces excellent, salable work, doesn't mind talking money, can (and will) execute queries and synopses, and perform market research, mailing, filing, and sales-conscious networking, you might not need to hire outside help. If not, you might want to focus on the work and find a good fit with a capable agent. Assess the time and stress spent against the 15% of your income most agents will charge. Then decide. Remember: No one will ever care about your career as much as you do, so stay involved. Track what is going on.

EMPLOYEE: If sales are to be in-house, at least at first, SCBWI and other writing organizations can save you years of wandering in the darkness. Handling your own sales effort can help you learn a great deal about the business. (*Accounting asks me to insert a reminder: Rejection slips are IRS-applicable documents. Keep receipts and records of costs: postage, letterhead paper; travel; phone, etc. Get advice from a tax expert and use every legal deduction you can find.*)

Don't waste your time and publishers' time sending work out blindly. To develop a sales sense and to form a network, talk management into sending you to as many conferences, workshops, and other book events as Accounting will approve. Talk to booksellers. Listen to editors' speeches carefully. Talk to teachers and librarians. Get as much information as you can. And don't lose sight of the needs of the Production Department. If sales is robbing the Production Department of time and energy it can't spare, find an agent.

PUBLICITY, PROMOTION & MARKETING

EMPLOYER: Finally! YouCorp sells its first book! It's time to celebrate. It's also time to think about promoting the book. Hiring a publicist from outside YouCorp is worth considering. For most writers though, it's too costly. Most children's authors end up setting up a Marketing Department. SCBWI and other organizations can help the staff get started with promotional ideas. Urge staff to get creative! If no one knows about your work, no one will buy it. This is a good time, when everyone at YouCorp is happy and excited, to break the best news of all: Author appearances are a staple of promotion.

Picture the staff lined up, facing the boss. Boss smiles: "Who likes to appear in public and give speeches?" (*no response*) ". . . Really?" (*no response*) "Well, draw straws or something because one of you has to learn . . ."

EMPLOYEE: The boss has made it pretty clear: You must find ways to make the public and the educational community aware of your published books and upcoming work. A website, postcards, appearances, and school visits are common promotional efforts. Read books about promotion and be creative. And learn to speak.

I had a 25-year history of panic attacks and was a two-puke speaker the first year—once before and once after. I am fine now, thanks. If I can learn to speak, you can. Join Toastmasters or another local group. Listen to others speak. Just as with writing, others' styles will inspire you to find your own. Find local speaking venues—volunteer at first to get practice gigs.

School visits are great fun. They can help pay the bills (Accounting will *like* that) and will help you build an audience (Promotion & Marketing will be happy.) Talking to readers will close the feedback loop. Kids will tell you what they love most about your work (R&D can use the information), and they will sometimes tell you things that spur book ideas (Production will thank you for that).

ACCOUNTING

EMPLOYER: YouCorp's Accounting Department will have to keep track of expenses; document travel, equipment, and promotion costs; and set some kind of budget for the year. Insist on sensible filing practices all year long. Without sacrificing a week of Production's working

---

The Five-Year Plan

The key to running a happy self-employment office is to be businesslike. Most businesses have a mission statement and a five-year plan. My mission statement is simple: I want to help children become and stay literate and leave the world a better place for my passing through it.

My first Five-Year Plan was three words: Make a living. My second Five-Year Plan: Continue to make a living. Get good at speaking and promote more. My third Five-Year Plan, written a few months ago: Write deeper and riskier. Continue to make a living.

Your goals and priorities are probably entirely different from mine. You can decide what is important to you and what is realistic. The sheer act of deciding, consciously, where you are headed, will help you get there.

time to worry about paper-sorting, accounting will have to prepare tax information, pay quarterly tax installments, and deal with other money and record keeping at YouCorp.

EMPLOYEE: Separate YouCorp from family/personal expenses. Open a bank account just for writing income—and the bank will keep income records you can rely on as a cross-check if needed. Consider using a single credit card for all your deductible costs: travel, entertainment, education, research, office supply/equipment, etc. Credit card companies sometimes provide a breakdown of expense categories at year's end.

Save *all* cash receipts in a file folder. I keep a folder for each trip I take. It holds receipts and badges, schedule, taxi receipts, plane tickets, log-notes, and so on, so that in the event of an audit, I have the original documentation to show. Contact a tax professional and learn what expenses are deductible—some may surprise you. If you work hard, work smart, and persist, YouCorp will prosper—and you will need all the deductions you can get!

Money Matters: Payment for Authors & Illustrators

BY JANIE BYNUM

After becoming published as a writer and illustrator, someone offered the advice "don't quit your day job." Wise words, but too late for me. I didn't hear—or appreciate—this sage advice until a couple of years *after* I started phasing out my freelance graphic design business to make more time for children's publishing projects. The bug had bitten.

I'm sure it wouldn't have mattered if I'd heard that advice at my first children's book illustration class or at my first SCBWI meeting. I tend to dive into a thing headlong if I'm passionate about it. No toe dipping. No gradual submersion. I like to think I can do almost anything I set my mind to. However, a payment schedule in the children's book industry is not something I can control.

If you must dive in, though (and if you are reading this, you are at least perched on the edge of that diving board), I will repeat that day job advice with conditions. Don't quit the job that provides dependable cash flow—*unless* you have an adequate financial cushion, enough paying projects underway, and/or some royalties coming in to sustain an existence you can live with.

THE WAITING BEGINS

So how does the Money Thing *really* work in children's publishing? When can you expect to get paid and by what type of schedule? There is no "regular" pay schedule, per se, in the children's book publishing industry (except for bi-annual royalty statements that—if you're lucky—come with attached checks). Each publisher has a slightly different method of handling contracts and payments, but with most, the basic process is similar.

Fingers crossed for a contract

Using fictitious Brilliant Publishing as an example, here is a general sequence of events that leads to an author or illustrator getting paid in trade picture book publishing.

First, you or your agent submit a manuscript to Brilliant Publishing. You wait. And maybe wait some more.

The Brilliant editor loves your story but there are a few things she would like you to revise before she takes it to a Brilliant Publishing acquisitions meeting. Up until a year ago, I had not been asked to revise a manuscript before a contract was offered; I am now. I'm hearing from other authors that this is happening to them, too, during these days of bottom-line book publishing. It even happens to more experienced authors with scores of titles.

This new practice of revisions-before-contract may be attributable to fall-out from the acquisition of publishing houses by bigger conglomerates who are putting more pressure on their editors to produce "blockbuster" books. As if there is some formula to a blockbuster. Predicting "winners" seems more like betting on a horse. You can do your best to breed a champion, then groom that horse for the big race, but it's anyone's guess as to who will place—let alone win.

JANIE BYNUM *is the self-supporting author and illustrator of* Altoona Baboona, Otis, *and* Pig Enough, *all from Harcourt. She has illustrated several picture books, including* Rock-A-Baby Band *and* Porcupining, A Prickly Love Story, *both from Little, Brown. Visit Janie's website: www.janiebynum.com.*

Janie Bynum kicked off the release of her latest book, *Pig Enough*, with a book signing at Barnes & Noble. In order to have any hope for success, authors and illustrators must be proactive in promoting their work. Bynum regularly participates in signings such as these, as well as school and library visits, to connect with her audience.

In the end, it's the Brilliant editor's job to sell your story to the rest of the publishing house. This is no small feat in today's publishing climate, even when armed with your great story and her innovative marketing ideas.

<u>You go back and forth via e-mail</u> (or overnight delivery, or, dread-of-dreads, snail mail). Finally, you and the Brilliant editor agree that this wonderful story is ready to go to the next acquisitions meeting. [Note: At many houses, acquisition meetings take place twice per month.] So, let's say the editor reads your story and the next meeting is a few days away. But many

other manuscripts are scheduled for presentation ahead of yours. So your story doesn't "go to acquisitions" until the next meeting.

Weeks later the Brilliant editor gets her chance to present your story and show her enthusiasm for it to the Brilliant Publishing acquisitions committee. This meeting may include: President, Publisher, Editor-in-Chief, Associate Editors, Editorial Assistants, Managing Editor, Art Director, Marketing Director, Sales Director, Special Sales Director, Subrights Manager, and Business (Financial) Manager. That's a big meeting of a lot of people who will help decide if your book meets their criteria for publishing.

Negotiation time

Finally, you get The Call (or your agent does) from the Brilliant editor. You are offered a contract of × amount. You (and your agent) consider the offer.

If the offer (advance plus terms) isn't quite as much as you or your agent expects, then it's negotiation time. Remember publishers are in this business to make a profit; it's how they afford to publish your book. They will make sure their assets are covered. And you need to do the same; this is your livelihood. You (with the help of a publishing attorney) or your agent negotiate the terms and come to a verbal agreement with Brilliant Publishing.

Brilliant Publishing has their Contracts Department draw up the contract. Most of the legalese is boilerplate (a standard contract they offer to all their authors and illustrators), but the specific points you negotiated (verbally, via phone or e-mail) will have been added or stricken (lines through those portions of the contract that you wanted removed).

Contract in hand

The contract arrives. You (or your agent) read the contract carefully to make sure all points are covered, all royalty and escalation numbers are correct, and all other terms are what you agreed upon. Escalation is the amount your royalties would increase should your book sell over a certain number of copies.

If the contract is acceptable, you sign the last page (initialing each page of the entire contract) and send it back to your editor at Brilliant Publishing (some publishers have you send directly to their contracts department).

Your Brilliant editor submits the contract to the contracts department who inspects it to ensure nothing has been changed since they issued the contract, all pages are initialed, and the last page is signed.

Show me the money

I'd like to tell you that an advance-upon-signing check is headed your way. And Brilliant Publishing usually sends payment immediately after the contract has been approved. But the staff member who handles the check disbursement could be on vacation. Or maybe your contract rests under twenty other contracts in this person's in-box. For authors and illustrators with literary agents, the check goes to the agency first so that they can deduct their fee. *Then*, that paycheck is sent to the creator of this Brilliant book.

So, up to this point, how much time has elapsed? You have no money in your pocket from this sale and no concrete idea of when a check will arrive. How do you budget your household expenses on such intangibles? This is where that financial cushion comes in handy. Ideally, when one starts a new business, it's smart to have six months' worth of income stashed away. Great plan, but few actually do it. Once the publishing bug bites, it's tough to wait until you have enough money to fund your new venture.

The check's in the mail

Congratulations! You received your first check! You've gotten either one-half or one-third of your advance on royalties (depending on the terms of your contract). An author/illustrator or illustrator-only could be paid another third upon acceptable finished sketches (which may take months since the revision/approval process varies) and another third upon acceptable finished art (more months). So, this Brilliant book project, from manuscript submission to last payment of the advance may have taken up to 18 months or more.

The illustrator's wait

Artists who illustrate for other authors bypass the original manuscript "selling" portion of the process, but have sometimes submitted portfolio samples to be kept on file in hopes that their style will fit the needs of the publisher—if not immediately, then in the future. The process of being selected to illustrate a book can take months or years.

In trade book publishing, authors who do not illustrate can wait years (yes, years) for an artist to begin illustrating their book. After an artist has been asked to read a manuscript and he or she accepts the job of illustrating it, a contract is usually negotiated shortly thereafter. So if we pick up the process at that stage, there are still many months from the acceptance call to money in the bank (not including the time the artist's samples may have been sitting in an art director's or editor's files).

Even after signing money is paid, maybe even after sketch money is paid, a project can get cancelled (or killed)—through no fault of the illustrator or author. If at all possible, try to get a kill fee guaranteed in your contract. And, make sure it's enough to cover your time should your project get canned. In today's volatile merger market and with some publishers filing for bankruptcy, as an illustrator, you don't want to be left holding the artwork for a project you cannot resell.

If you are an author/illustrator, you can submit that killed work elsewhere and possibly get it published. But, you spent a lot of time working on the project, possibly refusing other work so that you could focus on that project. So you should be compensated—fairly.

Then there are royalties (hopefully!) that are paid every six months—four to six months after a six-month sales period so that the publisher can account for possible returns. Returns are another challenging aspect of our industry. Megalo-bookstores can order huge quantities of books to fill their shelves, but if they over-supply and demand is too low (which frequently happens), they can return those books with no cost/loss to them. Any returns are deducted from actual sales made in the previous accounting period. Books that appear as "sold" on royalty statements may not have yet sold-*through* to the consumer. Until that book is in the hands of the consumer, it is not a completed sale.

Although it sounds a bit confusing, it's important for authors and illustrators to have a grasp of how the royalty system works. Don't rush out and put a down payment on that beach house just yet—at least not until you understand how the payout system works.

If you negotiated a higher advance for your book, it will take longer for the book to earn out the advance and begin generating royalties. If you received a lower advance, your book may earn out more quickly. But if the book doesn't sell, you will never make more than your advance. And, sales depend largely upon the marketing invested in a book—much of which is out of your control.

BOOSTING YOUR OWN BOTTOM LINE
Hit the road, Jack

An author or illustrator does have some influence in helping her books to sell, however. School and library visits expose your reading audience to you and your books. Speaking and signing books at state and national reading association conferences, teacher and librarian conferences, and booksellers' conventions helps get your books additional exposure and generates word-of-mouth buzz—all contributing to increased sales to some degree. Some editors say that they can look at an author or illustrator's book sales and tell whether and when they are doing visits—that there is a direct correlation between author or artist appearances and number of

Go with the Flow

One way to help keep the cash flowing as you illustrate a book is to invoice your editor or art director when you submit sketches or final art (according to how your pay-out is set up). While it's in your contract for your publisher to pay upon approval of art at these stages, editors and art directors juggle so many projects that a "reminder" can help keep the process moving.

If you're a casualty of the recent economic downturn and you don't have that day job to count on for financial security, or your career in children's publishing isn't established enough, you can find other sources of income that create quick cash flow—ideally doing what you love to do. Writers can freelance as copywriters for advertising and public relations firms or submit articles to magazines and anthologies that cover subjects they care about. Illustrators can freelance for these markets as well. Don't limit yourself to the children's market if you want to create faster and more cash flow. And, working in your field (art or writing, regardless of industry) helps hone your skills, making you a better writer and/or artist, and helping to increase your speed—which helps increase cash flow.

Many writers and illustrators work for educational publishers as well as producing trade books. In many cases, the jobs are fun and the writer or artist is paid well and swiftly. I love working on some of the quick assignments that can be completed in a much shorter time span than a 32-page picture book and where the check comes in just weeks after I complete the project. The focus of my career is trade book work, but these smaller projects and some graphic design work are what have helped keep my cash flowing.

books sold. (For tips on how to get school visit gigs see Get Booked: Creating Promotional Materials That Stand Out in a Crowd on page 81.)

Worldwide wonderful

Maintaining a well-designed, informative website helps your books reach even more people. Make sure you have your book covers displayed on your site at a size and quality that enables the viewer to enjoy the art and remember the title by visual association. If you make your covers too small (under 1½ inches, square), the book images may have little or no impact. However, you must make sure those images are optimized (Web lingo for as small as possible in actual file size, but retaining as much detail and information as to still be appealing), or your site will load slowly and many viewers just don't have the patience to wait. They'll move on.

Include links from your site to online booksellers (independents and the big guys) so that viewers become shoppers. Since many online purchases are made on impulse, linking to online booksellers is a great way to implement that process. (See What a Site! Creating Websites That Work on page 75 for more information.)

Plays well with publishers

Your publisher's marketing department will be happy to help with ideas to make your website a better marketing tool. Everyone supports increased book sales! If your editor hasn't given you a list of names within the company of who to contact for help with marketing, public relations, school visits, etc., just ask for one. Most maintain a printed reference sheet or an e-mail document with names, phone numbers, and e-mail addresses.

Publishers can also assist you in setting up paid appearances. Many publishers set up visits for you when they are contacted directly with a request for you to appear; some pass along the information for you to handle. But to make sure you get invited to speak at schools, libraries, etc., you need to advertise that you are available to do so. Many publishers have a visits brochure they make available to schools and libraries and/or a spot on their website; ask to be included. Also include visits information at your website. I've gotten many visit requests via my website.

While some aspects of this business are beyond your control, there is much you can do to help yourself and your bottom line. Learn to be a better contract negotiator. Help market your books. Rest assured; to publishers this is a business, not a hobby. It's your business, too. Money matters.

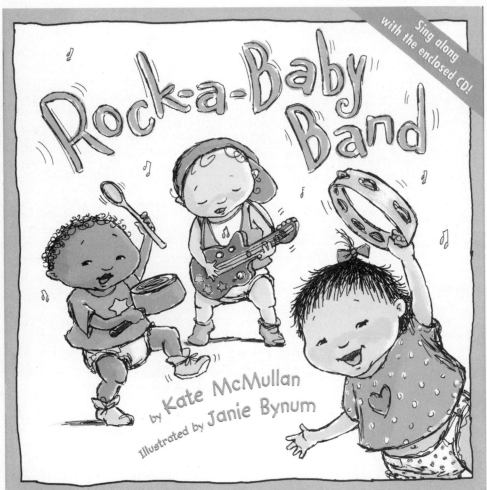

Wearing only her illustrator cap for the Megan Tingley release *Rock-a-Baby Band*, written by Kate McMullen, Janie Bynum bypassed much of the acquisitions process that happens when authors submit manuscripts to publishers. Generally, an illlustrator is commissioned only after the book has been accepted for publication.

Yellapalooza: Running a Successful Online Critique Group for Author/Illustrators

BY AGY WILSON

Some of my best friends, biggest cheerleaders, and most fault-finding critics are people I've never met. They are my on-the-Web critique group, The Yellowboard Community of Writers and Illustrators, or as we've lovingly dubbed ourselves, Yellapalooza.

At my dear husband's urging (or DH in computerese), I turned to the Web with the decision to fulfill my dream of writing and illustrating for children. The Internet is full of great resources and wonderful websites of authors and illustrators. I punched in names of my favorites. There are publishing companies' sites, writing and illustrating tutorial sites, as well as great online communities.

Among them is an informative site at www.write4kids.com, run by Jon Bard and Laura Backes of the *Children's Book Insider* newsletter. I found community on their message board. Ideas and information could be fast and furious, but rarely dull. Interesting discussions on "voice" and the various genres of children's literature, queries, cover letters, targeting submissions, *Children's Writer's & Illustrator's Market*, and critique groups all could be had there. And best of all, the people there shared my passions. In the beginning, I often felt like a mailroom kid listening to the V.P.s chat about how the company was run.

Illustrators even frequented and posted their work to the Yellowboard. It was a great mix from the well-published to the brand-newbie. I joined a few writing critique groups, and I also belonged to some illustrator critique groups. Still something was lacking. Megalomaniac that I am, I wanted to do it all. I wanted to write and illustrate.

GETTING STARTED

I'd actually tried another writing/illustrating group immediately prior to Yellapalooza. I didn't fit in with their working style and didn't care for the format. It was run as an e-mail group, which is not a bad thing. I was simply overwhelmed by the attachments and keeping track of the responses.

That's when it dawned on me: Dorothy, there's no place like home! The group of artists and wordsmiths frequenting the Yellowboard were already comfortable with each other. I feel computer-challenged on my best days. For our group to run smoothly, I knew it would be better to add a couple of other moderators to the mix. I recruited two other Yellowboard friends, Sarah Brannen (a featured SCBWI artist) and Elsbet Vance; we put a shout out and got a good response. We also invited a few members that we'd known from other areas of the Internet, and The Yellowboard Community of Writers and Illustrators was born.

AGY WILSON *writes midgrade and young adult stories and writes and illustrates picture books. She also co-moderates the critique group for writers who are illustrators (or is that illustrators who are writers?), Yellapalooza. For more information about the group and its process, check www.yellapalooza.com. She lives in Maine with her husband, two daughters, and a passel of pets.*

"Field Mouse Thanksgiving," a watercolor by Yellapalooza group member Sarah Brannen, was the Featured Artist Illustration for November/December 2002 on the Society of Children's Book Writers and Illustrators' website. Brannen was the runner-up for the 2003 Don Freeman Memorial Grant-in-Aid (given by SCBWI) for her book *Catsmill.*

We have three published members: Lisa Kopelke, author/illustrator of *Excuse Me!* (Simon & Schuster, 2003), Meghan McCarthy, author/illustrator of *George Upside Down* (Viking Children's Books, 2003. See First Books: Illustrators & Author/Illustrators on page 112.), and established illustrator Charles Jordan, with many credits to his name, including *Rough and Tough Charley*, by Verla Kay (Millbrook, 2004). Other members include Kathy Manchip, Rob Lak, Zeborah Loray, Kristie Anderson, Lauren Francis, Michelle Metty, Deanne Bellingham, Cindy Iannaccone, and moi.

Groups don't always gel; individual styles, goals, and characters vary. Trust is an issue, too. You're sharing your heart and life's work—and many creatives worry about copyright issues. When starting critique groups, there are also questions of how dedicated members will be and whether they'll get along personality-wise.

Because our group had prior online relationships, we knew some of these answers going in. We recognized everyone has strengths and weaknesses. When we formed our group, we didn't establish a prerequisite that members must be published and didn't need to review each other's work prior to acceptance. Most of us had already seen and read snippets of each other's work from the board. It's a personal decision whether a group has a skill litmus test. I like the gamut—a mix of abilities. Feedback from others experienced and new, especially viewpoints not constricted by too many "shoulds," can often lead to thinking outside the box—a desirable quality in this field.

The newbies get great hands-on experience, as well as a nudge—what I consider a self-directed nudge—to do their best. The more knowledgeable receive at least two things. Through sharing opinion and advice, veterans must think something through, explain, and show, which ultimately strengthens their own work as well as others'. The second benefit is invaluable personal contact. Most writers and illustrators lead a solitary life, so online communities and message boards become the virtual office cooler. Writing and illustrating is fraught with rejection, questions, and frustration at times, even if you're published. Having people who not only understand those issues but also might have a few solutions can mean the difference between continued success and finding a new career pursuit.

RUNNING THINGS

Once we assembled our group of illustrators/writers, the next step was to find the best way to conduct group business.

There are, of course, in-person crit groups. But with transportation, family, time, or place constraints, it's not always possible to join an in-person group. For our group, with far-flung members from New England to Nevada and Oregon to Canada, an in-person critique group was impossible.

For the day-to-day activities of our group, we use MSN groups. It's got great chat features for our chat needs, including a document section for writing and a picture section for our works-in-progress, and we can organize the message board into subcategories.

Lycos has groups features but is persnickety with uploading graphic files—not the best choice for a illustrator-oriented group.

Yahoo's plus sides are that you can keyword search the archives and hotlink a graphic file to the group. Their user service isn't as good as MSN, and the sites can go down for days. We are a small and fairly active group, so Yahoo's archives and graphics weren't as important to us as the organizational and chat features of MSN.

Some groups send attachments and place text (picture books are relatively short, the majority

Due out next year, *Show Dog* is the second installment in Meghan McCarthy's two-book deal with Viking. In addition to using input from Yellapalooza members, McCarthy relied heavily on research to get a feel for the book's subject matter. She watched dog show videos, read tons of dog books, and visited Internet sites. Read about her first publishing experience in First Books: Illustrators & Author/Illustrators on page 112.

being within the 100- to 1,000-word range) in the body of the e-mail. The drawbacks to this method are that it can clog up your e-mail, it can be difficult to keep straight, and it doesn't really encourage friendship and "chat."

There is no perfect way to run an online critique group, especially when dealing with graphics over the Web, so you have to pick the most effective or least frustrating for the needs and desires of your group.

ESTABLISHING RULES

Figuring out the rules for the day-to-day running of your group is an important step. These are our group rules:

1. Have fun!
2. No flaming. We ask that politics and religion not be discussed unless they pertain directly to the piece you are working on.
3. Criticism should be meant to help the artist/writer. The best way to critique work is to point out good aspects of the piece first and then give suggestions as to what could make it better or discuss what doesn't work and why. Be kind, but honest. Your true opinions will be more helpful than pats on the back.
4. Accept criticism with grace. You may hear things about your work that you don't like or don't want to hear, but if you can't handle gentle shredding from friends, this may not be the business you are meant to be in. Editors and agents will be shredding your manuscripts and artwork too, and they may have to be a lot more brutal.
5. Share what you can when you can, but please don't post something every day for the group to critique. Emergency crits are okay, but too many pieces at once can be overwhelming to the group. Please do your share and critique others as much as you ask for critiques.
6. The moderators reserve the right to silence or ban members who abuse the list or the other members on-or off-list. We want this to be a comfortable, safe place for everyone to share their work without fear.
7. Since ours is a closed, unlisted group, posting your work here does not constitute publication. Copyright of all posted work belongs to the author/illustrator. Posted work may not be copied or reproduced without express written permission of the author/illustrator.

By setting out the ground rules (many Internet communities have FAQs and manners and procedures they post on a regular basis) everyone knows what to expect going in. Perhaps your group would like to have a set time for critique, rules for what and how to submit, or a rule that each member needs to critique so many pieces a month to stay active. We prefer to be pretty laid back, and it's worked well for us.

WHEN CRITIQUERS CLICK

So how did we get from The Yellowboard Community of Writers and Illustrators to Yellapalooza? There's something magical that happens when a crit group "clicks." You become friends—support and resources, for sure; a shoulder to cry on; and people with whom you can share some of your sillier career fantasies and moments.

With two members' books making their debut simultaneously, it was easy to fantasize about success for all of us. Being writers, the "what-ifs" take over. What if we all had books published? What if we could all promote our books together? What if children loved our work as much as J.K. Rowling's—well, at least almost? Or better yet, what if we toured like all those rock groups for Lollapalooza (or, more aptly, Homer Simpson's Hullabalooza)? Thus, we became Yellapalooza. Silly, yes, but a great way to break up pre-publication jitters and keep us motivated.

The art is in the group's balance. We are focused on our goals, but we also care for each other, our successes, and difficulties. Seeing each others' foibles also has kept the newer writer/illustrators in the group from being awestruck with the more skilled members.

Lisa Kopelke was featured in the *2003 Children's Writer's & Illustrator's Market* First Books article for *Excuse Me!*, (Simon & Schuster Books for Young Readers) a colorful picture book that follows a loveable frog with a belching problem as he learns some manners. Frog and his friends return with the Fall 2004 release of her sequel, *Tissue Please!* Kopelke is still working on the illustrations, and describes *Tissue Please!* as "another humorous adventure in manners."

Yellapalooza co-founder Agy Wilson relies on feedback from her online author/illustrator critique group to help her perfect pieces like this colored pencil illustration, the last page of her unpublished work-in-progress called *After Everafter.* "It's kind of a Duc de Berry meets Chuck Jones fractured fairy tale," says Wilson.

© 2003 Agy Wilson. Reprinted with permission.

STAYING MOTIVATED

One of the hardest things to do in this business is to stay motivated, so as a group we provide optional monthly challenges. We switch back and forth from writing to illustrating, because as author/artists, we must be strong in both areas. Some of our challenges have included drawing body parts to express emotion, creating backgrounds only, and writing killer opening paragraphs. We also gear the challenges towards real-life projects, whether it's a member's deadline or a contest.

It's imperative to keep making new art, writing new pieces, and perfecting your craft. In tackling our monthly challenges, it's fun to see how different writers and illustrators interpret the same problem. It's also a great way to identify areas that need work and establish deadlines for new material. Motivation is easy; the group's energy keeps the momentum going.

We help each other look for legitimate contests, new contacts, and other opportunities. It's extremely difficult to make a living solely from your book proceeds. Some of us supplement with design work, architectural work, illustrating other's projects, author visits, and Web work. We bring those experiences and our editorial contacts to the group.

FROM CRIT GROUP TO PUBLISHER

All of our activities do no good unless we actually submit work to publishers. Our illustrations and manuscripts are stronger for having gone through the critique process. We share our dummy-making techniques and help each other find appropriate houses for each submission.

Being an author/artist is one of the hardest ways to break into the publishing business. But it can be done, as witnessed by some of our group's members and the close calls of others. How does one succeed? Do your homework. Make your submission the best you can make it. Let it sit for a while before you submit it. Luck, perseverance, and support all play a part. And of course, if you don't have a great crit group like mine, why not start one?

Crossing the Great Water:
Co-editing an Anthology from Afar
(& Other Collaborative Efforts)

BY ERZSI DEÀK

Setting out to compile an anthology can be a daunting task (starting any book can be daunting!), but sharing the job can make it easier, more rewarding—and present new challenges. Time difference and distance are but two of these challenges.

Today, you could put together a joint book project from anywhere in the world on your cell phone. And if books like M.T. Anderson's *Feed* foreshadow the truth, in a few years, you'll merely think and the computer chip in your brain will send your sentences and paragraphs to your collaborator and editor. We aren't there yet, but technology is zooming and making working together from afar easier than ever.

Little did Kristin Embry Litchman and I know when we prepared the proposal for *Period Pieces: Stories for Girls* (HarperCollins 2003), that our computers, the Internet, and each other would become our next of kin.

Collaboration is a kind of marriage. Kris and I, happily, enjoyed working together and produced a book we are proud of—and we still like each other! (See advice from Jane Yolen and others in the sidebar The Keys to Collaborating on page 73.)

We started working on *Period Pieces* after we met at a Society of Children's Book Writers and Illustrators (SCBWI) retreat in Texas. At one point during a break, discussion turned to life's landmark experiences. (If you get a group of women around a table talking about life, these things come up.) The stories were funny, poignant, horrifying.

Both Kris and I saw the beauty of the idea.

Back in Paris, I nagged everyone who'd told a story in Texas to send me a written version. Kris offered to co-edit. We were on our way.

THE INTERNET

How did writers ever survive without the Internet? It's about 4,000 miles from my apartment in Paris to Kristin's place in New Mexico. But I prefer to think in terms of hours and which day I'm operating in. France is eight hours later than New Mexico and six hours later than New York (where our editor Rosemary Brosnan was). During the making of *Period Pieces*, I was always a workday ahead of Kris and Rosemary. Happily, even with the miles and time differences, the Internet made collaboration between us more immediate. And, whether writing an

ERZSI DEÀK, *a journalist for more than twenty years, has covered fashion and children's features from Alaska to San Francisco to Paris. She has tramped the Alaska Pipeline looking for environmental problems; worked as a camp counselor managing the craft hut; and does dishes and windows, when she has to—always with a writer's eye. She is the International Coordinator for and sits on the Board of Advisors of the Society of Children's Book Writers and Illustrators. She lives in Paris, France, with her husband and three daughters. Most recently, her story, "Wild Strawberries," appeared in* Lines in the Sand: New Writing About War and Peace *(from Frances Lincoln UK and the Disinformation Company US).*

invitation letter to a potential contributor or negotiating a comma between the three of us, the Internet was key in making this project as seamless as it turned out to be. We were strewn around the world from Texas to Paris to New York to California to New Mexico, but today it doesn't matter if you are down the street or across oceans. Whether by modem or sophisticated satellite hookup, you are connected. For us, the Internet was our link to each other, all the writers, and the publisher.

A COLLECTIVE VISION

Kris and I both realized that women wanted to tell their stories and that girls and women of all ages wanted to hear them. On that premise, we sought stories that were timeless as well as giving a taste of days past (while I adore history, not all adolescents want to hear how it was when their parents were young). Originally we started out with short, thousand-word testimonials, but as the stories came in, we realized that the initial idea, the testimonial, was the kernel, the jumping-off point, and that the writers were diving into wonderful, full-bodied stories.

For the proposal, Kris and I bounced ideas around and edited the first submissions until we had a strong package. As Kris says, "We nagged and pushed, and finally got a group of eight stories together a year later to make up a proposal. We wrote our own stories and sent them to each other to edit, worked with the writers on their stories, and wrote a proposal letter and introduction. We did all this by e-mail—tremendous back-and-forth between Erzsi in Paris and me in New Mexico."

THE PROPOSAL

A year after that first meeting, we sent the proposal as a multiple submission to five editors. One house had a completely different vision (focusing on famous people). Another sent a rejection to "Mr. Deàk." Another never got back to us. Then it was between two publishers. Finally, Rosemary Brosnan at HarperCollins won the deal. Of the original eight stories in the proposal, only half were accepted by the publisher. From there, we invited other writers to participate. "It was like submitting artwork and text for a picture book," Kris says. "There's always the chance that one or the other might be accepted, but not both."

CONTRIBUTORS

Two years into the project, Kris and I met with Rosemary in New York to draw up a list of potential contributors. Initially, from the wish-list of authors, we were encouraged by the publisher to post letters to them. Then it was a year of eliciting submissions and swallowing rejections (from writers!). We found, however, that regular mail was too slow and we had a better percentage of acceptances from people we e-mailed—writers we knew, others who had worked with Rosemary, or those we had admired from afar. As soon as Rosemary was in the loop, our e-mail net grew. Aside from J.K. Rowling's gracious, "Sorry," and Joan Bauer winning a Newbery Honor so she had to bow out due to time constraints, we succeeded in interesting the majority of invited authors in the project.

And then there weren't any slots left.

We reveled in the empowering and often hilarious stories we received. "As the stories came to us," Kris says, "we made editorial suggestions and sent them to Rosemary. This process lopped over into the third year, which finished with lots of panicky rewrites, re-edits, line edits, galley proofs. We sent almost daily e-mails back and forth for about three years." It was only after the book was put to bed that I discovered the change-tracking options in Microsoft Word!

While we collaborated on any little written thing in the making of *Period Pieces*, as in any marriage, each of us had a different role in addition to editing and giving our opinions. Kris took on the administrative side of the anthology, as she was in the States and this was a book for the American market. She sent out all the snail mail—invitation letters and permission forms we cobbled together—and also handled the financial side, writing the checks and the 1099 tax

Period Pieces: Stories for Girls
STORIES FOR GIRLS
selected by **ERZSI DEÀK** and **KRISTIN EMBRY LITCHMAN**

"An honest, touching, sometimes hilarious collection," says *Booklist* about the new short story anthology *Period Pieces: Stories for Girls* spearheaded by Erzsi Deàk and Kristin Embry Litchman. Newbery Medal winner Linda Sue Park, Dian Curtis Regan, and Rita Williams-Garcia are among authors who shared short stories about girls' first periods. The seeds for the book were planted when Deàk and Litchman got to talking at a Society of Children's Book Writers and Illustrators retreat. What followed was a long distance collaboration across continents and oceans.

forms for each contributor. I was already working on publicity, marketing, and potential cooperative advertising approaches and preparing mailing lists and reviewer lists. (We were very happy with one such query that turned into a cooperative program with Proctor & Gamble's website, www.beinggirl.com.)

Throughout the entire project, Kris and I worked closely with Rosemary. Our official titles were "anthologists," rather than "editors." On the one hand, this was liberating, because Rosemary had the final say (though listened as carefully to us as we to her). On the other, Kris and I were forced to step back and allow the baby to grow as it would.

"As an editor, it was so interesting for me to work with anthologists who were, in effect, also acting as editors," says Rosemary. "Erzsi and Kris made very astute editorial comments and suggestions. And for me, working on the anthology offered an opportunity to see how two writers would approach editing various stories. Editors almost always work alone, and so collaborating provides a valuable experience for an editor. We get a chance to 'spy' on someone else's editorial work and learn from their opinions!"

Through collaboration, we drew on each other's strengths and made the strongest book possible.

COMPROMISE

Along the road to seeing *Period Pieces* in print, Kris and I spoke with one voice when discussing anything about the book. But compromises were necessary. Not so much between each other; throughout we were aware of our collective vision even when a couple of debates arose. It was more about seeing *Period Pieces* morph into the book it actually became. We had originally envisioned the book as a hands-on memoirs volume that would entertain and enlighten girls through the ages. But it was really when Rita Williams-Garcia's story came in that the potential for Story (with a capital S) became clear. From then on, it became a goal to provide more than anecdotal notes on the lives of oneself or others, to really provide a book with depth as well as humor and memoir. And the great stories kept coming in.

For a book that started out being about girls getting their first periods, the variety was enormous and emphasized the benefit of collaboration.

Period Pieces contributor Cynthia Leitich Smith notes: "I was glad to say 'yes' to submitting a story for consideration, and I made a point of telling my grandma about it in our weekly call. She said, 'Good heavens, child. You're going to write that and put it in a book? Why, in my day, nobody even talked about such things.' I very much wanted to do a story that involved a boy, perhaps because period-talk is usually reserved for women and I wanted to offer a different slant. Adolescence in all its awkwardness is, after all, a dual-gender experience."

Contributor Johanna Hurwitz points out an important quality of the writers in *Period Pieces*, who in many ways are all collaborators: "The contributors to *Period Pieces* have ages covering a large span of years. I'm one of the older authors in this volume because I grew up in the 1940s, long before people had TV in their homes or microwaves, computers, cell phones, CD players, etc. When I was growing up we lived in dread of contracting polio, and even measles and whooping cough could lead to disastrous complications. Times have certainly changed. But wherever and whenever a girl grew up, there is one common experience that she'll share with every other female on this planet—and that is getting her period. Not every woman will get married or have children. Not every woman will go to her senior prom or have siblings. But this one experience is a constant and will remain so forever. (Unless science has a surprise in store for all of us!)"

Getting boys into the stories notwithstanding, the biggest challenge and potential compromise was the title. At one point, noises were made for *Join the Club*, but Kris and I were stuck on *Period Pieces*. We were willing to contemplate compromise, however, so we drafted a list of some twenty other titles, but in the end, *Period Pieces*, with its double entendre, remained our top choice.

"Erzsi and I favored *Period Pieces* from the day we were swapping stories nearly four years before, but it took a while to convince some of the HarperCollins people (who were concerned that girls might be embarrassed to carry around a book with the word "period" in the title). They added *Stories for Girls* as a subtitle, and we were all happy!" says Kris. And, I like to add, the subtitle keeps the book out of the antique furniture section.

Most books show one author on the cover, sometimes two—an illustrator, a writer, possibly like Kris and me, co-anthologists. But books aren't borne alone. Behind every good writer there's a mother, a writing group, what happened at the office or the grocery store, or a best friend. Collaborating on an anthology leads the anthologists to a treasure trove of writers and their stories.

Behind every good book there is the writer (and her entourage), the editors, the publishers, the proofreaders, the designers, the printers, the artists, the marketing, publicity and sales teams, and the booksellers and librarians. Reading a book may be a solo act when read silently, but

The Keys to Collaborating

Whether you're collaborating on an anthology, novel, article, or other writing or illustrating project, there are a few simple keys to collaborating successfully:

A Collective Vision. Collaborating means cooperating, and the key to a collaboration is having a collective vision. Know what you and your collaborator want as an end product and work toward that goal.

Establish Roles. Decide who does what and when. Make a timeline, if that helps you.

Compromise. Be willing to give and take with the collective vision in mind.

Research. Before setting out to do an anthology, do your research: Look at market guides like the one in your hands. Check out catalogs, libraries, bookstores. Talk to librarians and knowledgeable book salespeople. A good librarian can tip you off on a great trail to follow or help keep you from wasting your precious time.

Leave Your Ego at the Door. Author and often-collaborator Jane Yolen has a good idea of what it takes to collaborate. Her words of wisdom? "Work out ego things ahead of time: whose name goes first, who has final pass, etc. Otherwise expect to forfeit a friendship. Be businesslike in the business arena and friends everywhere else. Don't hold back hurts. They fester and go gangrenous. Do find a friend and play. It is simply an exhilarating experience."

Bruce Coville and Yolen collaborated on the book *Armageddon Summer*. "I think one of the important things for us," says Coville, "was that we had clear boundaries, made easier by the fact that we were writing in two separate voices. So even though we were constantly reading and editing each other's work, we also had a measure of final say on our own sections. This is a very different style of collaboration than when you are both working on the same text, of course. Whichever kind of collaboration you engage in, mutual respect and a sense of humor will help you survive."

Revel in the Opportunity. Kris Litchman and I, along with editor Rosemary Brosnan, brought different talents and strengths to the editing table, just as two different writers will bring different slants and possibilities to the manuscript.

When Yolen and Coville collaborated, acknowledging the 500 miles between them, their plan was to communicate through e-mail as well as send chapters to each other through regular mail. Bruce did drive the distance to Jane's for a session of "dueling keyboards." This allowed the two voices to speak to each other even more immediately—and they managed to draft half the novel in one week's time. "Writing *Armageddon Summer*," says Coville, "was an incredibly exhilarating experience."

when read aloud, or passed from one to another, it becomes an ongoing collaborative work.

Collaborating with Kris and then with Rosemary and the writers on *Period Pieces* was one of the best editing experiences I've had wearing my professional editor's hat. It was a pleasure to share ideas, opinions, and comments in the process of collaboration. And despite the time differences and the miles between us, through collaboration we were able to bring together an anthology made richer from each individual's involvement—and a collection of stories woven into a fine latticework of tales relevant to girls ages eight and up.

What a Site! Creating Websites That Work

BY ROXYANNE YOUNG

I once had a woman tell me she would rather face a firing squad than build her own website. "No way I can do it," she said. "I don't know anything about building websites." Today, only six months later, she's managing her own online bookstore, and quite capably, too. How did she do it? Well, it didn't take a firing squad. She recognized that her business needed an online presence if it was going to grow, and because of that, she was willing to learn.

The same is true for any business, including children's writing and illustration. Ten years ago—even five years ago—it was enough for writers and illustrators to list their address, phone number, and maybe a fax number on their business cards and letterhead. Most were satisfied with a promotional postcard, one-page flyer, or a tri-fold brochure with a bio, a black & white picture, and a photocopy of their book cover (because, really, who can afford color copies?). These days, though, more and more writers and illustrators are finding that a professional website is a crucial element of their marketing efforts.

Anything you can put in a brochure, you can put on a website, but with more information and better quality graphics, including full-color pictures and book cover art. You can also change this information at will, so you can make sure your content is up to date without incurring new printing fees.

Websites are simply the most cost-effective means of self-promotion available to small business owners and professionals. The good news is that with all the new design tools available for nonprogrammers, the site you create can reflect your creative genius as much as anything you put on that blank page that faces you at the beginning of any new project.

Do you need a website?

One of the questions I'm asked most by newer writers and illustrators is "Do I need a website? My book won't be out until next year." I say yes, you do, but probably not until about six months before your book is scheduled for publication. That gives you time to get some relevant content up on your site, settle on a site design you like, and work out any kinks in the text or pictures. It also gives the search engines a chance to find you and get you listed in their databases. If you wait until your book is out, you're missing some prime promotional time, as the search engines can take several weeks to get your site listed, even when you submit your domain yourself. It also gives you time to get some reciprocal links set up. (More about these critical marketing tools later.)

Getting started: make a plan

The first thing you need to do is determine what you want your website to do. What do you want it to say about you? Who is the intended audience? What are they going to want from you? What do you need to give them in order to keep them coming back again and again?

ROXYANNE YOUNG *is Editorial Director of SmartWriters.com and co-founder of SmartReaders, Inc. and 2-Tier Software, Inc., where she was chief designer of the Professional Writers Website package. Contact her at Roxyanne@2-TierSoftware.com.*

Consider this a virtual professional résumé you're presenting to the world. You want it to be polished, organized, and informative. It should reflect your personality and prominently display your work for all the world to see. Visit other author and illustrator websites and take notes about the design elements you like and those you don't.

What is a professional website?

A professional website is your online résumé, an extension of your professional life, and as such, you should present your very best work in a sharp and easily navigable site. It can be as simple as a single page with a photo of you, your contact information, and a few samples of your work, or you can create an entire portfolio and add all sorts of dynamic applications, complete with a guestbook, calendar, opt-in newsletters for your fans, 360-degree view of your office, online games, and much more.

Above all, the focus must be on your content. You want site visitors to remember your work, not your cool page layout. If they come away with a bigger impression of your background graphics than your book titles, you've defeated your purpose.

CONTENT YOUR SITE MUST HAVE
Welcome/home page

This is your best chance to make a good first impression. You want it to immediately give your site visitors the impression of what they can expect from you and your website. It's a good idea to have some kind of photo of yourself and your latest book cover or the magazine cover where your most recent article is published, plus a brief list of site features they should be sure to see.

One important thing to remember about websites is that the shorter the text block, the more likely it is to be read. Web readers generally like bulleted lists and short paragraphs. It's just easier on the eyes. Not that you can't put longer text blocks on other pages, but try to keep the home page text short and simple to read.

Keep your power words up front. Make it easy for people to find the relevant content they're looking for.

Bio/About Me Page

The main reason people come to your site is to learn more about you. Maybe you do a lot of school visits—those students and teachers seek out your site to see what they're in for. Maybe a kid is doing a book report and wants to know more about why you write about dinosaurs or football or violence at home. Maybe someone just picked up your series on dragons and loved it and just wants to know more about how you came to be so darn creative.

List all of the cool stuff about you. Are you a rock climber, an adventurer, a world-traveler? Do you like to skateboard or take pictures? Did you win a contest for being the best kite flyer in the eighth grade? Your site visitors want to know about the things that inform your writing. This is your chance to make a more personal connection.

Portfolio/My Works Pages

It's a good idea to have a page dedicated to each work and work-in-progress. It helps you focus on promoting that particular work. Include what inspired the story or illustration, quirks of your research trips, photos and illustrations from the work, etc. Include a short excerpt if it's a work-in-progress. Point visitors to a site where they can buy the book, too.

Contact Page

Give your site visitors easy methods to contact you via e-mail, an online guestbook, through your publicist or publisher, or even via regular mail, although we caution people not to put a home address online.

Optional content

You can include, but are by no means limited to, the following:

- Sample chapters and book jacket art to promote your upcoming releases or backlist titles. Fans will put their favorite writer's next release date on their calendars months ahead of time. Be sure to get permission before posting any copyrighted content, like cover art, online.
- Links to professional colleagues, organizations, resource sites you've found helpful, etc. Make sure your professional colleagues link back to you, too; this is a reciprocal link and it helps you to rank higher in search engine results. The more reciprocal links you have coming in to your site, the higher your relevance rating, and the higher you will be listed on the results pages.
- A printable résumé or sample art sheet (saved as a PDF document).
- Educational supplements for your published works. If there is any chance your book could be used in the classroom as part of a curriculum unit, or even just for fun as supplemental reading material, put up a teacher's guide for it.
- Current writing credits. Freelancers take note: Editors actually do come and look when you send them a query letter with your Web address included, so make sure you've got a current list of writing credits posted, complete with links to any newspapers, literary journals, magazines, e-zines, or other online publications where your work appears. If you've got a rich and varied list, all the better.
- Games and other activities that have to do with your works for kids.
- Awards and honors you've received for your writing and illustration.
- Reviews of your work. Link to the actual online reviews if you can.
- FAQ/Fan Mail page. Maybe you're one of those lucky writers who gets lots of fan mail. Put up some of your favorites.
- School Visits/Book Signings/Special Appearances. Add a calendar listing all your special occasions that have to do with your work. Also, include a press kit for the people who are setting up these gigs so they'll be fully informed of what you expect and require.
- Policies and fees. Writers who do school visits should post their policies and fee schedule, along with glowing teacher reviews and thank-you notes received from students.

DESIGN ELEMENTS YOUR SITE MUST HAVE
Easy navigation

You should have consistent, easy-to-follow navigation for all top-level pages. Have a Home Page link on every page, too, and link your nameplate banner back to your home page.

Eye-catching graphics, yes, but . . .

Image Matters. Yes, the flashing gargoyle looks cool, but what does it have to do with your mid-grade biography of Albert Einstein? Watch out for flashy graphics that might be great for a gaming site, but do nothing to portray you or your professional body of work. Every page element should focus attention on your work.

Use well-lit, well-framed photographs—close ups are usually better—and be sure to identify everyone in the photo. One note: If you're using photos with kids in them, make sure you have their parent's permission and never put their whole names online or any information that might allow some weirdo to track them down. Make sure your website is compliant with the Children's Online Privacy Protection Act (COPPA-www.ftc.gov/ogc/coppa1.htm).

If you're using graphics created by someone else, you should give them some kind of attribution on your site. You can do this on a site credits page or in the footer. Some professional graphic artists have small banners they'll want you to put on your site to link back to theirs.

Be careful of basic design flaws like having the text and graphics centered on the page like a flyer, or having so much information on one page that your visitors have to scroll down and down and down to read it all. Or worse, the text is overlapping the onscreen tables and spilling into the margins, a sure sign of a beginner and absolutely not the polished, professional image you want. A good website layout will present a lot of information in a click-to-follow format, giving your visitors easy choices to find the information they need.

Meta Titles, Meta Tags/Keywords, Meta Descriptions

When constructing the site itself, use Meta Titles, Meta Descriptions, and Meta Tags or Keywords. The Meta Titles appear at the very top of browser windows. Meta Descriptions appear in search engine results—they're the 25-word paragraphs that draw people to your site. Meta Tags, also called Keywords, are what people will type into search engines in order to find you, even if they don't know they're looking for you in particular.

Include the ten or so most common words that are relevant to your web page right up front, then include common misspellings of your name or subject matter. For instance, if you're a children's writer, spell like a 10-year-old doing a book report.

Use words and phrases that will direct people to your site as a resource, and be page-specific if you can. Say you have written a book about twins and all the things that are special to their relationships. Now, searchers may never have heard of you, but they want to learn about twin telepathy or twin language. You'll want to have both of those listed in your keywords for the page on your twin book. When a searcher types in "twin telepathy" on her search engine, she'll get a link to your book page, even though she doesn't know you from Adam's housecat. Say you also have a book about oranges. You'll want the keywords on that page to reflect the content accurately.

SEARCH ENGINES

Search engines operate by their own rules. Some use programs called spiders that crawl the Web looking for new sites to catalog. When they hit your site, they catalog every term, every picture, every link. Then they follow every link on your site and catalog those sites. This is why reciprocal links are so important. It's imperative that people reciprocate links. It helps everyone involved rank higher in search engines.

High-quality links coming into your site, meaning those from sites that get a lot of traffic like SmartWriters.com, are actually more valuable than using appropriate Meta terms. The spiders will come to your site more often if you have a lot of high-traffic links coming in, moreso than if your Meta terms are relevant. The more often the spiders come to your site, the more often they have the chance to catalog any new information from you, and the more new information (including updated Meta terms, new page text, new photos, etc.), the higher your relevancy ranking will be. If you've got a stagnant site, they note that, too, and drop your ranking a bit.

Caution: Avoid submitting your site to search engines more than once a quarter, if that often. Too-frequent submissions can get you banned.

SECURITY

There's no real way to protect your online content 100%. When you put your text and images on your website, it is downloaded onto your visitors' computers. The best you can hope to do is put up roadblocks that will make it difficult for the average person to steal it. Some options:

- You can use a Java script that will disable the right click copy tool.
- You can put watermarks over images.
- You can digitally "sign" an image using special software that imbeds a piece of text in the image itself that is hidden from view, but is in the digital coding. This doesn't prevent theft, but does prove that it's yours.
- You can convert text into an image so it cannot be readily copied and pasted into another document.

Ruler of Your Domain:
How to Secure & Protect Your Domain Name

Okay, it's happened to the very best of us. Some of children's publishing's brightest stars and others new to the industry have lost their custom domain names, which usually get pointed to online malls of one sort or another in the hopes of drawing traffic to the new owner's products, whatever they may be. Maybe you've heard of the graphic designer who donated a bunch of promotional profile pages to 100 or so children's writers, and then lost his domain to a company that turned it into a porn portal, which sent all the site visitors for those children's writers to the pornography site. Horrifying, yes, but not especially uncommon.

Some of the original owners have gotten their domains back by paying the new owners' price, some have entered into legal action to try to reclaim their domain names, and others have chosen to let them go, not willing to deal with the domain snatchers.

There's one thing you need to know: Buying a lapsed domain name and charging the rightful owner to reclaim it is not illegal. Unethical? Probably. But it's also a thriving business. The people who do this are commonly called snappers (because they snap up domains as soon as the domain registration lapses), but they have also been referred to as domain pirates. They're people who are essentially just out to make some money from this incredible cyberland of opportunity called the Internet.

Buying and reselling domains is very much like buying and reselling items on eBay. Say you pick up a really pretty piece of costume jewelry at an estate sale for $20. Turns out it's real diamonds and you can resell it for a hundred times what you paid for it. It's the same concept in buying and reselling lapsed domain names, and those that are traffic magnets command a higher resale price.

So how do you buy and protect your domain name from lapsing and thereby hitting the open market for the snappers? Here are some tips:

- Deal with a reputable domain registrar that offers customer support to match your technological comfort level. My company, 2-Tier Software, Inc., has accounts with AllDomains.com and with GoDaddy.com. Both offer auto-renewals and domain locking.
- Only use registrars that offer auto-renewals. Set your domain name to auto-renew. This will automatically renew your domain name when the registration period is almost up, provided your credit card information is still current.
- Only use registrars that offer domain locking. This prevents your domain name from being transferred or modified without first being unlocked, which only the true owner can do.
- If you pay for website hosting and your host provider pays for your domain on your behalf, make sure they are using a reputable registrar that uses auto-renewals and domain locking. Also, follow up to make sure your provider actually renewed your domain.
- Keep your e-mail, contact, and credit card information current with your domain registrar. People change their e-mail addresses a lot, and now and then you have to change your credit card number (maybe you've lost your card and your credit card company changes the account number for your protection). If you don't notify the domain registrar of your new contact information, they won't be able to notify you that there's a problem processing your payment when the time comes, even if it's set to auto-renew. Bye-bye domain name.
- Take advantage of multi-year discounts. Network Solutions normally charges $35 per year, but I helped an author get a significant discount by paying for several years in advance, and she's assured that her domain is safe for the next decade.

- Don't put off renewing your domain registration. It's not like putting off your car registration, where you'd pay a fine and get to renew the tags anyway. If your domain name lapses, it could get snapped up in 30 days. Snappers use software that detects newly lapsed domains.
- Even if you don't have any immediate plans to build a website, go ahead and buy your custom domain if it's available, and buy alternative spellings, too, if you have an unusually spelled name. (I have RoxyanneYoung.com and RoxanneYoung.com, for instance.) You might be surprised how many professionals are entering the small business and entrepreneurial workforce, and they're all shopping for their own domain names for their websites. You may be the only person with your name that you know of, but chances are there's a Realtor in Florida or a lawyer in Kansas or a psychologist in Montana with the same name who's about to set up shop on the Web.

Ultimately it's your responsibility to protect your domain name. Only you can keep your account information up to date. The domain registrars aren't likely to go to any great lengths to find you; they may have millions of customers and rely heavily on electronic means of communication to confirm your existence. It's up to you to make sure that they can find you easily if there's a problem with your domain registration.

- Make sure there are copyright notices on every single page on your website. These should include the year, the name of the copyright holder, and a statement of the rights covered (i.e. Copyright © 2003 Smartwriters.com. All Rights Reserved.).

FINDING A SAFE HOSTING COMPANY OR DESIGNER

Talk with your friends and colleagues about their sites and what sort of service they've received from their designers and hosting companies. If the companies offer free trials, go try them on for size and see how the software fits.

Look for sites you like, then check near the bottom of the page for a "Site Designed by . . ." or "Powered by . . ." link. Designers welcome inquiries about their fees and design schedule. Check out their client list and contact those people directly via e-mail and ask if they're happy with the company or designer.

Above all, your website should be a reflection of you as a professional. It should present your site visitors with information that is both pertinent and entertaining, and it should work as a round-the-clock PR machine for your writing and illustration. It doesn't have to be expensive, but it shouldn't look cheap. You want people to take you seriously, and for that to happen, you need to take yourself seriously. A quality website can help you do just that.

Get Booked: Creating Promotional Materials That Stand Out in a Crowd

BY HOPE VESTERGAARD

So you've published your first book (or second, or seventh). Now you want to create a little book buzz. To visit or not to visit? School visits stimulate word-of-mouth attention and can increase book sales. But getting the visits takes a little work. And the impression you make on a school system or community begins the first time they open your mailing or visit your website.

Basic information

At the very least, you'll need a brochure. Include:

- Who you are: brief bio, photo
- What you do: titles and descriptions of your books; general descriptions of visits
- How to reach you: phone, address, e-mail (Some authors use a post office box to maintain privacy.)

Don't list fees, travel requirements, etc. on the brochure. Your fees will rise with demand and experience and you don't want to have to reprint the most expensive item in your packet. This is also strategic: Many buyers are turned off by price. Good salespeople don't start with price, but with selling points. Focus on your books, your credentials, and your style.

Booknotes should include covers, publishers, and positive review snippets. Credentials include teaching and speaking experience and educational background, if appropriate. Conveying style is a bit subtler. How might an audience describe your talk? Playful? Lively? Down-to-earth?

Program descriptions should include a catchy title, presentation length, target ages and group size, and a brief description of the content. Schools in search of speakers are generally looking for three broad categories of content: the writing life (how you got published, how you work, etc.); the craft of writing (how aspiring writers can hone their skills); and literacy topics (how parents and teachers encourage reading and/or use literature in the classroom). Make this a separate sheet on regular paper for easy e-mailing and editing. If possible, include quotes from satisfied customers.

To economize, do a broader brochure mailing and follow up promising leads with a smaller, more detailed packet that includes fees, program descriptions, and postcards or copies of your reviews. Author Shutta Crum (*Spitting Image*), includes copies of newspaper articles about her visits to other schools, which indicates satisfied customers and suggests that schools can turn her visit into a PR opportunity for their program.

Fees and travel expenses should be listed on a separate sheet from your brochure. Place them in the bottom of your materials (perhaps at the bottom of the page with your programs) so readers will see the price *after* you've piqued their interest. How to determine appropriate fees? Consider your record as a writer/illustrator and your skills and experience as a speaker. Survey

HOPE VESTERGAARD *is the author of seven picture books including* Hello, Snow *(FSG/Melanie Kroupa, Fall 2004),* Baby Love*;* Wake Up, Mama!*; and* Driving Daddy *(all with Dutton). She also freelances curricular materials for early childhood programs and has been known to armchair design a brochure or two for her writer friends. Visit her website: www.hopevestergaard.com.*

Two new picture books by
Hope Vestergaard

WAKE UP, MAMA!
by Hope Vestergaard
illustrations by Thierry Courtin

DRIVING DADDY
by Hope Vestergaard
illustrations by Thierry Courtin

Perfect for babies and toddlers!

Hope Vestergaard
Children's Book Author

Ann Arbor, Michigan, USA
www.hopevestergaard.com

Both from Dutton Children's Books:

DRIVING DADDY, illustrated by Thierry Courtin
ISBN: 0525470328

WAKE UP MAMA, illustrated by Thierry Courtin
ISBN: 0525470301

Art © 2003 Thierry Courtin. Reprinted with permission from Dutton Children's Books.

© Hope Vestergaard. Reprinted with permission.

Hope Vestergaard's promotional postcards stretch her promotional budget by featuring two book covers on the front. All other pertinent information, including author website, publisher, ISBN numbers, and copyright notes, appear on the reverse. The print size is large enough to be read easily but small enough to leave room for a personal note and/or event information. And she's made a point to leave the bottom edge and the "to" portion of the postcard blank to avoid confusing postal scanners and causing delivery delay.

the market in your area—what are other speakers charging? Don't forget what I call the aggravation factor: inevitable bumps and wrinkles along the way. Charge a fee that covers the costs for your time and that anticipates some difficulties.

Seasoned speaker tip: Rather than create a new presentation for each visit, develop several strong presentations that cover the range of your expertise. You can tweak them over time, but having pre-set talks and workshops makes it easier for buyers to find exactly what they need and will save you prep time in the long run.

As with any service transaction, the more specific you are about your fees, the more satisfied everyone will be. Give a breakdown along these general lines:

- One one-hour presentation for up to _____ students: $XXX
- Half-day visit (up to [2 or 3] [length of time] presentations: $XXX
- Full-day visit (up to [4-5] [length of time] presentations: $XXX

You may or may not want to include a volume discount. Doing several sessions in one location saves travel time and paper work; on the other hand, long days are draining.

Travel expenses are straightforward. Expect schools to pay travel, meals, and mileage (36¢/mile is the IRS rate for 2003). Indicate how far you're willing to drive without requiring an overnight stay. Use the contract to indicate specific preferences, such as whether you'll book flights and hotels yourself and be reimbursed or whether you prefer to have the host make your arrangements.

Savvy sales pitch: include a note with suggestions for economizing. This reduces haggling and puts the responsibility for making the visit affordable on the school's shoulders, rather than the author's. Here's what my note says:

I understand that cost is an issue for many programs. Consider finding another school or program in your area that would like to schedule a visit at the same time to save on travel expenses. Book sales are another option. Schools obtain books from the publisher or a distributor, pre-sell them, and retain all profits. Some schools use author visits as fundraisers. I entertain reasonable offers for schools in need and may have other suggestions for ways to make a visit affordable for your group or institution.

As soon as you do a mailing (or post your information on your website), be prepared for inquiries. A paper or computer spreadsheet works well to keep track of details as long as you update it diligently. Note contact information at each site, their interests, and dates. Also note how they found you—this information will help you better target your marketing efforts down the road.

Extras

Many authors and illustrators use postcards to alert friends and contacts to new releases and events. Two popular sources are www.modernpostcard.com and www.4over4.com; both will design a postcard for a modest fee. Put postcards in your contract pack so the school can make big posters of your book covers for the visit.

Bookmarks are another popular giveaway. They feature a book cover, titles of other books, and a review snippet or two. They're so inexpensive to get done professionally that you may save money going that route—you'll certainly save time. In addition to postcard producers, there are companies that specialize in bookmarks such as www.webcards.com. Author Alex Flinn (*Breathing Underwater*) gives bundles of bookmarks to reading groups that discuss her books.

Note to newbies: Even though online companies can pull photos and covers from a website, you'll get a crisper image if you send them your own high-resolution JPEG.

Educators particularly love activity guides and reading guides. An activity guide for a picture book can include related art activities and songs. More sophisticated guides describe cross-curricular activities that relate to your book. For chapter books and novels, readers' guides include questions about themes, characters, and plot. These are not quizzes on content, but discussion starters. If you'd like to write your own activity guides, study those posted at many author-illustrator websites.

Author Tracie Vaughn Zimmer (*Sketches from a Spy Tree*) has a collection of great guides on her website, www.tracievaughnzimmer.com. Illustrators can make coloring pages with characters or scenes from their books. If you're not up for an entire activity guide, pick one fun activity. Schools like cooking projects because they promote math, reading, science, and social skills. For Rhonda Gowler Greene's book, *At Grandma's*, we created recipes for two foods mentioned in the book. Four cards fit on a standard sheet; they can be printed on cardstock for cute giveaways, or schools and readers can download and copy them. Include your name and book title somewhere on every promotional piece.

Techno tip: Posting reproducible freebies on your website saves mailing costs and makes them available to readers who aren't yet in the market for a visit. PDF (portable document format) creators such as Adobe Acrobat make documents created in any program universally readable.

That's basically it for function. Now let's talk about form: Good information is even more impressive when it's wrapped up in a pretty package.

Desktop design on a dime

You don't need to hire a graphic designer to get an attractive brochure. Remember four basic goals as you design your promotional pieces:
- Your materials are the first indication of your professional personality. They should be consistent. Using the same colors, fonts, and tone across all your materials will present a memorable image.
- Materials should reflect your personal style. Playful? Serious? Zany? Whatever it is, don't let it overshadow your content.
- Content is key. Avoid the *me-me-me* syndrome. You may have numerous attributes and accomplishments, but your reader simply wants to know what you can do for her program. Explain what listeners will take away from your presentation.
- Polish, polish, polish. Beyond proofreading, have an independent reader check your materials for clarity and comprehensiveness.

Dealing with details

If it's worth having a brochure (or website), it's worth taking the time to make it good. (Besides, working on these extras is a great way to pass the time while you wait for your books to be published!)

Closing the Deal

To confirm a scheduled visit, you'll need to send the school a contract or review theirs. Toni Buzzeo, author of *Dawdle Duckling*, has examples of solid visit contracts on her website, www.tonibuzzeo.com. For convenience, include information about book sales: titles, publishers, prices, ISBN numbers, and ordering information (including required lead time). Author Rukhsana Khan (*Ruler of the Courtyard*) recently added this information to her website, www.rukhsanakhan.com, and received immediate positive feedback from booksellers and schools. Cynthia Leitich Smith's website, www.cynthialeitichsmith.com, has a great media guide. The easier it is for people to do something, the more likely they are to do it. When I return signed copies of contracts, I also include a photo and reproducible bio sheet to help promote the event.

Booknotes

BABY LOVE

illustrated by John Wallace ◆ Dutton Children's Books ◆ ISBN: 0-525-46902-8

Reviews

Booklist
"Vestergaard's first book is a profusion of wee, cheery poems for and about babies."
© American Library Association

Publishers Weekly
"...newcomer Vestergaard captures the nuances of life in this winsome collection of verse...these snapshots of an infant's endearing moments will appeal to baby lovers of all ages."   © Reed Business Information, Inc.

DRIVING DADDY and WAKE UP, MAMA

illustrated by Thierry Courtin ◆ Dutton Children's Books
DRIVING DADDY ISBN: 0-525-47032-8 ◆ WAKE UP, MAMA ISBN: 0-525-47030-1

Reviews

Booklist
"These pint-size companion books will delight active toddlers...The playful rhyming language is short and sweet, just right for the young target audience, and Courtin's childlike illustrations are also on the mark, providing comforting scenes of tender family fun that youngsters will page through on their own. "   —Lauren Peterson, © American Library Association

Children's Literature
"The bouncy rhyme is in sync with the story...With its warm and cozy feel, this will appeal to young children, especially those who have had the fun of waking a sleeping parent in the morning."   —Sharon Salluzzo, © Children's Literature

COMING FALL 2004: HELLO, SNOW! ◆ illustrated by Nadine Bernard Westcott
Melanie Kroupa Books/Farrar, Straus & Giroux

For activity guides, articles, and more information, please visit www.hopevestergaard.com

School Visits and Workshops

Hope Vestergaard

Children's Author

Presentations

Reaching Readers

These presentations are geared for adults.

Read to Your Babies: A discussion of the importance of reading, including brief statistics about literacy and strategies to nurture a life-long love for literature.

Revving Up Writers: Working on the mechanical aspects of reading and writing sometimes causes children to lose touch with their creative sides. Hope will share fuel-for-thought exercises to get reluctant writers' pencils racing across the page!

Get More Bang for Your Book! Hope describes creative strategies to incorporate books into all aspects of curriculum using webbing, long-term projects, and cross-discipline teaching.

For bookstores, libraries, and small groups:

Come Read With Me: Story hour for babies, toddlers, preschoolers and parents. Children bring their own dolls or lovies to cuddle as we read, sing, and move together!

Reading books together is a wonderful family tradition.

Art © 2002 John Wallace

The Writing Life

These programs are suitable for all ages.

Meet an Author—Show and Tell: Hope shares her writing, from grade school to the present. Includes sneak peeks at upcoming books and a question-and-answer session.

The Write Stuff: Learn the truth about what it takes to be a published author—the good, the bad, and the utterly ridiculous!

From Brainstorm to Book: Hope shares exercises for budding authors to strengthen their writing muscles.

Finding Your Voice: Hope describes concrete ways aspiring authors can find their own unique voices.

Picture Books 101: Publishing Peaks and Pitfalls. An intensive program perfect for anyone who's ever thought, "This idea might make a good book!" Hope will cover the *whos, whats, wheres, whens* and *whaaaas!* of getting a manuscript published.

....

Any of these programs can be tailored to fit your group's needs and interests. Contact Hope: hope@hopevestergaard.com.

Hope's Bio

When Hope Vestergaard was a child, she read everything she could get her hands on: cereal boxes, shopping lists, newspapers, encyclopedias and, yes... children's books.

Although Hope wore holes in her library cards and her teachers sent her to young authors conferences, it took a while for her to call herself a writer. She was an early childhood teacher and a center director for years before she started freelancing developmental materials and doing curriculum consulting.

The hundreds of books she read with infants, toddlers, and preschoolers inspired Hope to write her own books for children. To date, she has three picture books published with four more scheduled for future release.

Hope's informative and inspirational workshops help parents and teachers encourage young readers (and writers!) develop a life-long relationship with books.

While still relatively inexpensive to produce and easy to mail in a regular #10 envelope, author brochures allow more space with which to sell yourself than postcards. Hope Vestergaard sticks to the basics: bio, books, and presentations. She writes friendly, informative text that matches the tone of her speaking personality. She chooses font and design patterns that match her website to create a unified image. Her speaking presentation descriptions incorporate catchy titles (don't try to be *too* cute) with *brief* descriptions, while directing people to her website and giving her e-mail address for more detailed information.

When you choose a brochure format (size and layout), standard paper sizes make copying and mailing easier. Tri-fold brochures are popular because they're easy to mail and have built-in sections to help you organize information. Some authors use a flyer, or single standard page. Others choose an unusual shape to stand out in the pile. I made an $8\frac{1}{2} \times 5\frac{1}{2}$ double-sided card for author Lisa Wheeler (*One Dark Night*, Harcourt 2003); it fits into a standard "catalog" envelope.

For Shutta Crum, I made an accordion-fold 11×17 page which includes classroom suggestions for each of her books. This brochure does double-duty: Even if schools don't book her for a visit, they may use her activities and books in the classrooms. If you choose a brochure style that will be folded, be sure that none of the text or images is obscured by the creases.

Judicious use of fonts is one of the quickest ways to spruce up your image. Sans serif fonts (those that don't have the curlicue tails) are easier to read in dense text. Too many fonts give a cluttered, chaotic effect. Choose two, maybe three, fonts and stick to them in all your materials. Use one font for content and one for headings. They should complement each other and your "personality." Make sure your font size is legible. Use boldface, italics, and underlining sparingly and consistently. Steer clear of cutesy fonts.

Formatting text is one place that armchair graphic designers tend to fall down on the job. Take the time to learn how to use your program's formatting toolbars and shortcuts: indents, lists, line spacing, and tabs should not be a guessing game. If you position things by repeatedly hitting the space key or estimating when items are "centered" you will spend lots of time chasing down stray spaces and dangling punctuation. Try to avoid hyphenating words. Many programs allow users to turn off auto-hyphenation, which cleans up the look of text blocks. Don't leave a single line of text or word by itself; force a line break to leave two lines together or edit the text so the dangling word will fit in the previous column.

Clip art and borders are another sticky wicket. Art adds oomph, but it can also make a brochure too busy. Less is more—leave some white space. It's breathing room for your content; resist the temptation to fill it up with clip-art clutter. White space shapes your text blocks and gives eyes a rest from processing lines and images. Make sure any clip art is appropriate for your design and that all the clip art in a promo piece has similar lines. As you arrange art on the page, be sure to evenly distribute the "weight" of the whole brochure.

If you include photos or book covers, give proper credit. If you want to use art from inside your picture book, obtain permission from the artist and include a copyright notice with each piece. Professional photographers may require a fee (in addition to credit) to grant reproduction rights. Book covers for promo purposes are generally fair use, but you'll need to include the artist's copyright notice and the publisher's name. For best copy quality, photos should be high-contrast, high resolution (preferably 300 dpi; check your digital camera or scanner settings).

The materials you use to create your promotional items also make a statement. Office superstores sell everything from glossy brochure paper to heavyweight, textured cardstock. Splurge

Looking for Bookings?

Start with the libraries and schools in your town or metropolitan area; they're in the phone book. Another local resource: community childcare referral agencies. Join your state Reading Association (via the International Reading Association website, www.ira.org) to receive mailings for conference proposals and other events. If you write or illustrate young picture books, join the National Association for the Education of Young Children (www.naeyc.org). And if your book is topical, include any relevant organizations (adoption resources, for example) on your mailing list.

Once she's landed a presentation assignment, Hope Vestergaard uses handouts to help engage attendees and their children. Vestergaard's Storytime handout uses songs that directly relate to her books. Parents appreciate the added value of learning new songs and games to enjoy with their children *and* they take the handout, with Vestergaard's name, book titles, and website link, home with them.

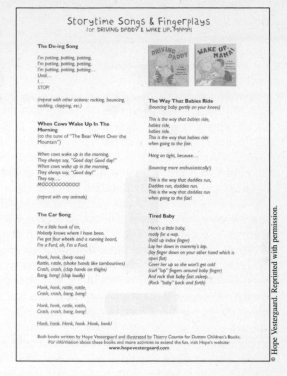

on good brochure paper, as this is the piece that most people will hang on to. Some authors and illustrators choose to print their own materials. Color inkjet cartridges can print a good number of brochures and are an affordable alternative to color photocopies if you have a good printer. Optimize your printer settings for color/photo printing and specialty papers. Another way to print an affordable, expensive-looking brochure is to use colored ink on nice paper. I have freelance items printed at a print shop: three colors on linen paper in quantities of 500-1,000 for under 20 cents per double-sided sheet. Pick a color that's dominant in your author photo or which complements it. If your photo's not in color, choose two complementary colors and stick to them throughout your materials.

Timesaving tip: Whether you print on demand or in volume, have a stash of at least 10 promo packets ready to mail out so you can send them right away when you get requests.

Don't forget the information superhighway

A website is one of the easiest ways to get author visits. (For more information see What a Site! Creating Websites That Work on page 75.) As with promotional materials, your website does not need to be high-tech or flashy to do its job. It does need to be attractive, informative, and easy to use. All of the content and design elements discussed above apply to Web pages. More considerations:

• **Domain name.** Before you do anything, register your domain name. There's a fee of about $30 per year to do so, and there are multiple services which will register your domain name for you. (I did it myself at www.register.com.)

• **Download speed.** Optimize your images so they don't take forever to load. If you work with a high-speed connection, test your site with a dial-up connection.

• **Search engines.** Search engines will find you . . .eventually. You can speed the process by registering (it's free) with the big ones: Yahoo, Google, and Alta Vista.

• **Metatags.** Help search engines find you. These are keywords built into your invisible Web page headers. Include words such as *children's author* or *illustrator*, your book titles, and content words. If you make your site content-rich (see below), include those words in your metatags, too.

• **Save all download documents as PDFs.** Material saved as PDFs is easily downloadable by website visitors. Otherwise, only people who have the programs used to create the documents will be able to read them. Macintosh OS9 has a built-in PDF creator. Adobe Acrobat is the best-known PDF program, but there are many pared-down versions that can be adequate for occasional users.

• **Links.** Format your website so when people follow any links you include, your site window doesn't close.

• **Consider the expiration date of your information.** If you can't or won't be updating frequently, don't post anything that will quickly go out of date. You should update periodically to maintain traffic to your site; even doing so quarterly helps.

Timesaver: To make updating more manageable, structure your content so that only one or two pages of the whole site will need regular attention.

There are dozens of do-it-yourself Web design programs available. Be sure that the domain host you select supports the program you want to use. If you have no interest in designing or maintaining a site, a skillful Web designer will know how to address these issues and even more. How to find a good designer? Find sites you like and ask who did them. Prices and quality of sites run the gamut. There are plenty of affordable designers and hosts. The Author's Guild offers site hosting and templates for members; www.smartwriters.com provides Web design and hosting service. If you plan to do your own site, allow time. It takes a while to become fluent in the do-it-yourself programs.

A website should include the content of a basic brochure, as well as information about visits. Post your programs and e-mail fees upon request. Content-rich websites offer information about getting published, about literacy, about the factual content of books, as well as activity guides and suggestions. Some authors include reading lists—favorite or related books. Posting content on your site will generate more traffic—and more exposure.

What's the bottom line? Schools get piles of promotional flyers for everything from jugglers to plays to exotic pets. How to rise to the top of *this* slush pile? Put your best face forward. Ensuring that your promotional materials are attractive, appropriate, and accurate will put you at the head of the class when it comes time for schools to plan literacy events.

Snazzy Sites

You don't need a lot of bells and whistles to build a good website. Here are some great examples of the features discussed above:

www.kathleenodell.com Basic, clean, personable website.

www.carolyncrimi.com Lots of personality shining through!

www.janiebynum.com Well-organized, playful illustrator site.

www.jenniferjacobson.com Content-rich author site, great visit info and resources.

The Children's Book Council site includes listings for many author and illustrator websites: **www.cbcbooks.org/html/links.html.** Be sure to register your site here.

Lights, Camera, Action:
The Mania of Books to Film

BY KELLY MILNER HALLS

Top-notch storytellers have at least one thing in common, regardless of medium—laser-fine creative vision. On paper or film, the process is painstaking and precise; every phrase, every frame selectively delivered. When the two art forms merge, the evolution can be magical—and lucrative.

But how does a story move from the printed page to Hollywood production? And how often does that creative union translate into creative bliss? Here, seven writers who have made the celluloid transition share their insights.

In 2002, *Life in the Fat Lane* authors **Cherie Bennett** and **Jeff Gottesfeld** joined the writing staff of *Smallville*, the WB network's teenage look at Superman's coming-of-age. But they were no strangers to the entertainment industry.

Meg Cabot knew her reluctant royal was a distinctive protagonist when she wrote *The Princess Diaries* for HarperCollins. But she never imagined Disney and Julie Andrews would so wholeheartedly agree.

Coming-of-age author **Chris Crutcher** has written eight novels, an autobiography, and one collection of short stories for Greenwillow, an imprint of HarperCollins. Almost every page he's written has been optioned for motion picture production. But only one project, *Angus*, has actually been captured on film. [Note: "Optioned" means they have paid for the "option" of making the story into a film or television project.]

Vision Quest starring Matthew Modine as Louden Swain was novelist **Terry Davis**' first big screen endeavor. It forever linked him with Madonna—she made her film debut alongside Modine—and launched his academic direction as a screenwriting professor.

Dying-young scenarios have made Random House novelist **Lurlene McDaniel** a healthy living for the past two decades. But a made-for-television translation of *Don't Die, My Love* (retitled *A Champion's Fight* by NBC) helped frost her literary cake.

Writing novelizations for films like *Addam's Family Values*, *Free Willy*, and *Ferris Bueller's Day Off* certainly helped make **Todd Strasser** a successful, full-time writer. But selling the rights to his original story, *Drive Me Crazy*, may have been a more cost-effective order.

With literally dozens and dozens of titles to her credit, few could dispute author **Jane Yolen**'s status as a children's book diva. But seeing actress Kirsten Dunst bring *The Devil's Arithmetic* protagonist Hannah to life in the Showtime production added another jewel to her crown.

KELLY MILNER HALLS *is a freelance writer in Spokane specializing in children's nonfiction and nonfiction about writing. She published more than 1,500 articles in* Highlights for Children, Teen PEOPLE, FamilyFun, Writer's Digest, Ask!, Dig, Boy's Life, U*S*Kids, The Chicago Tribune, The Washington Post, The Denver Post *and dozens of other publications. She has ten published children's books to her credit, including* Dinosaur Mummies: Beyond Bare-Bone Fossils *(Darby Creek Publishing, 2003). She has three more scheduled for release in 2004, including* The Jurassic Park Institute Dinosaur Travel Guide *(Random House, 2004) and* Girl Meets Boy, *a YA anthology (Simon & Schuster, 2004).*

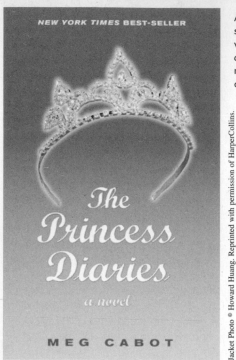

NEW YORK TIMES BEST-SELLER

The Princess Diaries

a novel

MEG CABOT

As a child in Bloomington, Indiana, Meg Cabot daydreamed that she really was a princess whose parents, the king and queen, would soon come for her. This childhood fantasy helped *The Princess Diaries* materialize. Cabot says she never dreamed her debut novel would become the popular Disney movie starring Julie Andrews.

Jacket Photo © Howard Huang. Reprinted with permission of HarperCollins.

When you write your manuscripts, do they unfold with cinematic potential in your minds? Can you see the film before it's conceptualized?

Cherie Bennett/Jeff Gottesfeld: Yes to the first, no to the second—except for *University Hospital*, which we wrote with the express idea that it could be easily ported over to TV. The more we work in the three main genres (TV, film, theater), the more we try to create stories that can work in all three arenas. For example, *Searching for David's Heart* started as a Scholastic novel (1998), then we turned it into a play (Dramatic, 2002). Now it's going to be a Disney Channel movie. I think our real strength is that we tend to write straightforward narratives with lots of plot twists and turns and strong characters, instead of strong descriptive passages. This helps when it comes to adaptation.

Terry Davis: I think because I grew up loving movies, I see stories in that "cinematic" way, that is, on the screen in my mind. So yes, I saw the people and events in *Vision Quest* like a movie. But I did not think of the book actually being made into a movie. Since the movie *was* made, I now see every moment in a story as a shot in a movie, hear every line as if it's coming out of speakers in a theatre. I imagine it this way because it's the best way for me to create. I throw it up there on the movie screen in my mind with all the richness I can create. I report it to the reader as richly and precisely as I can.

Lurlene McDaniel: Yes, but mostly because it helps me better "see" my scene, not because I actually believe it will go to film.

Todd Strasser: To be honest, I do not think of them cinematically. Were I to write a book with that thought, it would be very different. Lots more action, I would imagine. Cars would burst into flames even in the most minor of fender benders. Roads at night would always be wet.

When I am asked to take a book I've written and turn it into a script, I do begin to see it that way.

How important is writing a "visual" book to its successful conversion to film?

Bennett/Gottesfeld: I think that unless you've written a blockbuster like *Holes*, which got its film rights picked up in part on the strength of buzz, plot-centered/character-centered storytelling is key. *True Confessions*, Janet Tashjian's novel, just became a Disney Channel movie without being a blockbuster seller. And then, you can just think of all the huge sellers/award winners that have not become films or TV films. Now, the needed "visual-ness" can vary, depending on the particular outlet, for example Karen Cushman's *The Ballad of Lucy Whipple* worked well for CBS, but probably wouldn't have been a good candidate for Disney Channel.

Cabot: I don't know. I have seen books I never thought would translate to film made into great movies. I think it depends on the creativity of the filmmaker and screenwriter, and not so much on the book.

Crutcher: I really don't have any idea. It's the people who make the films that need to be visual. I've been told some of my stuff is, and I can see some of it I suppose, but I'm far more married to the words.

Davis: I don't think a book needs necessarily to be "visual" to make a good movie. I think it needs to, first, be highly and richly plotted. It's story that movie makers look for in books. Story first, last, and always. *They* will make it visual. That's the essence of what they're trained to do.

McDaniel: I think it's important. The more visual the project, the better its theatrical chances. That's why action books go to film most often. There's something for the camera to see. They aren't all cerebral, as are so many "think" books where the action happens in the character's head.

Yolen: Almost anything can be turned into a movie, but the operative word is "successful." Movies are best at delineating plot and counting on the actors to show character. But if something is mostly inward in a story, the moviemakers have to find some way to show an outward manifestation. Except for hokey voice-overs, it's hard to show inner thoughts.

How true to the books are most movie productions? What pushes a project off-track?

Bennett/Gottesfeld: So many things can go wrong. Script problems, director problems, actor problems, notes-from-studio problems. The list of book-to-film adaptations that actually work beautifully, as well as, or better than the underlying material, is pretty short. *One Flew Over the Cuckoo's Nest* is an example of an adaptation that knocked it out of the park. But there, everything came together magnificently. From our standpoint, the script is the bedrock on which everything else is built.

Cabot: People are surprised when they pick up the second book in The Princess Diaries series without having read the first and find that Mia's father, who was killed off in the film, is still alive.

Crutcher: I wasn't around for any of it, but I think *Angus* got pushed off track when they

Chris Crutcher's collection of short stories, *Athletic Shorts* was named a 1992 Best Book for Young Adult Readers by the American Library Association and Best of the Best in Young Adult Literature by the *School Library Journal*. The short story, "A Brief Moment in the Life of Angus Bethune," became the movie *Angus*, originally distributed by New Line Cinema. While Crutcher's short story addressed controversial issues such as gay parenthood, most of those references were omitted from the movie. Crutcher says it's important not to "take what the filmmakers do personally."

decided to make only one set of parents gay, then edited that out, and when they decided to make Angus younger.

Davis: For *Vision Quest*, the filmmakers wanted to make a commercial feature aimed at a young audience, and this is what they did with really phenomenal success. I mean, good God, the thing has been on TV every week for almost twenty years. The book, though, is richer, especially thematically and in terms of character. And I am proud of the work I did in the book's conclusion, whereas the film featured another concluding scene, which they surely had to do in view of their goals for the movie.

Strasser: From what I've seen, it is almost always trying to replicate the book story on the screen. I just don't think it can be done that way. To be successful you have to take the idea of the book, or even one idea in the book, and make a movie story out of it. One of my favorite movies is *McCabe and Mrs. Miller*, by Robert Altman. At some point I noticed that it was based on a book called *McCabe* by a writer named Edmund Naughton. For years I poked around used bookstores and libraries for the book. Finally a very kind librarian from Denver lent it to me. In the movie, the first three quarters of the story is about how McCabe builds this town out of almost nothing. The last quarter is about how it is taken away from him. The book was almost the opposite, a little bit about how he built it, but mostly about how it was taken away.

Yolen: First, I have to say that the movie is not the book. They made many changes in *The Devil's Arithmetic*. Some because their star (Kirsten Dunst) was four years older than my main character, and the difference between not quite 13 and over 17 is enormous. Second because the growth of character needs to be shown in outward action. And third, because moviemakers like to put their own stamp on a film. I think the movie works on its own terms. And I hadn't read the book myself carefully in ten years when the movie came out. So many kids who were more recently invested in the story didn't like it as well as I did.

How did you offer your book up for theatrical applications? Do you have a film agent?

Bennett/Gottesfeld: Yes. We've got an agent for fiction, and since we also write for TV and film, another agent for those mediums. Many YA writers have agents that "co-agent" with Los Angeles agencies on their work. Curtis Brown is very strong in this arena, but since their co-agenting doesn't extend to scriptwriters but only rights, we've elected to go with our own agency for that.

Cabot: My literary agent co-represented the book with a film agent she knew.

Crutcher: I do have a film agent.

Davis: I had an agent in New York, Liz Darhansoff, who had a partner in Hollywood, Lynn Pleshette. Lynn sold the book.

McDaniel: Yes, my agency works with Joel Gotler in Hollywood. He reps all their material.

Strasser: I don't. Right now I'm more or less content to be in limbo. It seems to me that most of the option money goes to pay for a lawyer, and since most options are never picked up, what's the point?

Yolen: I have a film/theatrical agent, but he tends to be reactive rather than proactive. In other

THE TRIUMPHANT
RE-RELEASE
OF THE CLASSIC
COMING-OF-AGE NOVEL

"THE TRUEST NOVEL ABOUT GROWING UP SINCE *CATCHER IN THE RYE*." —JOHN IRVING

TERRY DAVIS

WITH A NEW INTRODUCTION BY CHRIS CRUTCHER

© 2002 Eastern Washington University Press. Reprinted with permission.

First released in 1979 and regarded as a fresh and exciting new coming-of-age novel, Terry Davis gathered praise from authors such as John Irving, who compared *Vision Quest* to *The Catcher in the Rye* and *The World According to Garp*. *Vision Quest*, which is of the about-high-school-wrestling-but-not-really-all-about-wrestling variety, came out on film in 1985 starring Matthew Modine and Linda Fiorentino and is now counted among classic '80s movies.

words, he's not in Hollywood selling. People come to him. *The Devil's Arithmetic* had been optioned steadily for over ten years by five different groups. (Linda Lavin's production company tried twice to get the money to film it.) But it needed a Hollywood superstar—Dustin Hoffman—to get it into production.

How many production companies were interested in your project? And how do you decide who will win the bidding war?

Bennett/Gottesfeld: Several. How do you decide? You meet with the production companies. You look at the kind of work they've done. You see who you're simpatico with, who seems to at least get what you're trying to do in the underlying piece, and then, you pray. And money does enter into it, too.

Cabot: Gosh, I can't remember now. A few. As for how I decided, well, come on—it's *Disney*!

Crutcher: Actually I don't know how many were interested in *Angus*. There have been three with *Staying Fat for Sarah Byrnes*, but they have been interested at different times. The bidding war was for *Ironman*. I didn't have much information and wasn't in the business of thinking about screenplays then, so I just went with the money.

Davis: A number of individuals and production companies were interested in *Vision Quest*. We went with a fellow named Stan Weston because he seemed most enthusiastic, which made me think he had the best chance to actually get it made. Also, he agreed to let me write a screenplay for it. He immediately dealt the rights to Warner Brothers, who immediately got Gruber-Peters on it, who immediately got the director/writer team of Becker-Ponicson on it.

Yolen: It was actually optioned five separate times but no one could put all the parts together—interest, stars, production company, backing of a channel, and money.

Do you have other projects optioned by movie or television production companies now?

Bennett/Gottesfeld: Over the last several years, many different books and plays have been optioned. Here are some: Teen Angels series (Avon), first by Universal Family Television, then this past season by Spelling Entertainment for a UPN show. It went to pilot script for UPN, but alas, was not picked up. The University Hospital series (Berkley) was optioned by Tollin-Robbins Productions. Our Wild Hearts series (Pocket Books) was optioned by Lantana Productions. We wrote the script, they loved it. But the financing for the project fell apart at the last minute. *Good-bye, Best Friend* (HarperPaperbacks, 1993) was optioned by Jane Seymour's production company. *Life in the Fat Lane* is currently under option to Storyopolis and *Anne Frank and Me* to Gullane Entertainment. *Searching for David's Heart* is currently under option to Wildrice Productions; the script commissioned by Disney Channel for a Disney Channel TV movie for 2003. Yay!

Cabot: My teen paranormal series 1-800-WHERE-R-U is optioned by Lion's Gate, but not in production.

Crutcher: Yes, three.

Davis: None of my other books are optioned; none in production. I do believe, however, that *Mysterious Ways*, which came out in September, will be optioned. I am also trying to interest ESPN films in *If Rock and Roll Were a Machine*.

Strasser: I have a feeling it's two, but I'm really not sure. Due to some unfortunate contractual glitches, a number of my books are locked up even without an option.

Yolen: *Briar Rose*, Commander Toad books, and *Wizard's Hall* are all optioned. Others have been optioned and fallen through.

How common is it for books to be optioned, but never produced?

Bennett/Gottesfeld: It happens more often than not. In fact, *far* more often than not. As an example, according to a recent story in *Variety*, one of the major TV networks heard 1,200 pitches last year for TV shows for their upcoming season. They commissioned approximately 75 pilot scripts. They decided to shoot about 20 pilots. They'll choose maybe 4 hours of programming from those 20 pilots. This isn't exactly the same thing as book options turning into films, I know, but it's close enough in its principles. Just think of all the major YA blockbusters that haven't become films and have incredibly powerful titles—*Walk Two Moons, Staying Fat for Sarah Byrnes, Out of the Dust*. Walter Dean Myers' *Monster* is even written as a film script!

Davis: It is hugely common, most, most, most common for books to be optioned but not produced. I've read that something like only twenty percent of books optioned are ever produced. My guess is that the percentage is lower.

McDaniel: I know of optioned books that have languished for years without ever going to production. So many factors, including focus groups and detailed market research, often occur before a book is actually filmed or taped. If it doesn't test well, it's scrapped, but still tied up with option clause wording via a contract.

Jane Yolen's award-winning middle grade novel, *The Devil's Arithmetic*, invites readers along with 12-year-old Hannah, who, after complaining about her grandfather's incessant talk about Nazi-Germany, finds herself mysteriously transported to a small village in Poland in the 1940s. The book won the Sydney Taylor Award from the Association of Jewish Libraries, the Jewish Book Council Award, and was a Nebula Honor Book as well as an ALA Notable. Dustin Hoffman and Mimi Rogers created the movie version, which starred Kirsten Dunst, for Showtime.

Strasser: I hear it's pretty—no, check that—very common. Ironically, I've had four out of seven produced, but three were for TV. I generally assume the thing's not going to get made.

How long does it take the average produced book to move from page to screen?

Bennett/Gottesfeld: *Forrest Gump* took 10 years. Things *can* happen fast, à la *Harry Potter*. But there tends to be a driving reason for the process to get accelerated like that.

Cabot: *The Princess Diaries* took almost exactly a year. But that was fast-tracked by the studio. *All American Girl* is looking like it will be the same.

Crutcher: There is no set time. There are too many things that can hurry production up and *way* too many things that can slow it down.

Davis: A lot of books take many years from option to production to premier. I was astonishingly lucky with *Vision Quest*.

Strasser: I'm told mine (*Drive Me Crazy*) was done in record time—like a year or something. It showed in the final product.

Yolen: *The Devil's Arithmetic* took over ten years. How long does it take to make this transition? It takes as long as it takes. A bestseller can go quicker.

Have you tried to retain any degree of creative control? Should that matter to an author?

Bennett/Gottesfeld: Yes and no. Because we also write for the screen, and depending on the circumstances, we sometimes are the ones to do the adaptation. In that case, we'd have a lot of creative input. We're pretty much reconciled to the fact that when we're not writing the script, we have a voice but not a veto. And even when we are writing the script, there are going to be a lot of other voices, and the veto will be with the persons shelling out the millions of dollars it'll take to get the project made. That's just the way the business works.

Cabot: The producers kept in touch with me, and I certainly offered my advice, but when it comes to making movies, I know zero, so I felt comfortable with letting the project go.

Davis: I wish I'd retained some creative control when *Vision Quest* was made. I didn't have the personal maturity or the wisdom about story. I do now, however, and hope to be some part of the team, if another book of mine is ever filmed.

Any advice for writers looking towards Hollywood?

Bennett/Gottesfeld: Find an agent who's really active in the arena. Write story-driven books. Write even more story-driven books. Move to Los Angeles if you're really serious about doing more than simply letting the rights on your book go to a production company.

Cabot: I think if you are the kind of person who cannot stand to see someone else's interpretation of your characters/story, you are going to have a miserable time watching your project turned into a film. I think you just have to let it go, because no one is going to make a film that matches your vision. It isn't possible. And even if they do, it might not be such a great film. Case in point, *Harry Potter*, which I loved as a book, but as a film, it just didn't work for me; something got lost.

Crutcher: Decide whether or not you want to have a part in it, knowing it might not matter whether you do or not. And don't take what the filmmakers do personally. It's collaborative storytelling and that takes away a lot of the control and the creative process. If you're going to do it, realize what it is.

Davis: My advice to authors whose work is being optioned is to try to remember that the job of a filmmaker is to make the best movie he can, not to pay homage to a book. Pull yourself together, choose the best people you can to make your movie, then—if your opinion is not requested—shut the hell up, endorse the check, put it in the bank, and write another book.

McDaniel: The offers are usually few and far between. Be prepared to give up creative control. Unless you're Tom Clancy or Stephen King, the producers really don't want your opinions; neither do they care what you think. Take the money and wave goodbye!

Strasser: Never work for free, no matter what they promise you. Hire a really good entertainment attorney. Continue to write books.

Yolen: Cash the checks, and go on to write another book. Don't pin your hopes, your heart, or your mortgage on movies.

Lois Lowry: Natural Talent, Magical Gifts, Human Connections

BY LISA RONDINELLI ALBERT

Many of Lois Lowry's books revolve around a general theme: the importance of human connections. The roles people play and how relationships intertwine are main components of her fiction. Two-time winner of the prestigious Newbery Medal for her books *Number the Stars* and *The Giver*, Lowry has said, "Most serious writers use memories of turning points in their own past as a stimulus to explore, fictionally, the issues that such moments raise."

Over the past twenty-five years, Lowry has often turned to her own childhood emotions and events. Her first book for children, the moving *A Summer to Die*, is a fictionalized retelling of the loss of her sister, Helen, and the impact her death had on the family. Lowry was thirty-nine years old when she wrote the story.

Recollecting her young years, Lowry says, "I was a solitary child who lived in a world of books and my own imagination." Her love of words, language, and books began at a very early age when Helen, who was three years older, explained that letters had sounds and when the sounds were put together, they

Lois Lowry

Photo: Stephen Sheffield

formed words. It was one of several turning points in Lowry's journey toward becoming a writer.

When Lowry was three years old, her nursery school teacher sent a note home to her mother. It read: *She refuses to drink her milk at snack time and her unusual ability to read sets her apart from the other children.* "I can actually remember that—the feeling of being apart," she says. "Not having anything to do really with being able to read, but I never liked what seemed to me, at that very early age, some of the things you were required to do as children. In particular, they used to do this thing where they marched around holding their arms like trunks and were supposed to be elephants. I was supposed to be part of that but it was embarrassing to me," she

LISA RONDINELLI ALBERT *is co-chair for the Wisconsin SCBWI Spring Luncheon. This is her third contribution to the* Children's Writer's & Illustrator's Market. *She writes picture books, chapter books, middle grade, and young adult novels. Her YA novel,* Mercy Lily, *was a finalist in the 2001 SCBWI Work-in-Progress Grant for a Contemporary Novel for Young People and received Honorable Mention in* ByLine Magazine's *First Chapter of a Novel Contest. Visit her website: www.LisaAlbert.com.*

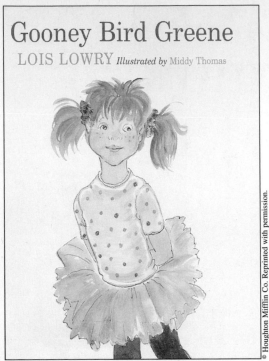

Gooney Bird Greene

LOIS LOWRY *Illustrated by* Middy Thomas

© Houghton Mifflin Co. Reprinted with permission.

Two-time Newbery Medal winner Lois Lowry released *Gooney Bird Greene* in 2002. Though written for a younger audience than is typical for Lowry, the book quickly became a favorite. *Horn Book* says: "Lowry displays a keen understanding of how second-grade classrooms operate." Keep an eye out for more Gooney books in the future.

recalls. "It's weird now thinking of it, that as a three-year-old I would feel that way, but I knew I wasn't an elephant. Clearly, that's imaginative play for most children, but I just wanted to sit in a corner and read a book. So, I can see why the teacher said it set me apart."

Being apart was natural for Lowry and exactly how she liked it. "Perhaps most children feel an individual sense of themselves, but I think for most, it comes later. For me, it was very early—that feeling of being an observer rather than a participant. I still feel that way. I don't know what that means, but it probably contributes to my being a writer."

Another contributing factor in Lowry's success was her family's recognition of her early enchantment with words and all that encompassed reading, writing, and books. "My mother had a keen sense of my need for privacy. Though she knew I spent my time writing and drawing, never once did she ask me to show her stuff that I was doing. Although, she wanted to," Lowry says.

Lowry also had an adoring grandfather who nurtured her need for language. "One evening he took me into his library. He took out a volume of poetry, opened it with a certain amount of ceremony, and then took me onto his lap in a blue wing chair, and read from it aloud." Being five at the time, Lowry didn't understand many of the words in the long poem. "But the cadence of it, and the sound, and the rapture of being on his lap, of being chosen—he had not invited my sister into the library—made me listen with a fascination that I had never brought to Christopher Robin."

Along with privacy and nurturing, Lowry was also given the means to create: "I had access to as much paper and as many pencils as I needed. I had my own desk and when I was thirteen years old, my father gave me a typewriter," Lowry says. "An astounding gift in 1950 for a child. Not only was it a typewriter but it was a brand new Smith-Corona. It was in a case that had a little silver plaque attached to it, which my father had had put on, with my name engraved on it. So, somehow, my parents knew what I liked and what I needed. Yet, it was something

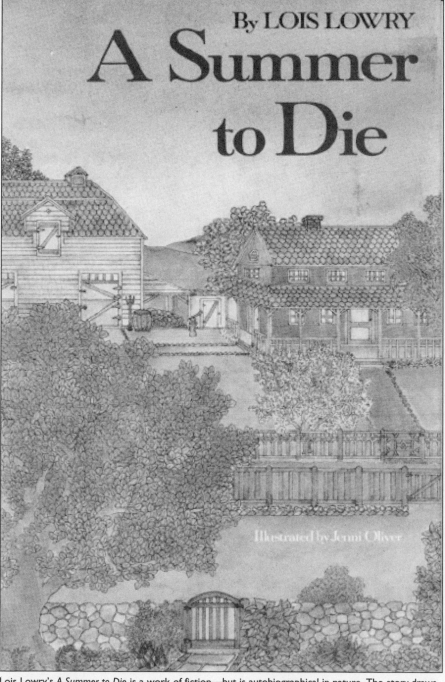

By LOIS LOWRY
A Summer to Die

Illustrated by Jenni Oliver

Lois Lowry's *A Summer to Die* is a work of fiction—but is autobiographical in nature. The story draws heavily on Lowry's own experience of her older sister's death when they were both still quite young. "Though like sisters we fought," she says. "Like Meg in that book, I would go on to miss my sister for the rest of my life."

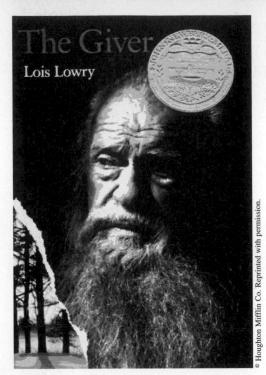

In Lois Lowry's second Newbery Medal-winning novel, *The Giver*, members of the community receive their "life assignments" each December. Lowry's fictional world almost seems utopian until the plot unravels and her main character discovers the truth about his society. The book explores the importance of community on a very personal level.

© Houghton Mifflin Co. Reprinted with permission.

that was never discussed or planned. It just sort of came naturally within the context of my family."

In college, Lowry majored in writing but left school during her sophomore year to get married. Years later, while in her thirties and after her children were grown, she returned to school to get her degree and began to write. Using the Smith-Corona she had received as a child, Lowry wrote *A Summer to Die*. It went on to receive the Children's Literature Award from the International Reading Association (IRA) in 1978. This would be the first of many awards she would receive for her writing and the first of many speeches she would give. It was a turning point.

At the National Council of Teachers of English Annual Convention in 1996, Lowry recounted that first award experience. "One spring day in 1978, I got a call from Mr. Ralph Steiger, president of the IRA, telling me that they had awarded *A Summer to Die* the IRA Children's Book Award. I didn't know who Ralph Steiger was, or what the IRA was, but I thanked him politely and hung up, a little mystified. I called my editor in Boston and asked him what it was all about. I told him that Mr. Steiger wanted me to go to Houston and I told him I would, but I was embarrassed because actually, I couldn't afford to go to Houston. My editor patiently explained that Houghton Mifflin would pay my way.

"And so I went to Houston to receive my award, which I thought would be a plaque or a certificate, maybe like the National Honor Society Award I had received in high school. When I arrived, my editor met me and took me to a luncheon at which there were 2,000 people. We sat at the head table, ate chicken, and listened to Mildred Taylor make an eloquent speech, during which I whispered to Walter, 'Do I have to make a speech?' He blanched and whispered back, 'You mean you don't have a speech?'" Lowry did give a speech that day and has since gone on to deliver many well-prepared lectures.

Now, Lowry starts each day by reading a poem to herself before settling in to write. "Most often, I sit down every day and reread at least the previous day's work, if not a whole lot more, just to get into it." She does not use outlines or character sketches. "I go about it very blindly, and this is not the best way to write but it's the one that works for me. I'm disorganized that way. I am capable of making an outline of an entire book but then, if I sit down to write the book, it hampers me to have an outline. It curtails the flow of imagination," she says. "I have in mind a main character, a vague setting, often a precipitating incident, which will begin the book. And a general sense of the meaning or what the point of the book is. That gives my imagination free reign. Each day I create what is happening, and the next day I have that to build on. What I've already put down is scaffolding on which to put more stuff. Plot is what most writers outline and plot is what I make up as I go along. I haven't any sense at all of what the plot is when I start."

Once a rough draft is complete, Lowry prints out a copy to read through. She allows herself time to think and only tweaks it here and there before returning to it for rewrite. Upon completion of a second draft, she sends it to her publisher. "I always like to think that is the final draft but, of course, the publisher comes back to me with suggestions and questions. Then I go to work again."

Though her characters often dictate what point of view their story should be told in, Lowry says, "I have two that I'm comfortable with, and one is the first person point of view. I'm very comfortable with that although it does have limitations. The point of view which I most use, and have for *The Giver* and *Gathering Blue*, is limited third person. I am not comfortable with an omniscient point of view; I think it detracts from a novel to use an omniscient narrator," she says. "However, *The Silent Boy* has an unusual point of view that I've used only once before in a book that goes way back, *Autumn Street*. It begins with an adult, looking back on her own childhood and telling a story of things that happened when she was young, using the child's perceptions but speaking in the adult voice. I'm not sure why I've loved using that point of view so much. It's hard to write that way."

In order to keep track of ideas, Lowry keeps notes in her computer. "I do not keep journals the way many writers do. I make a few notes. If something impresses me as potentially important, I do try to jot it down." She also has a file folder labeled "dreams," which she occasionally reads and finds inspiring. "Every now and then I have had a dream so vivid that I have written

Lois Lowry's Time Line & Reading List

1977 *A Summer to Die*
1978 *Find a Stranger, Say Goodbye*
1979 *Anastasia Krupkik*
1980 *Autumn Street*
1981 *Anastasia Again!*
1982 *Anastasia at your Service*
1983 *Taking Care of Terrific*
1983 *The One Hundredth Thing About Caroline*
1984 *Anastasia, Ask Your Analyst*
1984 *Us and Uncle Fraud*
1985 *Anastasia on Her Own*
1985 *Switcharound*
1986 *Anastasia Has the Answers*
1987 *Anastasia's Chosen Career*
1987 *RabbleStarkey*
1988 *All about Sam*

1989 *Number the Stars* (Newbery Medal winner)
1990 *Your Move, J.P.!*
1991 *Anastasia at This Address*
1992 *Attaboy, Sam!*
1993 *The Giver* (Newbery Medal winner)
1995 *Anastasia, Absolutely*
1996 *See You Around, Sam*
1997 *Stay! Keeper's Story*
1998 *Looking Back: A Book of Memories*
1999 *Zooman Sam*
2000 *Gathering Blue*
2002 *Gooney Bird Greene*
2003 *The Silent Boy*
2004 *Messenger*

Lois Lowry explores yet another alternative world view in her novel *Gathering Blue*, about a young orphan with disabilities in a world that sees the weak as extra baggage that should be thrown-away. Whether described as science fiction, speculative fiction, or allegory; countless reviews, teachers' lesson plans, and reader comments beg for investigation into the book's dark reality.

© Houghton Mifflin Co. Reprinted with permission.

it down. I'm not sure they contribute in any way to what I'm writing other than reflecting my great interest in trying to figure out what's going on in people's minds, including my own."

When Lowry's mother was hospitalized for a stroke, her mother began to cry one day and repeated, "Dorothy's baby has died. Dorothy's baby has died." Later, when Lowry's brother asked their mother if she had been actually seeing Dorothy or remembering Dorothy, their mother responded very clearly, "In the dream world, it doesn't matter." "I've remained fascinated by that," Lowry says. "That somewhere, there is a dream world, where everything is combined and it doesn't matter. Whether it's now or then or in the future or whether the people are gone, they're still there somewhere and there's this dream world, where things are all mixed up and it truly doesn't matter."

Lowry also uses daydreams to find out what's going on in her mind. "Subconscious is always there. I do a lot of waking dreaming, which I guess is another way of saying thinking. When I'm by myself, I sit at my desk, staring into space. I suppose anybody seeing me doing that would think, 'What a weird person. She sits there like a moron.' But I think so much and so much happens in my brain before I sit down and put it into the computer."

Considering her early appreciation for literature, and now her continued success, it's apparent Lowry has something in common with several of her characters. Much like Jonas in *The Giver* and Kira, Thomas, and Jo in *Gathering Blue*, Lowry's talent comes naturally, like a magical gift. Speaking of the comparison Lowry says, "In most of my books—I don't want to say all because I haven't thought through them all—the main character will be somebody who is very introspective and who feels set apart for some reason. I think that is a necessary component of most fiction because you need an introspective main character in order to invite the reader to be part of that character."

To date, Lowry has published twenty-nine books. Her endearingly popular Anastasia Krupnik series has humored readers since 1979 and continues to do so. She has written many serious novels with topics including death, mental illness, the Holocaust, and controlled societies.

Gooney Bird Greene, released in 2002, is a humorous story about a second grader who enchants her new classmates with "absolutely true" stories and a most unusual wardrobe. Lowry teamed up with long-time friend and illustrator Middy Thomas to bring Gooney Bird to life. There will be more of this eccentric little storyteller to come.

Released in April 2003, *The Silent Boy* is set in the early 1900s and tells the story of Katy

Thatcher, the daughter of the town doctor. Katy's desire to "know about people" leads to a friendship with Jacob, a farm boy who is "touched." Katy's ability to sense meaning behind Jacob's actions and sounds fuel their human connection. She sees there is more to the boy others call an imbecile. Katy's curious nature results in her deep understanding and subsequent defense of him.

Scheduled for publication in Spring 2004, *Messenger* is the highly anticipated novel that will complete the trilogy of *The Giver* and *Gathering Blue*. "The main character is Matt, from *Gathering Blue*," Lowry says. "He is about fifteen and has a gift of magical proportions."

Lowry skillfully creates realistic experiences for her characters and then sends them, along with her readers, on a journey. "I will tell you that in every book—in order for there to be a book, a story, a point, a reason for writing it—the main character takes a journey. Sometimes, very often in fact, it is an interior journey: a journey that does not involve geography, except the geography of the mind and heart. But there is always a going forth, a quest, a seeking of something, and a coming back, when something is found."

Coming back is just what Lowry's readers continue to do. And as she said so eloquently in a Brown University speech, "We all touch each other while we wait for what happens next." Again and again, readers will turn to her characters, her stories, to make that important connection—something that is always worth the wait.

Spirit à la Tomie dePaola: A Distinctive Force in Children's Literature

BY KELLY MILNER HALLS

According to legendary illustrator Tomie dePaola, angels flutter through his lively imagination with regularity and have since he was a small boy. Little wonder, if you consider the master's abundance of spirit. Miraculous entities surely recognize their own.

Too much, you say, to call dePaola a miracle? Perhaps. But children have gathered his books—better than 200 titles—like golden eggs for more than 30 years now. And as the time has flown by, they've added dePaola note cards, inkpads, fine art prints, book bags, stickers, and even videos to their cherished collections.

With his artistic anointing, book projects undeniably take flight. Like dePaola himself, they soar to what must surely be children's book heaven—the collective memory of young readers come and gone.

What makes this brilliant artist such a distinctive force in literature?

Skill is dePaola's magic, according to the *School Library Journal*. In describing *Adelita*, dePaola's retelling of Cinderella, they

Tomie dePaola

say, "Making perfect use of clear, warm hues, the full-color acrylic illustrations are a feast for the eye."

Or tenderness: "dePaola presents [*26 Fairmont Avenue*] with a keen understanding of the timeless concerns children share," also from the *School Library Journal*.

Or whimsy: Says *Kirkus* of *Holy Twins: Benedict and Scholastica*: "dePaola's inexhaustible

KELLY MILNER HALLS *is a freelance writer in Spokane specializing in children's nonfiction and nonfiction about writing. She has published more than 1,500 articles in* Highlights for Children, Teen PEOPLE, FamilyFun, Writer's Digest, Ask!, Dig, Boy's Life, U*S*Kids, The Chicago Tribune, The Washington Post, The Denver Post, *and dozens of other publications. She has ten published children's books to her credit, including* Dinosaur Mummies: Beyond Bare-Bone Fossils *(Darby Creek Publishing, 2003). She has three more scheduled for release in 2004, including* The Jurassic Park Institute Dinosaur Travel Guide *(Random House, 2004) and* Girl Meets Boy, *a YA anthology (Simon & Schuster, 2004).*

wellspring of creativity is never more evident than in ecclesiastical whimsy."

However his genius is described, one word can economically sum it up: Success. Tomie dePaola is an authentic, multigenerational bestseller. And this candid interview reveals a few of the secrets behind his prolific all-star children's literature career.

You were born in Connecticut and earned your BFA at the Pratt Institute in Brooklyn; a real east coast boy. How much culture shock did you experience when you went to graduate school in northern California?

I was ready for it. I'd gone to art school in New York in the '50s, left to teach in Vermont, then in Boston, then back to New York. Then, in 1967, I decided to go back to school to get my

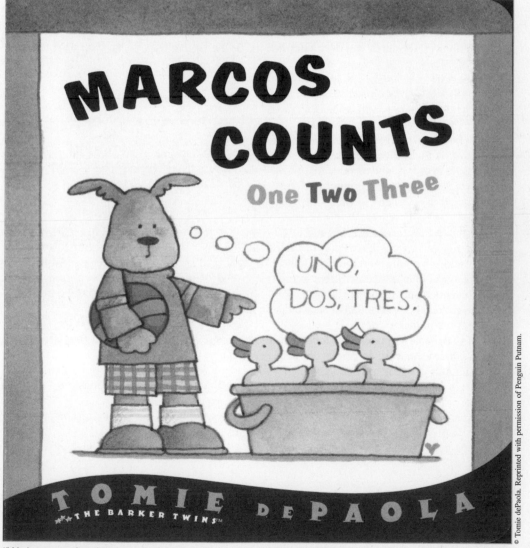

"We have to realize that we want children to be bilingual," said Tomie dePaola in an interview with Reading Rockets. A champion of multiculturalism, dePaola taught himself Italian words when writing *Strega Nona* and began teaching himself Spanish and Mexican to write *Adelita*. With board books like *Marcos Counts*, he practices his own Spanish while introducing bilingual books to beginning readers.

Masters. I didn't want to go back to Pratt, so I got myself a teaching job in Northern California. I found myself living in what was, at the time, the most beautiful city in the United States, the center of free speech in Berkeley. It was really possible then for young people, young art students, to be nonconformists. We didn't all look alike. It's harder today because of that insidious television, MTV. I was just at an event, a Youth Invasion party at the Warhol Museum in Pittsburgh, and the kids were trying so hard to be unique, but they all looked exactly alike.

Did your time in the Bay Area influence your illustrative style?

By the time I was doing my masters work, my style was pretty well established. In fact, when I asked one of my instructors at Pratt when we were going to learn about style, he said it wasn't something that could be taught. He said unless you were studying advertising design where you're required to be flexible with technique, style came from the inside, out. Style, he said, was about who you were. So I'm not sure it affected my style.

It did change my consciousness though, about feminism and race and war. All of those issues were so much a part of what was happening then. And there was more time to be spiritual because the pace was slower. I was introduced to a kind of Zen-like meditation there. And I'm a great believer in the idea that if you stay open as an artist and an illustrator, your life experiences will inform your work.

You loved California, and yet now you're at home in New Hampshire? What pulled you back?

I'd already started making children's books by then, and San Francisco was a long way from New York. There was no FedEx or Internet back then—only the telephone, letters, and telegrams. So I made a commitment to living back East. Besides, I missed the seasons.

How did your career as an illustrator begin?

I illustrated my first book in 1963, and it was published in 1965. That started it. I had graduated from art school in 1956 and was expecting to get my first book right away. But it was seven years coming. I finally met the woman who became my agent and she had my portfolio for about a month. I thought, "Nothing's going to happen." But the day before I was going to pick it up, she called and said, "Hi ho, hi ho, it's off to work we go." The name of the book was *Sound*, a picture book of science theories, written by a Denise Kohn.

One of your most famous book characters, Strega Nona, turned 25 a few years ago. Did you have any inkling she'd be so popular?

I had no idea Strega Nona would have a life of her own. That's one of the joys of being a children's book artist and author, the fact that our books stay in print a long time. And several years ago, *Nana Upstairs, Nana Downstairs* also celebrated its 25th anniversary. Then *The Clown of God* turned 25 recently. It's amazing that the books have stayed in print and found new fans for so long.

Where did *Strega Nona* come from?

I have no idea. She appeared on a doodle pad, full born, like Venus out of the sea. It was one of those things, very uncontrived and purely spontaneous. If you're interested, you can read the entire saga in Barbara Ellerman's book, *Tomie dePaola, His Art and His Stories*.

What's the trick to keeping subsequent *Strega Nona* stories engaging?

I always say I don't write *Strega Nona* books. I channel them. When I write a book with the same characters as were in a previous book, I always take it for granted that no one's read the previous book. It has to stand on its own.

Frida Kahlo: The Artist Who Painted Herself, written by Margaret Frith, is part of Grosset's Smart about Art series and was released in August, 2003. The book gives dePaola a chance to show off his long-time appreciation of the artist and her understanding of folk culture in Mexico. For the cover, dePaola made his goal to "saturate the page with color because Frida was all about color."

Did the Newbery Honor for 26 Fairmont Avenue surprise you?

I was totally surprised. It was never even in my mind that I might have a Newbery Honor book, because I never thought of myself as a writer of "literature." I was in my studio and I told my sister Maureen that I didn't want to be disturbed. She works for me. And they had a hard time getting past her. They finally said, "Oh, I think he'll want to take this call." That was a Monday morning in January, so I wasn't out in the garden.

Is Maureen pleased with the books, since she's one of your autobiographical characters?

Oh yes, she's thrilled. But she's been in a lot of my books actually. She was the subject matter of the picture book, *The Baby Sister*. She works with me and she was on the Barney TV show with me, so she's a superstar according to her grandchildren.

You touched on your spirituality earlier. You seem to write and illustrate a lot of books with spiritual or angelic themes, and yet they seldom seem judgmental or exclusive. How do you walk that line?

That's funny. I was actually working on an angel book when you called, a book called *Pasqual and the Kitchen Angels*. A Mexican friend of mine gave me a hand-carved piece and told me a little-known legend. Pasqual wanted to become a friar, but he wasn't educated. So they told him he couldn't be a friar, but could work as a layperson in the kitchen. He agreed, but he didn't know how to cook. So he prayed for angels to help him and they appeared and did all the cooking for him.

I was a very spiritual kid. I loved all that stuff and I won't deny it. It's part of me. But the last thing I want to do is spread propaganda about any church. That's not the point. The point is that these stories are as magical as any fairytale.

You worked on another surprising character recently—painter Frida Kahlo in the book Frida Kahlo: The Artist Who Painted Herself. How did that come about?

Grosset had a new series called Smart About Art. Margaret Frith, my semi-retired editor of 40 years at Putnam, had long been interested in Frida Kahlo. So Jane O'Conner, the series editor who is also semi-retired, asked Margaret if she'd write a book for the series. I've been in love with Frida for years because of Diego Rivera's work. I was introduced to her through him. So I had fun with illustrating that book. My art was more decorative. On the cover art, I wanted to saturate the page with color because Frida was all about color. She understood the depth of folk culture's impact in Mexico. Mexican natives use color, which comes from the Aztecs. You don't see anything like that in Spain. You see women dressed in black lace. But some of our Southwestern Native American tribes are very attracted to bright colors—same ancient influences.

From a sophisticated book topic to the simply sublime—you've also worked on some new board books lately, Marcos Colors and Marcos Counts.

I actually did several early on. I had such a wonderful time doing board books. I did a whole series of holiday titles for Putnam, things like *Baby's First Christmas*. Now I'm doing a group with the twins, the dog characters. And it's interesting that I can do this, but I can look at the books when they come, finished, and see them objectively. I said to my assistant, Bob, "These are so damn cute. So simple and colorful." That's the essence of a really good board book, I think—that it's really simple and bright.

The books are bilingual.

Yes, that's funny. I was trying to learn Spanish, so I thought, why not practice in these books. Now I know my colors and my numbers, at least.

Tomie dePaola's very first trip to Mexico inspired him to write the bilingual Mexican Cinderella story *Adelita*. Puebla, Mexico, called the City of Tiles and filled with elaborately tiled buildings, gave dePaola the idea to "hold the pictures in," using tile borders and themes throughout the book.

What advice do you have for would-be children's writers and illustrators?

Be a plumber? (laughter) No. My advice is to do your homework. Learn the professional way to submit the manuscript. And you can go to your library and there are plenty of very fine books that explain the process, that talk about how. Your local children's librarian is also a great resource.

Do you make a conscious effort to stay in touch with the child within yourself?

Yes, I do. And it took a long time to get back in touch with that child. I learned how to unlock the closet and let little Tomie out in therapy. And it's essential if you're going to create books for children that you are in touch with the feelings that you had as a child, good and bad.

How has the industry changed since you got your start?

When I started out, 30-some odd years ago, only 10 or 15% of all children's book sales were through bookstores. The rest were what they called "institutional sales"—sales to and through schools and libraries. Now it's probably 60 or 70% retail market. That's made a huge difference. It's made the industry harder for people to break into.

Have you seen any trends you find disturbing as a children's author/illustrator?

The only trends I find not so much disturbing as tiresome are the merchandise-driven books. For instance, when Disney's *The Lion King* came out as a film, there were suddenly 80-plus Lion King books out there, all from Disney. That takes up a lot of room in the market.

The other disturbing thing is that sometimes even a very unusual book doesn't get enough of a chance in today's market. Books go out of print much quicker than they used to. But, at the same time, I think there are more and more people who want to write children's books. And I have the faith that the truly good books will find their way and live for a long time.

First Books:
Illustrators & Author/Illustrators

BY MONA MICHAEL

The other night, I dreamed of a kangaroo that was really a piano—and it seemed natural for him, and he was quite friendly. I can't explain this adequately, so that you would understand. But if I were an illustrator, I could paint it for you, take the image from my head and place it onto paper. What magic!

I've come to believe that illustrators have a leg up on the rest of us—a key to a secret door, if you will, a way of seeing their world that the rest of us can only wonder at. Writers put ideas down on paper with words, but illustrators bring those words to life with watercolor, paper, and oil. That's what makes this year's First Book subjects special: All are illustrators; all are creators of picture books.

A ballerina with boat-sized feet, a canoe loaded with fauna, a sibling-stealing alligator, and a wrong-side-up boy usher this year's troop of creators into the club called "the published." All experienced shock at finally being noticed and joy at being asked to do what they would be doing anyway—making their imaginations come to life with the stroke of a brush.

AMY YOUNG
Belinda the Ballerina
(Viking)

Photo: Anna Pontoni

Amy Young's first book features an unlikely heroine: a ballerina with big feet. *Belinda the Ballerina* may dance like a swan, but all the judges see are the feet of an elephant. Discouraged by their criticism, Belinda tries to give up her dream and goes to work in a restaurant. There, she finds herself dancing blissfully to the music of the house band. Word travels fast in the city, and soon the restaurant overflows with people who have come to see Belinda dance.

Like her heroine, Young also spent some time trying to ignore her dreams. She began as a fine artist, earning her MFA in Painting from Indiana University in 1984. During that time though, "the reality of trying to make a living as a fine artist hit me," she says. Impossible, thought Young, that she could translate her training as a fine artist into a living for herself. So she decided to follow in her father's footsteps and go to law school. Just as Belinda found herself dancing in the restaurant, Young could never forget her true nature. She became the illustrating lawyer.

"I approached the Michigan Bar journal and asked if they would give me a chance. They did, and I did monthly illustrations for them over the course of many years. It was fun because my legal knowledge helped me to come up with appropriate concepts. They also didn't mind if I tried different styles and media, so it was a great place to learn and try new things. From there, I branched out into working for other magazines and newspapers and the occasional corporate

MONA MICHAEL *is assistant editor of* Children's Writer's & Illustrator's Market, Artist's & Graphic Designer's Market, *and is a freelance writing consultant.*

Amy Young began her children's publishing career to applause with a starred review in *Publishers Weekly* for her first book, *Belinda the Ballerina*, published by Viking. Readers and reviewers praise the picture book about a ballerina with big feet as a wonderful never-give-up-your-dreams tale. More than ten years passed though, from the time Young first conceived *Belinda* to her publication. Young even stopped submitting the manuscript at one point, calling it her "zombie story."

client." Eventually she tired of wearing two hats, when one clearly suited her better. "After seven years," she says. "I decided to 'retire' from law. It was a very difficult decision, but the only one I could make." She had been sending work out to magazines and establishing contacts already. So she went the next step and sent out promotional postcards, which she still does, using purchased mailing lists and directories, as well as *Children's Writer's & Illustrator's Market*.

The idea for *Belinda* came to Young all at once while enjoying a glass of wine with her husband after dinner. "I started to tell him the story, and then I had to draw it as I told it. And it all tumbled out, pictures and words together." She put together a dummy of the story and began sending it to publishers; she attended SCBWI conferences and got an invitation to submit it from contacts there. None of her efforts came to fruition though, and Young began to feel frustrated. "I started calling it my 'zombie story' because it wouldn't live and it wouldn't die. I even stopped submitting it," she says.

Then, when she was least expecting it . . .

"I was in New York showing my portfolio to art directors, along with a dummy and art samples for a new book (which a friend had written). The people at Viking liked the artwork but didn't think the story was right for them. They asked me what else I had, and I mentioned this story about a ballerina with big feet. They said 'Send it!' I tried to talk them out of it, saying 'You wouldn't like it, it just isn't right.' 'Send it!' they said. So I did, expecting the same sad course of events I had lived through so many times already. I did a few simple edits at their request, and when the editor called me to make an offer, I was dumbfounded. I don't think I ever really, truly believed it had happened until I got the bound book in my hands a year or so later."

Like many first-time authors and illustrators, Young was startled by the pace of the publishing process. "Two weeks is a luxury to crank out an editorial illustration. When I illustrate for *The New York Times*, I usually have only one or two days and deliver the final art by e-mail. In book publishing, it's not unusual for someone to hold onto a manuscript for months and months. Then even if you get a contract, you have to wait weeks or months for it to be delivered."

She's under contract to do two more books for Viking: a sequel to *Belinda the Ballerina* (Belinda will be heading to Paris) and another to follow. She's just finished illustrations for *Spike and Cubby's Ice Cream Island Adventure*, by Heather Sellers (Holt, Summer 2004) as well. With her big-footed ballerina in Paris and an uncertain but exciting future ahead, it looks like Amy Young has found her stage.

VICKY RUBIN
Ralphie and the Swamp Baby
(Henry Holt)

Photo: Julia Griner

"As a child I had an odd obsession with Snoopy," says Vicky Rubin, the author/illustrator whose first book, *Ralphie and the Swamp Baby*, is due for release by Holt in 2004. "And the worlds created in picture books have always been an oasis for me."

The idea for her own oasis originated from a children's market portfolio class. "I had this image of a mother alligator knitting a baby sweater and her husband looking flabbergasted. It took a long time for it to gel into a real story." *Ralphie and the Swamp Baby* turned out to be centered around a younger member of the alligator family, Ralphie, who feels threatened by the imminent arrival of a new sibling. And while Rubin describes her reaction to Holt's acceptance of the book "like seeing Santa come down the chimney after you've finally accepted he doesn't exist," her own story reads less like a fantasy made real and more like the culmination of a lot of very hard work.

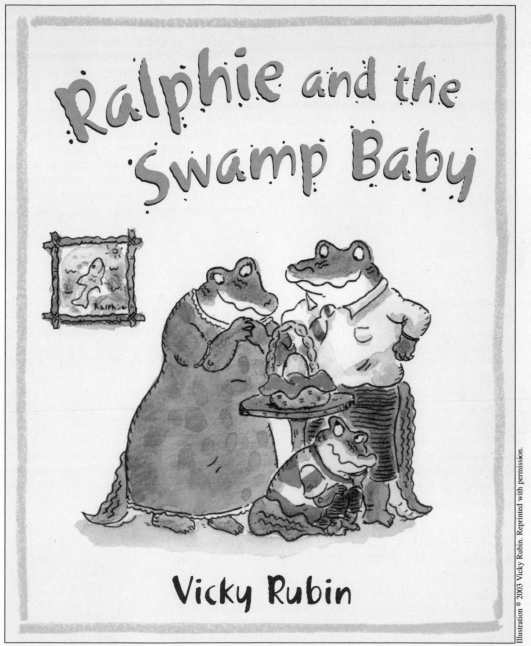

The idea for Vicky Rubin's first book, *Ralphie and the Swamp Baby* (Henry Holt, 2004) came to her during a children's market portfolio class as an image of a mother alligator knitting a baby sweater with her dismayed husband standing nearby. Many revisions, submissions, and rejections later, her new baby story centers around a young alligator dealing with the arrival of a new sibling.

A self-described compulsive student, she earned her undergraduate degree in history and post-graduate in art education—and she was just getting started. Looking for clues to the world she wished to enter, she enrolled in course after course, including private classes with Stuart Leeds, a *New Yorker* cartoonist; Writing for Children at the Writer's Voice of the West Side

YMCA; Anastasia Suen's online intensive picture book workshop; an online screenwriting class; and now an ongoing writing-for-children workshop with Marcia Savin. Her immersion in classes like these led to the discovery of "a whole children's book community," Rubin says.

Encouraged first by this new-found community and further by the sale of a couple of poems to *Cricket* and *Spider* magazines, Rubin began to feel at home in children's publishing. She joined the Children's Book Illustrator's Group (CBIG) organization in New York. Run by volunteers, the group added children's book editors and art directors to the widening circle of professionals she'd become acquainted with through her classes.

During one of CBIG's portfolio review days, Rubin found herself sitting across from Robbie Mayes, editor at Farrar, Straus & Giroux. Without much hope that he'd actually take a close look at her work, she showed Mayes a dummy she'd recently prepared. Mayes shocked her by asking to take the dummy with him. Rubin cut the meeting short—ending it after only six minutes of her ten minute allotment, saying "I was afraid he'd change his mind!" FSG kept the book for a year before they finally rejected it. The FSG editor suggested Rubin send the manuscript to Reka Simonsen at Holt. She did; and after editorial review, it was rejected there as well.

Not one to stand idle, Rubin had not stopped working while she waited for answers from the two publishers. By the time she received news of the Holt rejection, she was nearly ready with a dummy of an older story, one that began in a portfolio class. Disappointed by her previous rejections but not daunted, she finished *Ralphie and the Swamp Baby* and forwarded it to Mayes at FSG, ready to start the whole process again. The two wrote letters back and forth for a while, and Mayes "put stickies all over the dummy with suggestions for the illustrations," says Rubin. *Ralphie and the Swamp Baby* made its trip to committee, and was turned down without comment. Frustrated, Rubin took this rejection hard: "I felt discouraged and didn't do anything with it for a year."

Eventually, she found the courage to submit the book again, this time to Simonsen at Holt. To Rubin's surprise, Holt accepted the manuscript. "No requests for revisions or anything," she says. "That showed me that editors and houses are all different and if a book is rejected it may not be because of a problem with a story but just that it isn't right for that house. And each editor has a different vision."

With that in mind, Rubin is busy now working on new projects. A copyeditor by day at *BusinessWeek* magazine, she's learning to balance writing and illustration and has posted her work at both www.portfolios.com and www.picture-book.com. While she's not sure what will happen in the future, her first children's book publishing experience taught her at least one important lesson: "I'm learning to be patient."

MEGHAN McCARTHY
George Upside Down
(Viking)

Meghan McCarthy created her first picture book before she knew how to read. "I drew the pictures and dictated the words to my grandmother," she says. She remembers announcing at just seven years old that she wanted to publish a children's book. "But it wasn't until taking a class at Rhode Island School of Design that I learned how to put the writing and illustrating together— and it was two years after graduation before my skills were polished enough to make my dream a reality."

With her first published picture book, *George Upside Down* (Viking 2003) McCarthy played off another slightly less serious childhood dream. The main character in the book, George, is a spirited little fellow who wants nothing more than to live life upside down. "George was a culmination of my present imagination and my childhood fantasy," says McCarthy. George's world exists in bold, bright colors—and he drifts through his upside down world without a care. His creator has had a bit of a tougher time with him though.

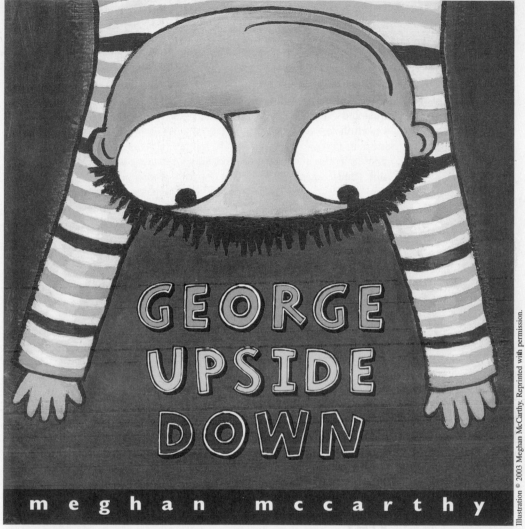

A rejection letter for an early version of *George Upside Down* convinced author/illustrator Meghan McCarthy that she needed to move from her home in Rhode Island to live in New York. Now she's made a new home for herself in the children's book world with her "day job" at Barnes & Noble, her online critique group, Yellapalooza (see article on page 63), and her two-part book deal with Viking. She suggests aspiring children's book creators save their pennies before trying to make ends meet solely with children's publishing.

McCarthy began submitting *George* while holding a job delivering pizzas shortly after she graduated college. She received a pile of rejections. However, hidden in that pile was at least one hopeful sentence. "I love the idea and illustrations," wrote Tracy Gates, then editor at Knopf. "But the story is slight. Give me a call when you're in NYC—I'd love to see your portfolio."

McCarthy considered that rejection as she delivered extra-pepperoni to lighted front porches late at night. Then, she made a decision. "I packed up my things and left my friends, family, and beautiful apartment behind," she says. Once she arrived in New York and recovered from the initial wave of culture shock, McCarthy began visiting publishers—portfolio in hand. After receiving enough positive responses to boost her confidence, if not land her an offer, she found the courage to call Tracy Gates, the editor whose invitation had spurred her into action. At their meeting Gates asked McCarthy how she liked New York. McCarthy told her she was close to running out of money, so was fairly certain she wouldn't be living in New York much longer. "I'll never forget her response," says McCarthy. "She said, 'Oh, I don't think you'll have to worry about that.' "

Two weeks later, McCarthy got the call—Gates wanted to publish her book. However the publishing process didn't move quite fast enough to relieve McCarthy's financial strain. So she found another way to pay the rent—at Barnes & Noble. "I took the job out of desperation. Contracts are slow. If I could tell my past self anything, it would be to save up $10,000 *then* (yeah, right), so *now* I wouldn't have to work seven days a week, get pizza without toppings, and buy used clothes from the sale bin."

While a typical day has McCarthy answering monotonous questions like, *Where's the bathroom?*, *Can I check this out?* and *How do I get back to the first floor?*, and struggling to get to work when she has a book due, being a bookseller does have advantages. "The bulk of my kid's book knowledge came from my job," she says. "I have an ample grasp of what sells and why. I've also stumbled on some invaluable opportunities."

One of those opportunities presented itself when McCarthy met the Barnes & Noble author promotions manager right before *George's* release. The promotions manager encouraged the fledgling author to do in-store events. Petrified of public speaking and filled with insecurity about her work, McCarthy hesitated—but eventually agreed. "I'm so glad I did! They've been great experiences for me. They've helped me get over some of my phobias, not to mention that I sold some books!"

Show Dog, the second part of her two-book deal with Viking, is due out next year. Besides that, she's working on her website, www.meghan-mccarthy.com, which features her portfolio, event listings, bio, information about her books, and will soon have a section devoted to the creation of picture books for new and experienced author/illustrators.

Always filled with new ideas, her latest bit of exciting news just arrived: "Two publishers have informed me they'd like to purchase the same manuscript. Yikes!" She still struggles to keep everything in line. "It's very difficult to work on a book and hold a full-time job," she says. "And I never would have dreamed that I'd be negotiating my own book contracts." However, she knows she still has a long way to go and doesn't plan on giving up anytime soon, admitting, "It takes a long time to make a living by creating children's books."

ARD HOYT
One-Dog Canoe
(Farrar, Strauss & Giroux)

Photo: Sonya Sones

Ard Hoyt, a graduate of The Art Center College of Design in Pasedena and father of "three terrific girls," has always dreamed of creating picture book illustrations. "Steven Kellogg's work; *The Story of Ferdinand*, by Munro Leaf; drawings by Robert Lawson; and H.A. Rey's *Curious George*—in these pictures, I was swimming with a beautiful fish, had the dog of my dreams and saw myself as a huge and muscular bull with a gentle heart. I knew from my first memories that I wanted to be part of this imaginative world. I feel honored to be on the shelf with those great ones."

Hoyt's first book, *One-Dog Canoe*, written by Mary Cassanova and published by Farrar, Straus & Giroux, arrived on those shelves in March 2003. And though Hoyt's goal has always been picture books, he's sometimes had to settle for less satisfying work. "From running the camel ride at the zoo to waiting tables," he says, "I have had nearly every kind of job imaginable. I was a graphic artist in a family printing business, designing everything from T-shirts to taco sauce labels. The toughest thing there was that I was constantly trying to infuse my character

Illustrator Ard Hoyt was once a pupil of Marla Frazee, illustrator, instructor, and winner of the 2002 Golden Kite Award. He counts her influence essential to his current success. It was Frazee who pointed Hoyt in the direction of the agent who eventually led him to his first book, *One-Dog Canoe*, written by Mary Cassanova (Farrar, Straus & Giroux, March 2003).

designs. And they were constantly telling me things like, 'What does this walrus have to do with beauty products?' "

While the jobs he held may have been less than ideal, Hoyt always found inspiration in the students and faculty at The Art Center College of Design. "Every day it seemed some fellow student would raise the bar to a new and higher level," he says. This was never more true than when he sought out an illustration class taught by Golden Kite Award-winner Marla Frazee (*The Seven Silly Eaters, Mrs. Biddlebox, Roller Coaster*). Only offered through the night program at the college, admission to Frazee's class required a lot of extra footwork. From the very first lesson, though, Hoyt knew it was worth it. "She read us a short passage from two books written for children. The first was apparently written by a board room of business types with the intent to make a mass market product. The next was from Beatrix Potter's *Peter Rabbit*. The difference, she explained, was motivation. One was written to make as much money as possible and the other was written to cheer up a sick child the author knew."

With his family, who puts "the steam" in his stride, and his desire to join the world of picture book illustration for motivation, Hoyt took Frazee's lessons to heart. His says his time at the college taught him that "talents are like fingerprints," and Frazee suggested he test his fingerprint on the outside world.

Frazee advised Hoyt to send some samples to an agent she knew and respected. With some hesitation, Hoyt gathered together some of his "best ideas in color copies" and sent them away. "You would have thought I was mailing away one of my children," he says. Later, when the agent called to tell Hoyt there was a possibility for a job illustrating a book for FSG, the illustrator discovered what he describes as the largest obstacle to being published: "convincing an editor you won't start something you can't finish."

FSG sent Hoyt a copy of the manuscript; he was to create some illustrations for it. After completing one set and sending them for consideration, Hoyt got word that the editor liked his work. However first he wanted a telephone interview, as well as some outside assurance that Hoyt would, in fact, finish the project. Hoyt credits Marla Frazee with aiding him on both fronts. "There is no value you can give a good and hard-earned reputation," he says. "Without her endorsement I would not be where I am today." With Frazee's assurances to the publisher, Hoyt only had to worry about the interview. "The interview was basically this: What's your motivation? And I was ready."

The publishing process itself added to Hoyt's education. His thoughts were listened to and considered—and his original sketches were always the starting point—so he always felt connected to the pictures. However, the process involved "a great deal of constructive alternatives to my initial thoughts on pretty much everything," he says. So much revision occurred that Hoyt wondered how they would ever meet the deadline. Through the process, he learned "to internalize every revision" and to "never look back or hold on to an idea too tightly."

The result is *One-Dog Canoe*, Hoyt's first book and an important building block to the reputation that is his career. "I am building that track record and reputation for finishing what I start with consistency and creativity," he says. Two more books already on the way speak to the success of that reputation. John Lithgow's *I'm a Manatee* (Simon & Schuster, September 2003), as well as *Ugly Pie*, by Lisa Wheeler (Harcourt, Inc., Spring 2004), will join *One-Dog Canoe* on the shelves along with the greats who first inspired Hoyt. And his motivation promises to see him through to many more.

"My father told me once," he says, " 'It's what you do with what you've got that counts.' I often ask myself, 'What have I done today with what I have available to me to get closer to my goals?' I think getting there often takes as much creativity as the job itself. You have a fingerprint. Find it and put it everywhere you can."

First Books Follow-up: Catherine Atkins

The first sale is the grand prize for beginning writers and illustrators. You've worked and worked, your first book collected awards from the American Library Association and Booklist and gathered praise from reviewers as well as readers—so, you've got it made now, right? Well, sort of. While many things have improved for her since we spoke to Catherine Atkins about her award-winning first book, *When Jeff Comes Home*, she still finds each sale a challenge. A debut publication is just that—the first—but it does not give you a magic ticket to the rest of your career. "What changes on being published is you gain a certain level of respect," says Atkins. "Editors give your work a careful read and you get thoughtful comments back, even on a rejection. What you don't get is a guaranteed sale."

Illustration © 2003 Mark Elliot. Reprinted with permission.

Atkins's second novel is *Alt Ed*, a funny, heart-wrenching look at high school, along with all the politics, pitfalls, and even a clueless school counselor. Reviewers from *The Horn Book* to *YM* have praised the fully drawn characters, and *Publishers Weekly* gave the book a starred review. However, *Alt Ed* "took a long time to sell," says Atkins. "It was rejected over and over and I didn't know why. I didn't know how to improve the manuscript, and I was blocked on writing anything else. This was the point when I joined my first critique group."

How did the critique group help? What role have groups played for you in the past?
Only my agent and editors saw *When Jeff Comes Home* before publication. I never considered sharing my work with other writers. The same approach wasn't working for *Alt Ed*.

At first I only read and commented on others' work. I didn't share my own—too chicken. They didn't push. I saw how they interacted and how they helped each other. I got the courage to send my work (this was all online), and they were kind and helpful. Their suggestions made sense. I rewrote and sent again to more readers—more help. It was a revelation that I could share my work and be affirmed by it at the same time I was hearing about the changes I needed to make. I began doing lots of critiques and I learned from that. It was a culture of improvement.

How was your approach and reaction to publication different the second time around?
When my first book was published, I wasn't working on anything else. I had writer's block. I had lost my agent and editor, both to retirement, and I wasn't sure if I would ever make another sale.

Flash forward to *Alt Ed*'s publication. As the reviews were rolling in, I was deep into the first draft of a contracted young adult novel. I had another contracted novel on deck. I was in touch with other writers, my encouraging agent, and an editor waiting for my work. Big changes, all positive.

What's been surprising for you about the writing/publishing world?
Everyone struggles. Everyone is insecure. No work is ever really finished. I guess I expected a certain level of confidence and a sense of, "I have arrived" among established writers. I haven't seen that, just a continuous asking of the question, "How can I do this better?"

When, why and how did you go about creating your website?
Self-promotion comes hard for me. I always felt a little guilty about not doing more to promote my first book. As publication time approached for the second book, I decided to put up a website as a quiet way of supporting my work. The website has done exactly what I hoped. Within days of its going live, I was receiving fan mail, comments, and questions from readers. I was happy to hear from them and in some cases modified the site thanks to their input. My goal is a reader-friendly and timely website.

I checked out lots of sites before deciding how I wanted to do mine. I knew I didn't want anything I couldn't maintain myself—no fancy stuff. I was searching for something simple and fun. I found it in Sara Ryan's site (www.sararyan.com). She is a young adult writer whose site at the time featured a bright yellow background, no pictures, and links to a variety of topics. I asked web designer Kelly Milner Halls to follow this style for my site. I e-mailed her the content to start. The only pictures we used were my book covers. I update the content every month. The pictures and background remain the same. Oh, self-promotion, right? Please visit my site: www.catherineatkins.com.

Can you tell me about your first speaking engagements and what you've learned about them since then?
Two ways to approach speaking engagements: Assume you are welcome and be responsive to your audience.

My first was at the California School Librarians' Association conference in Sacramento. I spoke at a breakout session to a crowd of about twenty-five on the topic of life as a young adult writer. I was very nervous leading up to the talk but comfortable once I got into it. The audience was receptive and friendly and not scary. Many were aspiring YA writers and they asked great questions. The experience made me want to speak more.

Your website says you read *The Only Girl in the Car*, by Kathy Dobie, as research for one of your characters. How do you use research to help develop your characters?
The Only Girl in the Car was an immense help in building the character of a school "slut." Dobie writes of how unaware she was of the way people were judging her, and also of her determination to be with these boys past all common sense. Her honesty gave me valuable perspective on the way Amber might be thinking.

Research is important and I am always looking for details. I think of it as having the antennae going (like a praying mantis, maybe, if you need a visual). I am a teacher, and I watch the way teens interact with each other and with teachers and staff.

Where does your inspiration for the honesty we see in your books come from?
I work in education, the land of euphemisms and buzzwords—alternative education at that, so honesty is always refreshing. School life often seems a "King of the Mountain" game, for students and staff, so I am interested in the idea of what someone does when they are already marked as unfit for the struggle.

What is the single most important thing you've learned that you didn't know before *When Jeff Comes Home* came out?
The value of critique.

Key to Symbols & Abbreviations

N Indicates a listing new in this edition.

Indicates a Canadian listing.

Indicates a listing is located in a country other than the U.S. or Canada.

Indicates a publisher produces educational material.

Indicates an electronic publisher or publication.

Indicates a book packager/producer.

Indicates a change to a company's mailing address since the 2003 edition.

A Indicates a publisher accepts agented submissions only.

Indicates an award-winning publisher.

● Indicates a comment from the editors of *Children's Writer's & Illustrator's Market*.

ms or **mss** Stands for manuscript or manuscripts.

SASE Refers to a self-addressed stamped envelope.

SAE Refers to a self-addressed envelope.

IRC Stands for International Reply Coupon. These are required with SAEs sent to markets in countries other than your own.

b&w Stands for black & white.

Important Listing Information

- Listings are based on questionnaires, phone calls, and updated copy. They are not advertisements nor are markets reported here necessarily endorsed by the editor of this book.
- Information in the listings comes directly from the companies and is as accurate as possible, but situations may change and needs may fluctuate between the publication of this directory and the time you use it.
- *Children's Writer's & Illustrator's Market* reserves the right to exclude any listing that does not meet its requirements.

Complaint Procedure

If you feel you have not been treated fairly by a listing in *Children's Writer's & Illustrator's Market*, we advise you to take the following steps:

- First try to contact the listing. Sometimes one phone call or a letter can quickly clear up the matter.
- Document all your correspondence with the listing. When you write to us with a complaint, provide the details of your submission, the date of your first contact with the listing, and the nature of your subsequent correspondence.
- We will enter your letter into our files and attempt to contact the listing.
- The number and severity of complaints will be considered in our decision whether or not to delete the listing from the next edition.

Markets

Book Publishers

There's no magic formula for getting published. It's a matter of getting the right manuscript on the right editor's desk at the right time. Before you submit it's important to learn publishers' needs, see what kind of books they're producing and decide which publishers your work is best suited for. *Children's Writer's & Illustrator's Market* is but one tool in this process. (Those just starting out, turn to Just Getting Started? Some Quick Tips, on page 2.)

To help you narrow down the list of possible publishers for your work, we've included several indexes at the back of this book. The **Subject Index** lists book and magazine publishers according to their fiction and nonfiction needs or interests. The **Age-Level Index** indicates which age groups publishers cater to. The **Photography Index** indicates which markets buy photography for children's publications. The **Poetry Index** lists publishers accepting poetry.

If you write contemporary fiction for young adults, for example, and you're trying to place a book manuscript, go first to the Subject Index. Locate the fiction categories under Book Publishers and copy the list under Contemporary. Then go to the Age-Level Index and highlight the publishers on the Contemporary list that are included under the Young Adults heading. Read the listings for the highlighted publishers to see if your work matches their needs.

Remember, *Children's Writer's & Illustrator's Market* should not be your only source for researching publishers. Here are a few other sources of information:

- The Society of Children's Book Writers and Illustrators (SCBWI) offers members an annual market survey of children's book publishers. (Members send a SASE with $1.06 postage or get the list for free online at www.scbwi.org. SCBWI membership information can also be found at www.scbwi.org.)
- The Children's Book Council website (www.cbcbooks.org) gives information on member publishers.
- If a publisher interests you, send a SASE for submission guidelines *before* submitting. To quickly find guidelines on the Internet, visit The Colossal Directory of Children's Publishers Online at www.signaleader.com/childrens-writers/.
- Check publishers' websites. Many include their complete catalogs which you can browse. Web addresses are included in many publishers' listings.
- Spend time at your local bookstore to see who's publishing what. While you're there, browse through *Publishers Weekly*, *The Horn Book* and *Riverbank Review*.

SUBSIDY & SELF-PUBLISHING

Some determined writers who receive rejections from royalty publishers may look to subsidy and co-op publishers as an option for getting their work into print. These publishers ask writers to pay all or part of the costs of producing a book. We strongly advise writers and illustrators to work only with publishers who pay them. For this reason, we've adopted a policy not to include any subsidy or co-op publishers in *Children's Writer's & Illustrator's Market* (or any other Writer's Digest Books market books).

If you're interested in publishing your book just to share it with friends and relatives, self-publishing is a viable option, but it involves a lot of time, energy and money. You oversee all book production details. Check with a local printer for advice and information on cost.

Whatever path you choose, keep in mind that the market is flooded with submissions, so it's important for you to hone your craft and submit the best work possible. Competition from thousands of other writers and illustrators makes it more important than ever to research publishers before submitting—read their guidelines, look at their catalogs, check out a few of their titles and visit their websites.

ADVICE FROM INSIDERS

For insight and advice on getting published from a variety of perspectives, be sure to read the Insider Reports in this section. Subjects include authors and illustrators **Ann Brashares** (page 132), **Bruce Balan** (page 152), **Kathi Appelt** (page 158), **Loreen Leedy** (page 163), **Ann Purmell** (page 176), **Mike Cressy** (page 192), and **Shana Corey** (page 200); and editors **Julie Strauss-Gabel** (page 146), and **Aimee Jackson** (page 182).

Information on book publishers listed in the previous edition but not included in this edition of *Children's Writer's & Illustrator's Market* may be found in the General Index.

ABINGDON PRESS, The United Methodist Publishing House, 201 Eighth Ave. S., Nashville TN 37203. (615)749-6384. Fax: (615)749-6512. E-mail: paugustine@umpublishing.org. **Acquisitions:** Peg Augustine, children's book editor. Estab. 1789. "Abingdon Press, America's oldest theological publisher, provides an ecumenical publishing program dedicated to serving the Christian community.
Fiction: All levels: multicultural, religion, special needs.
Nonfiction: All levels: religion.
How to Contact/Writers: Query; submit outline/synopsis and 1 sample chapter. Responds to queries in 3 months; mss in 6 months.
Illustration: Uses color artwork only. Reviews ms/illustration packages from artists. Query with photocopies only. Samples returned with SASE; samples not filed.
Photography: Buys stock images. Wants scenics, landscape, still life and multiracial photos. Model/property release required. Uses color prints. Submit stock photo list.
Terms: Pays authors royalty of 5-10% based on retail price. Work purchased outright from authors ($100-1,000).

HARRY N. ABRAMS BOOKS FOR YOUNG READERS 100 Fifth Ave., New York NY 1001. (212)206-7715. **Director, Children's Books:** Howard W. Reeves.
Fiction/Nonfiction: Picture books, young readers, middle readers, young adult.
How to Contact/Writers: Fiction/nonfiction: Submit cover letter and complete ms for picture books; query and sample chapter for nonfiction and longer works. Responds in 6 months only with SASE. Will consider multiple submissions.
Illustration: Illustrations only: Do not submit original material; copies only. Contact: Howard W. Reeves.

ABSEY & CO., 23011 Northcrest Dr., Spring TX 77389. (281)257-2340. Fax: (281)251-4676. E-mail: abseyandco@aol.com. Website: www.absey.com. **Publisher:** Edward Wilson. "We are looking primarily for education books, especially those with teaching strategies based upon research." Publishes hardcover, trade paperback and mass market paperback originals. Publishes 5-10 titles/year. 50% of books from first-time authors; 50% from unagented writers.
Fiction: "Since we are a small, new press, we are looking for good manuscripts with a firm intended audience." Recently published *Saving the Scrolls*, by Mary Kerry.
How to Contact/Writers: Fiction: Query with SASE. Nonfiction: Query with outline and 1-2 sample chapters. Does not consider simultaneous submissions. Responds to queries in 3 months.
Illustration: Reviews ms/illustration packages. Send photocopies, transparencies, etc.
Photography: Reviews ms/photo packages. Send photocopies, transparencies, etc.
Terms: Pays 8-15% royalty on wholesale price. Publishes book 1 year after acceptance of ms. Manuscript guidelines for #10 SASE.
Tips: "Absey publishes a few titles every year. We like the author and the illustrator working together to create something magical. Authors and illustrators have input into every phase of production."

ACTION PUBLISHING, P.O. Box 391, Glendale CA 91209. (323)478-1667. Fax: (323)478-1767. Website: www.actionpublishing.com. Book publisher. Estab. 1996. Publishes picture books and fiction. **Publisher:** Michael Metzler. **Art Acquisitions:** Art Director. Publishes 4 young readers/year; 2 middle readers/year; and 2 young adult titles/year.
Fiction: Picture book: fantasy. Young readers: adventure, fantasy. Middle readers: adventure. Recently published *The Family of Ree*, by Scott E. Sutton (ages 6-9, picture book).
How to Contact/Writers: Only interested in agented material. Current guidelines on website.
Illustration: Works with 4 illustrators/year. Reviews illustration packages from artists. Query. Contact: Publisher. Send

promotional literature. Contact: Art Director. Responds only if interested. Samples returned with SASE or kept on file if interested and OK with illustrator.

Photography: Buys stock and assigns work. Contact: Art Director. "We use photos on as-needed basis. Mainly publicity, advertising and copy work." Uses 35mm or 4×5 transparencies. Submit cover letter and promo piece.

Terms: Pays authors royalty based on wholesale price. Offers advances against royalties. Pays illustrators by the project or royalty. Pays photographers by the project or per photo Sends galleys to authors. Original art returned as negotiated depending on project.

N **ADVOCACY PRESS**, P.O. Box 236, Santa Barbara CA 93102. (805)962-2728. Fax: (805)963-3580. E-mail: advpress @impulse.com. Website: www.advocacypress.com. Division of The Girls Incorporated of Greater Santa Barbara. Book publisher. **Editorial Contact**: Ruth Vitale, curriculum specialist. Publishes 2-4 children's books/year.

Fiction: Picture books, young readers, middle readers: adventure, animal, concepts in self-esteem, contemporary, fantasy, folktales, gender equity, multicultural, nature/environment, poetry. "Illustrated children's stories incorporate self-esteem, gender equity, self-awareness concepts." Published *Father Gander Nursery Rhymes*, by Doug Larche, illustrated by Carolyn Blattel; *Minou*, by Mindy Bingham, illustrated by Itoko Maeno; *Time for Horatio*, by Penelope Paine, illustrated by Itoko Maeno. "Most publications are 32-48 page picture stories for readers 4-11 years. Most feature adventures of animals in interesting/educational locales."

Nonfiction: Middle readers, young adults: careers, multicultural, self-help, social issues, textbooks.

How to Contact/Writers: "Because of the required focus of our publications, most have been written in-house." Responds to queries/mss in 2 months. Include SASE.

Illustration: "Require intimate integration of art with story. Therefore, almost always use local illustrators." Average about 30 illustrations per story. Reviews ms/illustration packages from artists. Submit ms with dummy. Contact: Ruth Vitale. Responds in 2 months. Samples returned with SASE.

Terms: Authors paid by royalty or outright purchase. Pays illustrators by project or royalty. Book catalog and ms guidelines for SASE.

Tips: "We are not presently looking for new titles."

ALADDIN PAPERBACKS/SIMON PULSE PAPERBACK BOOKS, 1230 Avenue of the Americas, 4th Floor, New York NY 10020. Fax: (212) 698-7337. Website: www.simonsays.com. Paperback imprints of Simon & Schuster Children's Publishing Children's Division. Associate Vice President/Editorial Director: Ellen Krieger (middle grade/chapter books), Lisa Clancy (young adult), Julia Richardson (beginning readers, chapter books), Jennifer Klonsky (all areas), Bethany Buck, associate publisher. **Manuscript Acquisitions:** Attn: Submissions Editor. **Art Acquisitions:** Debra Sfetsios, Aladdin; Russel Gordon, Simon Pulse. Publishes 130 titles/year.

● Aladdin publishes primarily reprints of successful hardcovers from other Simon & Schuster imprints. They accept query letters with proposals for middle-grade series and single-title fiction, beginning readers, middle grade mysteries and commercial nonfiction. Simon Pulse primarily publishes Young Adult series and fiction, as well as reprints of successful hardcovers from other Simon & Schuster imprints. They accept query letters for young adult series and single-title fiction.

Fiction: Recently published The Unicorn series chapter book series by Kathleen Duey (ages 7-10, edited by Ellen Krieger; fantasy chapter books, Aladdin Paperbacks); *Pirate Hunter*, by Brad Strickland and Tom Fuller; and *Pendragon*, by D.J. MacHale (middle grade, fiction, edited by Lisa Clancy).

ALL ABOUT KIDS PUBLISHING, 6280 San Ignacio Ave., Suite D, San Jose CA 95119. (408)578-4026. Fax: (408)578-4029. E-mail: mail@aakp.com. Website: www.aakp.com. Estab. 1999. Specializes in fiction, educational material, multicultural material, nonfiction. Book publisher. **Manuscript Acquisitions:** Linda L. Guevara. **Art Acquisitions Editor:** Nadine Takvorian, art director. Publishes 10-20 picture books/year. 80% of books by first-time authors.

Fiction: Picture books, young readers: adventure, animal, concept, fantasy, folktales, history, humor, multicultural, nature/environment, poetry, religion, suspense/mystery. Average word length: picture books—450 words. Recently published *The Flight of the Sunflower*, by Melissa Bourbon-Ramirez (picture book).

Nonfiction: Picture books, young readers: activity books, animal, biography, concept, history, multicultural, nature/environment, religion. Average word length: picture books—450 words. Recently published *Fishes, Flowers & Fandangles*, by Hua Tao Zhang; *Activity Book to Teach Children Ages 5-12 Art For Teachers & Parents*.

How to Contact/Writers: Fiction: Submit complete ms. Nonfiction: Submit complete ms for picture books; outline synopsis and 2 sample chapters for young readers. Responds to mss in 3 months. Publishes a book 2-3 years after acceptance. Manuscript returned with SASE.

Illustration: Works with 20-30 illustrators/year. Reviews ms/illustration packages from artists. Submit ms with dummy or ms with 2-3 pieces of final art. Contact: Linda L. Guevara, editor. Illustrations only: Arrange personal portfolio review or send résumé, portfolio and client list. Contact: Nadine Takvorian, art director. Responds in 3 months. Samples returned with SASE; samples filed.

Photography: Works on assignment only. Contact: Linda L. Guevara, editor. Model/property releases required. Uses 35mm transparencies. Submit portfolio, résumé, client list.

Terms: Pays author royalty. Offers advances (Average amount: $1,000). Pays illustrators by the project (range: $3,000 minimum) or royalty of 3-5% based on retail price. Pays photographers by the project (range: $500 minimum) or royalty of 5% based on wholesale price. Sends galleys to authors; dummies to illustrators. All imprints included in a single catalog. Writer's, artist's and photographer's guidelines available for SASE.

Tips: "Write from the heart and for the love of children. Submit only one manuscript per envelope. Only one per month please."

N ALYSON PUBLICATIONS, INC., P.O. 4371, Los Angeles CA 90078. (323)860-6065. Fax: (323)467-0173. Book publisher. **Acquisitions:** Editorial Department. Publishes 1-3 picture books/year and 1-3 young adult titles/year.

Fiction: Will only consider submissions that deal with gay or lesbian topics. Young readers and middle readers: suspense, mystery. Teens: anthology.

Nonfiction: Teens: concept, social issues. "We like books that incorporate all racial, religious and body types. Books should deal with issues faced by kids growing up gay or lesbian." Published *Heather Has Two Mommies*, by Lesléa Newman; and *Daddy's Wedding*, by Michael Willhoite.

How to Contact/Writers: Submit outline/synopsis and sample chapters (young adults). Responds to queries/mss within 3 months. Include SASE.

Terms: Pays authors royalty of 8-12% based on wholesale price. "We *do* offer advances." Book catalog and/or ms guidelines free for SASE.

N AMERICAN BIBLE SOCIETY, 1865 Broadway, New York NY 10023-7505. Fax: (212)408-1305. Website: www.am ericanbible.org. Book publisher. Estab. 1816. **Art Acquisitions:** Charles Houser, director of editorial services. Publishes 1-2 picture books/year; 1 young reader/year; 1 youth activity/year; and 1 young adult/year. Publishes books with spiritual/ religious themes based on the Bible. "The purpose of the American Bible Society is to provide the Holy Scriptures to every man, woman and child in a language and form each can easily understand, and at a price each can easily afford. This purpose is undertaken without doctrinal note or comment." Please do not call. Submit all sample submissions, résumés, etc. for review via mail.

Nonfiction: All levels: activity books, multicultural, religion, self-help, reference, social issues and special needs. Multicultural needs include innercity lifestyle; African-American, Hispanic/Latino, Native American, Asian; mixed groups (such as choirs, classrooms, church events). "Unsolicited manuscripts will be returned unread! We prefer published writing samples with résumés so we can contact copywriters when an appropriate project comes up." Recently published *Experience Jesus Today*, a 248-page Bible storybook with prayers, discussion questions, and background information, full color (ages 7-11).

How to Contact/Writers: All mss developed in-house. Query with résumé and writing samples. Unsolicited mss rejected. No credit lines given.

Illustration: Works with 2-3 illustrators/year. Selects artists based on suitability to projects under development. Illustrations only: Query with samples; if interested, a personal interview will be arranged to see portfolio; send "résumés, tearsheets and promotional literature to keep; slides will be returned promptly." Responds to queries within 1 month. Samples returned; samples sometimes filed. Book catalog free on written request.

Photography: Buys stock and assigns work. Looking for "nature, scenic, multicultural, intergenerational people shots." Model/property releases required. Uses any size b&w prints; 35mm, 2¼×2¼ and 4×5 transparencies. Photographers should query with samples first. If interested, a personal interview will be set up to see portfolio; provide résumé, promotional literature or tearsheets.

Terms: Photographers paid by the project (range: $800-5,000); per photo (range $100-400). Credit line given on most projects. Most photos purchased for one-time use. Factors used to determine payment for ms/illustration package include "nature and scope of project; complexity of illustration and continuity of work; number of illustrations." Pays illustrators $200-1,000/illustration; based on fair market value. Sends 2 complimentary copies of published work to illustrators. ABS owns all publication rights to illustrations.

Tips: Illustrators and photographers: "Submit in a form that we can keep on file, if we like, such as tearsheets, postcards, photocopies, etc."

◘ AMIRAH PUBLISHING, P.O. Box 541146. Flushing NY 11354. Phone/fax: (718)321-9004. E-mail: amirahpbco@ao l.com. Website: www.ifna.net. Estab. 1992. Specializes in fiction, educational material, multicultural material. **Manuscript Acquisitions:** Yahiya Emerick. **Art Acquisitions:** Yahiya Emerick, president. Publishes 2 young readers/year; 5 middle readers; 3 young adult titles/year. 25% of books by first-time authors. "Our goal is to produce quality books for children and young adults with a spiritually uplifting application."

● Amirah accepts submissions only through e-mail.

Fiction: Picture books, young readers, middle readers, young adults: adventure, animal, history, multicultural, religion, Islamic. Average word length: picture books—200; young readers—1,000; middle readers—5,000; young adults—5,000. Recently published *Ahmad Deen and the Curse of the Aztec Warrior*, by Yahiya Emerick (ages 8-11); *Burhaan Khan*, by Qasim Najar (ages 6-8); *The Memory of Hands*, by Reshma Baig (ages 15 to adult).

Nonfiction: Picture books, young readers, middle readers, young adults: history, religion, Islamic. Average word length: picture books—200; young readers—1,000; middle readers—5,000; young adults—5,000. Recently published *Color and Learn Salah*, by Yahiya Emerick (ages 5-7, religious); *Learning About Islam*, by Yahiya Emerick (ages 9-11, religious); *What Islam Is All About*, by Yahiya Emerick (ages 14 and up, religious).

How to Contact/Writers: Fiction/nonfiction: Query via e-mail only. Responds to queries in 2 weeks; mss in 3 months. Publishes a book 6-12 months after acceptance. Will consider electronic submissions via disk or modem.

Illustration: Works with 2-4 illustrators/year. Reviews ms/illustration packages from artists. Query. Contact: Qasim Najar, vice president. Illustrations only: Query with samples. Contact: Yahiya Emerick, president. Responds in 1 month. Samples returned with SASE.

Photography: Works on assignment only. Contact: Yahiya Emerick, president. Uses images of the Middle East, children, nature. Model/property releases required. Uses 4×6, matte, color prints. Submit cover letter.

Terms: Work purchased outright from authors for $1,000-3,000. Pays illustrators by the project (range: $20-40). Pays photographers by the project (range: $20-40). Sends galleys to authors; dummies to illustrators. Originals returned to artist at job's completion. Book catalog available for SASE and 2 first-class stamps. All imprints included in a single catalog. Catalog available on website.

Tips: "We specialize in materials relating to the Middle East and Muslim-oriented culture such as stories, learning materials and such. These are the only types of items we currently are publishing."

ATHENEUM BOOKS FOR YOUNG READERS, 1230 Avenue of the Americas, New York NY 10020. (212)698-2715. Website: www.simonsayskids.com. Imprint of Simon & Schuster Children's Publishing Division. Book publisher. Vice President and Editorial Director: Ginee Seo. Estab. 1960. **Manuscript Acquisitions:** Send queries with SASE to: Ginee Seo, Anne Schwartz, editorial director of Anne Schwartz Books; Richard Jackson, editorial director of Richard Jackson Books; Caitlyn Dlouhy, executive editor. "All editors consider all types of projects." **Art Acquisitions:** Ann Bobco. Publishes 15-20 picture books/year; 4-5 young readers/year; 20-25 middle readers/year; and 10-15 young adults/year. 10% of books by first-time authors; 50% from agented writers. "Atheneum publishes original hardcover trade books for children from pre-school age through young adult. Our list includes picture books, chapter books, mysteries, biography, science fiction, fantasy, middle grade and young adult fiction and nonfiction. The style and subject matter of the books we publish is almost unlimited. We do not, however, publish textbooks, coloring or activity books, greeting cards, magazines or pamphlets or religious publications. Anne Schwartz Books is a highly selective line of books within the Atheneum imprint. The lists of Charles Scribner's Sons Books for Young Readers have been folded into the Atheneum program."

● Atheneum does not accept unsolicited manuscripts. Send query letter only. Atheneum title *The House of the Scorpion*, by Nancy Farmer, won a 2003 Printz Honor and a Newbery Honor. Ponder Goembel, illustrator for *Sailor Moo, Cow at Sea* won a 2002 Golden Kite Honor Book plaque. Their title *Six Days in October: The Stock Market Crash of 1929,* by Karen Blumenthal won a 2003 Robert F. Siebert Honor.

How to Contact/Writers: Send query letter and 3 sample chapters. Responds to queries in 1 month; requested mss in 3 months. Publishes a book 18-24 months after acceptance. Will consider simultaneous queries from previously unpublished authors and those submitted to other publishers, "though we request that the author let us know it is a simultaneous query."

Illustration: Works with 40-50 illustrators/year. Send art samples résumé, tearsheets to Ann Bobco, Design Dept. 4th Floor, 1230 Avenue of the Americas, New York NY 10020. Samples filed. Responds to art samples only if interested.

Terms: Pays authors in royalties of 8-10% based on retail price. Pays illustrators royalty of 5-6% or by the project. Pays photographers by the project. Sends galleys and proofs to authors; proofs to illustrators. Original artwork returned at job's completion. Manuscript guidelines for #10 SAE and 1 first-class stamp.

Tips: "Atheneum has a 40-year tradition of publishing distinguished books for children. Study our titles."

A/V CONCEPTS CORP., 30 Montauk Blvd., Oakdale NY 11769. (631)567-7227. Fax: (631)567-8745. E-mail: info@edcompublishing.com. Educational book publisher. **Manuscript Acquisitions:** Laura Solimene, editorial director. **Art Acquisitions:** Phil Solimene, president. Publishes 6 young readers/year; 6 middle readers/year; 6 young adult titles/year. 20% of books by first-time authors. Primary theme of books and multimedia is classic literature, math, science, language arts, self esteem.

Fiction: Middle readers: hi-lo. Young adults: hi-lo, multicultural, special needs. "We hire writers to adapt classic literature."

Nonfiction: All levels: activity books. Young adults: hi-lo, multicultural, science, self help, textbooks. Average word length: middle readers—300-400; young adults—500-950.

How to Contact/Writers: Fiction: Submit outline/synopsis and 1 sample chapter. Responds to queries in 1 month.

Illustration: Works with 4-6 illustrators/year. Reviews ms/illustration packages from artists. Submit ms with 3-4 pieces of final art. Illustrations only: Query with samples. "No originals; send nonreturnable material and samples only." Responds in 1 month. Samples returned with SASE; samples filed.

Photography: Submit samples.

Terms: Work purchased outright from authors (range $50-1,000). Pays illustrators by the project (range: $50-1,000). Pays photographers per photo (range: $25-250). Manuscript and art guidelines available for 9×12 SASE.

AVISSON PRESS, INC., 3007 Taliaferro Rd., Greensboro NC 27408. (336)288-6989. Fax: (336)288-6989. Estab. 1995. Specializes in multicultural material, nonfiction. **Manuscript Acquisitions:** Martin Hester, publisher. Publishes 5-7 young adult titles/year. 70% of books by first-time authors.

Nonfiction: Young adults: biography. Average word length: young adults—25,000. Recently published *Mum Bet: The Life and Times of Elizabeth Freeman*, by Mary Wilds; *Young Superstars of Tennis: The Venus and Serena Williams Story*, by Mike Fillon; *Here Comes Eleanor: A New Biography of Eleanor Roosevelt for Young People*, by Virginia Veeder Westervelt; *Eight Who Made a Difference: Pioneer Women in the Arts*, by Erica Stux.

How to Contact/Writers: Nonfiction: Submit outline/synopsis and 2 sample chapters. Responds to queries in 2 weeks; mss in 2 months. Publishes a book 9-12 months after acceptance. Will consider simultaneous submissions.

Terms: Pays author royalty of 8-10% based on wholesale price. Offers advances (Average amount: $400). Sends galleys to authors. Book catalog available for #10 SAE and 1 first-class stamp; ms guidelines available for SASE.

Tips: "We publish *only* YA biographies."

AVON BOOKS/BOOKS FOR YOUNG READERS, 1350 Avenue of the Americas, New York NY 10019. (212)261-6800. Fax: (212)261-6668. Website: www.harperchildrens.com. A division of HarperCollins Children's Book Group.

● Avon is not accepting unagented submissions. See listing for HarperCollins Children's Books.

AZRO PRESS, PMB 342 1704 Llano St. B, Santa Fe NM 87505. (505)989-3272. Fax: (505)989-3832. E-mail: books@azro press.com. Website: www.azropress.com. Estab. 1997. **Manuscript/Art Acquisitions:** Gae Eisenhardt, editor. Imprints: Green Knees (Jaenet Guggenheim, acquisitions editor). Publishes 6 picture books/year. 90% of books by first-time authors. "We publish illustrated children's books with a southwestern flavor."
Fiction: Picture books: animal, humor, multicultural. Average word length: picture books—1,000; young readers—1,500. Recently published *Watcha Doing?*, by Agatha Featherstone (ages 2-5); *One Bullfrog*, by Sid Hausman (age 5-10, illustrated song book with CD); *Lucy's Journey to the Wild West*, by Charlotte Piepmeier; and *Grow Grow Grow*, by Barbara Riley.
Nonfiction: Picture books: activity books, animals, science.
How to Contact/Writers: Fiction/nonfiction: Submit complete ms or outline/synopsis. Responds to queries in 2 weeks; mss in 3 months. Publishes a book 2 years after acceptance. Will consider simultaneous submissions.
Illustration: Works with 3-4 illustrators/year. Reviews ms/illustration packages from artists. Submit ms with 2-3 pieces of final art. Contact: Editor. Query with samples. Samples filed.
Terms: Pays authors royalty fo 5-10% based on wholesale price. Pays illustrators by the project (range: $3,000-4,000) or royalty of 5%. Sends galleys to authors; dummies to illustrators. Originals returned to artist at job's completion. Book catalog available for SASE. All imprints included in a single catalog. Manuscript guidelines available for SASE. Catalog available on website.
Tips: "Read our submission guidelines. Go to your local bookstore and library to see what is available."

N ⬚ BALLYHOO BOOKWORKS INC., P.O. Box 534, Shoreham NY 11792. E-mail: ballyhoo@optonline.net. Estab. 1986. Specializes in trade books, educational material. **Acquisitions:** Liam Gerrity, editorial director. Publishes 2 picture books/year; and 1 young readers/year. 30% of books by first-time authors. "We are a small press, but highly selective and want texts that flow from the tongue with clarity . . . and are infused with the author's passion for the piece."
Fiction: Young readers: animal, nature/environment. Average word length: picture books—to 500; young readers—to 1,000. Recently published *The Alley Cat* and *The Barnyard Cat*, by Brian J. Heinz, illustrated by June H. Blair (ages 5-9, picture books).
Nonfiction: Picture books: arts/crafts, how-to. Young readers, middle readers: activity books, arts/crafts, hobbies, how-to. Average word length: picture books—to 500; young readers—to 1,000; middle readers—to 10,000. Recently published *Metal Detecting for Treasure*, by Dorothy B. Francis (ages 10 and up, YA/how-to).
How to Contact/Writers: Accepts material from residents of US only. Fiction/nonfiction: Query or submit outline/synopsis or outline/synopsis and 2 sample chapters. Responds to queries in 1 month; mss in 2 months. Publishes book 12-18 months after acceptance. Will consider simultaneous submissions.
Illustration: Accepts material from residents of US only. Works with 2-3 illustrators/year. Reviews ms/illustration packages from artists. Query or send ms with dummy. Contact: Editorial Director. Illustrations only: Send résumé, promo sheet and tearsheets. "We file all samples for future reference."
Terms: Pays authors royalty of 5% based on retail price. Offers advances (Average amount $1,000-2,500). Pays illustrators 5% based on retail price. Sends galleys to authors. Originals returned to artist at job's completion. Manuscript guidelines available for SASE.
Tips: "We don't see any value in trends, only in good writing."

N ⬚ BANCROFT PRESS, P.O.Box 65360, Baltimore MD 21209. (410)358-0658. Fax: (410)637-7377. E-mail: bruceb @bancroftpress.com. Website: www.bancroftpress.com. Estab. 1988. Specializes in mass market books, fiction, nonfiction. We are an independent book packager/producer. **Manuscript Acquisitions:** Elly Zupko (fiction); Bruce Bortz (nonfiction). **Art Acquisitions:** Bruce Bortz, publisher. Publishes 1 middle readers/year; and 2-4 young adult titles/year.
Fiction: Middle readers, young adults: adventure, animal, contemporary, fantasy, humor, multicultural, problem novels, religion, science fiction, special needs, sports, suspense/mystery. Average word length: middle readers—50,000; young adults—50,000. Recently published *Uncovering Sadie's Secrets: A Bianca Balducci Mystery*, by Libby Sternberg (ages 10 and up); *Hank: The First Novel in the Gunpowder Trilogy*, by Arch Montgomery (ages 13 and up); and *The Reappearance of Sam Webber*, by Jonathon Scott Fuqua (ages 10 and up).
Nonfiction: Middle readers, young adults: animal, biography, concept, health, history, multicultural, music/dance, nature/environment, reference, religion, science, self help, social issues, special needs, sports, textbooks.
How to Contact/Writers: Fiction/nonfiction: Submit complete ms or submit submit outline/synopsis and 3 sample chapters. Responds to queries/mss in at least 6 months. Publishes book 18 months after acceptance. Will consider e-mail submissions, simultaneous submissions or previously published work.
Terms: Pays authors royalty of 8% based on retail price. Offers advances (Average amount: $1,000-3,000). Sends galleys to authors. Book catalog available for 6×9 SAE with 75¢ postage; ms guidelines available for SASE. All imprints included in a single catalog. Catalog available on website.
Tips: "We advise writers to visit our website, and also to be familiar with our previous work. Patience is the number one attribute contributors must have. It takes us a very long time to get through submitted material, because we are such a small company. Also, we only publish 4-6 books per year, so it may take a long time for your optioned book to be published. We like to be able to market our books to be used in schools and in libraries. We prefer fiction that bucks trends and moves in a new direction.We are especially interested in mysteries and humor (especially humorous mysteries)."

Ⓐ BANTAM BOOKS FOR YOUNG READERS, imprint of Random House Children's Books, 1745 Broadway, New York NY 10019. (212)354-6500. Website: www.randomhouse/kids.com. Book publisher.

● See listings for Random House Books for Young Readers Group, Delacorte, and Doubleday and Alfred A. Knopf and Crown Books for Young Readers.

☑ **BAREFOOT BOOKS**, 2067 Massachusetts Ave., 5th Floor, Cambridge MA 02140. (617)576-0660. Fax: (617)576-0049. Website: www.barefoot-books.com. Estab. 1993 in the UK; 1998 in the US. Specializes in fiction, trade books, multicultural material, nonfiction. **Manuscript/Art Acquisitions:** U.S. editor. Publishes 35 picture books/year; 10 anthologies/year. 40% of books by first-time authors. "The Barefoot child represents the person who is in harmony with the natural world and moves freely across boundaries of many kinds. Barefoot Books explores this image with a range of high-quality picture books for children of all ages. We work with artists, writers and storytellers from many cultures, focusing on themes that encourage independence of spirit, promote understanding and acceptance of different traditions, and foster a life-long love of learning."

● At presstime, Barefoot Books was not accepting submissions until early 2004. Check website for updates.

Fiction: Picture books, young readers: animal, anthology, concept, fantasy, folktales, multicultural, nature/environment, poetry, spirituality. Middle readers, young adults: anthology, folktales. Average word length: picture books—500-1,000; young readers—2,000-3,000; anthologies—10,000-20,000. Recently published *We All Went on Safari*, by Laurie Krebs, illustrated by Julia Cairns (ages 3-7, picture book); *Thesaurus Rex*, by Laya Steinberg, illustrated by Debbie Harter (ages 2-6, concept book); and *Goddesses: A World of Myth and Magic*, by Burleigh Mutén, illustrated by Rebecca Guay (ages 7 to adult, anthology).

How to Contact/Writers: Fiction: Submit query letter and one page of ms for picture books; outline/synopsis and 1 sample story for collections. Responds to queries in 2 months; mss in 3 months. Will consider simultaneous submissions and previously published work.

Illustration: Works with 20 illustrators/year. Uses color artwork only. Reviews ms/illustration packages from artists. Send query and art samples or dummy for picture books. Illustrations only: Query with samples or send promo sheet and tearsheets. Responds only if interested. Samples returned with SASE.

Terms: Pays author royalty of 5% based on retail price. Offers advances. Sends galleys to authors. Originals returned to artist at job's completion. Book catalog available for 9×12 SAE and 5 first-class stamps; ms guidelines available for SASE. Catalog available on website.

Tips: "We are looking for books that inspire, books that are filled with a sense of magic and wonder. We also look for strong stories from all different cultures, reflecting the ways of the individual culture while also touching deeper human truths that suggest we are all one. We welcome playful submissions for the very youngest children and also anthologies of stories for older readers, all focused around a universal theme. We encourage writers and artists to visit our website and read some of our books to get a sense of our editorial philosophy and what we publish before they submit to us. Always, we encourage them to stay true to their inner voice and artistic vision that reaches out for timeless stories, beyond the momentary trends that may exist in the market today."

⬚ **BARRONS EDUCATIONAL SERIES**, 250 Wireless Blvd., Hauppauge NY 11788. (800)645-3476, ext. 264. Fax: (631)434-3723. E-mail: waynebarr@barronseduc.com. Website: www.barronseduc.com. Book publisher. Estab. 1945. "Barrons tends to publish series of books, both for adults and children." **Manuscript Acquisitions:** Wayne R. Barr, acquisitions manager. **Art Acquisitions:** Bill Kuchler, art director. Publishes 20 picture books/year; 20 young readers/year; 20 middle reader titles/year; 10 young adult titles/year. 25% of books by first-time authors; 25% of books from agented writers.

Fiction: Picture books: animal, concept, multicultural, nature/environment. Young readers: Adventure, multicultural, nature/environment, fantasy, suspense/mystery. Middle readers: adventure, fantasy, horror, multicultural, nature/environment, problem novels, suspense/mystery. Young adults: horror, problem novels. Recently published *Everyday Witch*, by Sandra Forrester; *Word Wizardry* by Margaret and William Kenda.

Nonfiction: Picture books: concept, reference. Young readers: how-to, reference, self help, social issues. Middle readers: hi-lo, how-to, reference, self help, social issues. Young adults: biography, how-to, reference, self help, social issues, sports.

How to Contact/Writers: Fiction: Query via e-mail. Nonfiction: Submit outline/synopsis and sample chapters. "Submissions must be accompanied by SASE for response." Responds to queries in 2 months; mss in 4 months. Publishes a book 1 year after acceptance. Will consider simultaneous submissions.

Illustration: Works with 20 illustrators/year. Reviews ms/illustration packages from artists. Query first; 3 chapters of ms with 1 piece of final art, remainder roughs. Illustrations only: Submit tearsheets or slides plus résumé. Responds in 2 months.

Terms: Pays authors in royalties of 10-14% based on net price or buys ms outright for $2,000 minimum. Pays illustrators by the project based on retail price. Sends galleys to authors; dummies to illustrators. Book catalog, ms/artist's guidelines for 9×12 SAE.

Tips: Writers: "We publish preschool storybooks, concept books and middle grade and YA chapter books. No romance novels." Illustrators: "We are happy to receive a sample illustration to keep on file for future consideration. Periodic notes reminding us of your work are acceptable." Children's book themes "are becoming much more contemporary and relevant to a child's day-to-day activities, fewer talking animals. We have a great interest in children's fiction (ages 7-11 and ages 12-16) with New Age topics."

⬚ **BEBOP BOOKS**, Imprint of Lee & Low Books Inc., 95 Madison Ave., New York NY 10016-7801. (212)779-4400. Website: www.bebopbooks.com. Estab. 2000. **Acquisitions:** Jennifer Frantz. **Executive Editor:** Louise May. Publishes 10-15 educational market picture books/year. Many books by first-time authors. "Our goal is to publish child-centered stories that support literacy learning and provide multicultural content for children just beginning to learn to read. We make a special effort to work with writers and illustrators of diverse backgrounds. Current needs are posted on website."

Great characters, enthusiastic readers & magic pants

In an interview on her publisher's website, bestselling author Ann Brashares describes her favorite pair of pants: "At the moment, my favorite pair of pants are bright red," she says. "They are cropped, slightly flared summer pants. Like a good friend, they are flexible, forgiving, and boost my confidence even on really off days. They are low maintenance pants—never requiring dry cleaning or even ironing. The waistline is zippered and definite, so it doesn't have that subtly defeated quality of elastic. And these pants manage to make me feel loved even through major body transitions (like having a baby!)."

Ann Brashares

Photo: Jane Feldman

Who could want anything more in a pair of pants? But if I were Ann Brashares, no matter how much I loved those flattering red pants, my favorite pants would be the traveling pants—the pants she created as a vehicle for her debut book *The Sisterhood of the Traveling Pants* and it's sequel *The Second Summer of the Sisterhood.*

The books follow four lifelong friends, Tibby, Bridget, Lena and Carmen, as they spend summers apart, connected only by letters, e-mail, and, most importantly, by a "magic" pair of thrift store blue jeans that amazingly fits them all, and is ceremoniously passed from friend to friend following a set of agreed-upon rules. (#1. You must never wash the pants. #6. You must follow the procedures for documenting your time in the pants. #10. Remember: Pants = love. Love your pals. Love yourself.)

Brashares' two books have consistently helped fill out the top ten of both the New York Times and the Book Sense bestseller lists (just behind or sandwiched among the five Harry Potter titles and Louis Sachar's *Holes*).

With her Sisterhood books, Brashares, a former editor, has struck a chord with a receptive audience of tween and teen girls and enjoyed crossover success with twenty- and thirty-something readers. Her audience has been enthusiastic about her novels. Says one young Amazon.com reviewer about *The Second Summer*: "This book truly inspired me to take better care of my own friendships . . . and to remember that it's okay to lean on people sometimes."

"It's wonderful to think that you can affect other people's lives in a positive way," says Brashares of the reaction she's gotten from her readers. "It makes me feel I've found myself a really good job."

Brashares' former job as an editor at book packager 17th Street Productions (formerly Daniel Weiss Associates) was invaluable as she switched gears to writing fiction. "Before I began writing, I spent a long time thinking about books in an analytical way. In order to work effectively with writers, I felt I needed to find my way around their books, often to break troubled books down to their basic underlying structure in order to help the writers put them back together more solidly," she says. "I remember my father once telling me that his own father wouldn't let him get a car until he could take an engine apart and put it back together. (This was in the late '50s—it was possible then.) I almost felt like I couldn't really write until I learned to take a book apart."

After the bestseller-dom of the first book, re-entering the writing process for a sequel was a bit daunting for Brashares. "My expectations for my first novel were low, because I know how few books—even good books—succeed. My expectations for the second book were different, because I also know that once you find readers, they are yours to lose. And that's what made writing a sequel so hard, in a way," she says. "I didn't want to drive away the readers I had been lucky enough to find. Going into a second book, I felt more self-conscious, more blocked. But once I made my way back to the world of the characters, nearly all of that fell away."

It's Brashares' strong characters—Tibby, Bridget, Lena, and Carmen—that make her books so appealing. The girls possess quirks, fears, ideas and personalities all their own as their various stories are told chapter by chapter, and the pants are passed from girl to girl. "There's a little bit of me in each of them," confesses Brashares. There's also a little bit of who she isn't: "Carmen was the girl who said things I could never say and Bridget was the girl who did things I could never do."

The girls' strong friendship started from the time they were born. Their mothers became friends during their pregnancies, so Tibby, Bridget, Lena, and Carmen were literally together since birth. While *The Sisterhood of the Traveling Pants* focuses on the girls' friendship, *The Second Summer of the Sisterhood* goes beyond that, delving into the girls' relationships with their mothers. Brashares didn't go into the sequel intending to write a book about mothers and daughters, however.

The Second Summer
of the Sisterhood

~ANN BRASHARES~

Jacket photo: Jennifer Sargent/Alloy. Jacket design: Marci Senders. Reprinted with permission of Delacorte.

The Second Summer of the Sisterhood, the sequel to Ann Brashares' bestselling *The Sisterhood of the Traveling Pants* (Delacorte Press, 2001), continues to follow Carmen, Bridget, Tibby, and Lena (and their magic pair of thrift-store jeans) as they face their 16th summer—and their individual struggles with family, love, loss, identity, and change.

"It wasn't conscious at the very start," she explains. "Without meaning to, the first three characters I worked on seemed to be struggling with their mothers in different ways. When I realized where it was going, I decided I liked the theme. It gave the book a center of gravity, which I felt it needed. It also gave the book an identity distinct from the first book. And as far as subject matter goes, it's hard to beat the richness of the bond between mothers and daughters."

As friends, however, the mothers in Brashares' books have not fared as well as the daughters, having drifted apart over the years even as their daughters remain close as sisters. Brashares is at work on her third Sisterhood book (scheduled for a September 2004 release) which takes place during the last summer before Tibby, Bridget, Lena, and Carmen go off to college. "I think the girls are acutely aware of what their mothers lost when they let their friendship go," Brashares says. "They will fight hard not to let it happen to them—it certainly won't happen passively."

But what about the pants? Through all of this, through two books and a third on the way, there are the pants. The pants that have traveled to such far flung destinations as Mexico, Greece, and Alabama. The pants that fit just right over the curves or non-curves of the wearer. The pants that keep the four best friends linked to one another when they're apart. The pants that seemed not quite as magical in *The Second Summer*. In the words of a *Booklist* reviewer: "The pants are just pants, and life is just life, full of joys, sorrows, living, and dying."

—Alice Pope

Fiction: Picture books: adventure, concept, contemporary, hi-lo, multicultural, nature/environment, sports, culturally specific topics for young children.

Nonfiction: Picture books: arts/crafts, careers, concept, cooking, hi-lo, hobbies, how-to, multicultural, music/dance, nature/environment, social issues, sports.

How to Contact/Writers: Fiction/nonfiction: Submit complete ms. Responds to mss in up to 4 months; "manuscripts are acquired just once a year."

Illustration: Works with 10-15 illustrators/year. Uses color artwork only. Illustrations and photographs: Query with color samples and send client list or cover letter. Responds only if interested. Samples returned with SASE; samples filed. "We are especially interested in submissions from artists of color, and we encourage artists new to the field of children's books to send us samples of their work."

Terms: Pays authors royalty. Offers advances. Pays illustrators royalty and advance. Pays photographers royalty and advance. Book catalog available for 9×12 SAE and 89¢ postage, attn: Catalog Request. Catalog available on website.

Tips: "Bebop Books is currently specializing in emergent and beginning readers with multicultural themes. Often called 'little books,' they are used to help young children develop early reading skills and strategies. Each book is a small paperback, with full color illustrations and a story specifically written and illustrated to support beginning readers."

BEHRMAN HOUSE INC., 11 Edison Place, Springfield NJ 07081. (973)379-7200. Fax: (973)379-7280. Book publisher. Estab. 1921. Managing Editor: Bob Tinkham. **Acquisitions:** Editorial Department. Publishes 3 young reader titles/year; 3 middle reader titles/year; and 3 young adult titles/year. 12% of books by first-time authors; 2% of books from agented writers. Publishes books on all aspects of Judaism: history, cultural, textbooks, holidays. "Behrman House publishes quality books of Jewish content—history, Bible, philosophy, holidays, ethics—for children and adults."

Fiction: All levels: Judaism.

Nonfiction: All levels: Judaism, Jewish educational textbooks. Average word length: young reader—1,200; middle reader—2,000; young adult—4,000. Published *My Jewish Year*, by Adam Fisher (ages 8-9); *Partners with God*, by Gila Gevirtz (ages 8-9); and *It's a Mitzvah!*, by Bradley Artson (adult).

How to Contact/Writers: Fiction/Nonfiction: Submit outline/synopsis and sample chapters. Responds to queries in 1 month; mss in 2 months. Publishes a book 2½ years after acceptance. Will consider simultaneous submissions.

Illustration: Works with 6 children's illustrators/year. Reviews ms/illustration packages from artists. "Query first." Illustrations only: Query with samples; send unsolicited art samples by mail. Responds to queries in 1 month; mss in 2 months.

Photography: Purchases photos from freelancers. Buys stock and assigns work. Uses photos of families involved in Jewish activities. Uses color and b&w prints. Photographers should query with samples. Send unsolicited photos by mail. Submit portfolio for review.

Terms: Pays authors in royalties of 3-10% based on retail price or buys ms outright for $1,000-5,000. Offers advance.

Pays illustrators by the project (range: $500-5,000). Sends galleys to authors; dummies to illustrators. Book catalog free on request.

Tips: Looking for "religious school texts" with Judaic themes or general trade Judaica.

BENCHMARK BOOKS, Imprint of Marshall Cavendish, 99 White Plains Rd., Tarrytown NY 10591. (914)332-8888. Fax: (914)332-1888. E-mail: mbisson@marshallcavendish.com. Website: www.marshallcavendish.com. **Manuscript Acquisitions:** Michelle Bisson and Joyce Stanton. Publishes more than 100 young reader, middle reader and young adult books/year. "We look for interesting treatments of primarily nonfiction subjects related to elementary, middle school and high school curriculum."

Nonfiction: Most nonfiction topics should be curriculum related. Average word length for books: 4,000-20,000. All books published as part of a series. Recently published *Life in the Middle Ages* (series), *The City*, *The Countryside*, *The Church*, *The Castle*, by Kathryn Hinds; *Lifeways: The Abache*, *The Cheyenne*, *The Haida*, *The Huron*, by Raymond Bial.

How to Contact/Writers: Nonfiction: submit complete ms or submit outline/synopsis and 1 or more sample chapters. Responds to queries and mss in 3 months. Publishes a book 2 years after acceptance. Will consider simultaneous submissions.

Photography: Buys stock and assigns work.

Terms: Pays authors royalty based on retail price or buys work outright. Offers advances. Sends galleys to authors. Book catalog available. All imprints included in a single catalog.

⚏ THE BENEFACTORY, P.O. Box 128, Cohasset MA 02025. (781)383-8027. Fax: (781)383-8026. Website: www.readplay.com. Book publisher. Estab. 1990. **Manuscript/Art Acquisitions:** Cindy Germain, production manager. Publishes 6-12 picture books/year with the Humane Society of the United States; 6-12 picture books/year with Doris Day Animal Foundation. 50% of books by first-time authors. The Benefactory publishes "classic" true stories about real animals, through licenses with the Humane Society of the United States and Doris Day Animal Foundation. Each title is accompanied by a read-along audiocassette and a plush animal. A percentage of revenues benefits the licensor. Target age for DDAF titles: 4-7; for HSUS titles: 5-10.

Nonfiction: Picture books: nature/environment; young readers: animal, nature/environment. Average word length: HSUS titles: 1,200-1,500; DDAF titles: 700-800. Recently published *Chessie, the Travelin' Man*, written by Randy Houk, illustrated by Paula Bartlett (ages 5-10, picture book); *Condor Magic*, written by Lyn Littlefield Hoopes, illustrated by Peter C. Stone (ages 5-10, picture book); and *Caesar: On Deaf Ears*, written by Loren Spiotta-DiMare, illustrated by Kara Lee (ages 5-10, picture book).

How to Contact/Writers: Query only—does not accept unsolicited mss. Responds to queries in 6 weeks. Publishes a book 1 year after acceptance. Will consider simultaneous submissions. Send SASE for writer's guidelines.

Illustration: Works with 6-8 illustrators/year. Uses color artwork only. Reviews ms/illustration packages from artists. Query or send ms with dummy. Illustrations only: Send résumé, promo sheet and tearsheets to be kept on file. Responds in 6 months. Samples returned with SASE; samples filed. Send SASE for artist guidelines.

Terms: Pays authors royalty of 3-5% based on wholesale price. Offers advances (Average amount: $5,000). Pays illustrators royalty of 3-5% based on wholesale price. Sends galleys to authors; dummies to illustrators. Originals returned to artist at job's completion. Book catalog available for 8 1/2 × 11 SASE; ms and art guidelines available for SASE.

BETHANY HOUSE PUBLISHERS, 11400 Hampshire Ave. S., Minneapolis MN 55438-2852. (952)829-2500. Fax: (952)829-2768. Website: www.bethanyhouse.com. Book publisher. **Manuscript Acquisitions:** Youth Department. **Art Acquisitions:** Paul Higdon. Publishes 4 young readers/year; 18 middle-grade readers/year; and 8 young adults/year. "Bethany House Publishers is an evangelical Christian publisher seeking to publish imaginative, excellent books that reflect an evangelical worldview without being preachy." Publishes picture books under Bethany Backyard imprint.

Fiction: Children's and young adult fiction list is full.

Nonfiction: Young readers, middle readers, young adults: religion/devotional, self-help, social issues. Published *Get God*, by Kevin Johnson (young teen; discipleship); and *Hot Topics, Tough Questions*, by Bill Myers (young adult/teen, Biblically based advice).

How to Contact/Writers: Considers unsolicited 1-page queries sent by fax only. "Bethany House no longer accepts unsolicited manuscripts or book proposals." Responds in 4 months. Publishes a book 12-18 months after acceptance.

Illustration: Works with 12 illustrators/year. Reviews illustration samples from artists. Illustrations only: Query with samples. Responds in 2 months. Samples returned with SASE.

Terms: Pays authors royalty based on net sales. Pays illustrators by the project. Pays photographers by the project. Sends galleys to authors. Book catalog available for 11 × 14 SAE and 5 first-class stamps. Write "Catalog Request" on outside of envelope.

Tips: "Research the market, know what is already out there. Study our catalog before submitting material. We look for an evangelical message woven delicately into a strong plot and topics that seek to broaden the reader's experience and perspective."

BEYOND WORDS PUBLISHING, INC., 20827 N.W. Cornell Rd., Hillsboro OR 97124-1808. (503)531-8700. Fax: (503)531-8773. E-mail: info@beyondword.com. Website: www.beyondword.com. **Acquisitions:** Barbara Leese, managing editor children's division. Publishes 2-3 picture books/year and 7-9 nonfiction teen books/year. 50% of books by first-time authors. "Our company mission statement is 'Inspire to Integrity,' so it's crucial that your story inspires children in some way. Our books are high quality, gorgeously illustrated, meant to be enjoyed as a child and throughout life."

Fiction: Picture books: contemporary, feminist, folktales, history, multicultural, nature/environment. "We are looking for authors/illustrators; stories that will appeal and inspire." Average length: picture books—32 pages. Recently published

Abbie Against the Storm, by Marcia Vaughan, illustrated by Bill Farnsworth (all ages, historical fiction).
Nonfiction: Picture books, young readers: advice, biography, history, multicultural, nature/environment. *Girls Know Best* (compilation of 38 teen girls' writing—ages 7-15); *So, You Wanna Be a Writer?* (ages 9-16, advice/career).
How to Contact/Writers: Fiction: Submit complete ms. Nonfiction: Submit outline/synopsis. Responds to queries/mss in 6 months. Will consider simultaneous submissions and previously published work.
Illustration: Works with 4-6 illustrators/year. Reviews ms/illustration packages from artists. Submit ms with 2-3 pieces of final art. Illustrations only: Send résumé, promo sheet, "samples—no originals!" Responds in 6 months only if interested. Samples returned with SASE; samples filed.
Photography: Works on assignment only.
Terms: Sends galleys to authors; dummies to illustrators. Manuscript and artist's guidelines for SASE.
Tips: "Please research the books we have previously published. This will give you a good idea if your proposal fits with our company."

N BLOOMSBURY CHILDREN'S BOOKS, Imprint of Bloomsbury PLC, 175 Fifth Avenue, Suite 712, New York NY 10010. (212)674-5151. Fax: (212)982-2837. Website: www.bloomsbury.com/usa. Specializes in trade books, fiction, multicultural material. Publishes 25 picture books/year; 5 young readers/year; 10 middle readers/year; and 10 young adult titles/year. 25% of books by first-time authors.
Fiction: Picture books: adventure, animal, contemporary, fantasy, folktales, history, humor, multicultural, nature/environment, poetry, suspense/mystery. Young readers: adventure, animal, anthology, concept, contemporary, fantasy, folktales, history, humor, multicultural, nature/environment, poetry, suspense/mystery. Middle readers: adventure, animal, contemporary, fantasy, folktales, history, humor, multicultural, nature/environment, poetry, problem novels. Young adults: adventure, animal, anthology, contemporary, fantasy, folktales, history, humor, multicultural, nature/environment, poetry, problem novels, science fiction, sports, suspense/mystery. Recently published *The Frog Princes*, by E.D. Baker (ages 8-12, middle grade fairytale); *Mole and the Baby Bird*, by Marjorie Newman, illustrated by Patrick Benson (picture book); *Stravaganza: City of Masks*, by Mary Hoffman (young adult fantasy).
How to Contact/Writers: Submit complete ms. Responds to queries/mss in 6 months.
Illustration: Works with 15 illustrators/year. Reviews ms/illustration packages from artists. Query or Submit ms with dummy. Illustrations only: Query with samples. Responds in 6 months only if interested. Samples returned with SASE; samples filed.
Photography: Buys stock and assigns work. Uses color or b&w prints. Submit SASE.
Terms: Pays authors royalty or work purchased outright for jackets. Offers advances. Pays illustrators by the project or royalty. Pays photographers by the project or per photo. Sends galleys to authors; dummies to illustrators. Originals returned to artist at job's completion. Writer's and art guidelines available for SASE. Catalog available on website.
Tips: "Spend a lot of time in the bookstore and library to keep up on trends in market."

✓ BLUE SKY PRESS, 557 Broadway, New York NY 10012-3999. (212)343-6100. Fax: (212)343-4713. Website: www.scholastic.com. Book publisher. Imprint of Scholastic Inc. **Acquisitions:** Bonnie Verburg. Publishes 15-20 titles/year. 1% of books by first-time authors. Publishes hardcover children's fiction and nonfiction including high-quality novels and picture books by new and established authors.
  ● Blue Sky is currently not accepting unsolicited submissions due to a large backlog of books.
Fiction: Picture books: adventure, animal, concept, contemporary, fantasy, folktales, history, humor, multicultural, nature/environment, poetry. Young readers: adventure, contemporary, fantasy, folktales, history, humor, multicultural, nature/environment, poetry. Young adults: adventure, anthology, contemporary, fantasy, history, humor, multicultural, poetry. Multicultural needs include "strong fictional or themes featuring non-white characters and cultures." Does not want to see mainstream religious, bibliotherapeutic, adult. Average length: picture books—varies; young adults—150 pages. Recently published *To Every Thing There Is a Season*, illustrated by Leo and Diane Dillon (all ages, picture book); *Bluish*, by Virginia Hamilton; *No, David!*, by David Shannon; *The Adventures of Captain Underpants*, by Dav Pilkey; and *How Do Dinosaurs Say Good Night?*, by Jane Yolen, illustrated by Mark Teague.
How to Contact/Writers: "Due to large numbers of submissions, we are discouraging unsolicited submissions—send query with SASE only if you feel certain we publish the type of book you have written." Fiction: Query (novels, picture books). Responds to queries in 6 months. Publishes a book 1-3 years after acceptance; depending on chosen illustrator's schedule. Will not consider simultaneous submissions.
Illustration: Works with 10 illustrators/year. Reviews illustration packages "only if illustrator is the author." Submit ms with dummy. Illustrations only: Query with samples, tearsheets. Responds only if interested. Samples returned with SASE. Original artwork returned at job's completion.
Terms: Pays 10% royalty based on wholesale price split between author and illustrators. Advance varies.
Tips: "Read currently published children's books. Revise—never send a first draft. Find your own voice, style, and subject. With material from new people we look for a theme or style strong enough to overcome the fact that the author/illustrator is unknown in the market."

N BOLLIX BOOKS, 1609 W. Callender Ave., Peoria IL 61606. E-mail: editor@bollixbooks.com. Website: www.bollixbooks.com. **Manuscript/Art Acquisitions:** Staley Krause, publisher. Publishes 4 children's books/year. "Bollix wants to expose children to unusual, and unexpected art forms, and writing that is an alternative to mainstream children's books."
Fiction: Picture books, intermediate, young adult. "Not interested in stories about puppies or kittens or things cute or fuzzy. The literary quality of submissions should be high and if authors have had their work rejected by other published houses because it is too literary, Bollix might be a good house to consider." Visit website to read writers guidelines for

more information. Recently published *I Only Like What I Like*, written and illustrated by Julie Baer; and *Master Stitchum and the Moon*, by Mickle Mayer, illustrated by Spiro Dousias.

How to Contact/Writers: Fiction: Unsolicited submissions not accepted. Accepts e-mail query letters only. Responds to queries in 2 months.

Illustration: Accepts ms/illustration packages from artists. Query via e-mail with samples in 1 PDF file. Illustrations only: Query via e-mail with samples in 1 PDF file.

BOYDS MILLS PRESS, 815 Church St., Honesdale PA 18431. (800)490-5111 or (570)253-1164. Fax: (570)253-0179. Website: www.boydsmillspress.com. Imprint: Wordsong (poetry). Book publisher. **Manuscript Acquisitions:** Manuscript Coordinator. **Art Acquisitions:** Tim Gillner. 5% of books from agented writers. Estab. 1990. "We publish a wide range of quality children's books of literary merit, from preschool to young adult."

Fiction: All levels: adventure, contemporary, history, humor, multicultural, poetry. Picture books: animal. Young readers, middle readers, young adult: problem novels, sports. Multicultural themes include any story showing a child as an integral part of a culture and which provides children with insight into a culture they otherwise might be unfamiliar with. "Please query us on the appropriateness of suggested topics for middle grade and young adult. For all other submissions send entire manuscript." Does not want to see talking animals, coming-of-age novels, romance and fantasy/science fiction.

Nonfiction: All levels: nature/environment, science. Picture books, young readers, middle readers: animal, multicultural. Does not want to see reference/curricular text.

How to Contact/Writers: Fiction/Nonfiction: Submit complete ms or submit through agent. Query on middle reader, young adult and nonfiction. Responds to queries/mss in 1 month.

Illustration: Works with 25 illustrators/year. Reviews ms/illustration packages from artists. Submit complete ms with 1 or 2 pieces of art. Illustrations only: Query with samples; send résumé and slides. Responds only if interested. Samples returned with SASE. Samples filed. Originals returned at job's completion.

Photography: Assigns work.

Terms: Authors paid royalty or work purchased outright. Offers advances. Illustrators paid by the project or royalties; varies. Photographers paid by the project, per photo, or royalties; varies. Manuscripts/artist's guidelines available for #10 SASE.

Tips: "Picture books—with fresh approaches, not worn themes—are our strongest need at this time. Check to see what's already on the market before submitting your story."

BROADMAN & HOLMAN PUBLISHERS, LifeWay Christian Resources, 127 Ninth Ave. N., Nashville TN 37234-0115. Fax: (615)251-3752. Website: www.broadmanholman.com. Book publisher. **Contact:** Attn: Children's Area. Publishes 25-30 titles/year with majority being for younger readers. Only publish a few titles/year for ages 0-3 or 9-11. 10% of books by first-time authors. "All books have Christian values/themes."

Nonfiction: Picture books: religion. Young or middle readers: self-help, social issues, religion, contemporary. Recently published: *Manners Made Easy: A Workbook for Student Parent and Teacher*, by June Hines Moore, illustrated by Jim Osborn (ages 7-12); *The Great Adventure* and *Thank You*, by Stephen Elkins, illustrated by Ellie Colton (children's storybook with CD based on Dove-Award winning songs, age 5 and up); *Which Came First, the Chicken or the Egg?*, by Leslie Eckard, illustrated by Judy Sakaguchi (children's songbook, ages 5-8).

How to Contact/Writers: Only interested in agented material. Responds to queries/mss in 2 months. Publishes a book 1 year after acceptance. Will consider simultaneous submissions.

Illustration: Works with 5-6 illustrators/year. Samples returned with SASE; samples filed.

Terms: Pays authors royalty 10-18% based on wholesale price. Offers variable advance. Original artwork returned at job's completion. Book catalog available for 9 × 12 SAE and 2 first-class stamps. Manuscript guidelines available for SASE.

Tips: "We're looking for picture books with good family values; Bible story re-tellings; modern-day stories for younger readers based on Bible themes and principles. Write us to ask for guidelines before submitting."

CANDLEWICK PRESS, 2067 Massachusetts Ave., Cambridge MA 02140. (617)661-3330. Fax: (617)661-0565. E-mail: bigbear@candlewick.com. Children's book publisher. Estab. 1991. **Manuscript Acquisitions:** Karen Lotz, publisher; Liz Bicknell, editorial director; Joan Powers, editor-at-large; Mary Lee Donovan, executive editor; Kara LaReau, senior editor; Sarah Ketchersid, editor; Cynthia Platt, editor; Deborah Wayshak, editor; Jamie Michalak, associate editor. **Art Acquisitions:** Anne Moore. Publishes 160 picture books/year; 15 middle readers/year; and 15 young adult titles/year. 5% of books by first-time authors. "Our books are truly for children, and we strive for the very highest standards in the writing, illustrating, designing and production of all of our books. And we are not averse to risk."

● Candlewick Press is not accepting queries and unsolicited mss at this time. Candlewick title *Big Momma Makes the World*, by Phyllis Root, illustrated by Helen Oxenbury, won the 2003 Boston Globe-Horn Book Award for Picture Books; *The Jamie and Angus Stories*, by Anne Fine, illustrated by Penny Dale won the 2003 Boston Globe-Horn Book Award for Fiction and Poetry. *Feed*, by M.T. Anderson, was a 2003 Boston Globe-Horn Honor Book.

Fiction: Picture books: animal, concept, contemporary, fantasy, history, humor, multicultural, nature/environment, poetry. Middle readers, young adults: contemporary, fantasy, history, humor, multicultural, poetry, science fiction, sports, suspense/mystery. Recently published: *The Earth, My Butt, and Other Big Round Things*, by Carolyn Mackler (young adult fiction); *Seeing the Blue Between*, edited by Paul B. Janeczko (young adult poetry collection).

Nonfiction: Picture books: concept, biography, geography, nature/environment. Young readers: biography, geography, nature/environment. Recently published *To the Top*, by Stephen Venables (nonfiction).

Illustration: Works with 40 illustrators/year. "We prefer to see a variety of the artist's style." Reviews ms/illustration packages from artists. "General samples only please." Illustrations only: Submit résumé and portfolio to the attention of

Design Dept. Responds to samples in 6 weeks. Samples returned with SASE; samples filed.

Terms: Pays authors royalty of 2½-10% based on retail price. Offers advances. Pays illustrators 2½-10% royalty based on retail price. Sends galleys to authors; dummies to illustrators. Photographers paid 2½-10% royalty. Original artwork returned at job's completion.

CAPSTONE PRESS INC., 7825 Telegraph Rd., Minneapolis MN 55438. Fax: (952)933-2410. Website: www.capstone-press.com. Book publisher. Imprints: Capstone Press, Bridgestone Books, Pebble Books, Blue Earth Books, Life Matters, Edge Books, Capstone High-Interest Books, A + Books, Fact Finders, First Facts, Pebble Plus, Yellow Umbrella Books, Let Freedom Ring Books, Picture Window Books. "The mission of Capstone Press is to help people learn to read and read to learn. We publish and distribute accessible, accurate, attractive, and affordable books to serve the needs of readers, educators, and librarians."

• Capstone Press does not accept unsolicited manuscripts.

Nonfiction: Publishes only nonfiction books for emergent, early, challenged and reluctant readers. Currently looking for experienced authors to write on vehicle, military and sport topics; also science, social studies, and pleasure reading areas. All levels: animals, arts/crafts, biography, geography, health, history, hobbies, special needs. Young adults only: Hi-lo, cooking, self help. Recently published *Mummies* series (grades 3-9); *Do Cows Eat Cake? A Book About What Animals Eat*, by Michael Dahl, illustrated by Sandra D'Antonio (pre K-2); *Skateboard Greats: Champs of the Ramps*, by Angie Peterson Kaelberer (grades 3-9).

How to Contact/Writers: Does not accept submissions. Do not send mss. Instead, request author brochure with SASE, then send query letter, résumé and samples of nonfiction writing to be considered for assignment. Responds in 3 weeks.

Photographers: Buys stock and assigns work. Contact: Photo Research Manager. Model/property release required. Uses 35mm slides, 4×5, 8×10 transparencies. Submit slides, stock photo list.

Terms: Authors paid flat fee. Photographers paid by the project or per photo. Originals returned to artist at job's completion. Book catalog available for large format SAE.

Tips: "See website prior to sending query letter."

CAROLRHODA BOOKS, INC., Division of the Lerner Publishing Group, 241 First Ave. N., Minneapolis MN 55401. (612)332-3344 or (800)328-4929. Fax: (612)332-7615. Website: www.lernerbooks.com. Imprint of Lerner. Lerner's other imprints are Lerner Publications, Lerner Sports, LernerClassroom and First Avenue Editions. Book publisher. Estab. 1959. **Manuscript Acquisitions:** Jennifer Zimian (nonfiction) and Zelda Wagner (fiction). Publishes 50-60 titles/year. 10% of books by first-time authors. "Carolrhoda Books is a children's publisher focused on producing high-quality, socially conscious nonfiction and fiction books for young readers K through grade 12, that help them learn about and explore the world around them." List includes picture books, biographies, nature and science titles, multicultural and introductory geography books and fiction for beginning readers. Recently published *The War*, by Anais Vaugelade; *Little Wolf's Haunted Hall for Small Horrors*, by Ian Whybrow.

Nonfiction: Picture books, young readers, middle readers: arts/crafts, biography, geography, history, nature/environment, social issues, sports.

How to Contact/Writers: Submissions are accepted in the months of March and October only. Submissions received in any month other than March or October will be returned unopened to the sender. A SASE is required for all submissions. Responds in 6 months.

Terms: Pays authors royalty or purchases work outright.

Tips: Carolrhoda does not publish alphabet books, puzzle books, songbooks, textbooks, workbooks, religious subject matter or plays. Address requests for guidelines to: GUIDELINE REQUEST with #10 SASE. Address requests for catalogs to CATALOG REQUEST and include 9×12 SAE with $3.85 postage.

CARTWHEEL BOOKS, for the Very Young, Imprint of Scholastic Inc., 557 Broadway, New York NY 10012. (212)343-6200. Website: www.scholastic.com. Estab. 1991. Book publisher. Vice President/Editorial Director: Ken Geist. **Manuscript Acquisitions:** Grace Maccarone, executive editor; Melissa Torres, assistant editor; J. Elizabeth Mills, assistant editor. **Art Acquisitions:** Richard Deas, art director; Patti Ann Harris, assiciate art director. Publishes 25-30 picture books/year; 30-35 easy readers/year; 15-20 novelty/concept books/year. "With each Cartwheel list, we strive for a pleasing balance among board books and novelty books, hardcover picture books and gift books, nonfiction, paperback storybooks and easy readers. Cartwheel seeks to acquire novelties that are books first; play objects second. Even without its gimmick, a Cartwheel book should stand alone as a valid piece of children's literature. We want all our books to be inviting and appealing, and to have inherent educational and social value. We believe that small children who develop personal relationships with books and grow up with a love of reading, become book consumers, and ultimately better human beings."

Fiction: Picture books, young readers: humor, suspense/mystery. Average work length: picture books—1-3,000; easy readers—100-3,000.

Nonfiction: Picture books, young readers: animal, history, nature/environment, science, sports. "Most of our nonfiction is either written on assignment or is within a series. We do not want to see any arts/crafts or cooking." Average word length: picture books—100-3,000; young readers—100-3,000.

How to Contact/Writers: Cartwheel Books is no longer accepting unsolicited mss or queries. All unsolicited materials will be returned unread. Fiction/nonfiction: For previously published or agented authors, submit complete ms. Responds to mss in 6 months. Publishes a book within 2 years after acceptance. SASE required with all submissions.

Illustration: Works with 100 illustrators/year. Reviews ms/illustration packages from artists. Send ms with dummy. Illustrations only: Query with samples; arrange personal portfolio review; send promo sheet, tearsheets to be kept on file.

Contact: Art Director. Responds in 2 months. Samples returned with SASE; samples filed. Please do not send original artwork.

Photography: Buys stock and assigns work. Uses photos of kids, families, vehicles, toys, animals. Submit published samples, color promo piece.

Terms: Pays advance against royalty or flat fee. Sends galley to authors; dummy to illustrators. Originals returned to artist at job's completion. Book catalog available for 9×12 SAE and 2 first-class stamps; ms guidelines for SASE.

Tips: "Know what types of books we do. Check out bookstores or catalogs to see where your work would fit best."

CAVENDISH CHILDREN'S BOOKS, Imprint of Marshal Cavendish, 99 White Plains Rd., Tarrytown NY 10591-9001. (914)332-8888. Specializes in children's trade books. **Editorial Director:** Margery Cuyler. **Art Acquisitions:** Anahid Hamparian, art director. Publishes 20-25 books/year.

Fiction/Nonfiction: All levels.

How to Contact/Writers: Query nonfiction. Submit 3 chapters or more for fiction. No picture book submissions. Enclose SASE.

Illustration: Contact: Art Director.

Terms: Pays authors/illustrators advance and royalties.

CHARLESBRIDGE, 85 Main St., Watertown MA 02472. (617)926-0329. Fax: (617)926-5720. E-mail: tradeeditorial @charlesbridge.com. Website: www.charlesbridge.com. Book publisher. Estab. 1980. Imprints: Talewinds and Whispering Coyote. Publishes 60% nonfiction, 40% fiction picture books. Publishes nature, science, multicultural, social studies and fiction picture books. Charlesbridge also has an educational division. **Contact:** Trade Editorial Department, submissions editor or School Editorial Department.

Fiction: Picture books: "Strong, realistic stories with enduring themes." Considers the following categories: adventure, concept, contemporary, health, history, humor, multicultural, nature/environment, special needs, sports, suspense/mystery. Recently published: *The Wedding*, by Eve Bunting; and *Big Blue*, by Shelley Gill.

Nonfiction: Picture books: animal, biography, careers, concept, geography, health, history, multicultural, music/dance, nature/environment, religion, science, social issues, special needs, hobbies, sports. Average word length: picture books—1,500. Recently published: *How Do You Raise a Raisin*, by Pam Muñoz Ryan; and *Nature's Magnificient Flying Machines*, by Caroline Arnold.

How to Contact/Writers: Send ms and SASE. Accepts exclusive submissions only. Responds to mss in 3 months. Full mss only; no queries.

Illustration: Works with 5-10 illustrators/year. Uses color artwork only. Illustrations only: Query with samples; provide résumé, tearsheets to be kept on file. "Send no original artwork, please." Responds only if interested. Samples returned with SASE; samples filed. Originals returned at job's completion.

Terms: Pays authors and illustrators in royalties or work purchased outright. Manuscript/art guidelines available for SASE. Exclusive submissions only.

Tips: Wants "books that have humor and are factually correct. See our website for more tips."

CHICAGO REVIEW PRESS, 814 N. Franklin St., Chicago IL 60610. (312)337-0747. Fax: (312)337-5110. E-mail: publish@ipgbook.com. Website: www.ipgbook.com. Book publisher. Estab. 1973. **Manuscript Acquisitions:** Cynthia Sherry, executive editor. **Art Acquisitions:** Joan Sommers, art director. Publishes 3-4 middle readers/year and "about 4" young adult titles/year. 33% of books by first-time authors; 30% of books from agented authors. "Chicago Review Press publishes high-quality, nonfiction, educational activity books that extend the learning process through hands-on projects and accurate and interesting text. We look for activity books that are as much fun as they are constructive and informative."

Nonfiction: Picture books, young readers, middle readers and young adults: activity books, arts/crafts, multicultural, history, nature/environment, science. "We're interested in hands-on, educational books; anything else probably will be rejected." Average length: young readers and young adults—175 pages. Recently published *Oceans*, by Nancy Castaldo (ages 6-9); *The American Revolution for Kids*, by Janis Herbert (ages 9 and up); and *Monet and Impressionism for Kids*, by Carol Sabbeth (ages 9 and up).

How to Contact/Writers: Enclose cover letter and no more than table of contents and 1-2 sample chapters. Send for guidelines. Responds to queries/mss in 2 months. Publishes a book 1-2 years after acceptance. Will consider simultaneous submissions and previously published work.

Illustration: Works with 6 illustrators/year. Uses primarily b&w artwork. Reviews ms/illustration packages from artists. Submit 1-2 chapters of ms with corresponding pieces of final art. Illustrations only: Query with samples, résumé. Responds only if interested. Samples returned with SASE.

Photography: Buys photos from freelancers ("but not often"). Buys stock and assigns work. Wants "instructive photos. We consult our files when we know what we're looking for on a book-by-book basis." Uses b&w prints.

Terms: Pays authors royalty of $7\frac{1}{2}$-$12\frac{1}{2}$% based on retail price. Offers advances of $1,000-4,000. Pays illustrators by the project (range varies considerably). Pays photographers by the project (range varies considerably). Original artwork "usually" returned at job's completion. Book catalog/ms guidelines available for $3.

Tips: "We're looking for original activity books for small children and the adults caring for them—new themes and enticing projects to occupy kids' imaginations and promote their sense of personal creativity. We like activity books that are as much fun as they are constructive. Please write for guidelines so you'll know what we're looking for."

CHILD WELFARE LEAGUE OF AMERICA, Child & Family Press, 440 First St., NW, 3rd Floor, Washington DC 20001-2085. (202)942-0263. Fax: (202)638-4004. E-mail: ptierney@cwla.org. Website: www.cwla.org. The Child & Family

Press imprint was created in 1990. **Acquisitions:** Peggy Porter Tierney. Publishes 5 picture books/year; 1 middle reader/year. 50% books by first-time authors. "CWLA is the nation's oldest and largest membership-based child welfare organization. We are committed to engaging people everywhere in promoting the well-being of children, youth, and their families, and protecting every child from harm."

Fiction: Picture books: animal, concept, contemporary, health, multicultural, special needs. Recently published *A.D.D. not B.A.D.*, by Audrey Penn (ages 4-11, picture book); and *Coffee Can Kids*, by Jan Czech (ages 4-11, picture book).

Nonfiction: Picture books, young readers, middle readers, young adults: concept, multicultural, self-help, social issues, special needs (anything relating to child welfare). Recently published *Being Adopted*, by Stephanie Herbert (picture book, ages 4-8); *I Miss My Foster Parents*, by Stefan Herbert (picture book, 4-8); and *The Visit*, by Latisha Herbert (picture book, ages 4-8).

How to Contact/Writers: Fiction/nonfiction: Submit complete ms or submit outline/synopsis and 3-4 sample chapters. Responds in 6 months. Publishes a book 1 year after acceptance. Will consider simultaneous submissions.

Illustration: Works with 5 illustrators/year. Reviews ms/illustration packages from artists. Send ms with dummy or submit ms with 3-4 pieces of final art. Contact: Jennifer Geanakos, lead designer. Illustrations only: Query with samples. Contact: Peggy Porter Tierney, acquisitions. Responds in 3 months. "We prefer to keep samples on file in case suitable for future job." Samples returned with SASE.

Photography: Buys stock. Contact: Peggy Porter Tierney, acquisitions. Uses photos of children and families. Uses color or b&w prints and 35mm, $2\frac{1}{4} \times 2\frac{1}{4}$, 4×5 transparencies. Submit slides, client list, promo piece, published samples, stock photo list.

Terms: Pays authors royalty of 9-12% based on retail price. Pays illustrators royalties of 3-5% or by the project. Pays photographers by the project or per photo. Sends galleys to authors; dummies to illustrators. Catalog available on website.

Tips: "We are looking for upbeat, imaginative children's stories, particularly with some kind of message, but without being didactic. Authors do not need to worry about illustrations or formatting. In fact, a plain text to me is preferable to a manuscript set out in pages with very amateurish drawings. Do not call to propose an idea."

CHILDREN'S BOOK PRESS, 2211 Mission St., San Francisco CA 94110. (415)821-3080. Fax: (415)821-3081. E-mail: info@cbookpress.org. Website: www.cbookpress.org. **Acquisitions:** Submissions Editor. "Children's Book Press is a nonprofit publisher of multicultural and bilingual children's literature. We publish contemporary stories reflecting the traditions and culture of minorities and new immigrants in the United States. Our goal is to help broaden the base of children's literature in this country to include stories from the African-American, Asian-American, Latino/Chicano and Native American communities. Stories should encourage critical thinking about social and/or personal issues. These ideas must be an integral part of the story."

Fiction: Picture books, young readers: contemporary, history, multicultural, poetry. Average word length: picture books—800-1,600.

Nonfiction: Picture books, young readers: multicultural.

How to Contact/Writers: Submit complete ms to Submissions Editor. Responds to mss in roughly 4 months. "Please do not inquire about your manuscript. We can only return/respond manuscripts with a SASE." Publishes a book 1-2 years after acceptance. Will consider simultaneous submissions.

Illustration: Works with 4-5 illustrators/year. Uses color artwork only. Reviews ms/illustration packages from artists. Send ms with 3 or 4 color photocopies. Illustrations only: color copies preferable, slides if you must, no original artwork. Responds only if interested. Samples returned with SASE.

Terms: Original artwork returned at job's completion. Book catalog available; ms guidelines available via website or with SASE.

Tips: "Vocabulary level should be approximately third grade (eight years old) or below. Keep in mind, however, that many of the young people who read our books may be nine, ten, or eleven years old or older. Their life experiences are often more advanced than their reading level, so try to write a story that will appeal to a fairly wide age range. We are especially interested in humorous stories and original stories about contemporary life from the multicultural communities mentioned above by writers *from* those communities."

CHRISTIAN ED. PUBLISHERS, P.O. Box 26639, San Diego CA 92196. (858)578-4700. E-mail: jackelson@cehouse.com (writing); ckruger@cepub.com (illustration). Website: www.ChristianEdWarehouse.com. **Acquisitions:** Janet Ackelson, assistant editor; Carol Rogers, managing editor. Book publisher. Publishes 80 Bible curriculum titles/year. "We publish curriculum for children and youth, including program and student books (for youth) and take-home papers (for children)—all handled by our assigned freelance writers only."

Fiction: Young readers: contemporary. Middle readers: adventure, contemporary, suspense/mystery. "We publish fiction for Bible club take-home papers. All fiction is on assignment only."

Nonfiction: Publishes Bible curriculum and take-home papers for all ages. Recently published *All-Stars for Jesus*, by Treena Herrington and Letitia Zook, illustrated by Beverly Warren (Bible club curriculum for grades 4-6); and *Honeybees Classroom Activity Sheets*, by Janet Miller and Wanda Pelfrey, illustrated by Aiko Gilson and Terry Walderhaug (Bible club curriculum for ages 2-3).

How to Contact/Writers: Fiction/Nonfiction: Query. Responds to queries in 5 weeks. Publishes a book 1 year after acceptance. Send SASE for guidelines or contact Christian Ed. at slowe@cepub.com.

Illustration: Works with 6-7 illustrators/year. Uses b&w and 4-color artwork. Query; include a SASE; we'll send an application form. Contact: Clint Kruger, design coordinator (ckruger@cepub.com). Responds in 1 month. Samples returned with SASE.

Terms: Work purchased outright from authors for 3¢/word. Pays illustrators by the project (range: $300-400/book). Book

catalog available for 9×12 SAE and 4 first-class stamps; ms and art guidelines available for SASE.
Tips: "Read our guidelines carefully before sending us a manuscript or illustrations. All writing and illustrating is done on assignment only and must be age-appropriate (preschool-6th grade)."

CHRONICLE BOOKS, 85 Second St., 6th Floor, San Francisco CA 94105. (415)537-4422. Fax: (415)537-4415. Website: www.chroniclekids.com. Book publisher. **Acquisitions:** Victoria Rock, associate publisher, children's books. Publishes 35-60 (both fiction and nonfiction) books/year, 5-10% middle readers, young adult nonfiction titles. 10-25% of books by first-time authors; 20-40% of books from agented writers.
• Chronicle title *Stars in Darkness*, by Barbara Joose, illustrated by R. Gregory Christie won a 2002 Golden Kite Honor book plaque for picture book text.
Fiction: Picture books: animal, folktales, history, multicultural, nature/environment. Young readers: animal, folktales, history, multicultural, nature/environment, poetry. Middle readers: animal, history, multicultural, nature/environment, poetry, problem novels. Young adults: multicultural needs include "projects that feature diverse children in everyday situations." Recently published *Red is a Dragon*, by Roseanne Thong, illustrated by Grace Lin; *Bintou's Braids*, by Sylviane A. Dionf, illustrated by Shane W. Evans; *Twinkle Twinkle Little Star*, by Sylvia Long.
Nonfiction: Picture books: animal, history, multicultural, nature/environment, science. Young readers: animal, arts/crafts, cooking, geography, history, multicultural and science. Middle readers: animal, arts/crafts, biography, cooking, geography, history, multicultural and nature/environment. Young adults: biography and multicultural. Recently published *Story Painter: The Life of Jacob Lawrence*, by John Duggleby; *Seven Weeks on an Iceberg*, by Keith Potter (Doodlezoo series).
How to Contact/Writers: Fiction/Nonfiction: Submit complete ms (picture books); submit outline/synopsis and 3 sample chapters (for older readers). Responds to queries/mss in 4 months. Publishes a book 1-3 years after acceptance. Will consider simultaneous submissions, as long as they are marked "multiple submission." Will not consider submissions by fax or e-mail. Must include SASE or projects will not be returned.
Illustration: Works with 15-20 illustrators/year. Wants "unusual art, graphically strong, something that will stand out on the shelves. Either bright and modern or very traditional. Fine art, not mass market." Reviews ms/illustration packages from artists. "Indicate if project *must* be considered jointly, or if editor may consider text and art separately." Illustrations only: Submit samples of artist's work (not necessarily from book, but in the envisioned style). Slides, tearsheets and color photocopies OK. (No original art.) Dummies helpful. Résumé helpful. "If samples sent for files, generally no response—unless samples are not suited to list, in which case samples are returned. Queries and project proposals responded to in same time frame as author query/proposals."
Photography: Purchases photos from freelancers. Works on assignment only. Wants nature/natural history photos.
Terms: Generally pays authors in royalties based on retail price "though we do occasionally work on a flat fee basis." Advance varies. Illustrators paid royalty based on retail price or flat fee. Sends proofs to authors and illustrators. Book catalog for 9×12 SAE and 8 first-class stamps; ms guidelines for #10 SASE.
Tips: "Chronicle Books publishes an eclectic mixture of traditional and innovative children's books. We are interested in taking on projects that have a unique bent to them—be it in subject matter, writing style, or illustrative technique. As a small list, we are looking for books that will lend our list a distinctive flavor. Primarily we are interested in fiction and nonfiction picture books for children ages infant-8 years, and nonfiction books for children ages 8-12 years. We are also interested in developing a middle grade/YA fiction program, and are looking for literary fiction that deals with relevant issues. Our sales reps are witnessing a resistance to alphabet books. And the market has become increasingly competitive. The '80s boom in children's publishing has passed, and the market is demanding high-quality books that work on many different levels."

CLARION BOOKS, 215 Park Ave. S., New York NY 10003. (212)420-5800. Website: www.houghtonmifflinbooks.com/trade/. Imprint of Houghton Mifflin Company. Book publisher. Estab. 1965. **Manuscript Acquisitions:** Dinah Stevenson, associate publisher; Virginia Buckley, contributing editor; Jennifer Green, editor. **Art Acquisitions:** Joann Hill, art director.
• Clarion title *The Life and Death of Adolf Hitler*, by James Cross Giblin, won the 2003 Robert F. Sibert Medal. *To Fly: The Story of the Wright Brothers*, by Wendie C. Old, illustrated by Robert Andrew Parker was named a 2003 Boston Globe-Horn Honor book. Clarion is reading manuscripts but signing books for 2005 and beyond.
How to Contact/Writers: Fiction and picture books: Send complete mss. Nonfiction: Send query with up to 3 sample chapters. Must include SASE. Will accept simultaneous submission if informed.
Illustration: Send samples (no originals).
Terms: Pays illustrators royalty; flat fee for jacket illustration. Pays royalties and advance to writers; both vary.

CLEAR LIGHT PUBLISHERS, 823 Don Diego, Santa Fe NM 87505. (505)989-9590. Fax: (505)989-9519. Website: www.clearlightbooks.com. Book publisher. **Acquisitions:** Harmon Houghton, publisher. Publishes 4 middle readers/year; and 4 young adult titles/year.
Nonfiction: Middle readers and young adults: multicultural, American Indian and Hispanic only.
How to Contact/Writers: Fiction/Nonfiction: Submit complete ms with SASE. "No e-mail submissions. Authors supply art. Manuscripts not considered without art or artist's renderings." Will consider simultaneous submissions. Responds in 3 months. Only send *copies*.
Illustration: Reviews ms/illustration packages from artists. "No originals please." Submit ms with dummy and SASE.
Terms: Pays authors royalty of 10% based on wholesale price. Offers advances (average amount: up to 50% of expected net sales within the first year). Sends galleys to authors.
Tips: "We're looking for authentic American Indian art and folklore."

CONCORDIA PUBLISHING HOUSE, 3558 S. Jefferson Ave., St. Louis MO 63118. (314)268-1187. Fax: (314)268-1329. Website: cphmall.com. Book publisher. **Contact:** Peggy Kuethe. "Concordia Publishing House produces quality resources which communicate and nurture the Christian faith and ministry of people of all ages, lay and professional. These resources include curriculum, worship aids, books, multimedia products and religious supplies. We publish approximately 30 quality children's books each year. All are nonfiction based on a religious subject. We boldly provide Gospel resources that are Christ-centered, Bible-based and faithful to our Lutheran heritage."
Nonfiction: Picture books, young readers, middle readers, young adults: activity books, arts/crafts, concept, contemporary, religion. Picture books: poetry. "All books must contain explicit Christian content." Recently published *The Very First Christmas*, by Paul L Maier (picture book for ages 6-10); and *Running the Race of Faith*, by Pam Ausenhus (ages over 12, youth nonfiction).
How to Contact/Writers: Submit complete ms (picture books); submit outline/synopsis and sample chapters for longer mss. May also query. Responds to queries in 1 month; mss in 3 months. Publishes a book 2 years after acceptance. Will consider simultaneous submissions. "No phone queries."
Illustration: Works with 50 illustrators/year. Illustrations only: Query with samples. Contact: Ed Luhmann, art director. Responds only if interested. Samples returned with SASE; samples filed. Originals not returned at job's completion.
Terms: Pays authors in royalties based on retail price or work purchased outright ($750-2,000). Sends galleys to author. Manuscript guidelines for 1 first-class stamp and a #10 envelope. Pays illustrators by the project.
Tips: "Do not send finished artwork with the manuscript. If sketches will help in the presentation of the manuscript, they may be sent. If stories are taken from the Bible, they should follow the Biblical account closely. Liberties should not be taken in fantasizing Biblical stories."

CRICKET BOOKS, Imprint of the Cricket Magazine Group, 332 S. Michigan Ave., Suite 1100, Chicago IL 60604. (312)939-1500. E-mail: cricketBooks@caruspub.com. Website: www.cricketbooks.net. Imprint estab. 1999; Company estab. 1973. **Manuscript Acquisitions:** Carol Saller. **Art Acquisitions:** Tony Jacobson. Publishes 24 titles/year. "For 25 years we've published the best children's literary magazines in America, and we're looking for the same high-quality material for our book imprint."
   • Publisher Marc Aronson is publishing fiction and nonfiction for teenagers under his Marcato imprint.
Fiction: Young readers, middle readers, young adult/teen: adventure, animal, contemporary, fantasy, history, multicultural, humor, sports, suspense/mystery, science fiction, problem novels. Recently published *Breakout*, by Paul Fleischman; *Robert and the Weird & Wacky Facts*, by Barbara Seuling, illustrated by Paul Brewer.
How to Contact: Not accepting unsolicited mss. See website for details and updates on submissions policy.
Illustration: Works with 4 illustrators/year. Use color and b&w. Illustration only: submit samples, tearsheets. Contact: Tony Jacobson, 315 Fifth St., Peru IL 61354. Responds only if interested. Samples returned with SASE; sample filed.
Terms: Authors paid royalty of 7-10% based on retail price. Offers advances. Illustrators paid royalty of 3% based on retail price. Sends galleys to authors; dummies to illustrators. Originals returned to artist at job's completion. Writer's guidelines available for SASE. Catalog available at website.
Tips: "Primarily interested in chapter books, middle-grade fiction, and young adult novels, but will also consider picture books."

N CROCODILE BOOKS, 46 Crosby St., Northampton MA 01060. (413)582-7054. Fax: (413)582-7057. E-mail: interpg @aol.com. Imprint of Interlink Publishing Group, Inc. Book publisher. **Acquisitions:** Pam Thompson, associate publisher. Publishes 4 picture books/year. 25% of books by first-time authors.
   • Crocodile does not accept unsolicited mss.
Fiction: Picture books: animal, contemporary, history, spy/mystery/adventure.
Nonfiction: Picture book: history, nature/environment.
Terms: Pays authors in royalties.

N CSS PUBLISHING, 517 S. Main St., P.O. Box 4503, Lima OH 45802-4503. (419)227-1818. Fax: (419)222-4647. E-mail: acquisitions@csspub.com. Website: www.csspub.com. Book publisher. Imprints include Fairway Press and Express Press. **Manuscript Acquisitions:** Stan Purdum. Publishes books with religious themes. "We are seeking material for use by clergy, Christian education directors and Sunday school teachers for mainline Protestant churches. Our market is mainline Protestant clergy."
Fiction: Young readers, middle readers, young adults: religion, religious poetry and humor. Needs children's sermons (object lesson) for Sunday morning worship services; dramas for Advent, Christmas or Epiphany involving children for church services; activity and craft ideas for Sunday school or mid-week services for children (particularly pre-school and first and second grade). Published *That Seeing, They May Believe*, by Kenneth Mortonson (lessons for adults to present during worship services to pre-schoolers-third graders); *What Shall We Do With This Baby?*, by Jan Spence (Christmas Eve worship service involving youngsters from newborn babies-high school youth); and *Miracle in the Bethlehem Inn*, by Mary Lou Warstler (Advent or Christmas drama involving pre-schoolers-high school youth and adult.)
Nonfiction: Young readers, middle readers, young adults: religion. Young adults only: social issues and self help. Needs children's sermons (object lesson) for Sunday morning worship services; dramas for Advent, Christmas or Epiphany involving children for church services; activity and craft ideas for Sunday school or mid-week services for children (particularly pre-school and first and second grade). Published *Mustard Seeds*, by Ellen Humbert (activity/bulletins for pre-schoolers-first graders to use during church); and *This Is The King*, by Cynthia Cowen.
How to Contact/Writers: Responds to queries in 2 weeks; mss in 3 months. Publishes a book 9 months after acceptance. Will consider simultaneous submissions.

Terms: Work purchased outright from authors. Manuscript guidelines and book catalog available for SASE and on website.

N DARBY CREEK PUBLISHING, 7878 Industrial Pkwy., Plain City OH 43064. (614)873-7955. Fax: (614)873-7135. E-mail: info@darbycreekpublishing.com. **Manuscript/Art Acquisitions:** Tanya Dean, editorial director. Publishes 10 children's books/year.

Fiction: Middle readers, young adult. Recently published *The Warriors*, by Joseph Bruchac (ages 10 and up); and *Venus and the Comets*, by Erika Tamar (ages 8 and up).

Nonfiction: Middle readers: biography, history, science, sports. Recently published *Dinosaur Mummies*, by Kelly Milner Halls, illustrated by Rick Spears.

How to Contact/Writers: Accepts international material only with U.S. postage on SASE for return—no IRCs. Fiction/nonfiction: Submit publishing history and/or résumé and complete ms for short works or outline/synopsis and 2-3 sample chapters for longer works such as novels. Responds in 6 weeks. Does not consider previously published work.

Illustration: Illustrations only: Send photocopies and résumé with publishing history. "Indicate which samples we may keep on file and include SASE and appropriate packing materials for any samples you wish to have returned."

Terms: Offers advance against royalty contracts.

Tips: "We like to see nonfiction with a unique slant that is kid friendly, well-researched and endorsed by experts. We're interested in fiction or nonfiction with sports themes for future lists."

MAY DAVENPORT, PUBLISHERS, 26313 Purissima Rd., Los Altos Hills CA 94022-4539. (650)947-1275. Fax: (650)947-1373. E-mail: mdbooks@earthlink.net. Website: www.maydavenportpublishers.com. Independent book producer/packager. Estab. 1976. **Acquisitions:** May Davenport, editor/publisher. Publishes 1-2 picture books/year; and 2-3 young adult titles/year. 99% of books by first-time authors. Seeks books with literary merit. "We like to think that we are selecting talented writers who have something humorous to write about today's unglued generation in 30,000-50,000 words for teens and young adults in junior/senior high school before they become tomorrow's 'functional illiterates.' We are interested in publishing literature that teachers in middle and high schools can use in their Language Arts, English and Creative Writing courses. There's more to literary fare than the chit-chat Internet dialog and fantasy trips on television with cartoons or humanoids." This publisher is overstocked with picture book/elementary reading material.

Fiction: Young adults (15-18): contemporary, humorous fictional literature for use in English courses in junior-senior high schools in US. Average word length: 40,000-60,000. Recently published *The Lesson Plan*, by Irvin Gay (about an illiterate black boy who grows up to become a teacher, ages 15-18); *A Life on the Line*, by Michael Horton (about a juvenile delinquent boy who becomes a hero, ages 15-18); *Making My Escape*, by David Lee Finkle (about a young boy who daydreams movie-making in outer space to escape unhappy family life, ages 12-18).

Nonfiction: Teens: humorous. Recently published *The Runaway Game*, by Kevin Casey (a literary board game of street life in Hollywood, ages 15-18).

How to Contact/Writers: Fiction: Query. Responds to queries/mss in 3 weeks. "We do not answer queries or manuscripts which do not have SASE attached." Publishes a book 6-12 months after acceptance.

Illustration: Works with 1-2 illustrators/year. "Have enough on file for future reference." Responds only if interested. Samples returned with SASE; samples filed. Originals returned at job's completion.

Terms: Pays authors royalties of 15% based on retail price; negotiable. Pays "by mutual agreement, no advances." Pays illustrators by the project (range: $75-350). Book catalog, ms guidelines free on request with SASE.

Tips: "Create stories to enrich the non-reading high school readers. They might not appreciate your similies and metaphors and may find fault with your alliterations, but show them how you do it with memorable characters in today's society. Just project your humorous talent and entertain with more than two sentences in a paragraph."

DAWN PUBLICATIONS, 12402 Bitney Springs Rd., Nevada City CA 95959. (530)274-7775. Fax: (530)275-7778. E-mail: glenn@dawnpub.com. Website: www.dawnpub.com. Book publisher. Publisher: Muffy Weaver. **Acquisitions:** Glenn J. Hovemann, editor. Publishes works with holistic themes dealing with nature. "Dawn Publications is dedicated to inspiring in children a deeper appreciation and understanding of nature."

Nonfiction: Picture books: animal, nature/environment. Biographies of naturalists recently published *John Muir: My Life With Nature*, by Joseph Cornell (80-page biography); and *Do Animals Have Feelings Too?*, by David L. Rice (32-page picture book).

How to Contact/Writers: Nonfiction: Query or submit complete ms. Responds to queries/mss in 3 months maximum. Publishes a book 1 year after acceptance. Will consider simultaneous submissions.

Illustration: Works with 5 illustrators/year. Will review ms/illustration packages from artists. Query; send ms with dummy. Illustrations only: Query with samples, résumé.

Terms: Pays authors royalty based on wholesale price. Offers advance. Pays illustrators by the project or royalties based on wholesale price. Book catalog available online; ms guidelines available online.

Tips: Looking for "picture books expressing nature awareness with inspirational quality leading to enhanced self-awareness. Usually no animal dialogue."

DELACORTE AND DOUBLEDAY BOOKS FOR YOUNG READERS, (formerly Knopf Delacorte Dell Young Readers Group), 1745 Broadway, New York NY 10019. (212)782-9000. Website: www.randomhouse.com/kids. Imprints of Random House Children's Books. 90% of books published through agents.

   • See listings for Random House Golden Books for Young Readers and Alfred A. Knopf and Crown Books for Young Readers.

Fiction: Unsolicited mss are only being accepted as submissions to either the Marguerite de Angeli Contest for middle-grade contemporary or historical fiction or the Delacorte Press Contest for contemporary young adult fiction. Send a SASE for contest rules.

Illustration: Illustration only: Contact: Isabel Warren-Lynch, art director. Responds only if interested. Samples returned with SASE; samples filed.

Terms: Pays illustrators and photographers by the project or royalties. Original artwork returned at job's completion.

DIAL BOOKS FOR YOUNG READERS, Penguin Young Readers Group, 345 Hudson St., New York NY 10014. Website: www.penguin.com. Associate Publisher/Editorial Director: Lauri Hornik. **Acquisitions:** Nancy Mercado, editor; Cecile Goyette, senior editor; Karen Riskin, editor; Rebecca Waugh, editor. **Art Director:** Lily Malcom. Publishes 35 picture books/year; 3 young reader titles/year; 6 middle reader titles/year; and 9 young adult titles/year.

Fiction: Picture books, young readers: adventure, animal, contemporary, fantasy, folktales, history, humor, multicultural, poetry, sports. Middle readers, young adults: adventure, contemporary, fantasy, folktales, history, humor, multicultural, poetry, problem novels, science fiction, sports, mystery/adventure. Published *A Year Down Yonder*, by Richard Peck (ages 10 and up); *The Sea Chest*, by Toni Buzzeo, illustrated by Mary Grand Pre (all ages, picture book); *A Penguin Pup for Pinkerton*, by Steven Kellogg (ages 3-7, picture book).

   ● Dial title *Bronx Masquerade*, by Nikki Grimes won the 2003 Coretta Scott King Author Award.

Nonfiction: Will consider query letters for submissions of outstanding literary merit. Picture books, young readers, middle readers: biography, history, sports. Young adults: biography, contemporary, history, sports. Recently published *A Strong Right Arm*, by Michelle Y. Green (ages 10 and up) and *Dirt on their Skirts*, by Doreen Rappaport and Lyndall Callan (ages 4-8, picture book).

How to Contact/Writers: Accepts picture book ms and queries for longer works. Do not send more than 10 pages. Responds to queries/mss. in 3 months. "We do not supply specific guidelines, but we will send you a recent catalog if you send us a 9×12 SASE with four first-class stamps attached. Questions and queries should only be made in writing. We will not reply to anything without a SASE." No e-mail queries.

Illustration: Works with 35 illustrators/year. Art samples should be sent to Dial Design and will not be returned without a SASE. "No phone calls please. Only artists with portfolios that suit the house's needs will be interviewed."

Terms: Pays authors and illustrators in royalties based on retail price. Average advance payment "varies."

DK PUBLISHING, INC., DK Ink, 375 Hudson St., New York NY 10014. Website: www.dk.com. **Acquisitions:** submissions editor.

   ● DK Publishing does not accept unagented mss.

DNA PRESS, LLC, P.O. Box 572, Eagleville PA 19408. Fax: (501)694-5495. E-mail: dnapress@yahoo.com. Website: www.dnapress.net. Estab. 2000. Specializes in nonfiction, fiction, educational material. **Acquisitions:** Xela Schenk. Publishes 1 picture book/year; 2 middle readers/year; and 2 young adult titles/year. 75% of books by first-time authors.

Fiction: Picture books: health. Young adults: adventure, contemporary, fantasy.

Nonfiction: Picture books, young readers, middle readers, young adults: science.

How to Contact/Writers: Fiction/Nonfiction: Submit complete ms. Responds to queries in 1 month; mss in 6 weeks. Publishes book 6 months after acceptance.

Illustration: Works with 1 illustrator/year. Uses b&w artwork only. Reviews ms/illustration packages from artists. Send ms with dummy. Illustrations only: Send web page. Responds in 1 month. Samples not returned.

Terms: Pays authors royalty of 8-15% based on wholesale price. Pays illustrators and photographers by the project. Sends galleys to authors; dummies to illustrators.

Tips: Children's writers and illustrators should pay attention to "how-to books and books in which science knowledge is communicated to the reader. We focus on bringing science to the young reader in various forms of fiction and nonfiction books."

DOG-EARED PUBLICATIONS, P.O. Box 620863, Middletown WI 53562-0863. (608)831-1410. (608)831-1410. Fax: (608)831-1410. E-mail: field@dog-eared.com. Website: www.dog-eared.com. Book publisher. Estab. 1977. **Art Acquisitions:** Nancy Field, publisher. Publishes 2-3 middle readers/year. 1% of books by first-time authors. "Dog-Eared Publications creates action-packed nature books for children. We aim to turn young readers into environmentally aware citizens and to foster a love for science and nature in the new generation.

Nonfiction: Middle readers: activity books, animal, nature/environment, science. Average word length varies. Recently published *Discovering Sharks and Rays*, by Nancy Field, illustrated by Michael Maydak (middle readers, activity book); *Leapfrogging Through Wetlands*, by Margaret Anderson, Nancy Field and Karen Stephenson, illustrated by Michael Maydak (middle readers, activity book); *Ancient Forests*, by Margaret Anderson, Nancy Field and Karen Stephenson, illustrated by Sharon Torvik (middle readers, activity book).

How to Contact/Writers: Nonfiction: Currently not accepting unsolicited submissions.

Illustration: Works with 2-3 illustrators/year. Reviews ms/illustration packages from artists. Submit query and a few art samples. Illustrations only: Query with samples. Responds only if interested. Samples not returned; samples filed. "Interested in realistic, nature art!"

Terms: Pays authors royalty based on wholesale price. Offers advances (amount varies). Pays illustrators royalty based on wholesale price. Sends galleys to authors. Originals returned to artist at job's completion. Brochure available for SASE and 1 first-class stamp or on website.

N DOWN EAST BOOKS, P.O. Box 679, Camden, ME 04843-0679. (207)594-9544. Fax: (207)594-7215. E-mail: msteere@downeast.com. Book publisher. Senior Editor: Karin Womer. **Acquisitions:** Michael Steere, managing editor. Publishes 3-4 young readers and middle readers/year. 70% of books by first-time authors. "As a small regional publisher Down East Books specializes in non-fiction books with a Maine or New England theme. Down East Books' mission is to publish superbly crafted books which capture and illuminate the astonishing beauty and unique character of New England's people, culture and wild places; the very aspects that distinguish New England from the rest of the United States."
Fiction: Picture books, middle readers, young readers, young adults: animal, adventure, history, nature/environment. Young adults: suspense/mystery. Recently published *Miss Renee's Mice*, by Elizabeth Hoffman, illustrated by Dawn Pete.
Nonfiction: Picture books, middle readers, young readers, young adults: animal, history, nature/environment. Recently published *A Loon Alone*, by Pamela Love, illustrated by Shannon Sycks.
How to Contact/Writers: Fiction/Nonfiction: Query. Responds to queries/mss in 2 months. Publishes a book 6-18 months after acceptance. Will consider simultaneous and previously published submissions.
Illustration: Works with 2-3 illustrators/year. Reviews ms/illustration packages from artists. Query. Illustrations only: Query with samples. Responds in 2 months. Samples returned with SASE; samples filed sometimes. Originals returned at job's completion.
Terms: Pays authors royalty (7-12% based on net receipts). Pays illustrators by the project or by royalty (7-10% based on net receipts). Sends galleys to authors; dummies to illustrators. Original artwork returned at job's completion. Book catalog available. Manuscript guidelines available for SASE.

☑ ⊠ DUTTON CHILDREN'S BOOKS, Penguin Group (USA), 345 Hudson St., New York NY 10014-4502. (212)414-3700. Website: www.penguin.com. Book publisher. President and Publisher: Stephanie Owens Lurie. **Acquisitions:** Lucia Monfried (easy-to-read, middle-grade fiction); Meredith Mundy Wasinger (middle-grade fiction, picture books); Michele Coppola (picture books, middle-grade fiction); Julie Strauss-Gabel (picture books, middle-grade fiction, young adult); Alissa Heyman (all types fiction). **Art Acquisitions:** Sara Reynolds, art director. Publishes approximately 60 picture books/year; 6 young reader titles/year; 16 middle reader titles/year; and 12 young adult titles/year. 10% of books by first-time authors.

• Dutton is open to query letters only. Dutton title *Postcards from No Man's Land*, by Aidan Chambers won the 2003 Michael Printz award.

Fiction: Picture books: adventure, animal, history, humor, multicultural, nature/environment, poetry, contemporary. Young readers: adventure, animal, contemporary, fantasy. Middle readers: adventure, animal, contemporary, fantasy, history, multicultural, nature/environment. Young adults: adventure, animal, contemporary, fantasy, history, multicultural, nature/environment, poetry. Recently published *The The Boy Who Spoke Dog*, by Clay Morgan (middle-grade); *Skippyjon Jones*, by Judy Schachner (picture book); *PREP*, by Jake Coburn (young adult).
Nonfiction: Picture books. Recently published *Jack*, by Ilene Cooper; *Portraits of African American Heroes*, by Tonya Bolder.
How to Contact/Writers: Query only. Does not accept unsolicited mss. Responds to queries in 3 months. Publishes a book 12-18 months after acceptance. Will consider simultaneous submissions.
Illustration: Works with 40-60 illustrators/year. Reviews ms/illustration packages from artists. Query first. Illustrations only: Query with samples; send résumé, portfolio, slides—no original art please. Responds to art samples only if interested. Samples returned with SASE; samples filed. Original artwork returned at job's completion.
Terms: Pays authors royalties of 4-10% based on retail price or outright purchase. Book catalog, ms guidelines for SAE with 8 first-class stamps. Pays illustrators royalties of 2-5% based on retail price unless jacket illustration—then pays by flat fee. Pays photographers by the project or royalty based on retail price.
Tips: "Avoid topics that appear frequently. Illustrators: "We would like to see samples and portfolios from potential illustrators of picture books (full color), young novels (b&w) and jacket artists (full color)." Dutton is actively building its fiction lists, particularly upper YA titles. Humor welcome across all genres.

N □ EDUCATORS PUBLISHING SERVICE, Imprint of Delta Education, LLC, P.O. Box 9031, Cambridge MA 02139-9031. (617)547-6706. Fax: (617)547-3805. E-mail: epsbooks@epsbooks.com. Website: www.epsbooks.com. Estab. 1951. Specializes in educational material. **Manuscript Acquisitions:** Charlie Heinle. **Art Acquisitions:** Jan Shapiro, art director. Publishes 30-40 educational books/year. 50% of books by first-time authors.
How to Contact/Writers: Responds to queries/mss in 5 weeks. Publishes book 6-12 months after acceptance. Will consider e-mail submissions, simultaneous submissions, previously published work. See website for submission guidelines.
Illustration: Works with 6 illustrators/year. Reviews ms/illustration packages from artists. Query. Illustrations only: Query with samples; send promo sheet. Responds only if interested. Samples not returned; samples filed.
Photography: Buys stock and assigns work. Submit cover letter, samples.
Terms: Pays authors royalty of 5-12% based on retail price or work purchased outright from authors. Offers advances. Pays illustrators and photographers by the project. Sends galleys to authors. Book catalog free. All imprints included in a single catalog. Catalog available on website.
Tips: "We accept queries from educators writing for the school market, primarily in the reading and language arts areas, grades K-8. We are interested in materials that follow certain pedagogical constraints (such as decodable texts and leveled readers) and we would consider queries and samples from authors who might be interested in working with us on ongoing or future projects."

EERDMAN'S BOOKS FOR YOUNG READERS, an imprint of Eerdmans Publishing Company, 255 Jefferson Ave. SE, Grand Rapids MI 49503. (616)459-4591 or (800)253-7521. Website: www.eerdmans.com/youngreaders. Book publisher.

Finding the right fit in the children's publishing world

Julie Strauss-Gabel spent her adolescence balancing a love of reading, writing, and editing with a love of working with kids. But it wasn't until she took a children's literature class during her junior year in college that her passion for books and her commitment to studying child development came together. She earned a Master of Education degree before starting in publishing at Hyperion Books for Children in the subsidiary rights department. From there she joined Clarion Books as an Assistant Editor and rose to Associate Editor. She has been at Dutton Children's Books as Editor since March, 2002.

Photo: Ron Gabel

Julie Strauss-Gabel

Writers complain about the way editors play "musical chairs." Why do editors move frequently from house to house?

We move jobs just like any professional—to pursue opportunity and deepen our career experience. Finding a list that's the right fit is as critical for an editor as it is for a writer, and the process is not dissimilar from what we suggest to authors: look at catalogs, read the backlist, get to know the editors already at the house and find out what they're looking for, understand how that imprint fits into a larger house or stands on its own, understand the place that house holds in the industry and its reputation, know how books on the list are marketed and distributed.

It starts with the most basic questions: Do I want to be part of a trade hardcover, paperback, or mass market house? Big house or little house? Conglomerate or independent? Large list or small list? A lot of knowing the right fit when you find it is also knowing the kind of books you want to edit, much in the same way that authors must know where their manuscript fits into the publishing landscape and what it needs to survive in today's publishing market.

Do editors have pangs of guilt at leaving authors behind?

Editors must have faith in the skill of their colleagues to take care of authors and illustrators as they would have cared for them themselves. For me it was hard, but I knew that a move that was good for me was also a move that would be good for my authors and illustrators in the long run.

What made you want to work at Dutton?

I was interested in trying life at a larger house and was ready to build my own list of books. Being at Dutton allows me the freedom to aggressively pursue the books and the talent I am most passionate about—to build a list that reflects my style. The main question I ask myself now when I look at a manuscript for the first time is whether or not this is a "Julie" book.

That's an amazing freedom.

Then I ask myself if my vision fits into the overall list that we are building together as a house. A wonderful thing here at Dutton is the editorial collaborative. We each follow our own vision, but there's a support network in place for sharing work and brainstorming ideas. We challenge each other to challenge our authors and illustrators.

What are the steps you take in accepting a manuscript? You read a manuscript, you like it. Then what?

It varies from manuscript to manuscript, but here's a general outline. When I see something that I like—and often after I have done some revisions with the author—I share it with our publisher, Stephanie Owens Lurie. We also have regular editorial meetings that include all of the editors and our art director where we talk about projects under serious consideration. After we've discussed the projects as an editorial group, the publisher and I discuss whether the manuscript will fit with the Dutton list and if we will make an offer.

Do you go out looking for new writers?

Absolutely! I'm always excited to discover a new voice—someone I can build a list with. The best way I can do this is by reaching out through agents, interviews, conferences, and word of mouth to let people know the kinds of projects on my wish list. I always keep my eyes open for innovative work in magazines and journals or a talented writer from another field who might have an interest in writing for kids. Right now, I'm looking for picture books and especially fiction.

What makes you want to work with a writer?

Once I'm hooked by the writing, the author's ability to respond to queries and revise effectively is going to make a huge impression. The skill and commitment to make something good into something excellent and something excellent into something exceptional are qualities in a writer I'd want to work with.

What do you think an author should do in the way of promotion?

More and more it is critical to the success of a book—especially a first book—that authors get out and do as much on their own to promote the title as possible. School visits are a key part of this. So are using local connections and affiliations. Authors should target local book events and conferences, send out postcard mailings, look online, go to conferences. Not only do authors have the advantage of having the time to dedicate to their book exclusively, but they also best know the work and their market.

There is a growing list of books on self promotion and also freelance publicists who can help authors improve their self-promotional efforts either for a career or just for one title. Still, authors should be realistic about expectations, especially in the beginning, and not be afraid to ask the editor what's the norm. Be mindful that the relationships you're building in the field with local booksellers and librarians are going to be relationships for the whole of a career. You want to nurture and handle those relationships with care.

What would you change about the children's book publishing industry if you could?

I wish I could wave a magic wand and change the misperception that children's books are easier to create, less important. I'm sure that most editors—and authors—have encountered people who think writing for children is a passing hobby and that anyone could write a children's book in five minutes. Children's books play an unparalleled and critical role in educating us from childhood on how to draw strength from adversity, how to love others and ourselves, how to be citizens of the world, how to be human. I think writing well for children is one of the most challenging and most important creative endeavors, period.

What's your advice to writers, both new and previously published, who can't find a publisher now?

Keep writing, keep revising. It's important to move forward even while waiting on answers. Be open to constructive criticism and be aware of how the work can grow. Also be aware of the market and where your style fits in so you can better target submissions and also better understand why some manuscripts don't seem to be working. Be patient, always strive for the best. Nothing is ever going to be more important than the craft, so keep at it.

—*Anna Olswanger*

Manuscript Acquisitions: Judy Zylstra, editor-in-chief. **Art Acquisitions:** Matthew Van Zomeran. Publishes 12-15 books/year.

Fiction: Picture books, middle readers: parables, religion, retold Bible stories, child or family issues, historical fiction, art/artists, poetry. No science fiction.

Nonfiction: All levels: biography, religion.

How to Contact/Writers: Fiction/Nonfiction: Query with sample chapters (novels) or submit complete ms (picture books or middle readers under 200 pages). Always include cover letter. Responds to queries in 6 weeks; mss in 4 months.

Illustration: Works with 14-16 illustrators/year. Responds to ms/art samples in 3 months. Illustrations only: Submit résumé, slides or color photocopies. Samples returned with SASE; samples filed.

Terms: Pays authors and illustrators royalties of 5-7% based on retail price. Sends galleys to authors; dummies to illustrators. Original artwork returned at job's completion. Book catalog free on request with SASE (4 first class stamps, 9×12 envelope); ms and/or artist's guidelines free on request, with SASE.

Tips: "We are looking for material that will help children build their faith in God and explore God's world. We accept all genres. We will not accept or respond to manuscripts, proposals or queries sent by e-mail or fax."

ENSLOW PUBLISHERS INC., Box 398, 40 Industrial Rd., Berkeley Heights NJ 07922-0398. Website: www.enslow.com. Estab. 1978. **Acquisitions:** Brian D. Enslow, vice president. Imprint: MyReportLinks.com Books. Publishes 100 middle reader titles/year; and 100 young adult titles/year. 30% of books by first-time authors.

● Enslow Imprint MyReportLinks.com Books produces books on animals, states, presidents, continents, oceans and ancient civilizations for middle readers and young adults, and offers links to online sources of information on topics covered in books.

Nonfiction: Young readers, middle readers, young adults: animal, biography, careers, health, history, hobbies, nature/environment, social issues, sports. "Enslow is moving into the elementary (Grades 3-4) level and is looking for authors who can write biography and suggest other nonfiction themes at this level." Average word length: middle readers—5,000; young adult—18,000. Published *Louis Armstrong*, by Patricia and Fredrick McKissack (grades 2-3, biography); and *Lotteries: Who Wins, Who Loses?*, by Ann E. Weiss (grades 6-12, issues book).

How to Contact/Writers: Nonfiction: Send for guidelines. Query. Responds to queries/mss in 2 weeks. Publishes a book 18 months after acceptance. Will not consider simultaneous submissions.

Illustration: Submit résumé, business card or tearsheets to be kept on file.

Terms: Pays authors royalties or work purchased outright. Sends galleys to authors. Book catalog/ms guidelines available for $2, along with an 8½×11 SAE and $1.67 postage or via website.

☐ EVAN-MOOR EDUCATIONAL PUBLISHERS, 18 Lower Ragsdale Dr., Monterey CA 93940-5746. (831)649-5901. Fax: (831)649-6256. E-mail: main@evan-moor.com. Website: www.evan-moor.com. Book publisher. **Manuscript Acquisitions:** Acquisitions Editor. **Art Acquisitions:** Cheryl Pucket, art director. Publishes 30-50 books/year. Less than 10% of books by first-time authors. " 'Helping Children Learn' is our motto. Evan-Moor is known for high-quality educational materials written by teachers for use in the classroom and at home. We publish teacher resource and reproducible materials in most all curriculum areas and activity books (language arts, math, science, social studies). No fiction or nonfiction literature books."

Nonfiction: Recently published Readers Theater (6 book series, grades 1-6); History Pockets (8 books of projects on ancient cultures and past time periods); Basic Math Skills (6 books, practice based on NCTM standards, grades 1-6).

How to Contact/Writers: Query or submit outline, table of contents, and sample pages. Responds to queries in 2 months; mss in 4 months. Publishes a book 12-18 months after acceptance. Will consider simultaneous submissions if so noted. Submission guidelines available on our website. E-mail queries are responded to quickly. View our materials on our website to determine if your project fits in our product line.

Illustration: Works with 8-12 illustrators/year. Uses b&w artwork primarily. Illustrations only: Query with samples; send résumé, tearsheets. Contact: Art Director. Responds only if interested. Samples returned with SASE; samples filed.

Terms: Work purchased outright from authors, "dependent solely on size of project and 'track record' of author." Pays illustrators by the project (range: varies). Sends galleys to authors. Artwork is not returned. Book catalog available for 9×12 SAE; ms guidelines available for SASE.

Tips: "Writers—know the supplemental education or parent market. (These materials are *not* children's literature.) Tell us how your project is unique and what consumer needs it meets. Illustrators—you need to be able to produce quickly and be able to render realistic and charming children and animals."

[N] EXCELSIOR CEE PUBLISHING, P.O. Box 5861, Norman OK 73070-5861. (405)329-3909. Fax: (405)329-6886. E-mail: ecp@oecadvantage.net. Website: www.excelsiorcee.com. Book publisher. Estab. 1989. **Manuscript Acquisitions:** J.C. Marshall.

How to Contact/Writers: Nonfiction: Query or submit outline/synopsis. Responds to queries in 1 month. Publishes a book 1 year after acceptance. Will consider simultaneous submissions.

[N] FACTS ON FILE, 132 W. 31st St., New York NY 10001. (212)967-8800. Fax: (212)967-9196. Website: www.factsonfile.com. Book publisher. Editorial Director: Laurie Likoff. **Acquisitions:** Frank Darmstadt, science and technology/nature; Nicole Bowen, American history and studies; Jeff Soloway, language and literature; Owen Lancer, world studies; Jim Chambers, arts and entertainment. Estab. 1941. "We produce high-quality reference materials for the school library market and the general nonfiction trade." Publishes 25-30 young adult titles/year. 5% of books by first-time authors; 25% of books from agented writers; additional titles through book packagers, co-publishers and unagented writers.

Nonfiction: Middle readers, young adults: animal, biography, careers, geography, health, history, multicultural, nature/environment, reference, religion, science, social issues and sports.

How to Contact/Writers: Nonfiction: Submit outline/synopsis and sample chapters. Responds to queries in 10 weeks. Publishes a book 10-12 months after acceptance. Will consider simultaneous submissions. Sends galleys to authors. Book catalog free on request. Send SASE for submission guidelines.

Terms: Submission guidelines available via website or with SASE.

Tips: "Most projects have high reference value and fit into a series format."

FAITH KIDZ, (formerly Cook Communications Ministries), Imprint of Cook Communications Ministries, 4050 Lee Vance View, Colorado Springs CO 80918. (719)536-0100. Fax: (719)536-3296. Website: www.cookministries.com. Book publisher. **Acquisitions:** Heather Gemmen, acquisitions editor. Publishes 15-20 picture books/year; 6-8 young readers/year; and 6-12 middle readers/year. Less than 5% of books by first-time authors; 15% of books from agented authors. "All books have overt Christian values, but there is no primary theme."

● Cook accepts unsolicited mss, but prefers agented submissions.

How to Contact/Writers: Only accepts online submissions (www.cookministries.com/proposals).

Illustration: Works with 15 illustrators/year. "Send color material I can keep." Query with samples; send résumé, promo sheet, portfolio, tearsheets. Responds in 6 months only if interested. Samples returned with SASE; samples filed. Contact: Art Department.

Terms: Pays illustrators by the project, royalty or work purchased outright. Sends dummies to illustrators. Original artwork returned at job's completion. Manuscript guidelines available for SASE. Call ms hotline at (719)536-0100, ext. 3930.

[symbol] FARRAR, STRAUS & GIROUX INC., 19 Union Square W., New York NY 10003. (212)741-6900. Fax: (212)633-2427. Book publisher. Imprints: Frances Foster Books, Melanie Kroupa Books. Children's Books Editorial Director: Margaret Ferguson. **Manuscript Acquisitions:** Margaret Ferguson, editorial director; Frances Foster, publisher, Frances Foster Books; Melanie Kroupa, Melanie Kroupa Books; Beverly Reingold, executive editor; Wesley Adams, senior editor; Robbie Mayes, editor; Janine O'Malley, assistant editor. **Art Acquisitions:** Robin Gourley, art director, books for young readers. Estab. 1946. Publishes 40 picture books/year; 15 middle reader titles/year; and 15 young adult titles/year. 5% of books by first-time authors; 20% of books from agented writers.

● Farrar title *Hole in My Life*, by Jack Gantos won a 2003 Robert F. Sibert Honor and a 2003 Michael Printz Honor.

Fiction: All levels: all categories. "Original and well-written material for all ages." Recently published *Joey Piaza Loses Control*, by Jack Gantos (ages 10 up).

Nonfiction: All levels: all categories. "We publish only literary nonfiction."

How to Contact/Writers: Fiction/Nonfiction: Query with outline/synopsis and sample chapters. Do not fax submissions or queries. Responds to queries/mss in 3 months. Publishes a book 18 months after acceptance. Will consider simultaneous submissions.

Illustration: Works with 30-60 illustrators/year. Reviews ms/illustration packages from artists. Submit ms with 1 example of final art, remainder roughs. Do not send originals. Illustrations only: Query with tearsheets. Responds if interested in 2 months. Samples returned with SASE; samples sometimes filed.

Terms: "We offer an advance against royalties for both authors and illustrators." Sends galleys to authors; dummies to illustrators. Original artwork returned at job's completion. Book catalog available for 9×12 SAE and $1.87 postage; ms guidelines for 1 first-class stamp.

Tips: "Study our catalog before submitting. We will see illustrator's portfolios by appointment. Don't ask for criticism and/or advice—it's just not possible. Never send originals. Always enclose SASE."

FIESTA CITY PUBLISHERS, Box 5861, Santa Barbara CA 93150-5861. (805)681-9199. E-mail: fcooke3924@aol.com. Book publisher. **Acquisitions:** Frank Cooke, president. **Art Director:** Ann H. Cooke. Publishes 1 middle reader/year; 1 young adult/year. 25% of books by first-time authors. Publishes books about cooking and music or a combination of the two. "We are best known for children's and young teens' cookbooks and musical plays."
Fiction: Young adults: history, humor, musical plays.
Nonfiction: Young adult: cooking, how-to, music/dance, self-help. Average word length: 30,000. Does not want to see "cookbooks about healthy diets or books on rap music." Published *Kids Can Write Songs, Too!* (revised second printing), by Eddie Franck; *Bent-Twig*, by Frank E. Cooke, with some musical arrangements by Johnny Harris (a 3-act musical for young adolescents); *The Little Grammar Book*, by F. Cooke.
How to Contact/Writers: Query. Responds to queries in 4 days; mss in 1 month. Publishes a book 1 year after acceptance. Will consider simultaneous submissions.
Illustration: Works with 1 illustrator/year. Will review ms/illustrations packages (query first). Illustrations only: Send résumé. Samples returned with SASE; samples filed.
Terms: Pays authors 5-10% royalty based on retail price.
Tips: "Write clearly and simply. Do not write 'down' to young adults (or children). Looking for self-help books on current subjects, original and unusual cookbooks, and books about music, or a combination of cooking and music." Always include SASE.

圖 FIRST STORY PRESS, Imprint of Rose Book Group, P.O.Box 3755, Clarksville TN 37043. Publisher/Editor in Chief: Judith Pierson. **Contact:** Acquisitions Editor. Publishes 1 book/year. Publishes books on quilt themes only.
Fiction: Picture books. Average word length: picture books—700-1,500. Best seller of house: *Who's Under Grandma's Quilt*, by Rachel Waterstone.
How to Contact/Writers: Fiction: Submit complete ms. Send hard copy. Responds to queries/mss in 3 months.
Illustration: Reviews ms/illustration packages from artists. Send ms with dummy. Contact: Editor. Illustrations only: Send résumé, promo sheet and tearsheets to be kept on file. Contact: Editor. Responds only if interested. Samples returned with SASE; samples filed.
Terms: Manuscript guidelines available for SASE.
Tips: "SASE is always required. Do not send original artwork. Guidelines available—send SASE. Take a look at our books. We do not send out catalogs."

◘ ▢ FIVE STAR PUBLICATIONS, INC., P.O. Box 6698, Chandler AZ 85246-6698. (480)940-8182. Fax: (480)940-8787. E-mail: info@fivestarpublications.com. Website: www.fivestarpublications.com. Estab. 1985. Specializes in educational material, nonfiction. Independent book packager/producer. **Art Acquisitions:** Sue DeFabis. Publishes 7 middle readers/year.
Nonfiction: Recently published *Shakespeare for Children: The Story of Romeo & Juliet*, by Cass Foster; *The Sixty-Minute Shakespeare: Hamlet*, by Cass Foster; *The Sixty-Minute Shakespeare: Twelfth Night*, by Cass Foster.
How to Contact/Writers: Nonfiction: Query.
Illustration: Works with 3 illustrators/year. Reviews ms/illustration packages from artists. Query. Illustrations only: Query with samples. Responds only if interested. Samples filed.
Photography: Buys stock and assigns work. Works on assignment only. Submit letter.
Terms: Pays illustrators by the project. Pays photographers by the project. Sends galleys to authors; dummies to illustrators.

FORWARD MOVEMENT PUBLICATIONS, 412 Sycamore St., Cincinnati OH 45202. (513)721-6659. Fax: (513)721-0729. E-mail: orders@forwarddaybyday.com. Website: www.forwardmovement.org. **Acquisitions:** Edward S. Gleason, editor.
Fiction: Middle readers and young adults: religion and religious problem novels, fantasy and science fiction.
Nonfiction: Religion.
How to Contact/Writers: Fiction/Nonfiction: Query. Responds in 1 month. Does not accept mss via e-mail.
Illustration: Query with samples. Samples returned with SASE.
Terms: Pays authors honorarium. Pays illustrators by the project.
Tips: "Forward Movement is now exploring publishing books for children and does not know its niche. We are an agency of the Episcopal Church and most of our market is to mainstream Protestants."

圖 WALTER FOSTER PUBLISHING, 23062 La Cadena Dr., Laguna Hills CA 92653. (949)380-7510. Fax: (949)380-7575. Website: www.walterfoster.com. Estab. 1922. **Manuscript Acquisitions:** Sydney Sprague. **Art Acquisitions:** Pauline Foster, art director. Publishes 3-6 picture books/year; 3-6 young readers/year; 10-12 middle readers/year; 0-6 young adult titles/year. "We seek to provide quality art- and craft-related activity products that are instructional, innovative and competitively priced."
   ● Walter Foster Publishing is not accepting submissions at this time.

FREE SPIRIT PUBLISHING, 217 Fifth Ave. N., Suite 200, Minneapolis MN 55401-1299. (612)338-2068. Fax: (612)337-5050. E-mail: help4kids@freespirit.com. Website: www.freespirit.com. Book publisher. **Acquisitions:** Editor. Publishes 16-22 titles/year for children and teens, teachers and parents. "Free Spirit Publishing is the home of SELF-HELP FOR KIDS® and SELF-HELP FOR TEENS® nonfiction, issue-driven, solution-focused books and materials for children and teens, and the parents and teachers who care for them."
   ● Free Spirit no longer accepts fiction or storybook submissions.
Nonfiction: Areas of interest include emotional health, bullying and conflict resolution, tolerance and character develop-

ment, social and study skills, creative learning and teaching, special needs learning, teaching, and parenting (gifted & talented and LD), family issues, healthy youth development, challenges specific to boys (including the parenting and teaching of boys), classroom activities, and innovative teaching techniques. We do not publish fiction or picture storybooks, books with animal or mythical characters, books with religious or New Age content, or single biographies, autobiographies, or memoirs. We prefer books written in a natural, friendly style, with little education/psychology jargon. We need books in our areas of emphasis and prefer titles written by specialists such as teachers, counselors, and other professionals who work with youth." Recently published *When I Feel Afraid* and *Understand and Care*, by Cheri Meiners; *The Complete Guide to Service Learning*, by Cathryn Berger Kaye.

How to Contact/Writers: "Submissions are accepted from prospective authors, including youth ages 16 and up, or through agents. Please review our catalog and Author Guidelines (both available online) before submitting proposal." Responds to queries/mss in 4 months. "If you'd like materials returned, enclose a SASE with sufficient postage." Write or call for catalog and submission guidelines before sending submission. Accepts queries only by e-mail. Submission guidelines available online.

Illustration: Works with 5 illustrators/year. Submit samples to production manager for consideration. If appropriate, samples will be kept on file and artist will be contacted if a suitable project comes up. Enclose SASE if you'd like materials returned.

Photography: Submit samples to production manager for consideration. If appropriate, samples will be kept on file and photographer will be contacted if a suitable project comes up. Enclose SASE if you'd like materials returned.

Terms: Pays authors in royalties based on wholesale price. Offers advance. Pays illustrators by the project. Pays photographers by the project or per photo.

Tips: "Free Spirit is a niche publisher known for high-quality books featuring a positive and practical focus and jargon free approach. Study our catalog, read our author guidelines, and be sure your proposal is the right 'fit' before submitting. Our preference is for books that help parents and teachers help kids [and that help kids themselves] gain personal strengths, succeed in school, stand up for themselves and others, and otherwise make a positive difference in today's world."

FREESTONE/PEACHTREE, JR., Peachtree Publishers, 1700 Chattahooche Ave., Atlanta GA 30318-2112. (404)876-8761. Fax: (404)875-2578. Website: www.peachtree-online.com. Estab. 1977. **Manuscript Acquisitions**: Helen Harriss (children's, young adult). Publishes 4-8 young adult titles/year.
• Freestone & Peachtree, Jr. are imprints of Peachtree Publishers. See the listing for Peachtree for submission information. No e-mail or fax queries, please.

Fiction: Picture books, young readers, middle readers, young adults: adventure, contemporary, nature/environment, history, special needs, multicultural, sports.

Nonfiction: Picture books, young readers, middle readers, young adults: animal, health, history, multicultural, nature/environment, reference, science, social issues, special needs, sports.

How to Contact: Responds to queries/mss in 6 months.

Illustration: Works with 10-20 illustrators/year. Responds only if interested. Samples not returned; samples filed. Originals returned at job's completion.

Terms: Pays authors royalty. Payment to illustrators varies.

FRONT STREET BOOKS, 862 Haywood Rd., Asheville NC 28801. (828)236-3097. Fax: (828)236-3098. Fax: (828)236-3098. E-mail: contactus@frontstreetbooks.com Website: www.frontstreetbooks.com. Book publisher. Estab. 1995. **Acquistions:** Stephen Roxburgh, publisher; Joy Neaves, editor. Publishes 10-15 titles/year. "We are a small independent publisher of books for children and young adults. We do not publish pablum: we try to publish books that will attract, if not addict, children to literature and books that are a pleasure to look at and a pleasure to hold, books that will be revelations to young minds."
• See Front Street's website for submission guidelines and complete catalog. Front Street focuses on fiction, but will publish poetry, anthologies, nonfiction and high-end picture books. They are not currently accepting unsolicited picture book manuscripts. Front Street title *A Step from Heaven*, by An Na, won the 2002 Printz Award. Their title *Carver: A Life in Poems*, by Marilyn Nelson won a 2002 Newbery Honor and a 2002 Coretta Scott King Honor.

Fiction: Recently published: *Many Stones*, by Carolyn Coman; *Cut*, by Patricia McCormick; *A Step from Heaven*, by An Na; *Carver: A Life in Poems*, by Marilyn Nelson; *The Comic Book Kid*, by Adam Osterweil.

How to Contact/Writers: Fiction: Submit cover letter and complete ms if under 30 pages; submit cover letter, one or two sample chapters and plot summary if over 30 pages. Nonfiction: Submit detailed proposal and sample chapters. Poetry: Submit no more than 25 poems. Include SASE with submissions if you want them returned. "It is our policy to consider submissions in the order in which they are received. This is a time-consuming practice, and we ask you to be patient in awaiting our response."

Illustration "We do keep samples illustrations on file."

Terms: Pays royalties.

GIBBS SMITH, PUBLISHER, P.O. Box 667, Layton UT 84041. (801)544-9800. Fax: (801)544-5582. Website: gibbs-smith.com. **Manuscript Acquisitions:** Jennifer Grillone (picture books); Suzanne Taylor, editorial director (children's activity books). **Art Acquisitions:** Kurt Wahlner, art director. Imprint: Gibbs Smith. Book publisher; co-publisher of Sierra Club Books for Children. Publishes 2-3 books/year. 50% of books by first-time authors. 50% of books from agented authors. Mission Statement: "To enrich and inspire humankind."

Fiction: Picture books: adventure, contemporary, humor, multicultural, nature/environment, suspense/mystery, western. Average word length: picture books—1,000. Recently published *Bullfrog Pops!*, by Rick Walton, illustrated by Chris

insider report

Surviving a writer's hard times

Bruce Balan appeared on the children's book scene in 1988 when Green Tiger Press published his picture book *The Cherry Migration* and even made it the theme of its booth at the ABA (now the BEA) convention. Over the next ten years, he published picture books with Simon & Schuster, Random House, Viking, and ABC (London); six middle-grade novels in the Cyber.kdz series with Avalon Camelot; and a crossover book with Delacorte. He sold a novel to Bantam Doubleday Dell on the strength of a 40-page sample, and when his literary agent at the William Morris Agency left the business, he immediately got another agent who sold a picture book manuscript to Simon & Schuster. In Balan's own words, "I thought I had it made."

Bruce Balan

Photo: Dana Balan

   One year later, his editor had left Bantam Doubleday Dell, his new editor had rejected his novel, Simon & Schuster had canceled his picture book, he had parted ways with his agent and couldn't find another to represent him, and none of his books were in print. "It was awful, awful, awful," Balan says. Here, he talks about "hard times" and how a writer can survive them.

What do you think caused your hard times?
In 1999, with two books in production, I decided to fulfill a dream and move onto my sailboat. That meant I was out of the loop on what was happening with my books while I was sailing around Mexico for the greater part of two years. I relied on my agent to keep selling my manuscripts, but that didn't happen.

   What else? Bad luck. HarperCollins purchased Avon Camelot and that took the breath out of my already dying Cyber.kdz series. Delacorte went all out to market my crossover book, but it didn't catch on with readers. S&S trimmed its list and decided to cut my picture book because It was waiting for illustrations. My editor left Delacorte and I didn't click with the new one assigned to me. I was late delivering a manuscript to Random House. And finally, I must have been out of step with what editors were looking for because I had eight completed manuscripts that I couldn't sell.

What was your reaction?
I was reeling! I felt as though everything I had done for the last fourteen years was wasted. My self-image crashed big time.

Did you make a game plan at that point?
Yes. I started making calls and writing letters to round up flat-fee work. I decided I wouldn't turn down anything. I wasn't fond of the flat-fee work I produced, but it was important to me to get paid for my writing. Since I had no agent, I started sending my manuscripts out on my own.

Did the game plan work?

If you mean, am I able to support myself writing now, the answer is no. If you mean, does my game plan keep me moving forward and stop me from giving up, the answer is yes.

So you're still going through hard times?

I sold two books in the last year—one to Dial and one flat-fee to a Canadian educational publisher—but I still haven't found a new agent. Emotionally though, I'm surviving the hard times because I have faith that it will all work out in the end. The vagaries of our business require faith. Looking at what sells, what's popular, what the media covers, then comparing that to what I consider my best work would send me over the edge if it weren't for a deep sense that I'm supposed to be on this path and my writing has a purpose.

What have you learned from having gone through your hard times?

I thought that after achieving a certain degree of success, I was done with the struggling and the emotional turmoil it entails (rejections, doubt, more rejections, jealousy, more rejections). Surprise! I learned to be careful when choosing an agent. I learned that if you make the conscious decision to ignore the market and write what is in your heart, you need to be willing to reap what you sow. Like it or not, we are a market-driven business.

So were your early expectations about success unrealistic?

You don't hear speakers or read articles that say "I struggled for 15 years and still haven't published anything," or "I published 12 books and they all went out of print and I couldn't sell another thing." The articles talk about the first book that hit the bestseller list, or the writer who published slow and steady for twenty-five years and is now getting the recognition she deserves. In some ways it's good to hear these stories because they give us the hope we need to keep going. But they also give us a false sense of the level of success in the business, which makes it easy to feel we've failed when, in fact, we've done pretty well.

Buoy: Home at Sea (Delacorte Press), by Bruce Balan, a collection of vignettes featuring friends Buoy, Gull, and Seal and their oceanic home, was the recipient of the 1998 Parent's Choice Gold Medal for Picture Books. The book is being published in 12 languages.

Illustration © 1998 by Raúl Colón. Reprinted with permission.

How do you keep from feeling like you've failed?

I have railed against the stupidity of marketing departments, the ignorance of publishers, the injustice of rejections. I've wallowed in self-pity over the inane rejections of editors. All the while, I have a "second" job that pays the bills, food in my stomach, health, freedom, family and friends. I'm not saying we shouldn't strive for our goals and dreams with all our hearts. I'm not saying that we should be satisfied with what we have and not try to create something amazing with our writing. I'm saying that, when things don't go well, it's ridiculous to downplay what is wonderful in our lives. Forgetting to be grateful for our good fortune—that we can live decently and prosperously and relatively fearlessly—because we aren't selling enough books, is unconscionable.

How do you define success now?

Success is defined by the society we live in as financial reward and fame. Because of this, it's easy to forget that worth can be tied to something other than the judgment of others—especially when "others" means the vague, unknowable market for our books. There is honor in doing a good job, in penning a fine sentence, in creating a beautiful poem. Writing is not easy work and requires dedication and tenacity and pride in our skill. But, since the reason we write is to communicate, it's difficult to give ourselves credit if our work isn't published and, therefore, not communicated to others. It's good for me to remember that the giving of my time to a task I believe in is honorable.

Illustration © 1988 Dane Lane. Reprinted with permission

Bruce Balan's first children's book, *The Cherry Migration*, follows a jar of maraschino cherries in their quest for freedom and a safe home after escaping from certain culinary tragedy at the hands of a soda jerk. Originally published by Green Tiger Press in 1988, the book is now out of print, but Balan is looking for a new publisher for what he professes is his favorite published title.

What is your advice now to others who are going through hard times?

Don't forget that every day we make choices about what matters to us. Our focus and attitude can shift so quickly that we forget that we own our lives. One day I'm down because of a rejection letter from an agent. The next day, I'm enfolded by the glorious beauty of the ocean. These emotions don't just happen to me. I have a say. I am the one who chooses to crumple the rejection letter from the agent and I am the one who chooses to turn my head toward the sea. My advice to others is to find the worth in all your efforts.

So have you learned not to judge yourself?

Viktor Frankl wrote in *Man's Search for Meaning*: "Everything can be taken away from a man but one thing: the last of the human freedoms—to choose one's attitude in any given set of circumstances, to choose one's own way." I'm learning to choose my own way.

—*Anna Olswanger*

McAllister (ages 4-8); and *The Magic Boots*, by Scott Emerson, illustrated by Howard Post (ages 4-8).
Nonfiction: Middle readers: activity, arts/crafts, cooking, how-to, nature/environment, science. Average word length: up to 10,000. Recently published *Hiding in a Fort*, by G. Lawson Drinkard, illustrated by Fran Lee (ages 7-12); and *Sleeping in a Sack: Camping Activities for Kids*, by Linda White, illustrated by Fran Lee (ages 7-12).
How to Contact/Writers: Fiction/Nonfiction: Submit several chapters or complete ms. Responds to queries and mss in 2 months. Publishes a book 1-2 years after acceptance. Will consider simultaneous submissions. Manuscript returned with SASE.
Illustration: Works with 2 illustrators/year. Reviews ms/illustration packages from artists. Query. Submit ms with 3-5 pieces of final art. Illustrations only: Query with samples; provide résumé, promo sheet, slides (duplicate slides, not originals). Responds only if interested. Samples returned with SASE; samples filed.
Terms: Pays authors royalty of 2% based on retail price or work purchased outright ($500 minimum). Offers advances (average amount: $2,000). Pays illustrators by the project or royalty of 2% based on retail price. Sends galleys to authors; color proofs to illustrators. Original artwork returned at job's completion. Book catalog available for 9×12 SAE and postage. Manuscript guidelines available.
Tips: "We target ages 5-11. We do not publish young adult novels or chapter books."

[N] [○] GINGERBREAD HOUSE, 602 Montauk Highway, Westhampton Beach NY 11978. (631)288-5179. Fax: (631)288-5179. E-mail: GHBooks@optonline.net. Website: www.GingerbreadBooks.com. Estab. 2000. Specializes in trade books, Christian material, fiction, educational and multicultural material. Cannot accept submissions from writers. **Art Acquisitions:** Maria Nicotra, creative director. Publishes 2-4 picture books/year.
• While Gingerbread House is accepting submissions from artists, they currently publish only work written by Josephine Nobisso. Illustrators visit the website before submitting.
Fiction: Recently published *In English of Course*, by Josephine Nobisso, illustrated by Dasha Ziborova; *The Numbers Dance*, by Josephine Nobisso, illustrated by Dasha Ziborova; and *The Weight of a Mass, A Tale of Faith*, by Josephine Nobisso, illustrated by Katalin Szegedi.
Nonfiction: Recently published *Show; Don't Tell! Secrets of Writing*, by Josephine Nobisso, illustrated by Eva Montanari.
Illustration: Works with 3 illustrators/year. Uses color artwork only. Illustrations only: Send tearsheets. Responds only if interested. Samples not returned; samples filed.
Terms: Pays illustrators royalty of 5-6% based on retail price. Originals returned at job's completion. Catalog available on website.
Tips: "We will not be able to accept submissions for some time. When that policy changes, we will be sure to put out a call through the usual venues. Until then, manuscripts will be returned unread if there is an SASE, or discarded if not."

[A] DAVID R. GODINE, PUBLISHER, 9 Hamilton Place, Boston MA 02108. (617)451-9600. Fax: (617)350-0250. Website: www.godine.com. Book publisher. Estab. 1970. Publishes 1 picture book/year; 1 young reader title/year; 1 middle reader title/year. 10% of books by first-time authors; 90% of books from agented writers. "We publish books that matter for people who care."
• This publisher is no longer considering unsolicited manuscripts of any type.
Fiction: Picture books: adventure, animal, contemporary, folktales, nature/environment. Young readers: adventure, animal, contemporary, folk or fairy tales, history, nature/environment, poetry. Middle readers: adventure, animal, contemporary, folk or fairy tales, history, mystery, nature/environment, poetry. Young adults/teens: adventure, animal, contemporary, history, mystery, nature/environment, poetry. Recently published *A Cottage Garden Alphabet*, by Andrea Wisnewski (picture book); *Henrietta and the Golden Eggs*, by Hanna Johansen, illustrated by Kathi Bhënd.

Nonfiction: Picture books: alphabet, animal, nature/environment. Young readers: activity books, animal, history, music/dance, nature/environment. Middle readers: activity books, animal, biography, history, music/dance, nature/environment. Young adults: biography, history, music/dance, nature/environment.

How to Contact/Writers: Query. Publishes a book 3 years after acceptance. Include SASE for return of material.

Illustration: Only interested in agented material. Works with 4-6 illustrators/year. Reviews ms/illustration packages from artists. "Submit roughs and one piece of finished art plus either sample chapters for very long works or whole ms for short works." Illustrations only: "After query, submit slides, with one full-size blow-up of art." Please do not send original artwork unless solicited. "Almost all of the children's books we accept for publication come to us with the author and illustrator already paired up. Therefore, we rarely use freelance illustrators." Samples returned with SASE; samples filed (if interested).

Tips: "Always enclose a SASE. Keep in mind that we do not accept unsolicited manuscripts and that we rarely use freelance illustrators."

GOLDEN BOOKS, 1745 Broadway, New York NY 10019. (212)782-9000. Imprint of Random House Children's Books. **Editorial Directors:** Courtney Silk, color and activity; Chris Angelilli, storybooks. **Art Acquisitions:** Roberta Ludlow, art director.
  ● See listing for Random House/Golden Books for Young Readers Group.

How to Contact/Writers: Does not accept unsolicited submissions.

Fiction: They publish board books, novelty books, picture books, workbooks, series (mass market and trade).

GREENE BARK PRESS, P.O. Box 1108, Bridgeport CT 06601-1108. (203)372-4861. Fax: (203)371-5856. E-mail: greenebark@aol.com. Website: www.greenebarkpress.com. Book publisher. **Acquisitions:** Michele Hofbauer, associate publisher. Thomas J. Greene, publisher. Publishes 4-6 picture books/year. 40% of books by first-time authors. "We publish quality hardcover picture books for children. Our books and stories are selected for originality, imagery and colorfulness. Our intention is to capture a child's attention; to fire-up his or her imagination and desire to read and explore the world through books."

Fiction: Picture books, young readers: adventure, fantasy, humor. Average word length: picture books—650; young readers—1,400. Recently published *The Magical Trunk*, by Gigi Tegge; *Couldn't We Make A Difference*, by Michele Hofbauer; *Empty Pockets*, by Faye Van Wert; *To Know the Sea*, by Frances Gilbert.

How to Contact/Writers: Responds to queries in 2 months; mss in 6 months; must include SASE. No response without SASE. Publishes a book 18 months after acceptance. Will consider simultaneous submissions. Prefer to review complete mss with illustrations.

Illustrations: Works with 1-2 illustrators/year. Uses color artwork only. Reviews ms/illustration packages from artists. Submit ms with 3 pieces of final art (copies only). Illustrations only: Query with samples. Responds in 2 months only if interested. Samples returned with SASE; samples filed. Originals returned at job's completion.

Terms: Pays authors royalty of 10-12% based on wholesale price. Pays illustrators by the project (range: $1,500-3,000) or 5-7½% royalty based on wholesale price. No advances. Sends galleys to authors; dummies to illustrators. Book catalog available for $2.00 fee which includes mailing. All imprints included in a single catalog. Manuscript and art guidelines available for SASE or per e-mail request.

Tips: "As a guide for future publications do not look to our older backlist. Please no telephone, e-mail or fax queries."

GREENHAVEN PRESS, Imprint of the Gale Group, 10911 Technology Place, San Diego CA 92127. Website: www.gale.com/greenhaven. Book publisher. Estab. 1970. **Acquisitions:** Chandra Howard, acquisitions editor. Publishes 300 young adult titles/year. 35% of books by first-time authors. "Greenhaven continues to print quality nonfiction for libraries and classrooms. Our well known Opposing Viewpoints series is highly respected by students and librarians in need of material on controversial social issues. In recent years, Greenhaven has also branched out with a new series covering historical and literary topics."
  ● Greenhaven accepts no unsolicited manuscripts. All writing is done on a work-for-hire basis.

Nonfiction: Young adults (high school): biography, controversial topics, history, issues. Other titles "to fit our specific series."

How to Contact/Writers: Send query, résumé and list of published works.

Terms: Buys ms outright for $1,500-3,000. Sends galleys to authors. "No phone calls. Short writing samples are appropriate; long unsolicited manuscripts will not be read or returned."

Tips: "Review guidelines before submitting."

GREENWILLOW BOOKS, 1350 Avenue of the Americas, New York NY 10019. (212)261-6500. Website: www.harperchildrens.com. Imprint of HarperCollins. Book publisher. Vice President/Publisher: Virginia Duncan. **Art Acquisitions:** Paul Zakris, art director. Publishes 50 picture books/year; 5 middle readers books/year; and 5 young adult books/year. "Greenwillow Books publishes picture books, fiction for young readers of all ages, and nonfiction primarily for children under seven years of age."
  ● Greenwillow Books is currently accepting neither unsolicited mss nor queries. Unsolicited mail will not be opened and will not be returned. Call (212)261-6627 for an update. Greenwillow title *Amber Was Brave, Essie Was Smart*, by Vera B. Williams, won a 2002 Boston Globe-Horn Book Honor Award for Fiction and Poetry. Their title *Shaper*, by Jessie Haas, won a 2002 Golden Kite Honor Award for Fiction.

Illustration: Art samples (postcards only) should be sent in duplicate to Paul Zakris and Virginia Duncan.

Terms: Pays authors royalty. Offers advances. Pays illustrators royalty or by the project. Sends galleys to authors.

Ñ GREYCORE KIDS, Imprint of GreyCore Press, 2646 New Prospect Rd., Pine Bush NY 12566. (845)744-5081. Fax: (845)744-8081. E-mail: jschweighardt@hvc.rr.com. **Manuscript/Art Acquisitions:** Joan Schweighardt, publisher.
Fiction: Picture books. Recently published *When I Wished I Was Alone*, by David Cutler.
Nonfiction: Picture books.
How to Contact/Writers: Fiction/nonfiction. Query via e-mail. Responds only if interested.
Illustration: Illustrations only: Send photocopies.
Tips: "We are only interested in children's books for ages 2 through 8."

☐ GRYPHON HOUSE, P.O. Box 207, Beltsville MD 20704-0207. (301)595-9500. Fax: (301)595-0051. E-mail: kathyc @ghbooks.com. Website: www.gryphonhouse.com. Book publisher. **Acquisitions:** Kathy Charner, editor-in-chief.
Nonfiction: Parent and teacher resource books—activity books, textbooks. Recently published *First Art: Art Experiences for Toddlers and Twos*, by MaryAnn F. Kohl; *Games to Play with Babies Third Edition*, by Jackie Silberg; *Creating Readers*, by Pam Schiller.
How to Contact/Writers: Query. Submit outline/synopsis and 2 sample chapters. Responds to queries/mss in 6 months. Publishes a book 18 months after acceptance. Will consider simultaneous submissions, electronic submissions via disk or modem.
Illustration: Works with 4-5 illustrators/year. Uses b&w artwork only. Illustrations only: Query with samples, promo sheet. Responds in 2 months. Samples returned with SASE; samples filed.
Photography: Buys photos from freelancers. Buys stock and assigns work. Submit cover letter, published samples, stock photo list.
Terms: Pays authors royalty based on wholesale price. Offers advances. Pays illustrators by the project. Pays photographers by the project or per photo. Sends edited ms copy to authors. Original artwork returned at job's completion. Book catalog and ms guidelines available via website or with SASE.
Tips: "Send a SASE for our catalog and manuscript guidelines. Look at our books, then submit proposals that complement the books we already publish or supplement our existing books. We are looking for books of creative, participatory learning experiences that have a common conceptual theme to tie them together. The books should be on subjects that parents or teachers want to do on a daily basis."

GULLIVER BOOKS, 15 E. 26th St., New York NY 10010. (212)592-1000. Imprint of Harcourt, Trade Publishers. **Acquisitions:** Elizabeth Van Doren, editorial director; Kate Harrison, associate editor; Scott Piehl, art director. Publishes 25 titles/year.
• Gulliver only accepts manuscripts submitted by agents, previously published authors, or SCBWI members.
Fiction: Emphasis on picture books: animal, contemporary, history, humor, multicultural, poetry, sports. Also publishes middle grade and young adult.
Nonfiction: Publishes nonfiction. Picture books: animal, biography, history, multicultural. Also publishes some middle grade and young adult.
How to Contact/Writers: Only interested in agented material. Also accepts material from SCBWI members and previously published authors. Fiction/Nonfiction: Query or send ms for picture book. Resonds to queries/mss in 2 months.
Illustrations: Responds only if interested. Samples returned with SASE only; samples filed.
Terms: Authors and illustrators paid royalty.

HACHAI PUBLISHING, 156 Chester Ave., Brooklyn NY 11218-3020. (718)633-0100. Fax: (718)633-0103. E-mail: info@hachai.com. Website: www.hachai.com. Book publisher. **Manuscript Acquisitions:** Devorah Leah Rosenfeld, submissions editor. Publishes 3 picture books/year; 3 young readers/year; 1 middle reader/year. 75% of books published by first-time authors. "All books have spiritual/religious themes, specifically traditional Jewish content. We're seeking books about morals and values; the Jewish experience in current and Biblical times; and Jewish observance, Sabbath and holidays."
Fiction: Picture books and young readers: contemporary, historical fiction, religion. Middle readers: adventure, contemporary, problem novels, religion. Does not want to see fantasy, animal stories, romance, problem novels depicting drug use or violence. Recently published *Let's Go to Shul*, written and illustrated by Rikki Benenfeld (ages 2-5, picture book); *Get Well Soon*, by Dina Rosenfeld, illustrated by Rina Lyampe (ages 2-5, picture book); *Big Like Me! A New Baby Story*, by Ruth Finkelstein, illustrated by Esther Touson (ages 2-5, picture book); *Once Upon a Time*, by Draizy Zelcer, illustrated by Vitaliy Romanenko (ages 3-6, picture book); *The Great Potato Plan*, written and illustrated by Joy Nelkin Wieder (ages 7-10, short chapter book).
Nonfiction: Published *My Jewish ABC's*, by Draizy Zelcer, illustrated by Patti Nemeroff (ages 3-6, picture book); *Nine Spoons* by Marci Stillerman, illustrated by Pesach Gerber (ages 5-8).
How to Contact/Wrtiers: Fiction/Nonfiction: Submit complete ms. Responds to queries/mss in 6 weeks.
Illustration: Works with 4 illustrators/year. Uses primary color artwork, some b&w illustration. Reviews ms/illustration packages from authors. Submit ms with 1 piece of final art. Contact: Submissions Editor. Illustrations only: Query with samples; arrange personal portfolio review. Responds in 6 weeks. Samples returned with SASE; samples filed.
Terms: Work purchased outright from authors for $800-1,000. Pays illustrators by the project (range: $2,000-3,500). Book catalog, ms/artist's guidelines available for SASE.
Tips: "Write a story that incorporates a moral—not a preachy morality tale. Originality is the key. We feel Hachai publications will appeal to a wider readership as parents become more interested in positive values for their children."

Ñ HANDPRINT BOOKS, 413 Sixth Ave., Brooklyn NY 11215. E-mail: atobias@earthlink.net; publisher@handprintbo oks.com. Website: www.handprintbooks.com.

Teaching, storytelling & tapping into the sacred parts of ourselves

"The first time I gave serious thought to becoming a writer was early—in the first grade—when my teacher, Mrs. Beall, at Pearl Rucker Elementary School, told me she thought I'd be a writer when I grew up," says Kathi Appelt.

Kathi Appelt

Now a teacher herself, and mother of two, Appelt indeed proved Mrs. Beall right, going on to become an award-winning author of teen titles such as *Kissing Tennessee and Other Stories from the Stardust Dance; Just People & Paper/Pen/Poem: A Young Writer's Way to Begin*; and *Poems from Homeroom: A Writer's Place to Start*. Appelt has also penned numerous well-received picture books including *Oh My Baby, Little One*; *Bat Jamboree* (and its sequels); *Cut Down Shin Creek*; *Piggies in a Polka*; *The Best Kind of Gift*; *Incredible Me!*; *Alley Cat's Meow*; *Where, Where Is Swamp Bear?*; *Hushabye, Baby Blue*; and the Bubba and Beau series.

While Appelt spent some time dreaming of the theater (she minored in Theater Arts in college) and faced challenges from finding time to write with two young boys in the house, to finding stories for her characters, to battling her own "well-fed stable full of doubts, misgivings and worries," ultimately her formula for success is simple. "Eventually an idea or story or solution to a problem will show up if I just make myself sit down and work."

Read on for more insights from Appelt. And to learn more about her and her books, visit her website, kathiappelt.com.

What were your early challenges to finding success?
The biggest challenge was finding a balance between my family and my writing. When I began writing for kids, thanks to my kids, they were both very young. What I learned to do, and have practiced ever since, was to write in small snatches of time, five minutes here, five minutes there. It's amazing what you can do with a just a few minutes on your hands.

The other challenge was my own slow learning in regard to figuring what a story truly is. So much of my early writing suffered from lack of a real story. Even today, I struggle with the story line. I can cook up wonderful characters and settings, but then what?

How have you seen your writing evolve over the years? What new directions are interesting to you?
I hope my writing has become more "true." I constantly work to let my own voice shine through. Calling on voice is in some ways like calling on the muse. It's a slippery thing, and not a little magical. It has to do with passion and whether or not the subject you're writing about calls to you from somewhere deep, some profound place that means everything to you.

You have taught children's writing both in college classrooms and informal workshops. What draws you to the role of teacher?

Teaching is something I love to do. Writing is one of the most solitary professions, and sometimes that can get downright claustrophobic.

Teaching gives me a social circle, as well as a sense of "passing it on." I've had the great benefit of being taught by very generous teachers and it seems only right to me to carry that torch. And selfishly, I always feel that I bump up my own learning whenever I teach. Even if I never wrote another word, I would always want to teach.

Your writing shows tremendous range in age level, subject matter, and style. You do both fiction and nonfiction. Would you describe yourself as a confident writer, always ready to face the next challenge? Or do you have to psyche yourself up?

I'm way more comfortable in some genres than others; that's for sure. Though, I have lots of stories I want to write that I probably never will because I get in my own way. By that, I mean I put them off or find something else to take their place or convince myself I'm not the one to write those stories. I want to write a book about my grandmother, but so far I haven't found a way to "enter" that book, and so there it is, still just a dream. Dreams aren't worth much if they just stay in your head, are they?

***Kissing Tennessee and Other Stories from the Stardust Dance* was your first foray into young adult fiction. How did you enjoy the transition from children's to YA fiction? What were the special challenges in writing for an older audience?**

I loved the transition. It's funny, but most of my books are for toddlers, so here I was writing

Through the use of rhythm and rhyme, Kathi Appelt teaches young readers about various musical styles—like polka, rigadoon, and roundelay—in *Piggies in a Polka* (Harcourt 2003).

a book for teens. But what I decided is that toddlers and teens aren't so very different.

Our toddler years and our teen years are perhaps the most passionate times in our whole lives. At no other times do we yearn so much for things like independence, acceptance, responsibility, freedom, justice—all those things. So, I found myself dipping into the same emotional well for my older audience that I usually do for my younger audience. The difference is only in intensity—for the teens, I had to press myself to reach harder and deeper only because the situations are closer to the bone.

We've seen the toddler who feels passionately about tying his shoe; a teenager has the same passion about getting a driver's license. Both are intense, but the latter has bigger consequences. The intensity is the same, but the world is larger.

Are your two sons—one an older teen, the other a young man—an inspiration, a distraction, or both?

They are an inspiration, but mostly in the way that they remind me of my own experiences when I was their age. I've tried to use my boys as characters in my stories, but to no avail. It's always a mistake because I can't get inside their heads or their hearts no matter how much I want to. In the end, they will have to tell their own stories, without my interpretation.

The bigger gift to them would be to tell my stories, and let them figure out how they're going to tell theirs. Isn't that what all of us have to figure out, how to tell our stories? For some of us it shows up as music, for others art. Some of us express ourselves through science, math, engineering, dance. Our mission while we're here is to discover the vehicle we need for telling our stories. That's when we tap into the most sacred parts of ourselves.

What advice do you have for beginning writers?

Three things. First, read everything you can get your hands on. Second, if you intend to write for a child audience, find some kids to be around. And third, write every single day even if it's only your grocery list.

—*Cynthia Leitich Smith*

Illustration © 2003 Arthur Howard. Reprinted with permission of Harcourt, Inc.

Despite a long day of errands, Kathi Appelt's title characters in *Bubba and Beau Go Night-Night* (Harcourt 2003), aren't quite ready to surrender to the sandman. This bedtime tale with country-western flair is the sequel to *Bubba and Beau, Best Friends* (2002), which won School Library Journal's "Best Book of the Year" award.

A HARCOURT, INC., 525 B St., Suite 1900, San Diego CA 92101-4495. (619)699-6810. Fax: (619)699-6777. Children's Books Division includes: Harcourt Children's Books (Ms. Allyn Johnston, editorial director), Gulliver Books (Elizabeth Van Doren, editorial director), Voyager Paperbacks, Odyssey Paperbacks, and Red Wagon Books. Book publisher. **Art Acquisitions:** Art Director. Publishes 50-75 picture books/year; 5-10 middle reader titles/year; 10 young adult titles/year. 20% of books by first-time authors; 50% of books from agented writers. "Harcourt, Inc. owns some of the world's most prestigious publishing imprints—which distinguish quality products for the juvenile, educational and trade markets worldwide."

- The staff of Harcourt's children's book department is no longer accepting unsolicited manuscripts, queries or illustrations. Harcourt title *Little Rat Sets Sail*, by Monika Bang-Campbell, illustrated by Molly Bang, won a 2002 Boston Globe-Horn Book Honor Award for Picture Books.

Fiction: All levels: Considers all categories. Average word length: picture books—"varies greatly"; middle readers—20,000-50,000; young adults—35,000-65,000. Recently published *Home Run*, by Robert Burleigh, illustrated by Mike Wimmer (ages 6-10, picture book/biography); *Cast Two Shadows*, by Ann Rinaldi (ages 12 and up; young adult historical fiction); *Tell Me Something Happy Before I Go to Sleep*, by Joyce Dunbar, illustrated by Debi Gliori (ages 4-8, picture book).

Nonfiction: All levels: animal, biography, concept, history, multicultural, music/dance, nature/environment, science, sports. Average word length: picture books—"varies greatly"; middle readers—20,000-50,000; young adults—35,000-65,000. Recently published *Lives of the Presidents*, by Kathleen Krull; illustrated by Kathryn Hewitt (ages 8-12, illustrated nonfiction).

How to Contact/Writers: Only interested in agented material.

Illustration: Only interested in agented material.

Photography: Works on assignment only.

Terms: Pays authors and illustrators in royalty based on retail price. Pays photographers by the project. Sends galleys to authors; dummies to illustrators. Original artwork returned at job's completion. Book catalog available for 8×10 SAE and 4 first-class stamps; ms/artist's guidelines for business-size SASE. All imprints included in a single catalog.

A HARPERCOLLINS CHILDREN'S BOOKS, 1350 Avenue of the Americas, New York NY 10019. (212)261-6500. Website: www.harpercollins.com. Book publisher. Editor-in-Chief: Kate Morgan Jackson. Editorial Director: Maria Modugno. **Art Acquisitions:** Barbara Fitzsimmon, director. Imprints: Laura Geringer Books, Joanna Cotler Books, Greenwillow Books, Katherine Tegen Books, Julie Andrews Collection. Paperback Imprints: Harper Trophy, Harper Tempest, Avon. Merchandise Imprint: Harper Festival.

- HarperCollins is not accepting unsolicited and/or unagented mss not addressed to a specific editor. HarperCollins title *Mrs. Biddlebox*, by Linda Smith, illustrated by Marla Frazee, won a 2003 Golden Kite Award in picture book illustration. Their title *Surviving the Applewhites*, by Stephanie S. Tolan, won a 2003 Newbery Honor. Harper/Joanna Cotler Books title *I Stink*, by Kate McMullan, illustrated by Jim McMullan, won a 2002 Boston Globe-Horn Book Honor Award for Picture Books. Their title *The Stray Dog*, by Marc Simont, won a 2002 Caldecott Honor. Their title *Freewill*, by Chris Lynch, won a 2002 Printz Honor.

Fiction: Picture books: adventure, animal, anthology, concept, contemporary, fantasy, folktales, hi-lo, history, multicultural, nature/environment, poetry, religion. Middle readers: adventure, hi-lo, history, poetry, suspense/mystery. Young adults/teens: fantasy, science fiction, suspense/mystery. All levels: multicultural. "Artists with diverse backgrounds and settings shown in their work."

Nonfiction: Picture books: animal, arts/crafts, biography, geography, multicultural, nature/environment. Middle readers: how-to.

Illustration: Works with 100 illustrators/year. Responds only if interested. Samples returned with SASE; samples filed only if interested.

How to Contact/Writers: Nonfiction: Query with SASE only.

Terms: Art guidelines available for SASE.

A HARVEST HOUSE PUBLISHERS, 990 Owen Loop North, Eugene OR 97402. (541)343-0123. Fax: (541)302-0731. Website: www.harvesthousepublishers.com. Book publisher. Publishes 1-2 picture books/year and 2 young reader titles/year. Books follow a Christian theme.

- Harvest House no longer accepts unsolicited manuscripts.

How to Contact/Writers: Only interested in agented material. Accepts material from residents of the US only.

Illustration: Responds to solicited queries in 3 months. Samples returned with SASE. Originals returned at job's completion.

HAYES SCHOOL PUBLISHING CO. INC., 321 Pennwood Ave., Wilkinsburg PA 15221-3398. (412)371-2373. Fax: (800)543-8771. E-mail: chayes@hayespub.com. Website: www.hayespub.com. **Acquisitions:** Mr. Clair N. Hayes. Estab. 1940. Produces folders, workbooks, stickers, certificates. Wants to see supplementary teaching aids for grades K-12. Interested in all subject areas. Will consider simultaneous and electronic submissions.

How to Contact/Writers: Query with description or complete ms. Responds in 6 weeks. SASE for return of submissions.

Illustration: Works with 3-4 illustrators/year. Responds in 6 weeks. Samples returned with SASE; samples filed. Originals not returned at job's completion.

Terms: Work purchased outright. Purchases all rights.

HEALTH PRESS, P.O. Box 37470, Albuquerque NM 87176. (505)888-1394 or (877)411-0707. Fax: (505)888-1521. E-mail: goodbooks@healthpress.com. Website: www.healthpress.com. Book publisher. **Acquisitions:** Editor. Publishes 4 young readers/year; 4 middle readers/year. 100% of books by first-time authors.
Fiction: Young readers, middle readers: health, special needs. Average word length: young readers—1,000-1,500; middle readers—1,000-1,500. Recently published *Pennies, Nickels and Dimes*, by Elizabeth Murphy.
Nonfiction: Young readers, middle readers: health, special needs.
How to Contact/Writers: Submit complete ms. Responds in 1 month. Publishes a book 9 months after acceptance. Will consider simultaneous submissions.
Terms: Pays authors royalty. Sends galleys to authors. Book catalog available.

✓ **HENDRICK-LONG PUBLISHING COMPANY**, 10635 Tower Oaks, Suite D, Houston TX 77070. (832)912-READ. Fax: (832)912-7353. E-mail: hendrick-long@worldnet.att.net. Book publisher. Estab. 1969. **Acquisitions:** Vilma Long, vice president. Publishes 4 young reader titles/year; 4 middle reader titles/year. 20% of books by first-time authors. Publishes fiction/nonfiction about Texas of interest to young readers through young adults/teens.
Fiction: Middle readers: history books on Texas and the Southwest. No fantasy or poetry. Recently published *Young Pioneers in Texas*, written and illustrated by Betsy Warren (grades 4-6); *Maggie Houston, My Father's Honor*, by Jane Cook, illustrated by Janie Falcon (grades 4-6).
Nonfiction: Middle, young adults: history books on Texas and the Southwest, biography, multicultural. Recently published *Texas Brain Twisters*, by Jodie Weddle.
How to Contact/Writers: Fiction/Nonfiction: Query with outline/synopsis and sample chapter. Responds to queries in 1 month; mss in 2 months. Publishes a book 18 months after acceptance. No simultaneous submissions. Include SASE.
Illustration: Works with 2-3 illustrators/year. Uses primarily b&w interior artwork; color covers only. Illustrations only: Query first. Submit résumé or promotional literature or photocopies or tearsheets—no original work sent unsolicited. Responds only if interested.
Terms: Pays authors in royalty based on selling price. Advances vary. Pays illustrators by the project or royalty. Sends galleys to authors; dummies to illustrators. Manuscript guidelines for 1 first-class stamp and #10 SAE.
Tips "Material **must** pertain to Texas or the Southwest. Check all facts about historical figures and events in both fiction and nonfiction. Be accurate."

✓ **HOLIDAY HOUSE INC.**, 425 Madison Ave., New York NY 10017. (212)688-0085. Fax: (212)421-6134. Website: www.holidayhouse.com. Book publisher. Estab. 1935. Vice President/Editor-in-Chief: Regina Griffin. **Acquisitions:** Suzanne Reinoehl, editor. **Art Director:** Claire Counihan. Publishes 35 picture books/year; 3 young reader titles/year; 10 middle reader titles/year; and 3 young adult titles/year. 20% of books by first-time authors; 10% from agented writers. Mission Statement: "To publish high-quality books for children."
● Holiday House title *blues journey*, by Walter Dean Myers, illustrated by Christopher A. Myers won a 2003 Boston Globe-Horn Book Honor.
Fiction: All levels: adventure, contemporary, fantasy, folktales, ghost, historical, humor, multicultural, school, suspense/mystery, sports. Recently published *A Child's Calendar*, by John Updike, illustrated by Trina Schart Hyman; *I Was a Third Grade Science Project*, by M.J. Auch; and *Darkness Over Denmark*, by Ellen Levine.
Nonfiction: All levels: animal, biography, concept, contemporary, geography, historical, math, multicultural, music/dance, nature/environment, religion, science, social studies.
How to Contact/Writers: Send queries only to Editor. Responds to queries in 3 months; mss in 4 months. "If we find your book idea suited to our present needs, we will notify you by mail." Once a ms has been requested, the writers should send in the exclusive submission, with a SASE, otherwise the ms will not be returned.
Illustration: Works with 35 illustrators/year. Reviews ms illustration packages from artists. Send ms with dummy. Do not submit original artwork or slides. Color photocopies or printed samples are preferred. Responds only if interested. Samples filed.
Terms: Pays authors and illustrators an advance against royalties. Originals returned at job's completion. Book catalog, ms/artist's guidelines available for a SASE.
Tips: "Fewer books are being published. It will get even harder for first timers to break in."

✓ **HENRY HOLT & CO., LLC**, 115 W. 18th St., New York NY 10011. (212)886-9200. Website: www.henryholt.com. Book publisher. **Manuscript Acquisitions:** Laura Godwin, editor-in-chief/associate publisher of Books for Young Readers dept.; Nina Ignatowicz, executive editor; Christy Ottaviano, executive editor, Reka Simonsen, editor. Adriane Frye, associate editor; Kate Farrell, editor. **Art Acquisitions:** Patrick Collins, creative director. Publishes 20-40 picture books/year; 4-6 chapter books/year; 10-15 middle grade titles/year; 8-10 young adult titles/year. 15% of books by first-time authors; 40% of books from agented writers. "Henry Holt and Company Books for Young Readers is known for publishing quality books that feature imaginative authors and illustrators. We tend to publish many new authors and illustrators each year in our effort to develop and foster new talent."
● Holt title *Hondo & Fabian*, written and illustrated by Peter McCarty, won a 2003 Caldecott Honor.
Fiction: Picture books: animal, anthology, concept, folktales, history, humor, multicultural, nature/environment, poetry, special needs, sports. Middle readers: adventure, contemporary, history, humor, multicultural, special needs, sports, suspense/mystery. Young adults: contemporary, multicultural, problem novel, sports.
Nonfiction: Picture books: animal, arts/crafts, biography, concept, geography, history, hobbies, multicultural, music, dance, nature/environment, sports. Middle readers, young readers, young adult: biography, history, multicultural, sports.

'Look at My Book': imagination & inspiration for education

After receiving a general art degree from the University of Delaware in 1981, Loreen Leedy sought a way that she could integrate her varied talents in drawing, painting, and ceramics. She'd occasionally entertained thoughts of working on children's books, but since her university offered little relevant coursework, it didn't seem to be an attainable goal.

Photo: Andrew Schuerger

"My art training enabled me to draw realistically, but I hadn't figured out how to draw whimsical characters from my imagination," she says.

Leedy began making polymer clay jewelry and chess sets, which featured playful figures of pigs, cats, and dragons, and enjoyed great success selling them at craft shows. This creative outlet was just what she needed to spark her dormant imagina-

Loreen Leedy

tion, as the brightly colored pig pins, frog earrings, and dragon chess pieces allowed her to draw realistically from a three-dimensional model and then enhance the figures with a little artistic improvisation.

Leedy's publishing dream was revived in 1984 when a friend introduced her to Oliver Dunrea, a children's book author/illustrator. Dunrea gave her a behind-the-scenes look at the process of book creation, from rough sketches to finished art, and Leedy realized the task that had seemed so daunting before could be broken down into manageable steps. Suddenly, her jewelry and chess set "critters" began to take on lives of their own—on the pages of her own books. Dunrea showed a stack of Leedy's sketches to Margery Cuyler, then an editor at Holiday House in New York, and Cuyler was impressed with Leedy's dragon character.

"She then asked if I could write," remembers Leedy. "I thought back to the few creative writing experiences from my school days and thought it was worth a try. A couple of months later, I met with her and showed her three manuscripts and several new sketches. She thought the dragon-counting story was the closest to being publishable."

A week later the first pages for the book were on Cuyler's desk. In 1985, Leedy made her publishing debut with *A Number of Dragons*, a counting book written in verse. Once Leedy had this artistic breakthrough, she no longer needed the exercise of creating the polymer-clay figures to generate inspiration for her characters; the comical creatures now leapt directly from her mind to the page.

But the process of book creation still doesn't happen overnight: Writing and illustrating a book can take her anywhere from five months to over a year to complete. And, like any author/illustrator, she's still prone to the occasional creative block, though she relies on herself for motivation.

"Usually when I get about halfway through a project, I'm tired of it and think it's awful," she says. "But, since no one else is going to finish it for me, I just stay with it. By the time the book is finished, I love it again."

In addition to her own personal dedication, Leedy is motivated by her belief in the value of reading as an educational tool.

"My guiding philosophy is to create the kind of books I wish had been available when I was growing up. Then, I wanted to learn real things and used to read the encyclopedia and 'grown up' books. Now, I invent fun characters and write stories to put the topic area into context," she says. "Some people seem to think that children just want to be entertained all the time, but in actuality, they also want to find out about new things and master new skills."

And despite the fact that everything—even grade-school classrooms—seems to be going the way of the Web, Leedy still feels that books are a valuable medium through which children learn. "Kids relate to different media at various times, and there's a well-established place for

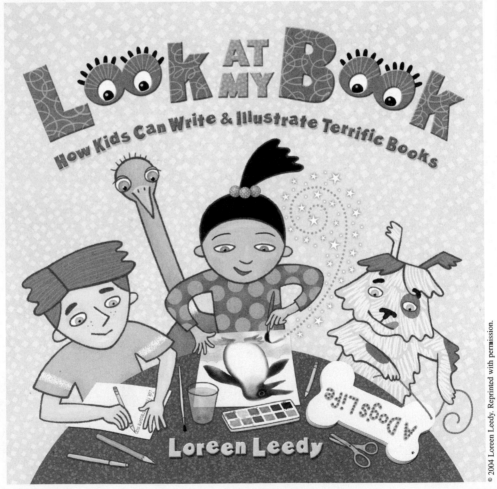

Many of Loreen Leedy's picture books seek to educate, in areas such as math, science and social studies, as well as entertain. Her latest project, *Look At My Book: How Kids Can Write & Illustrate Terrific Books* (Holiday House, 2004), joins *The Bunny Play* (1988), *The Furry News: How to Make a Newspaper* (1990), and *Messages in the Mailbox: How to Write a Letter* (1991) in her how-to set of language-arts titles.

books in their lives," she asserts. "The grade level when various topics are introduced to children in school seems to be getting younger all the time, and children need age-appropriate materials."

Her passion for and belief in children's books and creative writing originated in her own experience as a child. Leedy laments the fact that there was little or no integration of art and writing at her own elementary school, and she recalls that she was assigned no creative projects until around the sixth grade.

"I used to beg my English teachers year after year to do some creative writing in class, but somehow diagramming sentences was the priority," she remembers. "In short, I was a frustrated writer and didn't know how to progress on my own. There were many books about how to draw, but little or nothing about how to write existed that was suitable for my age level." As an adult, she still felt there was a need for children's instructional material on the art of putting their original writing and artwork together. Leedy was inspired to give to other "frustrated" young writer-illustrators what Dunrea had given to her years ago—a fun, encouraging, manageable how-to lesson.

In 1990, she produced *The Furry News: How to Make a Newspaper* (Holiday House), a picture book about a bear who decides to publish a neighborhood newspaper. The bear and his animal friends conduct interviews, write news and feature stories, sell ads, draw comics, and get their paper printed and distributed. The book even contains a glossary of twenty-one basic journalism terms. Now, she's tackling her own genre with *Look at My Book: How Kids Can Write & Illustrate Terrific Books* (Holiday House), scheduled to hit shelves in the spring of 2004. The book follows three characters—a boy, a girl, and a dog—as they go through the process of writing and illustrating their own books. The pages are divided by headlines, such as Ideas, Characters, Rough Draft, Revise, and Art, all the way to Binding.

Co-authored with Pat Street, *There's A Frog in My Throat! 440 Animal Sayings a Little Bird Told Me* (2003), explains the meanings of oft-uttered idioms like "his bark is worse than his bite," "something smells fishy," and "eager beaver" in addition to less well-known expressions like "mouse potato."

"I attempted to at least mention every facet of creating a book, such as thinking of a good title, but hopefully I kept it simple enough for elementary-age children. It's not a formula kind of thing where you follow step-by-step directions; it's a guide to the general process for young author/illustrators," explains Leedy.

And just to prove that she takes the work of her young protégés seriously, *Look at My Book* even contains a resource page for further information on writing, illustrating, and publishing.

After creating more than thirty picture books, Leedy gets her greatest inspiration from visiting schools and seeing what children are learning (or not learning) and at what grade level. With diligence like Leedy's, perhaps the next generation of creatives will be a little more inspired and a little less frustrated.

—*Lauren Mosko*

How to Contact/Writers: Fiction/Nonfiction: Submit complete ms with SASE. Responds in 3 months. Will not consider simultaneous or multiple submissions.

Illustration: Works with 50-60 illustrators/year. Reviews ms/illustration packages from artists. Random samples OK. Illustrations only: Submit tearsheets, slides. Do *not* send originals. Responds to art samples in 1 month. Samples returned with SASE; samples filed. If accepted, original artwork returned at job's completion.

Terms: Pays authors/illustrators royalty based on retail price. Sends galleys to authors; proofs to illustrators.

N **⬚** **HOT JAVA PRODUCTIONS, INC.**, P.O. Box 909, Kirkland WA 98083. (425)820-6848. Fax: (253)925-7209. E-mail: rom.author@juno.com. Website: www.hotjavaproductions.com. Estab. 1998. We are an independent book packager/producer. **Manuscript Acquisitions:** Nancy Radke, acquisitions editor. **Art Acquisitions:** Kyle Johnson, project manager. 90% of books by first-time authors. "We want good stories, plots; will help with editing."

Fiction: Picture books, young readers: adventure, animal, concept, contemporary, fantasy, folktales, health, hi-lo, history, humor, multicultural, nature/environment, poetry, religion, science fiction, special needs, sports, suspense/mystery. Middle readers, young adults: adventure, animal, concept, contemporary, fantasy, folktales, health, hi-lo, history, humor, multicultural, nature/environment, poetry, problem novels, religion, science fiction, special needs, sports, suspense/mystery. Average word length: young readers—7,000-10,000; middle readers—30,000; young adults—40,000-60,000.

Nonfiction: Picture books, young readers, middle readers, young adults: animal, arts/crafts, biography, careers, concept, cooking, geography, health, hi-lo, history, hobbies, how-to, multicultural, music/dance, nature/environment, reference, religion, science, self help, social issues, special needs, sports, textbooks. Average word length: young readers—7,000-10,000; middle readers—30,000; young adults—40,000-60,000.

How to Contact/Writers: Fiction/nonfiction: Submit outline/synopsis and 2 sample chapters. Responds to queries in 1 month; mss in 6 months. Publishes book 8 months after acceptance. Will consider simultaneous submissions, previously published work.

Illustration: Works primarily with in-house illustrators. Reviews ms/illustration packages from artists. Submit ms with dummy. Contact: Nancy Radke, senior editor. Illustrations only: Query with samples. Contact: Kyle Johnson. Responds in 2 months. Samples returned with SASE and a request; samples filed.

Terms: Pays authors royalty with graduated increase based on retail price. Offers advances (Average amount: $1,000). Pays illustrators by the project. Sends galleys to authors; dummies to illustrators. Writer's guidelines available for SASE. Catalog available on website.

Tips: "Writers: Write your story. Don't worry about formulas when submitting to us. Illustrators: All our our artwork eventually becomes digital. Keep it simple. Most of our work is done in-house; go to the website to see what we are doing. A 20,000 word story will have almost 2,000 illustrations. These are read-to-me books. Pay attention to how your book sounds. These books are sold on DVDs, to be viewed on a television screen, or other screen. The books are intensely illustrated and the script is both printed and read aloud."

⬚ **HOUGHTON MIFFLIN CO.**, Children's Trade Books, 222 Berkeley St., Boston MA 02116-3764. (617)351-5000. Fax: (617)351-1111. E-mail: childrens_books@hmco.com. Website: www.houghtonmifflinbooks.com. Book publisher. **Manuscript Acquisitions:** Hannah Rodgers, submissions coordinator. Kim Keller, managing editor; Ann Rider, Margaret Raymo, senior editors; Amy Flynn, editor; Eden Edwards, Sandpiper Paperback senior editor; Walter Lorraine, books editor; Kate O'Sullivan, editor. **Art Acquisitions:** Sheila Smallwood, creative director. Averages 60 titles/year. Publishes hardcover originals and trade paperback reprints and originals. Imprints include Walter Lorraine Books and Clarion Books. "Houghton Mifflin gives shape to ideas that educate, inform, and above all, delight."

● Houghton Mifflin title *My Heartbeat*, by Garret Freymann-Weyr, won a 2003 Michael Printz Honor. Their title *Black Potatoes: the Story of the Great Irish Famine*, by Susan Campbell Bartoletti, won the 2002 Robert F. Sibert Award.

Fiction: All levels: all categories except religion. "We do not rule out any theme, though we do not publish specifically religious material." *Zathura*, by Chris Van Allsburg (ages 4-8, picture book); *The Silent Boy*, by Lois Lowry (ages 10-14, novel); and *My Heartbeat*, by Garret Freymann-Weyr (ages 12 and up).

Nonfiction: All levels: all categories except religion. Recently published *What Do You Do With a Tail Like This?*, by Steve Jenkins (ages 6-10; picture book); *The Man-Eating Tigers of Sundarbans*, by Sy Montgomery (ages 4-8, photo); *The Sky's The Limit: Stories of Discovery by Women and Girls*, by Catherine Thimmesh, illustrated by Melissa Sweet (ages 8-12).

How to Contact/Writers: Fiction: Submit complete ms. Nonfiction: Submit outline/synopsis and sample chapters. Always include SASE. Responds within 4 months.

Illustration: Works with 60 illustrators/year. Reviews ms/illustration packages from artists. Manuscript/illustration packages or illustrations only: Query with samples (colored photocopies are fine); provide tearsheets. Responds in 4 months. Samples returned with SASE; samples filed if interested.

Terms: Pays standard royalty based on retail price; offers advance. Illustrators paid by the project and royalty. Manuscript and artist's guidelines available for SASE.

HUNTER HOUSE PUBLISHERS, P.O.Box 2914, Alameda CA 94501-0914. Fax: (510)865-5282. E-mail: acquisitions @hunterhouse.com. Website: www.hunterhouse.com. Book publisher. **Manuscript Acquisitions:** Jeanne Brondino. Publishes 0-1 titles for teenage women/year. 50% of books by first-time authors; 5% of books from agented writers.

Nonfiction: Young adults: self help, health, multicultural, violence prevention. "We emphasize that all our books try to take multicultural experiences and concerns into account. We would be interested in a self-help book on multicultural issues." Books are therapy/personal growth-oriented. Does *not* want to see books for young children; fiction; illustrated picture books; autobiography. Published *Turning Yourself Around: Self-Help Strategies for Troubled Teens*, by Kendall Johnson, Ph.D.; *Safe Dieting for Teens*, by Linda Ojeda, Ph.D.

How to Contact/Writers: Query; submit overview and chapter-by-chapter synopsis, sample chapters and statistics on your subject area, support organizations or networks and marketing ideas. "Testimonials from professionals or well-known authors are crucial." Responds to queries in 3 months; mss in 6 months. Publishes a book 18 months after acceptance. Will consider simultaneous submissions.

Terms: Payment varies. Sends galleys to authors. Book catalog available for 9×12 SAE and $1.25 postage; ms guidelines for standard SAE and 1 first-class stamp.

Tips: Wants therapy/personal growth workbooks; teen books with solid, informative material. "We do few children's books. The ones we do are for a select, therapeutic audience. No fiction! Please, no fiction."

HYPERION BOOKS FOR CHILDREN, 114 Fifth Ave., New York NY 10011-5690. (212)633-4400. Fax: (212)633-4833. Website: www.hyperionchildrensbooks.com. Trade imprint of Disney Publishing Worldwide. Book publisher. **Manuscript Acquisitions:** Liza Baker, editorial director. **Art Acquisitions:** Anne Diebel, art director. 10% of books by first-time authors. Publishes various categories.

● Hyperion title *Crispin: The Cross of Lead*, by Avi, won the 2003 Newbery Medal.

Fiction: Picture books, young readers, middle readers, young adults: adventure, animal, anthology (short stories), contemporary, fantasy, folktales, history, humor, multicultural, poetry, science fiction, sports, suspense/mystery. Middle readers, young adults: commercial fiction. Recently published *Emily's First 100 Days of School*, by Rosemary Wells (ages 3-6, *New York Times* bestseller); *Artemis Fowl*, by Eoin Colfer (YA novel, *New York Times* bestseller); *Dumpy The Dump Truck*, series by Julie Andrews Edwards and Emma Walton Hamilton (ages 3-7).

Nonfiction: All trade subjects for all levels.

How to Contact/Writers: Only interested in agented material.

Illustration: Works with 100 illustrators/year. "Picture books are fully illustrated throughout. All others depend on individual project." Reviews ms/illustration packages from artists. Submit complete package. Illustrations only: Submit résumé, business card, promotional literature or tearsheets to be kept on file. Responds only if interested. Original artwork returned at job's completion.

Photography: Works on assignment only. Publishes photo essays and photo concept books. Provide résumé, business card, promotional literature or tearsheets to be kept on file.

Terms: Pays authors royalty based on retail price. Offers advances. Pays illustrators and photographers royalty based on retail price or a flat fee. Sends galleys to authors; dummies to illustrators. Book catalog available for 9×12 SAE and 3 first-class stamps.

ILLUMINATION ARTS, P.O. Box 1865, Bellevue WA 98009. (425)644-7185. Fax: (425)644-9274. E-mail: liteinfo@illumin.com. Website: www.illumin.com. Book publisher. Estab. 1987. "All of our books are uplifting, inspirational/spiritual (nonreligious), hardcover, picture books. We specialize in children's books, but they are designed to appeal to all readers." **Acquisitions:** Ruth Thompson, editorial director.

Fiction: Word length: Prefer under 1,000, but will consider up to 1,500 words. Recently published *The Errant Knight*, by Ann Tompert, illustrated by Doug Keith; *In Every Moon There is a Face*, by Charles Mathes, illustrated by Arlene Graston; and *Inside Out*, by Wendy Stofan Halley, illustrated by Roberta Collier-Morales.

How to Contact/Writers: Fiction: Submit complete ms. Responds to queries in 3 months, with SASE only. **No electronic or CD submissions for text or art.** Publishes a book 1-2 years after acceptance. Will consider simultaneous submissions.

Illustration: Works with 3-5 illustrators/year. Uses color artwork only. Reviews ms/illustration packages from artists. Query or send ms with dummy. Illustrations only: Query with color samples, résumé and promotional material to be kept on file or returned with SASE only. Contact: Terri Cohlene, creative director. Responds in 1 month with SASE only. Samples returned with SASE or filed.

Terms: Pays authors and illustrators royalty based on wholesale price. Book fliers available for SASE.

Tips: "Read our books and follow our guidelines. Be patient. The market is competitive. We receive 2,000 submissions annually and publish 4-5 books a year. Sorry, we are unable to track unsolicited submissions."

IMPACT PUBLISHERS, INC., P.O. Box 6016, Atascadero CA 93423-6016. (805)466-5917. Fax: (805)466-5919. E-mail: info@impactpublishers.com. Website: www.impactpublishers.com. Estab. 1970. Nonfiction publisher. **Manuscript Acquisitions:** Melissa Froehner, children's editor. **Art Acquisitions:** Sharon Skinner, art director. Imprints: Little Imp Books, Rebuilding Books, The Practical Therapist Series. Publishes 1 young reader/year; 1 middle reader/year; and 1 young adult title/year. 20% of books by first-time authors. "Our purpose is to make the best human services expertise available to the widest possible audience. We publish only popular psychology and self-help materials written in everyday language by professionals with advanced degrees and significant experience in the human services."

Nonfiction: Young readers, middle readers, young adults: self-help. Recently published *The Divorce Helpbook for Kids*, by Cynthia MacGregor (ages 8-12, children's/divorce/emotions).

How to Contact/Writers: Nonfiction: Query or submit complete ms, cover letter, résumé. Responds to queries in 10 weeks; mss in 3 months. Will consider simultaneous submissions or previously published work.

Illustration: Works with 1 or less illustrator/year. Uses b&w artwork only. Reviews ms/illustration packages from artists. Query. Contact: Children's Editor. Illustrations only: query with samples. Contact: Sharon Skinner, production manager. Responds only if interested. Samples returned with SASE; samples filed. Originals returned to artist at job's completion.

Terms: Pays authors royalty of 10-12%. Offers advances. Pays illustrators by the project. Sends galleys to authors. Book catalog available for #10 SAE with 2 first-class stamps; ms guidelines available for SASE. All imprints included in a single catalog.

☐ INCENTIVE PUBLICATIONS, INC., 3835 Cleghorn Ave., Nashville TN 37215-2532. (615)385-2934. Fax: (615)385-2967. E-mail: info@incentivepublications.com. Website: www.incentivepublications.com. Estab. 1969. "Incentive publishes developmentally appropriate instructional aids for tots to teens." **Acquisitions:** Charlotte Bosarge. Approximately 20% of books by first-time authors. "We publish only educational resource materials for teachers and parents of children from pre-school age through high school. We publish *no fiction*. Incentive endeavors to produce developmentally appropriate research-based educational materials to meet the changing needs of students, teachers and parents. Books are written by teachers for teachers for the most part."

Nonfiction: Black & white line illustrated books, young reader, middle reader: activity books, arts/craft, multicultural, science, health, how-to, reference, animal, history, nature/environment, special needs, social issues, supplemental educational materials. "Any manuscripts related to child development or with content-based activities and innovative strategies will be reviewed for possible publication." Recently published Better Grades series (middle grade) and Ready to Learn series (8 books).

How to Contact/Writers: Nonfiction: Submit outline/synopsis, sample chapters and SASE. Responds to queries in 6 weeks; mss in 2 months. Typically publishes a book 18 months after acceptance. Will consider simultaneous submissions.

Illustration: Works with 2-6 illustrators/year. Responds in 1 month if reply requested (send SASE). Samples returned with SASE; samples filed. Need 4-color cover art; b&w line illustration for content.

Terms: Pays authors in royalties (5-10% based on wholesale price) or work purchased outright (range: $500-1,000). Pays illustrators by the project (range: $200-1,500). Pays photographers by the project. Original artwork not returned. Book catalog and ms and artist guidelines for SAE with $1.78 postage.

Tips: Writers: "We buy only educational teacher resource material that can be used by teachers and parents (home schoolers). Please do not submit fiction! Incentive Publications looks for a whimsical, warm style of illustration that respects the integrity and age of the child. We work primarily with local artists, but not exclusively."

☒ Ⓐ ☐ JALMAR PRESS, P.O. Box 1185, Torrance CA 90745-6329. (310)816-3085. Fax: (310)816-3092. E-mail: blwjalmar@att.net. Website: www.jalmarpress.com. Subsidiary of the B.L. Winch Group, Incorporated. Book publisher. Estab. 1971. **Acquisitions:** Bradley Winch, publisher; Cathy Winch, manager. Imprint: Personhood Press. Does not publish children's picture books or books for young readers. 10% of books by first-time authors. Publishes self-esteem (curriculum content related), character education, drug and alcohol abuse prevention, peaceful conflict resolution, stress management, virtues whole-brain learning, accelerated learning and emotional intelligence materials for counselors, teachers, and other care givers. "Our goal is to empower children to become personally and socially responsible through activities presented by teachers, counselors and other caregivers that allow them to experience being both successful and responsible. Our titles are activity-driven and develop social, emotional and ethical skills that lead to academic achievements."

• Jalmar's catalog is found on their website. Jalmar is now the exclusive distributor for Innerchoice Publishing's entire line of school counselor-oriented material (K-12).

Fiction: All levels: self-concept, self-esteem. Does not want to see "children's fiction books that have to do with cognitive learning (as opposed to affective learning) and autobiographical work." Published *Hilde Knows: Someone Cries for the Children*, by Lisa Kent, illustrated by Mikki Macklen (child abuse); and *Scooter's Tail of Terror: A Fable of Addiction and Hope*, by Larry Shles (ages 5-105). "All submissions must teach (by metaphor) in the areas listed above."

Nonfiction: All levels: activity books to develop social, emotional and ethical skills. Does not want to see autobiographical work. Published *Esteem Builders Program*, by Michele Borba, illustrated by Bob Burchett (for school use—6 books, tapes, posters).

How to Contact/Writers: Fiction/Nonfiction: Submit complete ms. Responds to queries/mss in 2 months. Publishes a book 12-18 months after acceptance. Will consider simultaneous submissions.

Illustration: Works with 2 illustrators/year. Responds in 1 week. Samples returned with SASE; samples filed.

Terms: Pays authors 7½-15% royalty based on net receipts. Average advance varies. Pays illustrators by the project on a bid basis. Pays photographers per photo on a bid basis. Book catalog/ms guidelines free on request.

Tips: Wants "thoroughly researched, tested, practical, activity-oriented, curriculum content and grade/level correlated books on self-esteem, peaceful conflict resolution, stress management, emotional intelligence, and whole brain learning and books bridging self-esteem to various 'trouble' areas, such as 'at risk,' 'dropout prevention,' etc. Illustrators—make artwork that can be reproduced. Emotional intelligence is becoming a 'hot' category, as is character education and morality-based education."

JAYJO BOOKS, L.L.C., A Guidance Channel Company, 135 Dupont St., P.O. Box 760, Plainview NY 11803-0760. (516)349-5520. Fax: (516)349-5521. E-mail: jayjobooks@guidancechannel.com. Website: www.jayjo.com. Estab. 1993. Specializes in educational material. Independent book packager/producer. **Manuscript Acquisitions:** Sally Germain. Publishes 3-5 illustrated, young readers/year. 25% of books by first-time authors. "Our goal is to provide quality children's health education through entertainment and teaching, while raising important funds for medical research and education."

Fiction: Young readers, middle readers: health, special needs, chronic conditions. Average word length: young readers—1,800; middle readers—1,800. Recently published *Taking Arthritis to School*, by Deedee L. Miller (ages 5-10); *Taking Depression to School*, by Kathy Khalsa (ages 5-10).

Nonfiction: Young readers, middle readers: health, special needs, chronic conditions. Average word length: young readers—1,500; middle readers—1,500.

How to Contact/Writers: Fiction/Nonfiction: Send query. Responds in 3 months. Publishes a book 2 years after acceptance. Will consider simultaneous submissions.

Illustration: Works with 2 illustrators/year. Uses color artwork only. Illustrations only: Query with samples. Responds in 3 months. Samples returned with SASE; samples filed.

Terms: Work purchased outright from authors. Pays illustrators by the project. Book catalog and guidelines available for #10 SAE and 1 first-class stamp. Manuscript guidelines for SASE.

Tips: "Send query letter. Since we only publish books adapted to our special format, we contact appropriate potential authors and work with them to customize manuscripts."

JEWISH LIGHTS PUBLISHING, P.O. Box 237, Rt. 4, Sunset Farm Offices, Woodstock VT 05091. (802)457-4000. Fax: (802)457-4004. E-mail: everyone@longhillpartners.com. Website: www.jewishlights.com. A division of LongHill Partners, Inc. Book publisher. Imprint: SkyLight Paths Publishing. President: Stuart M. Matlins. **Manuscript Acquisitions:** Submissions Editor. **Art Acquisitions:** Bridgett Taylor. Publishes 2 picture books/year; 1 young reader/year. 50% of books by first-time authors; 1% of books from agented authors. All books have spiritual/religious themes. "Jewish Lights publishes books for people of all faiths and all backgrounds who yearn for books that attract, engage, educate and spiritually inspire. Our authors are at the forefront of spiritual thought and deal with the quest for the self and for meaning in life by drawing on the Jewish wisdom tradition. Our books cover topics including history, spirituality, life cycle, children's, self-help, recovery, theology and philosophy. We do *not* publish autobiography, biography, fiction, *haggadot*, poetry or cookbooks. At this point we plan to do only two books for children annually, and one will be for younger children (ages 4-10)."

Fiction: Picture books, young readers, middle readers: spirituality. "We are not interested in anything other than spirituality." Recently published *God Said Amen*, by Sandy Eisenberg Sasso, illustrated by Avi Katz (ages 4-9, picture book); and *Cain and Abel*, by Sandy Eisenberg Sasso, illustrated by Joan Keller Rothenberg (ages 8 and up).

Nonfiction: Picture book, young readers, middle readers: activity books, spirituality. Recently published *When a Grandparent Dies: A Kid's Own Remembering Workbook for Dealing with Shiva and the Year Beyond*, by Nechama Liss-Levinson, Ph.D. (ages 7-11); and *Sharing Blessings: Children's Stories for Exploring the Spirit of the Jewish Holidays*, written by Rabbi Michael Klayman and Rahel Musleah, illustrated by Mary O'Keefe Young (ages 6-10, picture book).

How to Contact/Writers: Fiction/Nonfiction: Query with outline/synopsis and 2 sample chapters; submit complete ms for picture books. Include SASE. Responds to queries/mss in 4 months. Publishes a book 1 year after acceptance. Will consider simultaneous submissions and previously published work.

Illustration: Works with 2 illustrators/year. Reviews ms/illustration packages from artists. Query. Illustrations only: Query with samples; provide résumé. Samples returned with SASE; samples filed.

Terms: Pays authors royalty of 10% of revenue received. Offers advances. Pays illustrators by the project or royalty. Pays photographers by the project. Sends galleys to authors; dummies to illustrators. Book catalog available for 6½×9½ SAE and 59¢ postage; ms guidelines available for SASE.

Tips: "Explain in your cover letter why you're submitting your project to *us* in particular. (Make sure you know what we publish.)"

JOURNEYFORTH BOB JONES UNIVERSITY PRESS, Imprint of Bob Jones University Press, 1700 Wade Hampton Blvd., Greenville SC 29614. (803)242-5100, ext. 4350. E-mail: jb@bjup.com. Website: www.bjup.com/books/FreelanceOpportunities. Book publisher. Estab. 1974. **Acquisitions:** Mrs. Nancy Lohr, editor. Publishes 4 young reader titles/year; 4 middle reader titles/year; and 4 young adult titles/year. 30% of books by first-time authors. "Our books reflect the highest Christian standards of thought, feeling, and action, are uplifting or instructive and enhance moral purity. Themes advocating secular attitudes of rebellion or materialism are not acceptable. We are looking for books that present a fully developed main character capable of dynamic changes, who experiences the central conflict of the plot, which should have plenty of action and not be didactic in tone."

Fiction: Young readers, middle readers, young adults: adventure, animal, concept, contemporary, easy-to-read, fantasy, history, multicultural, nature/environment, sports, spy/mystery. Average word length: young readers—10,000; middle readers—30,000; young adult/teens—50,000. Published *The Case of the Sassy Parrot*, by Milly Howard (grades 2-4, adventure story); and *The Slide*, by Catherine Farnes (young adult, contemporary).

Nonfiction: Average word length: young readers—10,000; middle readers—30,000; young adult/teens—50,000. Published *Children of the Storm*, by Natasha Vins (young adult, autobiography); and *Someday You'll Write*, by Elizabeth Yates (how-to).

How to Contact/Writers: Fiction: Send the first 5 chapters and synopsis. "Do not send stories with magical elements. We are not currently accepting picture books. We do not publish these genres: romance, science fiction, poetry and drama." Nonfiction: Query or submit complete ms or submit outline/synopsis and sample chapters. Responds to queries in 3 weeks; mss in 3 months. Publishes book "approximately one year" after acceptance. Will consider simultaneous submissions.

Illustration: Works with 8 illustrators/year. Responds only if interested. Samples returned with SASE; samples filed.

Terms: Pays authors royalty based on wholesale price or work purchased outright. Pays illustrators by the project. Originals returned to artist at job's completion. Book catalog and ms guidelines free on request. Send SASE for book catalog and mss guidelines.

Tips: "Writers—give us original, well-developed characters in a suspenseful plot that has good moral tone. Artists—we need strong color as well as black & white illustrations. Looking for quality illustrations of people in action in realistic settings. Be willing to take suggestions and follow specific directions. We are committed to producing high-quality books for children."

JUST US BOOKS, INC., 356 Glenwood Ave., East Orange NJ 07017. (973)676-4345. Fax: (973)677-7570. Website: www.justusbooks.com. Imprint of Afro-Bets Series. Book publisher; "for selected titles" book packager. Estab. 1988. **Acquisitions:** Submissions Manager. **Art Director:** Cheryl Willis Hudson. Publishes 4-8 titles/year. . 33% of books by first-time authors. Looking for "queries for YA and middle reader fiction and nonfiction."

Fiction: Middle readers: contemporary (African-American themes). Young adults: concept, contemporary, history, humor, suspense/mystery. Average word length: "varies" per picture book; young reader—500-2,000; middle reader—5,000. Wants African-American themes. Gets too many traditional African folktales. Recently published *A Blessing In Disguise*, fiction (young adult novel); *Dear Corinne: Tell Somebody*, by Mari Evans (middle readers).

Nonfiction: Young adult: biography, concept, social issues (African-American themes). Recently published *Book of Black Heroes: Scientists Healers & Inventors* (ages 9 and up); *Langston's Legacy: 101 Ways to Celebrate the Life & Work of Langston Huges* (ages 9 and up, bio-activity book).

How to Contact/Writers: Fiction/Nonfiction: Query or submit outline/synopsis with SASE for proposed title. Responds to queries in 6 weeks only with SASE; unsolicited ms submissions in 4 months only with SASE. Publishes a book 12-18 months after acceptance. Will consider simultaneous submissions (with prior notice). All submissions must be accompanied by a SASE and must be sent via US mail only. *No faxes or e-mails.*

Illustration: Works with 4 illustrators/year. Reviews ms/illustration packages from artists ("but prefers to review them separately"). "Query first." Illustrations only: Query with samples; send résumé, promo sheet, slides, client list, tearsheets; arrange personal portfolio review. Responds only if interested. Samples not returned; samples filed. Original artwork returned at job's completion "depending on project."

Photography: Purchases photos from freelancers. Buys stock and assigns work. Wants "African-American and multicultural themes—kids age 10-13 in school, home and social situations."

Terms: Pays authors royalty and some work for hire depending on project. Pays illustrators by the project or royalty, or flat fee based on project. Sends galleys to authors; dummies to illustrators. Book catalog for business-size SASE and $1.06 postage; ms/artist's guidelines for business-size SASE and 37¢ postage.

Tips: "Multicultural books are tops as far as trends go. There is a great need for diversity and authenticity here. They will continue to be in the forefront of children's book publishing until there is more balanced treatment on these themes industry wide." Writers: "Keep the subject matter fresh and lively. Avoid 'preachy' stories with stereotyped characters. Rely more on authentic stories with sensitive three-dimensional characters." Illustrators: "Submit 5-10 good, neat samples. Be willing to work with an art director for the type of illustration desired by a specific house and grow into larger projects. All queries and submissions must be accompanied by a SASE to receive a response."

KAEDEN BOOKS, P.O. Box 16190, Rocky River OH 44116-6190. (440)617-1400. Fax: (440)617-1403. E-mail: curmston@kaeden.com. Website: kaeden.com. Book publisher. **Acquisitions:** Creative Vice President. 50% of books by first-time authors. "Kaeden Books produces high quality, pre-reader, emergent and early reader books for classroom and reading program educators."

Fiction: Young readers: adventure, animal, concept, contemporary, health, history, humor, multicultural, nature/environment, science fiction, sports, suspense/mystery. Average word length: picture books—20-150 words; young readers—20-150 words. Recently published *Moose's Loose Tooth*, by Nancy Louise Spinelle; *Another Sneeze, Louise!*, by Cheryl A. Potts; *Sammy's Moving*, by Kathleen Urmston and Karen Evans—all three titles illustrated by Gloria Gedeon.

Nonfiction: Young readers: activity books, animal, biography, careers, geography, health, history, hobbies, how-to, multicultural, music/dance, nature/environment, religion, science, sports. Multicultural needs include group and character diversity in stories and settings. Average word length: picture books—20-150 words; young readers—20-150 words.

How to Contact/Writers: Fiction/nonfiction: Query or submit complete ms. Do not send original transcripts. Responds to mss in 1 year. Will consider simultaneous submissions, electronic submissions via disk or modem.

Illustration: Works with 30 illustrators/year. Reviews ms/illustration packages from artists. Query. Submit art samples in color. Can be photocopies or tearsheets. Illustrations only: Query with samples. Send résumé, promo sheet, tearsheets, photocopies of work, preferably in color. Responds only if interested. Samples are filed.

Terms: Work purchased outright from authors. "Royalties to our previous authors." Offers negotiable advances. Pays

illustrators by the project (range: $50-150/page). Book catalog available for 8½×11 SAE and 2 first-class stamps.
Tips: "Our books are written for emergent and fluent readers to be used in the educational teaching environment. A strong correlation between text and visual is necessary along with creative and colorful juvenile designs."

KAMEHAMEHA SCHOOLS PRESS, 1887 Makuakane St., Honolulu HI 96817. (808)842-8719. Fax: (808)842-8895. E-mail: kspress@ksbe.edu. Website: www.ksbe.edu/kspress. Estab. 1933. Specializes in educational and multicultural material. **Manuscript Acquisitions:** Acquisitions Editor. "Kamehameha Schools Press publishes in the areas of Hawaiian history, Hawaiian culture, Hawaiian language and Hawaiian studies."
Nonfiction: Middle readers, young adults: biography, history, multicultural, Hawaiian folklore. Recently published *From the Mountains to the Sea: Early Hawaiian Life*, by Julie Stewart Williams, illustrated by Robin Yoko Racoma (pre-contact Hawaiian life and culture).
How to Contact/Writers: Query. Responds to queries in 2 months; mss in 3 months. Publishes a book 12-18 months after acceptance.
Illustration: Uses b&w artwork only. Illustrations only: Query with samples. Responds only if interested. Samples not returned.
Terms: Work purchased outright from authors. Pays illustrators by the project. Sends galleys to authors. Book catalog available for #10 SASE and 1 first-class stamp. All imprints included in a single catalog. Catalog available on website.
Tips: "Writers and illustrators *must* be knowledgeable in Hawaiian history/culture and be able to show credentials to validate their proficiency. Greatly prefer to work with writers/illustrators available in the Honolulu area."

KAR-BEN PUBLISHING, INC., a division of Lerner Publishing Group, 6800 Tildenwood Lane, Rockville MD 20852-4371. (301)984-8733. Fax: (301)881-9195. E-mail: karben@aol.com. Website: www.karben.com. Book publisher. Estab. 1975. **Manuscript Acquisitions:** Madeline Wikler and Judye Groner, editorial directors. Publishes 10-15 picture books/year; 20% of books by first-time authors. All of Kar-Ben Copies' books are on Jewish themes for young children and families.
Fiction: Picture books: adventures, concept, folktales, history, humor, multicultural, religion, special needs; *must be* on a Jewish theme. Average word length: picture books—2,000. Recently published *Too Much of A Good Thing*, by Mira Wasserman; *Lots of Latkes*, by Sandy Landon; *Sammy Spider's First Trip to Israel*, by Sylvia Rouss.
Nonfiction: Picture books, young readers: activity books, arts/crafts, biography, careers, concept, cooking, history, how-to, multicultural, religion, social issues, special needs; must be of Jewish interest. Recently published *Tasty Bible Stories*, by Tami Lehman-Wilzig; *Mitzvah Magic*, by Danny Siegel.
How to Contact/Writers: Fiction/nonfiction: Submit complete ms. Responds to queries/mss in 6 weeks. Publishes a book 18-24 months after acceptance. Will consider simultaneous submissions. "Story should be short, no more than 3,000 words."
Illustration: Works with 6-8 illustrators/year. Prefers "four-color art in any medium that is scannable." Reviews ms/illustration packages from artists. Submit whole ms and sample of art (no originals). Illustrations only: Submit tearsheets, photocopies, promo sheet "which show skill in children's book illustration." Enclose SASE for response. Responds to art samples in 2 weeks.
Terms: Pays authors in royalties of 5-6% of net against advance of $500-1,000; or purchases outright (range: $2,000-3,000). Offers advance (average amount: $1,000). Pays illustrators by the project (range: $2,000-5,000). Sends galleys to authors. Original artwork returned at job's completion. Book catalog free on request. Manuscript guidelines on website.
Tips: Looks for "books for young children with Jewish interest and content, modern, non-sexist, not didactic. Fiction or nonfiction with a *Jewish* theme—can be serious or humorous, life cycle, Bible story, or holiday-related."

KINGFISHER, Imprint of Houghton Mifflin Company, 215 Park Ave. South, New York NY 10003. (212)420-5800. Fax: (212)420-5899. Website: www.houghtonmifflinbooks.com/kingfisher. **Contact:** Phil Gray.
• Kingfisher is not currently accepting unsolicited mss. All solicitations must be made by a recognized literary agent. Kingfisher is an award-winning publisher of nonfiction and fiction for children of all ages. They publish high-quality books with strong editorial content and world class illustration at a competitive price, offering value to parents and educators.

ALFRED A. KNOPF AND CROWN BOOKS FOR YOUNG READERS, (formerly Crown Books for Young Readers), Imprint of Random House Children's Books, 1745 Broadway, New York NY 10019. (212)782-9000. Website: www.randomhouse.com/kids. See Random House and Delacorte and Doubleday Books for Young Readers listings. Book publisher.
• Knopf title *Hoot*, by Carl Hiassen, won a 2003 Newbery Honor Award.

WENDY LAMB BOOKS, Imprint of Random House, 1745 Broadway, New York NY 10019. Fax: (212)782-8234. Specializes in trade books, fiction, multicultural material. **Manuscript Acquisitions:** Wendy Lamb. Publishes 12 middle readers/year and young adult titles/year. 33% of books by first-time authors. Recently published *Island Boy*, by Graham Salisbury; *Pictures of Hollis Woods*, by Patricia Reilly; *Tribes*, by Arthur Slade.
• Wendy Lamb title *Pictures of Hollis Woods*, by Patricia Reilly Giff, won a 2003 Newbery Honor. Their title, *Fresh Girl*, by Jaïra Placide, won the 2002 Golden Kite Award for fiction.
How to Contact/Writers: Fiction/nonfiction: Query with SASE for reply. "A query letter should briefly describe the book you want to write, the intended age group, and your publishing credits, if any. If you like, you may send no more than 5 pages of the manuscript of shorter works (i.e. picture books) and a maximum of 10 pages of longer works (i.e. novels). *Please do not send more than the specified amount.* Also, do not send cassette tapes, videos, or other materials

along with your query or excerpt. Manuscript pages sent will not be returned. Do not send original art." Responds to queries in 6 weeks; mss in 4 months only with SASE. Publishes book 18 months after acceptance. Will consider electronic submissions via disk or e-mail; previously published work.

Illustration: Reviews ms/illustration packages from artists. Query with SASE for reply.

Tips: "Send query letters with a SASE (self addressed stamped envelope) for reply. If you do not live in the United States, you must send an international reply coupon. We recycle all letters and manuscripts without sufficient postage."

LEE & LOW BOOKS INC., 95 Madison Ave., New York NY 10016-7801. (212)779-4400. E-mail: info@leeandlow.com. Website: www.leeandlow.com. Book publisher. Estab. 1991. **Acquisitions:** Philip Lee, publisher; Louise May, executive editor. Publishes 12-14 picture books/year. 50% of books by first-time authors. Lee & Low publishes only picture books with multicultural themes. "One of our goals is to discover new talent and produce books that reflect the multicultural society in which we live."

- Lee & Low Books is dedicated to publishing culturally authentic literature. The company makes a special effort to work with writers and artists of color and encourages new voices. See listing for their imprint BeBop Books.

Fiction: Picture books: concept. Picture books, young readers: anthology, contemporary, history, multicultural, poetry. "We are not considering folktales or animal stories." Picture book, middle reader: contemporary, history, multicultural, nature/environment, poetry, sports. Average word length: picture books—1,000-1,500 words. Recently published *Love to Langston*, by Tony Medina, illustrated by R. Gregory Christie; *The Pot that Juan Built*, by Nancy Andrews-Goebel, illustrated by David Diaz; and *Love to Mamá*, edited by Pat Mora, illustrated by Pauls S. Barragán M.

Nonfiction: Picture books: concept. Picture books, middle readers: biography, history, multicultural, science and sports. Average word length: picture books—1,500. Recently published *Ray Charles*, by Sharon Bell Mathis, illustrated by George Ford; and *¡Béisbol! Latino Baseball Pioneers and Legends*, by Jonah Winter.

How to Contact/Writers: Fiction/Nonfiction: Submit complete ms. No e-mail submissions. Responds in 4 months. Publishes a book 1-2 years after acceptance. Will consider simultaneous submissions. Guidelines on website at leeandlow. com/editorial/wguide.html.

Illustration: Works with 12-14 illustrators/year. Uses color artwork only. Reviews ms/illustration packages from artists. Contact: Louise May. Submit ms with dummy. Illustrations only: Query with samples, résumé, promo sheet and tearsheets. Responds only if interested. Samples returned with SASE; samples filed. Original artwork returned at job's completion.

Photography: Buys photos from freelancers. Works on assignment only. Model/property releases required. Submit cover letter, résumé, promo piece and book dummy.

Terms: Pays authors royalty. Offers advances. Pays illustrators royalty plus advance against royalty. Photographers paid royalty plus advance against royalty. Sends galleys to authors; proofs to illustrators. Book catalog available for 9×12 SAE and $1.52 postage; ms and art guidelines available via website or with SASE.

Tips: "We strongly urge writers to visit our website and familiarize themselves with our list before submitting. Materials will only be returned with SASE."

LEGACY PRESS, Imprint of Rainbow Publishers, P.O. Box 261129, San Diego CA 92196. (858)668-3260. Book publisher. Estab. 1997. **Manuscript/Art Acquisitions:** Christy Scannell, editorial director. Publishes 3 young readers/year; 3 middle readers/year; 3 young adult titles/year. Publishes nonfiction, Bible-teaching books. "We publish growth and development books for the evangelical Christian—from a non-denominational viewpoint—that may be marketed primarily through Christian bookstores."

Nonfiction: Young readers, middle readers, young adults: reference, religion. Recently published *The Christian Girl's Guide to Friendship*, by Kathy Widenhouse, illustrated by Anita DuFalla.

How to Contact/Writers: Nonfiction: Submit outline/synopsis and 3-5 sample chapters. Responds to queries in 6 weeks; mss in 3 months. Publishes a book 18 months after acceptance. Will consider simultaneous submissions and previously published work.

Illustration: Works with 5 illustrators/year. Reviews ms/illustration packages from artists. Submit ms with 5-10 pieces of final art. Illustrations only: Query with samples to be kept on file. Responds in 6 weeks. Samples returned with SASE.

Terms: Pays authors royalty or work purchased outright. Offers advances. Pays illustrators by the project. Sends galley to authors. Book catalog available for business size SASE; ms guidelines for SASE.

Tips: "Get to know the Christian bookstore market. We are looking for innovative ways to teach and encourage children about the Christian life. No picture books please."

LERNER PUBLISHING GROUP, (formerly Lerner Publications Co.), 241 First Ave. N., Minneapolis MN 55401. (612)332-3344. Fax: (612)332-7615. E-mail: info@lernerbooks.com. Website: www.lernerbooks.com. Book publisher. Estab. 1959. **Manuscript Acquisitions:** Jennifer Zimian, nonfiction submissions editor and Zelda Wagner, fiction submissions editor. Primarily publishes books for children ages 7-18. List includes titles encompassing nature, geography, natural and physical science, current events, ancient and modern history, world art, special interest, sports, world cultures, and numerous biography series.

- See also listing for Carolrhoda Books.

How to Contact/Writers: Submissions are accepted in the months of March and October only. Lerner Publishing Group does not publish alphabet books, puzzle books, song books, textbooks, workbooks, religious subject matter or plays. Work received in any month other than March or October will be returned unopened. "A SASE is required for authors who wish to have their materials returned. Please allow 6 months for a response. No phone calls please."

🅰 🔽 **LITTLE, BROWN AND COMPANY CHILDREN'S BOOKS**, An AOL Time Warner Book Group Company, Time-Life Bldg., 1271 Avenue of the Americas, New York NY 10020. (212)522-8700. Website: www.lb-kids.com or www.lb-teens.com. Book publisher. Estab. 1837. **Editor-in-Chief:** Megan Tingley. Executive Editor: Andrea Spooner. **Art Director:** Alyssa Morris. Editorial Director of Megan Tingley Books: Megan Tingley; Senior Editor: Cynthia Eagan. Publishes picture books, board books, pop-up and lift-the-flap editions, chapter books and general fiction and nonfiction titles for middle and young adult readers.

● Little, Brown does not accept unsolicited mss or unagented material. Little, Brown title *Ansel Adams: America's Photographer*, by Beverly Gherman, won a 2002 Golden Kite Honor award for nonfiction.

Fiction: Picture books: adventure, animal, contemporary, fantasy, folktales, history, humor, multicultural, nature/environment. Young adults: contemporary, health, humor, multicultural, nature/environment, suspense/mystery. Multicultural needs include "any material by, for and about minorities." Average word length: picture books—1,000; young readers—6,000; middle readers—15,000-25,000; young adults—20,000-40,000. Recently published *Gossip Girl: All I Want is Everything*, by Cecily von Ziegesar; *The Family Book*, by Todd Parr; *Lookalike's Christmas*, by Joan Steiner.

Nonfiction: Middle readers, young adults: arts/crafts, history, multicultural, nature, self help, social issues, sports, science. Average word length: middle readers—15,000-25,000; young adults—20,000-40,000. Recently published *Cowboy's and Cowgirls*, by Gail Gibbons and *Hanukkah*, by Roni Schotter.

How to Contact/Writers: Only interested in solicited agented material. Fiction: Submit complete ms. Nonfiction: Submit cover letter, previous publications, a proposal, outline and 3 sample chapters. Do not send originals. Responds to queries in 2 weeks. Responds to mss in 2 months.

Illustration: Works with 55 illustrators/year. Illustrations only: Query art director or managing editor with b&w and color samples; provide résumé, promo sheet or tearsheets to be kept on file. Does not respond to art samples. Do not send originals; copies only.

Photography: Works on assignment only. Model/property releases required; captions required. Publishes photo essays and photo concept books. Uses 35mm transparencies. Photographers should provide résumé, promo sheets or tearsheets to be kept on file.

Terms: Pays authors royalties based on retail price. Pays illustrators and photographers by the project or royalty based on retail price. Sends galleys to authors; dummies to illustrators.

Tips: "Publishers are cutting back their lists in response to a shrinking market and relying more on big names and known commodities. In order to break into the field these days, authors and illustrators research their competition and try to come up with something outstandingly different."

LLEWELLYN WORLDWIDE LTD., P.O. Box 64383, St. Paul MN 55164-0383. (651)291-1970. Fax: (651)291-1908. E-mail: childrensbooks@llewellyn.com. Website: www.llewellyn. com. Estab. 1901. Specializes in trade books, nonfiction, fiction. **Manuscript Acquisitions:** Megan C. Atwood. 50% of books by first-time authors. "Our mission is to provide quality, well-written books that develop and introduce New Age, occult and/or metaphysical topics in an entertaining and edgy way, either in a fiction or nonfiction format, to both the 8- to 12-year-old and the 12- to 18-year-old demographic."

Fiction: Middle readers, young adults: New Age/metaphysical slant. Recently published *The Fortune Teller's Club: The Lost Girl*, by Dotti Enderle (middle grade, suspense/mystery); *Witches' Chillers: Witches' Night Out*, by Silver RavenWolf (young adult, suspense/mystery); *Seasons of Magic*, by Laurel Reinhardt (middle grade, religion).

Nonfiction: Middle readers, young adults: how-to, religion, self-help, New Age/metaphysical slant. Recently published *SpellCraft for Teens*, by Gwinevere Rain (young adult, how-to); *Teen Witch*, by Silver Raven Wolf (young adult, religion, how-to); *Teen Goddess*, by Catherine Wishart (young adult); *Blue is for Nightmares*, by Laurie Stolarz (young adult, fiction).

How to Contact/Writers: Fiction: Query or submit complete ms. Submit outline/synopsis and 1-2 sample chapters. Nonfiction: Query or submit complete ms or submit outline/synopsis and 1-2 sample chapters.

Responds to queries/mss in 2 months. Will consider simultaneous submissions, electronic submissions via e-mail—only for queries and proposals, previously published work.

Terms: Pays authors royalty of 10% based on wholesale price. Sends galleys to authors. Book catalog available for 9 × 12 SASE and 4 first-class stamps; ms guidelines available for SASE.

Tips: "Please be sure to only send in those submissions that hit the Middle Grade (ages 8-12) and Young Adult (ages 12-18) market. We do not accept any proposals for a younger audience at this time. We are interested in quality manuscripts specifically with a metaphysical or occult slant that fits our genre. Generally speaking, always request guidelines from a publishing company and follow the instructions before submitting. Also, be sure to familiarize yourself with a publishing company's repertoire of books to make sure that your proposal fits the company's genre."

LUCENT BOOKS, Imprint of The Gale Group, 10911 Technology Place, San Diego CA 92127. Fax: (858)485-8019. E-mail: chandra.howard@gale.com. Website: www.gale.com/lucent. **Acquisitions:** Chandra Howard (young adult nonfiction).

● See also listing for Greenhaven Press.

Nonfiction: Young readers: Animal, biography, nature/environment, science. Middle readers, young adults: biography, careers, geography, history, nature/environment, reference, religion, science, social issues. Recently published *A Worker on the Transcontinental Railroad*, by James Barter (Working Life series, young adult).

How to Contact/Writers: Responds to queries in 3 months.

Illustration: Returns samples with SASE only.

Terms: Work purchased outright from authors; writer-for-hire, flat fee.

MAGINATION PRESS, 750 First Street NE, Washington DC 20002-2984. Website: www.maginationpress.com. Book publisher. **Acquisitions:** Darcie Conner Johnston, managing editor. Publishes up to 10 picture books and young reader titles/year. "We publish books dealing with the psycho/therapeutic treatment or resolution of children's problems and psychological issues, many written by mental health professionals."

● Magination Press is an imprint of the American Psychological Association.

Fiction: All levels: concept, health, multicultural, special needs. Middle readers, some young adult titles. Recently published *Jenny Is Scared: When Sad Things Happen in the World*, by Carol Shuman, illustrated by Cary Pillo (ages 4-8); *Josh's Smiley Faces: A Story About Anger*, by Gina Ditta-Donahue, illustrated by Anne Catherine Blake (ages 3-6); *Why Are You So Sad? A Child's Book About Parental Depression*, by Beth Andrews, illustrated by Nicole Wong (ages 4-8) (all edited by Darcie Johnston).

Nonfiction: All levels: health, social issues, special needs, self help. Picture books, young readers, middle readers: activity.

How to Contact/Writers: Fiction/nonfiction: Submit complete ms. Responds in 6 months. Materials returned only with a SASE. Publishes a book 12-18 months after acceptance.

Illustration: Works with 10-15 illustrators/year. Reviews ms/illustration packages. Will review artwork for future assignments. Responds only if interested, or immediately if SASE or response card is included. We keep all samples on file.

How to Contact/Illustrators: Illustrations only: Query with samples. Original artwork returned at job's completion.

Terms: Pays authors 5-15% in royalties based on actual revenues (net). Pays illustrators by the project; royalties are negotiable. Book catalog and ms guidelines on request with SASE.

MAVAL PUBLISHING, INC., Imprint of Editora Maval, 567 Harrison St., Denver CO 80206. (303)338-8725. Fax: (303)745-6215. E-mail: maval@maval.com. Website: www.maval.com. Book publisher. Estab. 1991. **Acquisitions:** George Waintrub, manager; Mary Hernandez, manuscripts coordinator. Publishes 10 picture books/year. 50% of books by first-time authors.

Fiction: Picture books, young readers, middle readers: adventure, animal, anthology, contemporary, fantasy, health, history, multicultural, nature/environment. Picture books, young readers: concept. Picture books: folktales, sports.

Nonfiction Picture books, young readers, middle readers: adventure, animal, anthology, contemporary, fantasy, health, history, multicultural, nature/environment. Picture books, Young readers: concept. Picture books: folktales, sports.

How to Contact/Writers: Fiction/Nonfiction: Submit outline/synopsis and 1-2 sample chapters. Responds to queries/mss in 3 months. Publishes a book 6-12 months after acceptance. Will consider simultaneous submissions and previously published work.

Illustration: Works with 2 illustrators/year. Reviews ms/illustration packages from artists. Submit manuscript with 1-2 pieces of final art. Contact: George Waintrub, manager. Illustrations only: Query with samples. Contact: George Waintrub, manager. Responds in 2 months. Samples not returned.

Photography: Buys stock.

Terms: Pays authors royalty of 5-7% based on retail price. Pays illustrators royalty of 5-7%. Book catalog and writer's guidelines available for SASE. All imprints included in a single catalog. Catalog available on website.

MARGARET K. McELDERRY BOOKS, 1230 Avenue of the Americas, New York NY 10020. (212)698-7000. Fax: (212)698-2796. E-mail: childrens.submissions@simonandschuster.com. Website: www.simonsayskids.com. Imprint of Simon & Schuster Children's Publishing Division. Editor at Large: Margaret K. McElderry. **Manuscript Acquisitions:** Emma D. Dryden, vice president and editorial director. **Art Acquisitions:** Ann Bobco, executive art director. Publishes 10-12 picture books/year; 2-4 young reader titles/year; 8-10 middle reader titles/year; and 5-7 young adult titles/year. 10% of books by first-time authors; 33% of books from agented writers. "Margaret K. McElderry Books publishes original hardcover trade books for children from pre-school age through young adult. This list includes picture books, easy-to-read books, fiction for eight to twelve-year-olds, poetry, fantasy and young adult fiction. The style and subject matter of the books we publish is almost unlimited. We do not publish textbooks, coloring and activity books, greeting cards, magazines, pamphlets, or religious publications."

● Margaret K. McElderry Books is not currently accepting unsolicited mss. Queries are accepted via mail and e-mail. McElderry title *Saffy's Angel*, by Hilary McKay, won a 2002 Boston Globe-Horn Book Honor Award for Fiction and Poetry. Their title *The Life History of a Star*, by Kelly Easton, won a 2001 Golden Kite Honor.

Fiction: Young readers: adventure, contemporary, fantasy, history, poetry. Middle readers: adventure, contemporary, fantasy, humor, mystery. Young adults: contemporary, fantasy, mystery. "Always interested in publishing humorous picture books, original beginning reader stories, and strong poetry." Average word length: picture books—500; young readers—2,000; middle readers—10,000-20,000; young adults—45,000-50,000. Recently published *Bear Wants More*, by Karma Wilson, illustrated by Jane Chapman; *Mathmatickles*, by Betsy Franco, illustrated by Steven Salerno; *The Puppeteer's Apprentice*, by D. Anne Love; *Izzy's Place*, by Marc Kornblatt.

Nonfiction: Young readers, young adult teens, biography, history. Average word length: picture books—500-1,000; young readers—1,500-3,000; middle readers—10,000-20,000; young adults—30,000-45,000. Recently published *Shout, Sister, Shout!*, by Roxane Orgill.

How to Contact/Writers: Fiction/nonfiction: Submit query and 3 sample chapters with SASE; may also include brief résumé of previous publishing credits. Accepts queries through e-mail at childrens.submissions@simonandschuster.com. "Please clarify in the subject of your e-mail that your query is intended for Margaret K. McElderry Books." Responds to queries in 1 month; mss in 3 months. Publishes a book 18 months after contract signing. Will consider simultaneous submissions (only if indicated as such).

Illustration: Works with 20-30 illustrators/year. Query with samples; provide promo sheet or tearsheets; arrange personal portfolio review. Contact: Ann Bobco, executive art director. Responds to art samples in 3 months. Samples returned with SASE or samples filed.

Terms: Pays authors royalty based on retail price. Pays illustrators royalty based on retail price. Pays photographers by the project. Original artwork returned at job's completion. Manuscript guidelines free on request with SASE.

Tips: "We're looking for strong, original fiction. We are always interested in picture books for the youngest age reader."

MEADOWBROOK PRESS, 5451 Smetana Dr., Minnetonka MN 55343-9012. (952)930-1100. Fax: (952)930-1940. Website: www.meadowbrookpress.com. Book publisher. **Manuscript Acquisitions:** Submissions Editor. **Art Acquisitions:** Art Director. Publishes 1-2 middle readers/year; and 2-4 young readers/year. 20% of books by first-time authors; 10% of books from agented writers. Publishes children's activity books, arts-and-crafts books and how-to books.

- Meadowbrook does not accept unsolicited children's picture books, short stories or novels. They are primarily a nonfiction press. The publisher offers specific guidelines for children's poetry. Be sure to specify the type of project you have in mind when requesting guidelines.

Nonfiction: Young readers, middle readers: activity books, arts/crafts, how-to. Average word length: varies. Recently published *Arts and Crafts Busy Book*, by Trish Kieffer (activity book) and *Hocus Jokus*, by Steve Sharney.

How to Contact/Writers: Nonfiction: Query or submit outline/synopsis with SASE. Responds to queries in 3 months. Publishes a book 1-2 years after acceptance. Send a business-sized SASE and 2 first-class stamps for free writer's guidelines and book catalog before submitting ideas. Will consider simultaneous submissions.

Illustration: Works with 2 illustrators/year. Reviews ms/illustration packages from artists. Submit ms with 2-3 pieces of nonreturnable samples. Illustrations only: Responds only if interested. Samples filed.

Photography: Buys photos from freelancers. Buys stock. Model/property releases required. Submit cover letter.

Terms: Pays authors in royalties of 5-7½% based on retail price. Offers average advance payment of $2,000-4,000. Pays illustrators per project. Pays photographers by the project. Book catalog available for 5 × 11 SASE and 2 first-class stamps; ms guidelines and artists guidelines available for SASE.

Tips: "Illustrators and writers should send for our free catalog and guidelines before submitting their work to us. Also, illustrators should take a look at the books we publish to determine whether their style is consistent with ours. Writers should also note the style and content patterns of our books. Please correspond with us by mail before telephoning with questions about your submission. We work with the printed word and will respond more effectively to your questions if we have something in front of us."

MERIWETHER PUBLISHING LTD., 885 Elkton Dr., Colorado Springs CO 80907-3557. Fax: (719)594-9916. E-mail: merpeds@aol.com. Website: www.meriwetherpublishing.com. Book publisher. Estab. 1969. **Manuscript Acquisitions:** Ted Zapel, educational drama; Rhonda Wray, religious drama. "We do most of our artwork in-house; we do not publish for the children's elementary market." 75% of books by first-time authors; 5% of books from agented writers. "Our niche is drama. Our books cover a wide variety of theatre subjects from play anthologies to theatrecraft. We publish books of monologs, duologs, short one-act plays, scenes for students, acting textbooks, how-to speech and theatre textbooks, improvisation and theatre games. Our Christian books cover worship on such topics as clown ministry, storytelling, banner-making, drama ministry, children's worship and more. We also publish anthologies of Christian sketches. We do not publish works of fiction or devotionals."

Fiction: Middle readers, young adults: anthology, contemporary, humor, religion. "We publish plays, not prose-fiction."

Nonfiction: Middle readers: activity books, how-to, religion, textbooks. Young adults: activity books, drama/theater arts, how-to church activities, religion. Average length: 250 pages. Recently published *New 1-Act Plays for Acting Students* by Deb Bert and Norman Bert; and *Millenium Monologs*, by Gerald Lee Ratliff.

How to Contact/Writers: Nonfiction: Query or submit outline/synopsis and sample chapters. Responds to queries in 3 weeks; mss in 2 months. Publishes a book 6-12 months after acceptance. Will consider simultaneous submissions.

Illustration: Works with 2 illustrators/year. Query first. Query with samples; send résumé, promo sheet or tearsheets. Samples returned with SASE. Samples kept on file. Originals returned at job's completion.

Terms: Pays authors in royalties of 10% based on retail or wholesale price. Outright purchase $500-1,000. Royalties based on retail or wholesale price. Book catalog for SAE and $2 postage; ms guidelines for SAE and 1 first-class stamp.

Tips: "We are currently interested in finding unique treatments for theater arts subjects: scene books, how-to books, musical comedy scripts, monologs and short plays for teens."

N̄ ▢ MERKOS PUBLICATIONS, Imprint of Merkos L'Inyone; Chinuch, 291 Kingston Ave., Brooklyn NY 11213. (718)778-0226. Fax: (718)778-4148. E-mail: orders@kehotonline.com. Website: www.kehotonline.com. Estab. 1941. Specializes in Judaica, nonfiction, fiction, educational material. **Acquisitions:** Yonason Gordon, project coordinator. Imprints: Merkos Publications; Icehot Publication Society. Publishes 4 picture books/year; 4 young readers/year; 4 middle readers/ year; and 4 young adult titles/year. 30% of books by first-time authors. "A Jewish book publisher dedicated to fine Chasidic literature."

Fiction: Picture books, young readers, middle readers, young adults: religion. Recently published *The Money in the Honey*, by Aidel Buckmon (ages 9-11, picture book); *The Bat Mitzvah Club:Debbie's Story*, by Shayna Meiseles (ages 9-12, novel); and *A Touch of the High Holidays*, by Deborah Glazer (ages 0-3, board book).

Nonfiction: Picture books, young readers, middle readers, young adults: religion.

How to Contact/Writers: Fiction/nonfiction: Query. Responds to queries in 2 weeks; mss in 4 months. Publishes a book 6 months after acceptance.

Illustration: Uses color artwork only. Reviews ms/illustration packages from artists. Query. Illustrations only: query with samples. Responds in 2 weeks. Samples not returned; samples filed.

Terms: Payment negotiable. Originals returned at job's completion. Book catalog available online. All imprints included in a single catalog.

Tips: "We are the publishing house of Chabad-Lubavitch. As such, it's best to familiarize yourself with the material we put out either through our website or your local Lubavitch emissary."

insider report

'In desperate times, hold tight to your dreams'

In 1999, the only thing standing between Ann Purmell and her elementary education degree was the completion of her student teaching. That is, until Purmell herself became unable to stand when a rare incurable autoimmune disease left her bedridden. Amazingly, being struck by the disease eventually led to the publication of Purmell's first book, *Apple Cider Making Days*, illustrated by Joanne Friar (Millbrook Press)—the first of five picture books and counting.

Ann Purmell

Photo: Marcia Butterfield

As Purmell watched her dream of teaching dissolve, she turned to writing to work through her depression, piling her bed with legal pads that would become her journals. "In one of my darkest hours, I don't even know where it came from, I wrote 'In desperate times, hold tight to your dreams.'"

Purmell had loved writing her entire life, but never devoted herself to the task. Easily discouraged, she abandoned her writing projects at the first sign of rejection. "In the past I'd never written with a daily discipline, but with journaling I was doing it every single day."

Once Purmell's health improved a bit, so did her outlook. She turned her focus from personal writing to freelancing for her local newspaper and business magazine. "There was a period of time for about ten months where I was in a great deal of physical pain but not bedridden. I would sit down in front of the computer and write while my kids were in school, for five or six hours, and not feel any pain," she says.

"Now I look back on my life and realize I'd been given many opportunities to become a writer. But when I was young I pretty much turned up my nose at them because I knew writing jobs didn't pay well and I needed to make as much money as I could to put my husband through dental school. Plus I'd never taken a formal writing class. As I got older and my husband became well-established, I just couldn't believe my writing would be good enough that anyone would want to read, let alone pay for, what I wrote. So really I just fell into freelancing because there was nothing else I could do because of my illness."

In May 2000, at the height of what had become a successful freelancing career, Purmell experienced what she can only describe as "being hit by lightening" with the revelation that she didn't want to write local feature articles. She felt her true calling was to write for children.

"When I was younger I thought that having my own family, having my own kids, would be enough. I would be giving the world a couple of great kids and when I got old and died, that would be enough for me. Well, when I had to face death at the age of 45, I realized that wasn't enough. It just wasn't enough."

Purmell gave notice to the editor she worked for and spent the summer writing and submitting children's manuscripts—all of which were rejected. Then she got the idea to write from an experience she'd had on a field trip to an apple orchard with her daughter's class. "We had three classrooms of five-year-olds, and in the middle of it I looked around at all these little kids who had been really hyper. And everybody was standing still and listening. They were fascinated by the whole process of cider making."

She had written a business article on the orchard soon after her visit, and had talked to the cider mill's owner, who was worried that because of new pasteurization regulations, family-owned cider mills might start going out of business. "That was another thing that got me thinking about this book—if that was true, I want a record for future children so they could see what this life was about."

A year later, she found herself writing a picture book manuscript. It took only a week, but she spent the entire week revising and rewriting to get it as tight as she could. "I have always loved picture books—I own probably 600 or 700 of them. I bought them like crazy after my kids were born," she says.

When Purmell began to research her cover letter, she couldn't find even one other children's book on cider making. At that point she realized what had begun as writing from passion was unintentionally filling a niche. Having studied to be an elementary school teacher, she knew teachers usually did fall apple cider units. She included that angle in her cover letter, saying teachers or librarians could use this book if the students were unable to actually go out to a cider mill on a field trip. On Oct. 4, 2000, she sent the manuscript to a few publishers. She received a letter dated just nine days later from Millbrook Press proposing a contract to publish the book.

Ann Purmell's *Where Wild Babies Sleep* (Boyds Mills Press, 2003) is a natural bedtime story, letting readers explore the native nesting spots of baby animals like puffins, monkeys, and dormice, as they nestle in to rest for the night.

Illustration © 2002 Joanne Friar. Reprinted with permission.

Ann Purmell's first book, *Apple Cider Making Days* (Millbrook Press, 2002) is a pictorial tribute to the art of the independent cider press. Alex, Abigail, and the rest of the family help Grandpa with his harvest while also giving young readers a lesson in process from tree to market, making this book an autumn favorite of teachers and librarians.

Purmell became very involved in her book's production when she and her editor agreed that the success of the book hinged on accurate illustrations of the mill's equipment. She took pictures of the machinery and sent them to her editor, who forwarded them to the illustrator. Copies of each drawing were sent to Purmell for her approval throughout the illustration process. She loved having that kind of input, and now uses these preliminary drawings in the talks and readings she does in schools and libraries to promote her book.

"Essentially I'm physically disabled, so I cannot work, and having my own classroom is out of the question. It was very disappointing to me to lose that opportunity to be with children and to teach them. At a subconscious level I was probably also thinking if I somehow am able to publish a children's book then schools are going to invite me to come in."

While *Apple Cider Making Days* is Purmell's first success, it hasn't been her last. She's followed up with *Giraffes* (Random House), *Where Wild Babies Sleep* (Boyds Mills Press) and *Christmas Tree Farming* (Holiday House). And she has an agent who is circulating seven or eight more of her manuscripts. "Flabbergasted is the word that describes my whole writing career. I just can't believe what has happened and is happening for me."

The publication of her books carries deep meaning for Purmell. "I wanted something fairly permanent that was not ever going to get old, that was not ever going to get sick, that was not ever going to die," she says. "This is the only reason I became a writer. I used to be so sensitive about rejection. Now I realize, even if I do live to be 70, that my time—everyone's time—on earth is quite limited. That's what motivates me everyday to sit down and to write and to get as much written as I can. And I want to get as many books published as I possibly can."

Although Purmell fell into writing through her potentially fatal illness, with which she continues to struggle, she does have advice for aspiring authors: "Writing is a craft. You start as an apprentice and learn everything you can about the art of writing and the business of publishing. Get a mentor, someone who has published and is willing to guide you through the maze. A mentor is much more than a person to critique your work."

Today, the only thing standing between Purmell and a long successful career is her disease. Those words she wrote in her journal years ago still hang in her writing space to remind her of where she has been and where she is capable of going. "I kept thinking, if I could do anything in the world, my dream was to be a writer. And it really has come true."

—Jessica Yerega

MILKWEED EDITIONS, 1011 Washington Ave. S., Suite 300, Minneapolis MN 55415-1246. (612)332-3192. Fax: (612)215-2550. E-mail: editor@milkweed.org. Website: www.milkweed.org. Book Publisher. Estab. 1980. **Manuscript Acquisitions:** H. Emerson Blake, editor-in-chief. Publishes 3-4 middle readers/year. 25% of books by first-time authors. "Milkweed Editions publishes with the intention of making a humane impact on society, in the belief that literature is a transformative art uniquely able to convey the essential experiences of the human heart and spirit. To that end, Milkweed Editions publishes distinctive voices of literary merit in handsomely designed, visually dynamic books, exploring the ethical, cultural, and esthetic issues that free societies need continually to address."

Fiction: Middle readers: adventure, contemporary, fantasy, multicultural, nature/environment, suspense/mystery. Does not want to see anthologies, folktales, health, hi-lo, picture books, poetry, religion, romance, sports. Average length: middle readers—90-200 pages. Recently published *The Trouble with Jeremy Chance*, by George Harrar (historical), *The $66 Summer*, by John Armistead (multicultural, mystery); *The Ocean Within*, by V.M. Caldwell (contemporary, nature).

How to Contact/Writers: Fiction: Submit complete ms. Responds to mss in 6 months. Publishes a book 1 year after acceptance. Will consider simultaneous submissions.

Illustration: Works with 2-4 illustrators/year. Reviews ms/illustration packages from artists. Query; submit ms with dummy. Illustrations only: Query with samples; provide résumé, promo sheet, slides, tearsheets and client list. Samples filed or returned with SASE; samples filed. Originals returned at job's completion.

Terms: Pays authors royalty of 7½% based on retail price. Offers advance against royalties. Illustrators' contracts are decided on an individual basis. Sends galleys to authors. Book catalog available for $1.50 to cover postage; ms guidelines available for SASE or at website. Must include SASE with ms submission for its return.

◻ **THE MILLBROOK PRESS**, P.O. Box 335, 2 Old New Milford Rd., Brookfield CT 06804. (203)740-2220. Fax: (203)775-5643. Website: www.millbrookpress.com. Book publisher. Estab. 1989. **Manuscript Acquisitions:** Editorial Assistant. **Art Acquisitions:** Associate Art Director. Publishes 15 picture books/year; 30 young readers/year; 20 middle readers/year; and 15 young adult titles/year. 10% of books by first-time authors; 20% of books from agented authors. Publishes nonfiction, concept-oriented/educational books. Publishes under Twenty-First Century Books imprint also.

Nonfiction: Picture books: animal, biography, history, multicultural, nature/environment, science. Young readers: animal, arts/crafts, biography, careers, cooking, geography, health, hi-lo, history, multicultural, nature/environment, religion, science, sports. Middle readers: biography, careers, geography, health, hi-lo, history, multicultural, nature/environment, religion, science, social issues, sports. Young adults: biography, history, multicultural, nature/environment, reference, science, social issues. Average word length: young readers—5,000; middle readers—10,000; young adult/teens—20,000. Published *Wildshots: The World of the Wildlife Photographer*, by Nathan Aaseng (grades 5-8, nature and photography); *Meet My Grandmother: She's A Children's Book Author*, by Lisa Tucker McElroy, photographs by Joel Benjamin (grades 2-4, current events/history); *Little Numbers*, by Edward Packard, illustrated by Sal Murdocca (grades K-3, math/concepts); *Crafts From Your Favorite Children's Songs*, by Kathy Ross, illustrated by Vicky Enright (grades K-3, arts and crafts); *Adoption Today*, by Ann E. Weiss (grade 7-up, social studies). No fiction, picture books, activity books or other novelty submissions.

How to Contact/Writers: Send for guidelines with SASE *before* submitting. We do not accept unsolicited manuscripts, guidelines give specific instructions.

Illustration: Work with approximately 30 illustrators/year. Illustrations only: Query with samples; provide résumé, business card, promotional literature or tearsheets to be kept on file. No samples returned. Samples filed. Responds only if interested.

Photography: Buys stock.

Terms: Pays author royalty of 5-7½% based on wholesale price or work purchased outright. Offers advances. Pays illustrators by the project, royalty of 3-7% based on wholesale price. Sends galleys to authors. Manuscript and artist's guidelines by SASE. Address to: Manuscript Guidelines, The Millbrook Press . . . Book catalog for 9 × 11 SASE. Address to: Catalogues, The Millbrook Press . . .

◪ **MITCHELL LANE PUBLISHERS, INC.**, P.O. Box 196, Hockessin DE 19707. (302)834-9646. Fax: (302)834-4164. E-mail: mitchelllane@mitchelllane.com. Website: www.mitchelllane.com. Book publisher. **Acquisitons:** Barbara Mitchell, president. Publishes 20 young adult titles/year. "We publish multicultural biographies of role models for children and young adults."

Nonfiction: Young readers, middle readers, young adults: biography, multicultural. Average word length: 4,000-50,000 words. Recently published *Robert Jarvick and the First Artificial Heart*, by John Bankston (Unlocking the Secrets of Science); and *Francisco Vasquez de Coronado*, by Jim Whiting (Latinos in American History).

How to Contact/Writers: Most assignments are work-for-hire.

Illustration: Works with 2-3 illustrators/year. Reviews ms/illustration packages from artists. Query. Illustration only: query with samples; send résumé, portfolio, slides, tearsheets. Responds only if interested. Samples not returned; samples filed.

Photography: Buys stock images. Needs photos of famous and prominent minority figures. Captions required. Uses color prints or digital images. Submit cover letter, résumé, published samples, stock photo list.

Terms: Work purchased outright for $350-2,000. Pays illustrators by the project (range: $40-250). Sends galleys to authors.

Tips: "Most of our assignments are work-for-hire. Submit résumé and samples of work to be considered for future assignments."

◻ **MONDO PUBLISHING**, 980 Avenue of the Americas, New York NY 10018. (212)268-3560. Fax: (212)268-3561. Website: www.mondopub.com. Book publisher. **Acquisitions:** editorial staff. Publishes 60 picture and chapter books/year. 10% of books by first-time authors. Publishes various categories. "Our motto is 'creative minds creating ways to create lifelong readers.' We publish for both educational and trade markets, aiming for the highest quality books for both."

Fiction: Picture books, young readers, middle readers: adventure, animal, contemporary, fantasy, folktales, history, humor, multicultural, nature/environment, poetry, sports. Multicultural needs include: stories about children in different cultures or about children of different backgrounds in a US setting. Recently published *Herbert Fieldmouse: Secret Agent*, by Kevin O'Malley (ages 6-12); *Blueberry Mouse*, by Alice Low (ages 4-6); *Eaglesmount: The Silver Horn*, by Cherith Baldry (ages 8-12); *Right Outside My Window*, by Mary Ann Hoberman; *Jake Greenthumb*, by Loki (ages 4-8).

Nonfiction: Picture books, young readers, middle readers: animal, biography, geography, how-to, multicultural, nature/environment, science, sports. Recently published *Seahorses*, by Sylvia James; *How to Make a Collage*, by Sue and Will Johnson.

How to Contact/Writers: Fiction/Nonfiction: Query or submit complete ms. Responds to queries in 1 month; mss in 6 months. Will consider simultaneous submissions. Manuscripts returned with SASE. Queries must also have SASE.

Illustration: Works with 40 illustrators/year. Reviews ms/illustration packages from illustrators. Illustration only: Query with samples, résumé, portfolio. Responds only if interested. Samples returned with SASE; samples filed. Send attention: Art Deptartment.

Photography: Occasionally uses freelance photographers. Buys stock images. Uses mostly nature photos. Uses color prints, transparencies, slides or digital images.

Terms: Pays authors royalty of 2-5% based on wholesale/retail price for trade titles. Offers advance based on project. Pays illustrators by the project (range: 3,000-9,000), royalty of 2-4% based on retail price. Pays photographers by the project or per photo. Sends galleys to authors depending on project. Originals returned to artists at job's completion. Book catalogs available for 9×12 SASE with $3.20 postage.

Tips: "Prefer illustrators with book experience or a good deal of experience in illustration projects requiring consistency of characters and/or setting over several illustrations. Prefer manuscripts targeted to trade market plus crossover to educational market."

N MOREHOUSE PUBLISHING CO., 4775 Linglestown Rd., Harrisburg PA 17112. (717)541-8130. Fax: (717)541-8136. E-mail: dfarring@morehousegroup.com. Website: www.morehousegroup.com. Book publisher. Estab. 1884. **Manuscript Acquisitions:** Debra Farrington, editorial director. **Art Acquisitions:** Ryan Masteller, managing editor. Publishes 4 picture books/year. 25% of books by first-time authors.

Fiction: Picture Books: spirituality, religion. Wants to see new and creative approaches to theology for children. Recently published *Bless This Day*, by Anne E. Kitch, illustrated by Joni Oeltjenbruns.

Nonfiction: Picture Books: religion and prayers.

How to Contact/Writers: Fiction/nonfiction: Submit ms (1,500 word limit). Responds to mss in 2 months. Publishes a book 2 years after acceptance.

Illustration: Works with 2-3 illustrators/year. Reviews ms/illustration packages from artists. Submit résumé, tearsheets. Samples returned with SASE; samples filed.

Terms: Pays authors royalty based on net price. Offers modest advance payment. Pays illustrators royalty based on net price. Sends galleys to authors. Book catalog free on request if SASE ($2 postage) is supplied.

MORGAN REYNOLDS PUBLISHING, 620 S. Elm St., Suite 223, Greensboro NC 27406. (336)275-1311. Fax: (336)275-1152. E-mail: editorial@morganreynolds.com. Website: www.morganreynolds.com. **Acquisitions:** Elaine Hammer, editor. Book publisher. Publishes 24 young adult titles/year. 50% of books by first-time authors. Morgan Reynolds publishes nonfiction books for juvenile and young adult readers. We prefer lively, well-written biographies of interesting figures for our biography series. Subjects may be contemporary or historical. Books for our Great Events series should take an insightful and exciting look at critical periods.

Nonfiction: Middle readers, young adults/teens: biography, history. Average word length: 20,000-25,000. Recently published *Tycho Brahe: Mapping the Heavens*, by William J. Boerst; and *Great Communicator: The Story of Ronald Reagan*, by Jeff C. Young.

How to Contact/Writers: Prefers to see entire ms. Query; submit outline/synopsis with at least 1 sample chapter. Responds to queries/mss in 6 weeks. Publishes a book 1 year after acceptance. Will consider simultaneous submissions.

Terms: Pays authors negotiated price. Offers advances and royalties. Sends galleys to authors. Manuscript guidelines available for SASE. Visit website for complete catalog.

Tips: "Familiarize yourself with our titles before sending a query or submission. Visit our website."

MOUNT OLIVE COLLEGE PRESS, 634 Henderson St., Mount Olive NC 28365. (919)658-2502. Book publisher. Estab. 1990. **Acquisitions:** Pepper Worthington, editor. Publishes 1 middle reader/year. 85% of books by first-time authors.

Fiction: Middle readers: animal, humor, poetry. Average word length: middle readers—3,000 words.

Nonfiction: Middle readers: nature/environment, religion, self help. Average word length: middle readers—3,000 words.

How to Contact/Writers: Submit complete ms or outline/synopsis and 3 sample chapters. Responds to queries in 1-2 years.

Illustration: Uses b&w artwork only. Submit ms with 50% of final art. Contact: Pepper Worthington, editor. Responds in 6-12 months if interested. Samples not returned.

Terms: Payment negotiated individually. Book catalog available for SAE and 1 first-class stamp.

☑ TOMMY NELSON®, Imprint of Thomas Nelson, Inc., P.O. Box 141000, Nashville TN 37214. (615)889-9000. Fax: (615)902-2219. Website: www.tommynelson.com. Book publisher. **Acquisitions:** Dee Ann Grand, Vice President/associate publisher. Publishes 15 picture books/year; 20 young readers/year; and 25 middle readers/year. Evangelical Christian publisher.

Fiction: Picture books: concept, humor, religion. Young readers: adventure, concept, humor, religion. Middle readers:

adventure, humor, religion, sports, suspense/mystery. Young adults: adventure, problem novels, religion, sports, suspense/mystery. Recently published *Prayer of Jabez* series (4 books), and *Nightmare Academy*, by Frank Peretti.

Nonfiction: Picture books, young readers: activity books, religion, self help. Middle readers, young adults: reference, religion, self help. Recently published *He Chose You*, by Max Lucado.

How to Contact/Writers: Does not accept unsolicited mss, queries or proposals.

Illustration: Query with samples. Responds only if interested. Samples filed. Contact: Patti Evans, art director.

Tips: "Know the CBA market—and avoid preachiness."

NEW VOICES PUBLISHING, Imprint of KidsTerrain, Inc., P.O. Box 560, Wilmington MA 01887. (978)658-2131. Fax: (978)988-8833. E-mail: info@Kidsterrain.com. Website: www.kidsterrain.com. Estab. 2000. Specializes in fiction. **Manuscript/Art Acquisitions:** Book Editor. Publishes 2 picture books/year. 95% of books by first-time authors.

Fiction: Picture books, young readers: multicultural. Average word length: picture books—500; young readers—500-1,200. Recently published *Last Night I Left Earth for Awhile*, written and illustrated by Natalie L. Brown-Douglas (ages 4-8).

How to Contact/Writers: Fiction: No queries accepted until 2005. Publishes book 12-18 months after acceptance. Will consider simultaneous submissions.

Illustration: Works with 2 illustrators/year. Uses color artwork only. Reviews ms/illustration packages from artists. No queries accepted until 2005. Responds in 2 weeks. Samples returned with SASE.

Terms: Pays authors royalty of 10-15% based on wholesale price. Pays illustrators by the project or royalty. Sends galleys to authors. Offers writer's guidelines for SASE.

☑ Ⓐ 🏵 **NORTH-SOUTH BOOKS**, 875 Sixth Ave., Suite 1901, New York NY 10001. (212)706-4545. Website: www.northsouth.com. Imprint: Night Sky. U.S. office of Nord-Siid Verlag, Switzerland. Publishes 100 titles/year.

● North-South and its imprint do not accept queries or unsolicited manuscripts. Their title *Noah's Art*, written and illustrated by Jerry Pinkney won a 2003 Caldecott Honor.

☐ **NORTHWORD BOOKS FOR YOUNG READERS**, NorthWord Press, 18705 Lake Dr. E., Chanhassen MN 55317. (952)936-4700. Fax: (942)932-0386. Website: www.northwordpress.com. Specializes in mass market books, fiction, trade books, educational material, nonfiction. "Our mission at NorthWord Books for Young Readers is to publish books for children that encourage a love for the natural world." **Manuscript and Art Acquisitions:** Submissions Editor. Publishes 22 books/year—6-8 picture picture books (ages 3-5, 5-8), 12-14 nonfiction (ages 5-8, 7-11, 8-10).

Fiction: Picture books, young readers: animal, nature/environment. No novels. Average word length: picture books—1,000. Recently published *Anna's Table*, by Eve Bunting (ages 5-8); *The Day I Could Fly*, by Lynn Crosbie Loux (ages 4-7); *The Secret of the First One Up*, by Iris Hiskey Arno (ages 5-8).

Nonfiction: Picture books, young readers, middle readers: animal, arts/crafts, cooking, hobbies, how-to: all must relate to nature/environment. Recently published *Everything Dog* and *Everything Cat*, by Marty Crisp (2 titles) (ages 8-11, nonfiction books); *Let's Rock! Rock Painting for Kids*, by Linda Kranz (nonfiction series) and baby board book series: *Desert Babies*, *Forest Babies*, *Polar Babies* and *Prairie Babies*.

How to Contact/Writers: Picture books: Submit complete ms. All projects over 1,000 words: Query. Responds in 3 months. Publishes a book 2-3 years after acceptance. Will consider simultaneous submissions.

Illustration: Works with 10 illustrators/year. Uses color artwork only. Reviews ms/illustration packages from artists. Query. Illustrations only: Query with samples; send résumé and tearsheets. Responds in 3 months only if interested. Samples returned with SASE.

Photography: Buys stock images. Contact: Photo Editor. Uses photos of animals *wildlife and natural history*. "Film must be labeled with species (common and Latin names), the more information on photo the better." Uses 35mm, 2¼×2¼, 4×5 transparencies. Submit cover letter, published samples, stock photo list.

Terms: Payment depends on project—most nonfiction series is flat fee if commissioned by us—some (fiction, usually) is advance against royalty (usually list). Sends galleys for review; dummies to illustrators. Originals returned to artist at job's completion. Book catalog available with $1.06 SASE. Guidelines available with SASE.

Tips: "Always research the house you are submitting to. Make sure your work is appropriate for that house. *Always* include SASE with sufficient postage for all materials you'd like returned and for editor's response."

☐ **THE OLIVER PRESS, INC.**, Charlotte Square, 5707 W. 36th St., Minneapolis MN 55416-2510. (952)926-8981. Fax: (952)926-8965. E-mail: queries@oliverpress.com. Website: www.oliverpress.com. Book publisher. **Acquisitions:** Denise Sterling, Jenna Anderson. Publishes 8 young adult titles/year. 10% of books by first-time authors. "We publish collective biographies of people who made an impact in one area of history, including science, government, archaeology, business and crime. Titles from The Oliver Press can connect young adult readers with their history to give them the confidence that only knowledge can provide. Such confidence will prepare them for the lifelong responsibilities of citizenship. Our books will introduce students to people who made important discoveries and great decisions."

Nonfiction: Middle reader, young adults: biography, history, multicultural, social issues, history of science and technology. "Authors should only suggest ideas that fit into one of our existing series. We would like to add to our Innovators series on the history of technology and our Business Builders series on leaders of industry." Average word length: young adult—20,000 words. Recently published *Business Builders in Real Estate*, by Nathan Aaseng (ages 10 and up, collective biography); *Women with Wings*, by Jacqueline McLean (ages 10 and up, collective biography); *Space Flight: Crossing the Last Frontier*, by Jason Richie (ages 10 and up, collective biography); and *Ranchers, Homesteaders, and Traders: Frontiersmen of the South-Central States*, by Kieran Doherty (ages 10 and up, collective biography).

insider report

'We think nature is pretty cool'

Aimee Jackson

Picture book, beginning reader, young adult. History, fantasy, science fiction. As varied as children's books are, most writers have their favorites and this passion often guides the work they pursue.

The same holds true for editors. Large or small house, educational or regional publisher, editors' passions often affect where each editor chooses to work.

Such passion fueled Aimee Jackson's move from Rising Moon to NorthWord. "When I became the editor for Rising Moon, we were publishing titles for a national market," says Jackson. "After a management change, the company decided to stop publishing national titles and publish regionally-based titles only." But Jackson's desire to work on an imprint with a national list remained.

Then Creative Publishing International added the position of Executive Editor of Books for Young Readers to their NorthWord Press imprint. They approached Jackson who accepted the job, an opportunity to again pursue her passion. "NorthWord was a wonderful fit. We are a niche imprint," says Jackson, "but our titles are geared for a national audience. And even though NorthWord is part of a larger company, it is a very small, manageable imprint with editors who are passionate about the themes we publish."

Jackson's dedicated staff includes Kristen McCurry, Associate Editor, who edits most of the nonfiction. "Being small, we both do a little bit of everything!" says Jackson.

NorthWord offers benefits not available at a small press. "The good thing about being part of a larger company is having the marketing and sales backing that smaller companies sometimes lack," Jackson says. "We have a tremendous sales force with coverage in every possible sales channel. We are also an international publisher with reps who sell all over the world. Nature is a very universal theme, so our books travel very well." Here Jackson offers advice to writers passionate about nature.

How has NorthWord's list changed since your arrival?
NorthWord was primarily a nonfiction series publisher. These types of books continue to be our "bread and butter," but we have expanded our line and stretched the nature theme to include more traditional story picture books, books for younger children including preschool concept books, board books for babies and toddlers, and we have just published our first craft book. We also continue to add new series to the line that will have equal appeal in both the trade and school/library markets, and we have some interesting new books on the horizon that continue to stretch our animal and nature themes in new and exciting ways.

How do NorthWord's nature titles differ from those of other publishers?
A lot of others who publish books similar in theme to ours tend to focus more on the instit-

Kids'
FAQs

Everything
BUG

What Kids Really
Want to Know
About Insects
and Spiders

by
Cherie Winner

Cherie Winner's *Everything Bug: What Kids Really Want to Know About Insects and Spiders* (2004) is just one example of the nature-themed nonfiction books published by NorthWord Press, new home of editor Aimee Jackson. All the books in NorthWord's Kids' FAQs series, like *Everything Bug*, answer real questions from real kids culled from school visits—so they really know they're publishing what kids really want to know.

tional markets. While we strive for all our books to work well in the school and library markets, our first focus is trade. Our content is still full of information perfect for public and school libraries and in-classroom use, but our books tend to have more of a trade look and feel. We want them to be informational *and* fun for kids—the types of books they will pick up themselves in a bookstore or check out on their own at the library.

Given similar passions, what is the most important skill a writer can bring NorthWord?
Good writing. Good research skills.

How does this emphasis on research play into submitting nonfiction to NorthWord Press? Does the author need to be an expert on the topic they choose to write about?
We have authors who are scientists first and writers second; and we have authors who are children's book writers first who either have a passion for a particular animal or aspect of nature, or are tremendous researchers who can make any topic fascinating for kids. We love both types of writers!

If the writers are not experts in the field, we expect them to find expert readers to review their work, and we usually cite the expert readers in the credits to lend credibility to the material. I think any writer with a journalistic mentality (like a curious kid!) can write just about anything. It tends to be a very rewarding experience for everyone involved.

What is the quickest way for a new writer to make a good impression?
Professionalism, professionalism, professionalism! All romance aside, this is a business and we expect our authors to treat it as such. Author materials should be presented professionally, as though they were applying for a job. That includes both presentation and showing us that they've done the research—not just on the subject matter, but also on the competition and can show us what sets their book apart from others on the same subject.

Are you likely to request a rewrite on a manuscript that isn't quite right for your list?
We would only do so if it was something we thought we would seriously consider publishing. Even then, we wouldn't ask for an exclusive and we wouldn't make any promises that a rewrite would ensure a publishing spot with us. We might say, "If you choose to do a rewrite, we would love to reconsider it," or something like that. And when we say it, we really mean it. There's something there we like—the writing, the writing style, the authors credentials, the subject but maybe not the approach, etc.

What should an author inspire in your readers?
We hope our books inspire curiosity and interest and awe about the natural world, and in doing so, encourage a love and respect for our planet. Basically, we think nature is pretty cool, and we hope kids will think so too after they read our books.

Writers who can pass such a passion for nature on to their readers will find NorthWord Press editors eager to read their work.
—*Sue Bradford Edwards*

How to Contact/Writers: Nonfiction: Query with outline/synopsis. Responds in 6 months. Publishes a book approximately 1 year after acceptance.
Photography: Rarely buys photos from freelancers. Buys stock images. Looks primarily for photos of people in the news. Captions required. Uses 8×10 b&w prints. Submit cover letter, résumé and stock photo list.
Terms: Pays authors negotiable royalty. Work purchased outright from authors (fee negotiable). Pays photographers per photo (negotiable). Sends galleys to authors upon request. Book catalog and ms guidelines available online or for SASE.
Tips: "Authors should read some of the books we have already published before sending a query to The Oliver Press."

$□ ONSTAGE PUBLISHING, 214 E. Moulton St. NE, Decatur AL 35601. (256)308-2300, (888)420-8879. Website: www.onstagebooks.com. Estab. 1999. Specializes in mass market books, nonfiction, fiction, educational material. **Manuscript Acquisitions:** Dianne Hamilton. Publishes 1 picture book; 1 young readers; 2 middle readers; 1 young adult title/year. 80% of books by first-time authors.
Fiction: Picture books: adventure, contemporary, history, nature/environment, suspense/mystery. Young readers, middle readers: adventure, contemporary, fantasy, history, nature/environment, science fiction, suspense/mystery. Young adults: adventure, contemporary, fantasy, history, humor, science fiction, suspense/mystery. Average word length: picture books—50-100; young readers—100-300; middle readers—5,000 and up; young adults—25,000 and up. Recently published *The Secret of Crybaby Hollow*, by Darren Butler (a middle grade mystery book, ages 8-12, the Abbie Girl Spy adventures).
Nonfiction: All levels: animal, biography, history, music/dance, nature/environment, science, sports. Average word length: picture books—100-2,500; young readers—500-2,500; middle readers—1,000-3,000; young adults—5,000 and up. Recently published *Write Away*, by Margaret Green and Laurel Griffith (educational instruction book designed by elementary teacher that lays out a series of creative writing exercises for grades 1-6); *The Miracle at the Pump*, by Darren Butler, illustrated by Linda Lee (activity book for ages 5-8 based on the early life of Helen Keller).
How to Contact/Writers: Fiction/nonfiction: submit complete ms. Responds to queries/mss in 1 month. Publishes a book 2 years after acceptance. Will consider simultaneous submissions.
Illustration: Reviews ms/illustration packages from artists. Submit ms with 3 pieces of final art. Contact: Dianne Hamilton, senior editor. Illustrations only: arrange personal portfolio review. Responds in 6 weeks. Samples returned with SASE.
Photography: Works on assignment only. Contact: Art Department. Model/property releases required; captions required. Uses color, 5×7, semi gloss prints. Submit cover letter, published samples, stock photo list.
Terms: Pays authors/illustrators/photographers advance plus royalties. Sends galleys to authors; dummies to illustrators. Book catalog available for 9×12 SAE and 3 first-class stamps; ms guidelines available for SASE. Return of original artwork is negotiable. All imprints included in a single catalog. Catalog available on website.
Tips: "Study our catalog and get a sense of the kind of books we publish, so that you know whether your project is likely to be right for us. Electronic publishing will have an impact in the next five years, as choices, more information and more books will be accessible for the consumer. This is a market we are watching."

Ⓜ ORCHARD BOOKS, 557 Broadway, New York NY 10012. (212)343-6782. Fax: (212)343-4890. Website: www.scholastic.com. Imprint of Scholastic, Inc. Book publisher. Editorial Director: Ken Geist. **Manuscript Acquisitions:** Amy Griffin, senior editor. **Art Acquisitions:** David Saylor, art director. "We publish approximately 25 books yearly including fiction, poetry, picture books, and young adult novels." 10% of books by first-time authors.
  • Orchard is not accepting unsolicited manuscripts; query letters only. Orchard's title *Talkin' About Bessie: The Story of Aviator Elizabeth Coleman*, by Nikki Grimes, illustrated by E.B. Lewis, won a 2003 Coretta Scott King Award for illustration and Author Award Honor.
Fiction: All levels: animal, contemporary, history, humor, multicultural, nature/environment, poetry. Recently published *Stuart's Cape*, by Sara Pennypacker, illustrated by Martin Matje; *Giraffes Can't Dance*, by Giles Andreae, illustrated by Guy Parker-Rees; *Midnight for Charlie Bone*, by Jenny Nimmo.
Nonfiction: "We rarely publish nonfiction." Recently published *A Dragon in the Sky*, by Pringle Marshall.
How to Contact/Writers: Query only with SASE. Responds in 3 months.
Illustration: Works with 15 illustrators/year. Art director reviews ms/illustration portfolios. Submit "tearsheets or photocopies or photostats of the work." Responds to art samples in 1 month. Samples returned with SASE. No disks or slides, please.
Terms: Most commonly an advance against list royalties. Sends galleys to authors; dummies to illustrators. Original artwork returned at job's completion.
Tips: "Read some of our books to determine first whether your manuscript is suited to our list."

Ⓝ OUR CHILD PRESS, P.O. Box 4379, Philadelphia PA 19087-0074. Phone/fax: (610)407-0943. E-mail: ocp98@aol.com. Website: www.ourchildpress.com. Book publisher. **Acquisitions:** Carol Hallenbeck, president. 90% of books by first-time authors.
Fiction/Nonfiction: All levels: adoption, multicultural, special needs. Published *Don't Call Me Marda*, written and illustrated by Sheila Kelly Welch; *Is That Your Sister?* by Catherine and Sherry Burin; and *Oliver: A Story About Adoption*, by Lois Wichstrom.
How to Contact/Writers: Fiction/Nonfiction: Query or submit complete ms. Responds to queries/mss in 6 months. Publishes a book 6-12 months after acceptance.
Illustration: Works with 1 illustrator/year. Reviews ms/illustration packages from artists. Manuscript/illustration packages and illustration only: Query first. Submit résumé, tearsheets and photocopies. Responds to art samples in 2 months. Samples returned with SASE; samples kept on file.
Terms: Pays authors in royalties of 5-10% based on wholesale price. Pays illustrators royalties of 5-10% based on wholesale

price. Original artwork returned at job's completion. Book catalog for business-size SAE and 52¢ postage.
Tips: "Won't consider anything not related to adoption."

OUR SUNDAY VISITOR, INC., 200 Noll Plaza, Huntington IN 46750. (260)356-8400. Fax: (260)359-9117. E-mail: booksed@osv.com; jlindsey@osv.com; mdubruiel@osv.com; bmcnamara@osv.com. Website: www.osv.com. Book publisher. **Acquisitions:** Jacquelyn M. Lindsey, Michael Dubruiel, Beth McNamara. Art Director: Eric Schoenig. Publishes primarily religious, educational, parenting, reference and biographies. OSV is dedicated to providing books, periodicals and other products that serve the Catholic Church.

● Our Sunday Visitor, Inc., is publishing only those children's books that tie in to sacramental preparation. Contact the acquisitions editor for ms guidelines and a book catalog.

Nonfiction: Picture books, middle readers, young readers, young adults. Recently published *Just Like Mary*, by Rosemarie Gortler and Donna Piscitelli, illustrated by Mimi Sternhagen.
How to Contact/Writers: Query, submit complete ms, or submit outline/synopsis, and 2-3 sample chapters. Responds to queries/mss in 2 months. Publishes a book 18-24 months after acceptance. Will consider simultaneous submissions, electronic submissions via disk or modem, previously published work.
Illustration: Reviews ms/illustration packages from artists. Illustration only: Query with samples. Contact: Aquisitions Editor. Responds only if interested. Samples returned with SASE; samples filed. Original artwork returned at job's completion.
Photography: Buys photos from freelancers. Contact: Acquisitions Editor.
Terms: Pays authors royalty of 10-12% net. Pays illustrators by the project (range: $200-1,500). Sends galleys to authors; dummies to illustrators. Book catalog available for SASE; ms guidelines available for SASE.
Tips: "Stay in accordance with our guidelines."

THE OVERMOUNTAIN PRESS, P.O. Box 1261, Johnson City TN 37605. (423)926-2691. Fax: (423)929-2464. E-mail: bethw@overmtn.com. Website: www.overmountainpress.com or www.silverdaggermysteries.com. Estab. 1970. Specializes in regional history trade books. **Manuscript Acquisitions:** Jason Weems, senior editor. Publishes 3 picture books/year; 2 young readers/year; 2 middle readers/year. 50% of books by first-time authors. "We are primarily a publisher of southeastern regional history, and we have recently published several titles for children. We consider children's books about Southern Appalachia only!"
Fiction: Picture books: folktales, history. Young readers, middle readers: folktales, history, suspense/mystery. Average word length: picture books—800-1,000; young readers—5,000-10,000; middle readers—20-30,000. Recently published *Bloody Mary: The Mystery of Amanda's Magic Mirror*, by Patrick Bone (young, middle reader); *Bark and Tim*, by Ellen Gidaro and Audrey Vernick; and *Appalachian ABCs*, by Francie Hall, illustrated by Kent Oehm (pre-elementary, picture book).
Nonfiction: Picture books, young readers, middle readers: biography (regional), history (regional). Average word length: picture books—800-1,000; young readers—5,000-10,000; middle readers—20-30,000. Recently published *The Little Squash Seed*, written and illustrated by Gayla Dowdy Seale (preschool-elementary, picture book).
How to Contact/Writers: Fiction/Nonfiction: Submit outline/synopsis and 2 sample chapters. Responds to queries in 2 months; mss in 6 months. Publishes book 1 year after acceptance. Will consider simultaneous submissions and previously published work.
Illustration: Works with 4 illustrators/year. Uses color artwork only. Reviews ms/illustration packages from artists. Send ms with dummy with at least 3 color copies of sample illustrations. Illustrations only: Send résumé. Responds only if interested. Samples not returned; samples filed.
Terms: Pays authors royalty of 5-15% based on wholesale price. Pays illustrators royalty of 5-10% based on wholesale price or by author/illustrator negotiations (author pays). Sends galleys to authors; dummies to illustrators. Originals sometimes returned to artist at job's completion. Book catalog available for 8½ × 11 SAE and 4 first-class stamps; ms guidelines available for SASE. All imprints included in a single catalog. Catalog available on website.
Tips: "Because we are fairly new in the children's market, we will not accept a manuscript without complete illustrations. We are compiling a database of freelance illustrators which is available to interested authors. Please call if you have questions regarding the submission process or to see if your product is of interest. The children's market is huge! If the author can find a good local publisher, he or she is more likely to get published. We are currently looking for authors to represent our list in the new millennium. At this point, we are accepting regional (Southern Appalachian) manuscripts only. *Please* call if you have a question regarding this policy."

RICHARD C. OWEN PUBLISHERS, INC., P.O. Box 585, Katonah NY 10536. (800)336-5588. Fax: (914)232-3977. Website: www.rcowen.com. Book publisher. **Acquisitions:** Janice Boland, children's books editor/art director. Publishes 20 picture story books/year. 90% of books by first-time authors. We publish "child-focused books, with inherent instructional value, about characters and situations with which five-, six-, and seven-year-old children can identify—books that can be read for meaning, entertainment, enjoyment and information. We include multicultural stories that present minorities in a positive and natural way. Our stories show the diversity in America." Is not interested in lesson plans, or books of activities for literature studies or other content areas.
Fiction: Picture books, young readers: adventure, animal, contemporary, folktales, hi-lo, humor, multicultural, nature/environment, poetry, science fiction, sports, suspense/mystery. Does not want to see holiday, religious themes, moral teaching stories. "No talking animals with personified human characteristics, jingles and rhymes, alphabet books, stories without plots, stories with nostalgic views of childhood, soft or sugar-coated tales. No stereotyping." Average word length: under 500 words. Recently published *Digging to China*, by Katherine Goldsby, illustrated by Viki Woodworth; *The Red-*

Tailed Hawk, by Lola Schaefer, illustrated by Stephen Taylor; and *Dogs at School*, by Suzanne Hardin, illustrated by Jo-Ann Friar.

Nonfiction: Picture books, young readers: animals, careers, hi-lo, history, how-to, music/dance, geography, multicultural, nature/environment, science, sports. Multicultural needs include: "Good stories respectful of all heritages, races, cultural—African-American, Hispanic, American Indian." Wants lively stories. No "encyclopedic" type of information stories. Average word length: under 500 words. Recently published *New York City Buildings*, by Ann Mace, photos by Tim Holmstron.

How to Contact/Writers: Fiction/nonfiction: Submit complete ms and cover letter. Responds to mss in 1 year. Publishes a book 2-3 years after acceptance. See website for guidelines.

Illustration: Works with 20 illustrators/year. Uses color artwork only. Illustration only: Send color copies/reproductions or photos of art or provide tearsheets; do not send slides or originals. Include SASE and cover letter. Responds only if interested; samples filed.

Photography: Buys photos from freelancers. Contact: Janice Boland, art director. Include SASE and cover letter. Wants photos that are child-oriented; candid shots; not interested in portraits. "Natural, bright, crisp and colorful—of children and of interesting subjects and compositions attractive to children. If photos are assigned, we buy outright—retain ownership and all rights to photos taken in the project." Sometimes interested in stock photos for special projects. Uses 35mm, $2\frac{1}{4} \times 2\frac{1}{4}$, color transparencies.

Terms: Pays authors royalties of 5% based on wholesale price or outright purchase (range: $25-500). Offers no advances. Pays illustrators by the project (range: $100-2,500). Pays photographers by the project (range: $100-2,000) or per photo ($100-150). Original artwork returned 12-18 months after job's completion. Book brochure, ms/artists guidelines available for SASE.

Tips: Seeking "stories (both fiction and nonfiction) that have charm, magic, impact and appeal; that children living in today's society will want to read and reread; books with strong storylines, child-appealing language, action and interesting, vivid characters. Write for the ears and eyes and hearts of your readers—use an economy of words. Visit the children's room at the public library and immerse yourself in the best children's literature."

PACIFIC PRESS, P.O. Box 5353. Nampa ID 83653-5353. (208)465-2500. Fax: (208)465-2531. E-mail: booksubmissions @pacificpress.com. Website: www.pacificpress.com/writers/books.htm. Estab. 1874. Specializes in Christian material. **Manuscript Acquisitions:** Tim Lale. **Art Acquisitions:** Randy Maxwell, creative director. Publishes 1 picture book/year; 2 young readers/year; 2 middle readers/year. 5% of books by first-time authors. Pacific Press brings the Bible and Christian lifestyle to children.

Fiction: Picture books, young readers, middle readers, young adults: religion. Average word length: picture books—100; young readers—1,000; middle readers—15,000; young adults—40,000. Recently published *The Bandit of Benson Park*, by Charles Mills; *Elizabeth, an Adventist Girl*, by Kay Rizzo; *Flying High*, by Katy Pistole.

Nonfiction: Picture books, young readers, middle readers, young adults: religion. Average word length: picture books—100; young readers—1,000; middle readers—15,000; young adults—40,000. Recently published *Grandpa's Furry and Feathered Friends*, by Jan Doward; *Nibbles*, by Martha Myers; *Ellen White: Trailblazer for God*, by Paul Ricchiuti.

How to Contact/Writers: Fiction/Nonfiction: Query or submit outline/synopsis and 3 sample chapters. Responds to queries in 3 months; mss in 1 year. Publishes a book 6-12 months after acceptance. Will consider electronic submissions via disk or modem.

Illustration: Works with 2 illustrators/year. Uses color artwork only. Query. Responds only if interested. Samples returned with SASE.

Photography: Buys stock and assigns work. Model/property releases required.

Terms: Pays author royalty of 6-15% based on wholesale price. Offers advances (Average amount: $1,500). Pays illustrators royalty of 6-15% based on wholesale price. Pays photographers royalty of 6-15% based on wholesale price. Sends galleys to authors. Originals returned to artist at job's completion. Manuscript guidelines for SASE. Catalog available on website www.adventistbookcenter.com.

Tips: Pacific Press is owned by the Seventh-day Adventist Church. The Press rejects all material that is not Bible-based.

PACIFIC VIEW PRESS, P.O. Box 2657, Berkeley CA 94702. (510)849-4213. Fax: (510)843-5835. E-mail: PVP2@minds pring.com. Website: www.pacificviewpress.com. Book publisher. **Acquisitions:** Pam Zumwalt, president. Publishes 1-2 picture books/year. 50% of books by first-time authors. "We publish unique, high-quality introductions to Asian cultures and history for children 8-12, for schools, libraries and families. Our children's books focus on hardcover illustrated nonfiction. We look for titles on aspects of the history and culture of the countries and peoples of the Pacific Rim, especially China, presented in an engaging, informative and respectful manner. We are interested in books that all children will enjoy reading and using, and that parents and teachers will want to buy."

Nonfiction: Young readers, middle readers: Asia-related multicultural only. Recently published *Cloud Weavers: Ancient Chinese Legends*, by Rena Krasno and Yeng-Fong Chiang (all ages) and *Exploring Chinatown: A Children's Guide to Chinese Culture*, by Carol Stepanchuk (ages 8-12).

How to Contact/Writers: Query with outline and sample chapter. Responds in 3 months.

Illustration: Works with 2 illustrators/year. Responds only if interested. Samples returned with SASE.

Terms: Pays authors royalty of 8-12% based on wholesale price. Pays illustrators by the project (range: $2,000-5,000).

Tips: "We welcome proposals from persons with expertise, either academic or personal, in their area of interest. While we do accept proposals from previously unpublished authors, we would expect submitters to have considerable experience presenting their interests to children in classroom or other public settings and to have skill in writing for children."

□ PARENTING PRESS, INC., P.O. Box 75267, Seattle WA 98125. (206)364-2900. Fax: (206)364-0702. E-mail: office@parentingpress.com. Website: www.parentingpress.com. Book publisher. Estab. 1979. Publisher: Carolyn Threadgill. **Acquisitions:** Elizabeth Crary, (parenting) and Carolyn Threadgill (children and parenting). Publishes 4-5 books/year for parents or/and children and those who work with them. 40% of books by first-time authors. "Parenting Press publishes educational books for children in story format—no straight fiction. Our company publishes books that help build competence in parents and children. We are known for practical books that teach parents and can be used successfully by parent educators, teachers, and educators who work with parents. We are interested in books that help people feel good about themselves because they gain skills needed in dealing with others. We are particularly interested in material that provides 'options' rather than 'shoulds.'"

    ● Parenting Press's guidelines are available on their website.

Fiction: Picture books: concept. Publishes social skills books, problem-solving books, safety books, dealing-with-feelings books that use a "fictional" vehicle for the information. "We rarely publish straight fiction." Recently published *Heidi's Irresistible Hat, Willy's Noisy Sister, Amy's Disappearing Pickle*, by Elizabeth Crary, illustrated by Susan Avishai (ages 4-10); and *The Way I Feel*, written and illustrated by Janan Cain, a book that promotes emotional literacy.

Nonfiction: Picture books: health, social skills building. Young readers: health, social skills building books. Middle readers: health, social skills building. No books on "new baby; coping with a new sibling; cookbooks; manners; books about disabilities (which we don't publish at present); animal characters in anything; books that tell children what they should do, instead of giving options." Average word length: picture books—500-800; young readers—1,000-2,000; middle readers—up to 10,000. Published *Kids to the Rescue*, by Maribeth and Darwin Boelts (ages 4-12); *Bully on the Bus*, by Carl Bosch (ages 7-11).

How to Contact/Writers: Query. Responds to queries/mss in 3 months, "after requested." Publishes a book 18 months after acceptance. Will consider simultaneous submissions.

Illustrations: Works with 3-5 illustrators/year. Reviews ms/illustration packages from artists. "We do reserve the right to find our own illustrator, however." Query. Illustrations only: Submit "résumé, samples of art/drawings (no original art); photocopies or color photocopies okay." Responds only if interested. Samples returned with SASE; samples filed, if suitable.

Terms: Pays authors royalties of 3-8% based on wholesale price. Pays illustrators (for text) by the project; 3-5% royalty based on wholesale price. Pays illustrators by the project ($250-3,000). Sends galleys to authors; dummies to illustrators. Book catalog/ms/artist's guidelines for #10 SAE and 1 first-class stamp.

Tips: "Make sure you are familiar with the unique nature of our books. All are aimed at building certain 'people' skills in adults or children. Our publishing for children follows no trend that we find appropriate. Children need nonfiction social skill-building books that help them think through problems and make their own informed decisions. The traditional illustrated story book does not *usually* fit our requirements because it does all the thinking for the child."

PAULINE BOOKS & MEDIA, 50 St. Paul's Ave., Jamaica Plain MA 02130-3491. (617)522-8911. E-mail: editorial@paul ine.org. Website: www.pauline.org. Estab. 1932. Specializes in Christian material. **Manuscript Acquisitions:** Sr. Patricia Edward Jablonski, F.S.P. **Art Acquisitions:** Sr. Helen Rita Lane, FSP, art director. Publishes 2 picture books/year; 5 young readers/year; 3-5 middle readers/year; and 1-2 young adult titles/year. 20% of books by first-time authors. "We communicate the Gospel message through our lives and all available forms of media, responding to the needs and hopes of all people in the spirit of St. Paul."

Nonfiction: Picture books, young readers, middle readers, young adults: religion. Average word length: picture books—150-500; young readers—8,000-10,000; middle readers—15,000-25,000. Recently published *My Guardian Angel Coloring & Activity Book*, by D.Thomas Halpin, F.S.P., illustrated by Virginia Helen Richards, F.S.P. (ages 6-9); *The Rosary Comic Book*, written and illustrated by Gene Yang (ages 9-12); *When Should I Pray?*, by Nancy Pharr, illustrated by Heidi Rose (ages 4-7).

How to Contact/Writers: Nonfiction: Submit query letter with outline/synopsis and 3 sample chapters. Responds to queries in 2 months; mss in 4 months. Publishes book 2-3 years after acceptance. Will consider simultaneous submissions, electronic submissions via disk or modem.

Illustration: Works with 20-35 illustrators/year. Uses color artwork only. Illustrations only: Send résumé, promotional literature, client list or tearsheets. Responds only if interested. Samples returned with SASE only or samples filed.

Photography: Buys stock and assigns work. Looking for children, animals and nature (not New England) photos. Model/ property releases required; captions required. Uses color or b&w, 4×6, either matte or semigloss prints. Submit cover letter, résumé, client list, promo piece, published samples, stock photo list.

Terms: Pays authors royalty of 5-10% based on wholesale price. Offers advances (Average amount: $200). Pays illustrators by the project (range: $600-5,000) or royalty of 5-10% based on wholesale price. Pays photographers by the project, per photo or royalty depending on agreement. Sends galleys to authors. Book catalog available for 10½×13½ SAE and 7 first-class stamps; ms and art guidelines available for SASE. Catalog available on website.

Tips: "Please be sure that all material submitted is consonant with Christian teaching and values. We generally do not accept anthropomorphic stories, fantasy or poetry."

Ⓝ PAULIST PRESS, 997 Macarthur Blvd., Mahwah NJ 07430. (201)825-7300. Website: www.paulistpress.com. Book publisher. Estab. 1865. **Acquisitions:** Susan Heyboer O'Keefe, editor. Publishes 2-4 picture books/year; 6-8 young reader titles/year; and 4-6 middle reader titles/year. 80% of books by first-time authors; 10% of books from agented writers. "Our goal is to produce books on Christian and Catholic themes."

Fiction: "Almost none. Must have explicitly Christian or Catholic theme. No picture books on angels, adoption, grandparents, death, sharing, prejudice, or other general themes."

Nonfiction: All levels: concept, social issues, Catholic doctrine, prayers or customs. Published *What If the Zebras Lost Their Stripes*, by John Reitano, illustrated by Bill Haines (picture book); *It's Great to Be Catholic!*, by Susan Heyboer O'Keefe, illustrated by Patrick Kelley (picture book); *Hail Mary/Our Father*, illustrated by Vicki Pastore (picture book); *Great Women of Faith*, by Sue Stanton (young adult); *Martin de Porres*, by Joan Monahan (young adult).

How to Contact/Writers: Fiction/nonfiction: Submit complete ms for picture books; query and sample for longer works; include SASE with all submissions. Responds to queries/mss in 6 months. Publishes a book 2-3 years after acceptance.

Illustration: "Overstocked on samples right now. We tend to use artists we've used before."

Terms: Pays authors royalty of 4-8% based on net sales. Average advance payment is $500. Pays illustrators by flat fee, advance and by royalty, depending on the book.

Tips: "We receive too many inappropriate manuscripts. Please know our books, know our market, and submit accordingly. There should be a reason why you're submitting to a Catholic publisher and not a trade house."

PEACHTREE PUBLISHERS, LTD., 1700 Chattahoochee Ave., Atlanta GA 30318-2112. (404)876-8761. Fax: (404)875-2578. E-mail: hello@peachtree-online.com. Website: www.peachtree-online.com. Book publisher. Imprints: Peachtree Jr. and Freestone. Estab. 1977. **Acquisitions:** Helen Harriss. **Art Director:** Loraine Joyner. Production Manager: Melanie McMahon. Publishes 30-35 titles/year.

Fiction: Picture books, young readers: adventure, animal, concept, history, nature/environment. Middle readers: adventure, animal, history, nature/environment, sports. Young adults: fiction, mystery, adventure. Does not want to see science fiction, romance.

Nonfiction: Picture books: animal, history, nature/environment. Young readers, middle readers, young adults: animal, biography, nature/environment. Does not want to see religion.

How to Contact/Writers: Fiction/Nonfiction: Submit complete ms by postal mail only. Responds to queries/mss in 4 months. Publishes a book 1-2 years after acceptance. Will consider simultaneous submissions.

Illustration: Works with 8-10 illustrators/year. Illustrations only: Query production manager or art director with samples, résumé, slides, color copies to keep on file. Responds only if interested. Samples returned with SASE; samples filed.

Terms: "Manuscript guidelines for SASE, visit website or call for a recorded message. No fax or e-mail submittals or queries please."

PEEL PRODUCTIONS, P.O. Box 546, Columbus NC 28722. (828)894-8838. Fax: (801)365-9898. E-mail: editor@peelbooks.com. Website: www.peelbooks.com. Book publisher. **Acquisitions:** Susan Dubosque, editor. Publishes 1 picture book/year; and 5 how-to-draw books/year.

• Visit this company's website to see the types of books they publish.

Nonfiction: Young readers, middle readers: activity books (how to draw).

How to Contact/Writers: Nonfiction: Query first. Responds to queries in 2 months. Publishes a book 1 year after acceptance. Will consider simultaneous submissions.

Terms: Pays authors royalty. Offers advances. Sends galleys to authors. Book catalog available for SAE and 2 first-class stamps.

PELICAN PUBLISHING CO. INC., P.O. Box 3110, Gretna LA 70054-3110. (504)368-1175. Website: www.pelicanpub.com. Book publisher. Estab. 1926. **Manuscript Acquisitions:** Nina Kooij, editor-in-chief. **Art Acquisitions:** Tracey Clements, production manager. Publishes 22 young readers/year and 2 middle reader titles/year. 15% of books from agented writers. "Pelican publishes hardcover and trade paperback originals and reprints. Our children's books (illustrated and otherwise) include history, biography, holiday, and regional. Pelican's mission is to publish books of quality and permanence that enrich the lives of those who read them."

Fiction: Young readers: folktales, history, holiday, multicultural and regional. Middle readers: Louisiana history. Multicultural needs include stories about African-Americans, Irish-Americans, Jews, Asian-Americans, Cajuns and Hispanics. Does not want animal stories, general Christmas stories, "day at school" or "accept yourself" stories. Maximum word length: 1,100 young readers; middle readers—40,000. Recently published *Moon's Cloud Blanket*, by Rose Anne St. Romain (ages 5-8, folktale).

Nonfiction: Young readers: biography, history, multicultural. Middle readers: Louisiana history, multicultural, biography. Recently published *Huey P. Long: Talker and Doer*, by David R. Collins (ages 5-8, biography).

How to Contact/Writers: Fiction/Nonfiction: Query. Responds to queries in 1 month; mss in 3 months. Publishes a book 9-18 months after acceptance.

Illustration: Works with 18 illustrators/year. Reviews ms/illustration packages from artists. Query first. Illustrations only: Query with samples (no originals). Responds only if interested. Samples returned with SASE; samples kept on file.

Terms: Pays authors in royalties; buys ms outright "rarely." Sends galleys to authors. Illustrators paid by "various arrangements." Book catalog and ms guidelines available on website or for SASE.

Tips: "No anthropomorphic stories, pet stories (fiction or nonfiction), fantasy, poetry, science fiction or romance. Writers: Be as original as possible. Develop characters that lend themselves to series and always be thinking of new and interesting situations for those series. Give your story a strong hook—something that will appeal to a well-defined audience. There is a lot of competition out there for general themes. We look for stories with specific 'hooks' and audiences, and writers who actively promote their work."

PERFECTION LEARNING CORPORATION, Cover to Cover, 10520 New York, Des Moines IA 50322. (515)278-0133. Fax: (515)278-2980. E-mail: acquisitions@plconline.com. Website: www.perfectionlearning.com. Book publisher, independent book producer/packager. **Manuscript Acquisitions:** S. Thies (3-12 books), Rebecca Christian (curriculum). **Art Acquisitions:** Randy Messer, art director. Publishes 20 early chapter books/year; 40-50 middle readers/ year; 25 young adult titles/year.

 • Perfection Learning Corp. publishes *all* hi-lo children's books on a variety of subjects.

Fiction: Grades 3-12, ages 8-18: adventure, animal, contemporary, fantasy, folktales, history, humor, multicultural, nature/ environment, poetry, science fiction, special needs, sports, suspense/mystery. Average word length: early chapter books— 4,000; middle readers—10,000-14,000; young adults: 10,000-30,000. Recently published *Soccer Battles*; *The Club*, by Michael Strickland and Lisa Bahlinger.

Nonfiction: All levels: animal, biography, careers, geography, health, history, hobbies, multicultural, nature/environment, science, social issues, special needs, sports. Multicultural needs include contemporary fiction by authors who are of the culture. Does not want to see ABC or picture books. Average word length: early chapter books—4,000; middle readers— 10,000-14,000; young adults—10,000-14,000.

How to Contact/Writers: Fiction/Nonfiction: Submit a few sample chapters and synopsis. Responds to queries/mss in 3 months. Publishes a book 18 months after acceptance.

Illustration: Works with 15-20 illustrators/year. Illustration only: Query with samples; send résumé, promo sheet, client list, tearsheets. Responds only if interested. Samples returned with SASE; samples filed.

Photography: Buys photos from freelancers. Buys stock and assigns work. Uses children. Uses color or up to 8×10 b&w glossy prints; 2¼×2¼, 4×5 transparencies. Submit cover letter, client list, stock photo list, promo piece (color or b&w).

Terms: Pays authors "depending on going rate for industry." Offers advances. Pays illustrators by the project. Pays photographers by the project. Original artwork returned on a "case by case basis."

Tips: "Our materials are sold through schools for use in the classroom. Talk to a teacher about his/her needs."

PHILOMEL BOOKS, Penguin Putnam Inc., 345 Hudson St., New York NY 10014. (212)414-3610. Website: www.pengui nputnam.com. Putnam Books. Book publisher. Estab. 1980. **Manuscript Acquisitions:** Patricia Gauch, editorial director; Emily Heath, editor; Michael Green, executive editor. **Art Acquisitions:** Gina DiMassi, design assistant. Publishes 18 picture books/year; 2 middle-grade/year; 2 young readers/year; 4 young adult/year. 5% of books by first-time authors; 80% of books from agented writers. "We look for beautifully written, engaging manuscripts for children and young adults."

 • Philomel Books is not accepting unsolicited manuscripts.

Fiction: All levels: adventure, animal, anthology, contemporary, fantasy, folktales, hi-lo, history, humor, poetry, sports, multicultural. Middle readers, young adults: problem novels, science fiction, suspense/mystery. No concept picture books, mass-market "character" books, or series. Average word length: 1,000 for picture books; 1,500 young readers; 14,000 middle readers; 20,000 young adult.

Nonfiction: Picture books, young readers, middle readers: hi-lo. "Creative nonfiction on any subject." Average word length: 2,000 for picture books; 3,000 young readers; 10,000 middle readers.

How to Contact/Writers: Not accepting unsolicited mss. Fiction: Submit outline/synopsis and first two chapters. Nonfiction: Query. Responds to queries in 3 months; mss in 4 months.

Illustration: Works with 20-25 illustrators/year. Reviews ms/illustration packages from artists. Query with art sample first. Illustrations only: Query with samples. Send résumé and tearsheets. Responds to art samples in 1 month. Original artwork returned at job's completion. Samples returned with SASE or kept on file.

Terms: Pays authors in royalties. Average advance payment "varies." Illustrators paid by advance and in royalties. Sends galleys to authors; dummies to illustrators. Book catalog, ms guidelines free on request with SASE (9×12 envelope for catalog).

Tips: Wants "unique fiction or nonfiction with a strong voice and lasting quality. Discover your own voice and own story— and persevere." Looks for "something unusual, original, well-written. Fine art. The genre (fantasy, contemporary, or historical fiction) is not so important as the story itself and the spirited life the story allows its main character. We are also interested in receiving adolescent novels, particularly novels that contain regional spirit, such as a story about a young boy or girl written from a Southern, Southwestern or Northwestern perspective."

☑ ▢ **PHOENIX LEARNING RESOURCES**, 25 Third St., 2nd Floor, Stamford CT 06905. (203)353-1665. E-mail: john@phoenixlr.com. Website: www.phoenixlr.com. Book publisher. **Executive Vice President:** John A. Rothermich. Publishes 20 textbooks/year. Publisher's goal is to provide proven skill building materials in reading, language, math and study skills for today's student, grades K-adult.

Nonfiction: Middle readers, young readers, young adults: hi-lo, textbooks. Recently published *Reading for Concepts*, Third Edition.

How to Contact/Writers: Nonfiction: Submit outline/synopsis. Responds to queries in 2 weeks; mss in 1 month. Will consider simultaneous submissions and previously published work.

Photography: Buys stock. Uses color prints and 35mm, 2¼×2¼, 4×5 transparencies. Submit cover letter.

Terms: Pays authors royalty based on wholesale price or work purchased outright. Pays illustrators and photographers by the project. Sends galleys to authors. Book catalog available for SASE.

Tips: "We look for classroom-tested and proven materials."

▢ **PIANO PRESS**, P.O. Box 85, Del Mar CA 92014-0085. (619)884-1401. Fax: (858)755-1104. E-mail: PianoPress@aol. com. Website: www.pianopress.com. Estab. 1998. Specializes in music-related fiction, educational material, multicultural music material, nonfiction. **Manuscript Acquisitions:** Elizabeth C. Axford, M.A., editor. "We publish music-related books, either fiction or nonfiction, coloring books, songbooks and poetry."

Fiction: Picture books, young readers, middle readers, young adults: folktales, multicultural, poetry, music. Average word length: picture books—1,500-2,000. Recently published *Strum a Song of Angels*, by Linda Oatman High and Elizabeth C. Axford; *Music and Me*, by Kimberly White and Elizabeth C. Axford.

Nonfiction: Picture books, young readers, middle readers, young adults: multicultural, music/dance. Average word length: picture books—1,500-2,000. Recently published *The Musical ABC*, by Dr. Phyllis J. Perry and Elizabeth C. Axford; *Merry Christmas Happy Hanukkah—A Multilingual Songbook & CD*, by Elizabeth C. Axford.

How to Contact/Writers: Fiction/Nonfiction: Query. Responds to queries in 3 months; mss in 6 months. Publishes a book 1 year after acceptance. Will consider simultaneous submissions, electronic submissions via disk or modem.

Illustration: Works with 1 or 2 illustrators/year. Reviews ms/illustration packages from artists. Query. Illustrations only: Query with samples. Responds in 3 months. Samples returned with SASE; samples filed.

Photography: Buys stock and assigns work. Looking for music-related, multicultural. Model/property releases required. Uses glossy or flat, color or b&w prints. Submit cover letter, résumé, client list, published samples, stock photo list.

Terms: Pays author royalty of 5-10% based on retail price. Pays illustrators royalty of 5-10% based on retail price. Pays photographers royalty of 5-10% based on retail price. Sends galleys to authors; dummies to illustrators. Originals returned to artist at job's completion. Book catalog available for #10 SAE and 2 first-class stamps. All imprints included in a single catalog. Catalog available on website.

Tips: "We are looking for music-related material only for any juvenile market. Please do not send nonmusic-related materials. Query first before submitting anything."

Ⓝ PIÑATA BOOKS, Imprint of Arte Publico Press, University of Houston, 452 Cullen Performance Hall, Houston TX 77204-2004. (713)743-2843. Fax: (713)743-3080. E-mail: carmen.pena@mail.uh.edu. Website: www.artepublicopress.com. Estab. 1979. Specializes in trade books, fiction, multicultural material. **Manuscript Acquisitions:** Dr. Nicholas Kanellos. **Art Acquisitions:** Linda Garza, production manager. Publishes 6 picture books/year; 2 young readers/year; 5 middle readers/year; and 5 young adult titles/year. 80% of books are by first-time authors. "Arte Publico's mission is the publication, promotion and dissemination of Latino literature for a variety of national and regional audiences, from early childhood to adult, through the complete gamut of delivery systems, including personal performance as well as print and electronic media."

Fiction: Recently published *My Tata's Guitar/La Guitarra De Mi Tata*, by Ethriam Cash Brammer, illustrated by Daniel Lechon (ages 3-7); *Lorenzo's Revolutionary Quest*, by Lila and Rick Guzman (ages 11 and up); and *Teen Angel*, by Gloria Velasquez (ages 11 and up).

Nonfiction: Recently published *Cesar Chavez: The Struggle for Justice/Cesar Chavez: La Lucha Por La Justicia*, by Richard Griswold del Castillo, illustrated by Anthony Accardo (ages 3-7).

How to Contact/Writers: Accepts material from US/Hispanic authors only (living abroad OK). Fiction: Submit complete ms. Nonfiction: Query. Responds to queries in 2 months; mss in 8 months. Publishes a book 2 years after acceptance. Will sometimes consider previously published work.

Illustration: Works with 6 illustrators/year. Uses color artwork only. Reviews ms/illustration packages from artists. Query or send portfolio (slides, color copies). Illustrations only: Query with samples or send résumé, promo sheet, portfolio, slides, client list and tearsheets. Responds only if interested. Samples not returned; samples filed.

Terms: Pays authors royalty of 10% minimum based on wholesale price. Offers advances (Average amount $2,000). Pays illustrators advance and royalties of 10% based on wholesale price. Sends galleys to authors. Catalog available on website; ms guidelines available for SASE.

THE PLACE IN THE WOODS, "Different" Books, 3900 Glenwood Ave., Golden Valley MN 55422-5307. (763)374-2120. Fax: (952)593-5593. E-mail: placewoods@aol.com. Book publisher. **Acquisitions:** Roger Hammer, publisher/editor. Publishes 2 elementary-age titles/year and 1 middle readers/year; 1 young adult titles/year. 100% of books by first-time authors. Books feature primarily diversity/multicultural/disability themes, many by first-time authors and illustrators.

Fiction: All levels: adventure, animal, contemporary, fantasy, folktales, hi-lo, history, humor, poetry, multicultural, special needs. Recently published *Little Horse*, by Frank Minogue, illustrated by Beth Crire (young adult fiction); *Simon the Daredevil Centipede*, by Phil Segal, illustrated by Alisa Cajarelli (early elementary fiction).

Nonfiction: All levels: hi-lo, history, multicultural, special needs. Multicultural themes must avoid negative stereotypes. "Generally, we don't publish nonfiction, but we would look at these."

How to Contact/Writers: Fiction/Nonfiction: Submit complete ms. Responds to queries/mss in 1 month with SASE. "No multiple or simultaneous submissions. Please indicate a time frame for response."

Illustration: Works with 4 illustrators/year. Uses primarily b&w artwork only. Reviews ms/illustration packages from authors. Query; submit ms. Contact: Roger Hammer, editor. Illustration only: Query with samples. Responds in 1 month. Include SASE. "We buy all rights."

Photography: Buys photos from freelancers. Works on assignment only. Uses photos that appeal to children. Model/property releases required; captions required. Uses any b&w prints. Submit cover letter and samples with SASE.

Terms: Work purchased outright from authors ($50-250). Pays illustrators by the project (range: $10-500). Pays photographers per photo. For all contracts, "initial payment repeated with each printing." Original artwork not returned at job's completion. Guidelines available for SASE.

PLAYERS PRESS, INC., P.O. Box 1132, Studio City CA 91614-0132. (818)789-4980. Book publisher. Imprints: Showcase Publishing; Gaslight Productions; Health Watch Books. Estab. 1965. **Manuscript Acquisitions:** Robert W. Gordon, vice president/editorial director. **Art Acquisitions:** Attention: Art Director. Publishes 7-25 young readers dramatic plays and musicals/year; 2-10 middle readers dramatic plays and musicals/year; and 4-20 young adults dramatic plays and

insider report

Successful illustrator shares marketing secrets

Mike Cressy started drawing as soon as he could hold a pencil. "I remember being home sick when I was five years old, and my mother putting a stack of paper in front of me on a tray. I would draw all day long."

Mike Cressy

Basically a self-taught illustrator, Cressy has taken only one class in illustration, to learn a certain technique from an illustrator he I admired. He moved to California in pursuit of a career in art after spending several years working in auto factories in Detroit. "I wanted to be a comic strip artist," he says. "I got a job at a small animation studio and I was on my way. I did posters for theaters in L.A and then started getting work from the *L.A. Times* and other local publications by calling them up and making appointments to show my portfolio, being as persistent as I could be."

Cressy's career progressed into working for advertising agencies, national magazines, and children's books, including *Bugs*, by Patricia and Frederick McKissick (Children's Book Press); *Look! My Tooth is Loose*, by by Patricia Brennan Demuth (Grosset & Dunlap); and *The Great Show and Tell Disaster*, by Mike Reiss (Price Stern Sloan).

"One of the best things that happened to me was being asked to join Group West, a well-established illustration group in L.A. There were 12 well-known illustrators there and most of them were people I admired for their great work." he says. "They taught me so much about the business and how to keep the work coming in. I also learned how to illustrate in different styles, which I had to do there because sometimes other illustrators in the group would get too many jobs coming in at once and would end up farming out work to another illustrator who wasn't too busy to take on the overflow."

Through his experience in several areas of the illustration world and his contact with other successful illustrators, Cressy learned a lot about promoting himself to potential clients. An expert marketer, here he shares his self-promotion strategy, including advice on postcard campaigns, websites, and creating a signature style.

How did your marketing strategy evolve over the years?
About ten years ago I realized that just putting ads in annuals like *Showcase* or *WorkBook* wasn't the most effective way to get art directors to look at my work. I had heard from some other illustrators that they had been sending out postcards and getting more work because of that.

So I slowly started putting together a mailing list garnered from several different publications and then started printing postcards every three to six months and sending them out. Now, because every other illustrator is doing the same thing, I have to send them out more often and try to be more clever. I have an average of 2,500 people on the mailing list and it's constantly changing. You have to keep on top of it. People move from job to job and companies/magazines/advertising agencies come and go.

I've always been self-taught, so constantly checking out new ways to market myself is just part of what I do. I keep my eyes peeled to see what others are doing and try to figure out if it's really working for them and try to adapt it to my way of working. There are a few things that I've come up with on my own but mostly it's just seeing what works for people you see as being successful.

Your style is really recognizable. Did you consciously "brand" yourself?

I used to do mostly tight realistic illustration. Then it dawned on me that I could come up with something more fun and can play around more with metaphor and settings. It also dawned on me that I would be associated with that style, so that when some one saw one of my illustrations, they'd know who to blame.

My style is in the middle of changing as we speak. I've been working on something a little different using the same technique and I'll be sending out new cards soon with the first of that new direction. It's good to evolve.

Why did you decide to create your website (http://home.earthlink.net/~mikecressy)? Do you think this is something all illustrators need to do these days? What advice can you offer to other illustrators about creating websites?

Back in 1996 I was working for a software game company (taking a break from the freelance world for a few years and getting divorced), and the Internet was really starting to boom. I

Illustration ©Mike Cressy from *Look, My Tooth Is Loose* (Grosset & Dunlap). Reprinted with permission.

Mike Cressy's illustrations for *Look, My Tooth Is Loose!*, written by Patricia Brennen Demuth, survived major interruptions when his original editor/art director left and Cressy had little choice but to wait for a new person to fill the void. However, with six promotional mailings every year, Cressy found plenty to fill his time.

This illustration became the cover image for *Bugs!*, written by Patricia and Frederick McKissack, a 2000 Grolier release. Grolier (now a part of Scholastic Library Publishing along with Children's Press and Franklin Watts) was so pleased with Cressy's illustrations for the book that they invited him to do the catalog cover for that year.

got laid off in June of that year and thought right away that the Internet was the way to go. I put up my first version of my website by the end of that year.

I think it has been one of the best ways for potential and current clients to view my portfolio. No more mailing it around the country and possibly getting it lost—which has happened to so many illustrators. You announce your site with the postcards you send out and by alerting all the service sites on the web so that they list your website. The best thing an illustrator can do besides sending out postcards, calling clients, is creating a website. Get a simple program that will allow you to do the kind of site you need without having to read Klingon, and get it up on the Internet. Make it easy for clients to get around the site but put in enough depth to make it interesting so that they don't leave too quickly. Maybe throw in a few surprises like a secret link to a page that has some work you're proud of but doesn't quite fit with the style you're known for. In software game jargon, an Easter Egg.

You have a diverse client list. Does your strategy vary when contacting children's publishers vs. advertising clients?
I like working in different areas. I think it's good discipline for artists to constantly keep on their toes and be ready to effectively create something interesting in any area of media. It keeps you interested in the world. I am kind of lazy in that I approach each client, no matter the medium, the same way. I show them everything. Which is what the new version of my website is about and it should be up soon. I don't think that's the best way sometimes but I don't have enough extra time to put together individual presentations for each level of medium. You have to balance your life and make room for working on the art and experimenting. Being an artist is all-consuming. You have to give yourself to it all the way and it ends up being your life.

—*Alice Pope*

musicals/year. 35% of books by first-time authors; 1% of books from agented writers. Players Press philosophy is "to create is to live life's purpose."

Fiction: All levels: plays. Recently published *Play From African Folktales*, by Carol Korty (collection of short plays); *Punch and Judy*, a play by William-Alan Landes; and *Silly Soup!*, by Carol Korty (a collection of short plays with music and dance).

Nonfiction: Picture books, middle readers, young readers, young adults. "Any children's nonfiction pertaining to the entertainment industry, performing arts and how-to for the theatrical arts only." Needs include activity, arts/crafts, careers, history, how-to, music/dance, reference and textbook. Recently published *Scenery*, by J. Stell (How to Build Stage Scenery); *Monologues for Teens*, by Vernon Howard (ideal for teen performers); *Humorous Monologues*, by Vernon Howard (ideal for young performers); *Actor's Résumés*, by Richard Devin (how to prepare an acting résumé).

How to Contact/Writers: Fiction/nonfiction: Submit plays or outline/synopsis and sample chapters of entertainment books. Responds to queries in 1 month; mss in 1 year. Publishes a book 10 months after acceptance. No simultaneous submissions.

Illustration: Works with 2-6 illustrators/year. Use primarily b&w artwork. Illustrations only: Submit résumé, tearsheets. Responds to art samples in 1 week only if interested. Samples returned with SASE; samples filed.

Terms: Pays authors royalties based on wholesale price. Pay illustrators by the project (range: $5-5,000). Pays photographers by the project (up to 1,000); royalty varies. Sends galleys to authors; dummies to illustrators. Book catalog and ms guidelines available for 9×12 SASE.

Tips: Looks for "plays/musicals and books pertaining to the performing arts only. Illustrators: send samples that can be kept for our files."

◪ PLAYHOUSE PUBLISHING, 1566 Akron-Peninsula Rd., Akron OH 44313. (330)926-1313. Fax: (330)926-1315. E-mail: webmaster@playhousepublishing.com. Website: www.playhousepublishing.com. Specializes in mass market and educational material. **Acquisitions:** Submissions Editor. Imprints: Picture Me Books, Nibble Me Books. Publishes 10-15 novelty/board books/year, 1-3 picture books/year. 25% of books by first-time authors. "Playhouse Publishing is dedicated to finding imaginative new ways to inspire young minds to read, learn and grow—one book at a time."

Fiction: Picture books: adventure, animal, concept, fantasy, folktales, humor, nature/environment, sports. Average word length: board books—75; picture books—500. Recently published: *My Sparkle Purse*, by Cathy Hapka, illustrated by Lynne Schwaner; *My Vacation*, by Merry North, illustrated by Kim Petschauer; *My Sparkle Present*, by Jackie Wolf, illustrated by April Micozzi; *Picture Me Dinosaur*, by Eleanor Fremont, illustrated by April Roush; *Picture Me Christmas Princess*, by Cathy Hapka, illustrated by Heather Hill.

How to Contact/Writers: Fiction: Query or submit outline/synopsis via e-mail only. "All information must be contained in the body of the e-mail. Attachments will not be opened." Responds to queries/mss in 4 months. Publishes a book 18-24 months after acceptance. Will consider simultaneous submissions and electronic submissions via e-mail only.

Illustration: Works with 7 illustrators/year. Uses color artwork only. Reviews ms/illustration packages via e-mail or link to website only. Responds in 3 months. Items sent via postal mail will not be opened. Samples returned with SASE.

Photography: Works on assignment only. Model/property release required. Uses color prints.

Terms: Work purchased outright from authors. Illustrators and photographers paid by the project. Book catalog available for 9×12 SASE. All imprints included in single catalog. Catalog available online.

PLEASANT COMPANY PUBLICATIONS, 8400 Fairway Place, Middleton WI 53562-2554. (608)836-4768. Fax: (608)836-1999. Website: www.americangirl.com. Book publisher.**Manuscript Acquisitions:** Submissions Editor. Jodi Evert, editorial director fiction; Michelle Watkins, editorial director, American Girl Library. **Art Acquisitions:** Jane Varda, art director. Imprints: The American Girls Collection, American Girl Library, History Mysteries, AG Fiction, Girls of Many Lands. Publishes 30 middle readers/year. 10% of books by first-time authors. Publishes fiction and nonfiction for girls 7 and up. "Pleasant Company's mission is to educate and entertain girls with high-quality products and experiences that build self-esteem and reinforce positive social and moral values."

> ● Pleasant Company does not accept ideas or manuscripts for The American Girls Collection, but does accept manuscripts for stand-alone historical fiction, and is seeking manuscripts for AG fiction, its contemporary middle-grade fiction imprint for girls 10 and up. Request writers' guidelines for more information. Pleasant Company publishes *American Girl* magazine. See the listing for *American Girl* in the Magazines section.

Fiction: Middle readers: adventure, animal, contemporary, fantasy, suspense/mystery. Recently published *Meet Kit*, by Valerie Tripp, illustrated by Walter Rane (ages 7-12, historical fiction); *Smoke Screen*, by Amy Goldman Koss (ages 10 and up, contemporary fiction); *Trouble at Fort La Pointe*, by Kathleen Ernst (ages 10 and up, historical fiction/mystery).

Nonfiction: Middle readers: activity books, arts/crafts, cooking, history, hobbies, how-to, self help, sports. Recently published *Help! A Girl's Guide to Divorce and Stepfamilies*, by Nancy Holyoke, illustrated by Scott Nash (ages 8 and up; self-help); *Paper Punch Art*, by Laura Torres (ages 8 and up; craft); and *Quiz Book 2*, by Sarah Jane Brian, illustrated by Debbie Tilley (ages 8 and up; activity).

How to Contact/Writers: Fiction/nonfiction: Query or submit entire ms. Responds to queries/mss in 3 months. Will consider simultaneous submissions.

Illustration: Works with 10 illustrators/year. Reviews ms/illustration packages from artists. Illustrations only: Query with samples. Contact: Jane Varda, senior art director. Responds only if interested. Samples returned with SASE; copies of samples filed.

Photography: Buys stock and assigns work. Submit cover letter, published samples, promo piece.

Terms: Pays authors royalty or work purchased outright. Pays illustrators by the project. Pays photographers by the project. Sends galleys to authors; dummies to illustrators. Originals returned to artist at job's completion. Book catalog available for 8½×11 SAE and 4 first-class stamps. All imprints included in a single catalog.

N POLYCHROME PUBLISHING CORPORATION, 4509 N. Francisco, Chicago IL 60625. (773)478-4455. Fax: (773)478-0786. E-mail: polypub@earthlink.net. Website: www.polychromebooks.com. Book publisher. **Contact:** Editorial Board. **Art Director:** Brian Witkowski. Publishes 2-4 picture books/year; 1-2 middle readers/year; and 1-2 young adult titles/year. 50% of books are by first-time authors. Stories focus on children of Asian ancestry in the United States.

Fiction: All levels: adventure, contemporary, history, multicultural, problem novels, suspense/mystery. Middle readers, young adults: anthology. Multicultural needs include Asian American children's experiences. Not interested in animal stories, fables, fairy tales, folk tales. Published *Nene and the Horrible Math Monster*, by Marie Villanueva; *Stella: On the Edge of Popularity*, by Lauren Lee.

Nonfiction: All levels: multicultural. Multicultural needs include Asian-American themes.

How to Contact/Writers: Fiction/Nonfiction: Submit complete ms along with an author's bio regarding story background. Responds to queries in 4 months; mss in 6 months. Publishes a book 1-2 years after acceptance. Will consider simultaneous submissions.

Illustration: Works with 4-6 illustrators/year. Reviews ms/illustration packages from artists. Submit ms with bio of author, story background and photocopies of sample illustrations. Contact: Editorial Board. Illustrations only: Query with résumé and samples (can be photocopies) of drawings of multicultural children. Responds only if interested. Samples returned with SASE; samples filed "only if under consideration for future work."

Terms: Pays authors royalty of 2-10% based on wholesale price. Work purchased outright ($25 minimum). Pays illustrators 2-10% royalty based on wholesale price. Sends galleys to authors; dummies to illustrators. Book catalog available for #10 SAE and 34¢. Manuscript guidelines available for SASE.

Tips: Wants "stories about experiences that will ring true with Asian Americans, including tolerance and anti-bias that people of *ALL* colors can identify with."

PROMETHEUS BOOKS, 59 John Glenn Dr., Amherst NY 14228-2197. Fax: (716)564-2711. E-mail: editorial@prometheusbooks.com. Website: www.PrometheusBooks.com. Book publisher. Estab. 1969. **Acquisitions:** Steven L. Mitchell, editor-in-chief. Publishes 1-2 titles/year. 50% of books by first-time authors; 30% of books from agented writers. "We hope more books will be published that focus on real issues children face and real questions they raise. Our primary focus is to publish children's books with alternative viewpoints: humanism, free thought, skepticism toward the paranormal, moral values, critical reasoning, human sexuality, and independent thinking based upon science and reasoning. Our niche is the parent who seeks informative books based on these principles. We are dedicated to offering customers the highest-quality books. We are also committed to the development of new markets both in North America and throughout the world."

Nonfiction: All levels: sex education, moral education, critical thinking, nature/environment, science, self help, skepticism, social issues. Average word length: picture books—2,000; young readers—10,000; middle readers—20,000; young adult/teens—60,000. Recently published *A Solstice Tree For Jenny*, by Karen Shrugg (ages 4 and up); *All Families Are Different*, by Sid Gordon (ages 7 and up); and *Flat Earth? Round Earth?*, by Theresa Martin (ages 7 and up).

How to Contact/Writers: Submit complete ms with sample illustrations (b&w). Responds to queries in 3 weeks; mss in 1-2 months. Publishes a book 12-18 months after acceptance. SASE required for return of ms/proposal.

Illustration: Works with 1-2 illustrators/year. "We will keep samples in a freelance file, but freelancers are rarely used." Reviews ms/illustration packages from artists. "Prefer to have full work (manuscript and illustrations); will consider any proposal." Include résumé, photocopies.

Terms: Pays authors royalty of 5-15% based on wholesale price and binding. "Author hires illustrator; we do not contract with illustrators." Pays photographers per photo (range: $50-100). Sends galleys to author. Book catalog is free on request.

Tips: We do not accept projects with anthropomorphic characters. We stress realistic children in realistic situations. "Books should reflect secular humanist values, stressing nonreligious moral education, critical thinking, logic, and skepticism. Authors should examine our book catalog and website to learn what sort of manuscripts we're looking for."

PUFFIN BOOKS, Penguin Group (USA), Inc., 345 Hudson St., New York NY 10014-3657. (212)414-3600. Website: www.penguin.com/yreaders. Imprint of Penguin Young Readers Group. **Acquisitions:** Sharyn November, senior editor. Publishes trade paperback originals (very few) and reprints. Publishes 175-200 titles/year. Receives 600 queries and mss/year. 1% of books by first-time authors; 5% from unagented writers. "Puffin Books publishes high-end trade paperbacks and paperback originals and reprints for preschool children, beginning and middle readers, and young adults."

Fiction: Picture books, young adult novels, middle grade and easy-to-read grades 1-3. "We publish mostly paperback reprints. We publish few original titles." Recently published *Go and Come Back*, by Joan Ablelove; *Speak*, by Laurie Halse Anderson.

Nonfiction: Biography, children's/juvenile, illustrated book, young children's concept books (counting, shapes, colors). Subjects include education (for teaching concepts and colors, not academic), women in history. " 'Women in history' books interest us." Reviews artwork/photos. Send color photocopies. Recently published *Rachel Carson: Pioneer of Ecology*, by "Fadlinski" (history); *Grandma Moses*, by O'Neill Ruff (history). Publishes the Alloy Books series.

How to Contact/Writers: Fiction: Submit complete picture book ms or 3 sample chapters with SASE. Nonfiction: Submit 5 pages of ms with SASE. "It could take up to 5 months to get response." Publishes book 1 year after acceptance. Will consider simultaneous submissions, if so noted.

Terms: Pays royalty. Offers advance (varies). Book catalog for 9×12 SASE with 7 first-class stamps; send request to Marketing Department.

G.P. PUTNAM'S SONS, Penguin Putnam Books For Young Readers, 345 Hudson St., New York NY 10014. (212)414-3610. Website: www.penguinputnam.com. Book publisher. **Manuscript Acquisitions:** Kathy Dawson, executive editor; Susan Kochan, senior editor; John Rudolph, editor. **Art Acquisitions:** Cecilia Yung, art director, Putnam and Philomel. Publishes 30 picture books/year; 10 middle readers/year; and 2 young adult titles/year. 5% of books by first-time authors; 50% of books from agented authors.

Fiction: Picture books: animal, concept, contemporary, humor, multicultural, special needs. Young readers: adventure, contemporary, history, humor, multicultural, special needs, suspense/mystery. Middle readers: adventure, contemporary, history, humor, multicultural, problem novels, special needs, sports, suspense/mystery. Young adults: contemporary, history, problem novels, special needs. "Multicultural books should reflect different cultures accurately but unobtrusively." Regarding special needs, "stories about physically or mentally challenged children should portray them accurately and without condescension." Does not want to see series, romances. Average word length: picture books—200-1,500; middle readers—10,000-30,000; young adults—40,000-50,000. Recently published *Gumbrella*, by Barry Root (ages 4-8); and *Stand Tall*, by Joan Bauer (ages 10-14).

Nonfiction: Picture books: animal, concept, nature/environment. Subject must have broad appeal but inventive approach. Average word length: picture books—200-1,500. Recently published *Atlantic*, by G. Brian Karas (ages 4-8, 32 pages).

How to Contact/Writers: Fiction: Query with outline/synopsis and 1-3 sample chapters. Nonfiction: Query with outline/synopsis, 1 or 2 sample chapters and a table of contents. Unsolicited picture book mss only; do not send art unless requested. Responds to queries in 3 weeks; mss in 2 months. Publishes a book 2 years after acceptance. Will consider simultaneous submissions on queries only.

Illustration: Write for illustrator guidelines. Works with 40 illustrators/year. Reviews ms/illustration packages from artists. Manuscript/illustration packages and illustration only: Query. Responds only if interested. Samples returned with SASE; samples filed.

Terms: Pays authors royalty based on retail price. Pays illustrators by the project or royalty based on retail price. Sends galleys to authors. Original artwork returned at job's completion. Books catalog and ms and artist's guidelines available for SASE.

Tips: "Study our catalogs and get a sense of the kind of books we publish, so that you know whether your project is likely to be right for us.

RAINBOW PUBLISHERS, P.O. Box 261129, San Diego CA 92196. (858)668-3260. Website: www.rainbowpublishers.c om. Book publisher. Estab. 1979. **Acquisitions:** Christy Scannell, editorial director. Publishes 5 young readers/year; 5 middle readers/year; and 5 young adult titles/year. 50% of books by first-time authors. "Our mission is to publish Bible-based, teacher resource materials that contribute to and inspire spiritual growth and development in kids ages 2-12."
Nonfiction: Young readers, middle readers, young adult/teens: activity books, arts/crafts, how-to, reference, religion. Does not want to see traditional puzzles. Recently published *Worship Bulletins for Kids*, by Mary Rose Pearson and Jeanne Grieser (series of 2 books for ages 3-12).
How to Contact/Writers: Nonfiction: Submit outline/synopsis and 3-5 sample chapters. Responds to queries in 6 weeks; mss in 3 months. Publishes a book 18 months after acceptance. Will consider simultaneous submissions, submissions via disk and previously published work.
Illustration: Works with 2-5 illustrators/year. Reviews ms/illustration packages from artists. Submit ms with 2-5 pieces of final art. Illustrations only: Query with samples. Responds in 6 weeks. Samples returned with SASE; samples filed.
Terms: For authors work purchased outright (range: $500 and up). Pays illustrators by the project (range: $300 and up). Sends galleys to authors. Book catalog available for 10×13 SAE and 2 first-class stamps; ms guidelines available for SASE.
Tips: "Our Rainbow imprint carries reproducible books for teachers of children in Christian ministries, including crafts, activities, games and puzzles. Our Legacy imprint (new in '97) handles nonfiction titles for children in the Christian realm, such as Bible story books, devotional books, and so on. Please write for guidelines and study the market before submitting material."

☑ 🅰 💟 🖸 **RANDOM HOUSE GOLDEN BOOKS FOR YOUNG READERS GROUP**, 1745 Broadway, New York NY 10019. (212)782-9000. Random House, Inc. Book publisher. Estab. 1935. "Random House Books aims to create books that nurture the hearts and minds of children, providing and promoting quality books and a rich variety of media that entertain and educate readers from 6 months to 12 years." Publisher: Kate Klimo. Associate Publisher: Cathy Goldsmith.
Acquisitions: Easy-to-Read Books (step-into-reading and picture books): Heidi Kilgras, executive editor. Stepping Stones and middle grade fiction: Jennifer Dussling, senior editor. 100% of books published through agents; 2% of books by first-time authors.
   • Random House accepts only agented material. Random House title *Only Passing Through: The Story of Sojourner Truth*, illustrated by R. Gregory Christie (text by Anne Rockwell), won a 2001 Coretta Scott King Illustrator Honor Award.
How to Contact/Writers: Not accepting unsolicited mss and reserves the right not to return any work.
Illustration: Reviews ms/illustration packages from artists through agent only. Does not open or respond to unsolicited submissions.
Terms: Pays authors in royalties; sometimes buys mss outright. Sends galleys to authors. Book catalog free on request.

🅽 **RED RATTLE BOOKS**, Imprint of Soft Skull Press, 71 Bond St., Brooklyn NY 11217. Website: www.softskull.com. **Manuscript/Art Acquisitions:** Richard Eoin Nash, publisher. Publishes 4-6 children's books/year. Editorial philosophy: "to satisfy the need for socially award, nondidactic, sophisticated children's literature that's in line with the ideals of a new generation of parents."
Fiction: Picture books, young adult: graphic novels, poetry. Recently published *The Saddest Little Robot*, by Brian Gage.
How to Contact/Writers: Fiction: Submit cover letter with address information, phone and e-mail, outline/synopsis and sample chapter (no more than 30 pages). Responds only if interested and SASE included. Poetry: Submit "cover letter and no more than 10 pages."
Illustration: Accepts graphic novel submissions. Submit at least 5 "fully inked pages of art" with synopsis.
Tips: Do not send full mss unless requested. "We do not accept phone calls or e-mail manuscripts."

🖸 **RED WHEELBARROW PRESS, INC.**, E-mail: publisher@rwpress.com. Website: www.rwpress.com. Estab. 1997. Trade book publisher specializing in fiction (with slant) and educational material.
   • Red Wheelbarrow is currently not accepting submissions until further notice. Check their website for updates to this policy.

🖸 ▥ **RENAISSANCE HOUSE**, Imprint of Laredo Publishing, 9400 Lloydcrest Dr., Beverly Hills CA 90210. (800)547-5113. Fax: (310)860-9902. E-mail: laredo@renaissancehouse.net. Website: www.renaissancehouse.net. Estab. 1991. Specializes in trade books, educational, multicultural material. Independent book packager/producer. **Manuscript Acquisitions:** Raquel Benatar. **Art Acquisitions:** Sam Laredo. Publishes 5 picture books/year; 10 young readers/year; 10 middle readers/year; 5 young adult titles/year. 10% of books by first-time authors.
Fiction: Picture books: animal, folktales, multicultural. Young readers: animal, anthology, folktales, multicultural. Middle readers, young adult/teens: anthology, folktales, multicultural, nature/environment. Recently published *Isabel Allende, Memories for a Story* (English-Spanish, age 9-12, biography); *Stories of the Americas*, a series of legends by several authors (ages 9-12, legend).
How to Contact/Writers: Submit outline/synopsis. Responds to queries/mss in 3 weeks. Publishes a book 1 year after acceptance. Will consider simultaneous submissions, electronic submissions via disk or modem.
Illustration: Works with 25 illustrators/year. Uses color artwork only. Reviews ms/illustration packages from artists. Send ms with dummy. Contact: Sam Laredo. Illustrations only: Send tearsheets. Contact: Raquel Benatar. Responds in 3 weeks. Samples not returned; samples filed.
Terms: Pays authors royalty of 5-10% based on retail price. Pays illustrators by the project. Sends galleys to authors;

dummies to illustrators. Originals returned to artist at job's completion. Book catalog available for 9×12 SASE and $3 postage. All imprints included in a single catalog. Catalog available on website.

RISING MOON, P.O. Box 1389, Flagstaff AZ 86002-1389. (928)774-5251. Fax: (928)774-0592. E-mail: editorial@northl andpub.com. Website: www.northlandpub.com. Book publisher. **Manuscript Acquisitions:** Theresa Howell, editor. **Art Acquisitions:** Address to Art Director. Publishes 10-12 picture books/year; 10% of books by first-time authors. "Rising Moon is looking for exceptional bilingual (Spanish/English) stories about contemporary Latino American themes, stories about Latino role models, original stories with a Southwest flare, and Southwestern fractured fairy tales."

How to Contact/Writers: Rising Moon is accepting picture book mss from agented authors, previously published authors, and unsolicited picture book mss. We are no longer publishing middle-grade children's fiction. Please submit the entire ms for children's picture books, include a cover letter with information regarding any previously published work, and provide a self-addressed, stamped envelope (SASE) of adequate size and postage with your submission. No e-mail submissions.

Illustration: Works with 8-10 illustrators/year. Uses color artwork only. Reviews illustration packages from artists. Submit color samples (printed/color lasers) to art director with résumé, samples, promo sheet, slides, tearsheets. Samples returned with SASE only.

Terms: Pays authors royalty based on net. Pays illustrators by the project or royalty based on net. Sends galleys to authors; dummies to illustrators. Originals returned at job's completion. "Visit our website for writer's and artist's guidelines and complete catalog."

ROARING BROOK PRESS, Imprint of The Millbrook Press, 2 Old New Milford Rd., Brookfield CT 06804. (203)740-2220. Fax: (203)775-5643. Estab. 2000. Specializes in fiction, trade books. **Manuscript/Art Acquisitions:** Simon Boughton, publisher. Publishes approximately 40 titles/year. 1% of books by first-time authors. This publisher's goal is "to publish distinctive high-quality children's literature for all ages. To be a great place for authors to be published. To provide personal attention and a focused and thoughtful publishing effort for every book and every author on the list."

• Roaring Brook title *My Friend Rabbit*, written and illustrated by Eric Rohmann, won the 2003 Caldecott Medal. Their title *Action Jackson*, by Jan Greenberg and Sandra Jordan, illustrated by Robert Andrew Parker, won a 2003 Robert F. Siebert Honor.

Fiction: Picture books, young readers, middle readers, young adults: adventure, animal, contemporary, fantasy, history, humor, multicultural, nature/environment, poetry, religion, science fiction, sports, suspense/mystery. Recently published *Pool Boy*, by Michael Simmons.

How to Contact/Writer: Primarily interested in agented material. Not accepting unsolicited mss or queries. Will consider simultaneous submissions.

Illustration: Primarily interested in agented material. Works with 25 illustrators/year. Illustrations only: Query with samples. Do not send original art; copies only through the mail. Responds to agented queries/submissions in 1 month; unsolicited in 3 months. Samples returned with SASE.

Photography: Works on assignment only.

Terms: Pays authors royalty based on retail price. Pays illustrators royalty or flat fee depending on project. Sends galleys to authors; dummies to illustrators, if requested.

Tips: "You should find a reputable agent and have him/her submit your work."

THE ROSEN PUBLISHING GROUP INC., 29 E. 21st St., New York NY 10010. (212)777-3017. Fax: (212)777-0277. E-mail: rosened@erols.com. Website: www.rosenpub.com. **Art Acquisitions:** Cindy Reiman, photo director. Imprints: Rosen (Young Adult) (Iris Rosoff, editorial director); Rosen Central (Iris Rosoff, editorial director); PowerKids Press (Joanne Randolph, editorial director).

Nonfiction: Picture books: biography, health, hi-lo, nature/environment, science, self-help, social issues, special needs. Young readers: biography, health, hi-lo, multicultural, nature/environment, science, self-help, social issues, special needs. Middle readers: biography, careers, health, multicultural, nature/environment, science, self-help, social issues, special needs. Young adult: careers, health, multicultural, science, self-help, biography. Average word length: young readers—800-950; middle readers—5,000-7,500; young adults—between 8,000 and 30,000.

How to Contact/Writers: Nonfiction: Query with outline/synopsis and sample chapter as well as SASE. No unsolicited mss, no phone calls.

Photography: Buys stock and assigns work. Contact: Cindy Reiman, photo manager.

Terms: Pays flat fee or royalty, depending on book.

Tips: "Our list is specialized, and we publish only in series. Authors should familiarize themselves with our publishing program and policies before submitting."

ST. ANTHONY MESSENGER PRESS, 28 W. Liberty St., Cincinnati OH 45202-6498. (513)241-5615. Fax: (513)241-0399. E-mail: books@americancatholic.org. Website: www.AmericanCatholic.org. Book publisher. **Manuscript Acquisitions:** Lisa Biedenbach, editorial director. 25% of books by first-time authors. Imprints include Franciscan Communications (print and video) and Ikonographics (video). "Through print and electronic media marketed in North America and worldwide, we endeavor to evangelize, inspire and inform those who search for God and seek a richer Catholic, Christian, human life. We also look for books for parents and religious educators."

Nonfiction: Picture books, young readers, middle readers, young adults: religion. "We like all our resources to include anecdotes, examples, etc., that appeal to a wide audience. All of our products try to reflect cultural and racial diversity. All our books must be explicitly Catholic." Recently published *Friend Jesus: Prayers for Children*, by Gaynell Bordes Cronin;

insider report

From bloomers to baseball: an author celebrates courageous women

Amelia Bloomer isn't considered a proper lady because she wears pants. Katie Casey isn't good at being a girl and plays baseball. Milly misses the traditions of home, so she cooks up a brilliant plan with Mr. Macy. Bernice the bear cub lumps and tumbles rather than being a graceful ballerina, but still manages to steal the show. Besides being brave, spunky, and creative, what do these four characters have in common? They're all characters in books by children's writer Shana Corey.

"Most of my stories have similar threads running through them. I tend to be interested in girl main characters, and I'm fascinated by people who are confident enough to stand up for what they believe in," Corey says. "I think most people have that kind of confidence when they're young. When I was little, I always

Shana Corey

went around saying 'I want to be a movie star or an artist or a writer when I grow up.' But by the time I was in junior high, I stopped saying that. I even stopped thinking it! I lost that 'I can do anything' confidence that young kids have."

Courage and confidence are both themes that run through Corey's work, and even though her writing isn't autobiographical, it is a way for her to explore who she is and who she'd like to be. "What interests me is why and how some people—like Amelia Bloomer for instance—are able to keep that confidence into adulthood (something I certainly wish I could have done!). Wearing pants when the rest of the world says it's wrong, taking part in sports at a time when women weren't 'supposed' to be athletic—these are huge things."

Corey, herself, is no stranger to doing huge things. A successful writer of picture books and the series First Grader from Mars (illustrated by Mark Teague), she's also Assistant Editorial Director at Random House Children's Books. Corey started at Random House as an editorial assistant, helping to edit children's books, not write them. However, her sense of storytelling and her enthusiasm for women's history (along with the courage not to give up) led her down the writing path.

Along with creating inhouse copy, her duties as an editorial assistant for the Step into Reading line involved pitching book ideas for outside authors to write. Since she loved women's history, Corey pitched a number of related stories, but none were deemed right for the line. "Usually my boss would smile politely and say 'keep trying,' and that would be that."

Much like one of her determined heroines, Corey did keep trying, and eventually pitched an idea about Amelia Bloomer, a women's rights advocate for dress reform. While her supervisor didn't think the idea was right for the line, Corey couldn't stop thinking about Amelia, and with her supervisor's encouragement, she wrote the book herself. The finished manuscript still wasn't right for an early reader, but her supervisor suggested Corey pitch it to Tracy Mack, an editor at Scholastic. With her interest in fashion and feminism, Mack was a perfect match for the book. After she acquired it, she asked fashion illustrator Chesley McLaren to create the whimsical drawings that complete Corey's lively vision of Amelia's life. The result, named a Publishers Weekly Best Children's Book and a Booklist Editor's Choice, is a joyful celebration of personal freedom.

"I thought clothes were something everyone could relate to. Even very young kids can relate to how frustrating it can be to wear something uncomfortable. For me, Amelia's story (not the one I wrote but her actual story) is one of those wrinkles in time when something in the past comes to life and feels very up to date and connected to the present, and that absolutely thrills me."

Corey is skilled at finding these wrinkles, and making them come alive for today's readers. Her book *Milly and the Macy's Parade* (illustrated by Brett Helquist) is a fictional account of a young Polish girl who, through her ingenuity and love for her family, starts the Thanksgiving

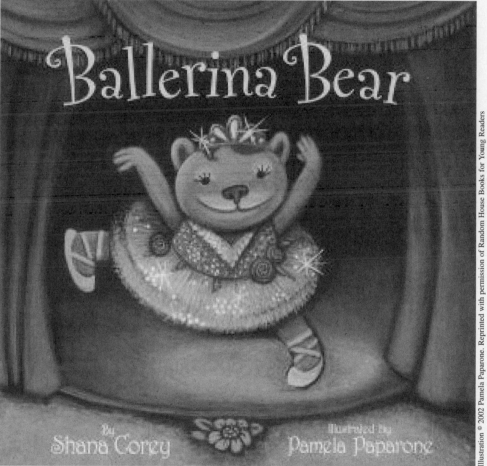

In *Ballerina Bear* (Random House, 2002), dancers Bernice and Bertram—the former is hopelessly clumsy and the latter is insufferably boring—team up, and the unlikely pair steals the stage. Like this book, all of Shana Corey's work encourages young readers to have self-confidence and determination.

day tradition. "With Milly, I came across a mention that the parade was started by immigrants who were homesick for the holiday customs of their homelands. That's such a wonderfully American beginning, it really stuck with me." However, Corey didn't have an actual historical figure to write about, so she researched around it. "I called Macy's and talked to their archivist. I researched what countries of origin were most common for New York immigrants at the time, what the holiday traditions were in those countries, what jobs immigrant employees might have been doing at Macy's. I also visited the tenement museum to get a sense of the times and took a tour of the old Macy's offices." Her research details helped her piece together the very real-life Milly.

Amelia Bloomer was a mid-nineteenth century temperance activist and publisher of *The Lily*. In addition to its other sociopolitical platforms, this monthly paper became a voice for change in women's clothing, specifically the abandonment of restrictive dresses in favor of shorter skirts and the knee-length undergarments that came to bear Amelia's surname. In *You Forgot Your Skirt, Amelia Bloomer!* (Scholastic, 2000), Shana Corey combines the historical and the whimsical to give modern readers an entertaining and informative picture of one our nation's early feminists and the fashion revolution she championed.

With *Players in Pigtails* (illustrated by Rebecca Gibbon), the story of the first women's baseball league, Corey had a different research challenge. She wanted to write a story about the league, but had *too many* amazing real-life histories to choose from and didn't know how to focus the tale. While researching, though, Corey had a breakthrough: She discovered that the lyrics for the baseball favorite "Take Me Out to the Ballgame," were, surprisingly, originally about a baseball fan named Katie Casey. "I've known that song my whole life, and not known that it was about a girl . . . it was that moment of 'a-ha!' Because for me, Katie's representative of all the women who played in the league—and really all women who love baseball!"

While Corey's ideas can originate from people who inspire her, they also grow out of quiet time. "If I find quiet time, stories come out of daydreaming—my mind wandering." In fact, Corey wrote the entire first draft of *Ballerina Bear* (illustrated by Pam Paparone), the story of the graceless but passionate dancer bear Bernice, on the subway. "For me, the subway is wonderful, because it's enforced space to daydream. My tendency when I have space or time is to fill it, but on the subway (especially if I'm stranded there without a book) gives me a couple of hours a day when there's nothing I can do except *think*."

Though she values solitary writing time, Corey recognizes the collaborative nature of the publishing process. Her editor at Scholastic is responsible for selecting each of Corey's illustrators, and the matches have added life and dimension to Corey's words. Corey is grateful for Mack's vision. "Tracy is encouraging. She finds wonderful illustrators, and she brings so much to my stories with her vision."

As a writer who's also an editor, Corey is in a unique position to appreciate the many sides of writing, from the genesis of ideas to the vision editors and illustrators bring to the work. Her writing ultimately grows from this energy. "I feel very lucky and thankful that the process is such a collaboration. When I'm surrounded by creative people, I get excited about ideas, and ideas can feed on each other."

—Meg Leder

Can You Find Jesus? Introducing Your Child to the Gospel, by Philip Gallery and Janet Harlow (ages 5-10); *People of the Bible: Their Life and Customs*, by Claire Musatti (ages 5-10).
How to Contact/Writers: Query or submit outline/synopsis and sample chapters. Responds to queries in 6 weeks; mss in 2 months. Publishes a book 12-18 months after acceptance.
Illustration: Works with 2 illustrators/year. "We design all covers and do most illustrations in-house, unless illustrations are submitted with text." Reviews ms/illustration packages from artists. Query with samples, résumé. Contact: Jeanne Kortekamp, art director. Responds to queries in 1 month. Samples returned with SASE; samples filed. Originals returned at job's completion.
Photography: Purchases photos from freelancers. Contact: Jeanne Kortekamp, art director. Buys stock and assigns work.
Terms: Pays authors royalties of 10-12% based on net receipts. Offers average advance payment of $1,000. Pays illustrators by the project. Pays photographers by the project. Sends galleys to authors. Book catalog and ms guidelines free on request.
Tips: "We do not publish fiction. We are slowing down publication of children's books. Know our audience—Catholic. We seek popularly written manuscripts that include the best of current Catholic scholarship. Parents, especially baby boomers, want resources for teaching children about the Catholic faith for passing on values. We try to publish items that reflect strong Catholic Christian values."

☒ ☐ SALINA BOOKSHELF, INC., 1254 W. University Ave., Suite 130, Flagstaff AZ 86001. (928)773-0066. Fax: (928)526-0386. E-mail: sales@salinabookshelf.com. Website: www.salinabookshelf.com. Estab. 1994. Specializes in educational and multicultural material. **Manuscript Acquisitions:** Jessie Ruffenach. **Art Acquisitions:** Art Department. Publishes 4 picture books/year; 4 young readers/year; and 1 young adult title/year. 50% of books are by first-time authors.
Fiction: Picture books, young readers, middle readers, young adults: adventure, animal, contemporary, folktales, multicultural.
Nonfiction: Picture books: multicultural. Young readers, middle readers, young adults: biography, history, multicultural.
How to Contact/Writers: Fiction/nonfiction: Query or submit complete ms. Responds to queries in 2 weeks; mss in 1 month. Publishes a book 1 year after acceptance. Will consider simultaneous submissions and previously published work.
Illustration: Accepts material from residents of the US only. Works with 5 illustrators/year. Reviews ms/illustration

packages from artists. Query. Illustrations only: Query with samples. Responds in 1 month. Samples returned with SASE; samples filed.

Photography: Buys stock and assigns work.

Terms: Pays authors royalty based on retail price. Offers advances (Average amount varies). Pays illustrators and photographers by the project. Originals returned to artist at job's completion. Catalog available for SASE or on website; ms guidelines available for SASE.

Tips: "Please note that all our books are Navajo oriented."

☑ ☑ SCHOLASTIC INC., 557 Broadway, New York NY 10012. (212)343-6100. Website: www.scholastic.com. Imprints: Cartwheel Books, Orchard Books, Scholastic Press.

● Scholastic does not accept unsolicited manuscripts. Their title *When Marian Sang*, by Pam Muñoz Ryan, illustrated by Brian Selznick, won a 2003 Robert F. Siebert Honor. *The Dinosaurs of Waterhouse Hawkins*, illustrated by Brian Selznick, text by Barbara Kerley, won a 2002 Caldecott Honor.

Illustration: Works with 50 illustrators/year. Does not review ms/illustration packages.Illustrations only: send promo sheet and tearsheets. Responds only if interested. Samples not returned. Original artwork returned at job's completion.

Terms: All contracts negotiated individually; pays royalty. Sends galleys to author; dummies to illustrators.

[N] SCHOLASTIC LIBRARY PUBLISHING, (formerly Grolier Publishing), 90 Sherman Turnpike, Danbury CT 06816. (203)797-3500. Book publisher. Vice President/Publisher: Phil Friedman. **Manuscript Acquisitions:** Kate Nunn, editor-in-chief. **Art Acquisitions:** Marie O'Neil, art director. Imprints: Grolier, Children's Press, Franklin Watts. Publishes more than 400 titles/year. 5% of books by first-time authors; very few titles from agented authors. Publishes informational (nonfiction) for K-12; picture books for young readers, grades 1-3.

Fiction: Publishes 1 picture book series, Rookie Readers, for grades 1-2. Does not accept unsolicited mss.

Nonfiction: Photo-illustrated books for all levels: animal, arts/crafts, biography, careers, concept, geography, health, history, hobbies, how-to, multicultural, nature/environment, science, social issues, special needs, sports. Average word length: young readers—2,000; middle readers—8,000; young adult—15,000.

How to Contact/Writers: Fiction: Does not accept fiction proposals. Nonfiction: Query; submit outline/synopsis, résumé and/or list of publications, and writing sample. SASE required for response. Responds in 3 months. Will consider simultaneous submissions. No phone or e-mail queries; will not respond to phone inquiries about submitted material.

Illustration: Works with 15-20 illustrators/year. Uses color artwork and line drawings. Illustrations only: Query with samples or arrange personal portfolio review. Responds only if interested. Samples returned with SASE. Samples filed. Do not send originals. No phone or e-mail inquiries; contact only by mail.

Photography: Contact: Caroline Anderson, Photo Manager. Buys stock and assigns work. Model/property releases and captions required. Uses color and b&w prints; $2\frac{1}{4} \times 2\frac{1}{4}$, 35mm transparencies, images on CD-ROM.

Terms: Pays authors royalty based on net or work purchased outright. Pays illustrators at competitive rates. Photographers paid per photo. Sends galleys to authors; dummies to illustrators.

☑ SCHOLASTIC PRESS, 557 Broadway, New York NY 10012. (212)343-6100. Website: www.scholastic.com. Book publisher. Imprint of Scholastic Inc. **Manuscript Acquisitions:** Dianne Hess, executive editor (picture book fiction/nonfiction); Lauren Thompson, senior editor (picture book fiction/nonfiction); Tracy Mack, executive editor (picture book, middle grade, YA). **Art Acquisitions:** David Saylor, all hardcover prints for Scholastic. Publishes 60 titles/year. 1% of books by first-time authors.

● Scholastic Press title *A Corner of the Universe*, by Ann M. Martin, won a 2003 Newbery Honor.

Fiction: Looking for strong picture books, middle grade novels (ages 8-11) and interesting and well written young adult novels.

Nonfiction: Interested "unusual and interesting approaches to commonly dry subjects, such as biography, math, history and science."

How to Contact/Writers: Fiction/nonfiction: "Send query with 1 sample chapter and synopsis. Don't call! Don't e-mail!" Picture books: submit complete ms.

Illustrations: Works with 30 illustrators/year. Uses both b&w and color artwork. Illustrations only: Query with samples; send tearsheets. Responds only if interested. Samples returned with SASE. Original artwork returned at job's completion.

Terms: Pays advance against royalty.

Tips: "Read *currently* published children's books. Revise, rewrite, rework and find your own voice, style and subject. We are looking for authors with a strong and unique voice who can tell a great story and have the ability to evoke genuine emotion. Children's publishers are becoming more selective, looking for irresistable talent and fairly broad appeal, yet still very willing to take risks, just to keep the game interesting."

SEEDLING PUBLICATIONS, INC., 4522 Indianola Ave., Columbus OH 43214-2246. (614)267-7333. Fax: (614)267-4205.Website: www.SeedlingPub.com. **Acquisitions:** Josie Stewart. 20% of books by first-time authors. Publishes books for the beginning reader in English. "Natural language and predictable text are requisite to our publications. Patterned text is acceptable, but must have a unique storyline. Poetry, books in rhyme, full-length picture books or chapter books are not being accepted at this time. Illustrations are not necessary."

Fiction: Beginning reader books: adventure, animal, fantasy, hi-lo, humor, multicultural, nature/environment, special needs. Multicultural needs include stories which include children from many cultures and Hispanic-centered storylines. Does not accept texts longer than 16 pages or over 150-200 words or stories in rhyme. Average word length: young readers—100.

Recently published *The Sleepy Red Ladybug*, by Clare Mishica; *Fish Money*, by Carmella Van Vleet; and *The Mat Maker*, by Pam Calvert.

Nonfiction: Beginning reader books: animal, concept, hi-lo, multicultural, music/dance, nature/environment, science, special needs, sports. Does not accept texts longer than 16 pages or over 150-200 words. Average word length: young readers—100. Recently published *Turtles Everywhere*, by Ryan Durney and *Scarlet Macaws*, by Dr. John Becker.

How to Contact/Writers: Fiction/Nonfiction: Submit complete ms. Responds in 6 months. Publishes a book 1-2 years after acceptance. Will consider simultaneous submissions.

Illustration: Works with 8-9 illustrators/year. Uses color artwork only. Reviews ms/illustration packages from artists. Submit ms with dummy. Illustrations only: Send color copies. Responds only if interested. Samples returned with SASE only; samples filed if interested.

Photography: Buys photos from freelancers. Works on assignment only. Model/property releases required. Uses color prints and 35mm transparencies. Submit cover letter and color promo piece.

Terms: Pays authors royalty of 5% based on retail price or work purchased outright. Pays illustrators and photographers by the project. Original artwork is not returned at job's completion.

Tips: "Follow our guidelines carefully and test your story with children and educators."

SILVER MOON PRESS, 160 Fifth Ave., New York NY 10010. (212)242-6499. Fax: (212)242-6799. E-mail: mail@sil vermoonpress.com. Website: www.silvermoonpress.com. Publisher: David Katz. Managing Editor: Hope Killcoyne. **Marketing Coordinator:** Karin Lillebo. Book publisher. Publishes 2 books for grades 4-6. 25% of books by first-time authors; 10% books from agented authors. "We publish books of entertainment and educational value and develop books which fit neatly into curriculum for grades 4-6. Silver Moon Press publishes mainly American historical fiction with a strong focus on the Revolutionary War and Colonial times. History comes alive when children can read about other children who lived when history was being made!"

Fiction: Middle readers: historical, multicultural and mystery. Average word length: 14,000. Recently published *A Silent Witness in Harlem*, by Eve Creary; *In the Hands of the Enemy*, by Robert Sheely; *Ambush in the Wilderness*, by Kris Hemphill; and *Race to Kitty Hawk*, by Edwina Raffa and Annelle Rigsby.

How to Contact/Writers: Fiction: Query. Send synopsis and/or a few chapters, along with a SASE. Responds to queries in 1 month; mss in 2 months. Publishes a book 1-2 years after acceptance. Will consider simultaneous submissions, or previously published work.

Illustration: Works with 2-3 illustrators/year. Reviews ms/illustration packages from artists. Query. Illustrations only: Query with samples, résumé, client list. Responds only if interested. Samples returned with SASE; samples filed. Original artwork returned at job's completion.

Photography: Buys photos from freelancers. Buys stock and assigns work. Uses archival, historical, sports photos. Captions required. Uses color, b&w prints; 35mm, 2¼×2¼, 4×5, 8×10 transparencies. Submit cover letter, résumé, published samples, client list, promo piece.

Terms: Pays authors royalty or work purchased outright. Pays illustrators by the project, no royalty. Pays photographers by the project, per photo, no royalty. Sends galleys to authors; dummies to illustrators. Book catalog available for 8½×11 SAE and 77¢ postage.

SIMON & SCHUSTER BOOKS FOR YOUNG READERS, 1230 Avenue of the Americas, New York NY 10020. (212)698-7000. Fax: (212)698-2796. E-mail: childrens.submissions@simonandschuster.com. Website: www.simonsayskids .com. Imprint of Simon & Schuster Children's Publishing Division. **Manuscript Acquisitions:** David Gale, editorial director, Kevin Lewis, senior editor; Paula Wiseman, editorial director, Paula Wiseman Books. **Art Acquisitions:** Dan Potash, art director. Publishes 75 books/year. "We publish high-quality fiction and nonfiction for a variety of age groups and a variety of markets. Above all we strive to publish books that will offer kids a fresh perspective on their world."

• Simon & Schuster Books for Young Readers does not accept unsolicited manuscripts. Queries are accepted via mail and e-mail. Their title *The Spider and the Fly*, illustrated by Toni DiTerlizzi, written by Mary Howitt, won a 2003 Caldecott Honor and *Chicken Soup by Heart*, by Esther Hershenhorn, illustrated by Rosanne Litziner, won the 2003 Sydney Taylor Award for Younger Readers.

Fiction: Picture books: animal, concept. Middle readers, young adult: adventure, suspense/mystery. All levels: anthology, contemporary, history, humor, poetry, nature/environment. Recently published *Giggle, Giggle, Quack*, by Doreen Cronin, illustration by Betsy Lewin (picture book, ages 3-7); *Gingerbread*, by Rachel Cohn (young adult fiction, ages 13 and up).

Nonfiction: All levels: biography, history, nature/environment. Picture books: concept. "We're looking for picture book or middle grade nonfiction that has a retail potential. No photo essays." Recently published *America: A Patriotic Primer*, by Lynne Cheney, illustrated by Robin Preiss Glasser (picture book nonfiction, all ages).

How to Contact/Writers: Accepting query letters only, preferably by e-mail at childrens.submissions@simonandschuste r.com. Please note the appropriate imprint in the subject line. Responds to queries/mss in 2 months. Publishes a book 4 years after acceptance. Will consider simultaneous submissions.

Illustration: Works with 70 illustrators/year. Do not submit original artwork. Editorial reviews ms/illustration packages from artists. Submit query letter to Submissions Editor. Illustrations only: Query with samples; samples filed. Provide promo sheet, tearsheets. Responds only if interested. Originals returned at job's completion.

Terms: Pays authors royalty (varies) based on retail price. Pays illustrators or photographers by the project or royalty (varies) based on retail price. Original artwork returned at job's completion. Manuscript/artist's guidelines available via website or free on request (call (212)698-2707).

Tips: "We're looking for picture books centered on a strong, fully-developed protagonist who grows or changes during the course of the story; YA novels that are challenging and psychologically complex; also imaginative and humorous middle-grade fiction. And we want nonfiction that is as engaging as fiction. Our imprint's slogan is 'Reading You'll Remember.' We aim to publish books that are fresh, accessible and family-oriented; we want them to have an impact on the reader."

SMALLFELLOW PRESS, Imprint of Tallfellow Press, 1180 S. Beverly Dr., Suite 320, Los Angeles CA 90035. E-mail: asls@pacbell.net; tallfellow@pacbell.net. Website: www.smallfellow.com. **Manuscript/Art Acquisitions:** Claudia Sloan.

Fiction: Picture books: humorous, whimsical. Recently published *The Enormous Mister Schumpsle*, by Joe Murray; *It's Spring*; *It's Summer*; *It's Fall*; *It's Winter*, all by Jimmy Pickering; and *Forever Friends*, by Barbara S. Cohen, illustrated by Dorothy Louise Hall.

How to Contact/Writers: Fiction: Query or submit complete ms. Include SASE.

Illustration: Send samples with SASE.

SMOOCH, Imprint of Dorchester Publishing, 276 Fifth Ave., Suite 1008, New York NY 10001. E-mail: lhulten@dorch esterpub.com. Website: www.dorchesterpub.com. **Manuscript Acquisitions:** Kate Seaver, editor. **Art Acquisitions:** Art Department. Specializes in mass market books. Publishes 12 young adult titles/year. Editorial Philosophy: "to bring the best fiction at the best value."

Fiction: Young adult: Contemporary, romance, paranormal. Word length: young adult titles—45,000. Recently published *The Year My Life Went Down the Loo*, by Katie Maxwell; *A Girl, A Guy & A Ghost*, by Sherrie Rose; and *My Life as a Snowbunny*, by Kaz Delaney.

How to Contact/Writers: Fiction: Submit 3 sample chapters. Responds in 8 months. Returns mss only with SASE.

Illustration: Illustrations only: Send tearsheets. No e-mails or portfolio reviews. Responds only if interested. Samples not returned.

Terms: Book catalog free. Call (800)481-9191 or visit website.

Tips: *Smooch* titles' word lengths' must be 45,000. "We prefer manuscripts to be written from the third-person point-of-view. Name, address, phone number and e-mail of the author should be on the first page of the manuscript, and a header for subsequent pages should contain the author's name and title. Retain a copy of all material sent in case the original gets lost in the mail. As our primary audience is girls ages 12-16, there should be no sex scenes."

SOUNDPRINTS, 353 Main Ave., Norwalk CT 06851-1552. (203)846-2274. Fax: (203)846-1776. E-mail: soundprints @soundprints.com. Website: www.soundprints.com. Estab. 1987. Specializes in trade books, educational material, multicultural material, fact-based fiction. **Manuscript Acquisitions:** Chelsea Shriver, assistant editor. **Art Acquisitions:** Marcin Pilchowski. Publishes 4 picture books/year; 8 young readers/year. Soundprints publishes children's books accompanied by plush toys and read-along cassettes that deal with wildlife, history and nature. All content must be accurate and realistic and is curated by experts for veracity. Soundprints will begin publishing early reader chapter books in the spring of 2002.

Fiction: Picture books: animal. Young readers: animal, multicultural, nature/environment. Middle readers: history, multicultural. .

Nonfiction: Picture books: animals. Young readers: animal, multicultural, nature/environment. Middle readers: history, multicultural. Published *Koala Country: Story of an Australian Eucalyptus Forest*, by Deborah Dennard, illustrated by James McKinnon (grades 1-4); *Box Turtle at Silver Pond*, by Susan Korman, illustrated by Stephen Marchesi (grades ps-2); *Bear on His Own*, by Laura Gales Gatvin (ages 18 months to 3 years).

How to Contact/Writers: Fiction/Nonfiction: Submit published writing samples. Responds in 3 months. Publishes book 2 years after acceptance.

Illustration: Works with 12 illustrators/year. Uses color artwork only. Query. Contact: Chelsea Shriver, assistant editor. Query with samples. Samples not returned.

Terms: Work purchased outright from authors for $1,000-2,500. Pays illustrators by the project. Book catalog available for 8½×11 SASE; ms and art guidelines available for SASE. Catalog available on website.

Tips: "As a small publisher with very specific guidelines for our well-defined series, we are not able to accept unsolicited manuscripts for publication. All of our authors are contracted on a 'work for hire basis,' meaning that they create manuscripts to our specifications, depending on our need. While we generally work with an established group of authors who know our needs as a publisher, we are always interested in reviewing the work of new potential authors. If you would like to submit some published writing samples, we would be happy to review them and keep them on file for future reference. Please send all writing samples to Chelsea Shriver, assistant editor."

SOURCEBOOKS, INC., 1935 Brookdale Rd., Suite 139, Naperville IL 60563-9245. (630)961-3900. Fax: (630)961-2168. Website: www.sourcebooks.com. Book publisher. **Manuscript Acquisitions:** Todd Stocke, editorial director; Hillel Black, agented manuscripts; Deborah Werksman, gift, humor, relationships. **Art Acquisitions:** Norma Fioretti, director of production.

How to Contact/Writers: Fiction/Nonfiction: Query or submit outline/synopsis. Responds to queries/mss in 3 months. Publishes a book 1 year after acceptance. Will consider simultaneous submissions, electronic submissions via disk and previously published work.

Illustration: Works with 10 illustrators/year. Reviews ms/illustration packages from artists. Query. Illustrations only: Query with samples. Samples returned with SASE; samples filed.

Photography: Buys stock.

Terms: Send galleys to authors. Originals returned to artist at job's completion. Book catalog for 9×12 SASE. All imprints included in a single catalog. Manuscript guidelines available for SASE or via website.

☐ **THE SPEECH BIN, INC.**, 1965 25th Ave., Vero Beach FL 32960. (561)770-0007. Fax: (561)770-0006. Book publisher. Estab. 1984. **Acquisitions:** Jan J. Binney, senior editor. Publishes 10-12 books/year. 50% of books by first-time authors; less than 15% of books from agented writers. "Nearly all our books deal with treatment of children (as well as adults) who have communication disorders of speech or hearing or children who deal with family members who have such disorders (e.g., a grandparent with Alzheimer's disease or stroke)."

• The Speech Bin is currently overstocked with fiction.

Fiction: Picture books: animal, easy-to-read, health, special needs. Young readers, middle readers, young adult: health, special needs, communication disorders.

Nonfiction: Picture books, young readers, middle readers, young adults: activity books, health, textbooks, special needs, communication disorders.

How to Contact/Writers: Fiction/Nonfiction: Query. Responds to queries in 6 weeks; mss in 3 months. Publishes a book 10-12 months after acceptance. "Will consider simultaneous submissions *only* if notified; too many authors fail to let us know if manuscript is simultaneously submitted to other publishers! We *strongly* prefer sole submissions. No electronic or faxed submissions."

Illustration: Works with 4-5 illustrators/year ("usually in-house"). Reviews ms/illustration packages from artists. Manuscript/illustration packages and illustration only: "Query first!" Submit tearsheets (no original art). SASE required for reply or return of material. No electronic or faxed submissions without prior authorization.

Photography: Buys stock and assigns work. Looking for scenic shots. Model/property releases required. Uses glossy b&w prints, 35mm or 2¼×2¼ transparencies. Submit résumé, business card, promotional literature or tearsheets to be kept on file.

Terms: Pays authors in royalties based on selling price. Pays illustrators by the project. Pays photographers by the project or per photo. Sends galleys to authors. Original artwork returned at job's completion. Book catalog for $1.43 postage and 9×12 SAE; ms guidelines for #10 SASE.

Tips: "No calls, please. All submissions and inquiries must be in writing."

STANDARD PUBLISHING, 8121 Hamilton Ave., Cincinnati OH 45231. (513)931-4050. Fax: (513)931-0950. E-mail: customerservice@standardpub.com. Website: www.standardpub.com. Book publisher. Estab. 1866. **Manuscript Acquisitions:** Diane Stortz, managing director consumer product. **Art Acquisitions:** Coleen Davis, art director; Rob Glover, consumer product senior designer. Many projects are written in-house. No juvenile or young adult novels. 25-40% of books by first-time authors; 1% of books from agented writers. Publishes picture books, board book, nonfiction, devotions and resources for teachers.

Fiction: Recently published *Jesus Must Be Really Special*, by Jennie Bishop, illustrated by Amy Wumman.

Nonfiction: Recently published *Playtime Devotions*, by Christine Tangvald, illustrated by Tamara Schmitz.

How to Contact/Writers: Responds in 6 weeks on queries, mss in 3 months.

Illustration: Works with 20 new illustrators/year. Illustrations only: Submit cover letter and photocopies. Responds to art samples only if interested. Samples returned with SASE; samples filed.

Terms: Pays authors royalties based on net price or work purchased outright (range varies by project). Pays illustrators (mostly) by project. Pays photographers by the photo. Sends galleys to authors on most projects. Book catalog available for $2 and 8½×11 SAE; ms guidelines for letter-size SASE.

Tips: "We look for manuscripts that help draw children into a relationship with Jesus Christ; help children develop insights about what the Bible teaches; make reading an appealing and pleasurable activity."

☒ **STARSEED PRESS**, Imprint of HJ Kramer, P.O. Box 1082. Tiburon CA 94920. (415)435-5367. Fax: (415)435-5364. Estab. 1984. **Manuscript Acquisitions:** Jan Phillips. **Art Acquisitions:** Linda Kramer, vice president. Publishes 2 picture books/year. 50% of books by first-time authors. "We publish 4-color, 32-page children's picture books dealing with self-esteem and positive values, with a non-denominational, spiritual emphasis."

Fiction: Picture books: adventure, multicultural, nature/environment. Average word length: picture books—500-1,500. Recently published *Thank You God*, by Holly Bea, illustrated by Kim Howard (ages 3-7, picture book).

Nonfiction: Picture books: multicultural, nature/environment.

How to Contact/Writers: Fiction/nonfiction: Submit outline/synopsis. Responds to queries/mss in 10 weeks. Publishes a book 18 months after acceptance. Will consider simultaneous submissions, previously published work.

Illustration: Works with 2 illustrators/year. Uses color artwork only. Illustrations only: Query with samples. Responds only if interested. Samples returned with SASE; samples filed.

Terms: Pays royalty of 6-20% (divided between author and illustrator—publisher's net receipts). Originals returned to artist at job's completion. Book catalog available for 9×11 SAE with $1.98 postage; ms and art guidelines available for SASE. All imprints included in a single catalog.

STEMMER HOUSE PUBLISHERS, INC., 2627 Caves Rd., Owings Mills MD 21117-9919. (410)363-3690. Fax: (410)363-8459. E-mail: stemmerhouse@home.com. Website: www.stemmer.com. Book publisher. Estab. 1975. **Acquisitions:** Barbara Holdridge, president. Publishes 1-3 picture books/year. "Sporadic" numbers of young reader, middle reader titles/year. 60% of books by first-time authors. "Stemmer House is best known for its commitment to fine illustrated books, excellently produced."

• Stemmer House is not currently accepting fiction.

Nonfiction: Picture books: animal, multicultural, nature. All level: animals, nature/environment. Multicultural needs include Native American, African. Recently published *Will You Sting Me? Will You Bite?*, by Sarah Swan Miller.

How to Contact/Writers: Fiction/Nonfiction: Query or submit outline/synopsis and sample chapters. Responds only with SASE. Responds to queries/mss in 1 week. Publishes a book 18 months after acceptance. Will consider simultaneous submissions. No submissions via e-mail.

Illustration: Works with 2-3 illustrators/year. Uses color artwork only. Reviews ms/illustration packages from artists. Query first with several photocopied illustrations. Illustrations only: Submit tearsheets and/or slides (with SASE for return). Responds in 2 weeks. Samples returned with SASE; samples filed "if noteworthy."

Terms: Pays authors royalties of 4-10% based on net sales price. Offers average advance payment of $300. Pays illustrators royalty of 4-10% based on net sales price. Pays photographers 4-10% royalty based on net sales price. Sends galleys to authors. Original artwork returned at job's completion. Book catalog and ms guidelines for 9×12 SASE or via website.

Tips: Writers: "Simplicity, literary quality and originality are the keys." Illustrators: "We want to see ms/illustration packages—don't forget the SASE!"

N STERLING PUBLISHING CO., INC., 387 Park Ave. S., New York NY 10016-8810. (212)532-7160. Fax: (212)981-0508. Website: www.sterlingpublishing.com. Specializes in trade books, nonfiction. **Manuscript Acquisitions:** Frances Gilbert. **Art Acquisitions:** Karen Nelson, creative director. Publishes 4 picture books/year; 50 young readers/year; 150 middle readers/year; and 10 young adult titles/year. 15% of books by first-time authors.

Nonfiction: Picture books: activity books, concept. Young readers: activity books, arts/crafts, cooking, hobbies, how-to, science. Middle readers, young adults: activity books, arts/crafts, hobbies, how-to, science, mazes, optical illusions, games, magic, math, puzzles.

How to Contact/Writers: Nonfiction: Submit outline/synopsis and 1 sample chapter. Responds to queries/mss in 6 weeks. Publishes book 1 year after acceptance. Will consider simultaneous submissions, previously pubilshed work.

Illustration: Works with 50 illustrators/year. Reviews ms/illustration packages from artists. Contact: Frances Gilbert, editorial director. Illustrations only: Send promo sheet. Contact: Karen Nelson, creative director. Responds in 6 weeks. Samples returned with SASE; samples filed.

Photography: Buys stock and assigns work. Contact: Karen Nelson.

Terms: Pays authors royalty or work purchased outright from authors. Offers advances (Average amount: $2,000). Pays illustrators by the project. Pays photographers by the project or per photo. Sends galleys to authors; dummies to illustrators. Originals returned to artist at job's completion. Offers writer's guidelines for SASE. Catalog available on website.

Tips: "We are primarily a nonfiction activities-based publisher. We do not publish fiction, but we are beginning to develop a picture book list. Our list is not trend-driven. We focus on titles that will backlist well."

N THE STORY PLACE, 1735 Brantley Rd., #1611, Ft. Myers FL 33902-3920. Fax: (775)206-7437. E-mail: tsp@thestoryplace.com. Website: www.thestoryplace.com. Estab. 1998. Specializes in mass market books, fiction, nonfiction. 100% of books by first-time authors. "The Story Place focuses on new and different ideas that fill the void in children's publishing today."

● The Story Place is currently going through reorganization and is not accepting submissions.

N SUNBELT MEDIA, INC./EAKIN PRESS, P.O. Box 90159, Austin TX 78709. (512)288-1771. Fax: (512)288-1813. E-mail: eakinpub@sig.net. Website: www.eakinpress.com. Book publisher. Estab. 1978. Publishes 25 books for young readers/year. 50% of books by first-time authors; 5% of books from agented writers.

Fiction: Picture books: animal. Middle readers, young adults: history, sports. Average word length: picture books—3,000; young readers—10,000; middle readers—15,000-30,000; young adults—30,000-50,000. "90% of our books relate to Texas and the Southwest."

Nonfiction: Picture books: animal. Middle readers and young adults: history, sports. Recently published *Ima & The Great Texas Ostrich Race*.

How to Contact/Writers: Fiction/Nonfiction: Query. Responds to queries in 2 weeks; mss in 6 weeks. Publishes a book 18 months after acceptance. Will consider simultaneous submissions.

Illustration: Reviews ms/illustration packages from artists. Query. Illustrations only: Submit tearsheets. Responds to art samples in 2 weeks.

Terms: Pays authors royalties of 10-15% based on net to publisher. Pays for separate authors and illustrators: "Usually share royalty." Pays illustrators royalty of 10-15% based on net to publisher. Sends galleys to authors. Book catalog $1 available via website or with SASE; writer guidelines available with SASE.

Tips: Writers: "Be sure all elements of manuscript are included—include bio of author or illustrator." Submit books relating to TX only.

A ☐ SUPER MANAGEMENT, Smarty Pants A/V, 15104 Detroit, Suite 2, Lakewood OH 44107-3916. (216)221-5300. Fax: (216)221-5348. Estab. 1988. Specializes in mass market books, fiction, educational material, Christian material, audio with each book. **Acquisitions:** S. Tirk, CEO/President. Publishes 12 young readers/year. 5% of books by first-time authors. "We do mostly the classics or well known names such as Paddington Bear."

Fiction: Picture books: adventure, animal, folktales, multicultural, nature/environment, poetry. Average word length: young readers—24 pages. Recently published *The Best of Mother Goose*, from the "Real M.G."; *Beatrix Potter, Paddington Bear*.

Nonfiction: Picture books, young readers: activity books, animal, music/dance, nature/environment. Average word length: picture books—24 pages; middle readers—24 pages.

How to Contact/Writers: Fiction: Submit complete ms. Responds in 3 weeks. Publishes a book 6-12 months after acceptance. Will consider simultaneous submissions and previously published work.

Illustration: Only interested in agented material. Works with several illustrators/year. Uses color artwork only. Reviews ms/illustration packages from artists. Submit ms with dummy with return prepaid envelope. Contact: S. Tirk, CEO/President. Illustrations only: send promo sheet. Responds in 3 weeks to queries. Samples returned with SASE.

Photography: Works on assignment only. Model/property releases required. Uses color prints. Submit color promo piece.

Terms: Pays author negotiable royalty. Buys artwork and photos outright. Manuscript and art guidelines available for SASE.

Tips: "We deal with mostly children's classics and well-known characters."

☑ ☐ ☐ **TEACHER IDEAS PRESS**, Libraries Unlimited, P.O. Box 6926, Portsmouth NH 03802. (800)541-2086. Fax: (603)431-7840. Website: www.teacherideaspress.com. Estab. 1965. Specializes in educational material, multicultural material. Independent book packager/producer.

Nonfiction: Young readers, middle readers, young adult: activity books, multicultural, reference, teacher resource books. Recently published *Science Through Children's Literature, 2002*, by Butzow (grades K-6, lit-based activity book); *More Novels & Plays: 30 Creative Teaching Guides for Grades 6-12*, by Worthington; and *Native American Today: Resources & Activities for Educators*, by Hirschfelder (grades 4-8).

How to Contact/Writers: Nonfiction: Query or submit outline/synopsis. Responds to queries in 6 weeks. Publishes a book 6-9 months after acceptance. Will consider simultaneous submission or electronic submissions via disk or modem.

Terms: Pays authors royalty of approximately 10%. Send galleys to authors. Book catalog available for 9 × 12 SAE and 2 first-class stamps. Writer's guidelines available for SASE. Catalog and ms guidelines available online at www.heinemann.com.

Tips: "We encourage queries from writers with classroom experience as teachers, although we will consider others. Activity Books, annotated bios, story collections with supplemental materials, and books with many reproducibles are welcome for consideration."

TILBURY HOUSE, PUBLISHERS, 2 Mechanic St., #3, Gardiner ME 04345. (207)582-1899. Fax: (207)582-8227. E-mail: tilbury@tilburyhouse.com. Website: www.tilburyhouse.com. Book publisher. **Publisher:** Jennifer Bunting. Publishes 1-3 young readers/year.

Fiction: Picture books, young readers, middle readers: multicultural, nature/environment. Special needs include books that teach children about tolerance and honoring diversity. Recently published *When the Bees Fly Home*, by Andrea Cheng, illustrated by Joline McFadden.

Nonfiction: Picture books, young readers, middle readers: multicultural, nature/environment. Recently published *Life Under Ice*, by Mary Cerullo, with photography by Bill Curtsinger; and *Saving Birds*, by Pete Salmansohn and Steve Kress.

How to Contact/Writers: Fiction/Nonfiction: Submit outline/synopsis. Responds to queries/mss in 1 month. Publishes a book 1-2 years after acceptance. Will consider simultaneous submissions "with notification."

Illustration: Works with 2 illustrators/year. Illustrations only: Query with samples. Responds in 1 month. Samples returned with SASE. Original artwork returned at job's completion.

Photography: Buys photos from freelancers. Works on assignment only.

Terms: Pays authors royalty based on wholesale price. Pays illustrators/photographers by the project; royalty based on wholesale price. Sends galleys to authors. Book catalog available for 6 × 9 SAE and 57¢ postage.

Tips: "We are primarily interested in children's books that teach children about tolerance in a multicultural society and honoring diversity. We are also interested in books that teach children about environmental issues."

Ⓐ **MEGAN TINGLEY BOOKS**, Imprint of Little, Brown and Company, Time and Life Building, 1271 Avenue of the Americas, New York NY 10020. (212)572-8700. Website: www.lb-kids.com or www.lb-teens.com. Estab. 2000. Specializes in trade books, nonfiction, fiction, multicultural material. **Manuscript Acquisitions:** Sara Morling, editorial assistant. **Art Acquisitions:** Managing Editor. Publishes 10 picture books/year; 1 middle readers/year; 1 young adult title/year. 2% of books by first-time authors.

● Megan Tingley Books accepts agented material only.

Fiction: Average word length: picture books—under 1,000 words. Recently published *You Read to Me, I'll Read to You: Very Short Stories to Read Together*, by Mary Ann Hoberman, illustrated by Michael Emberley (ages 4 and up, picture book); *It's Okay to be Different*, by Todd Parr (all ages, picture book); *Define Normal*, by Julie Peters.

Nonfiction: All levels: activity books, animal, arts/crafts, biography, concept, cooking, history, multicultural, music/dance, nature/environment, science, self help, social issues, special needs. Recently published *The Family Book*, by Todd Parr; *Sing Along Stories 2*, by Mary Ann Hoberman; and *Keeping You a Secret*, by Julie Peters.

How to Contact/Writers: Accepts agented material only. Query. Responds to mss in 3 months. Publishes a book 2 years after acceptance. Will consider simultaneous submissions, previously published work.

Illustration: Works with 15 illustrators/year. Reviews ms/illustration packages from artists. Query. Illustrations only: Query with samples. Contact: Editorial Assistant. Responds only if interested. Samples not returned; samples kept on file.

Photography: Buys stock images. Contact: Editorial Assistant. Submit cover letter, samples.

Terms: Pays authors royalty of 5% based on retail price or work purchased outright. Pays illustrators by the project, 5% royalty based on retail price. Pays photographers by the project, royalty 5% based on retail price. Sends galleys to authors. Originals returned to artist at job's completion. All imprints included in a single catalog. Book catalog and art guidelines available for SASE.

Ⓝ **TOR BOOKS**, Forge, Orb, Starscape, Tor Teen, 175 Fifth Ave., New York NY 10010-7703. Fax: (212)388-0191. Website: www.tor.com. **Publisher Starscape, Tor Teen, Children's and Young Adult Division:** Kathleen Doherty. Children's, Young Adult Starscape, Tor Teen Editor: Jonathan Schmidt. Educational Sales Coordinator: Christopher McDermott. Publishes 5-10 middle readers/year; 5-10 young adults/year.

• Tor Books is the "world's largest publisher of science fiction and fantasy, with strong category publishing in historical fiction, mystery, western/Americana, thriller, children's YA."

Fiction: Middle readers, young adult titles: adventure, animal, anthology, concept, contemporary, fantasy, history, humor, multicultural, nature/environment, problem novel, science fiction, suspense/mystery. "We are interested and open to books which tell stories from a wide range of perspectives. We are interested in materials that deal with a wide range of issues." Average word length: middle readers—30,000; young adults—60,000-100,000. Published *Hidden Talents, Flip,* by David Lubar (ages 10 and up); and *Briar Rose,* by Jane Yolen (ages 12 and up).

Nonfiction: Middle readers and young adult: geography, history, how-to, multicultural, nature/environment, science, social issues. Does not want to see religion, cooking. Average word length: middle readers—25-35,000; young adults—70,000. Published *Strange Unsolved Mysteries,* by Phyllis Rabin Emert; *Stargazer's Guide* (to the Galaxy), by Q.L. Pearce (ages 8-12, guide to constellations, illustrated).

How to Contact/Writers: Fiction/Nonfiction: Submit outline/synopsis and complete ms. Responds to queries in 1 month; mss in 6 months for unsolicited work; 1 month or less for agented submissions.

Illustration: Query with samples. Contact: Irene Gallo, art director. Responds only if interested. Samples kept on file.

Terms: Pays authors royalty. Offers advances. Pays illustrators by the project. Book catalog available for 9×12 SAE and 3 first-class stamps. Submission guidelines available with SASE.

Tips: "Know the house you are submitting to, familiarize yourself with the types of books they are publishing. Get an agent. Allow him/her to direct you to publishers who are most appropriate. It saves time and effort."

TRICYCLE PRESS, Imprint of Ten Speed Press, P.O. Box 7123, Berkeley CA 94707. (510)559-1600. Fax: (510)559-1637. Website: www.tenspeed.com. Estab. 1993. **Acquisitions:** Nicole Geiger, publisher. Publishes 12-14 picture books/year; 3 activity books/year; 2 middle readers/year; 1 'tween fiction/year; 4 board books/year. 25% of books by first-time authors. "Tricycle Press looks for something outside the mainstream; books that encourage children to look at the world from a different angle. Tricycle Press, like its parent company, Ten Speed Press, is known for its quirky, offbeat books. We publish high quality trade books."

• Tricycle Press title *George Hogglesberry, Grade School Alien,* by Sarah Wilson, illustrated by Chad Cameron, won the 2002 Golden Kite Award for picture book text.

Fiction: Board books, picture books, middle grade: adventure, animal, contemporary, fantasy, history, multicultural, nature, poetry, suspense/mystery. Picture books, young readers: concept. Middle readers: anthology, novels. Average word length: picture books—800. Recently published *Hey, Little Ant,* by Phil and Hannah Hoose (ages 5-8 picture book); *King and King,* by Linda de Haan and Stern Nijland.

Nonfiction: Picture books, middle readers: activity books, animal, arts/crafts, biography, careers, concept, cooking, history, how-to, multicultural, music/dance, nature/environment, science. Recently published *Q is for Quark Science: An Alphabet Book,* by David M. Schwartz (ages 9 and up, picture book); *Honest Pretzels and 64 Other Amazing Recipes for Cooks Ages 8 & Up,* by Mollie Katzen (activity book); and *The Young Adventurer's Guide to Everest,* by Jonathan Chester (ages 8 and up, nonfiction picture book).

How to Contact/Writers: Fiction: Submit complete ms for picture books. Submit outline/synopsis and 2-3 sample chapters for chapter book. "No queries!" Nonfiction: Submit complete ms. Responds to mss in 6 months. Publishes a book 1-2 years after acceptance. Welcomes simultaneous submissions and previously published work. Do not send original artwork; copies only, please. No electronic or faxed submissions.

Illustration: Works with 12 illustrators/year. Uses color and b&w. Reviews ms/illustration package from artists. Submit ms with dummy and/or 2-3 pieces of final art. Illustrations only: Query with samples, promo sheet, tearsheets. Responds only if interested. Samples returned with SASE; samples filed. Original artwork returned at job's completion unless work for hire.

Photography: Works on assignment only. Uses 35mm transparencies. Submit samples.

Terms: Pays authors royalty of 7½-8½% based on net receipts. Offers advances. Pays illustrators and photographers royalty of 7½-8½% based on net receipts. Sends galleys of novels to authors. Book catalog for 9×12 SASE (3 first-class stamps). Manuscript guidelines for SASE (1 first-class stamp). Guidelines available at website.

Tips: "We are looking for something a bit outside the mainstream and with lasting appeal (no one-shot-wonders)."

TROPHY/TEMPEST PAPERBACKS, (formerly Trophy Books), 1350 Avenue of the Americas, New York NY 10019. (212)261-6500. Fax: (212)261-6668. Website: www.harpercollins.com. Imprint of HarperCollins Children's Books Group. Book publisher. Publishes 6-9 chapter books/year, 25-30 middle grade titles/year, 20 reprint picture books/year, 10-15 young adult titles/year.

• Tempest is primarily a teen paperback reprint imprint. They publish a limited number of hardback and paperback originals each year.

How to Contact/Writers: Does not accept unsolicited or unagented mss.

TURTLE BOOKS, 866 United Nations Plaza, Suite 525, New York NY 10017. (212)644-2020. Website: www.turtlebooks.com. Book Publisher. Estab. 1997. **Acquisitions:** John Whitman. "Turtle Books publishes only picture books for young readers. Our goal is to publish a small, select list of quality children's books each spring and fall season. As often as possible, we will publish our books in both English and Spanish editions."

• Turtle does a small number of books and may be slow in responding to unsolicited manuscripts.

Fiction: Picture books: adventure, animal, concept, contemporary, fantasy, folktales, hi-lo, history, humor, multicultural, nature/environment, religion, sports, suspense/mystery. Recently published: *The Legend of Mexicatl*, by Jo Harper, illustrated by Robert Casilla (the story of Mexicatl and the origin of the Mexican people); *Vroom, Chugga, Vroom-Vroom*, by Anne Miranda, illustrated by David Murphy (a number identification book in the form of a race car story); *The Crab Man*, by Patricia VanWest, illustrated by Cedric Lucas (the story of a young Jamaican boy who must make the difficult decision between making an income and the ethical treatment of animals); *Prairie Dog Pioneers*, by Jo and Josephine Harper, illustrated by Craig Spearing (the story of a young girl who doesn't want to move, set in 1870s Texas); and *Keeper of the Swamp*, by Ann Garrett, illustrated by Karen Chandler (a dramatic coming-of-age story wherein a boy confronts his fears and learns from his ailing grandfather the secrets of the swamp); *The Lady in the Box*, by Ann McGovern, illustrated by Marni Backer (a modern story about a homeless woman named Dorrie told from the point of view of two children); and *Alphabet Fiesta*, by Anne Miranda, illustrated by young schoolchildren in Madrid, Spain (an English/Spanish alphabet story).

How to Contact/Writers: Send complete ms. "Queries are a waste of time." Response time varies.
Illustrators: Works with 6 illustrators/year. Responds to artist's queries/submissions only if interested. Samples returned with SASE only.
Terms: Pays royalty. Offers advances.

N A TYNDALE HOUSE PUBLISHERS, INC., 351 Executive Dr., P.O. Box 80, Wheaton IL 60189. (630)668-8300. Book publisher. Estab. 1962. **Manuscript Acquisitions:** Jan Axford. **Art Acquisitions:** Talinda Laubach.Publishes approximately 20 Christian children's titles/year.
   • Tyndale House no longer reviews unsolicited manuscripts. Only accepts agented material.
Fiction: Middle readers: adventure, religion, suspense/mystery.
Nonfiction: Picture books: religion. Young readers: Christian living, Bible, devotionals.
How to Contact/Writers: Only interested in agented material. "Request children's writer guidelines from (630)668-8310 ext. 836 for more information."
Illustration: Uses full-color for book covers, b&w or color spot illustrations for some nonfiction. Illustrations only: Query with photocopies (color or b&w) of samples, résumé.
Photography: Buys photos from freelancers. Works on assignment only.
Terms: Pay rates for authors and illustrators vary.
Tips: "All accepted manuscripts will appeal to Evangelical Christian children and parents."

UAHC PRESS, 633 Third Ave., New York NY 10017. (212)650-4120. Fax: (212)650-4119. E-mail: press@uahc.org. Website: www.uahc.press.com. Book publisher. Estab. 1876. **Manuscript/Art Acquisitions:** Rabbi Hara Person, editorial director. Publishes 4 picture books/year; 2 young readers/year; 2 middle readers/year; 2 young adult titles and 4 textbooks/year. "The Union of American Hebrew Congregations Press publishes textbooks for the religious classroom, children's tradebooks and scholarly work of Jewish education import—no adult fiction and no YA fiction."
Fiction: Picture books: religion. Average word length: picture books—1,500. Recently published *A Tree Trunk Seder*, written and illustrated by Camille Kress (toddler's board book); *Solomon and the Trees*, by Matt Biers-Ariel, illustrated by Esti Silverberg-Kiss (ages 4-8, picture book); *Sophie and the Shofar*, written by Fran Manuskin and illustrated by Rosalind Charney Kaye (ages 3-7, Jewish fiction).
Nonfiction: Picture books, young readers, middle readers: religion. Average word length: picture books—1,500. Recently published *My Jewish Holiday Fun Book*, written and illustrated by Ann Koffsky (ages 5-9, activity book); *Until the Messiah Comes*, by Kenneth Roseman (ages 10-13, do-it-yourself Jewish adventure); and *The Chocolate Chip Challah Activity Books*, written and illustrated by Lisa Rauchwerger (ages 5-10, activity book).
How to Contact/Writers: Fiction: Submit outline/synopsis and 2 sample chapters. Nonfiction: Submit complete ms. Responds to queries/ms in 4 months. Publishes a book 18-24 months after acceptance. Will consider simultaneous submissions.
Illustration: Works with 5 illustrators/year. Reviews ms/illustration packages from artists. Send ms with dummy. Illustrations only: Send portfolio to be kept on file. Responds in 2 months. Samples returned with SASE. Looking specifically for Jewish themes.
Photography: Buys stock and assigns work. Uses photos with Jewish content. Prefer modern settings. Submit cover letter and promo piece.
Terms: Offers advances. Pays photographers by the project (range: $200-3,000) or per photo (range:$20-100). Book catalog free; ms guidelines for SASE.
Tips: "Look at some of our books. Have an understanding of the Reform Jewish community. We sell mostly to Jewish congregations and day schools.' "

N UNITY HOUSE, 1901 NW Blue Pkwy., Unity Village MO 64065-0001. (816)524-3550, ext. 3190. Fax: (816)251-3552. Website: www.unityworldhq.org. Book publisher. Estab. 1896. Publishes "spiritual, metaphysical, new thought publications." **Manuscript Acquisitions:** Michael Maday. Other imprints: Wee Wisdom. Publishes 1 picture book every two years.
Fiction: All levels: religion. Recently published *I Turn to the Light*, by Connie Bowen (picture book); *Adventures of the Little Green Dragon*, by Mari Privette Ulmer, illustrated by Mary Maass (picture book anthology); and *The Sunbeam and the Wave*, by Harriet Hamilton, illustrated by Connie Bowen (picture book).
Nonfiction: All levels: religion.
How to Contact/Writers: Fiction/Nonfiction: Submit outline/synopsis and 1-3 sample chapters. Responds to queries/mss in 6 months. Publishes a book approximately 1 year after acceptance. Will consider simultaneous submissions or

previously self-published work. Writer's guidelines and catalog available upon request.

Illustration: Reviews ms/illustration packages from artists. Query.

Terms: Pays authors royalty of 10-15% based on net receipts or work purchased outright. Offers advances (Average amount: $1,500). Book catalog available.

Tips: "Read our Writer's Guidelines and study our catalog before submitting. All of our publications reflect Unity's spiritual teachings, but the presentations and applications of those teachings are wide open."

☑ **VIKING CHILDREN'S BOOKS**, Penguin Group Inc., 345 Hudson St., New York NY 10014-3657. (212)414-3600. Fax: (212)414-3399. E-mail: catherine.frank@us.penguingroup.com. Website: www.penguin.com. **Acquisitions:** Catherine Frank, associate editor, picture books, middle grade, and young adult fiction; Tracy Gates, executive editor, picture books, middle grade, and young adult fiction; Melanie Cecka, senior editor, picture books, middle grade, YA fiction; Jill Davis, senior editor picture books, middle grade, young adult, unique nonfiction; Anne Gunton, assistant editor, picture books, middle grade, young adult. **Art Acquisitions:** Denise Cronin, Viking Children's Books. Publishes hardcover originals. Publishes 80 books/year. Receives 7500 queries/year. 25% of books from first-time authors; 33% from unagented writers. "Viking Children's Books is known for humorous, quirky picture books, in addition to more traditional fiction and publishes the highest quality trade books for children including fiction, nonfiction, and novelty books for pre-schoolers through young adults." Publishes book 1-2 years after acceptance of artwork. Hesitantly accepts simultaneous submissions.

• Viking Children's Books is not accepting unsolicited submissions. Viking title *This Land Was Made for You and Me: The Life and Songs of Woody Guthrie*, by Elizabeth Partridge, won the 2002 Golden Kite Award for Nonfiction.

Fiction: All levels: adventure, animal, contemporary, fantasy, hi-lo, history, humor, multicultural, nature/environment, poetry, problem novels, religion, romance, science fiction, sports, suspense/mystery. Recently published *The Happy Hocky Family Moves to the Country*, by Lane Smith (ages 4-8, picture book); *The New Rules of High School*, by Blake Nelson (ages 12 and up).

Nonfiction: Picture books: activity books, animal, biography, concept. Young readers, middle readers, young adult: animal, biography, concept, geography, hi-lo, history, hobbies, multicultural, music/dance, nature/environment, reference, religion, science, sports. Recently published *Understanding September 11th*, by Mitch Frank (ages 12 and up, nonfiction).

Illustration: Works with 30 illustrators/year. Responds to artist's queries/submissions only if interested. Samples returned with SASE only or samples filed. Originals returned at job's completion.

How to Contact/Writers: Picture books: submit entire ms and SASE. Novels: submit outline with 3 sample chapters and SASE. Nonfiction: query with outline, one sample chapter and SASE. Responds to queries/mss in 6 months.

Terms: Pays 2-10% royalty on retail price or flat fee. Advance negotiable.

Tips: Mistake often made is that "authors disguise nonfiction in a fictional format."

WALKER AND COMPANY, Books for Young Readers, 435 Hudson St., New York NY 10014-3941. (212)727-8300. Fax: (212)727-0984. Website: www.walkeryoungreaders.com. Division of Walker Publishing Co. Inc. Book publisher. Estab. 1959. **Manuscript Acquisitions:** Emily Easton, publisher; Timothy Travaglini, editor. **Art Acquisitions:** Marlene Tungseth, art director. Publishes 20 picture books/year; 4-6 middle readers/year; 2-4 young adult titles/year. 5% of books by first-time authors; 65% of books from agented writers.

Fiction: Picture books: adventure, history, humor, poetry. Middle readers: adventure, contemporary, history, humor, multi-cultural, poetry. Young adults: adventure, contemporary, humor, historical fiction, suspense/mystery. Recently published *Mount Olympus Basketball*, by Kevin O'Malley (ages 6-10, edited by E. Easton, picture book); *Tulsa Burning* (ages 10-14, edited by E. Easton, middle grade novel); *All's Fair in Love, War, and High School*, by Janette Rallison (12 and up, edited by T. Travaglini, teen/young adult novel).

Nonfiction: Picture book, middle readers: biography, history. Recently published *Champion: The Story of Muhammad Ali*, by Jim Haskins, illustrated by Eric Velasquez (ages 6-10, edited by T. Travaglini, picture book, biography); *Fantastic Flights*, by Patrick O'Brien (ages 7-12, edited by T. Travaglini, picture book history); *The Signers*, by Dennis Fradin, illustrated by Michael McCurdy (10 and up, edited by E. Easton, illustrated nonfiction). Multicultural needs include "contemporary, literary fiction and historical fiction written in an authentic voice. Also high interest nonfiction with trade appeal."

How to Contact/Writers: Fiction/nonfiction: Submit outline/synopsis and sample chapters; complete ms for novels. Responds to queries/mss in 3 months. Send SASE for writer's guidelines.

Illustration: Works with 10-12 illustrators/year. Uses color artwork only. Editorial department reviews ms/illustration packages from artists. Query or submit ms with 4-8 samples. Illustrations only: Tearsheets. "Please do not send original artwork." Responds to art samples only if interested. Samples returned with SASE.

Terms: Pays authors royalties of 5-10%; pays illustrators royalty or flat fee. Offers advance payment against royalties. Original artwork returned at job's completion. Sends galleys to authors. Book catalog available for 9×12 SASE; ms guidelines for SASE.

Tips: Writers: "Make sure you study our catalog before submitting. We are a small house with a tightly focused list." Illustrators: "Have a well-rounded portfolio with different styles." Does not want to see folktales, ABC books, paperback series, genre fiction. "Walker and Company is committed to introducing talented new authors and illustrators to the children's book field."

☑ **WHAT'S INSIDE PRESS**, P.O. Box 29851, Atlanta GA 30359-0851. Fax: (800)856-2160. E-mail: submit@whatsinsidepress.com; art@whatsinsidepress.com. Website: www.zardwebdesign.com/wip/index.html. Estab. 1998. Specializes in fiction. What's Inside Press accepts e-mail queries only.

ALBERT WHITMAN & COMPANY, 6340 Oakton St., Morton Grove IL 60053-2723. (847)581-0033. Fax: (847)581-0039. Website: www.albertwhitman.com. Book publisher. Estab. 1919. **Manuscript Acquisitions:** Kathleen Tucker, editor-in-chief. **Art Acquisitions:** Carol Gildar, art director. Publishes 30 books/year. 20% of books by first-time authors; 15% of books from agented authors.

Fiction: Picture books, young readers, middle readers: adventure, concept (to help children deal with problems), fantasy, history, humor, multicultural, suspense. Middle readers: problem novels, suspense/mystery. "We are interested in contemporary multicultural stories—stories with holiday themes and exciting distinctive novels. We publish a wide variety of topics and are interested in stories that help children deal with their problems and concerns. Does not want to see "religion-oriented, ABCs, pop-up, romance, counting." Published *Birthday Zoo*, by Deborah Lee Rose, illustrated by Lynn Munsinger; *Mabela the Clever*, by Margaret Read MacDonald, illustrated by Tim Coffey; *Wanda's Monster*, by Eileen Spinelli, illustrated by Nancy Hayashi.

Nonfiction: Picture books, young readers, middle readers: animal, arts/crafts, health, history, hobbies, multicultural, music/dance, nature/environment, science, sports, special needs. Does not want to see "religion, any books that have to be written in or fictionalized biographies." Recently published *Shelter Dogs*, by Peg Kehret; *Apples Here!*, by Will Hubbell; and *The Riches of Oseola McCarty*, by Evelyn Coleman, illustrated by Daniel Minter.

How to Contact/Writers: Fiction/Nonfiction: Submit query, outline and sample chapter. For picture books send entire ms. Include cover letter. Responds to queries in 6 weeks; mss in 4 months. Publishes a book 18 months after acceptance. Will consider simultaneous submissions "but let us know if it is one."

Illustration: Do not send originals. Reviews ms/illustration packages from artists. Illustrations only: Query with samples. Send slides or tearsheets. Samples returned with SASE; samples filed. Originals returned at job's completion. Responds only if interested.

Photography: Publishes books illustrated with photos but not stock photos—desires photos all taken for project. "Our books are for children and cover many topics; photos must be taken to match text. Books often show a child in a particular situation (e.g., kids being home-schooled, a sister whose brother is born prematurely)." Photographers should query with samples; send unsolicited photos by mail.

Terms: Pays authors royalty. Pays illustrators and photographers royalty. Book catalog for 8×10 SAE and 3 first-class stamps.

Tips: "In both picture books and nonfiction, we are seeking stories showing life in other cultures and the variety of multicultural life in the U.S. We also want fiction and nonfiction about mentally or physically challenged children—some recent topics have been autism, stuttering, diabetes. Look up some of our books first, to be sure your submission is appropriate for Albert Whitman & Co."

JOHN WILEY & SONS, INC., 111 River St., Hoboken NJ 07030. (201)748-6000. Website: www.wiley.com. Book publisher. **Acquisitions:** Kate Bradford, senior editor. Publishes 18 middle readers/year; 2 young adult titles/year. 10% of books by first-time authors. Publishes educational nonfiction: primarily history, science, and other activities.

Nonfiction: Middle readers: activity books, arts/crafts, biography, cooking, geography, health, history, hobbies, how-to, nature/environment, reference, science, self help. Young adults: activity books, arts/crafts, health, hobbies, how-to, nature/environment, reference, science, self help. Average word length middle readers—20,000-40,000. Recently published: *Sports Science*, by Jim Wiese (ages 8-12, science/activity); *Outrageous Women of the American Frontier*, by Mary Forbee (ages 10-14, US history).

How to Contact/Writers: Query. Submit outline/synopsis, 2 sample chapters and an author bio. Responds to queries in 1 month; mss in 3 months. Publishes a book 1 year after acceptance. Will consider simultaneous and previously published submissions.

Illustration: Works with 6 illustrators/year. Uses primarily black & white artwork. Reviews ms/illustration packages from artists. Query. Illustrations only: Query with samples, résumé, client list. Responds only if interested. Samples filed. Original artwork returned at job's completion. No portfolio reviews.

Photography: Buys photos from freelancers.

Terms: Pays authors royalty of 10-12% based on wholesale price, or by outright purchase. Offers advances. Pays illustrators by the project. Photographers' pay negotiable. Sends galleys to authors. Book catalog available for SASE.

Tips: "We're looking for topics and writers that can really engage kids' interest—plus we're always interested in a new twist on time-tested subjects." Nonfiction submissions only; no picture books.

WILLIAMSON PUBLISHING CO., Box 185, Charlotte VT 05445. (802)425-2102. Fax: (802)425-2199. E-mail: susan @williamsonbooks.com. Website: www.williamsonbooks.com. Book publisher. Estab. 1983. **Manuscript Acquisitions:** Susan Williamson, editorial director. **Art Acquisitions:** Dana Pierson, production manager. Publishes 12-15 young readers titles/year. 50% of books by first-time authors; 10% of books from agented authors. Publishes "very successful nonfiction series (Kids Can!® Series) on subjects such as history, science, arts/crafts, geography. Successfully launched *Little Hands®* series for ages 2-6, *Kaleidoscope Kids®* series (age 7 and up) and *Quick Starts for Kids!®* series (ages 7 and up). "Our mission is to help every child fulfill his/her potential and experience personal growth."

Nonfiction: Hands-on active learning books, animals, African-American, arts/crafts, Asian, biography, careers, geography, health, history, hobbies, how-to, math, multicultural, music/dance, nature/environment, Native American, science, writing and journaling. Does not want to see textbooks, picture books, fiction. "Looking for historically accurate early reader and middle reader books, as well as biographies. We are looking for books in which learning and doing are inseparable." Recently published *Fizz Bubble, and Flash: Element Explorations & Atom Adventures for Hands-On Science Fun!*, by Anita Brandolini, Ph.D., illustrated by Michael Kline (ages 8 and up); *Ancient Rome! Exploring the Culture, People & Ideas of This Powerful Empire*, by Avery Hart, illustrated by Michael Kline (ages 7-14); and *The Kids' Book of Incredibly Fun Crafts*, by Roberta Gould, illustrated by Norma Jean Martin-Jourdenais (ages 7-14).

How to Contact/Writers: Query with annotated TOC/synopsis and 1 sample chapter. Responds to queries/mss in 4 months. Publishes book, "about 1 year" after acceptance. Writers may send a SASE for guidelines. Please do not query via e-mail.

Illustration: Works with at least 6 illustrators and 6 designers/year. "We're interested in expanding our illustrator and design freelancers." Uses primarily b&w artwork; some 2-color and 4-color. Responds only if interested. Samples returned with SASE; samples filed. Please do not send samples via e-mail.

Photography: Buys photos from freelancers; uses archival art and photos.

Terms: No advance. Pays authors royalty based on wholesale price or purchases outright. Pays illustrators by the project. Pays photographers per photo. Sends galleys to authors. Book catalog available for 8½×11 SAE and 6 first-class stamps; ms guidelines available for SASE.

Tips: "Please do not send any fiction or stories of any kind. We're interested in interactive learning books with a creative approach packed with interesting information, written for young readers ages 2-6 and 4-10. In nonfiction children's publishing, we are looking for authors with a depth of knowledge shared with children through a warm, embracing style. Our publishing philosophy is based on the idea that all children can succeed and have positive learning experiences. Children's lasting learning experiences involve participation."

☑ ▣ WINDSTORM CREATIVE LTD., P.O. Box 28, Port Orchard WA 98366. E-mail: wsc@windstormcreative.com. Website: www.windstormcreative.com. **Acquisitions:** Ms. Cris DiMarco, senior editor, young adult; Jennifer Anna, children's. Publishes trade paperback originals and reprints. Publishes 10 titles/year. 50% of books from first-time authors; 50% from unagented writers. WSC consists of the following imprints: Little Blue Works—Children's titles and young adult novels released in paper and on multimedia CD-ROM; Lightning Rod Ltd—Internet & Episode Guides; WSC—Cutting-edge fiction. Publishes genre fiction and poetry primarily in paper and on multimedia CD-ROM; RAMPANT Gaming—Role-playing and other games for ages 14 and—Paper Frog—theater and film, Orchard Academy—nonfiction, home school-based books and CD-ROMs; Full Spectrum—nonfiction. "We do not backlist. Ninety-five percent of our titles are still in print. We are an independent press with corporate synergy. We do not publish work that is racist, homophobic, sexist or graphically violent in content. All of our authors and artists should expect to be proactive in marketing their work. If you do not wish to read from and/or sign your books and/or artwork, you should not submit work to us."

Fiction: All levels: adventure, animal, fantasy, folktales, history, nature/environment, science fiction, suspense/mystery. Recently published *Yen Shei and the American Bonsai*, by Jennifer Anna/Karen Hallion (middle reader, Cris DiMarco, pre-chapter); *Mrs. Estronsky and the UFO*, by Pat Schmatz (junior high, Jennifer Anna).

Nonfiction: All levels: activity books, animal, how-to, multicultural.

How to Contact/Writers: "You must use the submission form plus label from the website. All queries or submissions *without* the label will be destroyed."

Illustration: Works with 20 illustrators/year. Visit website for guidelines. Responds to queries in 4 months, only if interested. Samples returned with SASE; samples filed. Originals returned at job's completion.

Photography: Buys photos from freelancers. See website.

Terms: Pays at least 15% royalty based on retail price. Will consider simultaneous submissions. Artists and photographers are paid flat fee for covers only. All other work is paid by the project ($200-1,000) or royalty basis. Royalty payment is 15% of gross monies received."

Tips: "We reserve the right to destroy any submissions that deviate from our format."

▢ WINDWARD PUBLISHING, Imprint of Finney Company, 3943 Meadowbrook Rd., Minneapolis MN 55426. (952)938-9330. Fax: (952)938-7353. E-mail: feedback@finney-hobar.com. Website: www.finney-hobar.com. Estab. 1947. Specializes in mass market books, trade books, nonfiction, educational material. **Manuscript/Art Acquisitions:** Alan E. Krysan. Publishes 1 picture book/year; 2-4 young readers, middle readers, young adult titles/year. 25% of books by first-time authors.

Fiction: Young readers, middle readers, young adults: adventure, animal, nature/environment. Recently published *Billy's Search for Florida Undersea Treasure*, illustrated by Russ Smiley (ages 5-10, story picture book).

Nonfiction: Young readers, middle readers, young adults: activity books, animal, careers, nature/environment, science. Young adults: textbooks. Recently published *Sea Turtles Hatching*, by Katherine Orr (ages 5-8, nature); *Occupational Guidance for Agriculture* (ages 12 and up, careers); *Reading a Ruler* (ages 12 and up, how-to).

How to Contact/Writers: Fiction: Query. Nonfiction: Submit outline/synopsis and 3 sample chapters. Responds to queries in 1 month; mss in 2 months. Publishes book 6-8 months after acceptance. Will consider simultaneous submissions and previously published work.

Illustration: Reviews ms/illustration packages from artists. Send ms with dummy. Query with samples. Responds in 2 months. Samples returned with SASE; samples filed.

Photography: Buys stock and assigns work. Photography needs depend on project—mostly ocean and beach subject matter. Uses color, 4×6, glossy prints. Submit cover letter, résumé, stock photo list.

Terms: Author's payment negotiable by project. Offers advances (Average amount: $500). Illustrators and photographers payment negotiable by project. Sends galleys to authors; dummies to illustrators. Originals returned to artist at job's completion. Book catalog available for 6×9 SAE and 3 first-class stamps; ms guidelines available for SASE. Catalog mostly available on website.

WM KIDS, Imprint of White Mane Publishing Co., Inc., P.O. Box, 708, 63 W. Burd St., Shippensburg PA 17257. (717)532-2237. Fax: (717)532-6110. E-mail: marketing@whitemane.com. Book publisher. Estab. 1987. **Acquisitions:** Harold Collier, acquisitions editor—White Mane Books, Burd Street Press, White Mane Kids, Ragged Edge Press. Publishes 10 middle readers/year. 50% of books are by first-time authors.

Fiction: Middle readers, young adults: history. Average word length: middle readers—30,000. Does not publish picture books. Recently published *Freedom Calls: Journey of a Slave Girl*, by Ken Knapp Sawyer (historical fiction, grades 5 and up); *Young Heroes of History*, by Alan Kay (grades 5 and up).

Nonfiction: Middle readers, young adults: history. Average word length: middle readers—30,000. Does not publish picture books. Recently published *Slaves Who Dared: The Story of Ten African American Heroes*, by Mary Garrison (young adult).

How to Contact/Writers: Fiction: Query. Nonfiction: Submit outline/synopsis and 2-3 sample chapters. Responds to queries in 1 month; mss in 3 months. Publishes a book 12-15 months after acceptance. Will consider simultaneous submissions.

Illustration: Works with 3 illustrators/year. Illustrations used for cover art only. Responds in 1 month. Samples returned with SASE.

Photography: Buys stock and assigns work. Submit cover letter and portfolio.

Terms: Pays authors royalty of 7-10%. Pays illustrators by the project. Pays photographers by the project. Sends galleys for review. Originals returned to artist at job's completion. Book catalog and writer's guidelines available for SASE. All imprints included in a single catalog.

N ☐ WORLD BOOK, INC., 233 N. Michigan Ave., #2000, Chicago IL 60601. (312)729-5800. Fax: (312)729-5612. Website: www.worldbook.com. Book publisher. **Manuscript Acquisitions:** Paul A. Kobasa, general managing editor. **Art Acquisitions:** Sandra Dyrlund, art/design manager. World Book, Inc. (publisher of *The World Book Encyclopedia*), publishes reference sources and nonfiction series for children in the areas of science, mathematics, English-language skills, basic academic and social skills, social studies, history, and health and fitness. We publish print and nonprint material appropriate for children ages 3 to 14. WBT does not publish fiction, poetry, or wordless picture books."

Nonfiction: Young readers: animal, arts/crafts, careers, concept, geography, health, reference. Middle readers: animal, arts/crafts, careers, geography, health, history, hobbies, how-to, nature/environment, reference, science. Young adult: arts/crafts, careers, geography, health, history, hobbies, how-to, nature/environment, reference, science.

How to Contact/Writers: Nonfiction: Submit outline/synopsis only; no mss. Responds to queries/mss in 2 months. Unsolicited mss will not be returned. Publishes a book 18 months after acceptance. Will consider simultaneous submissions.

Illustration: Works with 10-30 illustrators/year. Illustrations only: Query with samples. Responds only if interested. Samples returned with SASE; samples filed "if extra copies and if interested."

Photography: Buys stock and assigns work. Needs broad spectrum; editorial concept, specific natural, physical and social science spectrum. Model/property releases required; captions required. Uses color 8×10 gloss and matte prints, 35mm, 2¼×2¼, 4×5, 8×10 transparencies. Submit cover letter, résumé, promo piece (color and b&w).

Terms: Payment negotiated on project-by-project basis. Sends galleys to authors. Book catalog available for 9×12 SASE. Manuscript and art guidelines for SASE.

N ☐ THE WRIGHT GROUP, 19201 120th Ave. NE, Suite 100, Bothell WA 98011. Fax: (800)543-7323. Website: www.wrightgroup.com. Specializes in fiction and nonfiction educational and multicultural material. **Manuscripts Acquisitions:** Judy Sommer, vice president marketing. **Art Acquisitions:** Vicky Tripp, director of design. Publishes over 100 young readers, over 50 middle readers/year. "The Wright Group is dedicated to improving literacy by providing outstanding tutorials for students and teachers."

Fiction: Picture books, young readers: adventure, animal, concept, contemporary, fantasy, folktales, hi-lo, history, humor, multicultural, nature/environment, poetry, sports, suspense/mystery. Middle readers: adventure, animal, contemporary, fantasy, folktales, hi-lo, history, humor, multicultural, nature/environment, poetry, problem novels. Average word length: young readers—50-5,000; middle readers—3,000-10,000. Recenty published: *Wild Crayons*, by Joy Cowley (young reader fantasy); *The Gold Dust Kids*, by Michell Dionetti (historical fiction chapter book for young readers); and *Watching Josh*, by Deborah Eaton (middle reader mystery).

Nonfiction: Picture books, young readers, middle readers: animal, biography, careers, concept, geography, health, hi-lo, history, how-to, multicultural, nature/environment, science, sports. Average word length: young readers 50-3,000. Recently published: *Iditarod*, by Joe Ramsey (young reader); and *The Amazing Ant*, by Sara Sams (young reader); and *Chameleons*, by Nic Bishop (young reader).

How to Contact/Writers: Fiction/Nonfiction: Submit complete manuscript or submit outline/synopsis and 3 sample chapters. Responds to queries in 1 month; mss in 5 months. Publishes a book 8 months after acceptance. Will consider previously published work.

Illustration Query with samples. Responds only if interested. Samples kept on file.

Photography: Buys stock and assigns work. Model/property release and captions required. Uses 8½×11 color prints. Submit published samples, promo pieces.

Terms: Work purchased outright from authors ($500-2,400). Illustrators paid by the project. Photographers paid by the project ($3,500-5,000) or per photo ($300-350). Book catalog available online.

Tips: "Much of our illustration assignments are being done by offsite developers, so our level of commission in this area is minimal."

Canadian & International Book Publishers

While the United States is considered the largest market in children's publishing, the children's publishing world is by no means strictly dominated by the U.S. After all, the most prestigious children's book extravaganza in the world occurs each year in Bologna, Italy at the Bologna Children's Book Fair and some of the world's most beloved characters were born in the United Kingdom (i.e., Winnie-the-Pooh and Mr. Potter). We wanted *Children's Writer's & Illustrator's Market* to reflect this diversity. In this section you'll find book publishers from English-speaking countries around the world from Canada to Australia and New Zealand to the United Kingdom. The listings in this section look just like the U.S. Book Publishers section; and the publishers listed are dedicated to the same goal—publishing great books for children.

Like always, be sure to study each listing and research each publisher carefully before submitting material. Make certain the publisher is open to U.S. or international submissions, as many publishers accept submissions only from residents of their own country. Some publishers accept illustration samples from foreign artists, but do not accept manuscripts from foreign writers. Illustrators do have a slight edge in this category as many illustrators generate commissions from all around the globe. Visit publishers' websites to be certain they publish the sort of work you do. Visit online bookstores to see if the publishers' books are available there. Write or e-mail to request catalogs and submission guidelines.

When mailing requests or submissions out of the United States, remember that U.S. postal stamps are useless on your SASE. Always include International Reply Coupons (IRC's) with your SAE. Each IRC is good for postage for one letter. So if you want the publisher to return your manuscript or send a catalog, be sure to enclose enough IRC's to pay the postage. For more help visit the United State Postal Service website at www.usps.gov/global/welcome.htm. Visit www.timeanddate.com/worldclock and American Computer Resources, Inc.'s International Calling Code Directory at www.the-acr.com/codes/cntrycd.htm#a before calling or faxing internationally to make sure you're calling at a reasonable time and using the correct numbers.

As in the rest of *Children's Writer's & Illustrator's Market*, the maple leaf ♦ symbol identifies Canadian markets. Look for the Canadian ♦ and International ⊕ symbols throughout *Children's Writer's & Illustrator's Market* as well. Several of the Society of Children's Book Writers and Illustrator's (SCBWI) international conferences are listed this year in the Conferences & Workshops section along with other events in locations around the globe. Look for more information about SCBWI's international chapters on the organization's website, www.scbwi.org. You'll also find international listings in Magazines and Young Writer's & Illustrator's Markets. See Useful Online Resources on page 355 for sites that offer additional international information. And read French author and International SCBWI Regional Advisor Coordinator **Erzsi Deàk's** article on page 69 to learn how she collaborated with writers and editors from the U.S. in compiling the anthology *Period Pieces*.

To learn what it's like for a beginning author/illustrator in the United Kingdom, see the Insider Report with **Moira Munro** on page 222. For a Canadian perspective, hear from magazine writer **Fiona Bayrock** on page 266.

N ⊕ ♦ ALLEN & UNWIN, 406 Albert St., East Melbourne VIC 3002 Australia. E-mail: frontdesk@allenandunwin.com. Website: www.allenandunwin.com. **Contact:** Children's Editor.

● Allen & Unwin was voted Publisher of the Year by Australian booksellers in 1992, 1996, 2001, 2002.
Fiction: Average word length: young readers—20,000; young adults—40,000. Recently published *Looking for X*, by Deborah Ellis (junior fiction).
Nonfiction: Recently published *Written in Blood*, by Beverly MacDonald (YA, nonfiction).
How to Contact/Writers: Fiction: Submit complete ms (8,000 words or more) and SASE "of suitable size." Nonfiction: Send proposal and detailed chapter outline. Responds to mss in 4 months.
Tips: "Do not send e-mail submissions."

N 🌐 ANDERSEN PRESS LIMITED, Imprint of Random House, 20 Vauxhall Bridge Rd., London SW1V 2SA United Kingdom. (44) 020 7840 8703. Fax: (44) 020 7233 6263. Website: www.andersenpress.co.uk.
Fiction: Picture books, young readers, young adults. Average word length: picture books—under 2,000; young readers—3,000-5,000; young adults—15-30,000. Recently published *What Do You Remember?*, by Paul Stewart and Chris Riddell (ages 4 and up, picture book); *Millie's Big Surprise*, by Gerald Rose (ages 3 and up, picture book); *Last Seen Wearing Trainers*, by Rosie Pushton (ages 11 and up, fiction).
How to Contact/Writers: Accepts material from residents of United Kingdom only. Fiction: Submit complete ms and return postage for picture books; or submit outline/synopsis and 3 sample chapters and return postage for novels.
Tips: "Please note we do not publish poetry or short stories."

N 🔷 ANNICK PRESS LTD., 15 Patricia Ave., Toronto ON M2M 1H9 Canada. (416)221-4802. Fax: (416)221-8400. E-mail: annick@annickpress.com. Website: www.annickpress.com. Estab. 1975. Specializes in trade books, nonfiction, fiction, multicultural material. Does not accept unsolicited mss. **Creative Director:** Sheryl Shapiro. Publishes 8 picture books/year; 3 young readers/year; 3 middle readers/year; and 8 young adult titles/year. 25% of books by first-time authors. "Annick Press maintains a commitment to high-quality books that entertain and challenge. Our publications share fantasy and stimulate judgment and abilities."
Fiction: No unsolicited mss. Recently published *The Mole Sisters and the Cool Breeze*, by Roslyn Schwartz (ages 2-4, picture book); *The Losers' Club*, by John Lekich (ages 13 and up, young adult novel); and *Rocksy*, by Loris Lesynski (ages 4-8, picture book).
Nonfiction: Recently published *The Martial Arts Book*, by Laura Scandiffio, illustrated by Nicholas Debon (8 and up, middle readers and up); *Tunnels*, by Diane Swanson (8-12, middle readers); and *Ultra Hush Hush: Espionage and Special Missions*, by Stephen Shapiro and Tina Forrester, illustrated by David Craig (10 and up, middle reader).
How to Contact/Writers: Accepts material from residents of Canada only.
Illustration: Works with 20 illustrators/year. Illustrations only: Query with samples. Contact: Creative Director. Responds in 6 months with SASE. Samples returned with SASE or kept on file.
Terms: Pays authors royalty of 5-12% based on retail price. Offers advances (Average amount: $3,000). Pays illustrators royalty of 5% minimum. Originals returned to artist at job's completion. Book catalog available for 6×9 SASE. All imprints included in a single catalog. Artist's guidelines available on website.

🔷 BEACH HOLME PUBLISHERS, 2040 W. 12th Ave., Suite 226, Vancouver BC V6J 2G2 Canada. (604)733-4868, (888)551-6655 (orders). Fax: (604)733-4860. E-mail: bhp@beachholme.bc.ca. Website: www.beachholme.bc.ca. Book publisher. **Manuscript Acquisitions:** Michael Carroll, publisher. **Art Acquisitions:** Michael Carroll. Publishes 5-6 young adult titles/year and 7-8 adult literary titles/year. 40% of books by first-time authors. "We publish primarily regional historical fiction. We publish young adult novels for children aged 8-12. We are particularly interested in works that have a historical basis and are set in the Pacific Northwest, or northern Canada. Include ideas for teacher's guides or resources and appropriate topics for a classroom situation if applicable."
● Beach Holme *only* accepts work from Canadian writers.
Fiction: Young adults: contemporary, folktales, history, multicultural, nature/environment, poetry. Multicultural needs include themes reflecting cultural heritage of the Pacific Northwest, i.e., first nations, Asian, East Indian, etc. Does not want to see generic adventure or mystery with no sense of place. Average word length: middle readers—15-20,000; young adults/teens—30,000-40,000. Recently published *Tom Thomson's Last Paddle*, by Larry McCloskey (ages 9-13, young adult fiction); and *Criss Cross, Double Cross*, by Norma Charles (ages 8-13, young adult fiction).
How to Contact/Writers: Fiction: Submit outline/synopsis and 3 sample chapters. Responds to queries/mss in 6 months. Publishes a book 6 months-1 year after acceptance. No electronic or multiple submissions.
Illustration: Works with 4-5 Canadian illustrators/year. Responds to submissions in 2 months if interested. Samples returned with SASE; samples filed. Originals returned at job's completion. Works mainly with Canadian illustrators.
Terms: Pays authors 10% royalty based on retail price. Offers advances (average amount: $500). Pays illustrators by the project (range: $500-1,000). Pays photographers by the project (range: $100-300). Sends galleys to authors. Book catalog available for 9×12 SAE and 3 first-class Canadian stamps; ms guidelines available online at website.
Tips: "Research what we have previously published and view our website to familiarize yourself with what we are looking for. Please, be informed."

N 🔷 BOARDWALK BOOKS, Imprint of The Dundurn Group, 8 Market St., Suite 200, Toronto ON M5E 1M6 Canada. (416)214-5544. Fax: (416)214-5556. E-mail: editorial@dundurn.com. Website: www.dundurn.com. Estab. 1973. Specializes in fiction. **Manuscript Acquisitions:** Barry Jowett. Boardwalk Books is the YA imprint of The Dundurn Group. Publishes 6 young adult titles/year. 50% of books by first-time authors. "We aim to publish sophisticated literary fiction for youths aged 12 to 16."
Fiction: Young adults: contemporary, history, suspense/mystery. Average word length: young adults—40,000-45,000.

Recently published *Out of the Ashes*, by Valerie Sherrad (ages 12-16, fiction-mystery); *Shoulder the Sky*, by Leslie Choyce (ages 12-16, fiction); and *Seeds of Time*, by kc dyer (ages 12-16, fiction).

How to Contact/Writers: Accepts material from residents of Canada only. Fiction: Submit outline/synopsis and 3 sample chapters (or approximately 50 pages). Responds to queries/mss in 6 weeks. Publishes book 1 year after acceptance. Will consider simultaneous submissions.

Illustration: "We don't use children's illustrators."

Terms: Offers advances. Sends galleys to authors. Book catalog available for 9 × 12 SAE with sufficient Canadian postage or international coupon. All imprints included in a single catalog. Writer's guidelines available for SASE.

Tips: "Be sure your submission suits our list."

N **●** **BUSTER BOOKS**, Imprint of Michael O'Mara Books, 9 Lion Yard, Tremadoc Rd., London SW4 7NQ United Kingdom. E-mail: busterbooks@michaelomarabooks.com. Website: www.mombooks.com. "We are dedicated to providing irresistible and fun books for children of all ages."

Fiction: Picture books: concept, humor, interactive. Young readers/middle readers: humor. Recently published *Mouse Shops*, by Michelle Cartlidge; *StoryTime* (ages 3-8, anthology); *Secret Maths: Multiplication Tables*.

Nonfiction: Picture books, young readers, middle readers.

How to Contact/Writers: Fiction: Query or submit complete ms or submit outline/synopsis and 1 sample chapter. Responds to queries/mss in 6 weeks. Will consider e-mail submissions.

Tips: Visit website before submitting.

● **COTEAU BOOKS LTD.**, 401-2206 Dewdney Ave., Regina SK S4R 1H3 Canada. (306)777-0170. E-mail: coteau@co teaubooks.com. Website: www.coteaubooks.com. Thunder Creek Publishing Co-op Ltd. Book publisher. Estab. 1975. **Acquisitions:** Barbara Sapergia, children's editor. Publishes 8-10 juvenile and/or young adult books/year, 18-20 books/year. 40% of books by first-time authors. "Coteau Books publishes the finest Canadian fiction, poetry, drama and children's literature, with an emphasis on western writers."

   ● Coteau Books publishes Canadian writers and illustrators only; mss from the U.S. are returned unopened.

Fiction: Young readers, middle readers, young adults: adventure, contemporary, fantasy, history, humor, multicultural, nature/environment, science fiction, suspense/mystery. "No didactic, message pieces, nothing religious. No picture books. Material should reflect the diversity of culture, race, religion, creed of humankind—we're looking for fairness and balance." Recently published *Angels in the Snow*, by Wenda Young (ages 11-14); *Bay Girl*, by Betty Dorion (ages 8-11); and *The Innocent Polly McDoodle*, by Mary Woodbury (ages 8-12).

Nonfiction: Young readers, middle readers, young adult: biography, history, multicultural, nature/environment, social issues.

How to Contact/Writers: Fiction: Submit complete ms to acquisitions editor. Include SASE or send up to 20-page sample by e-mail, as an attached file, in the Mime protocol. Responds to queries/mss in 4 months. Publishes a book 1-2 years after acceptance.

Illustration: Works with 1-4 illustrators/year. Illustrations only: Submit nonreturnable samples. Responds only if interested. Samples returned with SASE; samples filed.

Photography: "Very occasionally buys photos from freelancers." Buys stock and assigns work.

Terms: Pays authors in royalties based on retail price. Pays illustrators and photographers by the project. Sends galleys to authors; dummies to illustrators. Original artwork returned at job's completion. Book catalog free on request with 9 × 12 SASE.

Tips: "Truthfully, the work speaks for itself! Be bold. Be creative. Be persistent! There is room, at least in the Canadian market, for quality novels for children, and at Coteau, this is a direction we will continue to take."

N **●** **FABER AND FABER**, 3 Queen Square, London WC1N 3AU United Kingdom. Website: www.faber.co.uk. Estab. 1929. **Contact:** The Editorial Department.

   ● Does not accept unsolicited submissions.

Fiction: Recently published *Heir of Mystery*, by Philip Ardagh (ages 8-11, fiction); *Virtutopia*, by Russell Stannard (ages 12 and up); and *Rocket Science*, by Jeanne Willis (ages 8-11).

Nonfiction: Recently published *The Spy's Handbook*, by Herbie Brennan; and *The Hieroglyph's Handbook*, by Philip Ardagh.

Tips: "Try to discern whether or not your work is suitable for our list by looking on our website or in bookshops at the types of books we publish. We do not, for example, publish in fields such as fantasy, science fiction, or photography, all of which we regularly receive."

N **●** **FENN PUBLISHING CO.**, 34 Nixon Rd., Bolton ON L7E-1W2 Canada. (905)951-6600. Fax: (905)951-6601. E-mail: fennpubs@hbfenn.com. Website: www.hbfenn.com. Estab. 1982. **Manuscript/Art Acquisitions:** C. Jordan Fenn, publisher. Publishes 35 books/year.

Fiction: Picture books: adventure, animal, folktales, multicultural, religion, sports. Young readers: adventure, animal, folktales, multicultural, religion. Middle readers: adventure, animal, health, history, multicultural, religion, special needs, sports. Young adults: adventure, animal, contemporary, folktales, health, history, multicultural, nature/environment, religion, science fiction, sports.

Nonfiction: Picture books, young readers, middle readers, activity books, animal, arts/crafts, geography, health, history, hobbies, how-to, multicultural, nature/environment, religion.

How to Contact/Writers: Fiction/Nonfiction: Query or submit complete ms. Responds to queries/mss in 2 months.

Illustration: Reviews ms/illustration packages from artists. Contact: C. Jordan Fenn, publisher. Responds only if interested. Samples not returned or filed.

Ⓝ Ⓐ 🔹 FITZHENRY & WHITESIDE LTD., 195 Allstate Pkwy., Markham ON L3R 4T8 Canada. (905)477-9700. Fax: (905)477-9179. Book publisher. President: Sharon Fitzhenry; Children's Publisher: Gail Winskill. Publishes 10 picture books/year; 5 early readers and early chapter books/year; 6 middle novels/year; 7 young adult titles/year. 10% of books by first-time authors. Publishes fiction and nonfiction—social studies, visual arts, biography, environment. Emphasis on Canadian authors and illustrators, subject or perspective.

● Fitzhenry & Whiteside does not accept unsolicited manuscripts. They prefer to work with agents.

How to Contact/Writers: Accepts agented material only. Fiction/Nonfiction. Publishes a book 12-18 months after acceptance. Will consider simultaneous submissions.

Illustration: Works with 15 illustrators/year. Reviews ms/illustration packages from artists. Submit outline and sample illustration (copy). Illustrations only: Query with samples and promo sheet. Responds in 3 months. Samples returned with SASE; samples filed if no SASE.

Photography: Buys photos from freelancers. Buys stock and assigns work. Captions required. Uses b&w 8×10 prints; 35mm and 4×5 transparencies. Submit stock photo list and promo piece.

Terms: Pays authors royalty of 10%. Offers "respectable" advances for picture books, 5% to author, 5% to illustrator. Pays illustrators by the project and royalty. Pays photographers per photo. Sends galleys to authors; dummies to illustrators.

Tips: "We respond to quality."

Ⓝ 🔹 GROUNDWOOD BOOKS, Imprint of Douglas & McIntyre, 720 Bathurst St., Suite 500, Toronto ON M5S 2R4 Canada. (416)537-2501. Fax: (416)537-4647. Website: www.groundwoodbooks.com. Specializes in trade books. **Manuscript Acquisitions:** Acquisitions Editor. **Art Acquisitions:** Art Director. Publishes 10 picture books/year; 3 young readers/year; 5 middle readers/year; and 5 young adult titles/year. 10% of books by first-time authors.

Fiction: "We will consider *Latino* books only—all categories." Recently published *The Breadwinner*, by Deborah Ellis (middle reader); *True Confessions of a Heartless Girl*, by Martha Brooks (young adult); and Stella & Sam series, by Marie-Louise Gay (picture book).

How to Contact/Writers: Fiction: Submit complete ms. Responds to queries in 2 months; mss in 4 months. Will consider simultaneous submissions.

Illustration: Works with 10-15 illustrators/year. Reviews ms/illustration packages from artists. Illustrations only: Send résumé, promo sheet, slides, and tearsheets. Responds only if interested. Samples not returned.

Terms: Offers advances. Pays illustrators by the project for cover art; otherwise royalty. Sends galleys to authors; dummies to illustrators. Originals returned to artist at job's completion. Book catalog available for SASE. "Visit our website for guidelines." Catalog available on website.

Tips: "Try to familiarize yourself with our list before submitting to judge whether your work is appropriate for our list."

Ⓝ 🔲 🌐 🔳 HINKLER BOOKS, 17-23 Redwood Dr., Dingley, Victoria Australia 3172. (61) 3 9552 1333. Fax: (61) 3 9552 2588. E-mail: tracey@hinkler.com.au. Website: www.hinklerbooks.com. Estab. 1993. Specializes in mass market books, educational material. We are an independent book packager/producer. **Acquisitions:** Tracey Ahern, publisher. "Hinkler Books publishes quality books affordable to the average family."

Ⓝ 🌐 Ⓐ HONNOCYF, Canolfan Merched y Wawr, Vulcan St., Aberystwyth, Ceredigion SY23 1JH Wales. Phone/fax: (44) 1970 623 150. E-mail: post@honno.co.uk. Website: www.honno.co.uk. Estab. 1986. Specializes in mass market books, fiction, multicultural. **Acquisitions:** Janet Thomas, acquisitions editor. Publishes 1-2 young readers/year; 2-3 middle readers/year; and possibly 1 young adult title/year. 30-50% of books by first-time authors. "We publish work by Welsh women authors—either women living in Wales now, regardless of where they were born, women born in Wales regardless of where they are living now, or women with another strong connection to the country. In children's, we are happy to look at a wide range of material—contemporary, historical and fantasy, not necessarily with a Welsh setting, though we do try to encourage work that tackles Welsh settings and concerns."

Fiction: Middle readers, young adults: animal, contemporary, fantasy, folktales, health, history, humor, multicultural, nature/environment, science fiction, special needs, sports, suspense/mystery. Average word length: middle readers—15-35,000; young adults—30-60,000. Recently published *The Dragonchild*, by Anne Lewis (ages 8-12, fantasy adventure); *Pwtyn and Pwtay Meet*, by Alys Jones (ages 4-7, animal story).

How to Contact/Writers: Only interested in agented material. "We don't accept work by a writer who has no connection to Wales. We are happy to accept work from an author not currently living in Wales." Fiction: Submit outline/synopsis and 3 sample chapters. Nonfiction: Submit outline/synopsis. Responds to queries in 1 month; mss in 3 months, hopefully. Publishes book 12-18 months after acceptance. Will consider simultaneous submissions or previously published work.

Illustration: Works with 3-4 illustrators/year. Primarily uses b&w artwork with color covers. Reviews ms/illustration packages from artists. Illustrations only: Query with samples. Illustrators must have some connection to Wales. Responds in 4 months. Samples returned with SASE; samples filed.

Photography: Buys stock and assigns work. Contact: Janet Thomas, editor. Uses cover material. All styles. Model/property releases required. Submit cover letter and published samples.

Terms: Payment depends on project. Offers advances "only a token amount of a few hundred pounds." Payment to illustrators "depends on amount of work needed. Illustrators rarely get royalty as we don't do fully illustrated color books. We only use photographs for covers, so no royalty." Sends galleys to authors; dummies to illustrators. Originals returned

to artist at job's completion. Book catalog available for A5 SAE and postage. All imprints included in a single catalog.
Tips: "We're a small press with limited time, so the proposal needs to be clear and to the point. We sell mostly within Wales and this is a tough market, where the books can easily be lost among the bigger UK publishers' work. So the book needs to have a strong selling point and we need to be very confident that a book can find its audience. (Sometimes some writers think a small press is less demanding, but in fact we have to be more.) There is alot of fantasy around, which is great, but I'd like to see some entertaining realistic fiction again that's not too 'issue driven.' It's difficult to do a good adventure story, for example, because you have to reflect the greatly reduced freedom children now, but an author who can find a way to do one would fill a great need in the market. Not that I'm not happy to see more fantasy."

HYPERION PRESS LIMITED, 300 Wales Ave., Winnipeg MB R2M 2S9 Canada. (204)256-9204. Fax: (204)255-7845. E-mail: tamos@escape.ca. Website: www.escape.ca/~tamos. Book Publisher. **Acquisitions:** Dr. M. Tutiah, editor. Publishes authentic-based, retold folktales/legends for ages 4-9. "We are interested in a good story or well researched how-to material."
Fiction: Young readers, middle readers: folktales/legends. Recently published *The Wise Washerman*, by Deborah Froese, illustrated by Wang Kui; *The Cricket's Cage*, written and illustrated by Stefan Czernecki; and *The Peacock's Pride*, by Melissa Kajpust, illustrated by Jo'Anne Kelly.
How to Contact/Writers: Fiction: Query. Responds in 3 months.
Illustration: Reviews ms/illustration packages from artists. Manuscript/illustration packages and illustration only: Query. Samples returned with SASE.
Terms: Pays authors royalty. Pays illustrators by the project. Sends galleys to authors; dummies to illustrators. Book catalog available for 8½ × 11 SAE and $2.00 postage (Canadian).

MILES KELLY PUBLISHING, The Bardfield Centre, Great Bardfield, Essex CM7 4SL 811309 United Kingdom. (44)1371 811309. Fax: (44)1731 811393. E-mail: info@mileskelly.net. Website: www.mileskelly.net. Estab. 1996. Specializes in trade books, nonfiction, fiction, educational material. We are an independent book packager/producer. **Art Acquisitions:** Jim Miles, director. Publishes 6 picture books/year; 30-40 young readers/year; 40-50 middle readers/year; and 3-6 young adult titles/year. Produces "top-quality illustration and design complementing sound and well-written information."
How to Contact/Writers: Responds to queries in 2 weeks.
Illustration: Works with 100 illustrators/year. Illustrations only. Contact: Jim Miles, director. Responds in 3 weeks only if interested.
Terms: Pays authors by the word only. Pays Illustrators £30 minimum. Catalog available online.
Tips: "Check our website first. Be aware that most UK publishers need international sales to make books viable—so appeal to international tastes."

KEY PORTER BOOKS, 70 The Esplanade, Toronto ON M5E 1R2 Canada. (416)862-7777. Fax: (416)862-2304. E-mail: jyoon@keyporter.com. Website: www.keyporter.com. Book publisher. Publishes 4 picture books/year; and 4 young readers/year. 30% of books by first-time authors. "Key Porter Books is the largest independent, 100% Canadian-owned trade publisher."
Fiction: Picture books, young readers, middle readers, young adult: adventure, animal, anthology, fantasy, folktales, sports. Does not want to see religious material. Average word length: picture books—1,500; young readers—5,000. Recently published *The Goodfellows Chronicles, Book 1: The Sacred Seal, Book 2: The Messengers*, by J.C. Mills (young adult fiction); *Rose in New York: Gotcha!*, by Carol Matas (young adult).
Nonfiction: Picture books: animal, arts/crafts, cooking, geography, nature/environment, reference, science. Middle readers: animal, nature/environment, reference, science. Average word length: picture books—1,500; middle readers—15,000. Recently published *The Dinosaur Atlas*, by Don Lessem (ages 8-12); *Rude Ramsey and The Roaming Radishes*, by Margaret Atwood (ages 4-7).
How to Contact/Writers: Only interested in agented material; *no unsolicited mss.* "Although Key Porter Books does not review unsolicited manuscript submissions, we do try and review queries and proposals." Responds to queries/proposals in 6 months.
Photography: Buys photos from freelancers. Buys stock and assigns work. Captions required. Uses 35mm transparencies. Submit cover letter, résumé, duplicate slides, stock photo list.
Tips: "Please note that all proposals and accompanying materials will be discarded unless sufficient postage has been provided for their return. Please do not send any original artwork or other irreplaceable materials. We do not accept responsibility for any materials you submit."

KOALA BOOKS, P.O. Box 626, Mascot NSW 1460 Australia. (61)02 9667-2997. Fax: (61)02 9667-2881. E-mail: admin@koalabooks.com.au. Website: www.koalabooks.com.au. **Manuscript Acquisitions:** Children's Editor. **Art Acquisitions:** Children's Designer. "Koala Books is an independent wholly Australian-owned children's book publishing house. Our strength is providing quality books for children at competitive prices."
Fiction: Picture books, young readers, middle readers.
Nonfiction: Looks for quirky nonfiction for primary readers.
How to Contact/Writers: Accepts material from residents of Australia only. Fiction and picture books only: Submit complete ms, blurb, synopsis, brief author biography, list of author's published works. Also SASE large enough for ms return. Responds to mss in 3 months.
Illustration: Accepts material from residents of Australia only. Illustrations only: Send cover letter, brief bio, list of

published works and samples (color photographs or photocopies) in "an A4 folder suitable for filing." Contact: Children's Designer. Responds only if interested. Samples not returned; samples filed.

Terms: Pays authors royalty of 10% based on retail price or work purchased outright occasionally (may be split with illustrator).

Tips: "Take a look at our website to get an idea of the kinds of books we publish. A few hours research in a quality children's bookshop would be helpful when choosing a publisher."

LIGHTWAVE PUBLISHING, 26275 98th Ave., Maple Ridge BC V2W 1K3 Canada. (604)462-7890. Fax: (604)462-8208. E-mail: mikal@lightwavepublishing.com. Website: www.lightwavepublishing.com. **Assistant:** Mikal Marrs. Estab. 1991. Independent book packager/producer specializing in Christian material. Publishes over 30 titles/year. "Our mission is helping parents pass on their Christian faith to their children."

Fiction: Picture books: religion adventure, concept. Young readers: concept, religion. Middle readers: adventure, religion. Young adults: religion.

Nonfiction: Picture books, young readers: activity books, concept, religion. Middle readers, young adults: concept, religion. Average word length: young readers—2,000; middle readers—20,000; young adults—30,000. Recently published *Focus On The Family's Guide to Spiritual Growth of Children*, edited by Osborne, Bruner, Trent; *The Memory Verse Bible*, by K. Christie Bowler.

How to Contact/Writers: Fiction/Nonfiction: Does not accept unsolicited mss. Only interested in writers who will work-for-hire. Query. Responds to queries in 6 weeks; mss in 2 months. Publishes book 1 year after acceptance.

Terms: Work purchased outright from authors. Payment varies. Book catalog available for SASE (Canadian postage or IRC). Writer's guidelines available for SASE (Canadian postage or IRC). Catalog available on website. Guidelines available on website.

Tips: "We only do work-for-hire. We have our own projects and ideas then find writers to help create them. No royalties. Interested writers are welcome to contact us. Please don't put U.S. stamps on SASE."

LION PUBLISHING plc, Imprint of Mayfield House, 256 Banbury Rd., Oxford OX2 7DH England. (44)1865 302750. Fax: (44)1865 302757. Website: www.lion-publishing.co.uk.

Fiction Picture books, young readers, middle readers: concept, fantasy, folktales, religion (Christian). Middle readers: adventure. Recently published *The Wolf Who Cried Boy*, by Bob Hartman, illustrated by Tim Raiglin (ages 5-8, picture books); *Telling the Sea*, by Pauline Flsk (ages 10-14); *The Dragon King Saga: Book 3*, by Stephan Lawhead (ages 11 and up).

Nonfiction: Picture books, young readers, middle readers: religion (Christian). Recently published *The Story of the Cross*, by Mary Joslin, illustrated by Gail Newey (ages 4-8); *The Book of Books*, by Trevor Dennis (ages 9 and up); and *My Very First Prayers*, by Lois Rock, illustrated by Alex Ayllffe (ages 0-4).

How to Contact/Writers: Accepts material from residents of England only. Fiction/nonfiction: Submit outline/synopsis with cover letter (include background information, previously published work, qualifications and experience). Responds to queries in 3 months.

Illustration: Accepts material from residents of England only. Manuscript/illustration packages should be submitted to Art Director at j.crawford@lion-publishing.co.uk. Illustrations only: E-mail or query with samples. Responds only if interested. Samples not returned.

Tips: "Online manuscript submissions are not accepted. Our children's fiction and poetry lists are strictly limited to **already-published authors**. We are **not** publishing fiction for teenagers. Please look through the Lion site. If the genre of book you have in mind does not appear on our site, then there is no point in submitting to us."

LITTLE TIGER PRESS, Imprint of Magi Publications, 1 The Coda Centre, 189 Munster Rd., London SW6 6AW United Kingdom.(44)20-7385 6333. Fax: (44)20 7385 7333. Website: www.littletigerpress.com. "Our aim is to create books that our readers will love as much as we do—helping them develop a passion for books that offer laughter, comfort, learning or exhilarating flights of the imagination!"

Fiction: Picture books: animal, concept, contemporary, humor. Average word length: picture books—1,000 words or less. Recently published *Cuddly Cuffs*, by Lucy Richards (ages 0-3, cloth, chewable, washable books); and *Quiet!*, by Paul Bright and Guy Parker-Rees (ages 3-7, picture book).

Nonfiction: Picture books. Average word length: picture books—1,000 words or less.

How to Contact/Writers: Fiction/nonfiction: Submit complete ms. Responds to queries/mss in 2 months.

Illustration: Illustrations only: Query with samples (include SASE with IRCs). Do not send originals. Color photocopies are best. Responds only if interested. Samples returned with SASE.

Tips: "Every reasonable care is taken of the manuscripts and samples we receive, but we cannot accept responsibility for any loss or damage. Try to read or look at as many books a publisher has published before sending in your material."

LOBSTER PRESS, 1620 Sherbrooke St. W., Suites C&D, Montréal QC H3H 1C9 Canada. (514)904-1100. Fax: (514)904-1101. E-mail: editorial@lobsterpress.com. Website: www.lobsterpress.com. Estab. 1997. **Editorial Manager:** Gabriella Mancini. Publishes 4 picture books/year; 4 young reader/year. "Driven by a desire to produce quality books that bring families together."

● Lobster Press is not currently accepting manuscripts or queries.

Fiction: Picture books, young readers, middle readers, young adults: adventure, animal, contemporary, health, history, multicultural, nature/environment, special needs, sports, suspense/mystery. Average word length: picture books—200-1,000. Recently published *How Hot Was It?*, by Jane Barclay, illustrated by Janice Donato (picture book); *Max the Mighty*

insider report

A U.K. perspective on approaching children's publishers

With a lifetime spent drawing but no formal education as an artist, Scottish illustrator Moira Munro approached London-based publisher Piccadilly Press, seeking an illustration commission. Piccadilly wanted her to write the book as well—thus Munro became author/illustrator of *Hamish, The Bear Who Found His Child*. Published in March 2003 by Piccadilly, the book tells the story of a teddy bear who goes from preferring his scooter to children, to wanting nothing more than to go home with a very special little girl who wanders into his toyshop.

Munro began her illustration career on her fortieth birthday after years of office-dwelling and drawing only occasional cartoons. At first she worried that she had neither the skill nor the speed to

Moira Munro

make it as a full-time illustrator. Eventually though, she realized that "I would improve with practice and I'd really had enough of sadistic managers, performance reviews and windowless offices."

Here, she shares some of her experiences as a beginning illustrator and author in the United Kingdom.

How did you choose what publishers to submit to? Did you submit only in the U.K. or did you submit to other countries as well?

In the U.K., the *Writers' & Artists' Yearbook* lists many publishers, though it doesn't tell you much about them. So I went through the list and picked those that sounded familiar. The *2001 Children's Writer's & Illustrator's Market* is the first book I got on the subject of children's books, and this gave me the confidence to approach publishers. I thought I'd stick to twenty U.K. publishers for my first mailing—and that one mailing, amazingly, led to my book. The advantage of sticking to your own country is you can research what style particular publishers go for; you can phone them up easily; you can get advice on contracts—everything seems a bit simpler. But your question reminds me I ought to try publishers from other countries. With the Internet, crossing frontiers isn't a big deal—and French is my mother tongue.

What do you include when you send samples? Has your process changed since you've been published?

In my first mailing I sent half a dozen pages of illustration samples and a cover letter making reference to my website. I included a stamped reply postcard on which I wrote the name of the publisher and of the person I was addressing my samples to. Then I printed several questions.

Not everyone returned my postcard, but from those who did, I got a bit more feedback than from a standard rejection letter.

After finishing my book, I did a new mailing with new illustration samples, making it clear in the very first paragraph that I am a published author/illustrator. I think your path is easier once you're published. I phoned some of the publishers who had given the best feedback after my first mailing, asking them if they had further advice. They told me my style had developed into something they could use and encouraged me to send stories. I said I was flying for a rare visit to London and met them. Because I had a personal contact with these art directors, I sent mainly story outlines. Publishers seem to have very specific reasons for not liking an idea, even before they see the writing style. So far, I've had no success with my proposals, but I've received

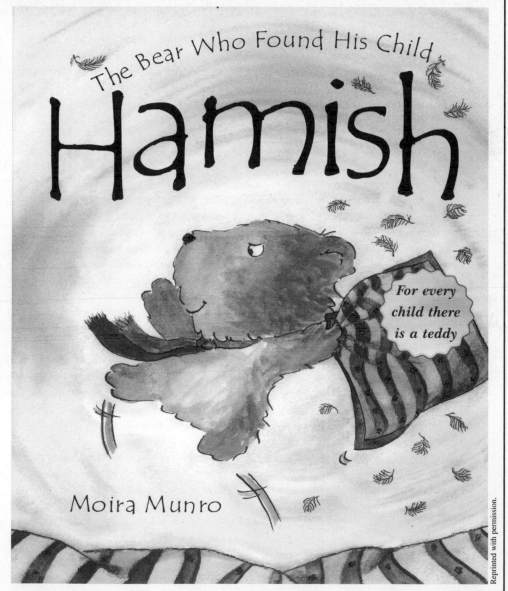

The Bear Who Found His Child

Hamish

For every child there is a teddy

Moira Munro

A handful of illustration samples, a cover letter, and a stamped reply postcard helped Moira Munro land the assignment for her first book, *Hamish, The Bear Who Found His Child* (Piccadilly Press, March 2003). Regular mailings, in addition to her website, www.moiramunro.com, have begun to create a steady flow of work for the artist, though she's still trying to sell the U.S. co-edition that is crucial for many U.K. publishers.

useful feedback. Every six months or so I do a new mailing—sometimes just a postcard with a new illustration and a brief handwritten note on the back. I did a separate mailing showing another style to a handful of educational publishers, and months later that yielded a really nice job (illustrations for a school book on theology).

What are the main differences between U.K. children's market and the U.S.?
In the U.K., publishers need international co-editions. The U.K. market is, I believe, not large enough to finance the many picture books released every year. So U.K. publishers mainly take on stories and illustration styles they think will be bought abroad. For instance, one publisher, leafing through my portfolio, pointed out pictures which "wouldn't sell in Europe." These were pen, ink and watercolor pictures. I've frequently heard of British publishers asking for changes to satisfy American co-publishers, always towards something more bland, sadly—such as a delightful manuscript about guinea pigs, which was rejected outright "because the Americans don't take to rodents, I'm afraid."

What made you decide to set up your website, www.moiramunro.com, and how did you begin it?
I thought a website would be a useful way to display my portfolio and I had fantasies that it would bring oodles of easy income selling stock (pictures previously published elsewhere), but that hardly ever happens. I didn't know how to get started, and a lovely friend insisted he'd do it for me for free. Problem was, this enthusiastic friend is also Mr. Unreliable. I egged him on for six months and then asked him to hand over whatever he'd done. I used the framework he'd created and a teach-yourself book to finish it off. It wasn't that hard.

So my website was up a couple of months after I became a freelance illustrator. It was another year before I looked into search engines and other ways for my site to be found, and the effort has paid off. Some publishers seem to hunt for new talent on the web—amazing when you think of all the submissions they receive. A large London publisher approached me that way and so did a Scottish publisher for whom I'm now illustrating some great children's books. I find that potential customers check my website before giving me work. My site also serves as a brochure on school visits—an unplanned source of income and fun now that my book has been published. A lot of work goes into keeping the site interesting, but it's well worth it.

You mention on your website your editor's repeated "slashing" of your story. Have you figured out any coping strategies for this?
My first reaction was always emotional and the only remedy was chocolate. After that I became rational, looked again, and admitted the editor had a point. A week later, I couldn't look at my original version without cringing. I'd be filled with gratitude that the editor had saved me from having such rubbish associated with my name. Quite often I didn't like the words put in by the editor—they didn't sound like my voice—so I'd make an alternative suggestion, which was usually accepted.

Are some chocolates better remedies than others?
Good question. If you'll excuse me I'm off to do some research.
    —Mona Michael

Superhero and *Max the Movie Director*, by Trina Wiebe, illustrated by Helen Flook (chapter books).

Nonfiction: Young readers, middle readers and adults/teens: animal, biography, careers, geography, hobbies, how-to, multicultural, nature/environment, references, science, self-help, social issues, sports, travel. Average word length: middle readers—40,000. Recently published *Make Things Happen: The Key to Networking for Teens*, by Lara Zielin (Millenium Generation).

How to Contact/Writers: "We are not accepting manuscripts at the moment. Please refer to our website for updates."

Illustration: Works with 5 illustrators/year. Uses line drawings and color artwork. Reviews ms/illustration packages from artists. Query with samples. Illustrations only: query with samples. Samples not returned; samples kept on file.

Terms: Pays authors 5-10% royalty based on retail price. Offers advances (average amount: $2,000-4,000). Pays illustrators by the project (range: $1,000-2,000) or 2-7% royalty based on retail price. Sends galleys to authors; dummies to illustrators. Originals returned to artist at job's completion. Writer's and artist's guidelines available on website.

Tips: "Please do not call and ask for an appointment. We do not meet with anyone unless we are going to use their work."

MANTRA LINGUA, 5 Alexandra Grove, London N12 8NU United Kingdom. (44)20 8445 5123. Fax: (44)20 8446 7445. E-mail: henri@mantralingua.com. Website: www.mantralingua.com. Specializes in multicultural material. **Manuscript Acquisitions:** Series Editor. Mantra Lingua "connects and transcends national differences in a way that is respectful and appreciative of local cultures."

• Mantra is currently seeking myths and folklore for picture books only.

Fiction: Picture books, young readers, middle readers: folktales, multicultural, myths. Average word length: picture books—1,000-1,500; young readers—1,000-1,500. Recently published *Beowulf—An Anglo-Saxon Epic*, retold by Henriette Barkow, illustrated by Alan Down (ages 9-13). *Jill and the Beanstalk*, by Manju Gregory (ages 3-8).

How to Contact/Writers: Accepts material from residents of United Kingdom only. Fiction: Myths only. Submit outline/synopsis (250 words, describe myth, "where it is from, whether it's famous or unknown, and why it would make a great picture book.") Will consider e-mail submissions only.

Illustration: Uses 2D animations for CD-ROMs. Query with samples. Responds only if interested. Samples not returned; samples filed.

MOOSE ENTERPRISE BOOK & THEATRE PLAY PUBLISHING, Imprint of Moose Hide Books, 684 Walls Rd., Sault St. Marie ON P6A 5K6 Canada. Phone/fax: (705)779-3331.E-mail: mooseenterprises@on.aibn.com. Estab. 1996. Specializes in mass market books, fiction, nonfiction, multicultural material. **Manuscript Acquisitions:** Edmond Alcid. Publishes 2 middle readers/year; and 2 young adult titles/year. 75% of books by first-time authors. Editorial philosophy: "To assist the new writers of moral standards."

• This publisher does not offer payment for stories published in its anthologies and/or book collections. Be sure to send a SASE for guidelines.

Fiction: Middle readers, young adults: adventure, fantasy, humor, suspense/mystery, story poetry. Recently published *Realm of the Golden Feather*, by C.R. Ginter (ages 12 and up, fantasy); *Tell Me a Story*, short story collection by various authors (ages 9-11, humor/adventure); and *Spirits of Lost Lake*, by James Walters (ages 12 and up, adventure).

Nonfiction: Middle readers, young adults: biography, history, multicultural.

How to Contact/Writers: Fiction/nonfiction: Query. Responds to queries in 1 month; mss in 3 months. Publishes book 1 year after acceptance. Will consider simultaneous submissions.

Illustration: Uses primarily black & white artwork. Illustrations only: Query with samples. Responds in 1 month, if interested. Samples returned with SASE; samples filed.

Terms: Originals returned to artist at job's completion. Manuscript and art guidelines available for SASE.

Tips: "Do not copy trends, be yourself, give me something new, something different."

ORCA BOOK PUBLISHERS, 1030 N. Park St., Victoria BC V8T 1C6 Canada. (250)380-1229. Fax: (250)380-1892. Website: www.orcabook.com. Book publisher. Estab. 1984. Publisher: R. Tyrrell. **Acquisitions:** Maggie deVries, children's book editor. Publishes 7 picture books/year; 16 middle readers/year; and 10 young adult titles/year. 25% of books by first-time authors. "We only consider authors who are Canadian or who live in Canada."

Fiction: Picture books: animals, contemporary, history, nature/environment. Middle readers: contemporary, history, fantasy, nature/environment, problem novels. Young adults: adventure, contemporary, history, multicultural, nature/environment, problem novels, suspense/mystery. Average word length: picture books—500-1,500; middle readers—20,000-35,000; young adult—25,000-45,000. Published *Tall in the Saddle*, by Anne Carter, illustrated by David McPhail (ages 4-8, picture book); *Me and Mr. Mah*, by Andrea Spalding, illustrated by Janet Wilson (ages 5 and up, picture book); and *Alone at Ninety Foot*, by Katherine Holubitsky (young adult).

How to Contact/Writers: Fiction: Submit complete ms if picture book; submit outline/synopsis and 3 sample chapters. "All queries or unsolicited submissions should be accompanied by a SASE." Responds to queries in 2 months; mss in 3 months. Publishes a book 18-36 months after acceptance. Submission guidelines available online.

Illustration: Works with 8-10 illustrators/year. Reviews ms/illustration packages from artists. Submit ms with 3-4 pieces of final art. "Reproductions only, no original art please." Illustrations only: Query with samples; provide résumé, slides. Responds in 2 months. Samples returned with SASE; samples filed.

Terms: Pays authors royalty of 5% for picture books, 10% for novels, based on retail price. Offers advances (average amount: $2,000). Pays illustrators royalty of 5% minimum based on retail price and advance on royalty. Sends galleys to authors. Original artwork returned at job's completion if picture books. Book catalog available for legal or 8½×11 manila SAE and $2 first-class postage. Manuscript guidelines available for SASE. Art guidelines not available.

Ⓝ ⊕ PICCADILLY PRESS, 5 Castle Rd., London NW1 8PR United Kingdom. (44)20 7267 4492. Fax: (44)20 7267 4493. E-mail: books@piccadillypress.co.uk. Website: www.piccadillypress.co.uk.
Fiction: Picture books: animal, contemporary, fantasy, nature/environment. Young adults: contemporary, humor, problem novels. Average word length: picture books—500-1,000; young adults—25,000-35,000. Recently published *Teen Queens & Has-beens*, by Cathy Hopkins (young adult); *Making Sense*, by Nadia Marks (young adult); and *Wilbie—Footie Mad*, by Sally Chambers (picture book).
Nonfiction: Young adults: self help (humorous). Average word length: young adults—25,000-35,000. Recently published *The Trouble with Boyfriends*, by Tricia Kreitman.
How to Contact/Writers: Accepts material from residents of United Kingdom only. Fiction: Submit complete ms for picture books or submit outline/synopsis and 2 sample chapters for YA. Enclose a brief cover letter and SASE for reply. Nonfiction: Submit outline/synopsis and 2 sample chapters. Responds to mss in approximately 6 weeks.
Illustration: Illustrations only: Query with samples (do not send originals).
Tips: "Keep a copy of your manuscript on file."

Ⓝ ⊕ PIPERS' ASH LTD., Church Rd., Christian Malford, Chippenham Wiltshire SN15 4BW United Kingdom. (44)1249 720563. Fax: (44)870 0568916. E-mail: pipersash@supamasu.com. Website: www.supamasu.com. Estab. 1976. Specializes in nonfiction, fiction. **Manuscript Acquisitions:** Manuscript Evaluation Desk. Publishes 1 middle readers/year; and 2 young adult titles/year. 90% of books by first-time authors. Editorial philosophy is "To discover new authors with talent and potential."
Fiction: Young readers, middle readers: adventure. Young adults: problem novels. Average word length: young readers—10,000; middle readers—20,000; young adults—30,000. Recently published *Free Wheeler*, by Shay Wilson (young readers); *Northern Lights*, by Anne Colledge (middle); and *Stay? No Way!*, by Vivienne Loranger (teens).
Nonfiction: Young readers: history, multicultural, nature/environment. Middle readers: biography, history, multicultural, nature/environment, sports. Young adults: self help, social issues, special needs. Average word length: young readers—10,000; middle readers—20,000; young adults—30,000. Recently published *SoU12BaPoet?*, by Bob Griffith; *In on the Act*, by Eve Blizzard; and *Write for the Stage*, by Eve Blizzard (all for teens and adults).
How to Contact/Writers: Fiction/nonfiction: Query. Responds to queries in 1 week; mss in 3 months. Publishes book 2 months after acceptance. Will consider e-mail submissions, previously published work.
Terms: Pays authors royalty of 10-15% based on wholesale price. Sends galleys to authors. Book catalog available for A5 SASE. Offers ms guidelines for SASE. "Include adequate postage for return of ms plus publisher's guidelines."
Tips: "Visit our website—note pages of hints, tips and guidelines."

Ⓝ ☐ ⊕ ☐ QUARTZ EDITIONS, Premier House, 112 Station Rd., Edgware, Middlesex HA8 7BJ United Kingdom. (44)208 951 5656. Fax: (44)208 381 2588. E-mail: quartzeditions@btconnect.com. Estab. 1993. Specializes in mass market books, trade books, nonfiction, fiction, educational material. We are an independent book packager/producer. **Manuscript/Art Acquisitions:** Susan Pinkus, managing director. Publishes more than 20 titles/year, but varies. "We aim to produce high-quality, lavishly illustrated titles for the international market, including translated editions for many countries—viz. France, Mexico, Russia, China, Japan, etc."
Fiction: Picture books: adventure, animal, fantasy, folktales, humor. Young readers, middle readers: adventure, animal, fantasy, folktales, humor, suspense/mystery. Young adults: adventure, animal, fantasy, folktales, humor, suspense/mystery, teen romance. Average word length: varies. Recently published *The Haunted School*, by C. Rose, illustrated by M. Dorey (ages 8-12).
Nonfiction: Picture books, young readers, middle readers, young adults: animal, careers, geography, health, history, how-to, nature/environment, religion, science, textbooks. Recently published Insects (8 titles), by T. Green (ages 9-14).
How to Contact/Writers: Fiction/nonfiction: Submit complete ms. Responds to queries/mss in 1 month. Will consider simultaneous submissions.
Illustration: Works with 6-10 illustrators/year. Reviews ms/illustration packages from artists. Submit ms/illustration package as complete as possible. Illustration only: send résumé, client list, tearsheets. Responds in 1 month. Samples filed.
Photography: Buys stock and assigns work. Uses mostly natural history. Model/property releases required; captions required. Uses color prints and transparencies. Submit cover letter, résumé, published samples, client list, stock photo list.
Terms: Work purchased outright from authors. Pays illustrators by the project. Pays photographers by the project. Book catalog available for 10×8 SASE. All imprints included in a single catalog.
Tips: "All submissions must be accompanied by stamped addressed envelope/packaging for return; otherwise no responsibility accepted. Please relate nonfiction titles to school curriculum as far as possible. Please do not send us the only copy of your manuscript. All manuscripts must be typed with double spacing."

Ⓝ ✴ RAINCOAST BOOKS, 9050 Shaughnessy St., Vancouver BC V6P 6E5 Canada. (604)323-7100. Fax: (604)323-2600. E-mail: info@raincoast.com. Website: www.raincoast.com. **Contact:** Editorial Department. Imprints: Polestar, Press Gang. Publishes 4 picture books/year; and 4 young adult titles/year
● Raincoast Books does not accept unsolicited manuscripts or e-mail queries.
Fiction: Picture books, young readers, young adults: contemporary, history. Recently published *Chimp and Zee and the Big Storm*, by Catherine and Laurence Anholt (picture book); *The Song within My Heart*, by David Bouchard, paintings by Allen Sapp (picture book); *Tess*, by Jocelyn Reekie (juvenile fiction).
Nonfiction: Picture books, young readers: science, sports, natural history. Recently published *Albertosaurus Death of a Predator*, by Monique Keiran; *A Young Dancer's Apprenticeship*, by Olympia Dowd.
How to Contact/Writers: Accepts material from residents of Canada only. Fiction/nonfiction: query letter with "details

about the work including word count, subject matter and your publication history for picture books and young readers." For young adult fiction submit query letter with list of publication credits plus 1-page outline of the plot. Responds to queries in 4 months. Will consider multiple submissions (indicate in query letter).

Illustration: Illustrations only: Query with samples; "no more than 10, nonreturnable color photocopies. Do not send original artwork or slides. Submit new samples to us as they become available." Contact: Creative Director. Responds only if interested. Samples not returned.

Terms: Book catalog available online.

Tips: "For older (teen readers) we're looking for subject matter that pushes the boundaries a little. For children's illustrative work, we are interested in illustrators who can successfully convey an artistic, painterly, whimsical style. Please refer to our catalogue for examples."

N ⊕ A RANDOM HOUSE CHILDREN'S BOOKS, 61-63 Uxbridge Rd., London W5 5SA England. Phone: (0208)231-6000. Fax: (0208)231-6737. E-mail: enquiries@randomhouse.co.uk. Imprints are Doubleday, Corgi Pups (ages 5-8), Young Corgi (ages 6-9), Corgi Yearling (ages 8-11), Corgi (ages 10 and up). Book publisher. Managing director: Philippa Dickinson. Publishes 120 picture books/year; 120 fiction titles/year.

Fiction: Picture books: adventure, animal, anthology, contemporary, fantasy, folktales, humor, multicultural, nature/environment, poetry, suspense/mystery. Young readers: adventure, animal, anthology, contemporary, fantasy, folktales, humor, multicultural, nature/environment, poetry, sports, suspense/mystery. Middle readers: adventure, animal, anthology, contemporary, fantasy, folktales, humor, multicultural, nature/environment, problem novels, romance, sports, suspense/mystery. Young adults: adventure, contemporary, fantasy, humor, multicultural, nature/environment, problem novels, romance, science fiction, suspense/mystery. Average word length: picture books—800; young readers—1,500-6,000; middle readers—10,000-15,000; young adults—20,000-45,000.

How to Contact/Writers: Only interested in agented material.

Illustration: Works with 50 illustrators/year. Reviews ms/illustration packages from artists. Submit ms with dummy. Contact: Penny Walker. Illustrations only: Query with samples. Responds in 1 month. Samples are returned with SASE (IRC).

Photography: Buys photos from freelancers. Contact: Tracey Hurst, art department. Buys stock images. Photo captions required. Uses color or b&w prints. Submit cover letter, published samples.

Terms: Pays authors royalty. Offers advances. Pays illustrators by the project or royalty. Pays photographers by the project or per photo.

📖 RED DEER PRESS, Rm 813, Mackimmie Library Tower, 2500 University Dr. NW, Calgary AB T2N 1N4 Canada. (403)220-4334. Fax: (403)210-8191. E-mail: rdp@ucalgary.ca. Website: www.reddeerpress.com. Imprints: Northern Lights Books for Children, Northern Lights Young Novels. Book publisher. Estab. 1975. **Manuscript/Art Acquisitions:** Peter Carver, children's editor. Publishes 3 picture books/year; 4 young adult titles/year. 20% of books by first-time authors. Red Deer Press is known for their "high-quality international children's program that tackles risky and/or serious issues for kids."

Fiction: Picture books, young readers: adventure, contemporary, fantasy, folktales, history, humor, multicultural, nature/environment, poetry; middle readers, young adult/teens: adventure, contemporary, fantasy, folktales, hi-lo, history, humor, multicultural, nature/environment, problem novels, suspense/mystery. Recently published *Courage to Fly*, by Troon Harrison, illustrated by Zhong-Yang Huung (ages 4-7, picture book); *Amber Waiting*, by Nan Gregory, illustrated by Macdonald Denton (ages 4-7, picture book); *Tom Finder*, by Martine Leavitt (14 and up).

How to Contact/Writers: Fiction/Nonfiction: Query or submit outline/synopsis. Responds to queries in 6 months; ms in 8 months. Publishes a book 18 months after acceptance. Will consider simultaneous submissions.

Illustration: Works with 4-6 illustrators/year. Illustrations only: Query with samples. Responds only if interested. Samples not returned; samples filed for six months. Canadian illustrators only.

Photography: Buys stock and assigns work. Model/property releases required. Submit cover letter, résumé and color promo piece.

Terms: Pays authors royalty (negotiated). Occasionally offers advances (negotiated). Pays illustrators and photographers by the project or royalty (depends on the project). Sends galleys to authors. Originals returned to artist at job's completion. Guidelines not available.

Tips: "Red Deer Press is currently not accepting children's manuscripts unless the writer is an established Canadian children's writer with an original project that fits its publishing program. Writers, illustrators and photographers should familiarize themselves with RD Press's children's publishing program."

📖 RONSDALE PRESS, 3350 W. 21st Ave., Vancouver BC V6S 1G7 Canada. (604)738-4688. Fax: (604)731-4548. E-mail: ronhatch@pinc.com. Website: ronsdalepress.com. Book publisher. Estab. 1988. **Manuscript/Art Acquisitions:** Veronica Hatch, children's editor. Publishes 2 children's books/year. 80% of titles by first-time authors. "Ronsdale Press is a Canadian literary publishing house that publishes 8 to 10 books each year, two of which are children's titles. Of particular interest are books involving children exploring and discovering new aspects of Canadian history."

Fiction: Young adults: Canadian historical novels. Average word length: for middle readers and young adults—50,000. Recently published *Adrift In Time*, by John Wilson (ages 9-14); *The Tenth Pupil*, by Constance Horne (ages 9-14); *Beginnings*, edited by Ann Walsh (anthology of short stories, ages 9 and up); *Eyewitness*, by Margaret Thompson (ages 8-14); and *Hurricanes over London*, by Charles Reid (ages 8-14).

Nonfiction: Middle readers, young adults: animal, biography, history, multicultural, social issues. Average word length: young readers—90; middle readers—90.

How to Contact/Writers: Accepts material from residents of Canada only. Fiction/Nonfiction: Submit complete ms. Responds to queries in 2 weeks; mss in 2 months. Publishes a book 1 year after acceptance. Will consider simultaneous submissions.

Illustrations: Works with 2 illustrators/year. Reviews ms/illustration packages from artists. Requires only cover art. Responds in 2 weeks. Samples returned with SASE. Originals returned to artist at job's completion.

Terms: Pays authors royalty of 10% based on retail price. Pays illustrators by the project $800-1,200. Sends galleys to authors. Book catalog available for 8½×11 SAE and $1 postage; ms and art guidelines available for SASE.

Tips: "Ronsdale Press publishes well-written books that have a new slant on things and that can take an age-old story and give it a new spin. We are particularly interested in novels for young adults with a historical component that offers new insights into a part of Canada's history. We publish only Canadian authors."

N ⊕ SCHOLASTIC AUSTRALIA, Imprint of Scholastic Inc., P.O. Box 579, Lindfield NSW 2070 Australia. (61)2 9416-4000. Fax: (61)2 9416-9877. Website: www.scholastic.com.au. **Manuscript Acquisitions:** Megan Fauvet, publishing secretary, Scholastic Press or Dyan Blacklock, publisher Omnibus Books. **Art Acquisitions:** Megan Fauvet, publishing secretary, Scholastic Press and Margaret Hamilton Books or Dyan Blacklock, publisher, Omnibus Books. Imprints: Scholastic Press (Margrete Lamond, acquisitions editor); Margaret Hamilton Books (Margrete Lamond, acquisitions editor); Omnibus Books (Dyan Bladdock). "Communicating with children around the world."

Fiction: Picture books, young readers. Recently published *After Alice*, by Jane Carroll (ages 8-12, fiction); *Amelia Ellicott's Garden*, by Lilianna Stafford, illustrated by Stephen Michael King (ages 5-7, picture book); and *An Ordinary Day*, by Libby Gleeson, illustrated by Armin Greder (ages 5-15, picture book).

Nonfiction: Omnibus and Scholastic Press will consider nonfiction. Recently published *Bass and Flinders*, by Cathy Dodson, illustrated by Roland Harvey (ages 9-12, history); *The Cartoon Faces Book*, by Robert Ainsworth (ages 7-14, art & craft); and *Excuse Me, Captain Cook, Who Did Discover Australia?*, by Michael Salmon (ages 7-12, history).

How to Contact/Writers: Accepts material from residents of Australia only. Fiction/nonfiction: Submit complete ms. For picture books, submit only ms, no art. Responds to mss in 2 months.

Illustration: Illustrations only: Send portfolio. Contact appropriate office for more information on what to include with portfolio.

Tips: "Scholastic Australia publishes books for children under three publishing imprints—Scholastic Press, Omnibus Books and Margaret Hamilton Books. To get a more specific idea of the flavor of each list, you will need to visit your local bookstore. Don't be too surprised or disappointed if your first attempts are not successful. Children's book publishing is a highly competitive field, and writing children's books is not quite as easy as some might imagine. But we are always ready to find the next Harry Potter or Paddington Bear, so if you believe you can write it, we're ready to hear from you."

◼ SCHOLASTIC CANADA LTD., 175 Hillmount Rd., Markham ON L6C 1Z7 Canada. (905)887-READ. Fax: (905)887-1131. Website: www.scholastic.ca; for ms/artist guidelines: www.scholastic.ca/guideline.html. Imprints: Scholastic Canada; North Winds Press; Les Éditions Scholastic. **Acquisitions:** Editor, children's books. Publishes hardcover and trade paperback originals. Publishes 30 titles/year; imprint publishes 4 titles/year. 3% of books from first-time authors; 50% from unagented writers. Canadian authors, theme or setting required.

Fiction: Children's/juvenile, young adult. Recently published *Dear Canada: With Nothing but Our Courage*, by Karleen Bradford (ages 9 and up); *After the War*, by Carol Matas (novel).

Nonfiction: Animals, history, hobbies, nature, recreation, science, sports. Reviews artwork/photos as part of ms package. Send photocopies. Recently published *Whose Bright Idea Was It?*, by Larry Verstraete (about amazing inventions).

How to Contact/Writers: Query with synopsis, 3 sample chapters and SASE. Nonfiction: Query with outline, 1-2 sample chapters and SASE (IRC or Canadian stamps only). Responds in 3 months. Publishes book 1 year after acceptance.

Terms: Pays 5-10% royalty on retail price. Offers advance: $1,000-5,000 (Canadian). Book catalog for 8½×11 SAE with 2 first-class stamps (IRC or Canadian stamps only).

N ⊕ SCHOLASTIC CHILDREN'S BOOKS UK, 1-19 New Oxford St., London WC1A 1NU United Kingdom. Website: www.scholastic.co.uk. **Manuscript Acquisitions:** The Editorial Department.

Fiction: Recently published *Dudley Top Dog*, by Jo Davies; *Partytime*, by Maureen Roffey; and *Catch*, by Trish Cooke.

Nonfiction: Recently published *My Story: Waterloo*, by Bryan Perrett; *Pickle Hill Primary: Miss Niles Mummy Lessons*, by Alan MacDonald; and *Horrible Histories: Ruthless Romans*, by Terry Deary.

How to Contact/Writers: Accepts material from residents of United Kingdom only. Fiction/nonfiction: Query or submit complete ms and SASE. Responds to queries/mss in 6 months.

Tip: "Do not be depressed if your work is not accepted. Getting work published can be a frustrating process, and it's often best to be prepared for disappointment."

N ◼ ◼ SECOND STORY PRESS, 720 Bathurst St., Suite 301, Toronto ON M5S 2R4 Canada. (416)537-7850. Fax: (416)537-0588. E-mail: info@secondstorypress.ca. Website: www.secondstorypress.on.ca.

● Second Story Press title *Hanna's Suitcase*, by Karen Levine, won the 2003 Sydney Taylor Award for Older Readers.

Fiction: Considers "nonsexist, nonracist and nonviolent stories, as well as historical fiction, chapter books." Picture books. Recently published *Pianomania*, by Manjusha Pawagi, illustrated by Liz Mikau; and *The Night Spies*, by Kathy Kacer.

Nonfiction: Picture books: biography.

How to Contact/Writers: Accepts material from residents of Canada only. Fiction: Submit complete ms or submit outline and sample chapters by postal mail only. No electronic submissions.

N 🌐 📖 **SIPHANO PICTURE BOOKS LTD.**, Regent's Place, 338 Euston Rd., London NW1 3BT United Kingdom. E-mail: info@siphano.com. Website: www.siphano.com. Specializes in fiction.We are an independent book packager/producer. **Manuscript Acquisitions:** The Editor. **Art Acquisitions:** The Art Editor. Publishes 10 picture books/year. 20% of books by first-time authors. Produces "likeable characters, humor, and imagination."

Fiction: Picture books, young readers: adventure, animal, contemporary, fantasy, humor. Average word length: picture books—800. Recently published *Excuse me . . . Are you a witch?*, by E. Horn, illustrated by Pawet Pawlak (ages 4-8, picture book).

How to Contact/Writers: Fiction: Submit complete ms. Responds to mss in 3 months. Will consider e-mail submissions, simultaneous submissions.

Illustration: Works with 5 illustrators/year. Uses color artwork only. Reviews ms/illustration packages from artists. Send ms with dummy or submit ms with 3 pieces of final art (no originals!) Illustrations only: Query with samples. Contact: art@siphano.com. Responds only if interested. Samples not returned; samples filed.

Terms: Payment varies. Originals returned to artist at job's completion. Book catalog available for SASE. Art guidelines available of SASE. Catalog available on website.

✂ Ⓐ **SOMERVILLE HOUSE INC.**, 24 Dinnick Crescent, Toronto ON M4N 1L5 Canada. Phone/fax: (416)487-2741 (call before faxing). E-mail: somer@sympatico.ca. Somerville publishes books and develops products and is an expert in merging media for the Youth and Family markets—the Web, wireless phones, pagers, electronic games, handheld personal computers, books and toys. **Acquisitions and Business Development:** Jane Somerville, publisher/president. Produces 5-10 titles/year in nonfiction and novelty formats.

- Somerville is currently accepting unsolicited mss in the areas of natural science, activities, sports and novelty formats.

Nonfiction: Recently published *The Hummingbird Book and Feeder*, by Neil Dawe; and *The Titantic Book and Submersible Model*, by Steve Santini.

How to Contact/Writers: Only interested in agented material. Responds to queries/mss in 3 months.

Illustration: Works with 20-30 illustrators/year. Responds only if interested. Samples not returned; samples filed.

✂ **THISTLEDOWN PRESS LTD.**, 633 Main St., Saskatoon SK S7H 0J8 Canada. (306)244-1722. Fax: (306)244-1762. E-mail: tdpress@thistledown.sk.ca. Website: www.thistledown.sk.ca. Book publisher. **Manuscript Acquisitions:** Patrick O'Rourke, editor-in-chief. **Art Acquisitions:** A.M. Forrie, art director. Publishes numerous middle reader and young adult titles/year. "Thistledown originates books by Canadian authors only, although we have co-published titles by authors outside Canada. We do not publish children's picture books."

Fiction: Young adults: adventure, anthology, contemporary, fantasy, humor, poetry, romance, science fiction, suspense/mystery, short stories. Average word length: young adults—40,000. Recently published *Up All Night*, edited by R.P. MacIntyre (young adult, anthology); *Offside*, by Cathy Beveridge (young adult, novel); *Cheeseburger Subversive*, by Richard Scarsbrook.

How to Contact/Writers: Submit outline/synopsis and sample chapters. Responds to queries in 1 month, mss in 6 months. Publishes a book about one year after acceptance. No simultaneous submissions.

Illustration: Prefers agented illustrators but "not mandatory." Works with few illustrators. Illustrations only: Query with samples, promo sheet, slides, tearsheets. Responds only if interested. Samples returned with SASE; samples filed.

Terms: Pays authors royalty of 10-12% based on retail price. Pays illustrators and photographers by the project (range: $250-750). Sends galleys to authors. Original artwork returned at job's completion. Book catalog free on request. Manuscript guidelines for #10 envelope and IRC.

Tips: "Send cover letter including publishing history and SASE."

N ✂ **TORMONT PUBLICATIONS**, 338 Saint Antoine St. E., Montreal QC H2Y 1A3 Canada. E-mail: info@tormont.ca. Website: www.tormont.com. Estab. 1984. "We specialize in producing high-quality novelty children's books at reasonable prices."

Fiction: Considers mass market books.

Nonfiction: Considers novelty books, games. Picture books, young readers, middle readers, young adults: activity books.

How to Contact/Writers: Accepts material from residents of Canada only. Fiction/nonfiction: Submit complete ms. Responds to mss in 2 months.

Illustration: Illustrations only: Send portfolio. Contact: Hélène Cousineau, art director. Responds in 2 months. Samples returned with SASE.

Tips: "Work submitted should be of the highest quality and the subject matter should 'travel well,'" that is, it should be of broad interest and relevance to the world children's market, since we publish internationally in well over a dozen languages. Please do not send any originals of your manuscripts, illustrations or prototypes, since we cannot be held responsible for lost or damaged materials. Send only photocopies. For US and international/submissions, include a Universal Postal Order for the cost of return postage."

✅ ✂ **TRADEWIND BOOKS**, 1809 Maritime Mews, Vancouver BC V6H 3W7 Canada.(604)662-4405. Fax: (604)730-0154. E-mail: tradewindbooks@eudoramail.com. Website: www.tradewindbooks.com. Estab. 1994. Trade book publisher. **Manuscript Acquisitions:** Michael Katz, publisher. **Art Acquisitions:** Carol Frank, art director. Publishes 3 picture books and 2 young adult titles/year. 25% of books by first-time authors.

Fiction: Picture books: adventure, animal, multicultural, folktales. Average word length: 900 words. Recently published

The Sea King, by Jane Yolen and Shulamith Oppenheim, illustrated by Stefan Czernecki; *The Alchemist's Portrait*, by Simon Rose.

Nonfiction: Picture books: animal and nature/environment.

How to Contact/Writers: Fiction: Submit complete ms. Will consider simultaneous submissions. Do not send query letter. Responds to mss in 6 weeks. Unsolicited submissions accepted only if authors have read a selection of books published by Tradewind Books. Submissions must include a reference to these books.

Illustration: Works with 3-4 illustrators/year. Uses color artwork only. Reviews ms/illustration packages from artists. Send ms with dummy. Illustrations only: Query with samples. Responds only if interested. Samples returned with SASE; samples filed.

Photography: Works on assignment only. Uses color prints.

Terms: Royalties negotiable. Offers advances against royalties. Originals returned to artist at job's completion. Book catalog available for 8×10 SAE and 3 first-class Canadian stamps. Catalog available on website.

N ⊕ ◻ USBOURNE PUBLISHING, 83-85 Saffron Hill, London EC1N 8RT United Kingdom. Website: www.usbor ne.com. Specializes in educational material. **Manuscript Acquisitions:** Fiction Editorial Director. **Art Acquisitions:** Usbourne Art Department. "Usbourne Publishing is a multiple-award winning, world-wide children's publishing company specializing in superbly researched and produced information on books with a unique appeal to young readers."

Fiction: Young readers: adventure, concept, fantasy, folktales, history, humor, science fiction, suspense/mystery. Middle readers: adventure, history, humor, multicultural, science fiction, suspense/mystery. Average word length: young readers—3,500-8,000; middle readers—10,000-30,000. Recently published *True Escape Stories* (ages 8 and up); *Dream Pony*, by S. Leigh; and *The Little Dragon*, by H. Amery, illustrated by S. Cartwright (picture book).

Nonfiction: Recently published *The Usbourne Internet-linked Encyclopedia of the Ancient World; Time Travellers: Viking Raiders*, by A. Civardi and G. Campbell; and *Greek Myths and Legends*, by C. Evans and A. Millaren, illustrated by R. Mathews.

How to Contact/Writers: Refer to guidelines on website or request from above address. Fiction: Submit 3 sample chapters and a full synopsis with SASE. Does not accept submissions for nonfiction. Responds to mss in 3 months.

Illustration: Illustrations only: Query with samples. Samples not returned.

Photography: Contact: Usbourne Art Department. Submit samples.

Tips: "Do not send any original work and, sorry, but we cannot guarantee a reply."

⬛ WHITECAP BOOKS, 351 Lynn Ave., North Vancouver BC V7J 2C4 Canada. (604)980-9852. E-mail: whitecap@whi tecap.ca. Website: www.whitecap.ca. Book publisher. Publishes 4 young readers and 2 middle readers/year.

Fiction: Picture books for children 3-7. Recently published *The Chinese Violin*, by Madeleine Thien and Joe Chang (ages 4-7).

Nonfiction: Young readers, middle readers: animal, nature/environment. Does not want to see text that writes down to children. Recently published *Welcome to the World of Frogs and Toads*, by Diane Swanson (ages 5-7); *Dot to Dot in the Sky: Stories in the Planets*, by Joan Marie Galat (ages 8-11); *Whose Teeth Are These*, by Wayne Lynch (ages 5-7).

How to Contact/Writers: Nonfiction: Query. Responds to queries in 1 month; ms in 3 months. Publishes a book 6 months after acceptance. Will consider simultaneous submissions. Please send international postal voucher if submission is from US. Mark envelopes "submissions." No e-mail submissions.

Illustration: Works with 1-2 illustrators/year. Reviews ms/illustration packages from artists. Query. Illustrations only: Query with samples—"never send original art." Contact: Robin Rivers. Samples returned with SASE with international postal voucher for Canada if requested.

Photography: Buys stock. "We are always looking for outstanding wildlife photographs." Uses 35mm transparencies. Submit cover letter, client list, stock photo list.

Terms: Pays authors a negotiated royalty or purchases work outright. Offers advances. Pays illustrators by the project or royalty (depends on project). Pays photographers per photo (depends on project). Originals returned to artist at job's completion unless discussed in advance. Manuscript guidelines available on website or for SASE with international postal voucher for Canada.

Tips: "Writers and illustrators should spend time researching what's already available on the market. Whitecap specializes in nonfiction for children and adults. Whitecap Children's Fiction focuses on humorous events or extraordinary animals. Please review previous publications before submitting."

Magazines

Children's magazines are a great place for unpublished writers and illustrators to break into the market. Illustrators, photographers, and writers alike may find it easier to get book assignments if they have tearsheets from magazines. Having magazine work under your belt shows you're professional and have experience working with editors and art directors and meeting deadlines.

But magazines aren't merely a breaking-in point. Writing, illustration and photo assignments for magazines let you see your work in print quickly, and the magazine market can offer steady work and regular paychecks (a number of them pay on acceptance). Book authors and illustrators may have to wait a year or two before receiving royalties from a project. The magazine market is also a good place to use research material that didn't make it into a book project you're working on. You may even work on a magazine idea that blossoms into a book project.

TARGETING YOUR SUBMISSIONS

It's important to know the topics typically covered by different children's magazines. To help you match your work with the right publications, we've included several indexes in the back of this book. The **Subject Index** lists both book and magazine publishers by the fiction and nonfiction subjects they're seeking.

If you're a writer, use the Subject Index in conjunction with the **Age-Level Index** to narrow your list of markets. Targeting the correct age group with your submission is an important consideration. Most rejection slips are sent because a writer has not targeted a manuscript to the correct age. Few magazines are aimed at children of all ages, so you must be certain your manuscript is written for the audience level of the particular magazine you're submitting to. Magazines for children (just as magazines for adults) may also target a specific gender.

If you're a poet, refer to the **Poetry Index** to find which magazines publish poems.

Each magazine has a different editorial philosophy. Language usage also varies between periodicals, as does the length of feature articles and the use of artwork and photographs. Reading magazines *before* submitting is the best way to determine if your material is appropriate. Also, because magazines targeted to specific age groups have a natural turnover in readership every few years, old topics (with a new slant) can be recycled.

If you're a photographer, the **Photography Index** lists children's magazines that use photos from freelancers. Using it in combination with the subject index can narrow your search. For instance, if you photograph sports, compare the Magazine list in the Photography Index with the list under Sports in the Subject Index. Highlight the markets that appear on both lists, then read those listings to decide which magazines might be best for your work.

Since many kids' magazines sell subscriptions through direct mail or schools, you may not be able to find a particular publication at bookstores or newsstands. Check your local library, or send for copies of the magazines you're interested in. Most magazines in this section have sample copies available and will send them for a SASE or small fee.

Also, many magazines have submission guidelines and theme lists available for a SASE. Check magazines' websites, too. Many offer excerpts of articles, submission guidelines and theme lists and will give you a feel for the editorial focus of the publication.

Watch for the Canadian ✖ and International ⊕ symbols. These publications' needs and requirements often differ from their U.S. counterparts. For insights into Canadian children's magazines turn to the Insider Report with **Fiona Bayrock**, Canadian children's magazine writer (page 266).

Information on magazines listed in the previous edition but not included in this edition of Children's Writer's & Illustrator's Market may be found in the General Index.

ADVENTURES, WordAction Publications, 6401 The Paseo, Kansas City MO 64131. (816)333-7000. Fax: (816)333-4439. E-mail: dfillmore@nazarene.org. **Editor:** Donna Fillmore. Weekly magazine. Circ. 45,000. "*Adventures* is a full-color story paper for first and second graders. It is designed to connect Sunday School learning with daily living experiences of the early elementary child. *Adventures'* target audience is children ages six to eight in the first and second grade. The readability goal should be at beginning readers level. The intent of *Adventures* is to: Provide a life-related paper enabling Christian values, encourage good choices and provide reinforcement for biblical concepts taught in WordAction Sunday School curriculum."
Fiction: Contemporary, inspirational, religious. "We need ethnic balance—stories and illustrations from a variety of experiences." Average word length: varies. Byline given.
How to Contact/Writers: Fiction: Send complete ms. Responds to queries/mss in 6 weeks. Send SASE for themes and guidelines.
Terms: Pays on acceptance. Pays variable amount for all rights.
Tips: Request guidelines.

☑ **ADVOCATE, PKA'S PUBLICATION**, PKA Publication, 1881 Little Westkill Rd., Prattsville NY 12468. (518)299-3103. **Publisher**: Patricia Keller. Bimonthly tabloid. Estab. 1987. Circ. 12,000. "*Advocate* advocates good writers and quality writings. We publish art, fiction, photos and poetry. *Advocate's* submitters are talented people of all ages who do not earn their livings as writers. We wish to promote the arts and to give those we publish the opportunity to be published."
 • Gaited Horse Association newsletter is now included in this publication. Horse-oriented stories, poetry, art and photos are currently needed.
Fiction: Middle readers and young adults/teens: adventure, animal, contemporary, fantasy, folktales, health, humorous, nature/environment, problem-solving, romance, science fiction, sports, suspense/mystery. Looks for "well written, entertaining work, whether fiction or nonfiction." Buys approximately 42 mss/year. Average word length: 1,500. Byline given. Wants to see more humorous material, nature/environment and romantic comedy.
Nonfiction: Middle readers and young adults/teens: animal, arts/crafts, biography, careers, concept, cooking, fashion, games/puzzles, geography, history, hobbies, how-to, humorous, interview/profile, nature/environment, problem-solving, science, social issues, sports, travel. Buys 10 mss/year. Average word length: 1,500. Byline given.
Poetry: Reviews poetry any length.
How to Contact/Writers: Fiction/nonfiction: send complete ms. Responds to queries in 6 weeks; mss in 2 months. Publishes ms 2-18 months after acceptance.
Illustration: Uses b&w artwork only. Uses cartoons. Reviews ms/illustration packages from artists. Submit a photo print (b&w or color), an excellent copy of work (no larger than 8 × 10) or original. Illustrations only: "Send previous unpublished art with SASE, please." Responds in 2 months. Samples returned with SASE; samples not filed. Credit line given.
Photography: Buys photos from freelancers. Model/property releases required. Uses color and b&w prints. Send unsolicited photos by mail with SASE. Responds in 2 months. Wants nature, artistic and humorous photos.
Terms: Pays on publication with contributor's copies. Acquires first rights for mss, artwork and photographs. Pays in copies. Original work returned upon job's completion. Sample copies for $4. Writer's/illustrator/photo guidelines for SASE.
Tips: "Artists and photographers should keep in mind that we are a b&w paper. Please do not send postcards. Use envelope with SASE."

AIM MAGAZINE, America's Intercultural Magazine, P.O. Box 1174, Maywood IL 60153-8174. Website: www.aimmagazine.org. **Contact:** Ruth Apilado (nonfiction), Mark Boone (fiction). **Photo Editor:** Betty Lewis. Quarterly magazine. Circ. 8,000. "Readers are high school and college students, teachers, adults interested in helping to purge racism from the human blood stream by the way of the written word—that is our goal!" 15% of material aimed at juvenile audience.
Fiction: Young adults/teens: adventure, folktales, humorous, history, multicultural, "stories with social significance." Wants stories that teach children that people are more alike than they are different. Does not want to see religious fiction. Buys 20 mss/year. Average word length: 1,000-4,000. Byline given.
Nonfiction: Young adults/teens: biography, interview/profile, multicultural, "stuff with social significance." Does not want to see religious nonfiction. Buys 20 mss/year. Average word length: 500-2,000. Byline given.
How to Contact/Writers: Fiction: Send complete ms. Nonfiction: Query with published clips. Responds to queries/mss in 1 month. Will consider simultaneous submissions.
Illustration: Buys 6 illustrations/issue. Preferred theme: Overcoming social injustices through nonviolent means. Reviews ms/illustration packages from artists. Query first. Illustrations only: Query with tearsheets. Responds to art samples in 1 month. Samples filed. Original artwork returned at job's completion "if desired." Credit line given.
Photography: Wants "photos of activists who are trying to contribute to social improvement."
Terms: Pays on acceptance. Buys first North American serial rights. Pays $15-25 for stories/articles. Pays in contributor copies if copies are requested. Pays $25 for b&w cover illustration. Photographers paid by the project. Sample copies for $5.
Tips: "Write about what you know."

AMERICAN CAREERS, Career Communications, Inc., 6701 W. 64th St., Overland Park KS 66202. (913)362-7788. Fax: (913)362-4864. Website: www.carcom.com. **Articles Editor:** Mary Pitchford. **Art Director:** Jerry Kanabel. Published

3 times/year. Estab. 1990. Circ. 400,000. Publishes career and education information for students in grades 8-10.

Nonfiction: Buys 20 mss/year. Average word length: 300-800. Byline given.

How to Contact/Writers: Nonfiction: Query with published clips. Responds to queries in 2 years. Will consider simultaneous submissions.

Terms: Pays on acceptance. Pays writers variable amount.

Tips: Send a query in writing with résumé and clips.

AMERICAN CHEERLEADER, Lifestyle Ventures LLC, 250 W. 57th St., Suite 420, New York NY 10107. (212)265-8890. Fax: (212)265-8908. E-mail: editors@americancheerleader.com. Website: www.americancheerleader.com. **Editorial Director:** Sheila Noone. **Managing Editor:** Marisa Walker. Bimonthly magazine. Estab. 1995. Circ. 200,000. Special interest teen magazine for kids who cheer.

Nonfiction: Young adults: biography, interview/profile (sports personalities), careers, fashion, beauty, health, how-to (cheering techniques, routines, pep songs, etc.), problem-solving, sports, cheerleading specific material. "We're looking for authors who know cheerleading." Buys 20 mss/year. Average word length: 750-2,000. Byline given.

How to Contact/Writers: Query with published clips. Responds to queries/mss in 3 months. Publishes ms 3 months after acceptance. Will consider electronic submission via disk or e-mail.

Illustration: Buys 2 illustrations/issue; 12-20 illustrations/year. Works on assignment only. Reviews ms/illustration packages from artists. Illustrations only: Query with samples; arrange portfolio review. Responds only if interested. Samples filed. Originals not returned at job's completion. Credit line given.

Photography: Buys photos from freelancers. Looking for cheerleading at different sports games, events, etc. Uses 35mm, 2¼×2¼ transparencies and 5x7 prints. Query with samples; provide résumé, business card, tearsheets to be kept on file. "After sending query, we'll set up an interview." Responds only if interested.

Terms: Pays on publication. Buys all rights for mss, artwork and photographs. Pays $100-500 for stories. Pays illustrators $50-200 for b&w inside, $100-300 for color inside. Pays photographers by the project $300-750; per photo (range: $25-100). Sample copies for $4.

Tips: "Authors: We invite proposals from freelance writers who are involved in or have been involved in cheerleading—i.e. coaches, sponsors or cheerleaders. Our writing style is upbeat, and 'sporty' to catch and hold the attention of our teen readers. Articles should be broken down into lots of sidebars, bulleted lists, etc. Photographers and illustrators must have teen magazine experience or high profile experience."

AMERICAN CHEERLEADER JUNIOR, Lifestyle Ventures, 250 W. 57th St., #420, New York NY 10107. (212)265-8890. Fax: (212)265-8908. Website: www.americancheerleaderjunior.com. **Articles Editor:** Sheila Noone. **Art Director:** Kristin Fennell. Quarterly magazine. Estab. 2001. "We celebrate the young cheerleaders across the country and provide ways to improve their abilities, friendships and community service." 95% of publication aimed at juvenile market.

Fiction: Middle readers: sports. Byline given.

Nonfiction: Picture-oriented, young readers, middle readers: arts/crafts, games/puzzles, health, how-to, humorous, sports. Average word length: 400. Byline given.

Poetry: Reviews poetry.

How to Contact/Writers: Fiction/nonfiction: Query with published clips. Responds in 2 months. Will consider electronic submission via disk or modem.

Illustration: Buys 2-4 illustrations/issue; 8-10 illustrations/year. Uses color artwork only. Works on assignment only. Reviews ms/illustration packages from artists. Contact: Kristin Fennell, art director. Illustrations only: query with samples, arrange portfolio review. Contact: Kristin Fennell. Responds only if interested. Samples not returned; samples filed. Credit line given.

Photography: Looking for photos depicting action, cheer, friendship. Model/property release required. Uses color prints and 35mm transparencies. Query with samples; arrange a personal interview to show portfolio. Responds only if interested.

Terms: Pays on publication. Buys exclusive magazine rights or negotiates for rights. Buys first rights for artwork; all rights for photos. Additional payment for ms/illustration packages and for photos accompanying articles. Payment for illustrators varies. Payment for photographers varies. Samples copies free for SAE. Writer's guidelines free for SASE.

Tips: "We look for fun, wholesome illustrations aimed at athletic and energetic kids."

AMERICAN GIRL, Pleasant Company, 8400 Fairway Place, P.O. Box 620986, Middleton WI 53562-0984. (608)836-4848. E-mail: im_agmag_editor@pleasantco.com. Website: www.americangirl.com. **Executive Editor:** Kristi Thom. **Managing Editor:** Barbara Stretchberry. **Contact:** Editorial Dept. Assistant. Bimonthly magazine. Estab. 1992. Circ. 750,000. "For girls ages 8-12. We use fiction and nonfiction."

Fiction: Middle readers: contemporary, multicultural, suspense/mystery, good fiction about anything. No romance, science fiction or fantasy. No preachy, moralistic tales or stories with animals as protagonists. Only a girl or girls as characters—no boys. Buys approximately 2 mss/year. Average word length: 2,300. Byline given.

Nonfiction: How-to, interview/profile, history. Any articles aimed at girls ages 8-12. Buys 3-10 mss/year. Average word length: 600. Byline sometimes given. No historical profiles about obvious female heroines—Annie Oakley, Amelia Earhart; no romance or dating.

How to Contact/Writers: Fiction: Query with published clips. Nonfiction: Query. Responds to queries/mss in 3 months. Will consider simultaneous submissions.

Illustration: Works on assignment only.

Terms: Pays on acceptance. Buys first North American serial rights. Pays $500 minimum for stories; $300 minimum for articles. Sample copies for $3.95 and 9 × 12 SAE with $1.93 in postage (send to Magazine Department Assistant). Writer's guidelines free for SASE.

Tips: "Keep (stories and articles) simple but interesting. Kids are discriminating readers, too. They won't read a boring or pretentious story. We're looking for short (maximum 175 words) how-to stories and short profiles of girls for 'Girls Express' section, as well as word games, puzzles and mazes."

ANALOG SCIENCE FICTION AND FACT, Dell Magazines, 475 Park Ave., New York NY 10016. (212)686-7188. Fax: (212)686-7414. E-mail: analog@dellmagazines.com. Website: www.analogsf.com. **Articles Editor:** Stanley Schmidt. **Fiction Editor:** Stanley Schmidt. **Art Director:** Victoria Green. Magazine published 11 times/year (one double issue). Estab. 1930. Circ. 50,000. "We publish science fiction and science fact articles aimed at intelligent scientifically literate adults. Some bright teenagers read us, but we are *not* a children's magazine."

Fiction: Young adults: science fiction. Buys 70 mss/year. Average word length: 80,000 maximum. "We use very few stories between 20,000 and 40,000 words; longer ones are occassionally serialized." Byline given.

Nonfiction: Young adults: nature/environment, science. Buys 11 mss/year. Average word length: 3,000-5,000.

How to Contact/Writers: Fiction: Query for serials (over 20,000 words) only. Send complete ms if under 20,000 words. Responds to /mss in 1 month. Publishes ms 1 year after acceptance.

Illustration: Buys 4 illustrations/issue; 45 illustrations/year. Works on assignment only. Illustrations only: Query with samples. Send portfolio, slides. Contact: Victoria Green, art director. Responds only if interested. Samples returned with SASE.

Terms: Pays on acceptance. Buys first North American serial rights, nonexclusive foreign serial rights. Pays $20-4,000 for stories. Sample copies for $5. Writer's/illustrators guidelines for SASE; also available on website.

Tips: "Read the magazine to get a feel for what our readers like."

APPLESEEDS The Magazine for Young Readers, Cobblestone Publishing, A Division of Carus Publishing, 140 E. 83rd St., New York NY 10028. E-mail: swbuc@aol.com. Website: www.cobblestonepub.com/pages/writersAPPguides.html. **Editor:** Susan Buckley. Magazine published monthly except June, July and August. *AppleSeeds* is a 36-page, multidisciplinary, nonfiction social studies magazine from Cobblestone Publishing for ages 8-10. Published 9 times/year.

• *AppleSeeds* is aimed toward readers ages 8-10. See website for current theme list.

How to Contact/Writers: Nonfiction: Query only. See website for submission guidelines and theme list. E-mail queries are preferred.

Tips: "Submit queries specifically focused on the theme of an upcoming issue. We generally work 6 months ahead on themes. We look for unusual perspectives, original ideas, and excellent scholarship. We accept no unsolicited manuscripts. Writers should check our website at cobblestonepub.com/pages/writersAPPguides/html for current guidelines, topics, and query deadlines. We use very little fiction. Illustrators should not submit unsolicited art."

ASK, Arts and Sciences for Kids, 332 S. Michigan Ave., Suite 1100, Chicago IL 60604. (312)939-1500. Fax: (312)939-8150. E-mail: ask@caruspub.com. Website: www.cricketmag.com. **AA Director:** Karen Kohn. Monthly magazine. Estab. 2002. "*ASK* encourages children between the ages of 7 and 10 to inquire about the world around them. Nonfiction articles, activities and reprints from trade books will be considered for publication."

Nonfiction: Young readers, middle readers: animal, arts/crafts, biography, careers, games/puzzles, geography, health, history, humorous, interview/profile, math, multicultural, nature/environment, problem-solving, science, social issues, sports. Buys 30-40 mss/year. Average word length: 250-900. Byline given.

How to Contact/Writers: Responds to mss in 3 months. Check website for theme list and guidelines. Will consider previously published work.

Illustration: Buys 10 illustrations/issue; 60 illustrations/year. Works on assignment only. Reviews ms/illustration packages from artists. Illustrations only: Query with samples.

BABYBUG, Carus Publishing Company, P.O. Box 300, Peru IL 61354. (815)224-5803 ext. 656. **Editor:** Paula Morrow. **Art Director:** Suzanne Beck. Published 10 times/year (monthly except for combined May/June and July/August issues). Estab. 1994. "A listening and looking magazine for infants and toddlers ages 6 to 24 months, *Babybug* is 6 ¼ × 7, 24 pages long, printed in large type (26-point) on high-quality cardboard stock with rounded corners and no staples."

Fiction: Looking for very simple and concrete stories, 4-6 short sentences maximum.

Nonfiction: Must use very basic words and concepts, 10 words maximum.

Poetry: Maximum length 8 lines. Looking for rhythmic, rhyming poems.

How to Contact/Writers: "Please do not query first." Send complete ms with SASE. "Submissions without SASE will be discarded." Responds in 3 months.

Illustration: Uses color artwork only. Works on assignment only. Reviews ms/illustration packages from artists. "The manuscripts will be evaluated for quality of concept and text before the art is considered." Contact: Suzanne Beck. Illustrations only: Send tearsheets or photo prints/photocopies with SASE. "Submissions without SASE will be discarded." Responds in 3 months. Samples filed.

Terms: Pays on publication for mss; after delivery of completed assignment for illustrators. Rights purchased vary. Original artwork returned at job's completion. Rates vary ($25 minimum for mss; $250 minimum for art). Sample copy for $5. Guidelines free for SASE.

Tips: "*Babybug* would like to reach as many children's authors and artists as possible for original contributions, but our standards are very high, and we will accept only top-quality material. Before attempting to write for *Babybug*, be sure to familiarize yourself with this age child." (See listings for *Cricket, Cicada, Ladybug, Muse* and *Spider*.)

Ⓝ ▣ **BIG COUNTRY PEACOCK CHRONICLE, Online Magazine**, RR1 Box 89k-112, Aspermont TX 79502. (806)254-2322. E-mail: publisher@peacockchronicle.com. Website: www.peacockchronicle.com. **Contact:** Audrey Yoeckel. Quarterly online magazine. Estab. 2000. "*The Big Country Peacock Chronicle* is a family magazine originally based on the traditional small town newspaper. It quickly evolved into a variety magazine. Our mission statement reads: Dedicated to the preservation of community values and folk cultures, this interactive e-zine focuses on traditional arts and crafts, artists, writer, information, resource links and mutual support. From our submission guidelines: *The Big Country Peacock Chronicle* is a children safe site. We will not publish any articles or items that promote hatred of any kind. We will always be on the lookout for items and sites that promote fellowship and solid community values." 25% of publication aimed at juvenile market.

Fiction: "As a family site, we look for fiction on any subject that can appeal to all or any age groups. As long as that material fits our (broad) guidelines, and is entertaining/informative it will be considered. Those that will not be considered are rejected based on excessive, graphic or inappropriate language or violence, or on a more subtle level, those that are disparaging of any race, religion, culture or social status." Uses 10-15 mss/year. Does not pay. Longer works can be serialised if necessary. Byline given.

Nonfiction: See guidelines for fiction. This is an unpaid market. "Currently, we are not a paying market. What we offer in exchange for nonexclusive e-rights is free promotion and marketing of an author's works. We have a strong interest in publishing illustrated works." Byline given.

Poetry: All forms are acceptable. Particularly interested in humor. Avoid overly negative poetry unless of exceptional quality. "Pieces longer than 40 lines should be single submissions." Limit submissions to 3 poems.

How to Contact/Writers: Fiction/nonfiction: Query. Responds to queries in 2 months; mss in 3 months. Publishes ms 1 month after acceptance. Will consider simultaneous submissions, electronic submissions via disk or modem, previously published work.

Illustration: "Although we have only occasionally used our own illustrations in the past, it has always been our intent to use them." Reviews ms/illustration packages from artists. Query. Illustrations only: Query with samples; via Internet, query only. Will provide further information for submitting work. Responds only if interested. Samples returned with SASE; samples filed. Credit line given.

Photography: Buys photos with accompanying ms only. Must be content related, humorous, those that reflect the mission statement. Manuscript may be in the form of captions (for multiple photo submissions) or history. Model/property release required; captions required. "Scanned, sized and optimized for webpages. (We can do this, if necessary.) 250 pixels wide, less than 9 kb weight (preferred). Uses color, b&w, 8×10 matte prints. Query with samples; via Internet, query only. Will provide further information for submitting work. Responds only if interested.

Terms: Does not pay. Manuscripts/artwork: Acquires nonexclusive e-rights. Originals returned at job's completion. "We are not currently a paying market. Will provide exposure and publication credits as well as free advertising in exchange for nonexclusive e-rights. In the case of illustrated written works, if the party/parties desire, will produce a downloadable free e-book with the author's/illustrator's contact information and bios. This would allow the creators to also distribute the book as they wish. (We do not furnish ISBN's)." Writer's guidelines free for SASE.

Tips: "The benefit from exposure in our publication should not be underestimated. Our readers are from all walks of life and age groups. Publishing your work on the web is a great way to test-market your work. Publishing your own pages requires knowledge of Internet promotion and marketing techniques which we provide when you publish with us. If you have access to the Internet, e-mail is the easiest way to communicate with us. If you do not have access, we'll work around it."

BOYS' LIFE, Boy Scouts of America, 1325 W. Walnut Hill Lane, Irving TX 75038. (972)580-2366. Website: www.boyslife. org. **Editor-in-Chief:** J.D. Owen. **Managing Editor:** W.E. Butterworth, IV. **Senior Editor:** Michael Goldman. **Fiction Editor:** Rich Haddaway. **Director of Design:** Joseph P. Connolly. **Art Director:** Scott Feaster. Monthly magazine. Estab. 1911. Circ. 1,300,000. *Boys' Life* is "a 4-color general interest magazine for boys 8 to 18 who are members of the Cub Scouts, Boy Scouts or Venturers; a 4-color general interest magazine for all boys."

Fiction: Middle readers: adventure, humor, science fiction, spy/mystery. Does not want to see "talking animals and adult reminiscence." Buys only 12-16 mss/year. Average word length: 1,000-1,500. Byline given.

Nonfiction: "Subject matter is broad. We cover everything from professional sports to American history to how to pack a canoe. A look at a current list of the BSA's more than 100 merit badge pamphlets gives an idea of the wide range of subjects possible. Even better, look at a year's worth of recent issues. Column headings are science, nature, earth, health, sports, space and aviation, cars, computers, entertainment, pets, history, music and others." Average word length: 500-1,500. Columns 300-750 words. Byline given.

How to Contact/Writers: Fiction: Send query or complete ms with cover letter and SASE to fiction editor. Nonfiction: Major articles query articles editor. Columns query associate editor with SASE for response. Responds to queries/mss in 2 months.

Illustration: Buys 10-12 illustrations/issue; 100-125 illustrations/year. Works on assignment only. Reviews ms/illustration packages from artists. "Query first." Illustrations only: Send tearsheets. Responds to art samples only if interested. Samples returned with SASE. Original artwork returned at job's completion. Credit line given.

Terms: Pays on acceptance. Buys first rights. Pays $750 and up for fiction; $400-1,500 for major articles; $150-400 for columns; $250-300 for how-to features. Pays illustrators $1,500-3,000 for color cover; $100-1,500 color inside. Sample copies for $3 plus 9×12 SASE. Writer's/illustrator's/photo guidelines available for SASE.

Tips: "We strongly urge you to study at least a year's issues to better understand the type of material published. Articles for *Boys' Life* must interest and entertain boys ages 8 to 18. Write for a boy you know who is 12. Our readers demand crisp, punchy writing in relatively short, straightforward sentences. The editors demand well-reported articles that demonstrate high standards of journalism. We follow *The New York Times* manual of style and usage. All submissions must be accompanied by SASE with adequate postage."

☑ **BOYS' QUEST**, P.O. Box 227, Bluffton OH 45817-0164. (419)358-4610. Fax: (419)358-5027. Website: boysquest.com. **Articles Editor:** Marilyn Edwards. **Art Submissions:** Anne Hohenbrink. Bimonthly magazine. Estab. 1995. "*Boys' Quest* is a magazine created for boys from 6 to 13 years, with youngsters 8, 9 and 10 the specific target age. Our point of view is that every young boy deserves the right to be a young boy for a number of years before he becomes a young adult. As a result, *Boys' Quest* looks for articles, fiction, nonfiction, and poetry that deal with timeless topics, such as pets, nature, hobbies, science, games, sports, careers, simple cooking, and anything else likely to interest a young boy."

Fiction: Picture-oriented material, young readers, middle readers: adventure, animal, history, humorous, multicultural, nature/environment, problem-solving, sports. Does not want to see violence, teenage themes. Buys 30 mss/year. Average word length: 200-500. Byline given.

Nonfiction: Picture-oriented material, young readers, middle readers: animal, arts/crafts, cooking, games/puzzles, history, hobbies, how-to, humorous, math, problem-solving, sports. Prefer photo support with nonfiction. Buys 30 mss/year. Average word length: 200-500. Byline given.

Poetry: Reviews poetry. Maximum length: 21 lines. Limit submissions to 6 poems.

How to Contact/Writers: All writers should consult the theme list before sending in articles. To receive current theme list, send a SASE. Fiction/Nonfiction: Query or send complete ms (preferred). Send SASE with correct postage. No faxed material. Responds to queries in 2 weeks; mss in 2 weeks (if rejected); 5 weeks (if scheduled). Publishes ms 3 months-3 years after acceptance. Will consider simultaneous submissions and previously published work.

Illustration: Buys 10 illustrations/issue; 60-70 illustrations/year. Uses b&w artwork only. Works on assignment only. Reviews ms/illustration packages from artists. Send ms with dummy. Illustrations only: Query with samples, arrange portfolio review. Send portfolio, tearsheets. Responds in 1 month only if interested and a SASE. Samples returned with SASE; samples filed. Credit line given.

Photography: Photos used for support of nonfiction. "Excellent photographs included with a nonfiction story is considered very seriously." Model/property releases required. Uses b&w, 5×7 or 3×5 prints. Query with samples; send unsolicited photos by mail. Responds in 3 weeks.

Terms: Pays on publication. Buys first North American serial rights for mss. Buys first rights for artwork. Pays 5¢/word for stories and articles. Additional payment for ms/illustration packages and for photos accompanying articles. Pays $150-200 for color cover; $25-35 for b&w inside. Pays photographers per photo (range: $5-10). "*Boys' Quest*, as a new publication, is aware that its rates of payment are modest at this time. But we pledge to increase those rewards in direct proportion to our success. Meanwhile, we will strive to treat our contributors and their work with respect and fairness. That treatment, incidentally, will include quick decision on all submissions." Originals returned to artist at job's completion. Sample copies for $4/each in US. Writer's/illustrator's/photo guidelines free for SASE.

Tips: "First be familiar with our magazines. We are looking for lively writing, most of it from a young boy's point of view—with the boy or boys directly involved in an activity that is both wholesome and unusual. We need nonfiction with photos and fiction stories—around 500 words—puzzles, poems, cooking, carpentry projects, jokes and riddles. Nonfiction pieces that are accompanied by black and white photos are far more likely to be accepted than those that need illustrations. We will entertain simultaneous submissions as long as that fact is noted on the manuscript." (See listing for *Hopscotch*.)

BREAD FOR GOD'S CHILDREN, Bread Ministries, Inc., P.O. Box 1017, Arcadia FL 34265-1017. (863)494-6214. Fax: (863)993-0154. E-mail: bread@sunline.net. Website: www.breadministries.org. **Editor:** Judith M. Gibbs. Bimonthly magazine. Estab. 1972. Circ. 10,000 (US and Canada). "*Bread* is designed as a teaching tool for Christian families." 85% of publication aimed at juvenile market.

Fiction: Young readers, middle readers, young adult/teen: adventure, religious, problem-solving, sports. Looks for "teaching stories that portray Christian lifestyles without preaching." Buys approximately 20 mss/year. Average word length: 900-1,500 (for teens); 600-900 (for young children). Byline given.

Nonfiction: Young readers, middle readers: animal. All levels: how-to. "We do not want anything detrimental to solid family values. Most topics will fit if they are slanted to our basic needs." Buys 3-4 mss/year. Average word length: 500-800. Byline given.

Illustration: "The only illustrations we purchase are those occasional good ones coming with a story we accept."

How to Contact/Writers: Fiction/nonfiction: Send complete ms. Responds to mss in 6 months "if considered for use." Will consider simultaneous submissions and previously published work.

Terms: Pays on publication. Pays $10-50 for stories; $25 for articles. Sample copies free for 9×12 SAE and 5 first-class stamps (for 2 copies).

Tips: "We want stories or articles that illustrate overcoming by faith and living solid, Christian lives. Know our publication and what we have used in the past . . . know the readership . . . know the publisher's guidelines. Stories should teach the value of morality and honesty without preaching. Edit carefully for content and grammar."

CADET QUEST, (formerly *Crusader*), Calvinist Cadet Corps, P.O. Box 7259, Grand Rapids MI 49510. (616)241-5616. Website: www.calvinistcadets.org. **Editor:** G. Richard Broene. **Art Director:** Robert de Jonge. Magazine published 7 times/year. Circ. 12,000. "Our magazine is for members of the Calvinist Cadet Corps—boys aged 9-14. Our purpose is to show how God is at work in their lives and in the world around them. Our magazine offers nonfiction articles and fast-moving fiction—everything to appeal to interests and concerns of boys, teaching Christian values subtly."

Fiction: Middle readers, boys/early teens: adventure, humorous, multicultural, problem-solving, religious, sports. Buys 12 mss/year. Average word length: 900-1,500.

Nonfiction: Middle readers, boys/early teens: arts/crafts, games/puzzles, hobbies, how-to, humorous, interview/profile, problem-solving, science, sports. Buys 6 mss/year. Average word length: 400-900.

How to Contact/Writers: Fiction/nonfiction: Send complete ms. Responds to queries in 1 month; mss in 2 months. Will consider simultaneous submissions.

Illustration: Buys 1 illustration/issue; buys 6 illustrations/year. Works on assignment only. Reviews ms/illustration packages from artists. Responds in 5 weeks. Samples returned with SASE. Originals returned to artist at job's completion. Credit line given.

Photography: Buys photos from freelancers. Wants nature photos and photos of boys.

Terms: Pays on acceptance. Buys first North American serial rights; reprint rights. Pays 4-5¢/word for stories/articles. Pays illustrators $50-200 for b&w/color cover or b&w inside. Sample copy free with 9×12 SAE and 4 first-class stamps.

Tips: "Our publication is mostly open to fiction; send SASE for a list of themes (available yearly in January). We use mostly fast-moving fiction that appeals to a boy's sense of adventure or sense of humor. Avoid preachiness; avoid simplistic answers to complicated problems; avoid long dialogue with little action. Articles on sports, outdoor activities, bike riding, science, crafts, etc. should emphasize a Christian perspective but avoid simplistic moralisms."

CALLIOPE, Exploring World History, Cobblestone Publishing Company, 30 Grove St., Suite C, Peterborough NH 03458. (603)924-7209. Fax: (603)924-7380. Website: www.cobblestonepub.com. **Managing Editor:** Lou Waryncia. **Co-editors:** Rosalie Baker and Charles Baker. **Art Director:** Ann Dillon. Magazine published 9 times/year. "*Calliope* covers world history (East/West), and lively, original approaches to the subject are the primary concerns of the editors in choosing material."

- *Calliope* themes for 2004-2005 include Qing Dynasty, Zoroastrianism, African Kingdom of Benin, Akbar of India, Shakespeare, Mexican Revolution. For additional themes and time frames, visit the website.

Fiction: Middle readers and young adults: adventure, folktales, plays, history, biographical fiction. Material must relate to forthcoming themes. Word length: up to 800.

Nonfiction: Middle readers and young adults: arts/crafts, biography, cooking, games/puzzles, history. Material must relate to forthcoming themes. Word length: 300-800.

Poetry: Maximum line length: 100. Wants "clear, objective imagery. Serious and light verse considered."

How to Contact/Writers: "A query must consist of the following to be considered (please use nonerasable paper): a brief cover letter stating subject and word length of the proposed article; a detailed one-page outline explaining the information to be presented in the article; an extensive bibliography of materials the author intends to use in preparing the article; a self-addressed stamped envelope. Writers new to *Calliope* should send a writing sample with query. If you would like to know if your query has been received, please also include a stamped postcard that requests acknowledgment of receipt. In all correspondence, please include your complete address as well as a telephone number where you can be reached. A writer may send as many queries for one issue as he or she wishes, but each query must have a separate cover letter, outline, bibliography and SASE. Telephone queries are not accepted. Handwritten queries will not be considered. Queries may be submitted at any time, but queries sent well in advance of deadline *may not be answered for several months*. Go-aheads requesting material proposed in queries are usually sent five months prior to publication date. Unused queries will be returned approximately three to four months prior to publication date."

Illustration: Illustrations only: Send tearsheets, photocopies. Original work returned upon job's completion (upon written request).

Photography: Buys photos from freelancers. Wants photos pertaining to any forthcoming themes. Uses b&w/color prints, 35mm transparencies. Send unsolicited photos by mail (on speculation).

Terms: Buys all rights for mss and artwork. Pays 20-25¢/word for stories/articles. Pays on an individual basis for poetry, activities, games/puzzles. "Covers are assigned and paid on an individual basis." Pays photographers per photo ($15-100 for b&w; $25-100 for color). Sample copy for $4.95 and SAE with $2 postage. Writer's/illustrator's/photo guidelines for SASE. (See listings for *AppleSeeds*, *Cobblestone*, *Faces*, *Footsteps* and *Odyssey*.)

CAMPUS LIFE, Christianity Today, International, 465 Gundersen Dr., Carol Stream IL 60188. (630)260-6200. Fax: (630)260-0114. E-mail: clmag@campuslife.net. Website: www.campuslife.net. **Articles and Fiction Editor:** Chris Lutes. Bimonthly magazine. Estab. 1944. Circ. 100,000. "Our purpose is to help Christian high school students navigate adolescence with their faith intact."

Fiction: Young adults: humorous, problem-solving. Buys 5-6 mss/year. Byline given.

Poetry: Reviews poetry.

How to Contact/Writers: Fiction/nonfiction: Query.

Illustration: Works on assignment only. Reviews illustration packages from artists. Contact: Doug Fleener, design director. Illustrations only: Query; send promo sheet. Responds only if interested. Credit line given.

Terms: Pays on acceptance. Original artwork returned at job's completion. Writer's/illustrator's/photo guidelines for SASE.

CAREER WORLD, General Learning Communications, 900 Skokie Blvd., Suite 200, Northbrook IL 60062-4028. (847)205-3000. Fax: (847)564-8197. **Articles Editor:** Carole Rubenstein. Monthly (school year) magazine. Estab. 1972. A guide to careers, for students grades 6-12.

Nonfiction: Young adults/teens: education, how-to, interview/profile, career awareness and development. Byline given.

How to Contact/Writers: Nonfiction: Query with published clips and résumé. "We do not want any unsolicited manuscripts." Responds to queries in 2 weeks.

Illustration: Buys 5-10 illustrations/year. Works on assignment only. Reviews ms/illustration packages from artists. Manuscript/illustration packages and illustration only: Query; send promo sheet and tearsheets. Credit line given.
Photography: Purchases photos from freelancers.
Terms: Pays on publication. Buys all rights for mss. Pays $150 and up for articles. Pays illustrators by the project. Writer's guidelines free, but only on assignment.

🅽 CAREERS & COLLEGES, Chalkboard Communications, LLC, P.O.Box 22, Keyport NJ 07735. (212)563-4688. (212)967-2531. Website: www.careersandcolleges.com. **Editorial Director:** Don Rauf. Magazine published 4 times during school year (September, November, January, March). Circ. 750,000. "*Careers & Colleges* provides juniors and seniors in high school with useful, thought-provoking, and hopefully entertaining reading on career choices, higher education and other topics that will help prepare them for life after high school. Each issue focuses on a specific single theme: How to Get Into College; How to Pay for College; Careers; and Life After High School."
Nonfiction: Young adults/teens: careers, college, health, how-to, humorous, interview/profile, personal development, problem-solving, social issues, sports, travel. Wants more celebrity profiles. Buys 20-30 mss/year. Average word length: 1,000-1,500. Byline given.
How to Contact/Writers: Nonfiction: Query. Responds to queries in 6 weeks. Will consider electronic submissions.
Illustration: Buys 8 illustrations/issue; buys 32 illustrations/year. Works on assignment only. Reviews ms/illustration packages from artists. Query first. Illustrations only: Send tearsheets, cards. Responds to art samples in 3 weeks if interested. Original artwork returned at job's completion. Credit line given.
Terms: Pays on acceptance plus 30 days. Buys first North American serial rights. Pays $100-600 for assigned/unsolicited articles. Additional payment for ms/illustration packages "must be negotiated." Pays $300-1,000 for color illustration; $200-700 for b&w/color inside illustration. Pays photographers by the project. Sample copy $5, writer's guidelines with SASE or via website.
Tips: "We look for articles with great quotes, good reporting, good writing. Articles must be rich with examples and anecdotes, and must tie in with our mandate to help our teenaged readers plan their futures. We are especially looking for the most current trends, policy changes and information regarding college admissions, financial aid, and career opportunities. Visit our website for a good sense of our magazine."

CARUS PUBLISHING COMPANY, P.O. Box 300, Peru IL 61354. See listings for *Babybug*, *Cicada*, *Cricket*, *Ladybug*, *Muse*, *Spider* and *ASK*.
 • Carus Publishing purchased Cobblestone Publishing, publisher of *AppleSeeds*, *Calliope*, *Cobblestone*, *Faces*, *Footsteps* and *Odyssey*.

CATHOLIC FORESTER, Catholic Order of Foresters, P.O. Box 3012, 355 Shuman Blvd., Naperville IL 60566-7012. (630)983-4900. E-mail: cofpr@aol.com. **Articles Editor:** Patricia Baron. **Art Director:** Keith Halla. Quarterly magazine. Estab. 1883. Circ. 100,000. Targets members of the Catholic Order of Foresters. In addition to the organization's news, it offers general interest pieces on health, finance, family life. Also use inspirational and humorous fiction.
Fiction: Buys 6-10 mss/year. Average word length: 500-1,500.
How to Contact/Writers: Fiction: Submit complete ms. Responds in 4 months. Will consider previously published work.
Illustration: Buys 2-4 illustrations/issue. Uses color artwork only. Works on assignment only.
Photography: Buys photos with accompanying ms only.
Terms: Pays on acceptance. Buys first North American serial rights, reprint rights, one-time rights. Sample copies for 9×12 SAE and 3 first-class stamps. Writer's guidelines free for SASE.

CELEBRATE, Word Action Publishing Co., Church of the Nazarene, 6401 The Paseo, Kansas City MO 64131. (816)333-7000, ext. 2358. Fax: (816)333-4439. E-mail: mhammer@nazarene.org. Website: www.wordaction.com. **Editor:** Melissa Hammer. **Editorial Assistant**: Andrea Callison. Weekly publication. Estab. 2001. Circ. 30,000. "This weekly take-home paper connects Sunday School learning to life for preschoolers (age 3 and 4), kindergartners (age 5 and 6) and their families." 75% of publication aimed at juvenile market; 25% parents.
Nonfiction: Picture-oriented material: arts/crafts, cooking, poems, action rhymes, piggyback songs (theme based). 50% of mss nonfiction. Byline given.
Poetry: Reviews poetry. Maximum length: 4-8 lines. Unlimited submissions.
How to Contact/Writers: Nonfiction: query. Responds to queries in 1 month. Responds to mss in 6 weeks. Publishes ms 1 year after acceptance. Will accept electronic submission via e-mail.
Terms: Pays on acceptance. Buys all rights, multi-use rights. Pays a minimum of $2 for songs and rhymes; 25¢/line for poetry; $15 for activities, crafts, recipes. Compensation includes 2 contributor copies. Sample copy for SASE.
Tips: "Limited acceptance at this time."

🅽 🌐 CHALLENGE, Pearson Education Australia, 95 Coventry St., South Melbourne VIC 3205 Australia. Phone: (61)03 9697 0666. Fax: (61)03 9699 2041. E-mail: magazines@pearsoned.com.au. Website: www.pearsoned.com.au/schoo ls. **Articles Editor:** Petra Poupa. **Fiction Editor:** Meredith Costain. Quarterly Magazine. Circ. 20,000. "Magazines are educational and fun. We publish mainly nonfiction articles in a variety of genres and text types. They must be appropriate, factually correct, and of high interest. We publish interviews, recounts, informational and argumentative articles."
 • *Challenge* is a theme based publication. Check the website to see upcoming themes and deadlines.
Fiction: Middle readers, young adults: adventure, animal, contemporary, fantasy, folktale, humorous, multicultural, problem-solving, science fiction, sports, suspense/mystery. Buys 12 mss/year. Average word length: 400-1,000. Byline given.

Nonfiction: Middle readers, young adults: animal, arts/crafts, biography, careers, cooking, fashion, geography, health, history, hobbies, how-to, humorous, interview/profile, math, multicultural, nature/environment, problem-solving, science, social issues, sports, travel (depends on theme of issue). Buys 100 ms/year. Average word length: 200-600. Byline given.

Poetry: Reviews poetry.

How to Contact/Writers: Fiction/nonfiction: Send complete ms. Responds to queries in 1 month; mss in 3 months. Publishes ms 3 months after acceptance. Will consider simultaneous submissions and electronic submissions via disk or e-mail.

Photography: Looking for photos to suit various themes; photos needed depend on stories. Model/property release required; captions required. Uses color, standard sized, matte prints and 35mm transparencies. Provide résumé, business card, promotional literature and tearsheets to be kept on file. Responds only if interested.

Terms: Pays on publication. Buys first Australian serial rights. Pays $80-200 (Australian) for stories; $100-220 (Australian) for articles. Additional payment for ms/illustration packages. Sample copies free for SAE. Writer's guidelines free for SASE.

Tips: "Check out our website for information about our publications." See listings for *Comet* and *Explore*.

CHICKADEE, The Owl Group, 49 Front St. E., 2nd Floor, Toronto ON M5E 1B3 Canada. (416)340-2700. Fax: (416)340-9769. E-mail: owl@owl.on.ca. Website: www.owlkids.com. **Contact:** Angela Keenlyside, managing editor. Magazine published 10 times/year. Estab. 1979. Circ. 110,000. "*Chickadee* is a hands-on publication designed to interest 6- to 9-year-olds in science, nature and the world around them. It features games, stories, crafts, experiments. Every effort is made to provide *Chickadee* readers with fresh ideas that are offered in an innovative and surprising way. Lively writing and a strong visual component are necessary strengths in any piece written for *Chickadee*."

Fiction: Picture-oriented material, new readers: animal, humorous, nature/environment. Does not want to see religious, anthropomorphic animal, romance material, material that talks down to kids. Buys 6 mss/year. Average word length: 800-900. Byline given.

Nonfiction: Picture-oriented material, new readers: animal (facts/characteristics), arts/crafts, games/puzzles, humorous, nature/environment, science. Does not want to see religious material. Buys 2-5 mss/year. Average word length: 300-800. Byline given.

Poetry: Limit submissions to 5 poems at a time.

How to Contact/Writers: Fiction/nonfiction: Send complete ms. SAE and international postage coupon for answer and return of ms. Responds to mss in 3 months unless return postage is missing. Will consider simultaneous submissions. "We prefer to read complete manuscript on speculation."

Illustration: Buys 3-5 illustrations/issue; 40 illustrations/year. Preferred theme or style: realism/humor (but not cartoons). Works on assignment only. Illustration only: Send promo sheet. Responds to art samples only if interested. Samples returned with SASE. Credit line given.

Photography: Looking for animal (mammal, insect, reptile, fish, etc.) and nature photos, kids, sports, science, bizarre, edgy. Uses 35mm and 2¼×2¼ transparencies. Write to request photo package for $1 money order, attention Rita Godlevskis, researcher.

Terms: Pays on publication. Buys all rights for mss. Buys one-time rights for photos. Original artwork returned at job's completion. Pays $10-250 for stories. Pays illustrators $100-650 for color inside, pays photographers per photo (range: $100-350). Sample copies for $4. Writer's guidelines free. All requests must include SAE and international postage coupon.

Tips: "The magazine publishes fiction and nonfiction that encourages kids to read and learn more about the world around them. The majority of *Chickadee*'s content is stories, puzzles, activities and observation games for young kids to enjoy on their own. Each issue also includes a longer story or poem that can be enjoyed by older kids." (See listings for *Chirp* and *OWL*.)

CHILD, Gruner & Jahr USA Pulishing, 375 Lexington Ave., New York NY 10017. (212)499-2000. Fax: (212)499-2038. Website: www.child.com. **Executive Editor:** Andrea Barbalich. **Photo Editor:** Topaz LeTourneau. Monthly magazine. Estab. 1984. Circ. 1 million. "Child provides parents of children from birth to age 12 with the newest thinking, information, and advice they need to raise their families in a constantly changing, time-pressed world."

Nonfiction: Freelance writers are invited to submit query letters and published clips only. The topics are children's health, nutrition and education, child behavior and development and personal essays pertaining to family life. Buys 75 mss/year.

How to Contact/Writers: Responds to queries in 10 weeks.

Illustration: Only interested in agented material.

Terms: Pays on acceptance. Buys first rights. Sample copies for $3.95. Writer's guidelines for SASE.

CHILDREN'S DIGEST, Children's Better Health Institute, 1100 Waterway Blvd., P.O. Box 567, Indianapolis IN 46206. (317)634-1100. Fax: (317)684-8094. Website: www.childrensdigestmag.org.

CHILDREN'S MAGIC WINDOW MAGAZINE, ProMark Publishing, P.O. Box 390, Perham MN 56573. (218)346-5696. Fax: (218)346-5829. E-mail: stories_illustrations@yahoo.com. Website: Childrensmagicwindow.com. **Articles Editor:** Joan Foster. **Fiction Editor:** Jeff Hoffman. **Art Director:** Mike Hoffman. Magazine published 6 times/year. Estab. 1999. Circ. 10,000. "*Children's Magic Window* is committed to restoring and advancing the diminishing interest in reading among our nation's youth. Featuring a something for everybody profile, *Magic Window* is a 100-page, full color, digest-sized, bi-monthly. Information should be challenging, but fun, aimed at 6 to 12 year olds. We avoid all pieces involving sex, drugs, alcohol, or violence. Exceptional articles or stories will be accepted without illustrations."

Fiction: Young readers, middle readers: adventure, animal, contemporary, fantasy, folktale, health, history, humorous, multicultural, nature/environment, problem-solving, science fiction, sports, suspense/mystery. Buys 50 mss/year. Average word length: up to 1,000 (maximum). Byline given.

Nonfiction: Young readers, middle readers: animal, arts/crafts, biography, careers, concept, cooking, games/puzzles, geography, health, history, hobbies, how-to, humorous, interview/profile, multicultural, nature/environment, problem-solving, science, sports, magic. Buys 50 mss/year. Average word length: up to 1,000. Byline given.

Poetry: Maximum length: 100 words. Limit submissions to 2 poems.

How to Contact/Writers: Send complete ms. Responds in 5 months. Publishes ms 3 months after acceptance. Will consider previously published work.

Illustration: Buys approximately 100 illustrations/issue; 500 illustrations/year. Uses color artwork only. Reviews ms/illustration packages from artists. Send ms with dummy. Contact: Jeff Hoffman, production director. Illustrations only: Query with samples, arrange portfolio for review; send promo sheet. Responds in 5 months. Samples returned with SASE. Credit line given.

Photography: Looking for color only, with a wide range of subject matter, depending on articles or stories to be published. Model release required; captions required. Uses color prints and 35mm, 2¼×2¼ transparencies. Query with samples. Provide business card, promotional literature.

Terms: Pays on publication. Buys first reprint rights, one-time rights or it depends on the article; some may require all rights. Original artwork returned at job's completion. Pays $400 maximum for stories and articles. Additional payment for photos accompanying articles. Pays up to $400/package for color inside. Pays photographers by the project (range: $40-200). Sample copies for $5. Writer's/illustrator's/photo guidelines for SASE.

Tips: "Familiarize yourself with our publication. Humor is always helpful. Fresh challenging, informative articles stand better chance. Only highest quality accepted. Work must require little, if any editing. Our readership is 6-12 year olds, but we use articles aimed at the 8-12 year olds. If the storyline is moderately entertaining to an adult, you are on the right track."

CHILDREN'S PLAYMATE, Children's Better Health Institute, 1100 Waterway Blvd., Box 567, Indianapolis IN 46206. (317)636-8881. Website: www.childrensplaymatemag.org. **Editor:** Terry Harshman. **Art Director:** Rob Falco. Magazine published 6 times/year. Estab. 1929. Circ. 135,000. For children ages 6-8 years; approximately 50% of content is health-related.

Fiction: Average word length: 100-300. Byline given.

Nonfiction: Young readers: easy recipes, games/puzzles, health, medicine, safety, science. Buys 16-20 mss/year. Average word length: 300-500. Byline given.

Poetry: Maximum length: 20-25 lines.

How to Contact/Writers: Fiction/nonfiction: Send complete ms. Responds to mss in 3 months. Do not send queries.

Illustration: Works on assignment only. Reviews ms/illustration packages from artists. Query first.

Terms: Pays on publication for illustrators and writers. Buys all rights for mss and artwork. Pays 17¢/word for stories. Pays minimum $25 for poems. Pays $275 for color cover illustration; $90 for b&w inside; $70-155 for color inside. Sample copy $1.75. Writer's/illustrator's guidelines for SASE. (See listings for *Child Life, Children's Digest, Humpty Dumpty's Magazine, Jack and Jill, Turtle Magazine* and *U*S* Kids*.)

Ⓝ CHRIST IN OUR HOME FOR FAMILIES WITH CHILDREN, Augsburg Fortress, 426 S. Fifth St., Box 1209, Minneapolis MN 55440. E-mail: hansonl@augsburgfortress.org. **Editor:** Laurie Hanson. Quarterly magazine. Circ. approximately 50,000. This is a booklet of interactive conversations and activities related to daily devotional material. Used primarily by Lutheran families with elementary school-aged children.

Fiction: Young readers, middle readers: adventure, contemporary, faith-related conversations, holidays and church seasons, nature/environment, problem-solving, religious, service activities. Byline given.

Nonfiction: Young readers, middle readers: devotional, faith-related conversations and activities, narrative, nature/environment, problem-solving, religious, social issues. Byline given.

How to Contact/Writers: Fiction/nonfiction: Query with published clips. Responds to unsolicited mss in 3 months. Manuscripts are accepted for review only. Published material is 100% assigned.

Terms: Pays on acceptance of final ms assignment. Buys all rights. Pays $40/printed page on assignment. Free sample and information for prospective writers. Include 6×9 SAE and postage.

Tips: "Pay attention to details in the sample devotional. Follow the process laid out in the information for prospective writers. Ability to interpret Bible texts appropriately for children is required."

CICADA, Carus Publishing Company, P.O. Box 300, 315 Fifth St., Peru IL 61354. (815)224-5803, ext. 656. Fax: (815)224-6615. E-mail: CICADA@caruspub.com. Website: www.cicadamag.com. **Editor-in-Chief:** Marianne Carus. **Executive Editor:** Deborah Vetter. **Associate Editor:** Tracy C. Schoenle. **Senior Art Director:** Ron McCutchan. Bimonthly magazine. Estab. 1998. *Cicada* publishes fiction and poetry with a genuine teen sensibility, aimed at the high school and college-age market. The editors are looking for stories and poems that are thought-provoking but entertaining.

Fiction: Young adults: adventure, animal, contemporary, fantasy, history, humorous, multicultural, nature/environment, romance, science fiction, sports, suspense/mystery, stories that will adapt themselves to a sophisticated cartoon, or graphic novel format. Buys up to 60 mss/year. Average word length: about 5,000 words for short stories; up to 15,000 for novellas only—we run one novella per issue.

Nonfiction: Young adults: first-person, coming-of-age experiences that are relevant to teens and young adults (example—life in the Peace Corps). Buys 6 mss/year. Average word length: about 5,000 words. Byline given.

Poetry: Reviews serious, humorous, free verse, rhyming (if done well) poetry. Maximum length: up to 25 lines. Limit submissions to 5 poems.

How to Contact/Writers: Fiction/nonfiction: send complete ms. Responds to mss in 3 months. Publishes ms 1-2 years after acceptance. Will consider simultaneous submissions if author lets us know.

Illustration: Buys 20 illustrations/issue; 120 illustrations/year. Uses color artwork for cover; b&w for interior. Works on assignment only. Reviews ms/illustration packages from artists. Send ms with 1-2 sketches and samples of other finished art. Illustrations only: Query with samples. Responds in 6 weeks. Samples returned with SASE; samples filed. Credit line given.

Photography: Wants documentary photos (clear shots that illustrate specific artifacts, persons, locations, phenomena, etc., cited in the text) and "art" shots of teens in photo montage/lighting effects etc. Uses b&w 4×5 glossy prints. Submit portfolio for review. Responds in 6 weeks.

Terms: Pays on publication. Rights purchased vary. Pays up to 25¢/word for mss; up to $3/line for poetry. Pays illustrators $750 for color cover; $50-150 for b&w inside. Pays photographers per photo (range: $50-150). Sample copies for $8.50. Writer's/illustrator's/photo guidelines for SASE.

Tips: "Please don't write for a junior high audience. We're looking for complex character development, strong plots, and thought-provoking themes for young people in high school and college. Don't forget humor! We're getting too many cancer-related stories and too much depressing fiction in general." (See listings for *Babybug, Cricket, Ladybug, Muse* and *Spider.*)

COBBLESTONE: Discover American History, Cobblestone Publishing Co., 30 Grove St., Suite C, Peterborough NH 03458. (603)924-7209. Fax: (603)924-7380. Website: www.cobblestonepub.com. **Editor:** Meg Chorlian. **Art Director:** Ann Dillon. **Managing Editor:** Lou Waryncia. Magazine published 9 times/year. Circ. 33,000. "*Cobblestone* is theme-related. Writers should request editorial guidelines which explain procedure and list upcoming themes. Queries must relate to an upcoming theme. It is recommended that writers become familiar with the magazine (sample copies available)."

- *Cobblestone* themes for 2004-2005 include The Electoral College, Colonial Philadelphia, George Rogers Clark/Revolutionary War in the West, Shays's Rebellion, Inventions/Industry in the 1800s, Women in the Civil War, The Muckrakers, Civilian Conservation Corp, Russian Americans. See website for deadlines.

Fiction: Middle readers, young adults: folktales, history, multicultural.

Nonfiction: Middle readers (school ages 8-14): arts/crafts, biography, geography, history (world and American), multicultural, social issues. All articles must relate to the issue's theme. Buys 120 mss/year. Average word length: 600-800. Byline given.

Poetry: Up to 100 lines. "Clear, objective imagery. Serious and light verse considered." Pays on an individual basis. Must relate to theme.

How to Contact/Writers: Fiction/nonfiction: Query. "A query must consist of all of the following to be considered: a brief cover letter stating the subject and word length of the proposed article, a detailed one-page outline explaining the information to be presented in the article, an extensive bibliography of materials the author intends to use in preparing the article, a self-addressed stamped envelope. Writers new to *Cobblestone* should send a writing sample with query. If you would like to know if your query has been received, please also include a stamped postcard that requests acknowledgment of receipt. In all correspondence, please include your complete address as well as a telephone number where you can be reached. A writer may send as many queries for one issue as he or she wishes, but each query must have a separate cover letter, outline, bibliography and SASE. Telephone queries are not accepted. Handwritten queries will not be considered. Queries may be submitted at any time, but queries sent well in advance of deadline *may not be answered for several months.* Go-aheads requesting material proposed in queries are usually sent five months prior to publication date. Unused queries will be returned approximately three to four months prior to publication date."

Illustration: Buys 5 color illustrations/issue; 45 illustrations/year. Preferred theme or style: Material that is simple, clear and accurate but not too juvenile. Sophisticated sources are a must. Works on assignment only. Reviews ms/illustration packages from artists. Query. Illustrations only: Send photocopies, tearsheets, or other nonreturnable samples. "Illustrators should consult issues of *Cobblestone* to familiarize themselves with our needs." Responds to art samples in 1 month. Samples are not returned; samples filed. Original artwork returned at job's completion (upon written request). Credit line given.

Photography: Photos must relate to upcoming themes. Send transparencies and/or color prints. Submit on speculation.

Terms: Pays on publication. Buys all rights to articles and artwork. Pays 20-25¢/word for articles/stories. Pays on an individual basis for poetry, activities, games/puzzles. Pays photographers per photo ($50-100 for color). Sample copy $4.95 with 7½×10½ SAE and 5 first-class stamps; writer's/illustrator's/photo guidelines free with SAE and 1 first-class stamp.

Tips: Writers: "Submit detailed queries which show attention to historical accuracy and which offer interesting and entertaining information. Study past issues to know what we look for. All feature articles, recipes, activities, fiction and supplemental nonfiction are freelance contributions." Illustrators: "Submit color samples, not too juvenile. Study past issues to know what we look for. The illustration we use is generally for stories, recipes and activities." (See listings for *AppleSeeds, Calliope, Dig, Faces, Footsteps* and *Odyssey.*)

COLLEGEBOUND TEEN MAGAZINE, (formerly *College Bound Magazine*), Ramholtz Publishing, Inc., 1200 South Ave., Suite 202, Staten Island NY 10314. (718)761-4800. 5700. Fax: (718)761-3300. E-mail: editorial@collegebound.net. Website: www.collegebound.net. **Articles Editor:** Gina LaGuardia. **Art Director:** Suzanne Vidal. Monthly magazine and website. Estab. 1987. Circ. 75,000 (regionals); 725,000 (nationals). *CollegeBound Teen Magazine* is written by college students (and those "young at heart") for high school juniors and seniors. It is designed to provide an inside view of college life, with college students from around the country serving as correspondents. The magazine's editorial content offers its teen readership personal accounts on all aspects of college, from living with a roommate, choosing a major, and joining a fraternity or sorority, to college dating, interesting courses, beating the financial aid fuss, and other college-bound concerns. *CollegeBound Teen Magazine* is published six times regionally throughout the tri-state area. Special issues include the National Editions (published each September and February) and Spring California, Illinois, Texas, Florida and New England issues. The magazine offers award-winning World Wide Web affiliates starting at *CollegeBound.NET*, at www.collegebound.net.

Nonfiction: Young adults: careers, college prep, fashion, health, how-to, interview/profile, problem-solving, social issues, college life. Buys 70 mss/year. Average word length: 400-1,100 words. Byline given.

How to Contact/Writers: Nonfiction: Query with published clips. Responds to queries in 2 months; mss in 10 weeks. Publishes ms 3-4 months after acceptance. Will consider electronic submission via disk or modem, previously published work (as long as not a competitor title).

Illustration: Buys 2-3 illustrations/issue. Uses color artwork only. Works on assignment only. Reviews ms/illustration packages from artists. Query. Illustrations only: Query with samples. Responds in 2 months. Samples kept on file. Credit line given.

Terms: Pays on publication. Buys first North American serial rights, all rights or reprint rights for mss. Buys first rights for artwork. Originals returned if requested, with SASE. Pays $25-100 for articles 30 days upon publication. All contributors receive 2 issues with payment. Pays illustrators $25-125 for color inside. Sample copies free for #10 SASE and $3 postage. Writer's guidelines for SASE.

Tips: "Review the sample issue and get a good feel for the types of articles we accept and our tone and purpose."

N̄ ⊕ COMET, Pearson Education Australia, 95 Coventry St., South Melbourne VIC Australia. Phone: (61)03 9697 0666. Fax: (61)03 9699 2041. E-mail: magazines@pearsoned.com.au. Website: www.pearsoned.com.au/schools. **Articles Editor:** Petra Poupa. **Fiction Editor:** Meredith Costain. Quarterly Magazine. Circ. 20,000. "Magazines are educational and fun. We publish mainly nonfiction articles in a variety of genres and text types. They must be appropriate, factually correct, and of high interest. We publish interviews, recounts, informational and argumentative articles."

● *Comet* is a theme based publication. Check the website to see upcoming themes and deadlines.

Fiction: Picture-oriented material, young readers: adventure, animal, contemporary, folktale, multicultural, nature/environment, problem solving. Young readers: fantasy, humorous, suspense/mystery. Average word length: 400-1,000. Byline given.

Nonfiction: Picture-oriented material, young readers: animal, arts/crafts, biography, careers, cooking, health, hobbies, how-to, interview/profile, math, multicultural, nature/environment, problem-solving, science, social issues, sports, travel. Picture-oriented material: geography. Young readers: games/puzzles, humorous. Average word length: 200-600. Byline given.

Poetry: Reviews poetry.

How to Contact/Writers: Fiction/nonfiction: Send complete ms. Responds to queries in 1 month; mss in 3 months. Publishes ms 3 months after acceptance. Will consider simultaneous submissions and electronic submissions via disk or e-mail.

Photography: Looking for photos to suit various themes; photos needed depend on stories. Model/property release required; captions required. Uses color, standard sized, matte prints and 35mm transparencies. Provide resume, business card, promotional literature and tearsheets to be kept on file. Responds only if interested.

Terms: Pays on publication. Buys first Australian rights. Pays $80-200 (Australian) for stories; $100-220 (Australian) for articles. Additional payment for ms/illustration packages. Sample copies free for SAE. Writer's guidelines free for SASE.

Tips: "Check out our website for information about our publications." See listings for *Challenge* and *Explore*.

CRICKET MAGAZINE, Carus Publishing, Company, P.O. Box 300, Peru IL 61354. (815)224-5803 ext. 656. Website: www.cricketmag.com. **Articles/Fiction Editor-in-Chief:** Marianne Carus. **Executive Editor:** Deborah Vetter. **Associate Editor:** Tracy Schoenle. **Associate Editor:** Julia M. Messina. **Senior Art Director:** Ron McCutchan. Monthly magazine. Estab. 1973. Circ. 72,000. Children's literary magazine for ages 9-14.

Fiction: Middle readers, young adults/teens: contemporary, fantasy, folk and fairy tales, history, humorous, science fiction, suspense/mystery. Buys 140 mss/year. Maximum word length: 2,000. Byline given.

Nonfiction: Middle readers, young adults/teens: adventure, architecture, archaeology, biography, foreign culture, games/puzzles, geography, natural history, science and technology, social science, sports, travel. Multicultural needs include articles on customs and cultures. Requests bibliography with submissions. Buys 40 mss/year. Average word length: 200-1,500. Byline given.

Poetry: Reviews poems, 1-page maximum length. Limit submissions to 5 poems or less.

How to Contact/Writers: Send complete ms. Do not query first. Responds to mss in 3 months. Does not like but will consider simultaneous submissions. SASE required for response.

Illustration: Buys 35 illustrations (14 separate commissions)/issue; 425 illustrations/year. Uses b&w and full-color work. Preferred theme or style: "strong realism; strong people, especially kids; good action illustration; no cartoons. All media, but prefer other than pencil." Reviews ms/illustration packages from artists "but reserves option to re-illustrate." Send complete ms with sample and query. Illustrations only: Provide tearsheets or good quality photocopies to be kept on file. SASE required for response/return of samples. Responds to art samples in 2 months.

Photography: Purchases photos with accompanying ms only. Model/property releases required. Uses color transparencies, b&w glossy prints.

Terms: Pays on publication. Rights purchased vary. Do not send original artwork. Pays up to 25¢/word for unsolicited articles; up to $3/line for poetry. Pays $750 for color cover; $75-150 for b&w, $150-250 for color inside. Pays $750 for color cover; $75-150 for b&w, $150-250 for color inside. Writer's/illustrator's guidelines for SASE.

Tips: Writers: "Read copies of back issues and current issues. Adhere to specified word limits. *Please* do not query." Illustrators: "Edit your samples. Send only your best work and be able to reproduce that quality in assignments. Put name and address on *all* samples. Know a publication before you submit—is your style appropriate?" (See listings for *Babybug*, *Cicada*, *Ladybug*, *Muse* and *Spider*.)

THE CRYSTAL BALL, The Starwind Press, P.O. Box 98, Ripley OH 45167. (937)392-4549. E-mail: susannah@techgallery.com. Articles/Fiction Editor: Marlene Powell. **Assistant Editor:** Susannah C. West. Quarterly magazine. Estab. 1997. Circ. 1,000. Publishes science fiction and fantasy for young adults.

Fiction: Young adults: fantasy, folktale, science fiction. Buys 8-12 mss/year. Average word length: 1,500-5,000. Byline given.

Nonfiction: Young adults: biography, how-to, interview/profile, science. Buys 8-12 mss/year. Average word length: 1,000-3,000.

Poetry: Only publishes poetry by kids.

How to Contact/Writers: Fiction: send complete ms. Nonfiction: query. Responds to queries and mss in 4 months. Publishes ms 6-12 months after acceptance. Will consider previously published work if published in noncompeting market.

Illustration: Buys 6-8 illustrations/issue; 24-32 illustrations/year. Uses b&w camera ready artwork only. Works on assignment only. Reviews ms/illustration packages from artists. Send ms with dummy. Contact: Marlene Powell, editor. Illustrations only: query with samples. Contact: Marlene Powell, editor. Responds in 4 months if SASE enclosed. Samples kept on file. Credit line given.

Photography: Looking for photos to illustrate nonfiction pieces. Uses b&w, line shots or already screened. Responds in 3 months.

Terms: Pays on acceptance. Buys first North American serial rights for mss, artwork and photos. Original artwork returned at job's completion if requested. Pays $5-20 for stories and articles. Additional payment for photos accompanying article. Pays illustrators $5-20 for b&w inside and cover. Pays photographers per photo (range: $5-20). Sample copies for $3. Writer's/illustrator's guidelines for SASE.

Tips: Be familiar with the science fiction/fantasy genre.

DANCE MAGAZINE, 111 Myrtle St., Suite 203, Oakland CA 94607. (510)839-6060. Fax: (510)839-6066. Website: www.dancemagazine.com. **Editor-in-Chief:** KC Patrick. **Art Director:** James Lambertus. Monthly magazine. Estab. 1927. Circ. 45,000. Covers "all things dance—features, news, reviews, calendar. We have a Young Dancer section." Byline given.

How to Contact: Query with published clips.

Photography: Uses dance photos.

Terms: Pays on publication. Buys first rights. Additional payment for ms/illustration packages and for photos accompanying articles. Pays photographers per photo. Sample copies for $4.95.

Tips: "Study the magazine for style."

DIG, Cobblestone Publishing, 30 Grove St., Suite C, Peterburough NH 03450. (603)924-7209. Fax: (603)924-7380. E-mail: cfbakeriii@meganet.net. Website: www.digonsite.com. **Editor:** Rosalie Baker. **Editorial Director:** Lou Waryncia. **Art Director:** Ann Dillon. Magazine published 9 times/year. Estab. 1999. Circ. 25,000. An archaeology magazine for kids ages 8-14. Publishes entertaining and educational stories about discoveries, artifacts, archaeologists.

• *Dig* was purchased by Cobblestone Publishing.

Nonfiction: Middle readers, young adults: biography, games/puzzles, history, science, archaeology. Buys 50 mss/year. Average word length: 400-800. Byline given.

How to Contact/Writers: Fiction/nonfiction: Query. "A query must consist of all of the following to be considered: a brief cover letter stating the subject and word length of the proposed article, a detailed one-page outline explaining the information to be presented in the article, an extensive bibliography of materials the author intends to use in preparing the article, and a SASE. Writers new to *Dig* should send a writing sample with query. If you would like to know if query has been received, include a stamped postcard that requests acknowledgement of receipt." Multiple queries accepted (include separate cover letter, outline, bibliography, SASE)—may not be answered for many months. Go-aheads requesting material proposed in queries are usually sent 5 months prior to publication date. Unused queries will be returned approximately 3-4 months prior to publication date.

Illustration: Buys 10-15 illustrations/issue; 60-75 illustrations/year. Uses color artwork only. Works on assignment only. Reviews ms/illustration packages from artists. Query. Illustrations only: Query with samples. Arrange portfolio review. Send tearsheets. Responds in 2 months only if interested. Samples not returned; samples filed. Credit line given.

Photography: Uses anything related to archaeology, history, artifacts and current archaeological events that relate to kids. Uses color prints and 35mm transparencies. Provide résumé, promotional literature or tearsheets to be kept on file. Responds only if interested.

Terms: Pays on publication. Buys all rights for mss. Buys first North American rights for photos. Original artwork returned at job's completion. Pays 20-25¢/word. Additional payment for ms/illustration packages and for photos accompanying articles. Pays per photo.

Tips: "We are looking for writers who can communicate archaeological concepts in a conversational, interesting, informative and *accurate* style for kids. Writers should have some idea where photography can be located to support their work."

DISCOVERIES, Children's Ministries, 6401 The Paseo, Kansas City MO 64131. (816)333-7000. Fax: (816)333-4439. E-mail: vfolsom@nazarene.org. **Editor**: Virginia Folsom. **Executive Editor**: Merritt J. Nielson. **Assistant Editor:** Julie J. Smith. Take-home paper. "*Discoveries* is a leisure-reading piece for third and fourth graders. It is published weekly by WordAction Publishing. The major purpose of the magazine is to provide a leisure-reading piece which will build Christian behavior and values and provide reinforcement for Biblical concepts taught in the Sunday School curriculum. The focus of the reinforcement will be life-related, with some historical appreciation. *Discoveries'* target audience is children ages eight to ten in grades three and four. The readability goal is third to fourth grade."

Fiction: Middle readers: adventure, contemporary, humorous, religious. "Fiction—stories should vividly portray definite Christian emphasis or character-building values, without being preachy. The setting, plot and action should be realistic." 500-word maximum. Byline given.

Nonfiction: Puzzles that fit the theme list and trivia (150 words) about any miscellaneous area of interest to 8- to 10-year-olds (hobbies, fun activities, to do in your spare time, interesting facts). Please document sources.

How to Contact/Writers: Fiction: Send complete ms. Responds to queries/mss in 1 month.

Terms: Pays "approximately one year before the date of issue." Buys multi-use rights. Pays $25 for stories; $15 for trivia, puzzles, and cartoons. Contributor receives 2 complimentary copies of publication. Sample copy free for #10 SASE with 1 first-class stamp. Writer's/artist's guidelines free with #10 SAE.

Tips: "*Discoveries* is committed to reinforcement of the Biblical concepts taught in the Sunday School curriculum. Because of this, the themes needed are mainly as follows: faith in God, obedience to God, putting God first, choosing to please God, accepting Jesus as Savior, finding God's will, choosing to do right, trusting God in hard times, prayer, trusting God to answer, importance of Bible memorization, appreciation of Bible as God's Word to man, Christians working together, showing kindness to others, witnessing. Because of this stories must follow our theme list. Please request one before attempting to submit copy." (See listing for *Passport*.)

DISCOVERY TRAILS, Gospel Publishing House, 1445 N. Boonville Ave., Springfield MO 65802-1894. (417)862-2781. E-mail: rl-discoverytrails@gph.org. Website: www.radiantlife.org. **Articles Editor:** Sinda S. Zinn. **Art Director:** David Bates. Quarterly take-home paper. Circ. 20,000. "*Discovery Trails* provides fiction stories that promote Christian living through application of biblical principles. Puzzles and activities are fun ways to learn more about God's Word and "bytes" of information are provided to inspire readers to be in awe of God's wonderful creation."

Fiction: Middle readers: adventure, animal, contemporary, humorous, nature/environment, problem-solving, religious, suspense/mystery. Buys 100 or less mss/year.

Nonfiction: Middle readers: animal, arts/crafts, how-to, humorous, nature/environment, problem-solving, religion. Buys 50-100 mss/year. Average word length: 200-500. Byline given.

Poetry: Reviews poetry. Limit submissions, at one time, to 2 poems.

How to Contact/Writers: Fiction/nonfiction: Send complete ms. Responds in 1 month. Publishes ms 15-24 months after acceptance. Will consider simultaneous submissions or previously published work. Please indicate such.

Illustration: Buys 1 illustration issue; 50-60 illustrations/year from assigned freelancers. Uses color artwork only. Works on assignment only. Send promo sheet, portfolio. Responds only if interested. Samples returned with SASE; samples filed. Credit line given.

Terms: Pays on acceptance. Pays authors 7-10¢ per word. Buys first rights or reprint rights for mss. Buys one-time rights for artwork. Original artwork returned at job's completion. Sample copies for 6×9 SAE and 2 first-class stamps. Writer's guidelines for SASE.

✓ **DOLPHIN LOG**, The Cousteau Society, 3612 E. Treemont, PMB 217, Throggs Neck NY 10465. (718)409-3770. Fax: (718)409-1677. E-mail: lisarao@aol.com. Website: www.dolphin.org. **Editor:** Lisa Rao. Bimonthly magazine for children ages 7-13. Circ. 80,000. Entirely nonfiction subject matter encompasses all areas of science, natural history, marine biology, ecology and the environment as they relate to our global water system. The philosophy of the magazine is to delight, instruct and instill an environmental ethic and understanding of the interconnectedness of living organisms, including people. Of special interest are articles on ocean- or water-related themes which develop reading and comprehension skills.

Nonfiction: Middle readers, young adult: animal, games/puzzles, geography, interview/profile, nature/environment, science, ocean. Multicultural needs include indigenous peoples, lifestyles of ancient people, etc. Does not want to see talking animals. No dark or religious themes. Buys 10 mss/year. Average word length: 500-700. Byline given.

How to Contact/Writers: Nonfiction: Query first. Unsolicited mss returned unopened. Responds to queries in 3 months; mss in 6 months.

Illustration: Buys 1 illustration/issue; buys 6 illustrations/year. Preferred theme: Biological illustration. Reviews ms/illustration packages from artists. Illustrations only: Query; send résumé, promo sheet, slides. Responds to art samples in 2 months only if interested. Credit line given to illustrators.

Photography: Wants "sharp, colorful pictures of sea creatures. The more unusual the creature, the better." Submit duplicate slides only. Query for submissions/rates.

Terms: Pays on publication. Buys first North American serial rights; reprint rights. Pays $75-250 for articles. Pays $100-400 for illustrations. Pays $75-200/color photos. Sample copy $2.50 with 9×12 SAE and 3 first-class stamps. Writer's/illustrator's guidelines free with #10 SASE.

Tips: Writers: "Write simply and clearly and don't anthropomorphize." Illustrators: "Be scientifically accurate and don't anthropomorphize. Some background in biology is helpful, as our needs range from simple line drawings to scientific illustrations which must be researched for biological and technical accuracy."

DRAMATICS, Educational Theatre Association, 2343 Auburn Ave., Cincinnati OH 45219. (513)421-3900. E-mail: dcorathers@edta.org. Website: www.edta.org. **Articles Editor:** Don Corathers. **Art Director:** William Johnston. Published monthly September-May. Estab. 1929. Circ. 35,000. "Dramatics is for students (mainly high school age) and teachers of theater. Mix includes how-to (tech theater, acting, directing, etc.), informational, interview, photo feature, humorous, profile, technical. "We want our student readers to grow as theater artists and become a more discerning and appreciative audience. Material is directed to both theater students and their teachers, with strong student slant."

Fiction: Young adults: drama (one-act and full-length plays.) Does not want to see plays that show no understanding of the conventions of the theater. No plays for children, no Christmas or didactic "message" plays. "We prefer unpublished scripts that have been produced at least once." Buys 5-9 plays/year. Emerging playwrights have better chances with résumé of credits.

Nonfiction: Young adults: arts/crafts, careers, how-to, interview/profile, multicultural (all theater-related). "We try to portray the theater community in all its diversity." Does not want to see academic treatises. Buys 50 mss/year. Average word length: 750-3,000. Byline given.

How to Contact/Writers: Send complete ms. Responds in 3 months (longer for plays). Published ms 3 months after acceptance. Will consider simultaneous submissions and previously published work occasionally.

Illustration: Buys 0-2 illustrations/year. Works on assignment only. Arrange portfolio review; send résumé, promo sheets and tearsheets. Responds only if interested. Samples returned with SASE; sample not filed. Credit line given.

Photography: Buys photos with accompanying ms only. Looking for "good-quality production or candid photography to accompany article. We very occasionally publish photo essays." Model/property release and captions required. Uses 5×7 or 8×10 b&w glossy prints and 35mm transparencies. Also uses high resolution digital files or Zip disk or CD (JPEG or TIFF files). Query with résumé of credits. Responds only if interested.

Terms: Pays on acceptance. Buys one-time rights, occasionally reprint rights. Buys one-time rights for artwork and photos. Original artwork returned at job's completion. Pays $100-500 for plays; $50-500 for articles; up to $100 for illustrations. Pays photographers by the project or per photo. Sometimes offers additional payment for ms/illustration packages and photos accompanying a ms. Sample copy available for 9×12 SAE with 4 ounces first-class postage. Writer's and photo guidelines available for SASE or via website.

Tips: "Obtain our writer's guidelines and look at recent back issues. The best way to break in is to know our audience—drama students, teachers and others interested in theater—and write for them. Writers who have some practical experience in theater, especially in technical areas, have an advantage, but we'll work with anybody who has a good idea. Some freelancers have become regular contributors."

☑ DYNAMATH, Scholastic Inc., 557 Broadway, Room 4052, New York NY 10012-3999. (212)343-6458. Fax: (212)343-4459. E-mail: dynamath@scholastic.com. Website: www.scholastic.com/dynamath. **Editor:** Matt Friedman. **Art Director:** Doreen Walsh. Monthly magazine. Estab. 1982. Circ. 200,000. Purpose is "to make learning math fun, challenging and uncomplicated for young minds in a very complex world."

Nonfiction: Middle readers: animal, arts/crafts, cooking, fashion, games/puzzles, health, history, hobbies, how-to, humorous, math, multicultural, nature/environment, problem-solving, science, social issues, sports—all must relate to math and science topics.

How to Contact/Writers: Nonfiction: Query with published clips, send ms. Responds to queries in 1 month; mss in 6 weeks. Publishes ms 4 months after acceptance. Will consider simultaneous submissions.

Illustration: Buys 4 illustrations/issue. Illustration only: Query first; send résumé and tearsheets. Responds on submissions only if interested. Credit line given.

Terms: Pays on acceptance. Buys all rights for mss, artwork, photographs. Originals returned to artist at job's completion. Pays $50-450 for stories.

N ⊕ EXPLORE, Pearson Education Australia, 95 Coventry St., South Melbourne VIC Australia. Phone: (61)03 9697 0666. Fax: (61)03 9699 2041. E-mail: magazines@pearsoned.com.au. Website: www.pearsoned.com.au/schools. **Articles Editor:** Petra Poupa. **Fiction Editor:** Meredith Costain. Quarterly Magazine. Circ. 20,000. "Magazines are educational and fun. We publish mainly nonfiction articles in a variety of genres and text types. They must be appropriate, factually correct, and of high interest. We publish interviews, recounts, informational and argumentative articles."

● *Explore* is a theme based publication. Check the website to see upcoming themes and deadlines.

Fiction: Young readers, middle readers: adventure, animal, contemporary, fantasy, folktale, humorous, multicultural, nature/environment, problem-solving, suspense/mystery. Middle readers: science fiction, sports. Average word length: 400-1,000. Byline given.

Nonfiction: Young readers, middle readers: animal, arts/crafts, biography, careers, cooking, health, history, hobbies, how-to, interview/profile, math, multicultural, nature/environment, problem-solving, science, social issues, sports, travel. Young readers: games/puzzles. Middle readers: concept, fashion, geography. Average word length: 200-600. Byline given.

Poetry: Reviews poetry.

How to Contact/Writers: Fiction/nonfiction: Send complete ms. Responds to queries in 1 month; mss in 3 months. Publishes ms 3 months after acceptance. Will consider simultaneous submissions and electronic submissions via disk or e-mail.

Photography: Looking for photos to suit various themes; photos needed depend on stories. Model/property release required; captions required. Uses color, standard sized, matte prints and 35mm transparencies. Provide résumé, business card, promotional literature and tearsheets to be kept on file. Responds only if interested.

Terms: Pays on publication. Buys first Australian rights. Pays $80-200 (Australian) for stories; $100-220 (Australian) for articles. Additional payment for ms/illustration packages. Sample copies free for SAE. Writer's guidelines free for SASE.

Tips: "Check out our website for information about our publications." (See listings for *Challenge* and *Comet*.)

FACES, People, Places & Cultures, Cobblestone Publishing Company, 30 Grove St., Peterborough NH 03458. (603)924-7209. Fax: (603)924-7380. E-mail: facesmag@yahoo.com. Website: www.cobblestonepub.com. **Editor**: Elizabeth Crooker Carpentiere. **Editorial Director**: Lou Warnycia. **Art Director**: Ann Dillon. Magazine published 9 times/year (September-May). Circ. 15,000. *Faces* is a theme-related magazine; writers should send for theme list before submitting ideas/queries. Each month a different world culture is featured through the use of feature articles, activities and photographs and illustrations.

• See website for 2004-2005 theme list.

Fiction: Middle readers, young adults/teens: adventure, folktales, history, multicultural, plays, religious, travel. Does not want to see material that does not relate to a specific upcoming theme. Buys 9 mss/year. Maximum word length: 800. Byline given.

Nonfiction: Middle readers and young adults/teens: animal, anthropology, arts/crafts, biography, cooking, fashion, games/puzzles, geography, history, how-to, humorous, interview/profile, nature/environment, religious, social issues, sports, travel. Does not want to see material not related to a specific upcoming theme. Buys 63 mss/year. Average word length: 300-600. Byline given.

Poetry: Clear, objective imagery; up to 100 lines. Must relate to theme.

How to Contact/Writers: Fiction/nonfiction: Query with published clips and 2-3 line biographical sketch. "Ideas should be submitted six to nine months prior to the publication date. Responses to ideas are usually sent approximately four months before the publication date." Guidelines on website.

Illustration: Buys 3 illustrations/issue; buys 27 illustrations/year. Preferred theme or style: Material that is meticulously researched (most articles are written by professional anthropologists); simple, direct style preferred, but not too juvenile. Works on assignment only. Roughs required. Reviews ms/illustration packages from artists. Illustrations only: Send samples of b&w work. "Illustrators should consult issues of *Faces* to familiarize themselves with our needs." Responds to art samples only if interested. Samples returned with SASE. Original artwork returned at job's completion (upon written request). Credit line given.

Photography: Wants photos relating to forthcoming themes.

Terms: Pays on publication. Buys all rights for mss and artwork. Pays 20-25¢/word for articles/stories. Pays on an individual basis for poetry. Covers are assigned and paid on an individual basis. Pays illustrators $50-300 for color inside. Pays photographers per photo ($25-100 for color). Sample copy $4.95 with 7½×10½ SAE and 5 first-class stamps. Writer's/illustrator's/photo guidelines via website or free with SAE and 1 first-class stamp.

Tips: "Writers are encouraged to study past issues of the magazine to become familiar with our style and content. Writers with anthropological and/or travel experience are particularly encouraged; *Faces* is about world cultures. All feature articles, recipes and activities are freelance contributions." Illustrators: "Submit b&w samples, not too juvenile. Study past issues to know what we look for. The illustration we use is generally for retold legends, recipes and activities." (See listings for *AppleSeeds*, *Calliope*, *Cobblestone*, *Footsteps* and *Odyssey*.)

Ⓝ FLORIDA LEADER, for high school students, Oxendine Publishing, Inc., P.O. Box 14081, Gainesville FL 32604-2081. (352)373-6907. Fax: (352)373-8120. E-mail: teresa@studentleader.com. Website: www.floridaleader.com. **Articles Editor**: Stephanie Reck. **Art Director**: Jeff Riemersma. Published 3 times/year. Estab. 1992. Circ. 25,000. "Magazine features articles focused on student leadership, current financial aid and admissions information, and stories on other aspects of college life for prospective college students." Audience includes ages 14-17.

Nonfiction: Young adult/teens: interview/profile (with student leaders), problem-solving, social issues, travel. Looking for "more advanced pieces on college preparation—academic skills, career exploration and general motivation for college." Buys 6-8 mss/year. Average word length: 800-1,000. 200-300 for columns.

How to Contact/Writers: Nonfiction: Query with published clips. Responds to queries/mss in 5 weeks. Publishes ms 3-5 months after acceptance. Will consider simultaneous submissions, electronic submissions, previously published work.

Illustration: Buys 5 illustrations/issue; 20 illustrations/year. Uses color artwork only. Works on assignment only. Reviews ms/illustration packages from artists. Query. Illustrations only: query with samples; send résumé, promo sheet, tearsheets. Responds only if interested. Samples returned with SASE; samples filed. Credit line given.

Photography: Buys photos from freelancers. Buys photos separately. Works on assignment only. Model/property release required. Uses color prints and 35mm, 2¼×2¼, 4×5 transparencies. Query with samples. Responds only if interested.

Terms: Pays on publication. Buys first North American serial rights, reprint rights for mss. Buys first-time rights for artwork and photos. Originals returned at job's completion. Pays $35-75 for articles. Pays first-time or less experienced writers or for shorter items with contribution copies or other premiums. Pays illustrators $75 for color inside. Pays photographers by the project (range: $150-300). Sample copies for $3.50. Writer's guidelines for SASE.

Tips: "Query first and review past issues for style and topics."

Focus on the Family CLUBHOUSE; Focus on the Family CLUBHOUSE JR., Focus on the Family, 8605 Explorer Dr., Colorado Springs CO 80920. (719)531-3400. Fax: (719)531-3499. Website: www.clubhousemagazine.org. **Editor:** Jesse Florea, *Clubhouse*; Annette Bourland, editor *Clubhouse Jr*. **Art Director:** Timothy Jones. Monthly magazine. Estab. 1987. Combined circulation is 210,000. "*Focus on the Family Clubhouse* is a 24-page Christian magazine, published monthly, for children ages 8-12. Similarly, *Focus on the Family Clubhouse Jr*. is published for children ages 4-8. We want fresh, exciting literature that promotes biblical thinking, values and behavior in every area of life."

Fiction: Young readers, middle readers: adventure, contemporary, multicultural, nature/environment, religious. Middle readers: history, sports, science fiction. Multicultural needs include: "interesting, informative, accurate information about other cultures to teach children appreciation for the world around them." Buys approximately 6-10 mss/year. Average word length: *Clubhouse*, 500-1,400; *Clubhouse Jr.*, 250-1,100. Byline given on all fiction and puzzles.

Nonfiction: Young readers, middle readers: arts/crafts, cooking, games/puzzles, how-to, multicultural, nature/environment, religion, science. Young readers: animal. Middle readers, young adult/teen: interview/profile. Middle readers: sports. Buys 3-5 mss/year. Average word length: 200-1,000. Byline given.

Poetry: *Clubhouse Jr.* wants to see "humorous or biblical" poetry for 4-8 year olds. Maximum length: 250 words. *Clubhouse* does not want poetry.

How to Contact/Writers: Fiction/nonfiction: send complete ms with SASE. Responds to queries/mss in 6 weeks.

Illustration: Buys 8 illustrations/issue. Uses color artwork only. Works on assignment only. Reviews ms/illustration packages from artists. Submit ms with rough sketches. Illustrations only: Query with samples, arrange portfolio review or send tearsheets. Responds in 3 months. Samples returned with SASE; samples kept on file. Credit line given.

Photography: Buys photos from freelancers. Uses 35mm transparencies. Photographers should query with samples; provide résumé and promotional literature or tearsheets. Responds in 2 months.

Terms: Pays on acceptance. Buys first North American serial rights for mss. Buys first rights or reprint rights for artwork and photographs. Original artwork returned at job's completion. Additional payment for ms/illustration packages. Pays writers $150-300 for stories; $50-150 for articles. Pays illustrators $300-700 for color cover; $200-700 for color inside. Pays photographers by the project or per photo. Sample copies for 9×12 SAE and 3 first-class stamps. Writer's/illustrators/ photo guidelines for SASE.

Tips: "Test your writing on children. The best stories avoid moralizing or preachiness and are not written *down* to children. They are the products of writers who share in the adventure with their readers, exploring the characters they have created without knowing for certain where the story will lead. And they are not always explicitly Christian, but are built upon a Christian foundation (and, at the very least, do not contradict biblical views or values)."

FOOTSTEPS, The Magazine of African American History, Cobblestone Publishing Co., 30 Grove St., Suite C, Peterborough NH 03458. (603)924-7204 or (800)821-0115. Fax: (608)924-7380. Website: www.cobblestonepub.com. **Editor:** Charles F. Baker. Magazine on African American history for readers ages 8-14.
  • *Footsteps*' themes for 2004-2005 include Black Inventors, Women Writers, and Sports Heroes. For additional themes and time frames, visit the website.

Fiction: Middle readers: adventure, history, multicultural. Word length: up to 700 words.

Nonfiction: Middle readers: history, interviews/profile. Word length: 300-750 words.

How to Contact/Writers: Query with cover letter, outline, bibliography and SASE. "All material must relate to the theme of a specific upcoming issue in order to be considered."

Terms: Writer's guidelines available on website.

Tips: "We are looking for articles that are lively, age-appropriate, and exhibit an original approach to the theme of the issue. Cultural sensitivity and historical accuracy are extremely important."

THE FRIEND MAGAZINE, The Church of Jesus Christ of Latter-day Saints, 50 E. North Temple, Salt Lake City UT 84150-3226. (801)240-2210. **Editor:** Vivian Paulsen. **Art Director:** Mark Robison. Monthly magazine for 3-11 year olds. Estab. 1971. Circ. 275,000.

Needs: Children's/true stories—adventure, ethnic, some historical, humor, mainstream, religious/inspirational, nature. Length: 1,000 words maximum. Publishes short stories length 250 words.

Poetry: Reviews poetry. Maximum length: 20 lines.

How to Contact/Writers: Send complete ms. Responds to mss in 2 months.

Illustration: Illustrations only: Query with samples; arrange personal interview to show portfolio; provide résumé and tearsheets for files.

Terms: Pays on acceptance. Buys all rights for mss. Pays 15¢/word for unsolicited fiction articles; $25 and up for poems; $25 for recipes, activities and games. Contributors are encouraged to send for sample copy for $1.50, 9×11 envelope and four 37¢ stamps. Free writer's guidelines.

Tips: "*The Friend* is published by The Church of Jesus Christ of Latter-day Saints for boys and girls up to twelve years of age. All submissions are carefully read by the *Friend* staff, and those not accepted are returned within two months when a self-addressed, stamped envelope is enclosed. Submit seasonal material at least eight months in advance. Query letters and simultaneous submissions are not encouraged. Authors may request rights to have their work reprinted after their manuscript is published."

☑ **FUN FOR KIDZ**, P.O. Box 227, Bluffton OH 45817-0164. (419)358-4610. Fax: (419)358-5027. Website: funforkidz.com. **Articles Editor:** Marilyn Edwards. Bimonthly magazine. Estab. 2002. "*Fun for Kidz* is a magazine created for boys and girls ages 6-13, with youngsters 8, 9, and 10 the specific target age. The magazine is designed as an activity publication to be enjoyed by both boys and girls on the alternative months of *Hopscotch* and *Boys' Quest* magazine."
  • *Fun for Kidz* is theme-oriented. Send SASE for theme list.

Fiction: Picture-oriented material, young readers, middle readers: adventure, animal, history, humorous, problem-solving, multicultural, nature/environment, sports. Average word length: 300-700.

Nonfiction: Picture-oriented material, young readers, middle readers: animal, arts/crafts, cooking, games/puzzles, history, hobbies, how-to, humorous, problem-solving, sports, carpentry projects. Average word length: 300-700. Byline given.

Poetry: Reviews poetry.

How to Contact/Writers: Fiction/nonfiction: Send complete ms. Responds to queries in 2 weeks; mss in 5 weeks. Will consider simultaneous submissions.

Illustration: Works on assignment mostly. "We are anxious to find artists capable of illustrating stories and features. Our inside art is pen & ink." Query with samples. Samples kept on file.

Photography: "We use a number of back & white photos inside the magazine; most support the articles used."

Terms: Pays on publication. Buys first American serial rights. Buys first American serial rights and photos for artwork. Pays 5¢/word; $10/poem or puzzle; $35 for art (full page); $25 for art (partial page). Pays illustrators $5-10 for b&w photos.

Tips: "Our point of view is that every child deserves the right to be a child for a number of years before he or she becomes a young adult. As a result, *Fun for Kidz* looks for activities that deal with timeless topics, such as pets, nature, hobbies, science, games, sports, careers, simple cooking, and anything else likely to interest a child."

GIRLS' LIFE, Monarch, 4517 Harford Rd., Baltimore MD 21214. (410)426-9600. Fax: (410)254-0991. Website: www.girls life.com. **Senior Editor**: Kelly White. **Creative Director**: Chun Kim. Bimonthly magazine. Estab. 1994. General interest magazine for girls, ages 10-15.

Fiction: Romance.

Nonfiction: Arts/crafts, fashion, interview/profile, social issues, sports, travel, hobbies. Buys appoximately 25 mss/year. Word length varies. Byline given. "No fiction!"

How to Contact/Writers: Nonfiction: Query with descriptive story ideas, résumé and published writing samples. Responds in 6 weeks. Publishes ms 3 months after acceptance. Will consider simultaneous submissions. No phone calls.

Illustration: Uses color artwork only. Works on assignment only. Reviews ms/illustration packages from artists. Send ms with dummy. Illustration only: Query with samples; send tearsheets. Contact: Chun Kim, creative director. Responds only if interested. Samples returned with SASE; samples filed. Credit line given.

Photography: Hires photographers. Send portfolio. Responds only if interested.

Terms: Pays on publication. Original artwork returned at job's completion. Pays $500-800 for features; $150-350 for departments. Sample copies available for $5. Writer's guidelines for SASE or via website.

Tips: "Don't call with queries. Make query short and punchy."

⬛ GO-GIRL.COM, The Collegebound Network, 1200 South Ave., Suite 202, Stanten Island NY 10314. (718)761-4800. Fax: (718)761-3300. E-mail: editorial@collegebound.net. Website: www.go-girl.com. **Articles Editor:** Gina LaGuardia. Weekly online magazine. Estab. 1997. "Go-Girl.com is one of The CollegeBound Network's affiliate of websites, and is devoted to empowering teen girls to become 'academic divas.' Student surfers have access to real people who guide them through their college and career choices. Our content is highly interactive—students can enter challenging contests, win scholarships and prizes, meet other students, and discover valuable information on academic and lifestyle issues of interest to them."

Nonfiction: Young adults: biography, careers, fashion, health, how-to, interview/profile, social issues, travel, celebrity education. Buys 25 mss/year. Average word length: 400-900. Byline given.

How to Contact/Writer: Nonfiction: Query. Responds to queries in 6 weeks; mss in 7 weeks. Publishes ms 2-3 months after acceptance. Will consider simultaneous submissions, electronic submission via disk or modem (upon acceptance).

Terms: Pays on publication. Buys first rights. Pays $50-100 for articles. Writer's guidelines for SASE.

GUIDE MAGAZINE, Review and Herald Publishing Association, 55 W. Oak Ridge Dr., Hagerstown MD 21740. (301)393-4038. Fax: (301)393-4055. E-mail: guide@rhpa.org. Website: www.guidemagazine.org. **Editor**: Randy Fishell. **Designer**: Brandon Reese. Weekly magazine. Estab. 1953. Circ. 32,000. "Ours is a weekly Christian journal written for middle readers and young teens (ages 10-14), presenting true stories relevant to the needs of today's young person, emphasizing positive aspects of Christian living."

Nonfiction: Middle readers, young adults/teens: adventure, animal, character-building, contemporary, games/puzzles, humorous, multicultural, problem-solving, religious. "We need true, or based on true, happenings, not merely true-to-life. Our stories and puzzles must have a spiritual emphasis." No violence. No articles. "We always need humor and adventure stories." Buys 150 mss/year. Average word length: 500-600 minimum, 1,200-1,300 maximum. Byline given.

How to Contact/Writers: Nonfiction: Send complete ms. Responds in 1 month. Will consider simultaneous submissions. "We can only pay half of the regular amount for simultaneous submissions." Responds to queries/mss in 6 weeks. Credit line given. "We encourage e-mail submissions."

Terms: Pays on acceptance. Buys first North American serial rights; first rights; one-time rights; second serial (reprint rights); simultaneous rights. Pays 6-12¢/word for stories and articles. "Writer receives several complimentary copies of issue in which work appears." Sample copy free with 6×9 SAE and 2 first-class stamps. Writer's guidelines for SASE.

Tips: "Children's magazines want mystery, action, discovery, suspense and humor—no matter what the topic. For us, truth is stronger than fiction."

⬛ GUIDEPOSTS FOR KIDS, 1050 Broadway, Suite 6, Chesterton IN 46304. Fax: (219)926-3839. E-mail: gp4k@guide posts.org. Website: www.gp4k.com. **Editor-in-Chief**: Mary Lou Carney. **Managing Editor**: Rosanne Tolin. **Art Director**: Mike Lyons. **Art Coordinator**: Rose Pomeroy. Electronic magazine. Estab. 1998. 95,000 plus unique visitors/month. "*Guideposts for Kids* online by Guideposts for kids 6-13 years old (emphasis on upper end of that age bracket). It is a value-centered, electronic magazine that is *fun* to visit. The site hosts a long list of interactive and editorial features including games, puzzles, how-tos, stories, poems, and facts and trivia.

• *Guideposts for Kids* is online only.

Fiction: Middle readers: adventure, animal, contemporary, fantasy, folktales, historical, humorous, multicultural, nature/environment, problem-solving, science fiction, sports, suspense/mystery. Multicultural needs include: Kids in other cultures—school, sports, families. Does not want to see preachy fiction. "We want real stories about real kids doing real things—conflicts our readers will respect; resolutions our readers will accept. Problematic. Tight. Filled with realistic dialogue and sharp imagery. No stories about 'good' children always making the right decision. If present at all, adults are minor characters and *do not* solve kids' problems for them." Buys approximately 25 mss/year. Average word length: 200-900. Byline given.

Nonfiction: Middle readers: animal, current events, games/puzzles, history, how-to, humorous, interview/profile, multicultural, nature/environment, problem-solving, profiles of kids, science, seasonal, social issues, sports. "Make nonfiction issue-oriented, controversial, thought-provoking. Something kids not only *need* to know but *want* to know as well." Buys 20 mss/year. Average word length: 200-1,300. Byline usually given.

How to Contact/Writers: Fiction: Send complete ms. Nonfiction: Query or send ms. Responds to queries/mss in 6 weeks.

Photography: Looks for "spontaneous, *real* kids in action shots."

Terms: Pays on acceptance. Buys electronic and nonexclusive print rights. "Features range in payment from $50-200; fiction from $75-250. We pay higher rates for stories exceptionally well-written or well-researched. Regular contributors get bigger bucks, too." Writer's guidelines free for SASE.

Tips: "Make your manuscript good, relevant and playful. No preachy stories about Bible-toting children. *Guideposts for Kids* is not a beginner's market. Study our e-zine magazine. (Sure, you've heard that before—but it's *necessary*!) Neatness *does* count. So do creativity and professionalism. SASE essential if sending a query by snail mail." (See listing for *Guideposts for Teens*.)

GUIDEPOSTS FOR TEENS, 1050 Broadway, Suite 6, Chesterton IN 46304. (219)929-4429. Fax: (219)926-3839. E-mail: gp4t@guideposts.org. Website: www.gp4teens.com. **Editor-in-Chief:** Mary Lou Carney. **Art Director:** Michael Lyons. **Art Coordinator:** Rose Pomeroy. Bimonthly magazine. Estab. 1998. "We are an inspirational magazine that offers teens advice, humor and true stories—lots of true stories. These first-person (ghostwritten) stories feature teen protagonists and are filled with action, adventure, overcoming adversity and growth—set against the backdrop of God at work in everyday life."

Nonfiction: Young adults: how-to, quizzes, celebrity interviews, true stories. Average word length: 300-2,000. Byline sometimes given.

How to Contact/Writers: Nonfiction: Query. Responds to queries/mss in 6 weeks. Will consider simultaneous submissions or electronic submission via disk or modem. Send SASE for writer's guidelines.

Illustration: Uses color artwork only. Works on assignment only. Reviews ms/illustration packages from artists. Query. Contact: Michael Lyons, art director. Illustrations only: Query with samples. Responds only if interested. Samples kept on file. Credit line given.

Photography: Buys photos separately. Wants location photography and stock; digital OK. Uses color prints and 35mm, $2\frac{1}{4} \times 2\frac{1}{4}$, 4×5 or 8×10 transparencies. Query with samples; provide web address. Responds only if interested.

Terms: Pays on acceptance. Buys all rights for mss. Buys one-time rights for artwork. Original artwork returned at job's completion. Pays $300-500 for true stories; $100-300 for articles. Additional payment for photos accompanying articles. Pays illustrators $125-1,500 for color inside (depends on size). Pays photographers by the project (range: $100-1,000). Sample copies for $4.50 from: Guideposts, 39 Seminary Hill Rd., Carmel NY 10512. Attn: Special Handling.

Tips: "Study our magazine! Language and subject matter should be current and teen-friendly. No preaching, please! (Your 'takeaway' should be inherent.) We are most in need of inspirational action/adventure, sports, and relationship stories. We also need short (250-word) true stories with a miracle/'aha' ending for our 'Soul Food' department. For illustrators: We get illustrators from two basic sources: submissions by mail and submissions by Internet. We also consult major illustrator reference books. We prefer color illustrations, 'on-the-edge' style. We accept art in almost any digital or reflective format."

HIGH ADVENTURE, Assemblies of God, 1445 N. Boonville Ave., Springfield MO 65802. (417)862-2781, Ext. 4177. Fax: (417)831-8230. E-mail: rangers@ag.org. Website: royalrangers.ag.org. **Editor:** Jerry Parks. Quarterly magazine. Circ. 86,000. Estab. 1971. Magazine is designed to provide boys ages 5-17—from kindergarten through high school age—with worthwhile, enjoyable, leisure reading; to challenge them in narrative form to higher ideals and greater spiritual dedication; and to perpetuate the spirit of Royal Rangers through stories, ideas and illustrations. 75% of material aimed at juvenile audience.

Fiction: Buys 100 mss/year; adventure, humorous, problem solving, religious, sports, travel. Maximum word length: 1,000. Byline given.

Nonfiction: Articles: Christian living, devotional, Holy Spirit, salvation, self-help, biography, missionary stories, news items, testimonies, inspirational stories based on true-life experiences; arts/crafts, games/puzzles, geography, health, hobbies, how-to, humorous, nature/environment, problem solving, sports, travel.

How to Contact/Writers: Fiction/nonfiction: Send complete ms. Responds to queries in 2 months. Will consider simultaneous submissions. Samples returned with SASE by request. Prefer hardcopy and media (3.5, Zip or Jaz).

Terms: Pays on publication. Buys first or all rights. Pays 6¢/word for articles ($30-35 for one page; 60-65 for two pages); $25-30 for cartoons; $15 for puzzles, $5 for jokes. Sample copy free with 9×12 SASE. Free writer's/illustrator's guidelines with SASE.

Tips: Obtain writer's guidelines. Articles are not subject to a theme-associated listing, but can be seasonal in nature or as described above.

HIGHLIGHTS FOR CHILDREN, 803 Church St., Honesdale PA 18431. (570)253-1080. E-mail: eds@highlights-corp.com. Website: www.highlights.com. **Contact:** Manuscript Coordinator. Editor: Christine French Clark. **Art Director:**

Janet Moir McCaffrey. Monthly magazine. Estab. 1946. Circ. 2.5 million. "Our motto is 'Fun With a Purpose.' We are looking for quality fiction and nonfiction that appeals to children, encourages them to read, and reinforces positive values. All art is done on assignment."

Fiction: Picture-oriented material, young readers, middle readers: adventure, animal, contemporary, fantasy, folktales, history, humorous, multicultural, problem-solving, sports. Multicultural needs include first person accounts of children from other cultures and first-person accounts of children from other countries. Does not want to see war, crime, violence. "We see too many stories with overt morals." Would like to see more contemporary, multicultural and world culture fiction, sports pieces, mystery stories, action/adventure stories, humorous stories, and fiction for younger readers. Buys 150 mss/year. Average word length: 400-800. Byline given.

Nonfiction: Picture-oriented material, young readers, middle readers: animal, arts/crafts, biography, careers, games/puzzles, geography, health, history, hobbies, how-to, interview/profile, multicultural, nature/environment, problem solving, science, sports. Multicultural needs include articles set in a country *about* the people of the country. Does not want to see trendy topics, fads, personalities who would not be good role models for children, guns, war, crime, violence. "We'd like to see more nonfiction for younger readers—maximum of 500 words. We still need older-reader material, too—500-800 words." Buys 200 mss/year. Maximum word length: 800. Byline given.

How to Contact/Writers: Send complete ms. Responds to queries in 1 month; mss in 6 weeks.

Illustration: Buys 25-30 illustrations/issue. Preferred theme or style: Realistic, some stylization. Works on assignment only. Reviews ms/illustration packages from artists. Illustrations only: photocopies, promo sheet, tearsheets, or slides. Résumé optional. Portfolio only if requested. Contact: Janet Moir McCaffrey, art director. Responds to art samples in 2 months. Samples returned with SASE; samples filed. Credit line given.

Terms: Pays on acceptance. Buys all rights for mss. Pays $50 and up for unsolicited articles. Pays illustrators $1,000 for color cover; $25-200 for b&w inside, $100-500 for color inside. Sample copies $3.95 and 9×11 SASE with 4 first-class stamps. Writer's/illustrator's guidelines free with SASE.

Tips: "Know the magazine's style before submitting. Send for guidelines and sample issue if necessary." Writers: "At *Highlights* we're paying closer attention to acquiring more nonfiction for young readers than we have in the past." Illustrators: "Fresh, imaginative work encouraged. Flexibility in working relationships a plus. Illustrators presenting their work need not confine themselves to just children's illustrations as long as work can translate to our needs. We also use animal illustrations, real and imaginary. We need crafts, puzzles and any activity that will stimulate children mentally and creatively. We are always looking for imaginative cover subjects. Know our publication's standards and content by reading sample issues, not just the guidelines. Avoid tired themes, or put a fresh twist on an old theme so that its style is fun and lively. We'd like to see stories with subtle messages, but the fun of the story should come first. Write what inspires you, not what you think the market needs."

☑ **HOPSCOTCH, The Magazine for Girls**, The Bluffton News Publishing and Printing Company, P.O. Box 164, Bluffton OH 45817-0164. (419)358-4610. Fax: (419)358-5027. Website: hopscotchmagazine.com. **Editor**: Marilyn Edwards. **Contact:** Diane Winebar, editorial assistant. Bimonthly magazine. Estab. 1989. Circ. 14,000. For girls from ages 6-12, featuring traditional subjects—pets, games, hobbies, nature, science, sports, etc.—with an emphasis on articles that show girls actively involved in unusual and/or worthwhile activities."

Fiction: Picture-oriented material, young readers, middle readers: adventure, animal, history, humorous, nature/environment, sports, suspense/mystery. Does not want to see stories dealing with dating, sex, fashion, hard rock music. Buys 30 mss/year. Average word length: 300-700. Byline given.

Nonfiction: Picture-oriented material, young readers, middle readers: animal, arts/crafts, biography, cooking, games/puzzles, geography, hobbies, how-to, humorous, math, nature/environment, science. Does not want to see pieces dealing with dating, sex, fashion, hard rock music. "Need more nonfiction with quality photos about a *Hopscotch*-age girl involved in a worthwhile activity." Buys 46 mss/year. Average word length: 400-700. Byline given.

Poetry: Reviews traditional, wholesome, humorous poems. Maximum word length: 300; maximum line length: 20. Will accept 6 submissions/author.

How to Contact/Writers: All writers should consult the theme list before sending in articles. To receive a current theme list, send a SASE. Fiction: Send complete ms. Nonfiction: Query or send complete ms. Responds to queries in 2 weeks; mss in 5 weeks. Will consider simultaneous submissions.

Illustration: Buys approximately 10 illustrations/issue; buys 60-70 articles/year. "Generally, the illustrations are assigned after we have purchased a piece (usually fiction). Occasionally, we will use a painting—in any given medium—for the cover, and these are usually seasonal." Uses b&w artwork only for inside; color for cover. Reviews ms/illustration packages from artists. Query first or send complete ms with final art. Illustrations only: Send résumé, portfolio, client list and tearsheets. Responds to art samples only if interested and SASE in 1 month. Samples returned with SASE. Credit line given.

Photography: Purchases photos separately (cover only) and with accompanying ms only. Looking for photos to accompany article. Model/property releases required. Uses 5×7, b&w prints; 35mm transparencies. Black & white photos should go with ms. Should show girl or girls ages 6-12.

Terms: For mss: pays on publication. For mss, artwork and photos, buys first North American serial rights; second serial (reprint rights). Original artwork returned at job's completion. Pays 5¢/word and $5-10/photo. "We always send a copy of the issue to the writer or illustrator." Text and art are treated separately. Pays $200 maximum for color cover; $25-35 for b&w inside. Sample copy for $4 and 8×12 SASE. Writer's/illustrator's/photo guidelines free for #10 SASE.

Tips: "Remember we publish only six issues a year, which means our editorial needs are extremely limited. Please look at our guidelines and our magazine . . . and remember, we use far more nonfiction than fiction. If decent photos accompany the piece, it stands an even better chance of being accepted. We believe it is the responsibility of the contributor to come up with photos. Please remember, our readers are 6-12 years—most are 7-10—and your text should reflect that. Many magazines try to entertain first and educate second. We try to do the reverse of that. Our magazine is more simplistic, like a book to be read from cover to cover. We are looking for wholesome, non-dated material." (See listing for *Boys' Quest*.)

HORSEPOWER, Magazine for Young Horse Lovers, Horse Publications Group, P.O. Box 670, Aurora ON L4G 4J9 Canada. (800)505-7428. Fax: (905)841-1530. E-mail: info@horse-canada.com. Website: www.horse-canada.com. **Editor:** Susan Stafford. Bimonthly magazine. Estab. 1988. Circ. 17,000. "*Horsepower* offers how-to articles and stories relating to horse care for kids ages 6-16, with a focus on safety."

Fiction: Middle readers, young adults: adventure, health, history, humorous, problem-solving sports. Buys 6-10 mss/year. Average word length: 500-1,000.

Nonfiction: Middle readers, young adults: arts/crafts, biography, careers, fashion, games/puzzles, health, history, hobbies, how-to, humorous, interview/profile, problem-solving, travel. Buys 6-10 mss/year. Average word length: 500-1,200. Byline given.

How to Contact/Writers: Fiction: query. Nonfiction: send complete ms. Responds to queries in 6 months; mss in 3 months. Publishes ms 6 months after acceptance. Will consider simultaneous submissions, electronic submission via disk or modem, previously published work.

Illustration: Buys 3 illustrations/year. Reviews ms/illustration packages from artists. Contact: Editor. Query with samples. Responds only if interested. Samples returned with SASE; samples kept on file. Credit line given.

Photography: Look for photos of kids and horses, instructional/educational, relating to riding or horse care. Uses b&w and color 4×6, 5×7, matte or glossy prints. Query with samples. Responds only if interested.

Terms: Pays on publication. Buys one-time rights for mss. Original artwork returned at job's completion if SASE provided. Pays $50-75 for stories. Additional payment for ms/illustration packages and for photos accompanying articles. Pays illustrators $25-50 for color inside. Pays photographers per photo (range: $10-15). Sample copies for $1. Writer's/illustrator's/photo guidelines for SASE.

Tips: "Articles must be easy to understand, yet detailed and accurate. How-to or other educational features must be written by, or in conjunction with, a riding/teaching professional. Fiction is not encouraged, unless it is outstanding and teaches a moral or practical lesson."

HULLABALOO, 954 Gayley Ave., Los Angeles CA 90024. (310)824-6566. E-mail: editor@hullabaloomagazine.com. Website: www.hullabaloomagazine.com. **Articles Editor:** Deidre Cutter. Bimonthly magazine. Estab. 2002. "*Hullabaloo* is a children's magazine featuring a different country with each issue. Through storytelling, fun facts, children's interviews and more, the reader explores the world from a child's perspective." 100% of publication aimed at juvenile market.

● See *Hullabaloo*'s website for a list of upcoming countries to be covered in the magazine. These include France, India, Finland, Egypt, Australia, China, and Brazil.

Fiction: Young readers: folktale. Middle readers: adventure, animal, contemporary, folktale, history, humorous, multicultural. Buys 18-24 mss/year. Average word length: 800-1,500. Byline given.

Nonfiction: Young readers: animal, arts/crafts, games/puzzles, math, travel. Middle readers: arts/crafts, biography, games/puzzles, geography, humorous, interview/profile, math, multicultural, science, travel. Buys up to 60 mss/year. Average word length: 400-750 or 50-200. Byline given.

Poetry: Accepts country-specific poems in style of country (ex: haiku) or regarding specific country. Maximum length: 16 lines.

How to Contact/Writers: Fiction: send complete ms. Nonfiction: query with published clips or send complete ms. Responds to queries in 3 weeks; mss in 6 weeks. Publishes ms 6 months after acceptance. Will consider simultaneous submissions, electronic submission via disk or previously published work.

Illustration: Buys 20 illustrations/issue; 120 illustrations/year. Works on assignment only. Reviews ms/illustration packages from artists. Send ms with dummy. Illustrations only: Query with samples; send tearsheets. Responds only if interested. Samples returned with SASE; samples kept on file. Credit line given.

Photography: Looking for country-specific photos of people, important places and landmarks, celebrations and festivals, daily life. Model/property release required. Uses color or b&w prints; 300 dpi digital photos; slides. Query with samples; send unsolicited photos by mail; provide résumé, promotional literature or tearsheets. Responds in 1 month if interested.

Terms: Pays on publication. Buys first North American serial rights. Buys first rights or reprint rights and promotional rights (for both). Original artwork returned at job's completion. Pays 20¢/word minimum for stories; 15¢/word minimum for articles. Additional payment for ms/illustration packages and for photos accompanying articles. Pays illustrators $300 and up for color cover; $25 and up for b&w, $75 and up for for color inside. Pays photographers per photo (range: $5 and up). Sample copies for $6. Writer's/illustrator's/photo guidelines for SASE.

Tips: "Know the magazine's style before submitting. All submissions should be specific to an upcoming country (see website or submission guidelines for list). We include many styles in the magazine—shorter nonfiction articles (50-200 words) are conversational 'sound-bytes' of interesting information for kids."

HUMPTY DUMPTY'S MAGAZINE, Children's Better Health Institute, 1100 Waterway Blvd., P.O. Box 567, Indianapolis IN 46206. (317)636-8881. Fax: (317)684-8094. Website: www.humptydumptymag.org. **Editor:** Phyllis Lybarger. **Art Director:** Rob Falco. Magazine published 6 times/year. *HDM* is edited for children ages 4-6. It includes fiction (easy-to-reads; read alouds; rhyming stories; rebus stories), nonfiction articles (some with photo illustrations), poems, crafts, recipes, and puzzles. Content encourages development of better health habits.

● *Humpty Dumpty's Magazine* is not currently accepting unsolicited manuscripts. *Humpty Dumpty's* publishes material promoting health and fitness with emphasis on simple activities, poems and fiction.

Fiction: Picture-oriented stories: adventure, animal, contemporary, fantasy, folktales, health, humorous, multicultural, nature/environment, problem-solving, science fiction, sports. Also, talking inanimate objects are very difficult to do well. Beginners (and maybe everyone) should avoid these." Buys 8-10 mss/year. Maximum word length: 300. Byline given.

Nonfiction: Picture-oriented articles: animal, arts/crafts, concept, games/puzzles, health, how-to, humorous, nature/environment, no-cook recipes, science, social issues, sports. Buys 6-10 mss/year. Prefers very short nonfiction pieces—200 words maximum. Byline given. Send ms with SASE if you want ms returned.

How to Contact/Writers: Send complete ms. Nonfiction: Send complete ms with bibliography if applicable. "No queries, please!" Responds to mss in 3 months. Send seasonal material at least 8 months in advance.

Illustration: Buys 5-8 illustrations/issue; 30-48 illustrations/year. Preferred theme or style: Realistic or cartoon. Works on assignment only. Illustrations only. Query with slides, printed pieces or photocopies. Samples are not returned; samples filed. Responds to art samples only if interested. Credit line given.

Terms: Writers: Pays on publication. Artists: Pays within 2 months. Buys all rights. "One-time book rights may be returned if author can provide name of interested book publisher and tentative date of publication." Pays up to 22¢/word for stories/articles; payment varies for poems and activities. 10 complimentary issues are provided to author with check. Pays $275 for color cover illustration; $35-90 per page b&w inside; $70-155 for color inside. Sample copies for $1.75. Writer's/illustrator's guidelines free with SASE.

☑ **I.D.**, Cook Communications Ministries, 4050 Lee Vance View, Colorado Springs CO 80918-7102. (719)536-0100. Fax: (719)536-3296. Website: www.cookministries.org. **Editor:** Gail Rohlfing. **Design Manager:** Paul Segsworgh. **Designer**: Kelly Robinson. Weekly magazine. Estab. 1991. Circ. 100,000. "*I.D.* is a class-and-home paper for senior high Sunday school students. Stories relate to Bible study."

Fiction: Young adults: religious.

How to Contact/Writers: Currently not accepting new submissions.

Illustrations: Buys 5 illustrations/year. Uses b&w and color artwork. Illustrations only: Query. Works on assignment only. Responds in 6 months. Samples returned with SASE.

Terms: Pays on acceptance. Pays $50-300 for stories and articles.

INSIGHT, Teens Meeting Christ, 55 W. Oak Ridge Dr., Hagerstown MD 21740. (301)393-4038. Fax: (301)393-4055. E-mail: insight@rhpa.org. Website: www.insightmagazine.org. **Contact:** Dwain Nielson Esmond. Weekly magazine. Estab. 1970. Circ. 20,000. "Our readers crave true stories written by teens or written about teens that convey a strong spiritual point or portray a spiritual truth." 100% of publication aimed at teen and college-age market.

Nonfiction: Young adults: animal, biography, fashion, health, humorous, interview/profile, multicultural, nature/environment, problem-solving, social issues, sports, travel: first-person accounts preferred. Buys 200 mss/year. Average word length: 500-1,500. Byline given.

Poetry: Reviews poetry. Publishes poems written by teens. Maximum length: 250-500 words.

How to Contact/Writers: Nonfiction: Send complete ms. Responds to queries in 2 months. Publishes ms 6-12 months after acceptance. Will consider simultaneous submissions, electronic submission via disk or modem, previously published work.

Illustration: Works on assignment only. Reviews ms/illustration packages from artists. Query. Illustrations only: Query with samples. Samples kept on file. Credit line given.

Photography: Looking for photos that will catch a young person's eye with unique elements such as juxtaposition. Model/property release required; captions not required but helpful. Uses color prints and 35mm, 2¼×2¼, 4×5, 8×10 transparencies. Query with samples; provide business card, promotional literature or tearsheets to be kept on file. Responds only if interested.

Terms: Pays on publication. Buys first North American serial rights for mss. Buys one-time rights for artwork and photos. Original artwork returned at job's completion. Pays $10-100 for stories/articles. Pays illustrators $100-300 for b&w (cover), color cover, b&w (inside), or color inside. Pays photographers by the project. Sample copies for 9×14 SAE and 4 first-class stamps.

Tips: "Do your best to make your work look 'hip,' 'cool,' appealing to young people."

INTEEN, Urban Ministries, Inc., 1551 Regency Ct., Calumet City IL 60409. (708)868-7100, ext. 239. Fax: (708)868-7105. E-mail: kawashington@urbanministries.com. **Editor:** Katara A. Washington. **Art Acquisitions:** Carla Branch. Quarterly magazine. Estab. 1970. "We publish Sunday school lessons for urban teens and features for the same group."

● Contact *Inteen* for guidelines. They work on assignment only—do not submit work.

Nonfiction: Young adults/teens: careers, games/puzzles, how-to, interview/profile, religion. "We make 40 assignments/year."

Terms: Pays $75-150 for stories.

JACK AND JILL, Children's Better Health Institute, 1100 Waterway Blvd., P.O. Box 567, Indianapolis IN 46206. (317)636-8881. Website: www.jackandjillmag.org. **Editor**: Daniel Lee. **Art Director**: Jennifer Webber. Magazine published 6 times/year. Estab. 1938. Circ. 360,000. "Write entertaining and imaginative stories *for* kids, not just *about* them. Writers should understand what is funny to kids, what's important to them, what excites them. Don't write from an adult 'kids are so cute' perspective. We're also looking for health and healthful lifestyle stories and articles, but don't be preachy."

Fiction: Young readers and middle readers: adventure, contemporary, folktales, health, history, humorous, nature, sports. Buys 30-35 mss/year. Average word length: 700. Byline given.

Nonfiction: Young readers, middle readers: animal, arts/crafts, cooking, games/puzzles, history, hobbies, how-to, humorous, interview/profile, nature, science, sports. Buys 8-10 mss/year. Average word length: 500. Byline given.

Poetry: Reviews poetry.

How to Contact/Writers: Fiction/nonfiction: Send complete ms. Responds to mss in 3 months. Guidelines by request with a #10 SASE.

Illustration: Buys 15 illustrations/issue; 90 illustrations/year. Responds only if interested. Samples not returned; samples filed. Credit line given.

Terms: Pays on publication; minimum 17¢/word. Pays illustrators $275 for color cover; $35-90 for b&w, $70-155 for color inside. Pays photographers negotiated rate. Sample copies $1.25. Buys all rights.

Tips: See listings for *Child Life*, *Children's Digest*, *Children's Playmate*, *Humpty Dumpty's Magazine*, *Turtle Magazine* and *U*S* Kids*. Publishes writing/art/photos by children.

THE KIDS HALL OF FAME NEWS, The Kids Hall of Fame, 3 Ibsen Court, Dix Hills NY 11746. (631)242-9105. Fax: (631)242-8101. E-mail: VictoriaNesnick@TheKidsHallofFame.com. Website: www.TheKidsHallofFame.com. **Publisher:** Victoria Nesnick. **Art/Photo Editor:** Amy Gilvary. Quarterly magazine. Estab. 1998. "We spotlight and archive extraordinary positive achievements of contemporary and historical kids internationally under age 20. Their inspirational stories are meant to provide positive peer role models and empower kids to say, 'If that kid can do it, so can I,' or 'I can do better.' Our magazine is the prelude to The Kids Hall of Fame set of books (one volume per year) and museum."

How to Contact/Writers: Query with published clips or send complete mss with SASE for response. Go to website for nomination form for The Kids Hall of Fame.

Tips: "Nomination stories must be positive and inspirational. See sample stories and nomination form on our website. Request writers' guidelines and list of suggested nominees. Evening telephone queries acceptable."

N KIDZ CHAT, Standard Publishing, 8121 Hamilton Ave., Cincinnati OH 45231. (513)931-4050. Website: www.standardpub.com/writers_guidelines.html. **Editor:** Elaina Meyers. Weekly magazine. Circ. 55,000.

  • *Kidz Chat®* has decided to reuse much of the material that was a part of the first publication cycle. They will not be sending out theme lists, sample copies or writers guidelines or accepting any unsolicited material because of this policy. See listing for *Live Wire*.

LADYBUG, The Magazine for Young Children, Carus Publishing Company, P.O. Box 300, Peru IL 61354. (815)224-5803 ext. 656. **Editor:** Paula Morrow. **Art Director:** Suzanne Beck. Monthly magazine. Estab. 1990. Circ. 130,000. Literary magazine for children 2-6, with stories, poems, activities, songs and picture stories.

Fiction: Picture-oriented material: adventure, animal, fantasy, folktales, humorous, multicultural, nature/environment, problem-solving, science fiction, sports, suspense/mystery. "Open to any easy fiction stories." Buys 50 mss/year. Average word length 300-850 words. Byline given.

Nonfiction: Picture-oriented material: activities, animal, arts/crafts, concept, cooking, humorous, math, nature/environment, problem-solving, science. Buys 35 mss/year.

Poetry: Reviews poems, 20-line maximum length; limit submissions to 5 poems. Uses lyrical, humorous, simple language.

How to Contact/Writers: Fiction/nonfiction: Send complete ms. Queries not accepted. Responds to mss in 3 months. Publishes ms up to 2 years after acceptance. Will consider simultaneous submissions if informed. Submissions without SASE will be discarded.

Illustration: Buys 12 illustrations/issue; 145 illustrations/year. Prefers "bright colors; all media, but use watercolor and acrylics most often; same size as magazine is preferred but not required." To be considered for future assignments: Submit promo sheet, slides, tearsheets, color and b&w photocopies. Responds to art samples in 3 months. Submissions without SASE will be discarded.

Terms: Pays on publication for mss; after delivery of completed assignment for illustrators. Rights purchased vary. Original artwork returned at job's completion. Pays 25¢/word for prose; $3/line for poetry. Pays $750 for color (cover) illustration, $50-100 for b&w (inside) illustration, $250/page for color (inside). Sample copy for $5. Writer's/illustrator's guidelines free for SASE.

Tips: Writers: "Get to know several young children on an individual basis. Respect your audience. We want less cute, condescending or 'preachy-teachy' material. Less gratuitous anthropomorphism. More rich, evocative language, sense of joy or wonder. Keep in mind that people come in all colors, sizes, physical conditions. Be inclusive in creating characters. Set your manuscript aside for at least a month, then reread critically." Illustrators: "Include examples, where possible, of children, animals, and—most important—action and narrative (i.e., several scenes from a story, showing continuity and an ability to maintain interest)." (See listings for *Babybug*, *Cicada*, *Cricket*, *Muse* and *Spider*.)

N THE LAMP-POST of the Southern California CS Lewis Society, 1106 W. 16th St., Santa Ana CA 92706. E-mail: dgclark@adelphia.net. **Articles Editor:** David G. Clark. **Art Director:** James Prothero. Quarterly magazine. Estab. 1986. "Main focus is upon C.S. Lewis and his circle of influence." 5% of publication aimed at juvenile market.

Fiction: Young adults: adventure, fantasy, religious. Average word length: 4,500 maximum.

Nonfiction: Young adults: religion.

Poetry: Reviews religion. Maximum length: 25-30 lines. Limit submissions to 4 or 5 poems (if short).

How to Contact/Writers: Fiction/Nonfiction: send complete ms via e-mail. Responds to queries/mss in 1 week. Publishes ms 1 year after acceptance. Will consider electronic submission via disk or modem.

Terms: Can't pay for work.

LISTEN, Drug-Free Possibilities for Teens, The Health Connection, 55 West Oak Ridge Dr., Hagerstown MD 21740. (301)393-4019. Fax: (301)393-3294. E-mail: listen@healthconnection.org. **Editor:** Anita Jacobs. Monthly magazine, 9 issues. Estab. 1948. Circ. 50,000. "*Listen* offers positive alternatives to drug use for its teenage readers. Helps them have a happy and productive life by making the right choices."

Fiction: Young adults: health, humorous, problem-solving peer pressure. Buys 50 mss/year. Average word length: 1,000. Byline given.

Nonfiction: Young adults: biography, games/puzzles, hobbies, how-to, health, humorous, problem solving, social issues, drug-free living. Wants to see more factual articles on drug abuse. Buys 50 mss/year. Average word length: 1,000. Byline given.

How to Contact/Writers: Fiction/nonfiction: Query. Responds to queries in 6 weeks; mss in 2 months. Will consider simultaneous submissions, e-mail and previously published work.

Illustration: Buys 8-10 illustrations/issue; 72 illustrators/year. Reviews ms/illustration packages from artists. Manuscript/illustration packages and illustration only: Query. Contact: Doug Bendall, designer. Responds only if interested. Originals returned at job's completion. Samples returned with SASE. Credit line given.

Photography: Purchases photos from freelancers. Photos purchased with accompanying ms only. Uses color and b&w photos; 35mm, 2¼×2¼. Query with samples. Looks for "youth oriented—action (sports, outdoors), personality photos."

Terms: Pays on acceptance. Buys exclusive magazine rights for mss. Buys one-time rights for artwork and photographs. Pays $50-200 for stories/articles. Pays illustrators $500 for color cover; $75-225 for b&w inside; $135-450 for color inside. Pays photographers by the project (range: $125-500); pays per photo (range: $125-500). Additional payment for ms/illustration packages and photos accompanying articles. Sample copy for $2 and 9×12 SASE and 2 first class stamps. Writer's guidelines free with SASE.

Tips: "*Listen* is a magazine for teenagers. It encourages development of good habits and high ideals of physical, social and mental health. It bases its editorial philosophy of primary drug prevention on total abstinence from tobacco, alcohol, and other drugs. Because it is used extensively in public high school classes, it does not accept articles and stories with overt religious emphasis. Four specific purposes guide the editors in selecting materials for *Listen*: (1) To portray a positive lifestyle and to foster skills and values that will help teenagers deal with contemporary problems, including smoking, drinking, and using drugs. This is *Listen*'s primary purpose. (2) To offer positive alternatives to a lifestyle of drug use of any kind. (3) To present scientifically accurate information about the nature and effects of tobacco, alcohol, and other drugs. (4) To report medical research, community programs, and educational efforts which are solving problems connected with smoking, alcohol, and other drugs. Articles should offer their readers activities that increase one's sense of self-worth through achievement and/or involvement in helping others. They are often categorized by three kinds of focus: (1) Hobbies. (2) Recreation. (3) Community Service."

N LIVE WIRE, Standard Publishing Co., 8121 Hamilton Ave., Cincinnati OH 45231. (513)931-4050. Fax: (513)931-0950. Website: www.standardpub.com. **Editor:** Elaine Meyers. Newspaper published quarterly in weekly parts. Estab. 1997. Circ. 40,000. "*Live Wire* is a weekly publication geared to preteens (10-12 year olds). 'who want to connect to Christ.' Articles are in a news brief format that feature current events and profiles. We publish true stories about kids, puzzles, activities, interviews."

- *Live Wire* has decided to reuse much of the material that was a part of the first publication cycle. They will not be sending out theme lists, sample copies or writers guidelines or accepting any unsolicited material because of this policy.

THE MAGAZINE OF FANTASY & SCIENCE FICTION, Spilogale, Inc., P.O. Box 3447, Hoboken NJ 07030. Phone/fax: (201)876-2551. E-mail: FandSF@aol.com. Website: www.fsfmag.com. **Articles/Fiction Editor:** Gordon Van Gelder. Estab. 1949. Circ. 50,000. "We are one of the longest-running magazines devoted to fantasy and science fiction."

Fiction: Young adults: fantasy, science fiction. "We have no formula for fiction. We are looking for stories that will appeal to science fiction and fantasy readers. The SF element may be slight, but it should be present. We prefer character-oriented stories. We receive a lot of fantasy fiction, but never enough science fiction or humor." Buys 80-120 mss/year. Average word length: 25,000 maximum. Byline given.

Nonfiction: Buys 0-1 ms/year. Byline given.

How to Contact/Writers: Fiction: Send complete ms. Responds to mss in up to 2 months. Publishes ms 9 months after acceptance. Will consider previously published work.

Illustration: Buys 1 illustration/issue; 11 illustrations/year. Uses color artwork only. Works on assignment only. Responds only if interested.

Terms: Pays on acceptance. Buys first North American serial rights. Original artwork returned at job's completion. Pays 5-8¢/word. Sample copies for $5. Writer's guidelines for SASE.

Tips: "We are not aimed primarily at young readers, but we value our young readers and we have published many works that have become classics for youngsters (such as Daniel Keyes's 'Flowers for Algernon' and 'The Brave Little Toaster', by Thomas M. Disch). Read a sample issue before submitting."

MUSE, Carus Publishing, 332 S. Michigan Ave, Suite 1100, Chicago IL 60604. (312)939-1500. Fax: (312)939-8150. E-mail: muse@caruspub.com. Website: www.cricketmag.com **Editor:** Diana Lutz. **Art Director:** Karen Kohn. **Photo Editor:** Carol Parden. Estab. 1996. Circ. 65,000. "The goal of *Muse* is to give as many children as possible access to the most important ideas and concepts underlying the principal areas of human knowledge. It will take children seriously as developing intellects by assuming that, if explained clearly, the ideas and concepts of an article will be of interest to them. Articles should meet the highest possible standards of clarity and transparency aided, wherever possible, by a tone of skepticism, humor, and irreverence."

- *Muse* is not accepting unsolicited mss or queries.

Nonfiction: Middle readers, young adult: animal, biography, history, interview/profile, math, multicultural, nature/environment, problem-solving, science, social issues.

Illustration: Buys 6 illustrations/issue; 40 illustrations/year. Uses color artwork only. Works on assignment only. Reviews ms/illustration packages. Send ms with dummy. Illustrations only: Query with samples. Send résumé, promo sheet and tearsheets. Responds only if interested. Samples returned with SASE. Credit line given.

Photography: Needs vary. Query with samples to photo editor.

Terms: Pays within 60 days of acceptance. Buys first publications rights; all rights for feature articles. Pays 50¢/word for assigned articles; 25¢/word for unsolicited manuscripts. Writer's guidelines and sample copy available for $5.

Tips: "*Muse* may on occasion publish unsolicited manuscripts, but the easiest way to be printed in *Muse* is to send a query. However, manuscripts may be submitted to the Cricket Magazine Group for review, and any that are considered suitable for *Muse* will be forwarded. Such manuscripts will also be considered for publication in *Cricket*, *Spider* or *Ladybug*." (See listings for *ASK*, *Babybug*, *Cricket*, *Ladybug* and *Spider*.)

MY FRIEND, The Catholic Magazine for Kids, Pauline Books & Media, 50 Saint Pauls Ave., Jamaica Plain, Boston MA 02130-3491. (617)522-8911. Fax: (617)541-9805. E-mail: myfriend@pauline.org. Website: www.myfriendmagazine.com. **Editor:** Sr. Maria Grace Dateno, FSP. **Art Director:** Sister Helen Lane, FSP. Monthly magazine. Estab. 1979. Circ. 12,000. "*My Friend* is a 32-page monthly Catholic magazine for boys and girls. Its goal is to communicate religious truths and positive values in an enjoyable and attractive way. Its pages are packed with fun, learning, new experiences, information, crafts, global awareness, friendships and inspiration. Together with its web page, *My Friend* provides kids and their families a wealth of information and contacts on every aspect of the Faith."

Fiction: Young readers, middle readers: adventure, Christmas, contemporary, humorous, multicultural, nature/environment, problem-solving, religious, sports. Buys 30 mss/year. Average word length: 750-1,100. Byline given.

Nonfiction: Young readers, middle readers: humorous, interview/profile, media literacy, problem-solving, religious, multicultural, social issues. Does not want to see material that is not compatible with Catholic values; no "New Age" material. Staff writes doctrinal articles and prepares puzzles. Buys 10 mss/year. Average word length: 450-750. Byline given.

How to Contact/Writers: Fiction/nonfiction: Send complete ms. Responds to queries/mss in 2 months.

Terms: Pays on acceptance for mss. Buys first rights for mss; variable for artwork. Original artwork returned at job's completion. Pays $80-150 for stories/articles. Sample copy $2 with 9 × 12 SAE and 4 first-class stamps. Writer's guidelines and theme list free with SASE.

Tips: Writers: "We are looking for stories that immediately grab the imagination of the reader. Good dialogue, realistic character development, and current lingo are necessary. Not all the stories of each issue have to be directly related to the theme. We continue to need stories that are simply fun and humorous. We also appreciate an underlying awareness of current events and current global tensions. Ever since September 11, kids are very sensitive to such realities."

NATIONAL GEOGRAPHIC KIDS, National Geographic Society, 1145 17th St. NW, Washington DC 20036-4688. (202)857-7000. Fax: (202)775-6112. Website: www.nationalgeographic.com/ngkids. **Editor:** Melina Bellows. **Art Director**: Jonathan Halling. **Photo Director**: Jay Sumner. Monthly magazine. Estab. 1975. Circ. 900,000.

NATURE FRIEND MAGAZINE, 2673 Twp. Rd., Sugarcreek OH 44681. (330)852-1900. Fax: (330)852-3285. **Articles Editor:** Marvin Wengerd. Monthly magazine. Estab. 1983. Circ. 10,000.

Fiction: Picture-oriented material, conversational, no talking animal stories.

Nonfiction: Picture-oriented material, animal, how-to, nature. No talking animal stories. No evolutionary material. Buys 50 mss/year. Average word length: 500. Byline given.

How to Contact/Writers: Nonfiction: Send complete ms. Responds to mss in 4 months. Will consider but must note simultaneous submissions.

Illustration: Buys approximately 8 illustrations/issue from freelancers; 96 illustrations/year. Responds to artist's submissions in 1 month. Works on assignment only. Credit line given.

Photography: Pays $75 for front cover, $50 for back cover, $75 for centerfold, $15-30 for text photos. Submit slides, transparencies or CD with color printout. Photo guidelines free with SASE.

Terms: Pays on publication. Buys one-time rights. Pays $15 minimum. Payment for illustrations: $15-80/b&w, $50-100/color inside. Two sample copies and writer's guidelines for $5 with 9 × 12 SAE and $2 postage.

Tips: Looks for "main articles, puzzles and simple nature and science projects. Needs conversationally-written stories about unique animals or nature phenomena. Please examine samples and writer's guide before submitting." Current needs: science and nature experiments for ages 8-12.

☑ NEW MOON: The Magazine For Girls & Their Dreams, New Moon Publishing, Inc., 34 E. Superior St., #200, Duluth MN 55803-3620. (218)728-5507. Fax: (218)728-0314. E-mail: girl@newmoon.org. Website: www.newmoon.org. **Managing Editor:** Julie Hoffer. Bimonthly magazine. Estab. 1992. Circ. 25,000. "*New Moon* is for every girl who wants her voice heard and her dreams taken seriously. *New Moon* portrays strong female role models of all ages, backgrounds and cultures now and in the past."

Fiction: Middle readers, young adults: adventure, animal, contemporary, fantasy, folktales, history, humorous, multicultural, nature/environment, problem-solving, religious, science fiction, sports, suspense/mystery, travel. Buys 3 mss/year from adults and 3 mss/year from girls. Average word length: 900-1,200. Byline given.

Nonfiction: Middle readers, young adults: animal, arts/crafts, biography, careers, cooking, games/puzzles, health, history, hobbies, humorous, interview/profile, math, multicultural, nature/environment, problem-solving, science, social issues, sports, travel, stories about real girls. Does not want to see how-to stories. Wants more stories about real girls doing real things written by girls. Buys 6-12 adult-written mss/year. 30 girl-written mss/year. Average word length: 600. Byline given.

How to Contact/Writers: Fiction/Nonfiction: Does not return or acknowledge unsolicited mss. Send only copies. Responds only if interested. Will consider simultaneous submissions and electronic submission e-mail.

Illustration: Buys 6-12 illustrations/year from freelancers. *New Moon* seeks 4-color cover illustrations as well as b&w illustrations for inside. Reviews ms/illustrations packages from artists. Query. Submit ms with rough sketches. Illustration only: Query; send portfolio and tearsheets. Samples not returned; samples filed. Responds in 6 months only if interested. Credit line given.

Terms: Pays on publication. Buys all rights for mss. Buys one-time rights, reprint rights, for artwork. Original artwork returned at job's completion. Pays 6-12¢/word for stories; 6-12¢/word for articles. Pays in contributor's copies. Pays illustrators $400 for color cover; $50-300 for b&w inside. Sample copies for $6.50. Writer's/cover art guidelines for SASE or available on website.

Tips: "Please refer to a copy of *New Moon* to understand the style and philosophy of the magazine. Writers and artists who understand our goals have the best chance of publication. We're looking for stories about real girls; women's careers, and historical profiles. We publish girl's and women's writing only." Publishes writing/art/photos by girls.

ODYSSEY, Adventures in Science, Cobblestone Publishing Company, 30 Grove St., Suite C, Peterborough NH 03458. (603)924-7209. Fax: (603)924-7380. E-mail: odyssey@cobblestonepub.com. Website: www.odysseymagazine.com. (Also see www.cobblestonepub.com.) **Editor:** Elizabeth E. Lindstrom. **Managing Editor:** Lou Waryncia. **Art Director**: Ann Dillon. Magazine published 9 times/year. Estab. 1979. Circ. 22,000. Magazine covers earth, general science and technology, astronomy and space exploration for children ages 10-16. All material must relate to the theme of a specific upcoming issue in order to be considered.

- *Odyssey* themes for 2004 include Court Room Science, The Coming Storm, Secret Agents: Understanding Bioterrorism, Future Power!, Weighing In, Wired, Wired World, Language of Cells, Mr. Feynman, Extreme Science.

Fiction: Middle readers and young adults/teens: science fiction, science, astronomy. Does not want to see anything not theme-related. Average word length: 900-1,200 words.

Nonfiction: Middle readers and young adults/teens: interiors, activities. Don't send anything not theme-related. Average word length: 750-1,200, depending on section article is used in.

How to Contact/Writers: "A query must consist of all of the following to be considered (please use nonerasable paper): a brief cover letter stating the subject and word length of the proposed article; a detailed one-page outline explaining the information to be presented in the article; an extensive bibliography of materials the author intends to use in preparing the article; a SASE. Writers new to *Odyssey* should send a writing sample with query. If you would like to know if your query has been received, please also include a stamped postcard that requests acknowledgment of receipt. In all correspondence, please include your complete address as well as a telephone number and e-mail address where you can be reached. A writer may send as many queries for one issue as he or she wishes, but each query must have a separate cover letter, outline, bibliography, and SASE. Telephone queries are not accepted. Handwritten queries will not be considered. Queries may be submitted at any time, but queries sent well in advance of deadline *may not be answered for several months.* Go-aheads requesting material proposed in queries are usually sent four months prior to publication date. Unused queries will be returned approximately three to four months prior to publication date."

Illustration: Buys 3 illustrations/issue; 27 illustrations/year. Works on assignment only. Reviews ms/illustration packages from artists. Query. Contact: Beth Lindstrom, editor. Illustration only: Query with samples. Send tearsheets, photocopies. Responds in 2 weeks. Samples returned with SASE; samples not filed. Original artwork returned upon job's completion (upon written request).

Photography: Wants photos pertaining to any of our forthcoming themes. Uses b&w and color prints; 35mm transparencies. Photographers should send unsolicited photos by mail on speculation.

Terms: Pays on publication. Buys all rights for mss and artwork. Pays 20-25¢/word for stories/articles. Covers are assigned and paid on an individual basis. Pays photographers per photo ($15-100 for b&w; $25-100 for color). Sample copy for $4.95 and SASE with $2 postage. Writer's/illustrator's/photo guidelines for SASE. (See listings for *AppleSeeds, Calliope, Cobblestone, Dig, Faces* and *Footsteps*.)

ON COURSE, A Magazine for Teens, General Council of the Assemblies of God, 1445 Boonville Ave., Springfield MO 65802-1894. (417)862-2781. Fax: (417)862-1693. E-mail: oncourse@ag.org. **Editor:** Amber Weigand-Buckley. **Art Director:** Jeff Fulton. Quarterly magazine. Estab. 1991. Circ. 180,000. *On Course* is a magazine to empower students to grow in a real-life relationship with Christ.

Fiction: Young adults: Christian discipleship, contemporary, humorous, multicultural, problem-solving, sports. Average word length: 1,000. Byline given.

Nonfiction: Young adults: careers, interview/profile, multicultural, religion, social issues, college life, Christian discipleship.

How to Contact/Writers: Works on assignment basis only. Résumés and writing samples will be considered for inclusion in Writer's File to receive story assignments.

Illustration: Buys 2 illustrations/issue; 8 illustrations/year. Uses color artwork only. Reviews ms/illustration packages from artists. Query. Illustration only: Query with samples or send résumé, promo sheet, slides, client list and tearsheets. Contact: Amber Weigand-Buckley. Responds if interested. Originals not returned at job's completion. Credit line given.

Photography: Buys photos from freelancers. "Teen life, church life, college life; unposed; often used for illustrative purposes." Model/property releases required. Uses color glossy prints and 35mm or 2¼×2¼ transparencies. Query with samples; send business card, promotional literature, tearsheets or catalog. Responds only if interested.

Terms: Pays on acceptance. Buys first or reprint rights for mss. Buys one-time rights for photographs. Pays 10¢/word for stories/articles. Pays illustrators and photographers "as negotiated." Sample copies free for 9×11 SAE. Writer's guidelines for SASE.

ON THE LINE, Mennonite Publishing Network, 616 Walnut Ave., Scottdale PA 15683. (724)887-8500. Fax: (724)887-3111. E-mail: otl@mph.org. **Editor:** Mary Clemens Meyer. Magazine published monthly. Estab. 1970. Circ. 5,500. "*On The Line* is a children's magazine for ages 9-14, emphasizing self-esteem and Christian values. Also emphasizes multicultural awareness, care of the earth and accepting others with differences."

Fiction: Middle readers, young adults: contemporary, history, humorous, nature/environment, problem-solving, religious, science fiction, sports. "No fantasy or fiction with animal characters." Buys 45 mss/year. Average word length: 1,000-1,800. Byline given.

Nonfiction: Middle readers, young adults: arts/crafts, biography, cooking, games/puzzles, health, history, hobbies, how-to, humorous, sports. Does not want to see articles written from an adult perspective. Average word length: 200-600. Byline given.

Poetry: Wants to see light verse, humorous poetry.

How to Contact/Writers: Fiction/nonfiction: Send complete ms. "No queries, please." Responds to mss in 1 month. Will consider simultaneous submissions. Prefers no e-mail submissions.

Illustration: Buys 5-6 illustrations/issue; buys 60 illustrations/year. "Inside illustrations are done on assignment only to accompany our stories and articles—our need for new artists is limited." Looking for new artists for cover illustrations—full-color work. Illustrations only: "Prefer samples they do not want returned; these stay in our files." Responds to art samples only if interested.

Terms: Pays on acceptance. For mss buys one-time rights; second serial (reprint rights). Buys one-time rights for artwork and photos. Pays 3-5¢/word for assigned/unsolicited articles. Pays $50 for full-color inside illustration; $150 for full-color cover illustration. Photographers are paid per photo, $25-50. Original artwork returned at job's completion. Sample copy—$2 plus 7×10 SAE. Writer's guidelines (SASE).

Tips: "We focus on the age 12-13 group of our age 9-14 audience."

OWL, The Discovery Magazine for Children, Bayard Press, 49 Front St. E, Toronto ON M5E 1B3 Canada. (416)340-2700. Fax: (416)340-9769. E-mail: owl@owl.on.ca. Website: www.owlkids.com. **Editor:** Marybeth Leatherdale. **Creative Director:** Barb Kelly. **Photo Editor:** Kim Gillingham. Monthly magazine. Circ. 75,000. "*OWL* helps children over eight discover and enjoy the world of science, nature and technology. We look for articles that are fun to read, that inform from a child's perspective, and that motivate hands-on interaction. *OWL* explores the reader's many interests in the natural world in a scientific, but always entertaining, way."

Nonfiction: Middle readers: animal, biology, games/puzzles, high-tech, humor, nature/environment, science, social issues, sports, travel. Especially interested in puzzles and game ideas: logic, math, visual puzzles. Does not want to see religious topics, anthropomorphizing. Buys 6 mss/year. Average word length: 500-1,500. Byline given.

How to Contact/Writers: Nonfiction: Query with published clips. Responds to queries/mss in 4 months. No e-mail submissions.

Illustration: Buys 3-5 illustrations/issue; 40-50 illustrations/year. Uses color artwork only. Preferred theme or style: lively, involving, fun, with emotional impact and appeal. "We use a range of styles." Works on assignment only. Illustrations only: Send tearsheets and slides. Responds to art samples only if interested. Original artwork returned at job's completion. No e-mail submissions.

Photography: Looking for shots of animals and nature. "Label the photos." Uses 2¼×2¼ and 35mm transparencies. Photographers should query with samples. No e-mail submissions.

Terms: Pays on publication. Buys first North American and world rights for mss, artwork and photos. Pays $200-500 (Canadian) for assigned/unsolicited articles. Pays up to $650 (Canadian) for illustrations. Photographers are paid per photo. Sample copies for $4.28. Writer's guidelines for SAE (large envelope if requesting sample copy) and money order for $1 postage (no stamps please).

Tips: Writers: "*OWL* is dedicated to entertaining kids with contemporary and accurate information about the world around them. *OWL* is intellectually challenging but is never preachy. Ideas should be original and convey a spirit of humor and liveliness." (See listing for *Chickadee*.)

PARENTING NEW HAMPSHIRE, Telegraph Publishing Co., P.O. Box 1291, Nashua NH 03061. (603)594-6434. Fax: (603)594-6565. E-mail: news@parentingnh.com. Website: www.parentingnh.com. **Articles Editor:** Beth Quarm Todgham. Purpose is "to provide news, information and resources to New Hampshire parents."

Nonfiction: Buys 10-12 mss/year. Average word length: 900-1,800. Byline given.

How to Contact/Writers: Nonfiction: Send complete ms. Responds to queries/mss in 6 months. Publishes ms 30 days after acceptance. Will consider simultaneous submissions, electronic submissions via disk or modem, previously pubished work.

Photography: Looks for photos related to children and families—primarily use as cover artwork. Uses color prints and 35mm, 2¼×2¼, 4× or 8×10 transparencies. Provide résumé, business card, promotional literature or tearsheets to be kept on file. Responds only if interested.

Terms: Pays on publication. Buys reprint rights, one-time rights, web rights for up to 1 year. Original artwork returned at job's completion. Pays $25-125 for stories. Additional payment for ms/illustration packages and for photos accompanying articles.   Sample copies for $1. Writer's guidelines for SASE.

☑ ▣ **PARENTS AND CHILDREN TOGETHER ONLINE, A magazine for parents and children on the World Wide Web**, EDINFO Press/Family Literary Centers, 2805 East 10th St., Suite 140, Bloomington IN 47408. (800)759-4723. E-mail: erices@indiana.edu. Website: http://eric.indiana.edu.pcto.html. **Editor-in-Chief:** Mei-Yu Lu. Quarterly online magazine. Estab. 1990 (in print format). Circ. 9,000 via worldwide web. "Our magazine seeks to promote family literacy by presenting original articles and stories for parents and children via the worldwide web." More than 75% of publication aimed at juvenile market.

Fiction: "We accept all categories. Would like to see stories on issues children are facing today. We welcome stories from all cultural backgrounds." Publishes 32 mss/year. Byline given.

Nonfiction: "All categories are examined and considered. We especially look for articles with photographs and/or illustrations included. We welcome articles about children and subjects that children will find interesting, and that reflect diverse cultural backgrounds." Publishes 24 mss/year. Byline given.

Poetry: Reviews poetry. "We accept poems written for children that children will enjoy—not poems about childhood by an adult looking back nostalgically."

How to Contact/Writers: Fiction/nonfiction: Send complete ms. Responds to queries in 1 week; mss in 3 months. Publishes ms 3-6 months after acceptance. Will consider simultaneous submissions, electronic submissions via disk or e-mail, and previously published work.

Illustration: Publishes 12 illustrations/issue; 48 illustrations/year. Reviews ms/illustration packages from artists. Query with ms dummy. Contact: Editor. Illustrations only: Query with samples. Contact: Editor. Responds to art samples within 1 month. Samples returned with SASE. Credit line given.

Photography: Looking for children and parents together, either reading together or involved in other literacy-related activities. Also, children with grandparents. Uses color prints and 35mm transparencies. Query with samples. Send unsolicited photos by mail. Responds in 1 month.

Terms: Buys first North American serial rights for mss. Art/photos use on web with copyright retained by artist/photographer. "We are a free online publication, and cannot afford to pay our contributors at present." Sample copies for $9. Writer's guidelines free for SASE.

Tips: "We are a good market for writers, artists and photographers who want their material to reach a wide audience. Since we are a free publication, available without charge to anyone with a web browser, we cannot offer our contributors anything more than a large, enthusiastic audience for their work. Our stories and articles are read by thousands of children and parents every month via their families' internet-connected computer."

Ⓝ PASSPORT, Sunday School Curriculum, 6401 The Paseo, Kansas City MO 64131-1284. (816)333-7000. Fax: (816)333-4439. Website: www.nazarene.org. **Editor:** Emily Freeburg. Weekly take-home paper. "*Passport* looks for a casual, witty approach to Christian themes. We want hot topics relevant to preteens."

Nonfiction: Middle readers, young adults: archaeological, biography, history, games/puzzles, how-to, interview/profile, problem-solving, multicultural, religion, social issues, travel. Multicultural needs include: ethnics and cultures—other world areas especially English-speaking.

How to Contact/Writers: Send complete ms. Responds to queries/mss in 2 months. Publishes ms 2 years after acceptance.

Terms: Pays on publication. "Payment is made approximately one year before the date of issue." Buys multiple use rights for mss. Also accepts cartoons; $15 for spot cartoon. Pays $15-30 for articles. Writer's guidelines for SASE.

Tips: Writers: "Follow our theme list; read the Bible verses that relate to the theme." (See listing for *Discoveries*.)

POCKETS, Devotional Magazine for Children, The Upper Room, 1908 Grand, P.O. Box 340004, Nashville TN 37203-0004. (615)340-7333. Fax: (615)340-7267. E-mail: pockets@upperroom.org. Website: www.upperroom.org/pockets. **Articles/Fiction Editor:** Lynn W. Gilliam. **Art Director:** Chris Schechner, 408 Inglewood Dr., Richardson TX 75080. Magazine published 11 times/year. Estab. 1981. Circ. 99,000. "*Pockets* is a Christian devotional magazine for children ages 6-12. Stories should help children experience a Christian lifestyle that is not always a neatly wrapped moral package but is open to the continuing revelation of God's will."

Fiction: Picture-oriented, young readers, middle readers: adventure, contemporary, occasional folktales, multicultural, nature/environment, problem-solving, religious. Does not accept violence or talking animal stories. Buys 40-45 mss/year. Average word length: 600-1,400. Byline given.

Nonfiction: Picture-oriented, young readers, middle readers: cooking, games/puzzles, interview/profile, religion. Does not accept how-to articles. "Our nonfiction reads like a story." Multicultural needs include: stories that feature children of various racial/ethnic groups and do so in a way that is true to those depicted. Buys 10 mss/year. Average word length: 400-1,000. Byline given.

How to Contact/Writers: Fiction/nonfiction: Send complete ms. "Do not accept queries." Responds to mss in 6 weeks. Will consider simultaneous submissions.

Illustration: Buys 40-50 illustrations/issue. Preferred theme or style: varied; both 4-color and 2-color. Works on assignment only. Illustrations only: Send promo sheet, tearsheets.

RANGER RICK, National Wildlife Federation, 11100 Wildlife Center Dr., Reston VA 20190. (703)438-6000. Website: www.nwf.org.
   ● Ranger Rick does not accept submissions.

READ, Weekly Reader Corporation, 200 First Stamford Place, P.O. Box 120023, Stamford CT 06912-0023. Fax: (203)705-1661. E-mail: sbarchers@weeklyreader.com. Website: www.weeklyreader.com. **Managing Editor:** Suzanne Barchers. Magazine published 18 times during the school year. Language arts periodical for use in classrooms for students ages 12-16; motivates students to read and teaches skills in listening, comprehension, speaking, writing and critical thinking.
Fiction: Wants short stories, narratives and plays to be used for classroom reading and discussions. Middle readers, young adult/teens: adventure, animal, contemporary, fantasy, folktales, history, humorous, multicultural, nature/environment, sports. Average word length: 1,000-2,500.
Nonfiction: Middle readers, young adult/teen: animal, games/puzzles, history, humorous, problem solving, social issues.
How to Contact: Responds to queries/mss in 6 weeks.
Illustration: Buys 2-3 illustrations/issue; 20-25 illustration jobs/year. Responds only if interested. Samples returned with SASE. Credit line given.
Terms: Pays on purchase. Rights purchased varies. Pays writers $100-800 for stories/articles. Pays illustrators $650-850 for color cover; $125-750 for b&w and color inside. Pays photographers by the project (range: $450-650); per photo (range: $125-650). Sample copies free for digest-sized SAE and 3 first-class stamps.
Tips: "We especially like plot twists and surprise endings. Stories should be relevant to teens and contain realistic conflicts and dialogue. Plays should have at least 12 speaking parts for classroom reading. Avoid formula plots, trite themes, underage material, stilted or profane language, and sexual suggestion. Get to know the style of our magazine as well as our teen audience. They are very demanding and require an engaging and engrossing read. Grab their attention, keep the pace and action lively, build to a great climax, and make the ending satisfying and/or surprising. Make sure characters and dialogue are realistic. Do not use cliché, but make the writing fresh—simple, yet original. Obtain guidelines first. Be sure submissions are relevant."

SCIENCE WEEKLY, Science Weekly Inc., P.O. Box 70638, Chevy Chase MD 20813. (301)680-8804. Fax: (301)680-9240. E-mail: sciencew@erols.com. Website: www.scienceweekly.com. **Editor:** Deborah Lazar. Magazine published 16 times/year. Estab. 1984. Circ. 200,000.
   • *Science Weekly* uses freelance writers to develop and write an entire issue on a single science topic. Send résumé only, not submissions. Authors must be within the greater DC, Virginia, Maryland area. *Science Weekly* works on assignment only.
Nonfiction: Young readers, middle readers, (K-8th grade): science/math education, education, problem-solving.
Terms: Pays on publication. Prefers people with education, science and children's writing background. *Send résumé* only. Samples copies free with SAE and 2 first-class stamps.

SCIENCE WORLD, Scholastic Inc., 555 Broadway, New York NY 10012-3999. (212)343-6299. Fax: (212)343-6333. E-mail: scienceworld@scholastic.com. **Editor:** Mark Bregman. **Art Director:** Felix Batcup. Magazine published biweekly during the school year. Estab. 1959. Circ. 400,000. Publishes articles in Life Science/Health, Physical Science/Technology, Earth Science/Environment/Astronomy for students in grades 7-10. The goal is to make science relevant for teens.
   • *Science World* publishes a separate teacher's edition with lesson plans and skills pages to accompany feature articles.
Nonfiction: Young adults/teens: animal, concept, geography, health, nature/environment, science. Multicultural needs include: minority scientists as role models. Does not want to see stories without a clear news hook. Buys 20 mss/year. Average word length: 800-1,000. Byline given. Currently does not accept unsolicited mss.
How to Contact/Writers: Nonfiction: Query with published clips and/or brief summaries of article ideas. Responds only if interested.
Illustration: Buys 2 illustrations/issue; 28 illustrations/year. Works on assignment only. Illustration only: Query with samples, tearsheets. Responds only if interested. Samples returned with SASE; samples filed "if we use them." Credit line given.
Photography: Model/property releases required; captions required including background information. Provide résumé, business card, promotional literature or tearsheets to be kept on file. Responds only if interested.
Terms: Pays on acceptance. Buys all rights for mss/artwork. Originals returned to artist at job's completion. For stories/articles, pays $200. Pays photographers per photo.

☑ **SEVENTEEN MAGAZINE**, Hearst Magazines, 1440 Broadway, 13th Floor, New York NY 10018. (212)204-4300. Fax: (212)204-3917. Website: www.seventeen.com. **Articles/Fiction Editor:** Jennifer Braunschweiger. **Art Director:** Meghan Smith. **Photo Editor:** Loraine Pavich. Monthly magazine. Estab. 1944. "We reach 14.5 million girls each month. Over the past five decades, *Seventeen* has helped shape teenage life in America. We represent an important rite of passage, helping to define, socialize and empower young women. We create notions of beauty and style, proclaim what's hot in popular culture and identify social issues."
Fiction: Young adults: contemporary, health, humorous, multicultural, problem-solving. "We consider all good literary short fiction." Buys 10-12 mss/year. Average word length: 2,000-3,000. Byline sometimes given.
Nonfiction: Young adults: careers, cooking, hobbies, how-to, humorous, interview/profile, multicultural, social issues. Buys 7-12 mss/year. Word length: Varies from 200-2,000 words for articles. Byline sometimes given.
How to Contact/Writers: Fiction: Send complete ms. Nonfiction: Query with published clips. "Do not call." Responds to queries/mss in 3 months. Will consider simultaneous submissions.
Illustration: Only interested in agented material. Buys 10 illustrations/issue; 120 illustrations/year. Works on assignment only. Reviews ms/illustration packages. Illustrations only: Query with samples. Responds only if interested. Samples not returned; samples filed. Credit line given.

Photography: Looking for photos to match current stories. Model/property releases required; captions required. Uses color, 8×10 prints; 35mm, 2¼×¼, 4×5 or 8×10 transparencies. Query with samples or résumé of credits, or submit portfolio for review. Responds only if interested.

Terms: Pays on publication. Buys first North American serial rights, first rights or all rights for mss. Buys exclusive rights for 3 months; online rights for photos. Original artwork returned at job's completion. Pays $1/word for articles/stories (varies by experience). Additional payment for photos accompanying articles. Pays illustrators/photographers $150-500. Sample copies not available. Writer's guidelines for SASE.

Tips: Send for guidelines before submitting.

SHARING THE VICTORY, Fellowship of Christian Athletes, 8701 Leeds, Kansas City MO 64129. (816)921-0909. Fax: (816)921-8755. Website: www.fca.org. **Articles/Photo Editor:** David Smale. **Art Director:** Frank Grey. Magazine published 9 times a year. Estab. 1982. Circ. 85,000. "Purpose is to present to coaches and athletes, and all whom they influence, the challenge and adventure of receiving Jesus Christ as Savior and Lord."

Nonfiction: Young adults/teens: religion, sports. Buys 30 mss/year. Average word length: 500-1,200. Byline given.

How to Contact/Writers: Nonfiction: Query with published clips. Responds in 6 weeks. Publishes ms 3 months after acceptance. Will consider simultaneous submissions, electronic submissions via disk or modem and previously published work. Writer's guidelines available on website.

Photography: Purchases photos separately. Looking for photos of sports action. Uses color prints and 35mm transparencies. E-mail electronic submissions.

Terms: Pays on publication. Buys first rights and second serial (reprint) rights. Pays $150-400 for assigned and unsolicited articles. Photographers paid per photo. Sample copies for 9×12 SASE and $1. Writer's/photo guidelines for SASE.

Tips: "Be specific—write short. Take quality, sharp photos." Wants interviews and features, articles on athletes with a solid Christian base; be sure to include their faith and testimony. Interested in colorful sports photos.

SHINE brightly, GEMS Girls' Clubs, Box 7259, Grand Rapids MI 49510. (616)241-5616. Fax: (616)241-5558. E-mail: sara@gemsgc.org. Website: www.gospelcom.net/gems. **Editor:** Jan Boone. **Managing Editor:** Sara Lynne Hilton. Monthly (with combined May/June/July/August summer issue) magazine. Circ. 16,000. "*Shine brightly* is designed to help girls ages 9-14 see how God is at work in their lives and in the world around them."

Fiction: Middle readers: adventure, animal, contemporary, health, history, humorous, multicultural, nature/environment, problem-solving, religious, sports. Does not want to see unrealistic stories and those with trite, easy endings. Buys 30 mss/year. Average word length: 400-900. Byline given.

Nonfiction: Middle readers: animal, arts/crafts, careers, cooking, fashion, games/puzzles, health, hobbies, how-to, humorous, nature/environment, multicultural, problem-solving, religious, social issues, sports, travel, also movies, music and musicians. Buys 9 mss/year. Average word length: 100-400. Byline given.

How to Contact/Writers: Send for annual update for publication themes. Fiction/nonfiction: Send complete ms. Responds to mss in 1 month. Will consider simultaneous submissions. Guidelines on website.

Illustration: Buys 3 illustrations/year. Prefers ms/illustration packages. Works on assignment only. Responds to submissions in 1 month. Samples returned with SASE. Credit line given.

Terms: Pays on publication. Buys first North American serial rights, first rights, second serial (reprint rights) or simultaneous rights. Original artwork not returned at job's completion. Pays 3-5¢/word, up to $35 for stories, assigned articles and unsolicited articles. Poetry is $5-15. Games and Puzzles are $5-10. "We send complimentary copies in addition to pay." Pays $25-75 for color cover illustration; $25-50 for color inside illustration. Pays photographers by the project ($20-50 per photo). Writer's guidelines for SASE.

Tips: Writers: "The stories should be current, deal with adolescent problems and joys, and help girls see God at work in their lives through humor as well as problem-solving."

SKATING, U.S. Figure Skating, 20 First St., Colorado Springs CO 80906. (719)635-5200. Fax: (719)635-9548. E-mail: skatingmagazine@usfsa.org. **Articles Editor:** Amy Partain. Magazine published 10 times/year. Estab. 1923. Circ. 45,000. "The mission of *SKATING* is to communicate information about the sport (figure skating) to the U.S. Figure Skating membership and figure skating fans, promoting U.S. Figure Skating programs, personalities, events and trends that affect the sport."

Nonfiction: Young readers, middle readers, young adults: biography, health, sports. Buys 30 mss/year. Average word length: 750-2,000. Byline given.

How to Contact/Writers: Nonfiction: Query with published clips. Responds to queries/mss in 1 month. Publishes ms 2 months after acceptance. Prefers electronic submissions via disk or e-mail.

Illustration: Buys 1 illustration/year. Works on assignment only. Reviews ms/illustration packages from artists. Query. Illustrations only: Query with samples. Responds only if interested. Samples returned with SASE; or filed. Credit line given.

Photography: Uses photos of kids learning to skate on ice. Model/property release required; captions required. Uses color most sizes glossy prints, 35mm transparencies. Contact by e-mail if interested in submitting. Responds only if interested.

Terms: Pays on publication. Buys first rights for mss, artwork and photos. Original artwork returned at job's completion. Pays $75-150 for stories and articles. Additional payment if photos are used. Pays photographers per photo (range: $15-35). Sample copies for SAE. Writer's/photo guidelines for SASE.

Tips: "*SKATING* covers Olympic-eligible skating, primarily focusing on the U.S. We do *not* cover professional skating. We are looking for fun, vibrant articles on U.S. Figure Skating members of all age levels and skills, especially synchronized skaters and adult skaters."

SKIPPING STONES, A Multicultural Children's Magazine, P.O. Box 3939, Eugene OR 97403. (541)342-4956. E-mail: editor@SkippingStones.org. Website: www.SkippingStones.org. **Articles/Photo/Fiction Editor:** Arun N. Toké. Bimonthly magazine. Estab. 1988. Circ. 2,500. *"Skipping Stones* is a multicultural, nonprofit children's magazine designed to encourage cooperation, creativity and celebration of cultural and ecological richness. We encourage submissions by minorities and under-represented populations."

  • Send SASE for *Skipping Stones* guidelines and theme list for detailed descriptions of the topics they're looking for.

Fiction: Middle readers, young adult/teens: contemporary, meaningful, humorous. All levels: folktales, multicultural, nature/environment. Multicultural needs include: bilingual or multilingual pieces; use of words from other languages; settings in other countries, cultures or multi-ethnic communities.

Nonfiction: All levels: animal, biography, cooking, games/puzzles, history, humorous, interview/profile, multicultural, nature/environment, creative problem-solving, religion and cultural celebrations, sports, travel, social and international awareness. Does not want to see preaching, violence or abusive language; no poems by authors over 18 years old; no suspense or romance stories for the sake of the same. Average word length: 500-750. Byline given.

How to Contact/Writers: Fiction: Query. Nonfiction: Send complete ms. Responds to queries in 1 month; mss in 4 months. Will consider simultaneous submissions; reviews artwork for future assignments. Please include your name on each page.

Illustration: Prefers color and/or b&w drawings, especially by teenagers and young adults. Will consider all illustration packages. Manuscript/illustration packages: Query; submit complete ms with final art; submit tearsheets. Responds in 4 months. Credit line given.

Photography: Black & white photos preferred, but color photos with good contrast are welcome. Needs: youth 7-17, international, nature, celebration.

Terms: Acquires first and reprint rights for mss and photographs. Pays in copies for authors, photographers and illustrators. Sample copies for $5 with SAE and 4 first-class stamps. Writer's/illustrator's guidelines for 4×9 SASE.

Tips: "We want material meant for children and young adults/teenagers with multicultural or ecological awareness themes. Think, live and write as if you were a child, tween or teen." Wants "material that gives insight on cultural celebrations, lifestyle, custom and tradition, glimpse of daily life in other countries and cultures. Photos, songs, artwork are most welcome if they illustrate/highlight the points. Translations are invited if your submission is in a language other than English. Upcoming themes will include cultural celebrations, living abroad, disability, hospitality customs of various cultures, cross-cultural understanding, African, Asian and Latin American cultures, humor, international, turning points and magical moments in life, caring for the earth, spirituality, and Multicutural Awareness."

[N] SPARKLE, GEMS Girls' Clubs, P.O. Box 7259, Grand Rapids MI 49510. (616)241-5616. Fax: (616)241-5558. E-mail: sara@gemsgc.org. Website: www.gemsgc.org. **Articles/Fiction Editor:** Sara Hilton. **Art Director/Photo Editor:** Tina DeKam. Magazine published 3 times/year. Estab. 2002. "We are a Christian magazine geared toward girls in the 1st-3rd grades. *Sparkle* prints stories, articles, crafts, recipes, games and more. The magazine is based on an annual theme."

Fiction: Young readers: adventure, animal, contemporary, health, humorous, multicultural, nature/environment, problem-solving, religious, sports, suspense/mystery. Buys 8 mss/year. Average word length: 100-400. Byline given.

Nonfiction: Young readers, middle readers: animal, arts/crafts, biography, careers, cooking, concept, fashion, games/puzzles, geography, health, history, hobbies, how-to, interview/profile, math, multicultural, nature/environment, problem-solving, science, social issues, sports, travel. Average word length: 100-400. Byline given.

How to Contact/Writers: Fiction/nonfiction: Send complete ms. Responds to ms in 1 month. Publishes ms 4-6 months after acceptance. Will consider previously published work.

Illustration: Buys 2 illustrations/issue; 6 illustrations/year. Uses color artwork only. Works on assignment only. Reviews ms/illustration packages from artists. Send ms with dummy. Contact: Sara Hilton, managing editor. Illustrations only: send promo sheet. Responds only if interested. Samples returned with SASE; samples filed. Credit line given.

Photography: Looking for close-up photos of girls, grades 1-3. Uses color prints. Send unsolicited photos by mail. Responds only if interested.

Terms: Pays on publication. Buys first North American serial rights for mss, artwork and photos. Pays $20 minimum for stories and articles. Pays illustrators $50-100 for color cover; $25-100 for color inside. Pays photographers per photo (range: $25-100). Additional payment for ms/illustration packages and for photos accompanying articles. Sample copies for $1. Writer's/illustrator/photo guidelines free for SASE.

SPIDER, The Magazine for Children, Carus Publishing Company, P.O. Box 300, Peru IL 61354. (815)224-5803, ext. 656. Website: www.cricketmag.com. **Editor-in-Chief:** Marianne Carus. **Editor:** Heather Delabre. **Art Director:** Tony Jacobson. Monthly magazine. Estab. 1994. Circ. 73,000. *Spider* publishes high-quality literature for beginning readers, primarily ages 6-9.

Fiction: Young readers: adventure, contemporary, fantasy, folktales, science fiction. "Authentic, well-researched stories from all cultures are welcome. No didactic, religious, or violent stories, or anything that talks down to children." Average word length: 300-1,000. Byline given.

Nonfiction: Young readers: animal, arts/crafts, cooking, games/puzzles, geography, history, math, multicultural, nature/environment, problem-solving, science. "Well-researched articles on all cultures are welcome. Would like to see more games, puzzles and activities, especially ones adaptable to *Spider's* takeout pages. No encyclopedic or overtly educational articles." Average word length: 300-800. Byline given.

Poetry: Serious, humorous, nonsense rhymes. Maximum length: 20 lines.

How to Contact/Writers: Fiction/nonfiction: Send complete ms with SASE. Do not query. Responds to mss in 3 months.

Publishes ms 2-3 years after acceptance. Will consider simultaneous submissions and previously published work.

Illustration: Buys 20 illustrations/issue; 240 illustrations/year. Uses color artwork only. "Any medium—preferably one that can wrap on a laser scanner—no larger than 20×24. We use more realism than cartoon-style art." Works on assignment only. Reviews ms/illustration packages from artists. Submit ms with rough sketches. Illustrations only: Send promo sheet and tearsheets. Responds in 6 weeks. Samples returned with SASE; samples filed. Credit line given.

Photography: Buys photos from freelancers. Buys photos with accompanying ms only. Model/property releases required; captions required. Uses 35mm or $2\frac{1}{4} \times 2\frac{1}{4}$ transparencies. Send unsolicited photos by mail; provide résumé and tearsheets. Responds in 6 weeks.

Terms: Pays on publication for text; within 45 days from acceptance for art. Rights purchased vary. Buys first and promotional rights for artwork; one-time rights for photographs. Original artwork returned at job's completion. Pays up to 25¢/word for previously unpublished stories/articles. Authors also receive 2 complimentary copies of the issue in which work appears. Additional payment for ms/illustration packages and for photos accompanying articles. Pays illustrators $750 for color cover; $200-300 for color inside. Pays photographers per photo (range: $25-75). Sample copies for $5. Writer's/ illustrator's guidelines for SASE.

Tips: Writers: "Read back issues before submitting." (See listings for *Babybug*, *Cicada*, *Cricket*, *Muse*, *Ladybug* and *ASK*.)

⬛ SPORTS ILLUSTRATED FOR KIDS, 135 W. 50th St., New York NY 10020-1393. (212)522-4876. Fax: (212)467-4247. Website: www.sikids.com. **Managing Editor:** Neil Cohen. **Art Director:** Beth Bugler. **Photo Editor:** Andrew McCloskey. Monthly magazine. Estab. 1989. Circ. 1,000,000. Each month *SI Kids* brings the excitement, joy, and challenge of sports to life for boys and girls ages 8-14 via: action photos, dynamic designs, interactive stories; a spectrum of sports: professional, extreme, amateur, women's and kids; profiles, puzzles, playing tips, sports cards; posters, plus drawings and writing by kids. 100% of publication aimed at juvenile and teen market.

Nonfiction: Middle readers, young adults: biography, games/puzzles, interview/profile, sports. Buys less than 20 mss/ year. Average word length: 500-700. Byline given.

How to Contact/Writers: Nonfiction: Query. Responds in 6 weeks. Will consider simultaneous submissions.

Illustration: Only interested in agented material. Buys 50 illustrations/year. Works on assignment only. Reviews ms/ illustration packages from artists. Submit ms/illustration package with SASE. Contact: Beth Bugler, art director. Illustrations only: Send promo sheet and samples. Contact: Beth Bugler, art director. Responds in 1 month. Samples kept on file. Credit line given.

Photography: Looking for action sports photography. Uses color prints and 35mm transparencies. Submit portfolio for review. Responds in 1 month.

Terms: Pays on acceptance. Buys all rights for mss. Buys all rights for artwork. Buys all rights for photos. Original artwork returned at job's completion. Pays $500 for 500-600 word articles. by the project—$400; $500/day; per photo (range: $75-1,000). Sample copies free for 9×12 SASE. Writer's guidelines for SASE or via website.

STORY FRIENDS, Mennonite Publishing Network, 616 Walnut Ave., Scottdale PA 15683. (724)887-8500. Fax: (724)887-3111. **Editor:** Susan Reith Swan. Estab. 1905. Circ. 6,000. Monthly magazine that reinforces Christian values for children ages 4-9.

Fiction: Picture-oriented material: contemporary, humorous, multicultural, nature/environment, problem-solving, religious, relationships. Multicultural needs include fiction or nonfiction pieces which help children be aware of cultural diversity and celebrate differences while recognizing similarities. Buys 45 mss/year. Average word length: 300-800. Byline given.

Nonfiction: Picture-oriented: animal, humorous, interview/profile, multicultural, nature/environment. Buys 10 mss/year. Average word length: 300-800. Byline given.

Poetry: Average length: 4-12 lines.

How to Contact/Writers: Fiction/nonfiction: Send complete ms. Responds to mss in 10 weeks. Will consider simultaneous submissions.

Illustration: Works on assignment only. Send tearsheets with SASE. Responds in 2 months. Samples returned with SASE; samples filed. Credit line given.

Photography: Occasionally buys photos from freelancers. Wants photos of children ages 4-8.

Terms: Pays on acceptance. Buys one-time rights or reprint rights for mss and artwork. Original artwork returned at job's completion. Pays 3-5¢/word for stories and articles. Pays photographers $15-30 per photo. Writer's guidelines $2; SAE and 2 first-class stamps.

Tips: "Become immersed in high quality children's literature."

TURTLE MAGAZINE, For Preschool Kids, Children's Better Health Institute, 1100 Waterway Blvd., P.O. Box 567, Indianapolis IN 46206-0567. (317)636-8881. Fax: (317)684-8094. Website: www.turtlemag.org. **Editor:** Terry Harshman. **Art Director:** Bart Rivers. Monthly/bimonthly magazine published 6 times/year. Circ. 300,000. *Turtle* uses read-aloud stories, especially suitable for bedtime or naptime reading, for children ages 2-5. Also uses poems, simple science experiments, easy recipes and health-related articles.

Fiction: Picture-oriented material: health-related, medical, history, humorous, multicultural, nature/environment, problem-solving, sports, recipes, simple science experiments. Avoid stories in which the characters indulge in unhealthy activities. Buys 20 mss/year. Average word length: 150-300. Byline given. Currently accepting submissions for Rebus stories only.

Nonfiction: Picture-oriented material: cooking, health, science, sports, simple science. "We use very simple experiments illustrating basic science concepts. These should be pretested. We also publish simple, healthful recipes." Buys 24 mss/ year. Average word length: 100-300. Byline given.

Poetry: "We're especially looking for short poems (4-8 lines) and slightly longer action rhymes to foster creative movement in preschoolers. We also use short verse on our inside front cover and back cover."

How to Contact/Writers: Fiction/nonfiction: "Prefer complete manuscript to queries." Responds to mss in 3 months.

Terms: Pays on publication. Buys all rights for mss. Pays up to 22¢/word for stories and articles (depending upon length and quality) and 10 complimentary copies. Pays $25 minimum for poems. Sample copy $1.75. Writer's guidelines free with SASE and on website.

Tips: "Our need for health-related material, especially features that encourage fitness, is ongoing. Health subjects must be age-appropriate. When writing about them, think creatively and lighten up! Always keep in mind that in order for a story or article to educate preschoolers, it first must be entertaining—warm and engaging, exciting, or genuinely funny. Here the trend is toward leaner, lighter writing. There will be a growing need for interactive activities. Writers might want to consider developing an activity to accompany their concise manuscripts." (See listings for *Child Life*, *Children's Digest*, *Children's Playmate*, *Humpty Dumpty's Magazine*, *Jack and Jill* and *U*S* Kids*.)

U*S* KIDS, Children's Better Health Institute, 1100 Waterway Blvd., P.O. Box 567, Indianapolis IN 46206. (317)636-8881. Website: www.uskidsmag.org. **Editor:** Daniel Lee. **Art Director:** Tim LaBelle. Magazine published 6 times a year. Estab. 1987. Circ. 230,000.

Fiction: Young readers: adventure, animal, contemporary, health, history, humorous, multicultural, nature/environment, problem-solving, sports, suspense/mystery. Buys limited number of stories/year. Query first. Average word length: 500-800. Byline given.

Nonfiction: Young readers: animal, arts/crafts, cooking, games/puzzles, health, history, hobbies, how-to, humorous, interview/profile, multicultural, nature/environment, science, social issues, sports, travel. Wants to see interviews with kids ages 5-10, who have done something unusual or different. Buys 30-40 mss/year. Average word length: 400. Byline given.

Poetry: Maximum length: 8-24 lines.

How to Contact/Writers: Fiction: Send complete ms. Responds to queries and mss in 3 months.

Illustration: Buys 8 illustrations/issue; 70 illustrations/year. Color artwork only. Works on assignment only. Reviews ms/illustration packages from artists. Query. Illustrations only: Send résumé and tearsheets. Responds only if interested. Samples returned with SASE; samples kept on file. Does not return originals. Credit line given.

Photography: Purchases photography from freelancers. Looking for photos that pertain to children ages 5-10. Model/property release required. Uses color and b&w prints; 35mm, 2¼×2¼, 4×5 and 8×10 transparencies. Photographers should provide résumé, business card, promotional literature or tearsheets to be kept on file. Responds only if interested.

Terms: Pays on publication. Buys all rights for mss. Purchases all rights for artwork. Purchases one-time rights for photographs. Pays 25¢/word minimum. Additional payment for ms/illustration packages. Pays illustrators $155/page for color inside. Photographers paid by the project or per photo (negotiable). Sample copies for $2.95. Writer's/illustrator/photo guidelines for #10 SASE.

Tips: "Write clearly and concisely without preaching or being obvious." (See listings for *Child Life*, *Children's Digest*, *Children's Playmate*, *Humpty Dumpty's Magazine*, *Jack and Jill* and *Turtle Magazine*.)

☑ ▢ **WEE ONES E-MAGAZINE**, 1011 Main St., Darlington MD 21034. E-mail: info@weeonesmag.com. Website: www.weeonesmag.com. **Editor:** Jennifer Reed. Monthly online magazine. Estab. 2001. "We are an online children's magazine for children ages 3-10. Our mission is to use the Internet to encourage kids to read. We promote literacy and family unity." 50% of publication aimed at juvenile market.

Fiction: Picture-oriented material: adventure, contemporary, health, history, humorous, multicultural, nature/environment, problem solving, sports, rebus with illustrations. Buys 60 mss/year. Average word length: up to 500. Byline given.

Nonfiction: Picture-oriented material: animal, arts/crafts, biography, concept, cooking, games/puzzles, geography, health, history, hobbies, how-to, humorous, multicultural, nature/environment, problem-solving, science, sports, travel. Buys 30 mss/year. Average word length: up to 500. Byline given.

Poetry: Uses rhyming poetry. Limit submissions to 3 poems.

How to Contact/Writers: Fiction/nonfiction: Send complete ms via e-mail. Responds to mss in 1 month. Publishes ms 6-12 months after acceptance. Will consider simultaneous submissions, electronic submissions via e-mail.

Illustration: Buys 6 illustrations/issue. Works on assignment only. Reviews ms/illustration packages from artists. Query. Contact: Jeff Reed, art editor. Illustrations only: Query with samples. Contact: Jeff Reed, art editor. Responds only if interested. Samples returned with SASE or kept on file. Credit line given.

Photography: Uses photos of children in various activities. Uses color b&w 4×6 prints. Responds only if interested.

Terms: Pays on publication. Buys one time electronic rights for mss, artwork and photos. Pays 3¢/word for stories and articles. Additional payment for ms/illustration packages and for photos accompanying articles. Pays $5-20 for b&w and color inside. Pays photographers per photo (range: $3). Writer's/illustrator's/photo guidelines for SASE.

Tips: "*Wee Ones* is the first online children's magazine. We are not in print! We reach over 80 countries and receive 35,000 hits per month. Study our magazine before submitting. Our guidelines are located on our site. Your chances on getting accepted depend widely only how well you follow our guidelines and submit *only* through e-mail."

▢ ▢ **WHAT IF?, Canada's Fiction Magazine for Teens**, What If Publications, 19 Lynwood Place, Guelph ON N1G 2V9 Canada. (519)823-2941. Fax: (519)823-8081. E-mail: whatif2003@hotmail.com. Website: whatifmagazine.ca. **Articles/Fiction Editor:** Mike Leslie. **Art Director:** Jean Leslie. Bimonthly magazine. Estab. 2003. Circ. 1,000. "The goal of *What If?* is to help young adults get published for the first time in a quality literary setting alongside more experienced and well-known Canadian writers."

Fiction: Young adults: adventure, contemporary, fantasy, folktale, health, humorous, multicultural, nature/environment, problem-solving, science fiction, sports, suspense/mystery. Buys 48 mss/year. Average word length: 500-3,000. Byline given.

Nonfiction: Young adults: editorial. "We publish editorial content from young adult writers only—similar to material seen on newspapers op-ed page." Average word length: 100-500. Byline given.

Poetry: Reviews poetry: all styles. Maximum length: 20 lines. Limit submissions to 4 poems.

How to Contact/Writers: Fiction/Nonfiction: Send complete ms. Responds to mss in 2 months. Publishes ms 4 months after acceptance. Will consider e-mail submissions, previously published work if the author owns all rights.

Illustration: Buys approximately 150 illustrations/year. Reviews ms/illustration packages from artists. Send ms with dummy. Query with samples. Contact: Jean Leslie, production manager. Responds in 1 month. Samples returned with SASE. Credit line given.

Terms: Pays on publication. Buys first rights for mss and artwork. Original artwork returned at job's completion. Pays 3 copies for stories; 1 copy for articles. "We are a new magazine and until we build our subscription and advertising base we pay in contributor's copies only." Pays illustrators 3 copies. Sample copies for $7.50 plus SAE with $1.60 Canadian postage or IRC. Writer's/illustrator's guidelines for SASE or available by e-mail.

Tips: "Read our magazine. The majority of the material we publish (60-70%) is by Canadian young adults. Another 20-30% is by Canadian Adults. We try to limit our foreign content to 10%. The majority of material we receive from young adults is contemporary, science fiction and fantasy. As an adult, avoid these genres."

WHAT MAGAZINE, What! Publishers Inc. 108-93 Lombard Ave., Winnipeg MB R3B 3B1 Canada. (204)985-8160. Fax: (204)957-5638. E-mail: l.malkin@m2ci.mb.ca. **Articles Editor:** Barb Chabai. **Art Director:** Brian Kauste. Magazine published 6 times/year. Estab. 1987. Circ. 250,000. "Informative and entertaining teen magazine for both genders. Articles deal with issues and ideas of relevance to Canadian teens. The magazine is distributed through schools so we aim to be cool and responsible at the same time."

Nonfiction: Young adults (13 and up): biography, careers, concept, health, how-to, humorous, interview/profile, nature/environment, science, social issues, sports. "No cliché teen stuff. Also, we're getting too many heavy pitches lately on teen pregnancy, AIDS, etc." Buys 8 mss/year. Average word length: 675-2,100. Byline given.

How to Contact/Writers: Nonfiction: Query with published clips. Responds to queries/mss in 2 months. Publishes ms 2 months after acceptance.

Terms: Pays on publication plus 30 days. Buys first rights for mss. Pays $100-500 (Canadian) for articles. Sample copies when available for 9×12 and $1.45 (Canadian). Writer's guidelines free for SASE.

Tips: "Teens are smarter today than ever before. Respect that intelligence in queries and articles. Aim for the older end of our age-range (14-19) and avoid cliché. Humor works for us almost all the time."

WINNER, The Health Connection, 55 W. OakRidge Dr., Hagerstown MD 21740. (301)393-4010. Fax: (301)393-3294. E-mail: Winner@healthconnection.org. Website: www.winnermagazine.org. **Articles Editor:** Anita Jacobs. **Art Director:** Doug Bendal. Monthly magazine (September-May). Estab. 1958. Publishes articles that will promote choosing a positive lifestyle for children in grades 4-6.

Fiction: Young readers, middle readers: contemporary, health, nature/environment, problem-solving, anti-tobacco, alcohol, and drugs. Byline sometimes given.

Nonfiction: Young readers, middle readers: biography, games/puzzles, health, hobbies, how-to, problem-solving, social issues. Buys 20 mss/year. Average word length: 600-650. Byline sometimes given.

How to Contact/Writers: Fiction/nonfiction: Query. Responds in 6 weeks. Publishes ms 6-12 months after acceptance. Will consider simultaneous submissions and e-mail submissions.

Illustration: Buys 3 illustrations/issue; 30 illustrations/year. Uses color artwork only. Works on assignment only. Reviews ms/illustration packages from artists. Send ms with dummy. Responds only if interested. Samples returned with SASE.

Terms: Pays on acceptance. Buys first rights for mss. Original artwork returned at job's completion. Additional payment for ms/illustration packages. Sometimes additional payment when photos accompany articles. Pays $200-400 for color inside. Writer's and illustrator's guidelines free for SASE. Sample magazine $2; include 9×12 envelope with 2 first-class stamps.

Tips: Keep material upbeat and positive for elementary age children.

WITH, The Magazine for Radical Christian Youth, Faith & Life Resources, 722 Main, P.O. Box 347, Newton KS 67114. (620)367-8432. Fax: (316)283-0454. E-mail: carold@mennoniteusa.org. **Editor:** Carol Duerksen. Published 6 times a year. Circ. 5,800. Magazine published for Christian teenagers, ages 15-18. "We deal with issues affecting teens and try to help them make choices reflecting a radical Christian faith."

Fiction: Young adults/teens: contemporary, fantasy, humorous, multicultural, problem-solving, religious, romance. Multicultural needs include race relations, first-person stories featuring teens of ethnic minorities. Buys 15 mss/year. Average word length: 1,000-2,000. Byline given.

Nonfiction: Young adults/teens: first-person teen personal experience (as-told-to), how-to, humorous, multicultural, problem-solving, religion, social issues. Buys 15-20 mss/year. Average word length: 1,000-2,000. Byline given.

Poetry: Wants to see religious, humorous, nature. "Buys 1-2 poems/year." Maximum length: 50 lines.

How to Contact/Writers: Send complete ms. Query on first-person teen personal experience stories and how-to articles. (Detailed guidelines for first-person stories, how-tos, and fiction available for SASE.) Responds to queries in 3 weeks; mss in 6 weeks. Will consider simultaneous submissions.

Illustration: Buys 6-8 assigned illustrations/issue; buys 64 assigned illustrations/year. Uses b&w and 2-color artwork only. Preferred theme or style: candids/interracial. Reviews ms/illustration packages from artists. Query first. Illustrations only:

Query with portfolio (photocopies only) or tearsheets. Responds only if interested. Credit line given.

Photography: Buys photos from freelancers. Looking for candid photos of teens (ages 15-18), especially ethnic minorities. Uses 8×10 b&w glossy prints. Photographers should send unsolicited photos by mail.

Terms: Pays on acceptance. For mss buys first rights, one-time rights; second serial (reprint rights). Buys one-time rights for artwork and photos. Original artwork returned at job's completion upon request. Pays 6¢/word for unpublished mss; 4¢/word for reprints. Will pay more for assigned as-told-to stories. Pays $10-25 for poetry. Pays $50-60 for b&w cover illustration and b&w inside illustration. Pays photographers per project (range: $120-180). Sample copy for 9×12 SAE and 4 first-class stamps. Writer's/illustrator's guidelines for SASE.

Tips: "We want stories, fiction or nonfiction, in which high-school-age youth of various cultures/ethnic groups are the protaganists. Stories may or may not focus on cross-cultural relationships. We're hungry for stuff that makes teens laugh— fiction, nonfiction and cartoons. It doesn't have to be religious, but must be wholesome. Most of our stories would not be accepted by other Christian youth magazines. They would be considered too gritty, too controversial, or too painful. Our regular writers are on the *With* wavelength. Most writers for Christian youth magazines aren't." For writers: "Fiction and humor are the best places to break in. Send SASE and request guidelines." For photographers: "If you're willing to line up models and shoot to illustrate specific story scenes, send us a letter of introduction and some samples of your work."

YES MAG, Canada's Science Magazine for Kids, Peter Piper Publishing Inc., 3968 Long Gun Place, Victoria BC V8N 3A9 Canada. Fax: (250)477-5390. E-mail: editor@yesmag.ca. Website: www.yesmag.ca. **Editor:** Shannon Hunt. **Art/Photo Director:** David Garrison. Managing Editor: Jude Isabella. Bimonthly magazine. Estab. 1996. Circ. 15,000. "*YES Mag* is designed to make science accessible, interesting, exciting, and FUN. Written for children ages 8 to 14, *YES Mag* covers a range of topics including science and technology news, environmental updates, do-at-home projects and articles about Canadian students and scientists."

Nonfiction: Middle readers: animal, health, math, nature/environment, science. Buys 70 mss/year. Average word length: 250-1,250. Byline given.

How to Contact/Writers: Nonfiction: Query with published clips or send complete ms (on spec only). Responds to queries/mss in 6 weeks. Generally publishes ms 3 months after acceptance. Will consider simultaneous submissions, previously published work.

Illustration: Buys 2 illustrations/issue; 10 illustrations/year. Uses color artwork only. Works on assignment only. Reviews ms/illustration packages from artists. Query. Illustration only: Query with samples. Responds in 6 weeks. Samples filed. Credit line given.

Photography: "Looking for science, technology, nature/environment photos based on current editorial needs." Photo captions required. Uses color prints. Provide résumé, business card, promotional literature, tearsheets if possible. Responds in 3 weeks.

Terms: Pays on publication. Buys one-time rights for mss. Buys one-time rights for artwork/photos. Original artwork returned at job's completion. Pays $25-125 for stories and articles. Sample copies for $4. Writer's guidelines for SASE.

Tips: "We do not publish fiction or science fiction. Visit our website for more information, sample articles and writers guidelines. We accept queries via e-mail. Articles relating to the physical sciences and mathematics are encouraged."

YM, 15 E. 26th St., 4th Floor, New York NY 10010. (646)758-0524. E-mail: ckelly@ym.com. **Executive Editor:** Tamara Glenny. **Editor-in-Chief:** Christina Kelly. "*YM* is a national magazine for girls ages 12-24 to help guide them through the joys and challenges of young adulthood."

Nonfiction: "*YM* covers dating, psychology, entertainment, friendship, self-esteem, human interest, beauty, fashion and news trends. All articles should be lively and empowering and include quotes from experts and real teens. We do publish fiction but not poetry." Word length: 800-2,000 words.

How to Contact/Writers: Nonfiction: Query with SASE. (Write "query"on envelope.) Responds to queries in 6 weeks; mss in 2 months. Send submissions to Jana Banin, jbanin@ym.com.

Terms: Pays on acceptance. Rates vary. Sample copies available for $2.99 with 8½×11 SASE.

YOUNG & ALIVE, Christian Record Services, P.O. Box 6097, Lincoln NE 68506. (402)488-0981. Fax: (402)488-7582. E-mail: editorial@christianrecord.org. Website: www.christianrecord.org. **Articles Editor:** Ms. Gaylena Gibson. Quarterly magazine. Estab. 1976. Circ. 28,000. "We seek to provide wholesome, entertaining material for young adults ages 12 through age 25."

Nonfiction: Young adult/teen: animal, biography, careers, games/puzzles, health, history, humorous, interview/profile, multicultural, nature/environment, problem-solving, religion ("practical Christianity"), sports, travel. Buys 40-50 mss/year from freelancers. Word length: 700-1,400. Byline given.

How to Contact/Writers: Send complete ms. Responds to queries in 2 months; mss in 2 years. Publishes a ms "at least 2 years" after acceptance. Considers simultaneous submissions and previously published work. "Please don't send the work as a previously published piece (tear sheet); send a clean copy."

Illustration: Works on assignment only. Reviews ms/illustration packages from artists. Send ms with dummy. Contact Gaylena Gibson, editor.

Photography: Buys photos with accompanying ms only. Model/property release required; captions required. Uses color or b&w 3×5 or 8×10 prints.

Terms: Pays on acceptance. Buys one-time rights for ms and photos. Original artwork returned at job's completion. Pays 4-5¢/word for stories/article. Pays $25-40 for b&w inside illustration. Pays photographers by the project ($25-75). Sample copies available for 8×10 SASE and 5 first-class stamps. Writers guidelines available for SASE.

insider report

Earthquakes are like Rice Krispies: writing science for kids

As a child, nonfiction writer Fiona Bayrock considered science a "two-dimensional, pencil and paper" subject. Growing up in what she called "the Dick and Jane era," before the likes of Bill Nye and the *Magic School Bus*, she had to rely on textbooks to learn the hard sciences.

Bayrock encountered a challenge, however, when her decision to homeschool her dyslexic son forced her to adjust the way she thought about—and explained—science to fit his kinesthetic learning style.

"He needed to learn with his body—doing, feeling, touching, building, pretending, modeling," she explains. "I had to come up with creative, hands-on ways for him to learn science."

As Bayrock and her eight-year-old son experimented and ex-

Fiona Bayrock

plored together, she realized that she was having just as much fun and asking just as many questions as her student. Her curiosity had been awakened and her passion for science was beginning to stir.

I can understand how you were inspired by your homeschooling experience with your son. How did it translate to your wanting to write? Had you always been a writer?
Yes. I'm one of those people who "needs to write"—have been for as long as I can remember. The homeschooling experience didn't motivate me to write, but it was instrumental in getting me interested in science, so that's what I chose to write about.

I think my writing nonfiction for kids was in the cards a long time ago. Two of us in my grade nine English class chose "make a children's book" as an optional assignment. I created a full-sized book about a child's first airplane ride, illustrating it with actual photos from my family's first plane trip. The other girl wrote a delightful fictional story about a family of bunnies. The teacher waved the other girl's book—palm-sized and illustrated in tiny, soft pastel drawings—and said something like, "Now *this* is a book made with children in mind," implying that my book with a true story and real photos was not. I couldn't understand where she was coming from. I knew some kids liked books about real things with real photos because I was one of them. And here I am, almost 30 years later, writing real stories with real photos!

How did you break into magazine writing?
I read everything I could get my hands on about freelance writing and children's nonfiction, as well as stacks of kids' magazines. I started with the magazines I admired and read back issues to find out which areas of the magazine were open to freelancers, the types of articles used, length, number of quotes, tone, target audience, etc. Then I sent away for writer's guidelines

and theme lists, wrote the best query I could, and sent it off. I thought my first topic was pretty cool—"Bowl of Earthquakes," a news item about how the physics of earthquakes and the noise of Rice Krispies cereal is the same—but the *YES Mag* editor rejected it. She did, however, mention she was in need of articles for the Math issue. My next query on number palindromes, targeted to this issue, was accepted. As soon as I'd turned in the article, I fired off another query before the editor forgot about me. As my relationship with *YES Mag* evolved into a regular assignment, I set my sights on *Odyssey* magazine, preparing for it as I had for the first. After a couple of queries, I was accepted there on a regular basis, too. Shortly after that, one market at a time, my clip file became broader.

When you began writing, did you find it difficult to cover complex science in a way that young minds could understand?
No, not really. At that point, I'd already been thinking in those terms with my own kids for several years, and I've always had a knack for that sort of thing, anyway. In a group, I tend to take on a distilling role—rewording, clarifying, and using analogies to get to a group understanding or consensus. This has served me well in writing for children.

What advice would you give writers who are struggling to make subject matter and vocabulary "digestible" without sounding condescending to kids?
In terms of subject matter, one of the best things is to link new information and concepts to something kids already know: Bat finger bones are like the spokes on an umbrella; the inner ear is the size of a pea. Simple activities and models are helpful, too. For example, steel wool, sand, and water rusting in a pie plate makes "Mars in a Dish"; sucking the juice from fruit and spitting out the pulp is eating like a fruit bat; and rubbing a finger on a balloon makes sound the same way as a violin. Humor and word play go a long way, too.

As for vocabulary, my kids happen to be the target age for most of what I write. When they ask what I'm working on, they become my own personal focus group. In casually explaining the science to them over supper or in the car, I can often see where I've oversimplified and what needs more explanation. If the kids aren't handy, I pretend I have a child the age of my intended audience that I'm explaining things to. I find that works wonders at keeping me at the right level of sophistication. Also, one of the steps in my revision process is to look at each sentence and ask myself if I can explain things in simpler terms or more clearly. I use "nickel words" instead of "dollar words" as much as possible, without shying away from challenging vocabulary if it's the right word for the job. Kids are pretty smart; I don't believe in "dumbing down."

Do you find that the scientists you interview are excited when they find out the audience for your articles is children? Or do they tend not to take your interview questions as seriously when you tell them you're writing for *Highlights* and not, say, *Time*?
At first, I thought scientists might brush me off once they discovered I was writing for children, but I found the exact opposite. They are excited to share their work with the next generation of scientists and often volunteer anecdotes and little pieces of information they think kids might be interested in.

I aim high and am constantly amazed at who will talk to me; I have spoken with the lead scientist for the Beagle2 lander mission to Mars and the scientists responsible for each of the battling theories about whether man evolved from Neanderthals. I'm also surprised at the

Canada's *YES Mag* was the first publication to which Fiona Bayrock submitted her writing, but now her science features, like her shark-anatomy article called "Sense-sational Survival Machines" (May/June 2003), appear regularly in the publication.

lengths to which some scientists will go to answer my questions. While researching an article on timbre—what gives each musical instrument its own unique sound—I asked a physicist what it was about the sound of nails on a chalkboard that was so universally grating. He didn't know and ended up running all over the physics building at his university, looking for a chalkboard so he could record the sound and run it through his instruments in order to figure it out.

Of course, I make sure my questions are thoughtful, so I'm not wasting anyone's time. By the time I do an interview, I've already done the research, and the information I ask for isn't readily available elsewhere.

What kinds of research do you conduct to generate story ideas?

Usually it's not *generating* ideas that's the problem, but rather deciding *which* idea to write about. It's very easy for me to become paralyzed, nose pressed to the glass, drinking in the possibilities.

I think this is the flip side of "insatiable curiosity," one of the reasons many writers are drawn to nonfiction and one of the qualities that leads to good nonfiction writing. The trick is allowing the curiosity to do its thing while avoiding inaction. I found limiting myself to a particular theme issue was helpful. To generate story ideas within a theme, I flip through kids' books on the subject or surf the Internet. Once I find a topic, I use adult materials for research purposes, but juvenile literature and the Web give me the big picture from which I can find a slice that sparks my interest.

What do you feel is the most important piece of advice you could give rookie writers?

I've been asked to present an entire workshop on this topic at the Surrey International Writers' Conference. Here it is in fast forward:

Be specific. Target the magazine you want to break into, learn it inside and out, and choose a topic that is narrow, specific, and tailored for that magazine. Write tight. Start your articles with a bang—hook the reader; get them asking questions right off the bat. Meet deadlines. Write about things that excite you; passion or lack of passion will shine through in your finished work. Look for the "Cool!" or unusual in a subject. Make sure your correspondence is clean and professional—no cutesy stuff. Read, read, read, in the genre you wish to write. Tie new information to something kids already know. Have fun; wiggle your funny bone. When selecting experts to interview, go for the best. Use reliable sources—primary when possible—and have at least two sources for everything. To see your work in print sooner, target magazines that use themes. Find the kid inside you.

—*Lauren Mosko*

YOUNG RIDER, The Magazine for Horse and Pony Lovers, Fancy Publications, P.O. Box 8237, Lexington KY 40533. (859)260-9800. Fax: (859)260-9814. Website: www.youngrider.com. **Editor:** Lesley Ward. Bimonthly magazine. Estab. 1994. "*Young Rider* magazine teaches young people, in an easy-to-read and entertaining way, how to look after their horses properly, and how to improve their riding skills safely."

Fiction: Young adults: adventure, animal, horses, horse celebrities, famous equestrians. Buys 10 mss/year. Average word length: 1,500 maximum. Byline given.

Nonfiction: Young adults: animal, careers, health (horse), sports, riding. Buys 8-10 mss/year. Average word length: 1,000 maximum. Byline given.

How to Contact/Writers: Fiction/nonfiction: Query with published clips. Responds to queries in 2 weeks. Publishes ms 6-12 months after acceptance. Will consider simultaneous submissions, electronic submissions via disk or modem, previously published work.

Illustration: Buys 2 illustrations/issue; 10 illustrations/year. Works on assignment only. Reviews ms/illustration packages from artists. Query. Contact: Lesley Ward, editor. Illustrations only: Query with samples. Contact: Lesley Ward, editor. Responds in 2 weeks. Samples returned with SASE. Credit line given.

Photography: Buys photos with accompanying ms only. Uses color, slides, photos—in focus, good light. Model/property release required; captions required. Uses color 4×6 prints, 35mm transparencies. Query with samples. Responds in 2 weeks. Digital images must be high-res.

Terms: Pays on publication. Buys first North American serial rights for mss, artwork, photos. Original artwork returned at job's completion. Pays $150 maximum for stories; $250 maximum for articles. Additional payment for ms/illustration packages and for photos accompanying articles. Pays $70-140 for color inside. Pays photographers per photo (range: $65-155). Sample copies for $3.50. Writer's/illustrator's/photo guidelines for SASE.

Tips: "Fiction must be in third person. Read magazine before sending in a query. No 'true story from when I was a youngster.' No moralistic stories. Fiction must be up-to-date and humorous, teen-oriented. Need horsey interest or celebrity rider features. No practical or how-to articles—all done in-house."

N YOUNG SALVATIONIST, The Salvation Army, 615 Slaters Lane, P.O. Box 269, Alexandria VA 22314-1112. (703)684-5500. Fax: (703)684-5534. E-mail: ys@usn.salvationarmy.org. Website: publications.salvationarmyusa.org. Published 10 times/year. Estab. 1984. Circ. 50,000. **Editor-in-Chief:** Lt. Colonel Marlene Chase. "We accept material with clear Christian content written for high school age teenagers. *Young Salvationist* is published for teenage members of The Salvation Army, an evangelical part of the Christian Church that focuses on living the Christian life."

Fiction: Young adults/teens: contemporary, humorous, problem-solving, religious. Buys 10-11 mss/year. Average word length: 750-1,200. Byline given.

Nonfiction: Young adults/teens: religious—careers, concept, interview/profile, how-to, humorous, multicultural, problem-solving, social issues, sports. Buys 40-50 mss/year. Average word length: 750-1,200. Byline given.

How to Contact/Writers: Fiction/nonfiction: Query with published clips or send complete ms. Responds to queries/mss in 1 month. Will consider simultaneous submissions.

Illustrations: Buys 3-5 illustrations/issue; 20-30 illustrations/year. Reviews ms/illustration packages from artists. Send ms with art. Illustrations only: Query; send résumé, promo sheet, portfolio, tearsheets. Responds only if interested. Samples returned with SASE; samples filed. Credit line given.

Photography: Purchases photography from freelancers. Looking for teens in action.

Terms: Pays on acceptance. Buys first North American serial rights, first rights, one-time rights or second serial (reprint) rights for mss. Purchases one-time rights for artwork and photographs. Original artwork returned at job's completion "if requested." For mss, pays 10-15¢/word; 10¢/word for reprints. Pays $60-150 color (cover) illustration; $60-150 b&w (inside) illustration; $60-150 color (inside) illustration. Pays photographers per photo (range: $60-150). Sample copy for 9×12 SAE and 4 first-class stamps. Writer's guidelines for #10 SASE.

Tips: "Ask for theme list/sample copy! Write 'up,' not down to teens. Aim at young *adults*, not children." Wants "less fiction, more 'journalistic' nonfiction."

Greeting Cards, Puzzles & Games

In this section you'll find companies that produce puzzles, games, greeting cards and other items (like coloring books, stickers and giftwrap) especially for kids. These are items you'll find in children's sections of bookstores, toy stores, department stores and card shops.

Because these markets create an array of products, their needs vary greatly. Some may need the service of freelance writers for greeting card copy or slogans for buttons and stickers. Others are in need of illustrators for coloring books or photographers for puzzles. Artists should send copies of their work that art directors can keep on file—never originals. Carefully read through the listings to find companies' needs, and send for guidelines and catalogs if they're available, just as you would for book or magazine publishers.

If you'd like to find out more about the greeting card industry beyond the market for children, there are a number of resources to help you. The Greeting Card Association is a national trade organization for the industry. For membership information, contact the GCA at 1156 15th St. NW, Suite 900, Washington DC 20005, (202)393-1778, www.greetingcard.org. *Greetings Etc.* (Edgel Communications), a quarterly trade magazine covering the greeting card industry, is the official publication of the Greeting Card Association. For information call (973)252-0100. Illustrators should check out *Greeting Card Design*, by Joanne Fink. For a complete list of companies, consult the latest edition of *Artist's & Graphic Designer's Market* (Writer's Digest Books). Writers should see *You Can Write Greeting Cards*, by Karen Ann Moore (Writer's Digest Books).

Information on greeting card, puzzle and game companies listed in the previous edition but not included in this edition of *Children's Writer's & Illustrator's Market* may be found in the General Index.

ABBY LOU ENTERTAINMENT, 1411 Edgehill Place, Pasadena CA 91103. (612)795-7334. Fax:(626)795-4013. E-mail: ale@full-moon.com. President: George LeFave. Estab. 1985. Animation production company and book publisher. "We are looking for top creative children's illustrators with classic artwork. We are a children's book publisher moving into greeting cards—nature illustrations with characters." Publishes greeting cards (Whispering Gardens), coloring books, puzzles, games, posters, calendars, books (Adventures in Whispering Gardens). 100% of products are made for kids or have kid's themes.

Writing: Needs freelance writing for children's greeting cards and other children's products. Makes 6 writing assignments/year. For greeting cards, accepts both rhymed and unrhymed verse ideas. Other needs for freelance writing include the theme of "Listen to your heart and you will hear the whispers." To contact, send cover letter, résumé, client list, writing samples. Responds in 2 weeks. Materials not returned; materials filed. For greeting cards, pays flat fee of $500, royalty of 3-10%; negotiable or negotiable advance against royalty. For other writing, payment is negotiated. Pays on acceptance. Buys one-time rights; negotiable. Credit line given.

Illustration: Need freelance illustration for children's greeting cards, posters and TV related property. Makes 12 illustration assignments/year. Prefers a "classical look—property that needs illustration is Adventures in Whispering Gardens and multidimentional entertainment property." Uses color artwork only. To contact send cover letter, published samples, slides, color photocopies and color promo pieces. Materials not returned; materials filed. For greeting cards and other artwork, payment is negotiable. Pays on acceptance or publication. Rights purchased are negotiable. Credit line given.

Tips: "Give clear vision of what you want to do in the business and produce top quality, creative work."

ARISTOPLAY, LTD., 8122 Main St., Dexter MI 48130. (734)424-0123. Fax: (734)424-0124. Website: www.aristoplay.com. Art Director: Doreen Consiglio. Estab. 1979. Produces educational board games and card decks, activity kits—all educational subjects. 100% of products are made for kids or have kids' themes.

Illustration: Needs freelance illustration and graphic designers (including art directors) for games, card decks and activity kits. Makes 2-4 illustration assignments/year. To contact, send cover letter, résumé, published samples or color photocopies.

Responds back in 1 month if interested. For artwork, pays by the project, $500-5,000. Pays on acceptance (½-sketch, ½-final). Buys all rights. Credit line given.
Photography: Buys photography from freelancers. Wants realistic, factual photos.
Tips: "Creating board games requires a lot of back and forth in terms of design, illustration, editorial and child testing; the more flexible you are, the better. Also, factual accuracy is important." Target age group 4-14. "We are an educational game company. Writers and illustrators working for us must be willing to research the subject and period of focus."

AVANTI PRESS, INC., 155 W. Congress, Suite 200, Detroit MI 48226. (313)961-0022. Submit duplicates to this address: Avanti, 6 W. 18th St., 12th Floor, New York NY 10011. (212)414-1025. Fax: (212)414-1055. Website: www.avantipress.com. **Photo Editors**: Bridget Hoyle and Judith Rosenbaum. Estab. 1979. Greeting card company. Publishes photographic greeting cards—nonseasonal and seasonal.
Photography: Purchases photography from freelancers. Buys stock and assigns work. Buys approximately 150 stock images/year. Makes approximately 150 assignments/year. Wants "narrative, storytelling images, graphically strong and colorful!" Accepts only photographs. Does not return images or photographs. Uses b&w/color prints; any size or format. Pays either a flat fee or a royalty which is discussed at time of purchase." Pays on acceptance. Buys exclusive product rights (world-wide card rights). Credit line given. Photographer's guidelines for SASE or via website.
Tips: At least 75% of products have kids' and pets themes. Submit seasonal material 9 months-1 year in advance. "All images submitted should express some kind of sentiment which either fits an occasion or can be versed and sent to the recipient to convey some feeling."

N **AVONLEA TRADITIONS, INC.**, 17075 Leslie St., Units 12-15, Newmarket ON L3Y 8E1 Canada. (905)853-1777. Fax: (905)853-1763. Website: www.avonlea-traditions.com and www.maplelea.com. President: Kathryn Morton. Estab. 1988. Giftware and doll designer, importer and distributor. Designs, imports and distributes products related to Canada's most famous storybook, *Anne of Green Gables*, and other Canadian themes. Creators of the New Maplelea Girls,™ 18″ vinyl doll play system which includes chapter books and journals.
Writing: (Girls) fiction.
Illustration: Needs freelance illustration for books, stationery and packaging. Makes 2-3 illustration assignments/month; 24/year. Prefers realistic style of artwork for chapter books. Also uses other youthful artwork styles. To contact, send color photocopies and promo pieces. Responds only if interested. Materials not returned; materials filed. For other artwork, pays by the hour (range: $20-30). Pays on publication. Buys all rights. Credit line sometimes given.
Photography: Sometimes uses stock photography of Canadian people and places.
Tips: "We only use artists/writers who are Canadian."

THE BEISTLE COMPANY, P.O. Box 10, Shippensburg PA 17257. (717)532-2131. Fax: (717)532-7789. E-mail: sales@beistle.com. Website: www.beistle.com. **Product Manager**: Rick Buterbaugh, art director. Estab. 1900. Paper products company. Produces decorations and party goods, posters—baby, baptism, birthday, holidays, educational, wedding/anniversary, graduation, ethnic themes, and New Year parties. 50% of products are made for kids or have kids' themes.
Illustration: Needs freelance illustration for decorations, party goods, school supplies, point-of-purchase display materials and gift wrap. Makes 100 illustration assignments/year. Prefers fanciful style, cute 4- to 5-color illustration in gouache and/or computer illustration. To contact, send cover letter, résumé, client list, promo piece. To query with specific ideas, phone, write or fax. Responds only if interested. Materials returned with SASE; materials filed. Pays by the project or by contractual agreement; price varies according to type of project. Pays on acceptance. Buys all rights. Artist's guidelines available for SASE.
Tips: Submit seasonal material 6 months in advance.

CARDMAKERS, P.O. Box 236, 66 High Bridge Rd., Lyme NH 03768-0236. (603)795-4422. Fax: (603)795-4222. E-mail: info@cardmakers.com. Website: cardmakers.com. Owner: Peter Diebold. Estab. 1978. "We publish whimsical greeting cards with an emphasis on Christmas and business-to-business."
Writing: To contact, send cover letter and writing samples with SASE. Responds in 3 months. Returns materials if accompanied by SASE. Pays on acceptance. Buys all rights. Credit line given. Writer's guidelines available for SASE.
Illustration: Needs freelance illustration for greeting cards. Makes 30-50 illustration assignments/year. Looking for happy holidays, "activity" themes—nothing with an "edge." To contact, send cover letter, published samples, color photocopies, promo pieces and SASE. Query with specific ideas, keep it simple. Responds in 3 months. Materials returned with SASE. For greeting cards, pays flat fee of $100-400. Pays on acceptance. Credit line given. Artist's guidelines available for SASE.
Photography: Buys stock images. Wants humor. To contact, send cover letter, published samples, SASE. Responds in 3 months. Returns material with SASE. Pays per photo (range: $100-400 for b&w, $100-400 for color). Pays on acceptance. Buys exclusive product rights. Credit line given. Guidelines available for SASE.
Tips: Submit seasonal material 9 months in advance. "Be brief. Be polite. We look at all our mail. No calls, no fax, no e-mails. E-mails, requests for catalogs will get no response. Contact us through the U.S. Postal Service only! Worst times to submit—September-December. The best submissions we see are simple, right to the point, color samples with a 'check-off' stamped, return postcard eliciting comments/expression of interest."

COURAGE CARDS AND GIFTS, 3915 Golden Valley Rd., Golden Valley MN 55422. (763)520-0211. Fax: (763)520-0299. E-mail: artsearch@courage.org. Website: www.couragecards.org. **Art and Production:** Laura Brooks. Estab. 1959. Nonprofit greeting card company. Courage Cards helps support Courage Center, a nonprofit provider of rehabilitation services for children and adults with disabilities. Published holiday/seasonal greeting cards. 10% of cards are made using kid art.

Illustration: Needs freelance illustration for children's greeting cards. Makes 40 illustration assignments/year. Prefers colorful Christmas, peace, international and fall/winter seasonal art for holiday cards. Uses color artwork only. To contact, download guidelines from website or request via e-mail or phone. Responds to submissions in 3 months. Returns materials if accompanied by SASE. For greeting cards, pays flat fee of $350. Pays on publication. Buys reprint rights. Artist photo and profile on the back of every card; credit line given. Guidelines and application for art search available on website.
Tips: "Please contact us for specific guidelines for the annual art search."

A CREATE-A-CRAFT, P.O. Box 941293, Plano TX 75094-1293. **Contact**: Editor. Estab. 1967. Greeting card company. Produces greeting cards (create-a-card), giftwrap, games (create-a-puzzle), coloring books, calendars (create-a-calendar), posters, stationery and paper tableware products for all ages.
Writing: Needs freelance writing for children's greeting cards and other children's products. Makes 5 writing assignments/year. For greeting cards, accepts both rhymed and unrhymed verse ideas. Other needs for freelance writing include rhymed and unrhymed verse ideas on all products. To contact, send via recognized agent only. Responds only if interested. Material not returned. For greeting cards, payment depends on complexity of project. Pays on publication. Buys all rights. Writer's guidelines available for SASE and $2.50—includes sample cards.
Illustration: Works with 3 freelance artists/year. Buys 3-5 designs/illustrations/year. Primary age concentration is 4-8 year old market. Prefers artists with experience in cartooning. Works on assignment only. Buys freelance designs/illustrations mainly for greetings cards and T-shirts. Also uses freelance artists for calligraphy, P-O-P displays, paste-up and mechanicals. Considers pen & ink, watercolor, acrylics and colored pencil. Prefers humorous and "cartoons that will appeal to families. Must be cute, appealing, etc. No religious, sexual implications or off-beat humor." Produces material for all holidays and seasons. Contact only through artist's agent. Some samples are filed; samples not filed are not returned. Responds only if interested. Write for appointment to show portfolio of original/final art, final reproduction/product, slides, tearsheets, color and b&w. Original artwork is not returned. "Payment depends upon the assignment, amount of work involved, production costs, etc. involved in the project." Pays after all sales are tallied. Buys all rights. For guidelines and sample cards, send $2.50 and #10 SASE.
Tips: Submit 6 months in advance. "Demonstrate an ability to follow directions exactly. Too many submit artwork that has no relationship to what we produce. No phone calls accepted. Follow directions given. Do not ignore them. We do not work with anyone who does not follow them."

N CREATIF LICENSING CORP., 31 Old Town Crossing, Mt. Kisco NY 10549. (914)241-6211. E-mail: art@creatifusa .com. Website: www.creatifusa.com. **President:** Paul Cohen. Estab. 1975. Gift industry licensing agency. Publishes greeting cards, puzzles, posters, calendars, fabrics, home furnishings, all gifts. 50% of products are made for kids or have kids' themes.
Illustration: Needs freelance illustration for children's greeting cards, all gift and home furnishings. Makes many illustration assignments/month. To contact, send cover letter, résumé, client list, published samples, photocopies, portfolio, promo piece and SASE. Responds in 1 month only if interested. Materials returned with SASE only; materials filed only if interested. For greeting cards, pays royalty and advance. For other artwork, pays royalty and advance. Pays on acceptance or publication. Artists and submission guidelines are available on website. Does not accept images via e-mail.
Tips: Submit seasonal material 8-12 months in advance.

DESIGN DESIGN INC., P.O. Box 2266, Grand Rapids MI 49501. (616)774-2448. Fax: (616)774-4020. Creative Director: Tom Vituj. Estab. 1986. Greeting card company. 5% of products are made for kids or have kids themes.
Writing: Needs freelance writing for children's greeting cards. Prefers both rhymed and unrhymed verse ideas. To contact, send cover letter and writing samples. Materials returned with SASE; materials not filed. For greeting cards, pays flat fee. Buys all rights or exclusive product rights; negotiable. No credit line given. Writer's guidelines for SASE.
Illustration: Needs freelance illustration for children's greeting cards and related products. To contact, send cover letter, published samples, color or b&w photocopies, color or b&w promo pieces or portfolio. Returns materials with SASE. Pays by royalty. Buys all rights or exclusive product rights; negotiable. Artist's guidelines available for SASE. Do not send original art.
Photography: Buys stock and assigns work. Looking for the following subject matter: babies, animals, dog, cats, humorous situations. Uses 4×5 transparencies or high quality 35mm slides. To contact, send cover letter with slides, stock photo list, color copies, published samples and promo piece. Materials returned with SASE; materials not filed. Pays royalties. Buys all rights or exclusive product rights; negotiable. Photographer's guidelines for SASE. Do not send original photography.
Tips: Seasonal material must be submitted 1 year in advance.

FAX-PAX USA, INC., 37 Jerome Ave., Bloomfield CT 06002. (860)242-3333. Fax: (860)242-7102. **Editor:** Stacey L. Savin. Estab. 1990. Buys 1 freelance project/year. Publishes art and history flash cards. Needs include US history, natural history.
Writing/Illustration: Buys all rights. Pays on publication. Cannot return material.
Tips: "We need concise, interesting, well-written 'mini-lessons' on various subjects including U.S. and natural history."

GREAT AMERICAN PUZZLE FACTORY, INC., 16 S. Main St., Norwalk CT 06854. (203)838-4240. Fax: (203)866-9601. E-mail: Frankd@greatamericanpuzzle.com. Website: www.greatamericanpuzzle.com. **Art Director:** Frank DeStefano. Estab. 1976. Produces puzzles. 70% of products are made for kids or have kids' themes.
Illustration: Needs freelance illustration for puzzles. Makes over 20 freelance assignments/year. To contact, send cover letter, color photocopies and color promo pieces (no slides or original art) with SASE. Responds in 1 month. Artists guidelines available for SASE. Rights purchased vary. Buys all rights to puzzles. Pays on publication. Payment varies.

Photography: Needs local cityscapes for regional puzzles. "Photos that we have used have been of wildlife. We do occasionally use city skylines. These are only for custom jobs, though, and must be 4×5 or larger format."

Tips: Targets ages 4-12 and adult. "Go to a toy store and look at puzzles. See what is appropriate. No slides. Send color copies (3-4) for style. Looking for whimsical, fantasy and animal themes with a bright, contemporary style. Not too washy or cute. No people, babies, abstracts, landscapes or still life. We often buy reprint rights to existing work. Graphic, children's-book style work is ideal for puzzles." Submit seasonal material 1 year in advance.

N INTERCONTINENTAL GREETINGS LTD., 176 Madison Ave., New York NY 10016. (212)683-5830. Fax: (212)779-8564. Art Director: Thea Groene. Estab. 1964. 100% of material freelance written and illustrated. Intended for greeting cards, scholastic products (notebook covers, pencil cases), novelties (gift bags, mugs), tin gift boxes, shower and bedding curtains. 30-40% of products are made for kids or have kids' themes.

Illustration: Needs illustrations for children's greeting cards, notebook covers, photo albums, gift products. Prefers primarily greeting card subjects, suitable for gift industry. To contact, send cover letter, client list and published samples (if available), photocopies, slides and/or CD's with SASE. Pays percentage on publication. Clients purchase temporary exclusive product rights for contract period of 3 years. Credit line sometimes given.

Photography: Needs stylized and interesting still lifes, studio florals, all themed toward the paper and gift industry. Guidelines available for SASE.

Tips: Target group for juvenile cards: ages 1-10. Illustrators: Use clean colors, not muddy or dark. Send a neat, concise sampling of your work. Include a SASE to issue return of your samples if wanted.

INTERNATIONAL PLAYTHINGS, INC., 75D Lackawanna Ave., Parsippany NJ 07054-1712. (973)316-2500. Fax: (973)316-5883. E-mail: irene.breznak@intplay.com. Website: www.intplay.com. Product Manager: Irene Breznak. Estab. 1968. Toy/game company. Distributes and markets children's toys, games and puzzles in specialty toy markets. 100% of products are made for kids or have kids' themes.

Illustration: Needs freelance illustration for children's puzzles and games. Makes 10-20 illustration assignments/year. Prefers fine-quality, original illustration for children's puzzles. Uses color artwork only. To contact, send published samples, slides, portfolio, or color photocopies or promo pieces. Responds in 1 month only if interested. Materials filed. For artwork, pays by the project (range: $500-2,000). Pays on publication. Buys one-time rights, negotiable.

Tips: "Mail correspondence only, please. No phone calls. Send child-themed art, not cartoon-y. Use up-to-date themes and colors."

N JILLSON & ROBERTS GIFT WRAPPINGS, 3300 W. Castor St., Santa Ana CA 92704-3908. (714)424-0111. Fax: (714)424-0054. Website: www.jillsonroberts.com. Art Director: Josh Neufeld. Estab. 1973. Paper products company. Makes gift wrap/gift bags. 20% of products are made for kids or have kids' themes.

Illustration: Needs freelance illustration for children's gift wrap. Makes 6-12 illustration assignments/year. Wants children/baby/juvenile themes. To contact, send cover letter. Responds in 1 month. Returns material with SASE; materials filed. For wrap and bag designs, pays flat fee (varies). Pays on publication. Rights negotiable. Artist's guidelines for SASE.

Tips: Seasonal material should be submitted up to 3½ months in advance. "We produce two lines of gift wrap per year: one everyday line and one Christmas line. The closing date for everyday is July 1 and Christmas is September 1."

☑ MEAD WESTVACL, (formerly AMCAL, INC.), Courthouse Plaza NE, Dayton OH 45463. (800)345-6323. Website: www.meadweb.com. **Contact:** Brent Bellinger, licensing account manager. Estab. 1975. Cards, calendars, desk diaries, boxed Christmas cards, journals, mugs, and other high quality gift and stationery products.

Illustration: Receives over 150 submissions/year. "Mead Westvacl publishes high quality full color, narrative and decorative art for a wide market from traditional to contemporary. "Currently we are seeking updated interpretations of classic subjects such as florals and animals, strong decorative icons that are popular in the market place as well as in country folk art and decorative styles. Know the trends and the market. Juvenile illustration should have some adult appeal. We sell to small, exclusive gift retailers and large chains. Submissions are always accepted for future lines." To contact, send samples, photocopies, slides and SASE for return of submission. Responds in approximately 1 month. Rights purchased negotiable. Guideline sheets for #10 SASE and 1 first-class stamp.

Tips: "To learn more about Mead Westvacl and our products, please visit our website."

NOVO CARD PUBLISHERS, INC., 3630 W. Pratt Ave., Lincolnwood IL 60712. (847)763-0077. Fax: (847)763-0020. E-mail: art@novocard.net. Website: www.novocard.net. **Contact:** Art Department. Estab. 1926. Greeting card company. Company publishes greeting cards, note/invitation packs and gift envelopes for middle market. Publishes greeting cards (Novo Card/Cloud-9). 40% of products are made for kids or have kids' themes.

Writing: Needs freelance writing for children's greeting cards. Makes 400 writing assignments/year. Other needs for freelance writing include invitation notes. To contact send writing samples. Responds in approximately 1 month only if interested. Materials returned only with SASE. For greeting cards, pays flat fee of $2/line. Pays on acceptance. Buys all rights. No royalties. Credit line sometimes given. Writer's guidelines available for SASE.

Illustration: Needs freelance illustration for children's greeting cards. Makes 500 illustration assignments/year. Prefers just about all types: traditional, humor, contemporary, etc. To contact, send published samples, slides and color photocopies. Responds in approximately 2 months if interested. Materials returned with SASE. For greeting cards, payment negotiable. Pays on acceptance. Buys all greeting card and stationary rights. Credit line sometimes given. Artist's guidelines available for SASE.

Photography: Buys stock and assigns work. Buys more than 100 stock images/year. Wants all types. Uses color and b&w prints; 35mm transparencies. To contact, send slides, stock photo list, published samples, paper copies acceptable. Responds in approximately 2 months. Materials returned with SASE. Pays negotiable rate. Pays on acceptance. Buys all greeting card and stationary rights. Credit line sometimes given. Guidelines for SASE.

Tips: Submit seasonal material 10-12 months in advance. "Novo has extensive lines of greeting cards: everyday, seasonal (all) and alternative lives (over 24 separate lines of note card packs and gift enclosures). Our lines encompass all types of styles and images."

NRN DESIGNS, 5142 Argosy Ave., Long Beach CA 92649. (714)898-6363. Fax: (714)898-0015. Website: nrndesigns .com. Art Director: Linda Braun. Estab. 1984. Paper products company. Publishes imprintables. 25% of products are made for kids or have kid's themes.

Illustration: Needs freelance illustration for children's imprintables. Uses color artwork only. To contact, send published samples. Materials filed.

Tips: Submit seasonal material anytime.

P.S. GREETINGS/FANTUS PAPER PRODUCTS, 5730 North Tripp Ave., Chicago IL 60646. (773)267-6069. Fax: (773)267-6055. Website: www.psgreetings.com. Send samples: Attn: Design Director. Estab. 1950. Greeting card company. Publishes boxed and individual counter greeting cards. Seasons include: Christmas, every major holiday and everyday. 30% of products are made for kids or have kid's themes. No phone calls please.

Writing: Needs freelance writing for children's greeting cards. Makes 10-20 writing assignments/year. To contact, send writing samples. Responds in 1 month. Material returned only if accompanied with SASE. For greeting cards, pays flat fee/line. Pays on acceptance. Buys exclusive greeting card rights. Writer's guidelines free with SASE.

Illustration: Needs freelance illustration for children's greeting cards. Makes about 30-50 illustration assignments/year. Open to all mediums, all themes. Uses primarily commissioned artwork. To contact, send published samples, color promo pieces and color photocopies only. Responds in 1 month. Material returned only if accompanied with SASE. Pays flat fee upon acceptance. Buys exclusive greeting card rights. Artist's guidelines free with SASE (speculative and on assignment).

Photography: Buys photography from freelancers. Speculative and on assignment. Prefers finished digital files. To contact, send slides or CD of work. Responds in 1 month. Materials returned only with SASE; materials filed. Pays flat fee upon acceptance. Buys exclusive greeting card rights. Photographer's guidelines free with SASE.

Tips: Seasonal material should be submitted 8 months in advance.

PANDA INK, P.O. Box 5129, West Hills CA 91308. (818)340-8061. Fax: (818)883-6193. E-mail: RuthLuuph@EarthL ink.Net. **Owner, Art/Creative Director:** Ruth Ann Epstein. Estab. 1981. Greeting card company and producer of clocks, magnets, bookmarks and miscellaneous gifts. Produces Judaica—whimsical, metaphysical, general, everyday. Publishes greeting cards. 15% of products are made for kids or have kid's themes.

Writing: Needs freelance writing for children's greeting cards. Makes 1-2 writing assignments/year. For greeting cards, accepts both rhymed and unrhymed verse ideas. Looks for greeting card writing which is Judaica or metaphysical. To contact, send cover letter and SASE. To query with specific ideas, write to request disclosure form first. Responds in 1 month. Materials returned with SASE; materials filed. For greeting cards, pays flat fee of $3-20. Pays on acceptance. Rights negotiable. Credit line sometimes given.

Illustration: Needs freelance illustration for children's greeting cards, magnets, bookmarks. Makes 1-2 illustration assignments/year. Needs Judaica (Hebrew wording), metaphysical themes. Uses color artwork only. To contact, send cover letter. Query with specific ideas. Responds in 2 months. Materials returned with SASE; materials filed. Payment is negotiable. Pays on acceptance. Rights negotiable. Credit line sometimes given. Submit seasonal material 1 year in advance.

Tips: "Always send SASE. Don't write for guidelines—we have no guidelines available. Send bright colored whimsical, good art."

PEACEABLE KINGDOM PRESS, 950 Gilman, Suite 200, Berkeley CA 94710. (510)558-2051. Fax: (510)558-2052. E-mail: pkp@pkpress.com. Website: www.pkpress.com. **Editors, Creative Development:** Helen Ring; Margaret Garrou. **Creative Director:** Suellen Ehnebuske. Estab. 1983. Produces posters, greeting cards, bookmarks and related products. Uses children's book illustrators exclusively, but not necessarily targeted only to children. 98% of products are made for kids or have kids' themes.

Writing: Needs freelance writing for children's greeting cards. Makes approximately 300 writing assignments/year. To contact, send cover letter, client list, writing samples. Responds in 2 months. Materials not returned; materials filed. For greeting cards, pays a flat fee of $50.

Illustration: Needs freelance illustration for children's greeting cards and posters. Makes 75 illustration assignments/year. "For specific occasions—Christmas, Valentine's Day, Mother's and Father's Days, etc., we look for visually sophisticated work with a narrative element." To contact, send cover letter, slides, promo pieces, published books or f&g's. and color photocopies. To query with specific ideas, submit 5×7 of same dimensions enlarged, vertical, plus ⅛, if full bleed color. Materials returned with SASE; materials not filed. Responds in 2 months. Pays on publication with advance and royalties. Buys first rights and reprint rights; negotiable for greeting cards. Buys rights to distribution worldwide. Artist's guidelines available for SASE.

Tips: "We only choose from illustrations that are from published children's book illustrators, or commissioned art by established children's book illustrators. Submit seasonal and everyday greeting cards one year in advance." (speculative and on assignment).

RECO INTERNATIONAL CORP., 138 Haven Ave., Pt. Washington NY 11050. (516)767-2400. Fax: (516)767-2409. E-mail: info@reco.com. Website: www.reco.com. President: Heio W. Reich. Estab. 1967. Collector's plate, giftware producer. 60% of products are made for kids or have kids' themes.

Illustration: Needs freelance illustration for collector's plates—children's subjects mainly, but also western, Indian, flowers, animals, fantasy and mystical. Makes 40 assignments/year. Uses color artwork only. To contact, send portfolio. Submit specific ideas. Responds in 1 month. Materials returned with SASE; materials filed. For greeting art licensed, pays flat fee and royalty. For other artwork, pays royalty and advance. Pays on acceptance. Buys exclusive product rights.

Photography: Buys photos at times. Wants good art photos.

Tips: Submit seasonal material 12-18 months in advance (although rarely uses seasonal work).

N̄ RED FARM STUDIO, 1135 Roosevelt Ave., P.O. Box 347, Pawtucket RI 02862. (401)728-9300. Contact: Production Coordinator. Estab. 1949. Greeting card company. Publishes coloring books and paintables. 20% of products are made for kids or have kids' themes.

Illustration: Needs freelance illustration for tweens' and teens' greeting cards, coloring books and paintables. Makes 1 illustration assignment/month; 6-12/year. Any medium accepted. For first contact, request art guidelines with SASE. Responds in 1 month. Returns materials with SASE. Appropriate materials are kept on file. "We work on assignment using ink line work (coloring books) or pencil renderings (paintables)." Buys all rights. Credit line given, and artist may sign artwork. Artist's guidelines for SASE.

Tips: Majority of freelance assignments made during January-May/yearly. "Research companies before sending submissions to determine whether your styles are compatible."

SHULSINGER JUDAICA, LTD., 799 Hinsdale St., Brooklyn NY 11207. (718)345-3300. Fax: (718)345-1540. **Merchandiser:** Raizy Lasker. Estab. 1979. Greeting card, novelties and paper products company. "We are a Judaica company, distributing products such as greeting cards, books, paperware, puzzles, games, novelty items—all with a Jewish theme." Publishes greeting cards, novelties, coloring books, children's books, giftwrap, tableware and puzzles. 60% of products are made for kids or have kids' themes to party stories, temples, bookstores, supermarkets and chain stores.

Writing: Looks for greeting card writing which can be sent by children to adults and sent by adults to children (of all ages). Makes 5-10 freelance writing assignments/year. To contact, send cover letter. To query with specific ideas, write to request disclosure form first. Responds in 2 weeks. Materials returned with SASE; materials filed. For greeting cards, pays flat fee (this includes artwork). Pays on acceptance. Buys exclusive product rights.

Illustration: Needs freelance illustration for children's greeting cards, books, novelties, games. Makes 15-25 illustration assignments/year. "The only requirement is a Jewish theme." To contact, send cover letter and photocopies, color if possible. To query with specific ideas, write to request disclosure form first. Responds in 2 weeks. Returns materials with SASE; materials filed. For children's greeting cards, pays flat fee (this includes writing). For other artwork, pays by the project. Pays on acceptance. Buys exclusive product rights. Credit line sometimes given. Artist's guidelines not available.

Tips: Seasonal material should be submitted 6 months in advance. "An artist may submit an idea for any item that is related to our product line. Generally, there is an initial submission of a portfolio of the artist's work, which will be returned at the artist's expense. If the art is appropriate to our specialized subject matter, then further discussion will ensue regarding particular subject matter. We request a sampling of at least 10 pieces of work, in the form of tearsheets, or printed samples, or high quality color copies that can be reviewed and then kept on file if accepted. If art is accepted and published, then original art will be returned to artist. Shulsinger Judaica, Ltd. maintains the right to re-publish a product for a mutually agreed upon time period. We pay an agreed upon fee per project."

N̄ STANDARD PUBLISHING, 8121 Hamilton Ave., Cincinnati OH 45231. (513)931-4050. Fax: (513)931-0950. E-mail: tneunschwander@standardpub.com. Website: www.standardpub.com. **Directors:** Paul Learned (youth-adult) and Ruth Frederick (children's resources). **Art Directors:** Coleen Davis. Estab. 1866. Publishes children's books and teacher helps for the religious market. 75% of products are made for kids or have kids' themes.

• Standard also has a listing in Book Publishers.

Writing: Responds in 3 months. Payment method varies. Credit line given.

Illustration: Needs freelance illustration for puzzle, activity books, teacher guides. Makes 6-10 illustration assignments/year. To contact, send cover letter and photocopies. Responds in 3 months if interested. Payment method varies. Credit line given.

Photography: Buys a limited amount of photos from freelancers. Wants mature, scenic and Christian themes.

Tips "Many of our projects are developed in-house and assigned. Study our catalog and products; visit Christian bookstores. We are currently looking for Bible-based word puzzles and activities."

TALICOR, INC., 14175 Telephone Ave., Suite A, Chino CA 91710. (909)517-1962. Fax: (909)517-1962. E-mail: webmaster@talicor.com. Website: www.talicor.com. **President:** Lew Herndon. Estab. 1971. Game and puzzle manufacturer. Publishes games and puzzles (adults' and children's). 70% of products are made for kids or have kids' themes.

Writing: Makes 1 writing assignment/month.

Illustration: Needs freelance illustration for games and puzzles. Makes 12 illustration assignments/year. To contact, send promo piece. Responds in 6 months. Materials returned with SASE; materials filed. For artwork, pays by the hour, by the project or negotiable royalty. Pays on acceptance. Buys negotiable rights.

Photography: Buys stock and assigns work. Buys 6 stock images/year. Wants photos with wholesome family subjects. Makes 6 assignments/year. Uses 4×5 transparencies. To contact, send color promo piece. Responds only if interested. Materials returned with SASE; materials filed. Pays per photo, by the hour, by the day or by the project (negotiable rates). Pays on acceptance. Buys negotiable rights.

Tips: Submit seasonal material 6 months in advance.

N: WARNER PRESS, P.O. Box 2499, Anderson IN 46018-9988. Fax: (765)640-8005. E-mail: krhodes@warnerpress.org. Website: www.warnerpress.com. **Senior Editor:** Karen Rhodes. Creative Director: John Silvey. Estab. 1880. Publishes church resources, coloring and activity books and children's supplies, all religious-oriented. 15% of products are made for kids.

Writing: To contact, request guidelines first (available for church resource products only). Contact: Jennie Bishop, senior editor. Responds in 2 months. Limited purchases of children's material right now. Materials may be kept on file for future use. Pays on acceptance. Buys all rights. Credit line sometimes given. E-mail for writer's guidelines or send SASE.

Illustration: We purchase a very limited amount of freelance art at this time, but we are always looking for excellent coloring book artists.

Photography: Buys photography from freelancers for church bulletin covers. Contact: John Silvey, creative director.

Tips: "Writers request guidelines for church resource products before submitting. No guidelines available for children's products at present. We purchase a very limited amount of children's material, but we may grow into more children's products and opportunities. Make sure to include SASE. Solicited material will not be returned without SASE. Unsolicited material that does not follow guidelines will not be reviewed."

Play Publishers & Producers

Writing plays for children and family audiences is a special challenge. Whether creating an original work or adapting a classic, plays for children must hold the attention of audiences that often include children and adults. Using rhythm, repetition and dramatic action are effective ways of holding the attention of kids. Pick subjects children can relate to, and never talk down to them.

Theater companies often have limited budgets so plays with elaborate staging and costumes often can't be produced. Touring companies want simple sets that can be moved easily. Keep in mind that they may have as few as three actors, so roles may have to be doubled up.

Many of the companies listed here produce plays with roles for adults and children, so check the percentage of plays written for adult and children's roles. Most importantly, study the types of plays a theater wants and doesn't want. Many name plays they've recently published or produced, and some have additional guidelines or information available. For more listings of theaters open to submissions of children's and adult material and information on contests and organizations for playwrights, consult *Dramatists Sourcebook* (Theatre Communications Group, Inc.).

Information on play publishers listed in the previous edition but not included in this edition of *Children's Writer's & Illustrator's Market* may be found in the General Index.

A.D. PLAYERS, 2710 W. Alabama, Houston TX 77098. (713)521-1475. Fax: (713)522-5475. E-mail: adplayer@hearn.org. Website: www.adplayers.org. Estab. 1967. Produces 4-5 children's plays/year in new Children's Theatre Series. Produces children's plays for professional productions.
Needs: 99-100% of plays/musicals written for adult roles; 0-1% for juvenile roles. "Cast must utilize no more than five actors. Need minimal, portable sets for arena stage with no fly space and no wing space." Does not want to see large cast or set requirements or New Age themes. Recently produced plays: *The Magician's Nephew*, by Aurand Harris; *Ruth*, by Jeannette Cliftgeorge (a new play on the Old Testament story of Ruth, musical).
How to Contact: See website for submission guidelines.
Terms: Buys some residual rights. Pay negotiated. Submissions returned with SASE.
Tips: "Children's musicals tend to be large in casting requirements. For those theaters with smaller production capabilities, this can be a liability for a script. Try to keep it small and simple, especially if writing for theaters where adults are performing for children. We are interested in material that reflects family values, emphasizes the importance of responsibility in making choices, encourages faith in God and projects the joy and fun of telling a story."

ALABAMA SHAKESPEARE FESTIVAL, #1 Festival Dr., Montgomery AL 36117. (334)271-5300. Fax: (334)271-5348. E-mail: asf@asf.net. Website: www.asf.net. **Literary Manager:** Gwen Orel. Estab. 1972. Produces 1 children's play/year.
Needs: Produces children's plays for professional LORT (League of Regional Theaters) theatre. 90% of plays/musicals written for adult roles; 10% for juvenile roles. Must have moderate sized casts (2-10 characters); have two stages (750 seat house/250 seat house). Interested in works for the Southern Writers' Project (contact ASF for information). Does not want to see plays exclusively for child actors. Recently produced plays: *Cinderella*, by Lynn Stevens (fairytale for elementary ages); *Wiley and the Hairy Man*, by Susan Zeder (southern folk tale for elementary ages).
How to Contact: Send full mss which meet/address the focus of the Southern Writers' Project. Musicals: Query with synopsis, character breakdown and set description; scripts which meet/address the focus of the Southern Writers' Project. Will consider simultaneous submissions and previously performed work. Responds in 1 year. Send submissions to Literary Manager.
Terms: Submissions returned with SASE.
Tips: "Created in 1991 by Artistic Director Kent Thompson, the Alabama Shakespeare Festival's Southern Writers' Project is an exploration and celebration of its rich Southern cultural heritage. In an attempt to reach this goal the project seeks: to provide for the growth of a 'new' voice for Southern writers and artists; to encourage new works dealing with Southern issues and topics including those that emphasize African American experiences; to create theatre that speaks in a special way to ASF's unique and racially diverse audiences. In this way the Southern Writers' Project strives to become a window

to the complexities and beauty found in this celebrated region of our country, the South."

AMERICAN STAGE, P.O. Box 1560, St. Petersburg FL 33731-1560. (727)823-1600. Fax: (727)821-2444. E-mail: info@americanstage.org. Website: www.americanstage.org. **Artistic Director:** Todd Olson. **Managing Director:** Lee Manwaring Lowry. Estab. 1977. Produces 3 children's plays/year. Produces children's plays for professional children's theater program, mainstage, school tour, performing arts halls.
Needs: Limited by "Small mainstage venue, 1 touring production conducive to small cast, light technical pieces." Subject matter: classics and original work for children (ages K-12) and families. Recently produced plays: *A Christmas Story*, by Philip Grecian, adapted from Jean Shepherd (nontraditional Christmas for all ages); *Dragon Fire* (multicultural stories for all ages). Does not want to see plays that look down on children. Approach must be that of the child or fictional beings or animals.
How to Contact: Query with synopsis, character breakdown and set description. Will consider simultaneous submissions and previously performed work.
Terms: Purchases "professional rights." Pays writers in royalties (6-8%); $25-35/performance. SASE for return of submission.
Tips: Sees a move in plays toward basic human values, relationships and multicultural communities.

ANCHORAGE PRESS PLAYS, INC., P.O. Box 2901, Louisville KY 40201-2901. (502)583-2288. Fax: (502)583-2281. E-mail: applays@bellsouth.net. Website: www.applays.com. **Publisher:** Marilee Miller. Estab. 1935. Publishes 6-8 children's plays/year; 2-3 children's musicals/year.
Needs: "There is no genre, subject of preferred interest. We want plays of high literary/theatrical quality. Like music, such material—by nature of the stage—will appeal to any age capable of following a story. Obviously some appeal more to primary ages, some secondary." Does not want send-ups or pedantic/subject matter. "Plays—like ice cream—work only if they are superb. Teaching is not the purpose of theatre—entertainment is, and that may include serious subjects fascinatingly explored." Recently produced plays: *Ezigbo the Spirit Child*, by Max Bush; *Paper Lanterns Paper Cranes*, by Brian Kral; *Amy Crocket: M.V.P.*, by Frumi Cohen.
How to Contact: Query for guidelines first. Will consider simultaneous submissions and previously performed work "essential to be proven." Responds in 6 months.
Terms: Buys all stage rights. Pays royalty (varies extensively from 50% minimum to 80%). Submissions returned with SASE.
Tips: "Get copy of play submissions guidelines from website. SASE essential."

APPLE TREE THEATRE, 595 Elm Place, Suite 210, Highland Park IL 60035. (847)432-8223. Fax: (847)432-5214. E-mail: appletreetheatre@yahoo.com. Website: www.appletreetheatre.com. Contact: Literary Manager. Produces 3 children's plays/year.
Needs: Produces professional, daytime and educational outreach programs for grades 4-9. 98% of plays written for adult roles; 2% for juvenile roles. Uses a unit set and limited to 9 actors. No musicals. Straight plays only. Does not want to see: "children's theater," i.e. Peter Rabbit, Snow White. Material *must* be based in social issues. Recently produced plays: *Diary of Anne Frank*, by Frances Goodrich and Albert Hackett (about the Holocaust, ages 10-up); *Roll of Thunder, Hear My Cry*, adapted from the novel by Mildred Taylor (about Civil rights, racial discrimination in Mississippi in 1930s, ages 10-up).
How to Contact: Query first. Query with synopsis, character breakdown and set description. Will consider simultaneous submissions and previously performed work. Responds in 2 months.
Terms: Payment negotiated per contract. Submissions returned with SASE.
Tips: "Never send an unsolicited manuscript. Include reply postcard for queries."

BAKER'S PLAYS, P.O. Box 699222, Quincy MA 02269-9222. (617)745-0805. Fax: (617)745-9891. E-mail: info@bakersplays.com. Website: www.bakersplays.com. **Associate Editor:** Kurt Gombar. Estab. 1845. Publishes 20 plays/year; 2 musicals/year.
Needs: Adaptations of both popular and lesser known folktales. Subject matter: "full lengths for family audience and full lengths and one act plays for teens." Recently published plays: *Fairy Tale Courtroom*, by Dana Proulx; *More Aesop's (oh so slightly) Updated Fables*, by Kim Esop-Wylie.
How to Contact: Submit complete ms, score and tape or CD of songs. Responds in 8 months.
Terms: Obtains worldwide rights. Pays writers in production royalties (amount varies) and book royalties.
Tips: "Know the audience you're writing for before you submit your play anywhere. 90% of the plays we reject are not written for our market. When writing for children, never be afraid to experiment with language, characters or story. They are fertile soil for fresh, new ideas."

BARTER THEATRE EDUCATION WING, P.O. Box 867, Abingdon VA 24212. (276)628-2281, ext. 318. Fax: (276)619-3335. E-mail: education@bartertheatre.com. Website: www.bartertheatre.com. **Artistic Director:** Richard Rose. Education Director: Tere Land. Estab. 1933. Produces 2-4 children's plays and 1 children's musical/year.
Needs: "We produce 'By Kids for Kids' productions as well as professional and semi-professional children's productions. 5-10% of plays/musicals written for adult roles; 90% written for juvenile roles. Recently produced plays: *Barnum* (musical); and *The Hobbit* (musical).
How to Contact: Query with synopsis, character breakdown and set description. Will consider simultaneous submissions and previously performed work. Responds only if interested.
Terms: Pays for performance ($20-60). Submissions returned with SASE.

Tips: "Find creative, interesting material for children K-12. Don't talk below the audience."

BILINGUAL FOUNDATION OF THE ARTS, 421 N. Avenue 19th, Los Angeles CA 90031. (323)225-4044. Fax: (323)225-1250. E-mail: bfa99@earthlink.net. Website: www.bfatheatre.org. Artistic Director: Margarita Galban. **Contact:** Estela Saarlata, production manager. Estab. 1973. Produces 1 children's play/year.
Needs: Produces children's plays for professional productions. 60% of plays/musicals written for adult roles; 40% for juvenile roles. No larger than 8 member cast. Recently produced plays: *Second Chance*, by A. Cardona and A. Weinstein (play about hopes and fears in every teenager for teenagers); *Choices*, by Gannon Daniels (violence prevention, teens); *Fool 4 Kool*, Leane Schirmer and Guillermo Reyes.
How to Contact: Plays: Query with synopsis, character breakdown and set description and submit complete ms. Musicals: Query with synopsis, character breakdown and set description and submit complete ms with score. Will consider simultaneous submissions and previously performed work. Responds in 6 months.
Terms: Pays royalty; per performance; buys material outright; "different with each play."
Tips: "The plays should reflect the Hispanic experience in the U.S."

BIRMINGHAM CHILDREN'S THEATRE, P.O. Box 1362, Birmingham AL 35201-1362. (205)458-8181. Fax: (205)458-8895. E-mail: bertb@bct123.org. Website: www.bct123.org. **Managing Director:** Bert Brosowsky. Estab. 1947. Produces 8-10 children's plays/year; some children's musicals/year.
Needs: "BCT is an adult professional theater performing for youth and family audiences September-May." 99% of plays/musicals written for adult roles; 1% for juvenile roles. "Our 'Wee Folks' Series is limited to 4-5 cast members and should be written with preschool-grade 1 in mind. We prefer interactive plays for this age group. We commission plays for our 'Wee Folks' Series (preschool-grade 1), our Children's Series (K-6) and our Young Adult Series (6-12)." Recently produced plays: *Our Town*, by Thornton Wilder (YA series); *The Wizard of Oz*, by L. Frank Baum, adapted by R. Eugene Jackson (children's series); *Three Billy Goats Gruff*, by Jean Pierce (Wee Folks' Series). No adult language. Will consider musicals, interactive theater for Wee Folks Series. Prefer children's series and young adult series limited to 4-7 cast members.
How to Contact: Query first, query with synopsis, character breakdown and set description. Responds in 4 months.
Terms: Buys negotiable rights. Submissions returned with SASE.
Tips: "We would like our commissioned scripts to teach as well as entertain. Keep in mind the age groups (defined by each series) that our audience is composed of. Send submissions to the attention of Bert Brosowsky, managing director."

BOARSHEAD THEATER, 425 S. Grand Ave., Lansing MI 48933. (517)484-7800. Fax: (517)484-2564. **Artistic Director:** John Peakes. **Director of P.R., Marketing and Outreach:** Carey McConkey. Estab. 1966. Produces 3 children's plays/year.
Needs: Produces children's plays for professional production. Majority of plays written for young adult roles. Prefers 5 characters or less for touring productions, 5 plus characters for mainstage productions; one unit set, simple costumes. Recently produced plays: *The Lion, the Witch & the Wardrobe*, by Joseph Robinette (fantasy for ages 6-12); *1,000 Cranes*, by Katharine Schultz Miller; *The Planet of the Perfectly Awful People*; and *Patchwork*. Does not want to see musicals.
How to Contact: Query with synopsis, character breakdown and set description. Send to Education Director. Include 10 pages of representative dialogue. Will consider previously performed work. Responds in 2 weeks on queries; 4 months "if we ask for submissions."
Terms: Submissions returned with SASE. If no SASE, send self-addressed stamped postcard for reply.

CALIFORNIA THEATRE CENTER, P.O. Box 2007, Sunnyvale CA 94087. (408)245-2979. Fax: (408)245-0235. E-mail: ctc@ctcinc.org. Website: www.ctcinc.org. **General Director:** Gayle Cornelison. Estab. 1975. Produces 15 children's plays and 1 musical for professional productions.
Needs: 75% of plays/musicals written for adult roles; 20% for juvenile roles. Prefers material suitable for professional tours and repertory performance; one-hour time limit, limited technical facilities. Recently produced *Most Valuable Player*, by Mary Hall Surface (U.S. history for grades 3 and up); *Sleeping Beauty*, by Gayle Cornelison (fairy tale for ages K-5).
How to Contact: Query with synopsis, character breakdown and set description. Send to: Will Huddleston. Will consider previously performed work. Responds in 6 months.
Terms: Rights negotiable. Pays writers royalties; pays $35-50/performance. Submissions returned with SASE.
Tips: "We sell to schools, so the title and material must appeal to teachers who look for things familiar to them. We look for good themes, universality. Avoid the cute. We also do a summer conservatory that requires large cast plays."

CHILDREN'S STORY SCRIPTS, Baymax Productions, PMB 130, 2219 W. Olive Ave., Burbank CA 91506-2648. (818)787-5584. E-mail: baymax@earthlink.net. **Editor:** Deedra Bebout. Estab. 1990. Produces 1-10 children's scripts/year.
Needs: "Except for small movements and occasionally standing up, children remain seated in Readers Theatre fashion." Publishes scripts sold primarily to schools or wherever there's a program to teach or entertain children. "All roles read by children except K-2 scripts, where kids have easy lines, leader helps read the narration. Prefer multiple cast members, no props or sets." Subject matter: scripts on all subjects that dovetail with classroom subjects. Targeted age range—K-8th grade, 5-13 years old. Recently published plays: *A Clever Fox*, by Mary Ellen Holmes (about using one's wits, grades 2-4); *Memories of the Pony Express*, by Sharon Gill Askelson (grades 5-8). No stories that preach a point, no stories about catastrophic disease or other terribly heavy topics, no theatrical scripts without narrative prose to move the story along, no monologues or 1-character stories.
How to Contact: Submit complete ms. Will consider simultaneous submissions and previously performed work (if rights are available). Responds in 2 weeks.
Terms: Purchases all rights; authors retain copyrights. "We add support material and copyright the whole package." Pays

writers in royalties (10-15% on sliding scale, based on number of copies sold). SASE for reply and return of submission. **Tips:** "We're only looking for stories related to classroom studies—educational topics with a freshness to them. Our scripts mix prose narration with character dialogue—we do not publish traditional, all-dialogue plays." Writer's guidelines packet available for business-sized SASE with 2 first-class stamps. Guidelines explain what Children's Story Scripts are, give 4-page examples from 2 different scripts, give list of suggested topics for scripts.

CIRCA '21 DINNER THEATRE, P.O. Box 3784, Rock Island IL 61204-3784. (309)786-2667. Fax: (309)786-4119. Website: circa21.com. **Producer:** Dennis Hitchcock. Estab. 1977. Produces 3 children's musicals/year.
Needs: Produces children's plays for professional productions. 95% of musicals written for adult roles; 5% written for juvenile roles. "Prefer a cast of four to eight—no larger than ten. Plays are produced on mainstage sets." Recently produced plays: *Jungle Book*, by Ty Stover and Michael Hoagland (ages 8-adult); *Jack & The Beanstalk*, by Prince Street Players (ages 4-adult).
How to Contact: Send complete script with audiotape of music. Responds in 3 months.
Terms: Payment negotiable.

I.E. CLARK PUBLICATIONS, P.O. Box 246, Schulenburg TX 78956-0246. (979)743-3232. Fax: (979)743-4765. E-mail: ieclark@cvtv.net. **General Manager:** Donna Cozzaglio. Estab. 1956. Publishes 3 or more children's plays/year; 1 or 2 children's musicals/year.
Needs: Publishes plays for all ages. Published plays: *Little Women*, by Thomas Hischak (dramatization of the Alcott novel for family audiences); *Heidi*, by Ann Pugh, music by Betty Utter (revision of our popular musical dramatization of the Johanna Spyri novel). Does not want to see plays that have not been produced.
How to Contact: Submit complete ms and audio or video tape. Will consider simultaneous submissions and previously performed work. Responds in 4 months.
Terms: Pays writers in negotiable royalties. SASE for return of submission.
Tips: "We publish only high-quality literary works. Request a copy of our writer's guidelines before submitting. Please send only one manuscript at a time and be sure to include videos and audiotapes."

COLUMBIA ENTERTAINMENT COMPANY, % Betsy Phillips, 309 Parkade, Columbia MO 65202-1447. (573)874-5628. Website: cec.missouri.org. **Contest Director:** Betsy Phillips. Estab. 1988. Produces 0-2 children's plays/year; 0-1 children's musicals/year.
Needs: "We produce children's theatre plays. Our theatre school students act all the roles. We cast adult and children roles with children from theatre school. Each season we have 5 plays done by adults (kid parts possible)—up to 3 theatre school productions. We need large cast plays—more than 20, as plays are produced by theater school classes (ages 5-14). We also consider small cast (7 characters) plays that might work with an individual class. Any set changes are completed by students in the play." Musical needs: Musicals must have songs written in ranges children can sing. Recently produced: *Mississippi Odyssey*, by Mary Barile (retelling of story set in Lewis & Clark era, family audience 5-100).
How to Contact: Plays: Submit complete ms; use SASE to get form. Musicals: Submit complete ms and lead sheets. Score required if play is produced. CD or tape of music must be included, use SASE to get entry form. Will consider simultaneous submissions and previously performed work. Responds within 3 months of June 1st deadline. All scripts are read by a minimum of 3 readers. The authors will receive a written evaluation of the strengths and weaknesses of the play.
Terms: "We have production rights sans royalties for one production. Production rights remain with author." Pays $500 1st prize. Submissions returned with SASE.
Tips: "Please write a play/musical that appeals to all ages. We like plays that audiences of all ages will enjoy. We always need lots of parts, especially for girls."

CONTEMPORARY DRAMA SERVICE, Division of Meriwether Publishing Ltd., 885 Elkton Dr., Colorado Springs CO 80907-3557. (719)594-4422. Fax: (719)594-9916. E-mail: merpcds@aol.com. Website: www.meriwetherpublishing.com. **Associate Editor:** Arthur L. Zapel. Estab. 1979. Publishes 60 children's plays/year; 15 children's musicals/year.
Needs: Prefer shows with a large cast. 50% of plays/musicals written for adult roles; 50% for juvenile roles. Recently published plays: *Pecos Bill, Slue Foot Sue and the Wing Dang Doo!*, by Arthur Zapel and Bill Francoeur (a musical); *Cinderella*, by Kirk Buis (a comedy spoof); *The Night the Animals Sang*, by Katherine Babb (a Christmas play). "We publish church plays for elementary level for Christmas and Easter. Most of our secular plays are for teens or college level." Does not want to see "full-length, three-act plays unless they are adaptations of classic works or have unique comedy appeal."
How to Contact: Query with synopsis, character breakdown and set description; "query first if a musical." Will consider simultaneous submissions or previously performed work. Responds in 1 month.
Terms: Purchases first rights. Pays writers royalty (10%) or buys material outright for $200-1,000. SASE for return of submission.
Tips: "If the writer is submitting a musical play, an audiocassette of the music should be sent. We prefer plays with humorous action. We like comedies, spoofs, satires and parodies of known works. A writer should provide credentials of plays published and produced. Writers should not submit items for the elementary age level."

☑ **DALLAS CHILDREN'S THEATER**, 5938 Skillman, Dallas TX 75231-7608. Fax: (214)978-0118. E-mail: family@dct.org. Website: www.dct.org. **Artistic Associate:** Artie Olaisen. Estab. 1984. Produces 8-10 children's plays/year. Produces 1-2 children's musicals/year.
Needs: Produces children's plays for professional theater. 80% of plays/musicals written for adult roles; 20% for juvenile roles. Prefer cast size between 8-12. Musical needs: "We do produce musical works, but prefer non-musical. Availability

of music tracks is a plus." Does not want to see: anything not appropriate for a youth/family audience. Recently produced plays: *Holes*, by Louis Sachar (based on popular book, darkly humorous tale of crime, punishment and redemption for ages 8 and older; *Coyote Tales*, by Linda Daugherty (lively telling of traditional folk stories of Mexico for all ages).

How to Contact: Plays: Query with synopsis, character breakdown and set description. Musicals: Query with synopsis, character breakdown and set description. Will consider previously performed work. Responds in up to 1 year. Please, no phone calls; no unsolicited scripts.

Terms: Rights are negotiable. Payment is negotiable. Submissions returned with SASE. All scripts should be sent to the attention of Artie Olaisen.

Tips: "We are only interested in full-length substantive works. Please no classroom pieces. Our mainstage season serves a multi-generational family audience."

DRAMATIC PUBLISHING, INC., 311 Washington St., Woodstock IL 60098. (815)338-7170. Fax: (815)338-8981. E-mail: plays@dramaticpublishing.com. Website: www.dramaticpublishing.com. **Acquisitions Editor:** Linda Habjan. Estab. 1885. Publishes 10-15 children's plays/year; 4-6 children's musicals.

Needs: Recently published: *Anastasia Krupnik*, by Meryl Friedman, based on the book by Lois Lowry; *A Village Fable*, by James Still, adapted from *In the Suicide Mountain*, by John Gardner; *The Little Prince*, adapted by Rick Cummins and John Scoullar.

How to Contact: Submit complete ms/score and CD/videotape (if a musical); include SASE if materials are to be returned. Responds in 3 months. Pays writers in royalties.

Tips: "Scripts should be from ½ to 1½ hours long and not didactic or condescending. Original plays dealing with hopes, joys and fears of today's children are preferred to adaptations of old classics. No more adapted fairytales."

DRAMATICS, 2343 Auburn Ave., Cincinnati OH 45219-2815. (513)421-3900. Fax: (513)421-7077. Website: www.edta.org. **Editor:** Don Corathers. Estab. 1929. Publishes 7 young adult plays/year.

Needs: Most of plays written for high school actors. 14-18 years old (grades 9-12) appropriate for high school production and study. "We prefer not to receive plays geared for young children." Recently produced plays: *Nine Ten*, by Warren Leight (life in NYC before September 11, as seen at jury duty, ages 15 and up); *Reese and Babe* (a woman apologizes to a clown for killing his monkey, after the woman's husband buries her car, ages 15 and up).

How to Contact: Plays: Submit complete ms. Musicals: Not accepted. Will consider simultaneous submissions, electronic submissions via disk/modem, previously performed work. Responds in 6 months.

Terms: Buys one-time publication rights. Payment varies. Submissions returned with SASE.

Tips: Our readers are savvy theater makers. Give them more than stereotypes and fairy tales to work with.

EARLY STAGES CHILDREN'S THEATRE @ STAGES REPERTORY THEATRE, 3201 Allen Parkway, Suite 101, Houston TX 77019. (713)527-0220. Fax: (713)527-8669. E-mail: rbundy@stagestheatre.com. Website: www.stagestheatre.com. **Artistic Director:** Rob Bundy. Estab. 1978. Produces 5 children's plays/year.

Needs: In-house professional children's theatre. 100% of plays/musicals written for adult roles. Cast size must be 8 or less. Performances are in 2 theaters—Arena has 230 seats; Thrust has 180 seats. Musical needs: Shows that can be recorded for performance; no live musicians. Touring Needs: Small cast (no more than 5) addressing relevant issues for middle and high school students and teachers—2003 tour of *In Between*, by R.N. Sandberg. Recently produced plays: *Cinderella*, by Sidney Berger, music by Rob Laudes, *The Courage of Mandy Kate Brown*, by Kate Pogue (a tale of the Underground Railroad).

How to Contact: Plays/musicals: Query with synopsis, character breakdown and set description. Will consider simultaneous submissions and previously performed work. Responds only if interested.

Terms: Manuscripts optioned exclusively. Pays 3-8% royalties. Submissions returned with SASE.

Tips: "Select pieces that are intelligent, as well as entertaining, and that speak to a child's potential for understanding. We are interested in plays/musicals that are imaginative and open to full theatrical production."

EL CENTRO SU TEATRO, 4725 High, Denver CO 80216. (303)296-0219. Fax: (303)296-4614. E-mail: elcentro@suteatro.org. Website: www.suteatro.org. **Artistic Director:** Anthony J. Garcia. Estab. 1971. Produces 2 children's plays/year.

Needs: "We are interested in plays by Chicanos or Latinos that speak to that experience. We do not produce standard musicals. We are a culturally specific company." Recently produced *Joaquim's Christmas*, by Anthony J. Garcia (children's Christmas play for ages 7-15); and *The Dragonslayer*, by Silviana Woods (young boy's relationship with grandfather for ages 7-15); *And Now Miguel*, by Jim Krungold. Does not want to see "cutesy stuff."

How to Contact: Query with synopsis, character breakdown and set description. Will consider simultaneous submissions and previously performed work. Responds in 9 months. Buys regional rights.

Terms: Pays writers per performance: $35 1st night, $25 subsequent. Submissions returned with SASE.

Tips: "People should write within their realm of experience but yet push their own boundaries. Writers should approach social issues within the human experience of their character."

ELDRIDGE PUBLISHING CO. INC., P.O. Box 14367, Tallahassee FL 32317. (800)447-8243. Fax: (800)453-5179. E-mail: info@histage.com. Website: www.histage.com or www.95church.com. **Editor:** Nancy Vorhis. Estab. 1906. Publishes approximately 25 children's plays/year; 4-5 children's musicals/year.

Needs: "We publish for junior and high school, community theater and children's theater (adults performing for children), all genres, also religious plays." Recently published plays: *A Midsummer Night's Dream—A Musical*, adapted by Wade Bradford with music by Rachel Greenlee. Prefers work which has been performed or at least had a staged reading.

"WE WANT TO PUBLISH YOUR WORK."

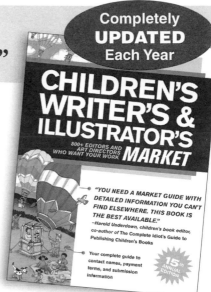

You would give anything to hear an editor speak those six magic words. So you work hard for weeks, months, even years to make that happen. You create a brilliant piece of work and a knock-out presentation, but there's still one vital step to ensure publication. You still need to submit your work to the right buyers. With rapid changes in the publishing industry, it's not always easy to know who those buyers are. That's why each year thousands of writers just like you turn to the most current edition of this indispensable market guide.

Keep ahead of the changes by ordering *2005 Children's Writer's & Illustrator's Market* today! You'll save the frustration of getting manuscripts returned in the mail stamped MOVED: ADDRESS UNKNOWN, and of NOT submitting your work to new listings because you don't know they exist. All you have to do to order next year's edition — at this year's price — is complete the attached order card and return it with your payment. Lock in the 2004 price for 2005 — order today!

2005 Children's Writer's & Illustrator's Market will be published and ready for shipment in November 2004.

Turn Over for More Great Books to Help You Get Published! ➤

Get Your Children's Stories Published with Help from These Writer's Digest Books!

Grammatically Correct
by Anne Stilman

Make sure your writing is smooth, clear, graceful — and correct. With this easy-to-use reference, you can quickly master the building blocks that make up good writing — including punctuation, spelling, style, usage and more. Complete with exercises and examples!

#10529-K/$19.99/352 p/hc

Children's Writer's Word Book
by Alijandra Mogilner

This quick-reference guide helps you write in the language of your young audience. Learn what words are appropriate when, see samples of writing for each reading level, and get ideas for new stories. Plus, *Children's Writer's Word Book* contains a thesaurus and a list of specific vocabulary words introduced in 7 different grade levels (K-6).

#10649-K/$16.99/352 p/pb

2004 Novel & Short Story Writer's Market
edited by Anne Bowling

Discover buyers hungry for your work! You'll find the names, addresses, pay rates, and editorial needs of thousands of fiction publishers, including many prestigious non-paying markets not listed in *Writer's Market*. Plus, articles and interviews with professionals who know what it takes to get published!

#10855-K/$24.99/690 p/pb

Snoopy's Guide to the Writing Life
edited by Barnaby Conrad with a forward by Monte Schulz

Thirty famous writers, including Ray Bradbury, Sue Grafton and Fannie Flagg, respond to their favorite "Snoopy-at-the-typewriter" strips. Each strip inspires a reflection on some aspect of the writing life — from getting rejected to the search for new ideas. The essays are light and sometimes humorous, but they all reveal the wisdom behind the world's most literary beagle.

#10856-K/$19.99/192 p/hc

How to Write and Illustrate Children's Books And Get Them Published
edited by Treld Pelkey Bicknell & Felicity Trotman

Advice and insider tips from some of the finest talents in children's publishing are collected in this must-have guide for success in writing and illustrating in the children's market. You'll find inspiring and insightful instruction from experts in the field to help you get your work published.

#10694-K/$19.99/144p/pb

Picture Writing
A new approach to writing for kids and teens
by Anastasia Suen

Learn to create evocative characters, setting and plots fueled by the power of vivid description. You'll discover how to optimize the five senses, and how to recognize what type of descriptive words work best for various age groups.

#10755-K/$16.99/224p/pb

Pick up these helpful references today at your local bookstore, use the handy Order Card on the reverse side, or visit the Web site: www.writersdigest.com/store/books.asp.

How to Contact: Submit complete ms, score and tape of songs (if a musical). Will consider simultaneous submissions if noted. Responds in 3 months.

Terms: Purchases all dramatic rights. Pays writers royalties of 50%; 10% copy sales; buys material outright for religious market.

Tips: "Try to have your work performed, if at all possible, before submitting. We're always on the lookout for comedies which provide a lot of fun for our customers. But other more serious topics that concern teens, as well as intriguing mysteries and children's theater programs are of interest to us as well. We know there are many new talented playwrights out there, and we look forward to reading their fresh scripts."

ENCORE PERFORMANCE PUBLISHING, P.O. Box 692, Orem UT 84059. (902)527-3524. Fax: (902)543-6156. E-mail: encoreplay@aol.com. Website: www.Encoreplay.com. **Contact:** Mike Perry. Estab. 1978. Publishes 20-30 children's plays/year; 10-20 children's musicals/year.

Needs: Prefers close to equal male/female ratio if possible. Adaptations for K-12 and older. 60% of plays written for adult roles; 40% for juvenile roles. Recently published plays: *Boy Who Knew No Fear*, by G. Riley Mills/Mark Levenson (adaptation of fairy tale, ages 8-16); *Two Chains*, by Paul Burton (about drug abuse, ages 11-18).

How to Contact: Query first with synopsis, character breakdown, set description, production history, and song list if musical. Will only consider previously performed work. Responds in 2 months.

Terms: Purchases all publication and production rights. Author retains copyright. Pays writers in royalties (50%). SASE for return of submission.

Tips: "Give us issue and substance, be controversial without offense. Use a laser printer! Don't send an old manuscript. Make yours look the most professional."

THE ENSEMBLE THEATRE, 3535 Main, Houston TX 7002. (713)520-0055, ext.317. Fax: (713)520-1269. **Artistic Director:** Jackson Randolph. Estab. 1976. Produces 4 children's plays/year; 1 children's musical/year.

Needs: Produces children's plays for professional productions (in-house and touring). 70% of plays/musicals written for adult roles; 30% for juvenile roles. Limited to cast of 6 or less, with limited staging, costuming and props. Musical needs: appropriate for limited or recorded accompaniment. Recently published *Coolsuit*, by Lauren Mayer; *On Stage*, by Nancy Zelenak, music and lyrics by C. Michael Perry.

How to Contact: Plays: Query with synopsis, character breakdown and set description; submit complete ms. Musicals: Query with synopsis, character breakdown and set description. Will consider simultaneous submissions and previously performed work. Responds only if interested.

Terms: Pays $20-75/performance.

Tips: "Entertain, educate and enlighten."

FLORIDA STUDIO THEATRE, 1241 N. Palm Ave., Sarasota FL 34236. (941)366-9017. Fax: (941)955-4137. E-mail: james@fst2000.org. Website: www.fst2000.org. **Artistic Director:** Richard Hopkins. **Coordinator:** James Ashford. Estab. 1973. Produces 3 children's plays/year.

Needs: Produces children's plays for professional productions. "Prefer small cast plays (5-8 characters) that use imagination more than heavy scenery." Will consider new plays and previously performed work.

How to Contact: Query with synopsis, character breakdown, 5 pages of sample dialogue; Attn: James Ashford. Responds in 1 month to queries. Rights negotiable. Payment negotiable. Submissions returned with SASE.

Tips: "Children are a tremendously sophisticated audience. The material should respect this."

THE FOOTHILL THEATRE COMPANY, P.O. Box 1812, Nevada City CA 95959-1812. (530)265-9320. Fax: (530)265-9325. E-mail: info@foothilltheatre.org. Website: www.foothilltheatre.org. **Literary Manager:** Gary Wright. Estab. 1977. Produces 0-2 children's plays/year; 0-1 children's musicals/year. Professional nonprofit theater.

Needs: 95% of plays/musicals written for adult roles; 5% for juvenile roles. "Small is better, but will consider anything." Produced *Peter Pan*, by J.M. Barrie (kids vs. grownups, for all ages); *Six Impossible Things Before Breakfast*, by Lee Potts & Marilyn Hetzel (adapted from works of Lewis Carroll, for all ages). Does not want to see traditional fairy tales.

How to Contact: Query with synopsis, character breakdown and set description. Will consider simultaneous submissions and previously performed work. Responds in 6 months.

Terms: Buys negotiable rights. Payment method varies. Submissions returned with SASE.

Tips: "Trends in children's theater include cultural diversity, real life issues (drug use, AIDS, etc.), mythological themes with contemporary resonance. Don't talk down to or underestimate children. Don't be preachy or didactic—humor is an excellent teaching tool."

N: THE FREELANCE PRESS, P.O. Box 548, Dover MA 02030. (508)785-8250. **Managing Editor:** Narcissa Campion. Estab. 1979.

Needs: Casts are comprised of young people, ages 8-15, and number 25-30. "We publish original musicals on contemporary topics for children and adaptations of children's classics (e.g., Rip Van Winkle)." Published plays: *The Tortoise and the Hare* (based on story of same name, for ages 8-12); *Monopoly*, 3 (young people walk through board game, for ages 11-15).

● The Freelance Press does not accept plays for adult performers.

How to Contact: Submit complete ms and score with SASE. Will consider simultaneous submissions and previously performed work. Responds in 3 months.

Terms: Pays writers 10% royalties on book sales, plus performance royalties. SASE for return of submission.

SAMUEL FRENCH, INC., 45 W. 25th St., New York NY 10010. (212)206-8990. Fax: (212)206-1429. **Senior Editor:** Lawrence Harbison. Estab. 1830. Publishes very few children's plays/year; "variable number of musicals."

Needs: Subject matter: "all genres, all ages. No puppet plays. No adaptations of any of those old 'fairy tales.' No 'Once upon a time, long ago and far away.' No kings, princesses, fairies, trolls, etc."

How to Contact: Submit complete ms and demo tape (if a musical). Responds in "minimum of 2 months."

Terms: Purchases "publication rights, amateur and professional production rights, option to publish next 3 plays." Pays writers "book royalty of 10%; variable royalty for professional and amateur productions. SASE for return of submissions.

Tips: "Most of our recent children's plays have been published by our London affiliate, Samuel French, or by our subsidiary, Baker's Plays."

THE GROWING STAGE THEATRE, In Residence at the Palace, Rt. 183, Netcong NJ 07857. (973)347-4946. Fax: (973)691-7069. **Executive Director:** Stephen L. Fredericks. Estab. 1982. Produces 5 mainstage children's shows, a summer production for the whole family and 3 children's musicals/year. Equity touring production to schools and other organizations. Professional actors work with community actors.

Needs: 60% of plays/musicals written for adult roles; 40% for juvenile roles. Produced: *Snow White*, by Stephen L. Fredericks (adaptation of classic tale, ages 5-up); *The Hobbit*, by Thomas Olsen (Tolkien classic, for ages 10-up). Plays for young audiences only.

How to Contact: Query with synopsis, character breakdown and set description. Will consider previously performed work. Responds in 2 months.

Terms: "Contracts are developed individually." Pays $25-75/performance. Submissions returned with SASE.

Tips: "There's an overabundance on issue-oriented plays. Creativity, quality, the standards we place on theater aimed at adults should not be reduced in preparing a script for young people. We, together, are forming the audience of tomorrow. Don't repel young people by making the theater another resource for the infomercial—nurture, challenge and inspire them. Never write down to your intended audience."

HAYES SCHOOL PUBLISHING CO. INC., 321 Pennwood Ave., Pittsburgh PA 15221. (412)371-2373. Fax: (412)371-6408. Website: www.hayespub.com. Contact: Mr. Clair N. Hayes III. Estab. 1940.

Needs: Wants to see supplementary teaching aids for grades K-12. Interested in all subject areas, especially music, foreign language (French, Spanish, Latin), early childhood education.

How to Contact: Query first with table of contents or outline and 3-4 sample pages. Will consider simultaneous and electronic submissions. Responds in 6 weeks.

Terms: Purchases all rights. Work purchased outright. SASE for return of submissions.

HEUER PUBLISHING COMPANY, P.O. Box 248, Cedar Rapids IA 52406. (319)364-6311. Fax: (319)364-1771. E-mail: editor@hitplays.com. Website: www.hitplays.com. **Associate Editor:** Geri Albrecht. Estab. 1928. Publishes 10-15 plays/year for young audiences and community theaters; 5 musicals/year.

Needs: "We publish plays and musicals for schools and community theatres (amateur)." 100% for juvenile roles. Single sets preferred. Props should be easy to find and costumes, other than modern dress, should be simple and easy to improvise. Stage effects requiring complex lighting and/or mechanical features should be avoided. Musical needs: "We need musicals with large, predominantly female casts. We publish plays and musicals for middle, junior and senior high schools." Recently published plays: *Pirate Island*, by Martin Follose (popular for all producing groups); *Virgil's Wedding*, by Eddie McPherson (delightful characters and non-stop laughter).

How to Contact: Plays/musicals: Query with synopsis. Will consider simultaneous submissions and previously performed work. Responds in 2 months.

Terms: Buys amateur rights. Pays royalty or purchases work outright. Submissions returned with SASE.

Tips: "We sell almost exclusively to junior and smaller senior high schools so the subject matter and language should be appropriate for schools and young audiences."

LAGUNA PLAYHOUSE YOUTH THEATRE, P.O. Box 1747, Laguna Beach CA 92652. (949)497-2787. Fax: (949)497-7109. E-mail: jlauderdale@lagunaplayhouse.com; dinglima@lagunaplayhouse.com. Website: www.lagunaplayho use.com. **Artistic Director:** Joe Lauderdale. Estab. 1986. Produces 4 mainstage (including musical) and 3 touring shows/year.

Needs: The Laguna Playhouse is a LORTB theater company with TYA contract for touring shows and nonprofessionals in mainstage shows. 40% of plays/musicals written for adult roles; 60% for juvenile roles. Musical needs: Small combos of 4-7 people with some doubling of instruments possible. Recently produced plays: *The Adveutures of Tom Sawyer*, by Joe Lauderdale and Mark Turnbull; *The Wrestling Season*, by Laurie Brooks; and *The Wizard of Oz*, Royal Shakespeare version.

How to Contact: Submit letter of intent and synopsis. Musicals should also submit recording. Responds in 8 months.

Terms: Pays 4-6% royalties.

Tips: "Three of our mainstage works are literary based. The fourth mainstage show is targeted for teens and deals with appropriate issues. Touring shows have small casts (4-6 people) and are on Carlifornia Reading Curriculum lists."

MERRY-GO-ROUND YOUTH THEATRE, P.O. Box 506, Auburn NY 13021. (315)255-1305. Fax: (315)252-3815. E-mail: youthmgr@dreamscape.com. Website: www.merry-go-round.com. **Producing Director:** Ed Sayles. Estab. 1958. Produces 10 children's plays/year; 3 children's musicals/year.

Needs: 100% of plays/musicals written for adult roles. Cast maximum, 4 and staging must be tourable. Recently produced plays: *Seagirl*, by Francis Elitzig (Chinese folktale); *There Once Was a Longhouse, Where Now There is Your House*, by Rick Balian (Native Americans of New York state).

How to Contact: Plays/musicals: query with synopsis, character breakdown and set description; submit complete ms and score. Will consider simultaneous submissions, electronic submissions via disk/e-mail and previously performed work. Responds in 2 months.

Terms: "Realize that our program is grade/curriculum specific. And understanding of the NYS Learning Standards may help a writer to focus on a point of curriculum that we would like to cover."

NEBRASKA THEATRE CARAVAN, 6915 Cass St., Omaha NE 68132. (402)553-4890, ext. 154. Fax: (402)553-6288. E-mail: caravan@omahaplayhouse.com. Website: www.omahaplayhouse.com. **Director:** Richard L. Scott. Estab. 1976. Produces 3-4 children's plays/year; 1-2 children's musicals/year.

Needs: Produces children's plays for professional productions with a company of 5-6 actors touring. 100% of plays/musicals written for adult roles; setting must be adaptable for easy touring. 65 minute show for grades 7-12; 60 minutes for elementary. Musical need: 1 piano or keyboard accompaniment. Recently produced plays: *A Thousand Cranes*, by Kathryn Schultz Miller (Sadako Susaki, for ages K-8).

How to Contact: Plays: query with synopsis, character breakdown and set description. Musicals: query first. Will consider simultaneous submissions and previously performed work. Responds in 3 months.

Terms: Pays $35-40/performance; pays commission—option 1—own outright, option 2—have right to produce at any later date—playwright has right to publish and produce. Submissions returned with SASE.

Tips: "Be sure to follow guidelines."

THE NEW CONSERVATORY THEATRE CENTER, 25 Van Ness Ave., San Francisco CA 94102-6033. (415)861-4914. Fax: (415)861-6988. E-mail: email@nctcsf.org. Website: www.nctcsf.org. **Executive Director:** Ed Decker. Estab. 1981. Produces 5-7 children's plays/year; 1 children's musical/year.

Needs: Limited budget and small casts only. Produces children's plays as part of "a professional theater arts training program for youths ages 4-19 during the school year and 2 summer sessions. The New Conservatory also produces educational plays for its touring company. We do not want to see any preachy or didactic material." Recently produced plays: *Aesop's Funky Fables*, adapted by Dyan McBride (fables, for ages 4-9); *A Little Princess*, by Frances Hodgson Burnett, adapted by June Walker Rogers (classic story of a young girl, for ages 5-10).

How to Contact: Query with synopsis, character breakdown and set description, or submit complete ms and score. Responds in 3 months.

Terms: Rights purchased negotiable. Pays writers in royalties. SASE for return of submission.

Tips: "Wants plays with name recognition, i.e., *The Lion, the Witch and the Wardrobe* as well as socially relevant issues. Plays should be under 50 minutes in length."

NEW PLAYS INCORPORATED, P.O. Box 5074, Charlottesville VA 22905-0074. (434)979-2777. Fax: (434)984-2230. E-mail: patwhitton@aol.com. Website: www.newplaysforchildren.com. **Publisher:** Patricia Whitton Forrest. Estab. 1964. Publishes 3-4 plays/year; 1 or 2 children's musicals/year.

Needs: Publishes "generally material for kindergarten through junior high." Recently published: *Everyman in the Circus of Life*, by Travis Tyre (contemporary adaptation of the medieval classic); *Buried Treasure*, by Tom Ballmar (adventure play for upper elementary/junior high).

How to Contact: Submit complete ms and score. Will consider simultaneous submissions and previously performed work. Responds in 2 months (usually).

Terms: Purchases exclusive rights to sell acting scripts. Pays writers in royalties (50% of production royalties; 10% of script sales). SASE for return of submission.

Tips: "Write the play you really want to write (not what you think will be salable) and find a director to put it on."

Ⓝ THE OPEN EYE THEATER, P.O. Box 959, Margaretville NY 12455. Phone/fax: (845)586-1660. E-mail: openeye@catskill.net. Website: www.theopeneye.org. **Producing Artistic Director:** Amie Brockway. Estab. 1972 (theater). Produces 3 plays/year for a family audience. Most productions are with music but are not musicals.

Needs: "Casts of various sizes. Technical requirements are kept to a minimum." Produces professional productions combining professional artists and artists-in-training (actors of all ages). Recently produced plays: *Gary Grinkle's Battles with Wrinkles and Other Troubles in Mudgeville* (musical), by Stefan Lanfer, music by Scott MacKenzie; *Tomato Plant Girl*, by Wesley Middleton.

How to Contact: "No videos or cassettes. Letter of inquiry only." Will consider previously performed work. Responds in 6 months.

Terms: Rights agreement negotiated with author. Pays writers one-time fee or royalty negotiated with publisher. SASE for return of submission.

Tips: "Send letter of inquiry only. We are interested in plays for a multigenerational audience (8-adult)."

PHOENIX THEATRE'S COOKIE COMPANY, 100E. McDowell, Phoenix AZ 85004. (602)258-1974. Fax: (602)253-3626. E-mail: phoenixtheatre@yahoo.com. Website: phoenixtheatre.net. **Artistic Director:** Alan J. Prewitt. Estab. 1980. Produces 4 children's plays/year.

Needs: Produces theater with professional adult actors performing for family audiences. 95% of plays/musicals written for adult roles; 5% for juvenile roles. Requires small casts (4-7), small stage, mostly 1 set, flexible set or ingenious sets for a small space. Short musicals accepted. Does not want to see larger casts, multiple sets, 2 hour epics. Recently produced *Holidays on the Prairie*, by Alan J. Prewitt (a single mother with children faces the Santa Fe Trail, for ages 4-12); *The*

Sleeping Beauty, by Alan J. Prewitt (classic tale gets "truthful parent" twist, for ages 4-12).
How to Contact: Plays/musicals: Query with synopsis, character breakdown and set description. Will consider simultaneous submissions. Responds only if interested within 1 month.
Terms: Submissions returned with SASE.
Tips: "Only submit innovative, imaginative work that stimulates imagination and empowers the child. We specialize in producing original scripts based on classic children's literature."

PIONEER DRAMA SERVICE, P.O. Box 4267, Englewood CO 80155-4267. (303)779-4035. Fax: (303)779-4315. E-mail: editors@pioneerdrama.com. Website: www.pioneerdrama.com. **Submissions Editor:** Lori Conary. Publisher: Steven Fendrich. Estab. 1960. Publishes more than 10 new plays and musicals/year.
Needs: "We are looking for plays up to 90 minutes long, large casts and simple sets." Publishes plays for ages middle school-12th grade and community theatre. Recently published plays/musicals: *We the People—The Musical*, by Pat Cook, music and lyrics by Bill Francoeu; *Chateau La Roach*, by Lauren Wilson. Wants to see "script, scores, tapes, pics and reviews."
How to Contact: Query with synopsis, character breakdown, running time and set description. Submit complete ms and cassette or CD of music (if a musical) with SASE. Will consider simultaneous submissions, e-mail submissions, previously performed work. Contact: Submissions Editor. Responds in 4 months. Send for writer's guidelines.
Terms: Purchases all rights. Pays writers in royalties (10% on sales, 50% royalties on productions). Research Pioneer through catalog and website.
Tips: "Research the company. Include a cover letter and a SASE."

N PLAYERS PRESS, INC., P.O. Box 1132, Studio City CA 91614-0132. (818)789-4980. **Vice President:** R. W. Gordon. Estab. 1965. Publishes 10-20 children's plays/year; 3-12 children's musicals/year.
Needs: Subject matter: "We publish for all age groups." Recently published: *African Folk Tales*, by Carol Korty (for ages 10-14).
How to Contact: Query with synopsis, character breakdown and set description; include #10 SASE with query. Considers previously performed work only. Responds to query in 1 month; submissions in 1 year.
Terms: Purchases stage, screen, TV rights. Payment varies; work purchased possibly outright upon written request. Submissions returned with SASE.
Tips: "Submit as requested—query first and send only previously produced material. Entertainment quality is on the upswing and needs to be directed at the world, no longer just the U.S. Please submit with two #10 SASEs plus ms-size SASE. Please do not call."

N PLAYS, The Drama Magazine for Young People, P.O. Box 600160, Newton MA 02460. E-mail: lpreston@playsm ag.com. Website: www.playsmag.com. **Editor:** Elizabeth Preston. Estab. 1941. Publishes 70-75 children's plays/year.
Needs: "Props and staging should not be overly elaborate or costly. There is little call among our subscribers for plays with only a few characters; ten or more (to allow all students in a class to participate, for instance) is preferred. Our plays are performed by children in school from lower elementary grades through junior-senior high." 100% of plays written for juvenile roles. Subject matter: Audience is lower grades through junior/senior high. Recently published plays: *The Three-Sided Coin*, by John Tissot (Will first-year teacher be able to stand his ground against a powerful parent with political connections?); *To Dine Alone*, by Martin A. Follose (Grandma plays matchmaker); *Besieged*, by Craig Sodaro (The attack on Vicksburg forces a family underground . . . and one of them faces harsh truths about herself); *The Red Door*, by Kevin Stone (Strange noises, a door that won't stay shut, ghostly figures give Joanna's birthday party a spooky feel); *Catch the Morning*, by Eric Alter (Young medical student tries to make sense of the world, post-September 11th). "Send nothing downbeat—no plays about drugs, sex or other 'heavy' topics."
How to Contact: Query first on adaptations of folk tales and classics; otherwise submit complete ms. Responds in 3 weeks.
Terms: Purchases all rights. Pay rates vary. Guidelines available; send SASE. Sample copy $4.
Tips: "Get your play underway quickly. Keep it wholesome and entertaining. No preachiness, heavy moral or educational message. Any 'lesson' should be imparted through the actions of the characters, not through unbelievable dialogue. Use realistic situations and settings without getting into downbeat, depressing topics. No sex, drugs, violence, alcohol."

N RIVERSIDE CHILDREN'S THEATRE, 3280 Riverside Park Dr., Vero Beach FL 32963. (561)234-8052. Fax: (561)234-4407. E-mail: rct@riversidetheatre.com. Website: www.riversidetheatre.com. **Education Director:** Linda Downey. Estab. 1980. Produces 4 children's plays/year; 2 children's musicals/year.
Needs: Produces amateur youth productions. 100% of plays/musicals written for juvenile roles. Musical needs: For children ages 6-18. Produced plays: *The Beloved Dently*, by Dory Cooney (pet bereavement, general); *Taming of the Shrew*, by Shakespeare (general).
How to Contact: Plays/musicals: Query with synopsis, character breakdown and set description. Will consider simultaneous submissions, electronic submissions via disk/modem and previously performed work. Responds only if interested.
Terms: Pays royalty or $40-60 per performance. Submissions returned with SASE.
Tips: "Interested in youth theatre for children ages 6-18 to perform."

SEATTLE CHILDREN'S THEATRE, 201 Thomas St., Seattle WA 98109. Fax: (206)443-0442. Website: www.sct.org. **Literary Manage:** Madeleine Oldham. Estab. 1975. Produces 5 full-length children's plays/year; 1 full-length children's musical/year. Produces children's plays for professional productions (September-June).
Needs: "We generally use adult actors even for juvenile roles." Produced plays: *The King of Ireland's Son*, by Paula Wing

(mythology and Hero Quest for ages 8 and older); *Pink and Say*, by Oyamo (adaptation from Patricia Polacco); *Holes*, by Louis Sacher. Does not want to see anything that condescends to young people—anything overly broad in style.

How to Contact: Accepts agented scripts or those accompanied by a professional letter of recommendation (director or dramaturg). Responds in 1 year.

Terms: Rights vary. Payment method varies. Submissions returned with SASE.

Tips: "Please *do not* send unsolicited manuscripts. We prefer sophisticated material (our weekend performances have an audience that is half adults)."

TADA!, 15 W. 28th St., 3rd Floor, New York NY 10001. (212)252-1619. Fax: (212)252-8763. E-mail: tada@tadatheater.c om. Website: www.tadatheater.com. **Artistic Director:** Janine Nina Trevens. Estab. 1984. Produces 5 staged readings of children's plays and musicals/year; 0-5 children's plays/year; 2-3 children's musicals/year.

Needs: "All actors are children, ages 8-17." Produces children's plays for professional, year-round theater. 100% of plays/ musicals written for juvenile roles. Recently produced musicals: *Sleepover*, by Phillip Freedman and James Belloff (peer acceptance, for ages 3 and up); *The Little House of Cookies*, by Janine Nina Trevens and Joel Gelpe (international communication and friendship). Does not want to see fairy tales or material that talks down to children.

How to Contact: Query with synopsis, character breakdown and set description; submit complete ms, score and tape of songs (if a musical). Responds in 1 year "or in October following the August deadline for our Annual Playwriting Competition. (Send two copies of manuscript if for competition)."

Terms: Rights purchased "depend on the piece." Pays writers in royalties of 1-6% and/or pays commissioning fee. SASE a must for return of submissions.

Tips: "For plays for our Annual Playwriting Competition, submit between January and August 15. We're looking for plays with current topics that specific age ranges can identify with, with a small cast of children and one or two adults. Our company is multi-racial and city-oriented. We are not interested in fairy tales. We like to produce material that kids relate to and that touches their lives today."

N: THEATRE FOR YOUNG AMERICA, 5909 Johnson Dr., Mission KS 66202. (913)831-2131. **Artistic Director:** Gene Mackey. Estab. 1974. Produces 9 children's plays/year; 3-5 children's musicals/year.

Needs: "We use a small cast (4-7), open thrust stage." Theatre for Young America is a professional equity company. 90% of plays/musicals written for adult roles; 10% for juvenile roles. Produced plays: *The Wizard of Oz*, by Jim Eiler and Jeanne Bargy (for ages 6 and up); *A Partridge in a Pear Tree*, by Lowell Swortzell (deals with the 12 days of Christmas, for ages 6 and up); *Three Billy Goats Gruff*, by Gene Mackey and Molly Jessup (Norwegian folk tales, for ages 6 and up).

How to Contact: Query with synopsis, character breakdown and set description. Will consider simultaneous submissions and previously performed work. Responds in 2 months.

Terms: Purchases production rights, tour rights in local area. Pays writers in royalties or $10-50/performance.

Tips: Looking for "cross-cultural material that respects the intelligence, sensitivity and taste of the child audience."

THEATREWORKS/USA, 151 W. 26th, 7th Floor, New York NY 10001. (212)647-1100. Fax: (212)924-5377. E-mail: info@theatreworksusa.org. Website: www.theatreworks.org. **Artistic Director:** Barbara Pasternack. **Assistant Artistic Director:** Michael Alltop. Estab. 1960. Produces 3-4 children's plays and musicals/year.

Needs: Cast of 5 or 6 actors. Play should be 1 hour long, tourable. Professional children's theatre comprised of adult equity actors. 100% of shows are written for adult roles. Produced plays: *The Mystery of King Tut*, by Mindi Dickstein and Daniel Messé (Ancient Egypt); *Sarah, Plain and Tall*, by Larry O'Keefe, Nell Benjamin and Julia Jordan (adaptation).

How to Contact: Query first with synopsis, character breakdown and sample songs. Will consider previously performed work. Responds in 3 months.

Terms: Pays writers royalties of 6%. SASE for return of submission.

Tips: "Plays should be not only entertaining, but 'about something.' They should touch the heart and the mind. They should not condescend to children."

Young Writer's & Illustrator's Markets

The listings in this section are special because they publish work of young writers and artists (under age 18). Some of the magazines listed exclusively feature the work of young people. Others are adult magazines with special sections for the work of young writers. There are also a few book publishers listed that exclusively publish the work of young writers and artists. Many of the magazines and publishers listed here pay only in copies, meaning authors and illustrators receive one or more free copies of the magazine or book to which they contributed.

As with adult markets, markets for children expect writers to be familiar with their editorial needs before submitting. Many of the markets listed will send guidelines to writers. Guidelines state exactly what the markets need and how to submit it. You can often get these by sending a request with a self-addressed, stamped envelope (SASE) to the magazine or publisher, or by checking a publication's website (a number of listings include web addresses). In addition to obtaining guidelines, read through a few copies of any magazines you'd like to submit to—this is the best way to determine if your work is right for them.

A number of kids' magazines are available on newsstands or in libraries. Others are distributed only through schools, churches or home subscriptions. If you can't find a magazine you'd like to see, most editors will send sample copies for a small fee.

Before you submit your material to editors, take a few minutes to read Before Your First Sale on page 8 for more information on proper submission procedures. You may also want to check out two other sections—Contests & Awards and Conferences & Workshops. Some listings in these sections are open to students (some exclusively)—look for the phrase **open to students** in bold. Additional opportunities for writers can be found in *The Young Writers Guide to Getting Published* (Writer's Digest Books) and *A Teen's Guide to Getting Published: the only writer's guide written by teens for teens*, by Danielle and Jessica Dunn (Prufrock Press). More information on these books are given in the Helpful Resources section in the back of this book.

For more insight and tips for getting started, see **The market for young writers** on page 292.

Information on companies listed in the previous edition but not included in this edition of *Children's Writer's & Illustrator's Market* may be found in the General Index.

THE ACORN, 1530 Seventh St., Rock Island IL 61201. (309)788-3980. Newsletter. Estab. 1989. **Editor:** Betty Mowery. Audience consists of "teachers, parents, young authors." Purpose in publishing works for children: "to provide a showcase for young authors. We hope to publish material other publications won't." Children must be K-12 (put name, address, grade on manuscripts). Guidelines and contest rules available for SASE.
Magazines: 100% of magazine written by children. Uses 6 fiction pieces (500 words); 20 pieces of poetry (32 lines). No payment; purchase of a copy isn't necessary to be printed. Sample copy $3. Subscription $10 for 4 issues. Submit mss to Betty Mowery, editor. Send complete ms. Will accept typewritten, legibly handwritten and/or computer printout. Include SASE. Responds in 1 week. Will not respond without SASE.
Artwork: Publishes artwork by children. Looks for "all types; size 4×5. Use black ink in artwork." No cash payment or copy. Submit artwork either with ms or separately to Betty Mowery. Include SASE. Responds in 1 week.
Tips: "Always include SASE and put name on manuscripts. When submitting to contests send SASE plus entry fee of six (6) 37¢ stamps."

AMERICAN GIRL, 8400 Fairway Place, Middleton WI 53562. (608)836-4848. Fax: (608)831-7089. Website: www.americangirl. **Contact:** Magazine Department Assistant. Bimonthly magazine. Audience consists of girls ages 8-12 who are joyful about being girls. Purpose in publishing works by young people: "self-esteem boost and entertainment for readers. *American Girl* values girls' opinions and ideas. By publishing their work in the magazine, girls can share their thoughts with other girls! Young writers should be 8-12 years old. We don't have writer's guidelines for children's submissions. Instruction for specific solicitations appears in the magazine."

Magazines: 20% of magazine written by young people. "A few pages of each issue feature articles that include children's answers to questions or requests that have appeared in a previous issue of *American Girl*." Pays in copies. Submit to address listed in magazine. Will accept legibly handwritten ms. Include SASE. Responds in 3 months.

Tips: "Please, no stories, poems, etc. about American Girls Collection Characters (Felicity, Samantha, Molly, Kirsten, Addy, Josefina or Kit). Inside *American Girl*, there are several departments that call for submissions. Read the magazine carefully and submit your ideas based on what we ask for."

BEYOND WORDS PUBLISHING, INC., 20827 NW Cornell Rd., Suite 500, Hillsboro OR 97124-9808. (503)531-8700. Fax: (503)531-8773. Website:www.beyondword.com. Book publisher. **Managing Editor of Children's Division:** Barbara Leese. Publishes 2-3 picture books/year; 4-6 YA nonfiction books. Looks for "books that inspire integrity in children ages 5-15 and encourage creativity and an appreciation of nature." Wants to "encourage children to write, create, dream and believe that it is possible to be published. The books must be unique, be of national interest, and the author must be personable and promotable." Writer's guidelines available with SASE.

Books: Holds yearly writing contests for activity/advice books written by and for children/teens. Publishes historical fiction and multicultural picture books. Also publishes nonfiction advice books for children, such as guides for kids about pertinent concerns. Responds in 6 months.

Artwork/Photography: Submit artwork to Managing Editor.

Tips: "Write about issues that affect your life. Trust your own instincts. You know best!"

BLUEJEANONLINE.COM, (formerly *Blue Jean Online*), P.O. Box 67111, Chestnut Hill MA 02132. (877)FOR-BLUE. E-mail: editors@bluejeanonline.com. Website: www.bluejeanonline.com. Bluejeanonline.com, "The only website written and produced by young women around the world" showcases the writing, artwork and creativity of young women around the world. Our cover stories profile interesting and exciting teen girls and young women in action. You will find no supermodels, tips on dieting or fashion spreads on our pages. We publish young-women-produced poetry, artwork, photography, fiction and much more!" Audience is young women ages 14-22. Bluejeanonline.com showcases work by young women: "to stay true to what really matters, which is publishing what young women are thinking, saying and doing." Writer's guidelines available online by clicking the "Who Are We?" link or on request for SASE.

Magazine: 100% of website is written by young people. Uses 5 fiction stories; 8-14 nonfiction stories (250-3,000 words); 5-10 commentary and opinion pieces, 10-12 feature articles; 10-12 book, music and other media reviews; and 1-3 poems. Does not publish work by adult freelancers. Submit complete mss per submission guidelines. Will accept typewritten mss. Include SASE. Responds in 4 months at most. "Many times within two months."

Artwork: Publishes artwork, crafts, and photography by young women. Will consider a variety of styles! Artwork must be submitted by an artist (ages 14-22). Submit artwork and photography between 2 pieces of cardboard. Include SASE with enough postage for return. Responds in 4 months.

Tips: "View submission guidelines on website and click on the 'submit' link. Publishes many first-time young women authors and artists. Select articles and reviews are republished on Knight Ridder/Tribune Newswire appearing in newspapers across America, reaching millions of readers each week. Do not inquire about your work by calling. Replies guaranteed when material sent through mail with SASE."

CHICKADEE, 49 Front St. Toronto, ON M5E 1B3 Canada. (416)340-2700. Fax: (416)340-9769. E-mail: owl@ow l.on.ca. Website: www.owlkids.com. **Editor:** Hilary Bain. Magazine published 9 times/year. "*Chickadee* is for children ages 6-9. Its purpose is to entertain and educate children about science, nature and the world around them. We publish children's drawings to give readers the chance to express themselves. Drawings must relate to the topics that are given in the 'All Your Own' section of each issue."

Artwork: Publishes artwork by children. No payment given. Mail submissions with name, age and return address for thank you note. Submit to Mitch Butler, All Your Own Editor. Responds in 4 months. Does not accept e-mail submissions.

CHILD LIFE, Children's Better Health Institute, P.O. Box 567, Indianapolis IN 46206. Parcels and packages: please send to 1100 Waterway Blvd., 46202. (317)634-1100. Fax: (317)684-8094. Website: www.childlifemag.org. **Editor:** Jack Gramling. **Art Director:** Greg Vanzo. Magazine published 6 times/year. Estab. 1921. Circ. 30,000. Targeted toward kids ages 9-11. Focuses on health, sports, fitness, nutrition, safety, academic excellence, general interests, and the nostalgia of *Child Life's* early days. "We publish jokes, riddles and poems by children." Kids should include name, address, phone number (for office use) and school photo. "No mass duplicated, multiple submissions."

• *Child Life* is no longer accepting manuscripts for publication. See listings for *Children's Playmate, Humpty Dumpty's Magazine, Jack And Jill, Turtle Magazine* and *U*S*Kids*.

Tips: "We use kids' submissions from our age range—9 to 11. Those older or younger should try one of our sister publications: *Children's Digest, Children's Playmate, Humpty Dumpty's Magazine, Jack And Jill, Turtle Magazine, U*S*Kids.*"

CHIXLIT, the literary 'zine for chicks ages 7 to 17, P.O. Box 12051, Orange CA 92859. E-mail: submit@chixlit.c om. Website: www.chixlit.com. Magazine ("more of a 'zine really.") "Published bimonthly but we're working up to monthly within a year, we hope. *chixLIT* is intended to give girls a place to express themselves and help coax along their emerging talent and emotions. We want to share writing techniques and feelings and let each other know we are not alone.

Our audience is also teachers, librarians and scout leaders who want to encourage writing and confidence-building, as well as children's book authors who want to know what's going on in our heads! There are plenty of places for grownups, but we wanted a place for chix like us! Writers must be female and age 7 to 17. Anywhere in the world is OK, but writing must be in English. We like a parent or adult guardian to tap with us and let us know it's honest work and OK to print." Writer's guidelines available on request and on website.

Magazines: 80% of magazine written by young people. "We publish poems, short stories, reviews, rants, raves, love letters, song lyrics, journal entries and more." Pays 1 free copy of the 'zine and a discount on the subscription rate. "We sometimes will 'pay' little gifts or small cash prizes in a contest." Submit complete ms. Will accept typewritten form. Accepts e-mail submissions "in the body of an e-mail (no attachments!). Must be in English. We are planning a Spanish-language edition for 2004-05." Include SASE only if you want your submission back or an answer by snail mail (i.e., if you have no e-mail. But we prefer e-mail). Responds in 10 weeks.

Artwork: Publishes artwork and photography by girls. Looks for "photos of chix or things that chix like, artwork of chix or things that make you think of chix. We are open to individual expression, but it has to be by girls, and it has to be flat and scannable and look decent in black & white." Pays 1 free issue for any artwork used and a small gift prize for any chosen for the cover. "We prefer submission of a piece of work (or a good color or b&w copy) in an envelope (not rolled) and sent to our P.O. Box (so it can't be too big either)."

Tips: "Look at everything as an object of potential beauty, if beauty is defined as anything with passion. Don't just read books or look at art, but ask yourself how you feel when you look at/read it and why. Then go your own way. Buy a subscription and back issues to see what we're about and what other chix are up to."

CICADA, Carus Publishing Company, P.O. Box 300, Peru IL 61354. (815)224-5803, ext. 656. Fax: (815)224-6615. E-mail: cicada@caruspub.com. Website: www.cicadamag.com. **Editor-in-Chief:** Marianne Carus. Executive Editor: Deborah Vetter. Associate Editor: Tracy Schoenle. Senior Art Director: Ron McCutchan. Bimonthly magazine.

• *Cicada* publishes work of writers and artists of high-school age (must be at least 14 years old). See the *Cicada* listing in the magazines section for more information, or check their website or copies of the magazine.

THE CLAREMONT REVIEW, 4980 Wesley Rd., Victoria, BC Canada V8Y 1Y9. (250)658-5221. Fax: (250)658-5387. E-mail: susan_field@sd63.bc.ca. Website: www.theClaremontReview.com. Magazine. Publishes 2 books/year by young adults. Publishes poetry and fiction with literary value by students aged 13-19 anywhere in English-speaking world. Purpose in publishing work by young people: to provide a literary venue. Sponsors annual poetry contest.

Magazines: Uses 10-12 fiction stories (200-2,500 words); 30-40 poems. Pays in copies. Submit mss to editors. Submit complete ms. Will accept typewritten mss. SASE. Responds in 6 weeks (except during the summer).

Artwork: Publishes artwork by young adults. Looks for b&w copies of imaginative art. Pays in copies. Send picture for review. Negative may be requested. Submit art and photographs to editors. SASE. Responds in 6 weeks.

Tips: "Read us first—it saves disappointment. Know who we are and what we publish. We're closed July and August. SASE a must. American students send I.R.C.'s as American stamps *do not* work in Canada."

CREATIVE KIDS, P.O. Box 8813, Waco TX 76714-8813. (800)998-2208. Fax: (254)756-3339. E-mail: creative_kids @prufrock.com. Website: www.prufrock.com. **Editor:** Libby Goolsby. Magazine published 4 times/year. Estab. 1979. "All material is by children, for children." Purpose in publishing works by children: "to create a product that provides children with an authentic experience and to offer an opportunity for children to see their work in print. *Creative Kids* contains the best stories, poetry, opinion, artwork, games and photography by kids ages 8-14." Writers ages 8-14 must have statement by teacher or parent verifying originality. Writer's guidelines available on request with SASE.

Magazines: Uses "about 6" fiction and nonfiction stories (800-900 words); poetry, plays, ideas to share (200-750 words) per issue. Pays "free magazine." Submit mss to submissions editor. Will accept typewritten mss. Include SASE. Responds in 1 month.

Artwork/Photography: Publishes artwork and photos by children. Looks for "any kind of drawing, cartoon, or painting." Pays "free magazine." Send original or a photo of the work to submissions editor. Include SASE. Responds in 1 month.

Tips: "*Creative Kids* is a magazine by kids, for kids. The work represents children's ideas, questions, fears, concerns and pleasures. The material never contains racist, sexist or violent expression. The purpose is to provide children with an authentic experience. A person may submit one piece of work per envelope. Each piece must be labeled with the student's name, birth date, grade, school, home address and school address. Include a photograph, if possible. Recent school pictures are best. Material submitted to *Creative Kids* must not be under consideration by any other publication. Items should be carefully prepared, proofread and double checked (perhaps also by a parent or teacher). All activities requiring solutions must be accompanied by the correct answers. Young writers and artists should always write for guidelines and then follow them."

CREATIVE WITH WORDS, Thematic anthologies, Creative with Words Publications, P.O. Box 223226, Carmel CA 93922. Fax: (831)655-8627. E-mail: cwwpub@usa.net. Website: members.tripod.com/CreativeWithWords. **Editor:** Brigitta Geltrich. Nature Editor: Bert Hower. Publishes 12 anthologies/year. Estab. 1975. "We publish the creative writing of children (2 anthologies written by children; 2 anthologies written by adults; 6-8 anthologies written by all ages)." Audience consists of children, families, schools, libraries, adults, reading programs. Purpose in publishing works by children: to offer them an opportunity to get started in publishing. "Work must be of quality, typed, original, unedited, and not published before; age must be given (up to 19 years old) and home address." SASE must be enclosed with all correspondence and mss. Writer's guidelines and theme list available on request with SASE, via e-mail or on website.

Books: Considers all categories except those dealing with sensationalism, death, violence, pornography and overly religious.

Uses fairy tales, folklore items (up to 800 words) and poetry (not to exceed 20 lines, 46 characters across). Published *Nature Series: Seasons, Nature, School, Love* and *Relationships* (all children and adults). Pays 20% discount on each copy of publication in which fiction or poetry by children appears. Submit mss to Brigitta Geltrich, editor. Query; child, teacher or parent can submit; teacher and/or parents must verify originality of writing. Will accept typewritten and/or legibly handwritten mss. SASE. "Will not go through agents or overly protective 'stage mothers'." Responds in 1 month after deadline of any theme.

Artwork/Photography: Publishes b&w artwork, b&w photos and computer artwork created by children (language art work). No already existing computer artwork. Pays 20% discount on every copy of publication in which work by children appears. Submit artwork to Brigitta Geltrich, editor, and request info on payment.

Tips: "Enjoy the English language, life and the world around you. Look at everything from a different perspective. Look at the greatness inside all of us. Be less descriptive and use words wisely. Let the reader experience a story through a viewpoint character, don't be overly dramatic. Match illustrations/photos to the meaning of the story or poem."

THE CRYSTAL BALL, The Starwind Press, P.O. Box 98, Ripley OH 45167. (937)392-4549. E-mail: susannah@techgallery.com. Articles/Fiction Editor: Marlene Powell. **Assistant Editor:** Susannah C. West. Quarterly magazine. Estab. 1997. Circ. 1,000. Publishes science fiction and fantasy for young adults.

Fiction: Young adults: fantasy, folktale, science fiction. Buys 8-12 mss/year. Average word length: 1,500-5,000. Byline given.

Nonfiction: Young adults: biography, how-to, interview/profile, science. Buys 8-12 mss/year. Average word length: 1,000-3,000.

Poetry: Only publishes poetry by kids.

N: FREE SPIRIT PUBLISHING INC., 217 Fifth Ave. N, Suite 200, Minneapolis MN 55401-1299. (612)338-2068. Fax: (612)337-5050. E-mail: help4kids@freespirit.com. Website: www.freespirit.com. Book publisher. **Acquisitions:** Editor. Publishes 16-22 titles/year for children and teens, teachers and parents. "Free Spirit Publishing is the home of SELF-HELP FOR KIDS® and SELF-HELP FOR TEENS® nonfiction, issue-driven, solution-focused books and materials for children and teens, and the parents and teachers who care for them."

• Free Spirit no longer accepts fiction or storybook submissions.

Books: Publishes nonfiction. "Submissions are accepted from prospective authors, including youth ages 16 and up, or through agents. Please review our catalog and Author Guidelines (both available online) before submitting proposal." Responds to queries/mss in 4 months. "If you'd like materials returned, enclose a SASE with sufficient postage." Write or call for catalog and submission guidelines before sending submission. Accepts queries only by e-mail. Submission guidelines available online.

Tips: "We do not publish fiction or picture storybooks, books with animal or mythical characters, books with religious or New Age content, or single biographies, autobiographies, or memoirs. We prefer books written in a natural, friendly style."

GREEN KNEES, Imprint of Azro Press, PMB 342, 1704 Llano St. B, Santa Fe NM 87505. (505)989-3272. Fax: (505)989-3832. E-mail: books@azropress.com. Website: www.greenknees.com. Book. Publishes 1 book/year by children. "Green Knees is primarily interested in picture books and easy readers written and illustrated by children who are 13 years old or younger." The book must have been written by a child under 13 and illustrations done by the author or children in the same grade or school. Writer's guidelines available on request.

Books: Publishes picture books and young readers; interested in animal stories and humor. Length: 1,000 words for fiction. Submit mss to Jaenet Guggenheim. Query or submit complete ms or synopsis and sample illustration (if longer than 40 pages). Send a copy of the ms, do not send original material. Will accept typewritten or electronically (disk or e-mail). Include SASE. Responds in 2 months.

Artwork/Photography: Publishes artwork by children.

HIGH SCHOOL WRITER, P.O. Box 718, Grand Rapids MN 55744-0718. (218)326-8025. Fax: (218)326-8025. E-mail: writer@mx3.com. Editor: Barbara Eiesland. Magazine published 6 times during the school year. "The *High School Writer* is a magazine written *by* students *for* students. All submissions must exceed contemporary standards of decency." Purpose in publishing works by young people: to provide a real audience for student writers—and text for study. Submissions by junior high and middle school students accepted for our junior edition. Senior high students' works are accepted for our senior high edition. Students attending schools that subscribe to our publication are eligible to submit their work." Writer's guidelines available on request.

Magazines: Uses fiction, nonfiction (2,000 words maximum) and poetry. Submit mss to editor. Submit complete ms (teacher must submit). Will accept typewritten, computer-generated (good quality) mss.

Tips: "Submissions should not be sent without first obtaining a copy of our guidelines (see page 2 of every issue). Also, submissions will not be considered unless student's school subscribes."

HIGHLIGHTS FOR CHILDREN, 803 Church St., Honesdale PA 18431. (570)253-1080. Magazine. Published monthly. "We strive to provide wholesome, stimulating, entertaining material that will encourage children to read. Our audience is children ages 2-12." Purpose in publishing works by young people: to encourage children's creative expression.

Magazines: 15-20% of magazine written by children. Uses stories and poems. Also uses jokes, riddles, tongue twisters. Features that occur occasionally: "What Are Your Favorite Books?" (8-10/year), Recipes (8-10/year), "Science Letters" (15-20/year). Special features that invite children's submissions on a specific topic occur several times per year. Recent examples include "Pet Stories," "Favorite Songs," "Kids at Work," and "Help the Cartoonists." Pays in copies. Submit complete ms to the editor. Will accept typewritten, legibly handwritten and computer printout mss. Responds in 6 weeks.

insider report

The market for young writers

The market for young writers is a strange and challenging obstacle course, but the prize for completion is wonderful. No thrill could rival opening your contributor's copy and finding your story or poem smack in the middle of page 42 and knowing others will find it (and read it), too.

This is probably what drove writers like Ernest Hemingway, Sylvia Plath, Langston Hughes, and Louisa May Alcott to publish work before they reached their 18th birthdays (Plath when she was only 8). If your 8th year has already come and gone, don't panic; French poet Arthur Rimbaud didn't publish his first piece until he was 16, only to retire from writing at age 20.

How can *you* get started? Get to know the publishing opportunities available to young writers, including the raft of sites online, and investigate their age requirements. You'll find most of those journals and websites welcome submissions from teen writers exclusively, while a handful accept submissions from pre-teens only. Rarely will you find a magazine that accepts work from both age groups.

Editors whose magazines consider and publish work by young writers—including *Claremont Review*, *Merlyn's Pen*, *Stone Soup*, and *Word Dance*—can select the best work submitted by the best young writers, and the quality of their magazines shows that they do. This means you're in for some stiff competition when you submit to these markets.

Stone Soup, for example, publishes only writers aged 8 through 13, yet editor Gerry Mandel is flooded with more submissions than she can possibly use. "At *Stone Soup* we get 300 submissions a week—that's 15,000 a year," says Mandel. She regularly receives phone calls from 14-year-olds, begging the magazine to let them submit their work. She usually directs them to the links page on the *Stone Soup* website, which lists several children- and teen-friendly markets.

When searching for publishing opportunities, Kathy Henderson, author of *The Young Writer's Guide to Getting Published*, says, "Look locally. Kids who are beginning should look to local groups and newspapers." Her own local paper prints a weekly column that frequently publishes poetry by kids, for example.

If you're serious about your writing, you strive to make each piece its best, and you're ready for a challenge, perhaps it's time to approach adult-level magazines. Remember, though, your writing will be judged against work submitted by adults, who are probably more experienced and skilled. However, Henderson points out, "I've been working with some nine- and ten-year-olds who can write the pants off some adults."

Whether you're submitting work for local publication, submitting to magazines for and by kids, or submitting to adult literary journals, you're in competition with other writers. Aside from excellent writing, what gives you the edge over other young writers? Over adults?

First, remember this: The quickest path to rejection is an unprofessional-looking manuscript. Check out the formatting instructions in Before Your First Sale on page 8. Unless a magazine's guidelines tell you differently, use our suggested format to set up your manuscript.

A neat, professional manuscript really does make a difference. Let's say an editor receives a brilliant story. At least he *thinks* it's brilliant—smeared ballpoint ink makes the tiny handwriting impossible to read. The story's sort of scrawled on a piece of lined paper ripped from a spiral-bound notebook. There's no cover letter with the submission, no SASE, just a name and a phone number squeezed into the bottom corner of the page.

Quite simply, the editor's not going to publish that piece. Despite its brilliance, such a submission falls squarely into the too-much-trouble-to-bother-with category. No matter where you're submitting your work, do it right. Make sure your manuscript is neatly typed or computer-generated on white paper, with no typos or painful grammatical mistakes, and with your contact information presented clearly.

Wait, back up to those "magazine guidelines" mentioned above. What are those? Guidelines spell out all the requirements for submission: word or line count, format, and other important information. Guidelines may be available from a magazine for a SASE (self-addressed stamped envelope) or on the magazine's website. "Find out the individual guidelines," Henderson recommends. "You'll get further along that way than by breaking the rules."

Guidelines can only tell you so much about a journal, though. It's an excellent idea to purchase a sample copy of a publication, primarily to see if your writing would suit it—but also to see if the journal suits your writing. Shelling out two or three dollars for a sample copy (usually a back issue) will be worth it if you wind up deciding you don't want your work to appear in a journal that's been photocopied badly and paper-clipped together. (If a journal that interests you isn't available in your local bookstore or at the library, check online for ordering information.)

The preceding rules apply to adult as well as young writers, but there's one area that generally doesn't concern adults: Should you include your age in the cover letter? One school of thought is that editors might give special attention, advice or encouragement to young writers—even if they don't publish their work. Also, editors, if they choose to publish a piece, need to know if they must get a parent's permission before publishing the work of a young writer.

Henderson, however, advises kids, and their teachers and parents, not to tell their age unless guidelines specify they should. "Editors want good work, not good work by 9-year-olds or good work by 35-year-olds." If a story is accepted, *then* tell the editors your age.

"Have your parents' support and permission from the beginning," Henderson advises. That way, if your work is accepted and the editor of the journal *does* want your parents' okay, you can take care of everything professionally, without any fuss. There's no need to include your parents' permission with your manuscript (unless the guidelines expressly instruct you to). If your work is accepted, you might need to have your parents write you a note or fill out a contract. Then again, you might not need them to do anything at all except sit back and wait for your contributor's copy to arrive.

If you're 13 or older, you're the one who should handle the actual submission process. As far as who submits the actual work to *Stone Soup*, Mandel says it "runs the whole gamut. More teachers and kids, though, than parents."

Henderson is adamant about copyright for kids when the adults get involved. "I am totally against parents and teachers sending work in without the writer's permission," she says. "If you're squeamish about someone reading your work, then don't publish it." Seeking publication should be the writer's choice and no one else's.

Henderson says if you're submitting a classroom exercise to an editor, either with the rest of your class or on your own, "Keep in mind that when teachers are reviewing writing, they're judging by completely different criteria than a magazine editor. You receive an A for understanding the concepts and putting them into practice, but your friend—who maybe doesn't shine grammatically—is published in venues everywhere because he's taking risks, writing from his heart, trying new things, pushing boundaries in his writing." Henderson points out the difference between writing for school and writing for yourself or for publication: "School is about learning how to do it; art is about learning how to do it better."

Whether you're looking to publish to satisfy a class assignment or to take your first steps on the path to a writing career, submit only work you are proud of. Even if your work is not accepted, mastering the submission process puts you light years ahead of your peers and is an accomplishment in itself.

—*Vanessa Lyman*

Artwork: Publishes artwork by children. Pays in copies. No cartoon or comic book characters. No commercial products. Submit b&w or color artwork for "Our Own Pages." Features include "Creatures Nobody Has Ever Seen" (5-8/year) and "Illustration Job" (18-20/year). Responds in 6 weeks.

INSIGHT, Teens Meeting Christ, 55 W. Oak Ridge Dr., Hagerstown MD 21740. (301)393-4038. Fax: (301)393-4055. E-mail: insight@rhpa.org. Website: www.insightmagazine.org. **Contact:** Dwain Nielson Esmond. Weekly magazine. Estab. 1970. Circ. 20,000. "Our readers crave true stories written by teens or written about teens that convey a strong spiritual point or portray a spiritual truth." 100% of publication aimed at teen and college-age market.

Nonfiction: Young adults: animal, biography, fashion, health, humorous, interview/profile, multicultural, nature/environment, problem-solving, social issues, sports, travel: first-person accounts preferred. Buys 200 mss/year. Average word length: 500-1,500. Byline given.

KWIL KIDS PUBLISHING, The Little Publishing Company That Kwil Built, Kwilville, P.O. Box 29556, Maple Ridge, BC V2X 2V0 Canada. E-mail: kmarquis@sd42.ca. Publishes weekly column in local paper, four quarterly newsletters. "*Kwil Kids* come in all ages, shapes and sizes—from 4-64 and a whole lot more! Kwil does not pay for the creative work of children but provides opportunity/encouragement. We promote literacy, creativity and written 'connections' through written and artistic expression and publish autobiographical, inspirational, stories of gentleness, compassion, truth and beauty. Our purpose is to foster a sense of pride and enthusiasm in young writers and artists, to celebrate the voice of youth and encourage growth through joy-filled practice and cheerleading, not criticism." Must include name, age, address and parent signature (if a minor). Will send guidelines upon request."

Books: Publishes autobiographical, inspirational, creative stories (alliterative, rhyming refrains, juicy words) fiction; short rhyming and non-rhyming poems (creative, fun, original, expressive, poetry). Length: 500 words for fiction; 8-16 lines for poetry. No payment—self-published and sold "at cost" only (1 free copy). Submit mss to Kwil or Mr. Marquis. Submit complete ms; send copy only—expect a reply but will not return ms. Will accept typewritten and legibly handwritten mss and e-mail. Include SASE or enclose IRC or $1 for postage as US stamps may not be used **from** Canada. Responds in April, August and December.

Newsletter: 95% of newsletter written by young people. Uses 15 short stories, poems (20-100 words). No payment—free newsletters only. Submit complete ms. Will accept typewritten and legibly handwritten mss and e-mail. Kwil answers every letter in verse. Responds in April, August and December.

Artwork: Publishes artwork and photography by children with writing. Looks for black ink sketches to go with writing and photos to go with writing. Submit by postal mail only; white background for sketches. Submit artwork/photos to Kwil publisher. Include SASE. Responds in 3 months.

Tips: "We love stories that teach a lesson or encourage peace, love and a fresh, new understanding. Just be who you are and do what you do. Then all of life's treasures will come to you."

MERLYN'S PEN: Fiction, Essays, and Poems by America's Teens, P.O. Box 910, East Greenwich RI 02818. (800)247-2027. Fax: (401)885-5199. Website: www.merlynspen.org. Magazine. Published annually. "By publishing student writing, *Merlyn's Pen* seeks to broaden and reward the young author's interest in writing, strengthen the self-confidence of beginning writers and promote among all students a positive attitude toward literature. We publish 75 manuscripts annually by students in grades 6-12. The entire magazine is dedicated to young adults' writing. Our audience is classrooms, libraries and students from grades 6-12." Writers must submit via website only. When a student is accepted, he/she, a parent and a teacher must sign a statement of originality. Writer's guidelines available at website.

Magazines: Published authors receive $10-100. Submit 1 title at a time. Responds in 6 weeks.

Tips: "You must visit our website and use the form there to submit."

NATIONAL GEOGRAPHIC KIDS, 1145 17th St. NW, Washington DC 20036-4688. (202)857-7000. Fax: (202)775-6112. Website: www.nationalgeographic.com/ngkids. Magazine published 10 times/year. Photo-driven magazine for ages 8-14. Purpose in publishing work for young people: to entertain while educating and exciting them about their world.

• *National Geographic Kids* does not accept unsolicited manuscripts.

Tips: Publishes art, letters, games, riddles, jokes and craft ideas by children in mailbag section only. No payment given. Send by mail to: Submissions Committee. "Sorry, but we cannot acknowledge or return your contributions."

NEW MOON: The Magazine For Girls & Their Dreams, New Moon Publishing, Inc., P.O. Box 3620, Duluth MN 55803-3620. (218)728-5507. Fax: (218)728-0314. E-mail: girl@newmoon.org. Website: www.newmoon.org. **Managing Editor:** Julie Hoffer. Magazine. Published bimonthly. *New Moon's* primary audience is girls ages 8-14. "We publish a magazine that listens to girls." More than 70% of *New Moon* is written by girls. Purpose in publishing work by children/teens: "We want girls' voices to be heard. *New Moon* wants girls to see that their opinions, dreams, thoughts and ideas count." Writer's guidelines available for SASE or online.

• See listing in Magazines section.

Magazine: Buys 3 fiction mss/year (900-1,200 words); 30 nonfiction mss/year (600 words). Submit to Julie Hoffer, managing editor. Submit query, complete mss for fiction and nonfiction. "We do not return or acknowledge unsolicited material. Do not send originals—we will not return any materials." Responds in 6 months if interested.

Artwork/Photography: Publishes artwork and photography by girls. "We do not return unsolicited material."

Tips: "Read *New Moon* to completely understand our needs."

☑ **POTLUCK CHILDREN'S LITERARY MAGAZINE**, P.O. Box 546, Deerfield IL 60015 (847)948-1139. Fax: (847)317-9492. E-mail: submissions@potluckmagazine.org or susan@potluckmagazine.org. Website: www.potluckmagazine.org. A not-for-profit quarterly magazine for and by writers/artists ages 8-16. "We look for works with imagery, humor and human truths. Editors are available to assist in editing and to answer any questions the writer may have concerning his or her work. The purpose of *Potluck* is to educate today's young writers, to encourage creative expression and to provide a professional forum in which their voices can be heard. Educational articles are written by guest authors, teachers and writing instructors, to help them enrich their writing skills, and to prepare them for the adult markets of their future." Writer's guidelines available on request with a SASE or online.

Magazines: 99% of magazine written by young people. Uses fiction (1,000 words); nonfiction (1,000 words); poetry (30 lines); book reviews (250 words). Pays with copy of issue published. Submit mss to Susan Napoli Picchietti, editor-in-chief. Submit complete ms; teacher may send en masse, but must review all work to ensure it complies with guidelines. Include a SASE for reply. Will accept typewritten and e-mailed mss (No attachments—place work within body of e-mail). Include SASE. Responds 6 weeks after deadline.

Artwork/Photography: Publishes artwork by young artists. Looks for all types of artwork—no textured works. 8½×11 preferred. Pays in copies. Do not fold submissions. Include proper postage and envelope for return of original artwork. Color photo copy accepted. Submit artwork to Susan Napoli Picchietti, editor-in-chief. Include SASE. Responds in 6 weeks.

Tips: "Relax, observe and acknowledge all that is around you. Life gives us a lot to draw on. Don't get carried away with, 'style' let your words speak for themselves. If you want to be taken seriously as a writer, you must take yourself seriously. The rest will follow. Enjoy yourself and take pride in every piece, even the bad—they keep you humble."

☑ **SKIPPING STONES**, Multicultural Children's Magazine, P.O. Box 3939, Eugene OR 97403. (541)342-4956. E-mail: editor@SkippingStones.org. Website: www.SkippingStones.org. **Articles/Poems/Fiction Editor:** Arun N. Toké. 5 issues a year. Estab. 1988. Circulation 2,500. "*Skipping Stones* is a multicultural, nonprofit, children's magazine to encourage cooperation, creativity and celebration of cultural and environmental richness. It offers itself as a creative forum for communication among children from different lands and backgrounds. We prefer work by children under 18 years old. International, minorities and under-represented populations receive priority, multilingual submissions are encouraged."

• *Skipping Stones'* theme for the 2004 Youth Honor Awards is multicultural/international understanding and nature awareness. Send SASE for guidelines and more information on the awards. *Skipping Stones* is winner of the AME and Ed Press awards.

Magazines: 50% written by children and teenagers. Uses 5-10 fiction short stories and plays (500-750 words); 5-10 nonfiction articles, interviews, letters, history, descriptions of celebrations (500-750 words); 15-20 poems, jokes, riddles, proverbs (250 words or less) per issue. Pays in contributor's copies. Submit mss to editor. Submit complete ms for fiction or nonfiction work; teachers and parents can also submit their contributions. Submissions should include "cover letter with name, age, address, school, cultural background, inspiration piece, dreams for future." Will accept typewritten, legibly handwritten and computer/word processor mss. Include SASE. Responds in 4 months. Accepts simultaneous submissions.

Artwork/Photography: Publishes artwork and photography for children. Will review all varieties of ms/illustration packages. Wants comics, cartoons, b&w photos, paintings, drawings (preferably ink & pen or pencil), 8×10, color photos OK. Subjects include children, people, celebrations, nature, ecology, multicultural. Pays in contributor's copies.

Terms: "*Skipping Stones* is a labor of love. You'll receive complimentary contributor's (up to four) copies depending on the extent/length of your contribution. We may allow others to reprint articles and art or photographs." Responds to artists in 4 months. Sample copy for $5 and 4 first-class stamps.

Tips: "Let the 'inner child' within you speak out—naturally, uninhibited." Wants "material that gives insight on cultural celebrations, lifestyle, custom and tradition, glimpse of daily life in other countries and cultures. Please, no mystery for the sake of mystery! Photos, songs, artwork are most welcome if they illustrate/highlight the points. Upcoming features: Living abroad, turning points, inspirations and magical moments in life, cultural celebrations around the world, folktales, caring for the earth, endangered species, your dreams and visions, heroes, kid-friendly analysis of current events, and minority experiences."

🅽 **SPRING TIDES**, 824 Stillwood Dr., Savannah GA 31419. (912)925-8800. Annual magazine. Audience consists of children 5-12 years old. Purpose in publishing works by young people: to promote and encourage writing. Requirements to be met before work is published: must be 5-12 years old. Writers guidelines available on request.

Magazines: 100% of magazine written by young people. Uses 5-6 fiction stories (1,200 words maximum); autobiographical experiences (1,200 words maximum); 15-20 poems (20 lines maximum) per issue. Writers are not paid. Submit complete ms or teacher may submit. Will accept typewritten mss. SASE.

Artwork: Publishes artwork by children. "We have so far used only local children's artwork because of the complications of keeping and returning pieces."

STONE SOUP, The Magazine by Young Writers and Artists, Children's Art Foundation, P.O. Box 83, Santa Cruz CA 95063. (831)426-5557. Fax: (831)426-1161. E-mail: editor@stonesoup.com. Website: www.stonesoup.com. **Articles/ Fiction Editor, Art Director:** Ms. Gerry Mandel. Magazine published 6 times/year. Circ. 20,000. "We publish fiction, poetry and artwork by children through age 13. Our preference is for work based on personal experiences and close observation of the world. Our audience is young people through age 13, as well as parents, teachers, librarians." Purpose in publishing works by young people: to encourage children to read and to express themselves through writing and art. Writer's guidelines available upon request with a SASE.

Magazines: Uses animal, contemporary, fantasy, history, problem-solving, science fiction, sports, spy/mystery/adventure fiction stories. Uses 5-10 fiction stories (100-2,500 words); 5-10 nonfiction stories (100-2,500 words); 2-4 poems per issue. Does not want to see classroom assignments and formula writing. Buys 65 mss/year. Byline given. Pays on publication. Buys all rights. Pays $40 each for stories and poems, $40 for book reviews. Contributors also receive 2 copies. Sample copy $4. Free writer's guidelines. "We don't publish straight nonfiction, but we do publish stories based on real events and experiences." Send complete ms to editor. Will accept typewritten and legibly handwritten mss. Do not include SASE. Send copies, not originals. If we are interested in publishing your work, you will hear from us in 6 weeks. If you don't hear from us, it means we could not use your work. Don't be discouraged. Try again.

Artwork/Photography: Does not publish artwork other than illustrations. Pays $25 for color illustrations. Contributors receive 2 copies. Sample copy $4. Free illustrator's guidelines. Send color copies, not originals. If you would like to illustrate for *Stone Soup*, send us 2 or 3 samples (color copies) of your work, along with a letter telling us what kinds of stories you would like to illustrate. We are looking for artists who can draw complete scenes, including the background. Send submissions to editor. Include SASE. Responds in 6 weeks. All artwork must be by children through age 13.

Tips: "Be sure to enclose a SASE with artwork; not with stories and poems. Only work by young people through age 13 is considered. Whether your work is about imaginary situations or real ones, use your own experiences and observations to give your work depth and a sense of reality. Read a few issues of our magazine to get an idea of what we like."

WHAT IF?, Canada's Magazine for Teens, 19 Lynwood Place, Guelph ON N1G 2V9 Canada, (519)823-2941. Fax: (519)823-8081. E-mail: Whatif2003@hotmail.com. Magazine. Published bimonthly. Writer's guidelines available on request.

• See full listing in Magazines section.

Magazines: 60-70% of magazine written by young people. Pays in copies. Submit mss to Mike Leslie, managing editor. Submit complete ms. Responds in 2 months.

Artwork: Publishes artwork by young adults. Submit artwork to Jean Leslie, production manager. Include SASE for return of samples. Responds in 1 month.

WHOLE NOTES, P.O. Box 1374, Las Cruces NM 88004-1374. (505)541-5744. E-mail: rnhastings@zianet.com. **Editor:** Nancy Peters Hastings. Magazine published twice yearly. "We encourage interest in contemporary poetry by showcasing outstanding creative writing. We look for original, fresh perceptions in poems that demonstrate skill in using language effectively, with carefully chosen images and clear ideas. Our audience (general) loves poetry. We try to recognize excellence in creative writing by children as a way to encourage and promote imaginative thinking." Writer's guidelines available for SASE.

Magazines: Every fourth issue is 100% by children. Writers should be 21 years old or younger. Uses 30 poems/issue (length open). Pays complimentary copy. Submit mss to editor. Submit complete ms. "No multiple submissions, please." Will accept typewritten and legibly handwritten mss. SASE. Responds in 2 months.

Artwork/Photography: Publishes artwork and photographs by children. Looks for b&w line drawings which can easily be reproduced; b&w photos. Pays complimentary copy. Send clear photocopies. Submit artwork to Nancy Peters Hastings, editor. SASE. Responds in 2 months.

Tips: Sample issue is $3. "We welcome translations. Send your best work. Don't send your only copy of your poem. Keep a photocopy."

WORD DANCE, Playful Productions, Inc., P.O. Box 10804, Wilmington DE 19850-0804. (302)894-1950. Fax: (302)894-1957. E-mail: playful@worddance.com. Website: www.worddance.com. **Director:** Stuart Unger. Quarterly magazine. "We're a magazine of creative writing and art that is for *and* by children in kindergarten through grade eight. We give children a voice."

Magazines: Uses adventure, fantasy, humorous, etc. (fiction); travel stories, poems and stories based on real life experiences (nonfiction). Publishes 250 total pieces of writing/year; maximum length: 3 pages. Submit mss to Stuart Ungar, articles editor. Sample copy $3. Free writer's guidelines and submissions form. Include a SASE. Responds in 9 months.

Artwork: Illustrations accepted from young people in kindergarten through grade 8. Accepts illustrations of specific stories or poems and other general artwork. Must be high contrast. Query. Submit complete package with final art to art director. SASE. Responds in 8 months.

Tips: "Submit writing that falls into one of our specific on-going departments. General creative writing submissions are much more competitive."

☑ **THE WRITERS' SLATE**, (The Writing Conference, Inc.), P.O. Box 669, Ottawa KS 66067. Phone/fax: (785)242-1995. E-mail: jbushman@writingconference.com. Website: www.writingconference.com. Magazine. Publishes 3 issues/year. *The Writers' Slate* accepts original poetry and prose from students enrolled in kindergarten-12th grade. The audience is students, teachers and librarians. Purpose in publishing works by young people: to give students the opportunity to publish and to give students the opportunity *to read* quality literature written by other students. Writer's guidelines available on request.

Magazines: 90% of magazine written by young people. Uses 10-15 fiction, 1-2 nonfiction, 10-15 other mss per issue. Submit mss to Shelley McHerney, editor, 7619 Hemlock St., Overland Park KS 66204. Submit complete ms. Will accept typewritten mss. Responds in 1 month. Include SASE with ms if reply is desired.

Artwork: Publishes artwork by young people. Bold, b&w, student artwork may accompany a piece of writing. Submit to Shelley McHerney, editor. Responds in 1 month.

Tips: "Always accompany submission with a letter indicating name, home address, school, grade level and teacher's name. If you want a reply, submit a SASE."

Ⓝ **YOUNG VOICES MAGAZINE**, P.O. Box 2321, Olympia WA 98507. (360)357-4683. E-mail: support@youngvoices magazine.com. Website: www.youngvoicesmagazine.com. Magazine published quarterly. "*Young Voices* is by elementary and high school students for people interested in their work." Purpose in publishing work by young people: to provide a forum for their creative work. "Home schooled writers *definitely* welcome, too." Writer's guidelines available on request with SASE and on website.

Magazines: Uses 15 fiction stories, 5 reviews, 10 essays and 15 poems per issue (lengths vary). Pays $5-10 on acceptance (more depending on the length and quality of the writing). Submit mss to Steve Charak. Query first. Will accept typewritten and legibly handwritten mss and e-mail submission. SASE. Responds in 2 months.

Artwork/Photography: Publishes artwork and photography by children. "Prefer work that will show up in black and white." Pays $5 on acceptance. Submit artwork to Steve Charak. SASE. Responds in 2 months.

Tips: "Please read one or more issues before submitting work."

Resources

Agents & Art Reps

This section features listings of literary agents and art reps who either specialize in or represent a good percentage of children's writers or illustrators. While there are a number of children's publishers who are open to nonagented material, using the services of an agent or rep can be beneficial to a writer or artist. Agents and reps can get your work seen by editors and art directors more quickly. They are familiar with the market and have insights into which editors and art directors would be most interested in your work. Also, they negotiate contracts and will likely be able to get you a better deal than you could get on your own.

Agents and reps make their income by taking a percentage of what writers and illustrators receive from publishers. The standard percentage for agents is 10-15 percent; art reps generally take 25-30 percent. We have not included any agencies in this section that charge reading fees.

WHAT TO SEND

When putting together a package for an agent or rep, follow the guidelines given in their listings. Most agents open to submissions prefer initially to receive a query letter describing your work. For novels and longer works, some agents ask for an outline and a number of sample chapters, but you should send these only if you're asked to do so. Never fax or e-mail a query letter or sample chapters to agents without their permission. Just as with publishers, agents receive a large volume of submissions. It may take them a long time to reply, so you may want to query several agents at one time. It's best, however, to have a complete manuscript considered by only one agent at a time. Always include a self-addressed, stamped envelope (SASE).

For initial contact with art reps, send a brief query letter and self-promo pieces. Again, follow the guidelines given in the listings. If you don't have a flier or brochure, send photocopies. Always include a SASE.

For those who both write and illustrate, some agents listed will consider the work of author/illustrators. Read through the listings for details.

As you consider approaching agents and reps with your work, keep in mind that they are

---

An Organization for Agents

In some listings of agents you'll see references to AAR (The Association of Authors' Representatives). This organization requires its members to meet an established list of professional standards and code of ethics.

The objectives of AAR include keeping agents informed about conditions in publishing and related fields; encouraging cooperation among literary organizations; and assisting agents in representing their author-clients' interests. Officially, members are prohibited from directly or indirectly charging reading fees. They offer writers a list of member agents on their website. They also offer a list of recommended questions an author should ask an agent. They can be contacted at AAR, P.O. Box 237201, Ansonia Station NY 10003. Website: www.aar-online.org.

very choosy about who they take on to represent. Your work must be high quality and presented professionally to make an impression on them. For additional listings of art reps see *Artist's & Graphic Designer's Market* (Writer's Digest Books).

Information on agents and art reps listed in the previous edition but not included in this edition of *Children's Writer's & Illustrator's Market* may be found in the General Index.

AGENTS

N̄ ALLRED & ALLRED, 7834 Alabama Ave., Canoga Park CA 91304-4905. (818)346-4313. **Contact:** Robert Allred and Kim Allred. Seeking both new and established writers. Estab. 1991. Represents 8 clients. 75% of clients are new/previously unpublished writers. 25% of material handled is books for young readers. Staff includes Robert Allred, Kim Allred.
Represents: Considers fiction, nonfiction, middle grade, young adult textbooks. Handles all and any material except picture books.
How to Contact: Send outline and first 2 sample chapters. Considers simultaneous queries and submissions. Responds in 1 month to queries; 2 months to mss. Returns material only with SASE. Obtains clients through queries/solicitations.
Recent Sales: Sold 2 books for young readers in the last year. *Red Fox & Grey Fox*, by Heidi Mueller (Everyday).
Terms: Agent receives 10% on domestic sales; 20% on foreign sales. Offers written contract, binding for 1 year. 1-month notice must be given to terminate contract.

BOOKS & SUCH, 4788 Carissa Ave., Santa Rosa CA 95405. (707)538-4184. Fax: (626)398-0246. E-mail: jkgbooks@aol.com. **Contact:** Janet Kobobel Grant. Estab. 1996. Associate member of CBA. Represents 40 clients. 8% of clients are new/unpublished writers. Specializes in "the Christian booksellers market but places some projections in the ABA market."
   • Before becoming an agent, Janet Kobobel Grant was an editor for Zondervan and managing editor for *Focus on the Family*.
Represents: 15% juvenile books. Considers: nonfiction, fiction, picture books, young adult.
How to Contact: Query with SASE. Considers simultaneous queries. Responds in 1 month to queries; 6 weeks to mss. Returns material only with SASE.
Recent Sales: *Hand Over the Moon* (Tyndale).
Needs: Actively seeking "material that deslights and charms the reader." Obtains new clients through recommendations and conferences.
Terms: Agent receives 15% commission on domestic and foreign sales. Offers written contract. 2 months notice must be given to terminate contract. Charges for postage, photocopying, fax and express mail.
Tips: "The heart of my motivation is to develop relationships with the authors I serve, to do what I can to shine the light of success on them, and to help be a caretaker of their gifts and time."

N̄ BOOKSTOP LITERARY AGENCY, 67 Meadow View Rd., Orinda CA 94563. Website: www.bookstopliterary.com. Seeking both new and established writers. Estab. 1983. 100% of material handled is books of young readers.
Represents: Considers fiction, nonfiction, picture books, middle grade, young adult. "Special interest in Hispanic writers and illustrators for children."
How to Contact: Send entire ms with SASE. Considers simultaneous submissions. Responds in 6 weeks. Responds and returns material only with SASE.
Terms: Agent receives 15% commission on domestic sales. Offers written contract, binding for 1 year.

N̄ ANDREA BROWN LITERARY AGENCY, INC., 1076 Eagle Dr., Salinas CA 93095. (831)422-5925. E-mail: ablit@redshift.com. **President:** Andrea Brown. Estab. 1981. Member of SCBWI and WNBA. 10% of clients are new/previously unpublished writers. Specializes in "all kinds of children's books—illustrators and authors."
   • Prior to opening her agency, Andrea Brown served as an editorial assistant at Random House and Dell Publishing and as an editor with Alfred A. Knopf.
Member Agents: Andrea Brown, president; Laura Rennert, vice president.
Represents: 98% juvenile books. Considers: nonfiction (animals, anthropology/archaeology, art/architecture/design, biography/autobiography, current affairs, ethnic/cultural interests, history, how-to, nature/environment, photography, popular culture, science/technology, sociology, sports); fiction (historical, science fiction); picture books, young adult.
How to Contact: Query. Responds in 3 months to queries and mss. E-mail queries only.
Needs: Mostly obtains new clients through recommendations, editors, clients and agents.
Recent Sales: *Figure Skating*, by Sasha Cohen (HarperCollins); *Tequilla Worm*, by Viola Lanates (Wendy Lamb Books-Random House); *Big Blue Pick-Up Truck*, by Candice Ransom (Walker).
Terms: Agent receives 15% commission on domestic sales; 20% on foreign sales. Written contract.
Writers' Conferences: Agents at Andrea Brown Literary Agency attend Austin Writers League; SCBWI, Columbus Writers Conference, Willamette Writers Conference, Orange County Conferences; Mills College Childrens Literature Conference (Oakland CA); Asilomar (Pacific Grove CA); Maui Writers Conference, Southwest Writers Conference; San Diego State University Writer's Conference; Big Sur Children's Writing Workshop (Director).

Tips: Query first. "Taking on very few picture books. Must be unique—no rhyme, no anthropomorphism. Do not call, or fax queries or manuscripts."

RUTH COHEN, INC. LITERARY AGENCY, P.O. Box 2244, LaJolla CA 92038-2244. (858)456-5805. **Contact:** Ruth Cohen. Currently accepting new clients. Estab. 1982. Member of AAR, Authors Guild, Sisters in Crime, Romance Writers of America, SCBWI. Represents 45 clients. 15% of clients are new/previously unpublished writers. Specializes in "quality writing in contemporary fiction; women's fiction; mysteries; thrillers and juvenile fiction."

● Prior to opening her agency, Ruth Cohen served as directing editor at Scott Foresman & Company (now HarperCollins).

Represents: 40% juvenile. Considers: fiction, picture books, middle grade, young adult. Does not want to see poetry or scripts.

How to Contact: *No unsolicited mss.* Accepts queries by mail only. Send outline plus 2 sample chapters. "Please indicate your phone number or e-mail address." *Must include SASE.* Responds in 3 weeks on queries.

Needs: Obtains new clients through recommendations from others and through submissions.

Terms: Agent receives 15% commission on domestic sales; 20% on foreign sales, "if a foreign agent is involved." Offers written contract, binding for 1 year "continuing to next." Charges for foreign postage, phone calls, photocopying submissions and overnight delivery of mss when appropriate.

Tips: "As the publishing world merges and charges, there seem to be fewer opportunities for new writers to succeed in the work that they love. We urge you to develop the patience, persistence and perseverance that have made this agency so successful. Prepare a well-written and well-crafted manuscript, and our combined best efforts can help advance both our careers."

DUNHAM LITERARY, INC., 156 Fifth Ave., Suite 625, New York NY 10010-7002. Website: www.dunhamlit.com. **Contact:** Jennie Dunham. Seeking both new and established writers but prefers to work with established writers. Estab. 2000. Member of AAR, signatory of SCBWI. Represents 50 clients. 15% of clients are new/previously unpublished writers. 50% of material handled is books of young readers.

Represents: Considers fiction, picture books, middle grade, young adult. Most agents represent children's books or adult books, and this agency represents both. Actively seeking mss with great story and voice. Not looking for activity books, workbooks, educational books, poetry.

How to Contact: Query with SASE. Consider simultaneous queries and submissions. Responds in 1 week to queries; 2 months to mss. Returns material only with SASE. Obtains clients through recommendations from others.

Recent Sales: Sold 30 books for young readers in the last year. *The Night Before Christmas*, by Robert Sabuda (Little Simon); *Clever Beatrice*, illustrated by Heather Solomon (Atheneum); *Gauchada*, by C. Drew Lamm (Knopf); *Dahlia*, by Barbara McClintock (Farrar, Straus & Giroux); *Who Will Tell My Brother?*, by Marlene Carvell (Hyperion).

Terms: Agent receives 15% commission on domestic sales; 20-25% on foreign sales. Offers written contract. 60 days notice must be given to terminate contract.

Fees: The agency takes expenses from the clients' earnings for specific expenses documented during the marketing of a client's work in accordance with the AAR (Association of Authors' Representatives) Canon of Ethics. For example, photocopying, messenger, express mail, UPS, etc. The client is not asked to pay for these fees up front.

☑ **DWYER & O'GRADY, INC.**, P.O. Box 790, Cedar Key FL 32625. (352)543-9307. Fax: (603)375-5373. **Contact:** Elizabeth O'Grady. Estab. 1990. Member of SCBWI. Represents 25 clients. Represents both writers and illustrators.

● Dwyer & O'Grady is currently not accepting new clients.

Member Agents: Elizabeth O'Grady (children's books); Jeff Dwyer (children's books).

Represents: 95% juvenile books. Considers: nonfiction, fiction, picture books, young adult.

Needs: Obtains new clients through referrals or direct approach from agent to writer whose work they've read. Does not accept unsolicited mss.

Terms: Agent receives 15% commission on domestic sales; 20% on foreign sales. Offers written contract. Thirty days notice must be given to terminate contract. Charges for "photocopying of longer manuscripts or mutually agreed upon marketing expenses."

Tips: Agents from Dwyer & O'Grady attend Book Expo; American Library Association; Society of Children's Book Writers & Illustrators conferences. Clients include: Kim Ablon Whitney, Tom Bodett, Odds Bodkin, Donna Clair, Leonard Jenkins, Steve Schuch, Virginia Stroud, Natasha Tarpley, Zong-Zhou Wang, Peter Sylvada, Mary Azarian, E.B. Lewis, Rich Michelson, Barry Moser, Stan Fellows, Lynda Jones, James Charlesworth, Irving Toddy and Tom Sanders.

🄽 🄳 **EDUCATIONAL DESIGN SERVICES INC.**, P.O. Box 253, Wantagh NY 11793. E-mail: linder.eds@juno.com. **Contact:** B. Linder or E. Selzer. Handles only certain types of work. Estab. 1981. 80% of clients are new/previously unpublished writers.

Represents: Considers text materials for K-12 market. "We specialize in educational materials to be used in classrooms, in class sets." Actively seeking educational, text materials. Not looking for picture books, story books, any fiction, no illustrators.

How to Contact: Query with SASE or send outline and 1 sample chapter. Considers simultaneous queries and submissions if so indicated. Responds in 2 months to queries/mss. Returns material only with SASE. Obtains clients through recommendations from others, queries/solicitations, or through conferences.

Recent Sales: *Nueva Historia de los Estados Unidos*, by Parker Hall (Minerva Books); *Reviewing U.S. & NYS History*, by Farran-Ricci (Amsco); *A World History*, by Lind-Selz-Berk (McDougal-Littell).

Terms: Agent receives 15% commission on domestic sales; 25% on foreign sales. Offers written contract, binding until any party opts out. Terminate contract through certified letter.

ETHAN ELLENBERG LITERARY AGENCY, 548 Broadway, #5-E, New York NY 10012. (212)431-4554. Fax: (212)941-4652. E-mail: agent@ethanellenberg.com. Website: EthanEllenberg.com. **Contact:** Ethan Ellenberg or Michael Psaltis. Estab. 1983. Represents 80 clients. 10% of clients are new/previously unpublished writers. Children's books are an important area for us.

- ● Prior to opening his agency, Ethan Ellenberg was contracts manager of Berkley/Jove and associate contracts manager for Bantam.

Represents: "We do a lot of children's books." Considers: nonfiction, fiction, picture books, young adult.

How to Contact: Children's submissions—send full ms. Young adults—send outline plus 3 sample chapters. Accepts queries by e-mail; does not accept attachments to e-mail queries or fax queries. Considers simultaneous queries and submissions. Responds in 10 days to queries; 1 month to mss. Returns materials only with SASE.

Terms: Agent receives 15% on domestic sales; 10% on foreign sales. Offers written contract, "flexible." Charges for "direct expenses only: photocopying, postage."

Tips: "We do consider new material from unsolicited authors. Write a good clear letter with a succinct description of your book. We prefer the first three chapters when we consider fiction, but for children's book submissions, we prefer the full manuscript. For all submissions you must include SASE for return or the material is discarded. It's always hard to break in, but talent will find a home. We continue to seek natural storytellers and nonfiction writers with important books." This agency sold over 100 titles in the last 3 years, including the 2003 Caldecott winner *My Friend Rabbit*, by Eric Rohman.

N: FLANNERY LITERARY, 1140 Wickfield Court, Naperville IL 60563-3300. (630)428-2682. Fax: (630)428-2683. **Contact:** Jennifer Flannery. Estab. 1992. Represents 33 clients. 50% of clients are new/previously unpublished writers. Specializes in children's and young adult, juvenile fiction and nonfiction.

- ● Prior to opening her agency, Jennifer Flannery was an editorial assistant.

Represents: 100% juvenile books. Considers: nonfiction, fiction, picture books, middle grade, young adult.

How to Contact: Query. Responds in 2 weeks to queries; 5 weeks to mss.

Needs: Obtains new clients through referrals and queries.

Terms: Agent receives 15% commission on domestic sales; 20% on foreign sales. Offers written contract, binding for life of book in print, with 30 day cancellation clause. 100% of business is derived from commissions on sales.

Tips: "Write an engrossing succinct query describing your work." Flannery Literary sold 20 titles in the last year.

BARRY GOLDBLATT LITERARY AGENCY INC., 320 Seventh Ave., #266, Brooklyn NY 11215. (718)832-8787. Fax: (718)832-5558. E-mail: bgliterary@earthlink.net. **Contact:** Barry Goldblatt. Estab. 2000. Member of SCBWI. Represents 30 clients. 40% of clients are new/previously unpublished writers. 100% of material handled is books for young readers. Staff includes Barry Goldblatt (picture books, middle grade and young adult novels).

Represents: Considers picture books, fiction, middle grade, young adult.

How to Contact: Send entire ms for picture books; outline and 3 sample chapters for fiction. Prefers to read material exclusively. Responds in 3 weeks to queries; 2 months to mss. Returns material only with SASE. Obtains clients through recommendations from others.

Recent Sales: Sold 30 books for young readers in the last year.

Terms: Agent receives 15% commission on domestic sales; 20% on foreign and dramatic sales.

Tips: "I structure my relationship with each client differently, according to their wants and needs. I'm mostly hands-on, but some want more editorial input, others less. I'm pretty aggressive selling work, but I'm fairly laid back in how I deal with clients. I'd say I'm quite friendly with most of my clients, and I like it that way. To me this is more than just a simple business relationship."

KIRCHOFF/WOHLBERG, INC., AUTHORS' REPRESENTATION DIVISION, 866 United Nations Plaza, #525, New York NY 10017. (212)644-2020. Fax: (212)223-4387. Director of Operations: John R. Whitman. Estab. 1930s. Member of AAR. Represents 50 authors. 10% of clients are new/previously unpublished writers. Specializes in juvenile through young adult trade books and textbooks.

Member Agents: Liza Pulitzer-Voges (juvenile and young adult authors).

Represents: 80% juvenile books, 20% young adult. "We are interested in any original projects of quality that are appropriate to the juvenile and young adult trade book markets. But we take on very few new clients as our roster is full."

How to Contact: "Send a query that includes an outline and a sample; SASE required." Responds in 1 month to queries; 2 months to mss. Please send queries to the attention of Liza Pulitzer-Voges.

Needs: "Usually obtains new clients through recommendations from authors, illustrators and editors."

Terms: Agent receives standard commission "depending upon whether it is an author only, illustrator only, or an author/illustrator book." Offers written contract, binding for not less than 1 year.

Tips: "Kirchoff/Wohlberg has been in business since 1930 and sold over 50 titles in the last year."

BARBARA S. KOUTS, LITERARY AGENT, P.O. Box 560, Bellport NY 11713. (631)286-1278. **Contact:** Barbara Kouts. Currently accepting new clients. Estab. 1980. Member of AAR. Represent 50 clients. 10% of clients are new/previously unpublished writers. Specializes in children's books.

Represents: 100% juvenile books. Considers: nonfiction, fiction, picture books, ms/illustration packages, middle grade, young adult.

How to Contact: Accepts queries by mail only. Responds in 1 week to queries; 6 weeks to mss.

Needs: Obtains new clients through recommendations from others, solicitation, at conferences, etc.

Recent Sales: *Sacajawea*, by Joseph Bruchac (Harcourt); *Born Blue*, by Han Nolan (Harcourt); *Froggy Plays in the Band*, by Jonathan London (Viking).

Terms: Agent receives 15% commission on domestic sales; 20% on foreign sales. Charges for photocopying.

Tips: "Write, do not call. Be professional in your writing."

GINA MACCOBY LITERARY AGENCY, P.O. Box 60, Chappaqua NY 10514. (914)238-5630. **Contact:** Gina Maccoby. Estab. 1986. Represents 35 clients. Represents writers and illustrators of children's books.

Represents: 50% juvenile books. Considers: nonfiction, fiction, young adult.

How to Contact: Query with SASE. "Please, no unsolicited mss." Considers simultaneous queries and submisssions. Responds to queries in 2 months. Returns materials only with SASE.

Needs: Usually obtains new clients through recommendations from own clients and/or editors.

Terms: Agent receives 15% commission on domestic sales; 25% on foreign sales. Charges for photocopying. May recover certain costs such as airmail postage to Europe or Japan or legal fees.

Tips: This agency sold 18 titles last year including *The Crying Rocks*, by Janet Taylor Lisle.

N MCINTOSH & OTIS, INC., 353 Lexington Ave., New York NY 10016. (212)687-7400. Fax: (212)687-6894. **Contact:** Tracey Adams. Seeking both new and established writers. Estab. 1927. Member of AAR and SCBWI. 20% of clients are new/previously unpublished writers. 100% of material handled is books for young readers.

Represents: Considers fiction, nonfiction, picture books, middle grade, young adult. "McIntosh & Otis has a long history of representing authors of adult and children's books. The children's department is a separate division." Actively seeking "books with memorable characters, distinctive voice, and a great plot." Not looking for educational, activity books, coloring books.

How to Contact: Query with SASE. Send entire ms if picture book. Prefers to read material exclusively. Responds in 1 month to queries; 6 weeks to mss. Returns material only with SASE. Obtains clients through recommendations from others or through conferences.

Terms: Agent receives 15% commission on domestic sales; 20% on foreign sales.

Writers' Conferences: Attends Bologna Book Fair, in Bologna Italy in April, SCBWI Conference in New York in February, and regularly attends other conferences and industry conventions.

ERIN MURPHY LITERARY AGENCY, P.O. Box 2519, Flagstaff AZ 86003-2519. (928)525-2056. Closed to unsolicited queries and submissions. Considers both new and established writers, by referral or personal contact (such as conferences) only. Estab. 1999. Member of SCBWI. Represents 40 clients. 80% of clients are new/previously unpublished writers. 100% of material handled is books of young readers.

  • Prior to opening her agency, Erin Murphy was editor-in-chief at Northland Publishing/Rising Moon. Agency is not currently accepting unsolicited queries or submissions.

Represents: Fiction, nonfiction, picture books, middle grade, young adult.

Terms: Agent receives 15% commission on domestic sales; 20% on foreign sales. Offers written contract. 30 days notice must be given to terminate contract.

N ALISON PICARD, LITERARY AGENT, P.O. Box 2000, Cotuit MA 02635. Phone/fax: (508)477-7192. E-mail: ajpicard@aol.com. **Contact:** Alison Picard. Seeking both new and established writers. Estab. 1985. Represents 50 clients. 40% of clients are new/previously unpublished writers. 20% of material handled is books for young readers.

  • Prior to opening her agency, Alison Picard was an assistant at a large New York agency before co-founding Kidde, Hoyt & Picard in 1982. She became an independent agent in 1985.

Represents: Considers nonfiction, fiction, a very few picture books, middle grade, young adult. "I represent juvenile and YA books. I do not handle short stories, articles, poetry or plays. I am especially interested in commercial non-fiction, romances and mysteries/suspense/thrillers. I work with agencies in Europe and Los Angeles to sell foreign and TV/film rights." Actively seeking middle grade fiction. Not looking for poetry or plays.

How to Contact: Query with SASE. Accepts queries by e-mail with no attachments. Considers simultaneous queries and submissions. Responds in 1 week to queries; 3 months to mss. Returns material only with SASE. Obtains clients through queries/solicitations.

Recent Sales: Sold 8 books for young readers in the last year. *2030*, by Amy Zuckerman and Jim Daly (Dutton); *The Great Receiver*, by Elena Yates Eulo (Holiday House); *Stanislawski the Great*, by Mary Bartele (Henry Holt); and *The Boldness of Boys*, by Susan Strong (Andrews McMeel).

Terms: Receives 15% commission on domestic sales; 20-25% on foreign sales. Offers written contract, binding for 1 year. 1-week notice must be given to terminate contract.

N PUBLISHERS GRAPHICS INC., 231 Judd Rd., Easton CT 06612. (203)445-1511. Fax: (203)445-1411. Website: publishersgraphics.com. **Contact:** Paige Gillies. Not currently seeking new clients. Estab. 1972. Member of SCBWI. Represents 11 clients. 100% of material handled is books of young readers.

Represents: Considers fiction, nonfiction, picture books, middle grade. "Our specialty is honest service to clients and publishers. We have thirty years experience and know that personal contact beats hundreds of thousands in ad and marketing dollars."

How to Contact: "My portfolio is closed. Do not send queries or mss."

Recent Sales: Sold books for young readers in the last year.

Terms: Agent receives 25% commission on domestic sales; 25% on foreign sales. Offers written contract, binding for 3 years with automatic renewal. 1 month notice must be given to terminate contract

Tips: "My interest is in the artistic development of the individual artist to enhance their satisfaction with their work and the assignments they receive. The client chooses my level of involvement in their process and in their life. I am straightforward and pragmatic."

N ANN TOBIAS—A LITERARY AGENCY FOR CHILDREN'S BOOKS, 520 E. 84th St., Apt. 4L, New York NY 10028. E-mail: atobias@earthlink.net. **Contact:** Ann Tobias. Seeking both new and established writers. Handles only certain types of work. Estab. 1988. Represents 25 clients. 50% of clients are new/previously unpublished writers. 100% of material handled is books for children.

• Prior to opening her agency, Ann Tobias worked as a children's book editor at Harper, William Morrow, Scholastic.

Represents: Fiction, nonfiction, middle grade, picture books, poetry, young adult, young readers.

How to Contact: Send entire ms for picture books; 30 pages and synopsis for longer works. No e-mail, fax or phone queries. Accepts simultaneous submissions. Responds to queries only if interested; 2 months to mss. Returns material only with SASE. Obtains clients through recommendations from editors.

Recent Sales: Sold 23 titles in the last year.

Terms: Agent receives 15% commission on domestic sales; 20% on foreign sales.

Tips: "Read at least 200 children's books in the age group and genre in which you hope to be published. Follow this by reading another 100 children's books in other age groups and genres so you will have a feel for the field as a whole."

SCOTT TREIMEL NY, 434 Lafayette St., New York NY 10003. (212)505-8353. Fax: (212)505-0664. E-mail: ST.NY@Verizon.net. **Contact:** Scott Treimel. Currently seeking established writers or artists only. Estab. 1995. Represents 33 clients. 10% of clients are new/unpublished writers. Specializes in children's books, all genres: tightly focused segments of the trade and, to a lesser extent, educational markets. Member AAR, Author's Guild, SCBWI.

• Prior to opening his agency, Scott Treimel was an assistant to Marilyn E. Marlow of Curtis Brown; a rights agent for Scholastic, Inc.; a book packager and rights agent for United Feature Syndicate; the founding director of Warner Bros. Worldwide Publishing, a freelance editor; and a rights consultant for HarperCollins Children's Books.

Represents: 100% juvenile books. Considers middle grade, young adult and ms/illustration packages. No religious books.

How to Contact: Accepts queries by postal mail only. Query with SASE. For picture books, send entire ms (no more than 2). Does not accept queries by fax or e-mail. No multiple submissions. Requires "90-day exclusivity on all submissions." Replies to submissions only with SASE, otherwise discards.

Needs: Interested in seeing picture book author-illustrators, first chapter books, middle-grade fiction and teen fiction. Obtains most clients through recommendations. Prefers published authors and illustrators.

Recent Sales: Sold 20 titles in the last year. *Please is a Good Word to Say*, by Barbara Joosse (Philomel); *A Pieplate in the Sky*, by Alice Luv (Holiday House); *Playing in Traffic*, by Gail Giles (Roaring Brook Press).

Terms: Agent receives 15-20% commission on domestic sales; 20-25% on foreign sales. Offers verbal or written contract, binding on a "contract-by-contract basis." Charges for photocopying, overnight/express postage, messengers and books ordered for subsidiary rights sales. Offers editorial guidance selectively, if extensive charges higher commission.

Writer's Conferences: Attends Society of Children's Book Writers & Illustrators Conferences, participates in panel discussions.

Tips: Do not pitch; let your work speak for itself.

WECKSLER-INCOMCO, 170 West End Ave., New York NY 10023. (212)787-2239. Fax: (212)496-7035. E-mail: jacinny@aol.com. **Contact:** Sally Wecksler. Estab. 1971. Represents 30 clients. 50% of clients are new/previously unpublished writers. "However, I prefer writers who have had something in print." Specializes in nonfiction with illustrations (photos and art).

• Prior to becoming an agent, Sally Wecksler was an editor at *Publishers Weekly*; publisher with the international department of R.R. Bowker; and international director at Baker & Taylor.

Member Agents: Joann Amparan-Close (general, children's books), S. Wecksler (general, foreign rights/co-editions, fiction, illustrated books, children's books).

Represents: 25% juvenile books. Considers: nonfiction, fiction, picture books.

How to Contact: Query with outline plus 3 sample chapters. Include brief bio. Responds in 1 month on queries; 3 months on mss.

Needs: Actively seeking "illustrated books for adults or children with beautiful photos or artwork." Does not want to receive "science fiction or books with violence." Obtains new clients through recommendations from others and solicitations.

Terms: Agent receives 15% commission on domestic sales; 20% on foreign sales. Offers written contract, binding for 3 years.

Tips: "Make sure a SASE is enclosed. Send three chapters and outline, clearly typed or word processed manuscript, double-spaced, written with punctuation and grammar in approved style. *We do not like to receive presentations by fax or e-mail.*"

WRITERS HOUSE, 21 W. 26th St., New York NY 10010. (212)685-2400. Fax: (212)685-1781. Estab. 1974. Member of AAR. Represents 280 clients. 50% of clients were new/unpublished writers. Specializes in all types of popular fiction and nonfiction. No scholarly, professional, poetry or screenplays.

Member Agents: Amy Berkower (major juvenile authors); Merrilee Heifetz (quality children's fiction); Susan Cohen

(juvenile and YA authors and illustrators), Jodi Reamer (juvenile and young adult fiction and nonfiction); Steven Malk (quality YA fiction and picture books); Robin Rue (YA fiction).
Represents: 35% juvenile books. Considers: nonfiction, fiction, picture books, young adult.
How to Contact: Query. Responds in 1 month on queries.
Needs: Obtains new clients through recommendations from others.
Terms: Agent receives 15% commission on domestic sales; 20% on foreign sales. Offers written contract, binding for 1 year.
Tips: "Do not send manuscripts. Write a compelling letter. If you do, we'll ask to see your work."

WRITERS HOUSE, (West Coast Office), 3368 Governor Dr., #224F, San Diego CA 92122. (858)678-8767. Fax: (858)678-8530. **Contact:** Steven Malk.
• See Writers House listing above for more information.
Represents: Nonfiction, fiction, picture books, young adult.

WYLIE-MERRICK LITERARY AGENCY, 1138 S. Webster St., Kokomo IN 46902. (765)459-8258. E-mail: smartin@w ylie-merrick.com or rbrown@wylie-merrick.com. Website: www.wylie-merrick.com. **Contact:** Sharene Martin or Robert Brown. Seeking both new and established writers. Estab. 1999. Member of SCBWI and Mystery Writers of America (MWA). Represents 12 clients. 50% of clients are new/previously unpublished writers. 60% of material handled is books for young readers. Staff includes Sharene Martin (picture books, middle-grade and young adult novels), Robert Brown (young adult novels).
• Prior to opening their agency, Sharene Martin worked as an English teacher, grades 8-adult; writer; and educational technology consultant. Robert Brown worked as an engineer; dance instructor; and writer.
Represents: Considers genre fiction, nonfiction, picture books, middle grade, young adult. "We are very focused on representing quality literature; our agency represents a true passion for 'good reads.' We work closely with our clients to develop their potential to the greatest extent possible. If we request a writer's work, we try to give him/her a critique and some suggestions on improving the project's marketability even if we don't represent it." Actively seeking genre fiction: mystery, science fiction/fantasy; novels depicting strong relationships, romance, sports, and/or Christian themes. Not looking for poetry.
How to Contact: For novels submit first 10 pages and synopsis; submit entire ms for picture books. Consider simultaneous queries and submissions. Responds in 1 month to queries; 3 months to mss. Returns material only with SASE. Obtains clients through recommendations from others, queries/solicitations, conferences.
Recent Sales: *How I Fell in Love and Learned to Shoot Free Throws* (Roaring Brook Press); *Death for Dessert* (Fivestar).
Terms: Agent receives 15% commission on domestic sales; 20% on foreign sales. Offers written contract binding on all sales even after canceled. 10 days notice must be given to terminate contract.
Writers' Conferences: Attended Wilamette Writers Conference in Portland, OR, August 2003; Surrey International Writers Conference in Surrey, BC, October 2003; will attend Aspiring Authors Conference in Plymouth, IN (local high school event ONLY) April, 2004.
Tips: "We are a small, low-key agency that works closely with its clients. We do edit some material for clients (no charge) and request revisions as needed. We are excited about the projects we represent, and we enjoy working with our authors to develop great literature for children and young adults."

ART REPS

ART FACTORY, (formerly Nachreiner Boie Art Factory), 925 Elm Grove Rd., Elm Grove WI 53122. (262)785-1940. Fax: (262)785-1611. E-mail: tstocki@artfactoryltd.com. Website: www.artfactoryltd.com. **Contact:** Tom Stocki. Commercial illustration representative. Estab. 1978. Represents 9 illustrators. 10% of artwork handled is children's book illustration. Currently open to illustrators seeking representation. Open to both new and established illustrators.
Handles: Illustration.
Recent Sales: Represents Tom Buchs, Tom Nachreiner, Todd Dakins, Linda Godfrey, Larry Mikec, Bill Scott, Amanda Aquino, Gary Shea, Terry Herman, Troy Allen.
Terms: Receives 25-30% commission. Offers written contract. Advertising costs are split: 75% paid by illustrators; 25% paid by rep. "We try to mail samples of all our illustrators at one time and we try to update our website; so we ask the illustrators to keep up with new samples." Advertises in *Picturebook*, *Workbook*.
How to Contact: For first contact, send query letter, tearsheets. Responds only if interested. Call to schedule an appointment. Portfolio should include tearsheets. Finds illustrators through queries/solicitations.
Tips: "Have a unique style."

ASCIUTTO ART REPS., INC., 1712 E. Butler Circle, Chandler AZ 85225. (480)899-0600. Fax: (480)899-3636. E-mail: Aartreps@cox.net. **Contact:** Mary Anne Asciutto. Children's illustration representative. Estab. 1980. Member of SPAR, Society of Illustrators. Represents 12 illustrators. 99% of artwork handled is children's book illustration. Specializes in children's illustration for books, magazines, posters, packaging, etc. Markets include: publishing/packaging/advertising.
• Asciutto is now representing children's book writers as well as illustrators.
Handles: Stories and illustration for children only.
Recent Sales: *Bats*, illustrated by Henderson (Boyd's Mill's Press).
Terms: Rep receives 25% commission. No geographic restrictions. Advertising costs are split: 75% paid by talent; 25%

paid by representative. For promotional purposes, talent should provide "prints (color) or originals within an $8\frac{1}{2} \times 11$ size format."

How to Contact: Send printed materials, tearsheets, photocopies and/or ms in a SASE. Responds in 2 weeks. After initial contact, send appropriate materials if requested. Portfolio should include original art on paper, tearsheets, photocopies or color prints of most recent work. If accepted, materials will remain for assembly.

Tips: In obtaining representation "be sure to connect with an agent who handles the kind of accounts you (the artist/writer) *want*."

CAROL BANCROFT & FRIENDS, 121 Dodgingtown Rd., P.O. Box 266, Bethel CT 06801. (203)748-4823 or (800)720-7020. Fax: (203)748-4581. E-mail: artists@carolbancroft.com. Website: www.carolbancroft.com. **Owner:** Carol Bancroft. Illustration representative for children's publishing. Estab. 1972. Member of SPAR, Society of Illustrators, Graphic Artists Guild, SCBWI. Represents 40 illustrators. Specializes in illustration for children's publishing—text and trade; any children's-related material. Clients include Scholastic, Houghton Mifflin, HarperCollins, Dutton, Harcourt Brace.

Handles: Illustration for children of all ages. Seeking multicultural and fine artists.

Terms: Rep receives 25-30% commission. Advertising costs are split: 75% paid by talent; 25% paid by representative. For promotional purposes, talent must provide "laser copies (not slides), tearsheets, promo pieces, good color photocopies, etc.; 6 pieces or more is best; narrative scenes and children interacting." Advertises in *RSVP*, *Picture Book*, *Directory of Illustration*.

How to Contact: "Send 2-3 samples by e-mail only and include website address."

SHERYL BERANBAUM, 75 Scenic Dr., Warwick RI 02886. (401)737-8591. Fax: (401)739-5189. E-mail: sheryl@beranbaum.com. Website: www.beranbaum.com. Commercial illustration representative. Estab. 1985. Member of Graphic Artists Guild. Represents 17 illustrators. 75% of artwork handled is children's book illustration. Currently open to illustrators seeking representation. Open to both new and established illustrators. Submission guidelines available by phone.

Handles: Illustration. "My illustrators are diversified and their work comes from a variety of the industry's audiences."

Terms: Receives 30% commission. Charges marketing plan fee or web only fee. Offers written contract. Advertising costs are split: 75% paid by illustrators; 25% paid by rep. Requires Itoya portfolio; postcards only for promotion. Advertises in *Creative Black Book*.

How to Contact: For first contact, send direct mail flier/brochure, tearsheets, photocopies. Responds only if interested. Portfolio should include photocopies.

SAM BRODY, ARTISTS & PHOTOGRAPHERS CONSULTANT, 77 Winfield St., Apt. 4, E. Norwalk CT 06855-2138. Phone/fax: (203)854-0805 (for fax, add 999). E-mail: sambrody@bigplanet.com. **Contact:** Sam Brody. Commercial illustration and photography broker. Estab. 1948. Member of SPAR. Markets include: advertising agencies; corporations/client direct; design firms; editorial/magazines; publishing/books; sales/promotion firms.

Handles: Consultant.

Terms: Agent receives 30% commission. For promotional purposes, talent must provide back-up advertising material, i.e., cards (reprints—*Workbook*, etc.) and self-promos.

How to Contact: For first contact, send bio, direct mail flier/brochure, tearsheets. Responds in 3 days or within 1 day if interested. After initial contact, call for appointment or drop off or mail in appropriate materials for review. Portfolio should include tearsheets, slides, photographs. Obtains new talent through recommendations from others, solicitation.

Tips: Considers "past performance for clients that I check with and whether I like the work performed."

☑ **PEMA BROWNE LTD.**, 22284 Avenue San Luis, Woodland Hills CA 91364. (818)340-4302. **Contact:** Pema Browne. Estab. 1966. Represents 6 illustrators. Specializes in general commercial. Markets include: all publishing areas; children's picture books; advertising agencies. Clients include HarperCollins, Thomas Nelson, Bantam Doubleday Dell, Nelson/Word, Hyperion, Putnam. Client list available upon request.

Handles: 30% Illustration; 15% writers. Looking for "professional and unique" talent.

Terms: Rep receives 30% commission. Exclusive area representation is required. For promotional purposes, talent must provide color mailers to distribute. Representative pays mailing costs on promotion mailings.

How to Contact: For first contact, send query letter, direct mail flier/brochure and SASE. If interested will ask to mail appropriate materials for review. Portfolios should include tearsheets and transparencies or good color photocopies, plus SASE. Obtains new talent through recommendations and interviews (portfolio review).

Tips: "We are doing more publishing—all types—less advertising." Looks for "continuity of illustration and dedication to work."

CATUGEAU: ARTIST AGENT, 110 Rising Ridge Rd., Ridgefield CT 06877. (203)438-7307. Fax: (203)984-1993. E-mail: chris@catugeau.com. Website: www.CATugeau.com. **Owner:** Chris Tugeau. Children's publishing—trade, mass market, educational. Estab. 1994. Member of SPAR, SCBWI, Graphic Artists Guild. Represents 40 illustrators. 90% of artwork handled is children's book illustration. Staff includes Chris Tugeau, owner.

● Not accepting new artists presently.

Handles: Illustration.

Terms: Receives 25% commission. "Artists responsible for providing samples for portfolios, promotional books and mailings." Exclusive representation required. Offers written contract. Advertises in *Picturebook*, *RSVP*, *Directory of Illustration*.

How to Contact: For first contact, send SASE, direct mail flier/brochure, photocopies. Responds ASAP. Portfolio should include tearsheets, photocopies. Finds illustrators through recommendations from others, conferences, personal search. No CDs!

Tips: "Do research, look at artists' websites, talk to other artists—make sure you're comfortable with personality of rep. Be professional yourself . . . know what you do best and be prepared to give rep what they need to present you!"

CORNELL & MCCARTHY, LLC, 2-D Cross Hwy., Westport CT 06880. (203)454-4210. Fax: (203)454-4258. E-mail: cmartreps@aol.com. Website: www.cornellandmccarthy.com. **Contact:** Merial Cornell. Children's book illustration representatives. Estab. 1989. Member of SCBWI and Graphic Artists Guild. Represents 30 illustrators. Specializes in children's books: trade, mass market, educational.
Handles: Illustration.
Terms: Agent receives 25% commission. Advertising costs are split: 75% paid by talent; 25% paid by representative. For promotional purposes, talent must provide 10-12 strong portfolio pieces relating to children's publishing.
How to Contact: For first contact, send query letter, direct mail flier/brochure, tearsheets, photocopies and SASE. Responds in 1 month. Obtains new talent through recommendations, solicitation, conferences.
Tips: "Work hard on your portfolio."

[N] CREATIVE FREELANCERS, INC., 99 Park Ave., #210A, New York NY 10016. (800)398-9544. Fax: (203)532-2927. Website: www.freelancers.com. **Contact:** Marilyn Howard. Commercial illustration representative. Estab. 1988. Represents 30 illustrators. "Our staff members have art direction, art buying or illustration backgrounds." Specializes in children's books, advertising, architectural, conceptual. Markets include: advertising agencies; corporations/client direct; design firms; editorial/magazines; paper products/greeting cards; publishing/books; sales/promotion firms.
Handles: Illustration. Artists must have published work.
Terms: Rep receives 30% commission. Exclusive area representation is preferred. Advertising costs are split: 75% paid by talent; 25% paid by representative. For promotional purposes, talent must provide "printed pages to leave with clients. Co-op advertising with our firm could also provide this. Transparency portfolio preferred if we take you on, but we are flexible." Advertises in *American Showcase*, *Workbook*.
How to Contact: For first contact, send tearsheets or "whatever best shows work." Responds back only if interested.
Tips: Looks for experience, professionalism and consistency of style. Obtains new talent through "word of mouth and website."

DIMENSION, 1500 McAndrew Rd. W, #217, Burnsville MN 55337. (952)201-3981. Fax: (952)892-1722. E-mail: jkeltes @dimensioncreative.com. Website: www.dimensioncreative.com. **Contact:** Joanne Koltes. Commercial illustration representatiave. Estab. 1982. Member of MN Book Builder. Represents 12 illustrators. 45% of artwork handled is children's book illustration. Staff includes Joanne Koltes.
Terms: Advertises in *Picturebook*.
How to Contact: Responds only if interested.

[✓] DWYER & O'GRADY, INC., P.O. Box 790, Cedar Key FL 32625-0790. (352)543-9307. Fax: (603)375-5373. E-mail: eogrady@dwyerogrady.com. Website: www.dwyerogrady.com. **Contact:** Elizabeth O'Grady. Agents for children's artists and writers—"small career development agents." Estab. 1990. Member of Society of Illustrators, SCBWI, ABA. Represents 18 illustrators and 7 writers. Staff includes Elizabeth O'Grady, Jeffrey Dwyer. Specializes in children's books (middle grade and young adult). Markets include: publishing/books, audio/film.
  • Dwyer & O'Grady is currently not accepting new clients.
Handles: Illustrators and writers of children's books.
Recent Sales: *See You Down the Road*, by Kim Ablon Whitney (Knopf Books for Young Readers); *Norman On the Last Frontier*, by Tom Bodett (Knopf); *Happy Feet*, by R. Michelson, illustrated by E.B. Lewis (Harcourt).
Terms: Receives 15% commission domestic, 20% foreign. Additional fees are negotiable. Exclusive representation is required (world rights). Advertising costs are paid by representative.
How to Contact: For first contact, send query letter by postal mail only.

HANNAH REPRESENTS, 14431 Ventura Blvd., #108, Sherman Oaks CA 91423. (818)378-1644. E-mail: hannahreprese nts@yahoo.com. **Contact:** Hannah Robinson. Literary representative for illustrators. Estab. 1997. Represents 8 illustrators. 100% of artwork handled is children's book illustration. Looking for established illustrators only.
Handles: Manuscript/illustration packages. Looking for illustrators with book already under contract.
Terms: Receives 15% commission. Offers written contract. Advertises in *Picturebook*.
How to Contact: For first contact, send SASE and tearsheets. Responds only if interested. Call to schedule an appointment. Portfolio should include photocopies. Finds illustrators through recommendations from others, conferences, queries/solicitations, international.
Tips: "Present a carefully developed range of characterization illustrations that are world-class enough to equal those in the best children's books."

[N] HERMAN AGENCY, 350 Central Park West, New York NY 10025. (212)749-4907. Fax: (212)662-5151. E-mail: HermanAgen@aol.com. Website: HermanAgencyInc.com. **Contact:** Ronnie Ann Herman. Commercial illustration and text representative. Estab. 1999. Member of SCBWI. Represents 30 illustrators, 7 authors. 100% of artwork handled is children's book illustration and related markets. Staff includes Ronnie Ann Herman and Ruth Roemer, assistant. Currently open to illustrators and authors seeking representation who are widely published by trade publishing houses. Looking for established illustrators only.

Handles: Illustration, illustration/manuscript packages and mss.

Recent Sales: Represents illustrators: Joy Allen, Dawn Apperley, Tom Arma, Mary Bono, Seymour Chwast, Pascale Constantin, Rebecca Dickinson, Doreen Gay-Kassel, Jan Spivey Gilchrist, Barry Gott, Steve Haskamp, Aleksey Ivanov, Gideon Kendall, Ana Martin Larranaga, Mike Lester, Scott McDougall, Bob McMahon, Alexi Natchev, Jill Newton, John Nez, Anna Nilsen, Betina Ogden, Tamara Petrosino, Lynn Rowe Reed, Michael Rex, Ken Robbins, Wendy Rouillard, David Sheldon, Mark Weber, Nick Zarin-Ackerman, Deborah Zemke. Represents authors: Anne Foster, Deloris Jordan, Bobbi Miller, Jill Robinson, Brian Yansky.

Terms: Receives 25% commission for illustration assignments; 15% for mss assignments. Artists pay 75% of costs for promotional material—about $300 a year. Exclusive representation usually required. Offers written contract. Advertising costs are split: 75% paid by illustrator; 25% paid by rep. Advertises in *Picturebook*, *Directory of Illustration*, *Promo Pages*.

How to Contact: For first contact, send samples, SASE, direct mail flier/brochure, tearsheets, photocopies. Responds in 1 month or less. I will contact you if I like your samples. Portfolio should include tearsheets, photocopies, books, dummies. Finds illustrators and authors through recommendations from others, conferences, queries/solicitations.

☑ **HK PORTFOLIO**, 10 E. 29th St., 40G, New York NY 10016. (212)689-7830. E-mail: mela@hkportfolio.com. Website: www.hkportfolio.com. **Contact:** Harriet Kasak or Mela Bolinao. Commercial illustration representative. Estab. 1986. Member of SPAR, Society of Illustrators and Graphic Artists Guild. Represents 43 illustrators. Specializes in illustration for juvenile markets. Markets include: advertising agencies; editorial/magazines; publishing/books.

Handles: Illustration.

Recent Sales: *What's That Noise*, illustrated by Paul Meisel (Candlewick); *The Secret of the Great Houdini*, illustrated by Leonid Gore (Simon & Schuster); *My Last Chance Brother*, illustrated by Jack E. Davis (Dutton).

Terms: Rep receives 25% commission. No geographic restrictions. Advertising costs are split: 75% paid by talent; 25% paid by representative. Advertises in *Picturebook* and *Workbook*.

How to Contact: No geographic restrictions. For first contact, send query letter, direct mail flier/brochure, tearsheets, slides, photographs or color copies and SASE. Responds in 1 week. After initial contact, send in appropriate materials for review. Portfolio should include tearsheets, slides, photographs or photocopies.

Tips: Leans toward highly individual personal styles.

KIRCHOFF/WOHLBERG, ARTISTS' REPRESENTATION DIVISION, 866 United Nations Plaza, #525, New York NY 10017. (212)644-2020. Fax: (212)223-4387. Website: www.kirchoffwohlberg.com. **Director of Operations:** John R. Whitman. Estab. 1930. Member of SPAR, Society of Illustrators, AIGA, Association of American Publishers, Bookbuilders of Boston, New York Bookbinders' Guild. Represents over 50 illustrators. Artist's Representative: Elizabeth Ford. Specializes in juvenile and young adult trade books and textbooks. Markets include: publishing/books.

Handles: Illustration and photography (juvenile and young adult).

Terms: Rep receives 25% commission. Exclusive representation to book publishers is usually required. Advertising costs paid by representative ("for all Kirchoff/Wohlberg advertisements only"). "We will make transparencies from portfolio samples; keep some original work on file." Advertises in *American Showcase*, *Art Directors' Index*, *Society of Illustrators Annual*, children's book issues of *Publishers Weekly*.

How to Contact: Please send all correspondence to the attention of Elizabeth Ford. For first contact, send query letter, "any materials artists feel are appropriate." Responds in 6 weeks. "We will contact you for additional materials." Portfolios should include "whatever artists feel best represents their work. We like to see children's illustration in any style. To see illustrators currently represented, visit website."

LEVY CREATIVE MANAGEMENT, 300 E. 46th St., Suite 8E, New York NY 10017. (212)687-6465. Fax: (212)661-4839. E-mail: info@levycreative.com. Website: www.levycreative.com. **Contact:** Sari Levy. Estab. 1998. Member of Society of Illustrators, Graphic Artists Guild, Art Directors Club. Represents 13 illustrators. 30% of artwork handled is children's book illustration. Currently open to illustrators seeking representation. Open to both new and established illustrators. Submission guidelines available on website.

Handles: Illustration, manuscript/illustration packages.

Recent Sales: Represents Alan Dingman, David Cooper, Max Gafe, Liz Lomax, Oren Sherman, Jason Tharp.

Terms: Receives 25% commission. Exclusive representation required. Offers written contract. Advertising costs are split: 75% paid by illustrators; 25% paid by rep. Advertises in *Picturebook*, *American Showcase*, *Workbook*, *Alternative Pick Contact*.

How to Contact: For first contact, send tearsheets, photocopies, SASE. "See website for submission guidelines." We will contact only if interested. Portfolio should include professionally presented materials. Finds illustrators through recommendations from others, word of mouth, competitions.

☑ **LINDGREN & SMITH**, 630 Ninth Ave., New York NY 10036. (212)397-7330. Fax: (212)397-7334. E-mail: inquiry@lindgrensmith.com. Website: www.lindgrensmith.com. **Contact:** Pat Lindgren, Piper Smith. Illustration representative. Estab. 1984. Member of SCBWI. Markets include children's books, advertising agencies; corporations; design firms; editorial; publishing.

Handles: Illustration.

Recent Sales: *The Trellis & the Seed*, by Jan Karon, illustrated by Robert Gantt Steele (Viking).

Terms: Exclusive representation is required. Advertises in *American Showcase*, *The Workbook*, *The Black Book*.

How to Contact: For first contact, send postcard. "We will respond by mail or phone—if interested."

Tips: "Check to see if your work seems appropriate for the group. We only represent experienced artists who have been professionals for some time."

MARLENA AGENCY, INC., 145 Witherspoon St., Princeton NJ 08542. (609)252-9405. Fax: (609)252-1949. E-mail: marzena@bellatlantic.net. Website: www.marlenaagency.com. Commercial illustration represenative. Estab. 1990. Member of Society of Illustrators. Represents 25 illustrators. Staff includes Marlena Torzecka, Greta T'Jonck, Ella Lupo. Currently open to illustrators seeking representation. Open to both new and established illustrators. Submission guidelines available for #10 SASE.

Handles: Illustration.

Recent Sales: *Pebble Soup*, by Marc Monqeau (Rigby); *Sees Behind Trees*, by Linda Helton (Harcourt Brace & Company); *New Orleans Band*, by Marc Monqeau (Scott Foresman); and *My Cat*, by Linda Helton (Scholastic). Represents Marc Mongeau, Gerard Dubois, Linda Helton, Cyril Cabry, Martin Jarrie, Serge Bloch and Ferrucio Sardella.

Terms: Exclusive representation required. Offers written contract. Advertising costs are split: 70% paid by illustrator; 30% paid by rep. Requires printed portfolios, transparencies, direct mail piece (such as postcards) printed samples. Advertises in *Picturebook, American Showcase, Creataive Black Book, Workbook.*

How to Contact: For first contact, send tearsheets, photocopies. Responds only if interested. Drop off or mail portfolio, photocopies. Portfolio should include tearsheets, photocopies. Finds illustrators through queries/solicitations, magazines and graphic design.

Tips: "Be creative and persistent."

⬛ THE NEIS GROUP, P.O. Box 174, 11440 Oak Dr., Shelbyville MI 49344. (269)672-5756. Fax: (269)672-5757. E-mail: neisgroup@wmis.net. Website: www.neisgroup.com. **Contact:** Judy Neis. Commercial Illustration representative. Estab. 1982. Represents 45 illustrators. 60% of artwork handled is children's book illustration. Currently open to illustrators seeking representation. Looking for established illustrators only.

Handles: Illustration, photography and calligraphy/manuscript packages.

Recent Sales: Represents Lyn Boyer, Pam Thomson, Dan Sharp, Terry Workman, Liz Conrad, Garry Colby, Clint Hansen, Don McLean, Julie Borden, Margo Burian, Erica LeBarre, Joel Spector, John White, Neverne Covington and Ruth Pettis.

Terms: Receives 25% commission. Advertising costs are split: 75% paid by illustrator; 25% paid by rep. "I prefer porfolios on CD, color printouts and e-mail capabilities whenever possible." Advertises in *Picturebook, American Showcase, Creative Black Book,* and *Directory of Illustration.*

How to Contact: For first contact, send bio, tearsheets, direct mail flier/brochure. Responds only if interested. After initial contact, drop off portfolio of non-returnables. Portfolio should include tearsheets, photocopies. Obtains new talent through recommendations from others and queries/solicitations.

⬛ WANDA NOWAK/CREATIVE ILLUSTRATION AGENCY, 231 E. 76th St., 5D, New York NY 10021. (212)535-0438. Fax: (212)535-1629. E-mail: wandanowak@aol.com. Website: www.wandanow.com. **Contact:** Wanda Nowak. Commercial illustration representative. Estab. 1996. Member of Graphic Artists Guild. Represents 16 illustrators. 25% of artwork handled is children's book illustration. Staff includes Wanda Nowak. Open to both new and established illustrators.

Handles: Illustration. Looking for "unique, individual style."

Recent Sales: Represents Martin Matje, Emilie Chollat, Herve Blandon, Thea Kliros, Pierre Pratt, Frederique Bertrand, Ilja Bereznickas, Boris Kulikov, Yayo, Laurence Cleyet-Merh, E. Kerner, Ellen Usdi Biros Kulike, Stephane Jorisch.

Terms: Receives 30% commission. Exclusive representation required. Offers written contract. Advertising costs are split: 70% paid by illustrators; 30% paid by rep. Advertises in *Picturebook, Workbook, The Alternative Pick, Black Book.*

How to Contact: For first contact, send SASE. Responds only if interested. Drop off portfolio. Portfolio should include tearsheets. Finds illustrators through recommendations from other, sourcebooks like *CA, Picture Book, Black Book,* exhibitions.

Tips: "Develop your own style, send a little illustrated story, which will prove you can carry a character in different situations with facial expressions etc."

⬛ THE PENNY & STERMER GROUP, 2031 Holly Dr., Prescott AZ 86305. (928)708-9446 (West Coast); (212)505-9342 (East Coast). Fax: (928)708-9447. Website: www.pennystermergroup.com. **Contact:** Carol Lee Stermer. Commercial illustration representative. Estab. 1978.

REMEN-WILLIS DESIGN GROUP, 2964 Colton Rd., Pebble Beach CA 93953. (831)655-1407. Fax: (831)655-1408. E-mail: AnnRWillis@aol. Website: www.Picture-book.com. Childrens' book illustration trade/education. Estab. 1984. Member of SCBWI. Represents 15 illustrators. 100% of artwork handled is children's book illustration.

Recent Sales: List of illustrators represented available upon request.

Terms: Offers written contract. Advertising costs are split: 50% paid by illustrators; 50% paid by rep. Illustrator must provide small precise portfolio for promotion. Advertises in *Picturebook, Workbook.*

How to Contact: For first contact, send tearsheets, photocopies. Responds in 1 week. To set up an interview or portfolio review mail portfolio. Portfolio should include tearsheets, photocopies.

Tips: "Send samples of only the type of work you are interested in receiving. Check out rep's forte first."

RENAISSANCE HOUSE, 9400 Lloydcrest Dr., Beverly Hills CA 90210. (800)547-5113. Fax: (310)860-9902. E-mail: info@renaissancehouse.net. Website: www.renaissancehouse.net. **Contact:** Raquel Benatar. Children's, educational, and textbooks, advertising rep. Estab. 1991. Represents 80 illustrators. 95% of artwork handled is children's book illustration. Currently open to illustrators seeking representation. Open to both new and established illustrators.

Handles: Illustration.

Recent Sales: Pablo Torrecilla (Lee & Low, Scholastic); Ana Lopez (Scholastic); Ruth Araceli (Houghton Mifflin); Vivi Escrivā (Albert Whitman); Marie Jara (Sparknotes); Sheli Petersen (McGraw-Hill).

Terms: Exclusive representation required. Illustrators must provide scans of illustrations. Advertises in *Picturebook*, *Directory of Illustration*, own website and *Catalog of Illustrators*.

How to Contact: For first contact send tearsheets. Responds in 2 weeks. Finds illustrators through recommendations from others, conferences, direct contact.

S.I. INTERNATIONAL, 43 E. 19th St., New York NY 10003. (212)254-4996. Fax: (212)995-0911. E-mail: info@si-i.com. Website: www.si-i.com. Commercial illustration representative. Estab. 1983. Member of SPAR, Graphic Artists Guild. Represents 50 illustrators. Specializes in license characters, educational publishing and children's illustration, digital art and design, mass market paperbacks. Markets include design firms; publishing/books; sales/promotion firms; licensing firms; digital art and design firms.

Handles: Illustration. Looking for artists "who have the ability to do children's illustration and to do license characters either digitally or reflectively."

Terms: Rep receives 25-30% commission. Advertising costs are split: 70% paid by talent; 30% paid by representative. "Contact agency for details. Must have mailer." Advertises in *Picturebook*.

How to Contact: For first contact, send query letter, tearsheets. Responds in 3 weeks. After initial contact, write for appointment to show portfolio of tearsheets, slides.

LIZ SANDERS AGENCY, 2415 E. Hangman Creek Lane, Spokane WA 99224. E-mail: liz@lizsanders.com. Website: www.lizsanders.com. Commercial illustration representative. Estab. 1985. Represents 15 illustrators. Currently open to illustrators seeking representation. Open to both new and established illustrators.

Handles: Illustration. Markets include publishing, entertainment, giftware and advertising.

Recent Sales: Represents Amy Ning, Tom Pansini, Chris Lensch, Bachrun Lomele, Susan Synarski, Kari Kroll and more.

Terms: Receives 30% commission against pro bono mailing program. Offers written contract. Advertises in *Picturebook*, *American Showcase*, *Workbook*, *Directory of Illustration*. No geographic restrictions.

How to Contact: For first contact, send tearsheets, direct mail flier/brochure, color copies, —nonreturnables. Responds only if interested. After initial contact, submit portfolio. Portfolio should include tearsheets, photocopies. Obtains new talent through recommendations from others, conferences and queries/solicitations, Literary Market Place.

GWEN WALTERS ARTIST REPRESENTATIVE, 1801 S. Flagler Dr., #1202, W. Palm Beach FL 33401. (561)848-3362. E-mail: artincgw@aol. Website: www.gwenWaltersartrep.com. Commercial illustration representative. Estab. 1976. Represents 18 illustrators. 90% of artwork handled is children's book illustration. Currently open to illustrators seeking representation. Looking for established illustrators only.

Handles: Illustration.

Recent Sales: Sells to "All major book publishers."

Terms: Receives 30% commission. Artist needs to supply all promo material. Offers written contract. Advertising costs are split: 70% paid by illustrator; 30% paid by rep. Advertises in *Picturebook*, *RSVP*, *Directory of Illustration*.

How to Contact: For first contact, send tearsheets. Responds only if interested. Finds illustrators through recommendations from others.

Tips: "Go out and get some first-hand experience. Learn to tell yourself to understand the way the market works."

WENDYLYNN & CO., 504 Wilson Rd., Annapolis MD 21401. (401)224-2729. Fax: (410)224-5832. E-mail: wendy@wendylynnandco.com. Website: wendylynnandco.com. **Contact:** Wendy Mays. Children's illustration representative. Estab. 2002. Member of SCBWI. Represents 18 illustrators. 100% of artwork handled is children's book illustration. Staff includes Wendy Mays, Janice Onken. Currently open to illustrators seeking representation. Open to both new and established illustrators. Submission guidelines available via e-mail.

Handles: Illustration.

Terms: Receives 25% commission. Exclusive representation required. Offers written contract. Requires 10-15 images submitted on disk. Advertises in *Picturebook*.

How to Contact: For first contact, e-mail or send color photocopies or tearsheets with bio; e-mail is preferred. Responds ASAP. After initial contact mail artwork on CD and send tearsheets. Portfolio should include tearsheets and photocopies. Finds illustrators through recommendations from others.

Tips: "Show a character developed consistently in different settings in a series of illustrations interacting with other children, animals or adults."

DEBORAH WOLFE LTD., 731 N. 24th St., Philadelphia PA 19130. (215)232-6666. Fax: (215)232-6585. E-mail: inquiry@illustrationOnline.com. Website: www.illustrationOnline.com. **Contact:** Deborah Wolfe. Commercial illustration representative. Estab. 1978. Member of Graphic Artist Guild. Represents 30 illustrators. Currently open to illustrators seeking representation.

Handles: Illustration.

Terms: Receives 25% commission. Exclusive representation required. Offers written contract. Advertising costs are split: 75% paid by illustrators; 25% paid by rep. Advertises in *Picturebook*, *American Showcase*, *Directory of Illustration*, *The Workbook*.

How to Contact: Responds in 2 weeks. Portfolio should include "anything except originals." Finds illustrators through queries/solicitations.

Clubs & Organizations

Contacts made through organizations such as the ones listed in this section can be quite beneficial for children's writers and illustrators. Professional organizations provide numerous educational, business and legal services in the form of newsletters, workshops or seminars. Organizations can provide tips about how to be a more successful writer or artist, as well as what types of business records to keep, health and life insurance coverage to carry and competitions to consider.

An added benefit of belonging to an organization is the opportunity to network with those who have similar interests, creating a support system. As in any business, knowing the right people can often help your career, and important contacts can be made through your peers. Membership in a writer's or artist's organization also shows publishers you're serious about your craft. This provides no guarantee your work will be published, but it gives you an added dimension of credibility and professionalism.

Some of the organizations listed here welcome anyone with an interest, while others are only open to published writers and professional artists. Organizations such as the Society of Children's Book Writers and Illustrators (SCBWI, www.scbwi.org) have varying levels of membership. SCBWI offers associate membership to those with no publishing credits, and full membership to those who have had work for children published. International organizations such as SCBWI also have regional chapters throughout the U.S. and the world. Write or call for more information regarding any group that sounds interesting, or check the websites of the many organizations that list them. Be sure to get information about local chapters, membership qualifications and services offered.

Information on organizations listed in the previous edition but not included in this edition of *Children's Writer's & Illustrator's Market* may be found in the General Index.

AMERICAN ALLIANCE FOR THEATRE & EDUCATION, Theatre Department, Arizona State University, P.O. Box 872002, Tempe AZ 85287-2002. (480)965-6064. Fax: (480)965-5351. E-mail: aate.info@asu.edu. Website: www.aate.com. **Administrative Director:** Christy M. Taylor. Purpose of organization: to promote standards of excellence in theatre and drama education. We achieve this by assimilating quality practices in theater and theater education, connecting artists, educators, researchers and scholars with each other, and by providing opportunities for our members to learn, exchange and diversify their work, their audiences and their perspectives. Membership cost: $110 annually for individual in US and Canada, $160 annually for organization, $60 annually for students, $70 annually for retired people; add $30 outside Canada and US. Annual conference. Newsletter published quarterly (on website only). Contests held for unpublished play reading project and annual awards in various categories. Awards plaque and stickers for published playbooks. Publishes list of unpublished plays deemed worthy of performance in newsletter and press release and staged readings at conference. **How to Contact/Writers:** Manuscripts should be 8-10 pages, or 2,000 words. Manuscripts may include lesson plans, interviews, Coda Essays, and reviews of computer software, books, and plays (as scripts or in performance). A three-sentence biographical statement should also be included with a SASE.

AMERICAN SOCIETY OF JOURNALISTS AND AUTHORS, 1501 Broadway, Suite 302, New York NY 10036. E-mail: staff@asja.org. Website: www.asja.org. **Executive Director:** Brett Harvey. Qualifications for membership: "Need to be a professional nonfiction writer. Refer to website for further qualifictions." Membership cost: Application fee—$25; annual dues—$195. Group sponsors national conferences; monthly workshops in New York City. Workshops/conferences open to nonmembers. Publishes a newsletter for members that provides confidential information for nonfiction writers.

CANADIAN SOCIETY OF CHILDREN'S AUTHORS, ILLUSTRATORS AND PERFORMERS, (CANS-CAIP), 104-40 Orchard View Blvd., Toronto ON M4R 1B9 Canada. (416)515-1559. Fax: (416)515-7022. E-mail: office@canscaip.org. Website: www.canscaip.org. **Office Manager:** Lena Coakley. Purpose of organization: development of Canadian children's culture and support for authors, illustrators and performers working in this field. Qualifications for membership: Members—professionals who have been published (not self-published) or have paid public performances/records/tapes to their credit. Friends—share interest in field of children's culture. Membership cost: $75 (members dues), $35 (friends dues),

$75 (institution dues). Sponsors workshops/conferences. Publishes newsletter: includes profiles of members; news round-up of members' activities countrywide; market news; news on awards, grants, etc; columns related to professional concerns.

LEWIS CARROLL SOCIETY OF NORTH AMERICA, P.O. Box 204, Napa CA 94559. E-mail: hedgehog@napanet.net. Website: www.lewiscarroll.org/lcsna.html. **Secretary:** Cindy Watter. "We are an organization of Carroll admirers of all ages and interests and a center for Carroll studies." Qualifications for membership: "An interest in Lewis Carroll and a simple love for Alice (or even the Snark)." Membership cost: $20/year. There is also a contributing membership of $50. Publishes a quarterly newsletter.

THE CHILDREN'S BOOK COUNCIL, INC., 12 W. 37th St., 2nd Floor, New York NY 10018. (212)966-1990. Fax: (212)966-2073. E-mail: info@cbcbooks.org. Website: www.cbcbooks.org. **President:** Paula Quint. Purpose of organization: "A nonprofit trade association of children's and young adult publishers and packagers, CBC promotes the enjoyment of books for children and young adults and works with national and international organizations to that end. The CBC has sponsored National Children's Book Week since 1945 and Young People's Poetry Week since 1999." Qualifications for membership: US trade publishers and packagers of children's and young adult books and related literary materials are eligible for membership. Publishers wishing to join should e-mail membership@cbcbooks.org or contact the CBC for dues information." Sponsors workshops and seminars for publishing company personnel. Individuals wishing to receive the CBC semi-annual journal, *CBC Features* with articles of interest to people working with children and books and materials brochures, may be placed on CBC's mailing list for a one-time-only fee of $60. Sells reading encouragement posters and graphics and informational materials suitable for libraries, teachers, booksellers, parents, and others working with children.

FLORIDA FREELANCE WRITERS ASSOCIATION, Cassell Network of Writers, P.O. Box A, North Stratford NH 03590. (603)922-8338. E-mail: danakcnw@ncia.net. Websites: www.writers-editors.com; www.ffwamembers.com. **Executive Director:** Dana K. Cassell. Purpose of organization: To act as a link between Florida writers and buyers of the written word; to help writers run more effective communications businesses. Qualifications for membership: "None. We provide a variety of services and information, some for beginners and some for established pros." Membership cost: $90/year. Publishes a newsletter focusing on market news, business news, how-to tips for the serious writer. Non-member subscription: $39—does not include Florida section—includes national edition only. Annual *Directory of Florida Markets* included in FFWA newsletter section and electronic download. Publishes annual *Guide to CNW/Florida Writers*, which is distributed to editors around the country. Sponsors contest: annual deadline March 15. Guidelines on website. Categories: juvenile, adult nonfiction, adult fiction and poetry. Awards include cash for top prizes, certificate for others. Contest open to non-members.

GRAPHIC ARTISTS GUILD, 90 John St., Suite 403, New York NY 10038. (800)500-2672. E-mail: membership@gag.org. Website; www.gag.org. **President:** Lloyd Dangle, CAE. Purpose of organization: "to promote and protect the economic interests of member artists. It is committed to improving conditions for all creators of graphic arts and raising standards for the entire industry." Qualification for full membership: 50% of income derived from the creation of artwork. Associate members include those in allied fields, students and retirees. Initiation fee: $25. Full memberships $130, $175, $230, $290; student membership $55/year. Associate membership $140/year. Publishes *Graphic Artists Guild Handbook, Pricing and Ethical Guidelines* (free to members, $34.95 retail). "The Guild UAW Local 3030 is a national union that embraces all creators of graphic arts intended for presentation as originals or reproductions at all levels of skill and expertise. The long-range goals of the Guild are: to educate graphic artists and their clients about ethical and fair business practices; to educate graphic artists about emerging trends and technologies impacting the industry; to offer programs and services that anticipate and respond to the needs of our members, helping them prosper and enhancing their health and security; to advocate for the interests of our members in the legislative, judicial and regulatory arenas; to assure that our members are recognized financially and professionally for the value they provide; to be responsible stewards for our members by building an organization that works efficiently on their behalf."

HORROR WRITERS ASSOCIATION, P.O. Box 50577, Palo Alto CA 94303. E-mail: hwa@horror.org. Website: www.horror.org. **Office Manager:** Nancy Etchemendy. Purpose of organization: To encourage public interest in horror and dark fantasy and to provide networking and career tools for members. Qualifications for membership: Anyone who can demonstrate a serious interest in horror may join as an affiliate. Any non-writing professional in the horror field may join as an associate. (Booksellers, editors, agents, librarians, etc.) To qualify for full active membership, you must be a published, professional writer of horror. **Open to students** as affiliates, if unpublished in professional venues. Membership cost: $65 annually in North America; $75 annually elsewhere. Holds annual Stoker Awards Weekend and HWA Business Meeting. Publishes monthly newsletter focusing on market news, industry news, HWA business for members. Sponsors awards. We give the Bram Stoker Awards for superior achievement in horror annually. Awards include a handmade Stoker trophy designed by sculptor Stephen Kirk. Awards open to non-members.

INTERNATIONAL READING ASSOCIATION, 800 Barksdale Rd., P.O. Box 8139, Newark DE 19714-8139. (302)731-1600 ext. 293. Fax: (302)731-1057. E-mail: pubinfo@reading.org. Website: www.reading.org. **Public Information Associate:** Janet Butler. Purpose of organization: "Formed in 1956, the International Reading Association seeks to promote high levels of literacy for all by improving the quality of reading instruction through studying the reading process and teaching techniques; serving as a clearinghouse for the dissemination of reading research through conferences, journals, and other publications; and actively encouraging the lifetime reading habit. Its goals include professional development; enhance and improve professional development, advocacy, partnerships, research and global literacy development. **Open to students.** Basic membership: $36. Sponsors annual convention. Publishes a newsletter called "Reading Today." Sponsors a number of awards and fellowships. Visit the IRA website for more information on membership, conventions and awards.

THE INTERNATIONAL WOMEN'S WRITING GUILD, P.O. Box 810, Gracie Station, New York NY 10028. (212)737-7536. **Executive Director and Founder:** Hannelore Hahn. IWWG is "a network for the personal and professional empowerment of women through writing." Qualifications: open to any woman connected to the written word regardless of professional portfolio. Membership cost: $45 annually. "IWWG sponsors several annual conferences a year in all areas of the US. The major conference is held in August of each year at Skidmore College in Saratoga Springs NY. It is a week-long conference attracting over 500 women internationally." Also publishes a 32-page newsletter, *Network*, 6 times/year; offers health insurance at group rates, referrals to literary agents.

LEAGUE OF CANADIAN POETS, 920 Young St., Suite 608, Toronto ON M4W 3C7 Canada. (416)504-1657. Fax: (416)504-0096. Website: www.poets.ca or www.ryoungpeets.ca. **Executive Director:** Edita Page. President: Matt Robinson. Inquiries to Program Manager: Joanna Poblocka. The L.C.P. is a national organization of published Canadian poets. Our constitutional objectives are to advance poetry in Canada and to promote the professional interests of the members. Qualifications for membership: full—publication of at least 1 book of poetry by a professional publisher; associate membership—an active interest in poetry, demonstrated by several magazine/periodical publication credits, student—an active interest in poetry, 12 sample poems required; supporting—any friend of poetry. Membership fees: full—$175/year, associate—$60, student—$20, supporting—$100. Holds an Annual General Meeting every spring; some events open to nonmembers. "We also organize reading programs in schools and public venues. We publish a newsletter which includes information on poetry/poetics in Canada and beyond. Also publish the books *Poetry Markets for Canadians*; *Who's Who in the League of Canadian Poets*; *Poets in the Classroom* (teaching guide), and online publications. The Gerald Lampert Memorial Award for the best first book of poetry published in Canada in the preceding year and The Pat Lowther Memorial Award for the best book of poetry by a Canadian woman published in the preceding year. Deadline for awards November 31. Send SASE for more details. Sponsors youth poetry competition. Deadline December 1 of each year. Send SASE for details.

LITERARY MANAGERS AND DRAMATURGS OF THE AMERICAS, P.O. Box 728, Village Station NY 10014. E-mail: lmda@lmda.org. Website: www.lmda.org. LMDA is a not-for-profit service organization for the professions of literary management and dramaturgy. Student Membership: $25/year. Open to students in dramaturgy, performing arts and literature programs, or related disciplines. Proof of student status required. Includes national conference, New Dramaturg activities, local symposia, job phone and select membership meetings. Active Membership: $60/year. Open to full-time and part-time professionals working in the fields of literary management and dramaturgy. All privileges and services including voting rights and eligibility for office. Associate Membership: $45/year. Open to all performing arts professionals and academics, as well as others interested in the field. Includes national conference, local symposia and select membership meetings. Institutional Membership: $135/year. Open to theaters, universities, and other organizations. Includes all privileges and services except voting rights and eligibility for office. Publishes a newsletter featuring articles on literary management, dramaturgy, LMDA program updates and other articles of interest.

THE NATIONAL LEAGUE OF AMERICAN PEN WOMEN, 1300 17th St. N.W., Washington D.C. 20036-1973. (202)785-1997. Fax: (202)452-6868. E-mail: nlapw1@juno.com. Website: www.americanpenwomen.org. **President:** Dr. Bernice Strand Reid. Purpose of organization: to promote professional work in art, letters, and music since 1897. Qualifications for membership: An applicant must show "proof of sale" in each chosen category—art, letters, and music. Membership cost: $40 ($10 processing fee and $30 National dues); Annual fees—$30 plus Branch/State dues. Different levels of membership include: Active, Associate, International Affiliate, Members-at-Large, Honorary Members (in one or more of the following classifications: Art, Letters, and Music). Holds workshops/conferences. Publishes magazine 6 times a year titled *The Pen Woman*. Sponsors various contests in areas of Art, Letters, and Music. Awards made at Biennial Convention. Biannual scholarships awarded to non-Pen Women for mature women. Awards include cash prizes—up to $1,000. Specialized contests open to non-members.

NATIONAL WRITERS ASSOCIATION, 3140 S. Peoria St., #295PMB, Aurora CO 80014. (303)841-0246. Fax: (303)751-8593. E-mail: ExecDirSandyWhelchel@nationalwriters.com. Website: www.nationalwriters.com. **Executive Director:** Sandy Whelchel. Purpose of organization: association for freelance writers. Qualifications for membership: associate membership—must be serious about writing; professional membership—must be published and paid writer (cite credentials). Membership cost: $65-associate; $85-professional; $35-student. Sponsors workshops/conferences: TV/screenwriting workshops, NWAF Annual Conferences, Literary Clearinghouse, editing and critiquing services, local chapters, National Writer's School. Open to non-members. Publishes industry news of interest to freelance writers; how-to articles; market information; member news and networking opportunities. Nonmember subscription $20. Sponsors poetry contest; short story contest; article contest; novel contest. Awards cash for top 3 winners; books and/or certificates for other winners; honorable mention certificate places 11-20. Contests open to nonmembers.

NATIONAL WRITERS UNION, 113 University Place, 6th Floor, New York NY 10003. (212)254-0279. Website: www.nwu.org. **Open to students.** Purpose of organization: Advocacy for freelance writers. Qualifications for membership: "Membership in the NWU is open to all qualified writers, and no one shall be barred or in any manner prejudiced within the Union on account of race, age, sex, sexual orientation, disability, national origin, religion or ideology. You are eligible for membership if you have published a book, a play, three articles, five poems, one short story or an equivalent amount of newsletter, publicity, technical, commercial, government or institutional copy. You are also eligible for membership if you have written an equal amount of unpublished material and you are actively writing and attempting to publish your work." Membership cost: annual writing income under $5,000—$95/year; annual writing income $5,000-25,000—$155/year; annual writing income $25,000-50,000—$210/year; over $50,000—$260/year. Holds workshops throughout the country. Offers national union newsletter quarterly, *American Writer*, issues related to freelance writing and to union organization for members. Offers contract and grievance advice.

PEN AMERICAN CENTER, 568 Broadway, New York NY 10012. (212)334-1660. Fax: (212)334-2181. E-mail: jm@pen .org. Website: www.pen.org. Purpose of organization: "To foster understanding among men and women of letters in all countries. International PEN is the only worldwide organization of writers and the chief voice of the literary community. Members of PEN work for freedom of expression wherever it has been endangered." Qualifications for membership: "The standard qualification for a writer to join PEN is that he or she must have published, in the United States, two or more books of a literary character, or one book generally acclaimed to be of exceptional distinction. Editors who have demonstrated commitment to excellence in their profession (generally construed as five years' service in book editing), translators who have published at least two book-length literary translations, and playwrights whose works have been professionally produced, are eligible for membership." An application form is available upon request from PEN Headquarters in New York. Candidates for membership should be nominated by 2 current members of PEN. Inquiries about membership should be directed to the PEN Membership Committee. Friends of PEN is also open to writers who may not yet meet the general PEN membership requirements. PEN sponsors public events at PEN Headquarters in New York, and at the branch offices in Boston, Chicago, New Orleans, San Francisco and Portland, Oregon. They include tributes by contemporary writers to classic American writers, dialogues with visiting foreign writers, symposia that bring public attention to problems of censorship and that address current issues of writing in the United States, and readings that introduce beginning writers to the public. PEN's wide variety of literary programming reflects current literary interests and provides informal occasions for writers to meet each other and to welcome those with an interest in literature. Events are all open to the public. The Children's Book Authors' Committee sponsors biannual public events focusing on the art of writing for children and young adults and on the diversity of literature for juvenile readers. The PEN/Phyllis Naylor Working Writer Fellowship was established in 2001 to assist a North American author of fiction for children or young adults. Pamphlets and brochures all free upon request. Sponsors several competitions per year. Monetary awards range from $2,000-20,000.

N: ⊕ PLAYMARKET, P.O. Box 9767, Te Aro Wellington New Zealand. Phone/fax: (64)4 3828461. Website: www.play market.org.nz. **Director:** Dilys Grant. Administrator: Laura Hill. Script Advisor: Susan Wilson. Purpose of organization: funded by the Arts Council of New Zealand, Playmarket serves as New Zealand's script advisory service and playwrights agency. Playmarket offers script assessment, development and agency services to help New Zealand playwrights secure professional production for their plays. Playmarket runs the NZ Young Playwrights Competition, The Aoteanoa Playwrights Conference and the Adam Playreading Series and administers the annual Bruce Mason Playwrighting Award.

PUPPETEERS OF AMERICA, INC., P.O. Box 29417, Parma OH 44129-0417. (888)568-6235. Fax: (440)843-7867. E-mail: pofajoin@puppeteers.org. Website: www.puppeteers.org. **Membership Officer:** Joyce and Chuck Berty. Purpose of organization: to promote the art of puppetry as a means of communications and as a performing art. Qualifications for membership: interest in the art form. Membership cost: single adult, $40; youth member, $20 (6-17 years of age); full-time college student, $25; retiree, $25 (65 years of age); family, $60; couple, $50. Membership includes a bimonthly newsletter (*Playboard*). Discounts for workshops/conferences, access to the Audio Visual Library & Consultants in many areas of Puppetry. *The Puppetry Journal*, a quarterly periodical, provides news about puppeteers, puppet theaters, exhibitions, touring companies, technical tips, new products, new books, films, television, and events sponsored by the Chartered Guilds in each of the 8 P of A regions. *The Puppetry Journal* is the only publication in the United States dedicated to puppetry in the United States. Subscription: $35 (libraries only). The Puppeteers of America sponsors an annual National Day of Puppetry the last Saturday in April.

N: SCIENCE-FICTION AND FANTASY WRITERS OF AMERICA, INC., P.O. Box 877, Chestertown MD 21620. E-mail: execdir@sfwa.org. Website: www.sfwa.org. **Executive Director:** Jane Jewell. Purpose of organization: to encourage public interest in science fiction literature and provide organization format for writers/editors/artists within the genre. Qualifications for membership: at least 1 professional sale or other professional involvement within the field. Membership cost: annual active dues—$50; affiliate—$35; one-time installation fee of $10; dues year begins July 1. Different levels of membership include: active—requires 3 professional short stories or 1 novel published; accociate—requires 1 professional sale; or affiliate—which requires some other professional involvement such as artist, editor, librarian, bookseller, teacher, etc. Workshops/conferences: annual awards banquet, usually in April or May. Open to nonmembers. Publishes newsletter, *The Bulletin*. Nonmember subscription: $18/year in US. Sponsors SFWA Nebula™ Awards for best published science fiction in the categories of novel, novella, novelette and short story. Awards trophy.

SOCIETY OF CHILDREN'S BOOK WRITERS AND ILLUSTRATORS, 8271 Beverly Blvd., Los Angeles CA 90048. (323)782-1010. E-mail: info@scbwi.org (autoresponse). Website: www.scbwi.org. **President:** Stephen Mooser. Executive Director: Lin Oliver. Chairperson, Board of Advisors: Sue Alexander. Purpose of organization: to assist writers and illustrators working or interested in the field. Qualifications for membership: an interest in children's literature and illustration. Membership cost: $50/year. Plus one time $10 initiation fee. Different levels of membership include: full membership—published authors/illustrators; associate membership—unpublished writers/illustrators. Holds 100 events (workshops/conferences) worldwide each year. National Conference open to nonmembers. Publishes a newsletter focusing on writing and illustrating children's books. Sponsors grants for writers and illustrators who are members.

✔ SOCIETY OF ILLUSTRATORS, 128 E. 63rd St., New York NY 10021-7303. (212)838-2560. Fax: (212)838-2561. E-mail: info@societyillustrators.org. Website: www.societyillustrators.org. **Director:** Terrence Brown. Purpose of organization: to promote interest in the art of illustration for working professional illustrators and those in associated fields. Membership cost: Initiation fee—$250. Annual dues for non-resident members (those living more than 125 air miles from SI's headquarters) are $287. Dues for Resident Artist Members are $475 per year; Resident Associate Members $552. Different levels of membership: *Artist Members* "shall include those who make illustration their profession" and through which they earn at least 60% of their income. *Associate Members* are "those who earn their living in the arts or who have made a substantial contribution to the art of illustration." This includes art directors, art buyers, creative supervisors, instructors, publishers and like categories. The candidate must complete and sign the application form which requires a brief biography, a listing of schools attended, other training and a résumé of his or her professional career." Candidates for *Artist* membership, in addition to the above requirements, must submit examples of their work. Sponsors "The Annual of American Illustration." Awards include gold and silver medals. Open to nonmembers. Deadline: October 1. Sponsors "The Original Art: The Best of Children's Book Illustration." Deadline: mid-August. Call for details.

SOCIETY OF MIDLAND AUTHORS, % SMA, P.O. 10419, Chicago IL 60610-0419. Website: www.midlandauthors.c om. **Membership Secretary:** Thomas Frisbie. Purpose of organization: create closer association among writers of the Middle West; stimulate creative literary effort; maintain collection of members' works; encourage interest in reading and literature by cooperating with other educational and cultural agencies. Qualifications for membership: author or co-author of a book demonstrating literary style and published by a recognized publisher and be identified through residence with Illinois, Indiana, Iowa, Kansas, Michigan, Minnesota, Missouri, Nebraska, North Dakota, Ohio, South Dakota or Wisconsin. Membership cost: $35/year dues. Different levels of membership include: regular—published book authors; associate, nonvoting—not published as above but having some connection with literature, such as librarians, teachers, publishers and editors. Program meetings held 5 times a year, featuring authors, publishers, editors or the like individually or on panels. Usually second Tuesday of October, November, February, March and April. Also holds annual awards dinner in May. Publishes a newsletter focusing on news of members and general items of interest to writers. Non-member subscription: $5. Sponsors contests. "Annual awards in six categories, given at annual dinner in May. Monetary awards for books published which premiered professionally in previous calendar year. Send SASE to contact person for details." Categories include adult fiction, adult nonfiction, juvenile fiction, juvenile nonfiction, poetry, biography. No picture books. Contest open to non-members. Deadline for contest: January 30.

SOCIETY OF SOUTHWESTERN AUTHORS, P.O. Box 30355, Tucson AZ 85751-0355. Fax: (520)296-5562. E-mail: wporter202@aol.com. Website: www.azstarnet.com/nonprofit/ssa. **President:** Penny Porter. Purpose of organization: to promote fellowship among members of the writing profession, to recognize members' achievements, to stimulate further achievement, and to assist persons seeking to become professional writers. Qualifications for membership: proof of publication of a book, articles, TV screenplay, etc. Membership cost: $25 initiation plus $25/year dues. The Society of Southwestern Authors has annual 2-day Writers' Conference held the next to last weekend in January (check website for updated information). Publishes a bimonthly newsletter, *The Write Word*, about members' activities, achievements, and up to the minute trends in publishing and marketing. Yearly writing contest open to all writers. Applications are available in September. Send SASE to the P.O. Box, Attn: Contest.

☑ TEXT AND ACADEMIC AUTHORS ASSOCIATION, University of South Florida, 140 Seventh Ave. S., St. Petersburg FL 33701. (727)553-1195. E-mail: taa@bayflash.stpt.usf.edu. Website: www.taaonline.net. **President:** Michael Sullivan. Purpose of organization: to address the professional concerns of text and academic authors, to protect the interests of creators of intellectual property at all levels, and support efforts to enforce copyright protection. Qualifications for membership: all authors and prospective authors are welcome. Membership cost: $30 first year; $75 per year following years. Workshops/conferences: June each year. Newsletter focuses on all areas of interest to text authors.

Ⓝ VOLUNTEER LAWYERS FOR THE ARTS, 1 E. 53rd St., 6th Floor, New York NY 10022-4201. (212)319-2787 ext. 10 (administration); ext.9 (the Art Law Line). Fax: (212)752-6575. E-mail: askvla@vlany.org. Website: www.vlany.org. **Executive Director:** Elena M. Paul. Purpose of organization: Volunteer Lawyers for the Arts is dedicated to providing free arts-related legal assistance to low-income artists and not-for-profit arts organizations in all creative fields. Over 800 attorneys in the New York area donate their time through VLA to artists and arts organizations unable to afford legal counsel. There is no membership required for our services. Everyone is welcome to use VLA's Art Law Line, a legal hotline for any artist or arts organization needing quick answers to arts-related questions. VLA also provides clinics, seminars and publications designed to educate artists on legal issues which affect their careers. Membership is through donations and is not required to use our services. Members receive discounts on publications and seminars as well as other benefits. Some of the many publications we carry are *All You Need to Know About the Music Business*; *Business and Legal Forms for Fine Artists, Photographers & Authors & Self-Publishers*; *Contracts for the Film & TV Industry*, plus many more.

WESTERN WRITERS OF AMERICA, INC., 1012 Fair St., Franklin TN 37064-2718. (615)791-1444. Fax: (615)791-1444. E-mail: candywwa@aol.com; tncrutch@aol.com. Website: www.westernwriters.org. **Secretary/Treasurer:** James A. Crutchfield. **Open to students.** Purpose of organization: to further all types of literature that pertains to the American West. Membership requirements: must be a *published* author of Western material. Membership cost: $75/year ($90 foreign). Different levels of membership include: Active and Associate—the two vary upon number of books published. Holds annual conference. The 2003 conference held in Helena, MT. Publishes bimonthly magazine focusing on western literature, market trends, book reviews, news of members, etc. Non-members may subscribe for $30 ($50 foreign). Sponsors contests. Spur awards given annually for a variety of types of writing. Awards include plaque, certificate, publicity. Contest open to nonmembers.

DISCOVER
A WORLD OF
WRITING
SUCCESS

Are you ready to be praised, published, and paid for your writing? It's time to invest in your future with *Writer's Digest*! Beginners and experienced writers alike have been enjoying *Writer's Digest*, the world's leading magazine for writers, for more than 80 years — and it keeps getting better! Each issue is brimming with:

Get 2 FREE ISSUES of Writer's Digest!

- Inspiration from writers who have been in your shoes
- Detailed info on the latest contests, conferences, markets, and opportunities in every genre
- Tools of the trade, including reviews of the latest writing software and hardware
- Writing prompts and exercises to overcome writer's block and rekindle your creative spark
- Expert tips, techniques, and advice to help you get published
- And so much more!

That's a lot to look forward to every month. Let *Writer's Digest* put you on the road to writing success!

NO RISK!
Send No Money Now!

☐ **Yes!** Please rush me my 2 FREE issues of *Writer's Digest* — the world's leading magazine for writers. If I like what I read, I'll get a full year's subscription (12 issues, including the 2 free issues) for only $19.96. That's 67% off the newsstand rate! If I'm not completely happy, I'll write "cancel" on your invoice, return it and owe nothing. The 2 FREE issues are mine to keep, no matter what!

Name_____

Address_____

City_____

State_____ZIP_____

Annual newsstand rate is $59.88. Orders outside the U.S. will be billed an additional $10 (includes GST/HST in Canada.) Please allow 4-6 weeks for first-issue delivery.

www.writersdigest.com

TFCM3

Get 2 FREE TRIAL ISSUES of Writer's® Digest

Packed with creative inspiration, advice, and tips to guide you on the road to success, *Writer's Digest* will offer you everything you need to take your writing to the next level! You'll discover how to:

- Create dynamic characters and page-turning plots
- Submit query letters that publishers won't be able to refuse
- Find the right agent or editor for you
- Make it out of the slush-pile and into the hands of the right publisher
- Write award-winning contest entries
- And more!

See for yourself by ordering your 2 FREE trial issues today!

RUSH! 2 Free Issues!

N̄ ☘ **WRITERS' FEDERATION OF NEW BRUNSWICK**, Box 37, Station A, 404 Queen St., Fredericton NB E3B 4Y2 Canada. (506)459-7228. E-mail: wfnb@nb.aibn.com. Website: www.sjfn.nb.ca/~wfnb/index.htm. **Executive Director:** Mary Hutchman. Purpose of organization: "to promote New Brunswick writing and to help writers at all stages of their development." Qualifications for membership: interest in writing. Membership cost: $30, basic annual membership; $40, family membership; $50, institutional membership; $100, sustaining member; $250, patron; and $1,000, lifetime member. Holds workshops/conferences. Publishes a newsletter with articles concerning the craft of writing, member news, contests, markets, workshops and conference listings. Sponsors annual literary competition (for New Brunswick residents). Categories: fiction, poetry, children's literature—3 prizes per category of $150, $75, $50; Alfred Bailey Prize of $400 for poetry ms; The Richards Prize of $400 for short novel, collection of short stories or section of long novel; The Sheree Fitch Prize for writing by young people (14-18 years of age). Contest open to nonmembers (residents of Canada only).

N̄ ☘ **WRITERS GUILD OF ALBERTA**, 11759 Groat Rd., Edmonton AB T5M 3K6 Canada. (780)422-8174. Fax: (780)422-2663. E-mail: mail@writersguild.ab.ca. Website: www.writersguild.ab.ca. **Executive Director:** Diane Walton. Purpose of organization: to provide meeting ground and collective voice for the writers in Alberta. Membership cost: $60/year; $30 for seniors/students. Holds workshops/conferences. Publishes a newsletter focusing on markets, competitions, contemporary issues related to the literary arts (writing, publishing, censorship, royalties etc.). Nonmembers may subscribe to newsletter. Subscription cost: $60/year. Sponsors annual literary awards program in 7 categories (novel, nonfiction, short fiction, children's literature, poetry, drama, best first book). Awards include $500, leather-bound book, promotion and publicity. Open to nonmembers.

WRITERS OF KERN, P.O. Box 6694, Bakersfield CA 93386-6694. (661)399-0423. Open to published writers and any person interested in writing. Dues: $45/year, $20 for students. Types of memberships: professional, writers with published work; associate—writers working toward publication, affiliate—beginners and students. Monthly meetings held on the third Saturday of every month. Bi- or tri-annual writers' workshops, with speakers who are authors, agents, etc., on topics pertaining to writing; critique groups for several fiction genres, poetry, children's, nonfiction, journalism and screenwriting which meet bimonthly. Members receive a monthly newsletter with marketing tips, conferences and contests; access to club library; discount to annual CWC conference.

Conferences & Workshops

Writers and illustrators eager to expand their knowledge of the children's publishing industry should consider attending one of the many conferences and workshops held each year. Whether you're a novice or seasoned professional, conferences and workshops are great places to pick up information on a variety of topics and network with experts in the publishing industry, as well as your peers.

Listings in this section provide details about what conference and workshop courses are offered, where and when they are held, and the costs. Some of the national writing and art organizations also offer regional workshops throughout the year. Write or call for information.

Writers can find listings of more than 1,200 conferences (searchable by type, location and date) at The Writer's Digest/Shaw Guides Directory to Writers' Conferences, Seminars and Workshops—www.writersdigest.com/conferences.

Members of the Society of Children's Book Writers and Illustrators can find information on conferences in national and local SCBWI newsletters. Nonmembers may attend SCBWI events as well. SCBWI conferences are listed in the beginning of this section under a separate subheading. For information on SCBWI's annual national conferences, contact them at (323)782-1010 or check their website for a complete calendar of national and regional events (www.scbwi.org).

Information on conferences listed in the previous edition but not this edition of *Children's Writer's & Illustrator's Market* **may be found in the General Index.**

SCBWI CONFERENCES

SCBWI; ANNUAL CONFERENCES ON WRITING AND ILLUSTRATING FOR CHILDREN, 8271 Beverly Blvd., Los Angeles CA 90048. (323)782-1010. Fax: (323)782-1892. E-mail: scbwi@scbwi.org. Website: www.scbwi.org. **Conference Director:** Lin Oliver. Writer and illustrator workshops geared toward all levels. **Open to students.** Covers all aspects of children's book and magazine publishing—the novel, illustration techniques, marketing, etc. Annual conferences held in August in Los Angeles and in New York in February. Write for more information or visit website.

[N] SCBWI—ALASKA; RAVEN UNDER THE NORTHERN LIGHTS—CHILDREN'S WRITER'S & ILLUS-TRATOR'S CONFERNCE, P.O. Box 84988, Fairbanks AK 99708-4988. (907)474-2138. (Please note Alaska time is 1 hour before Pacific Time.) E-mail: stihlerunits@mosquitonet.com. Website: www.scbwialaska.org. **Conference Organizer:** Cherie Stihler. Writer and illustrator workshops geared toward all levels. **Open to students.** Sample of sessions: Putting Together Your Portfolio; Developing Your Voice; Steps to Illustrate a Children's Picture Book; Self-Publishing; Writing for Christian Markets; Breaking into Children's Nonfiction Magazine Writing; Conducting and Organizing Research; Story Mapping; Creating Memorable Characters; Watercolor Workshop (all skill levels); "Okay I've Turned in the Final Draft-Now What Do I Do?". Conference held every 3 years. Next conference held March 26-28, 2004. Writing facilities available: portfolio and ms consultation (additional fee), art show and sale, book sales, school visits. "See website for details." Cost of conference: $199 (Early Bird Registration); includes registration, materials and handouts, Welcome Bag, breakfast at conference site, Welcome Reception, and the opportunity to meet, mingle and network with your peers in Alaska. "Please e-mail or visit our website. We invite you to come on up to Alaska and experience what magic folks have been 'raven' about for centuries. Come take a dog sled ride, marvel at the majestic Northern Lights, view colossal sculptures made of ice, enjoy a Native dance performance and join in the fun. Hotel, airfare and rental car discounts available. Authors' Luncheon (Saturday) and Book Brunch (Sunday) for an additional fee."

[N] SCBWI—ARIZONA; 2004 EVENTS, P.O. Box 26384, Scottsdale AZ 85255-0123. E-mail: rascbwiaz@aol.com. Website: www.scbwiaz.addr.com. **Regional Advisor:** Michelle Parker-Rock. "SCBWI Arizona will offer a variety of workshops, retreats, conferences, meetings and/or industry-related events throughout 2004. Open to members and nonmembers, published and nonpublished." Registration usually limited. Pre-registration always required. Visit website, write or e-mail for more information.

[N] [⊕] SCBWI—BRITISH ISLES; ILLUSTRATOR'S DAY (Spring)/WRITER'S DAY (Fall), (44)208 671 7539. E-mail: scbwi_bi@hotmail.com. Website: www.wordpool.co.uk/scbwi. SCBWI British Isles Regional Advisor: Natascha

Biebow. SCBWI Illustrator Coordinator: Anne-Marie Perks. Writer and illustrator conference geared toward beginner, intermediate and advanced levels. **Open to students.** Writer's Day: Sessions include for What to Write Down, What to Throw Out—Selection & Revision, Visual Thinking for Picture Book Writers, Creative Ways Into Non-Fiction: Non-fiction for Storytellers, Approaching Publishers and Handling Rejections, Novelties and Picture Books—Publishing Opportunities with a Packager, Tickling Funny Bones: Capturing & Creating Memorable Characters, Getting Your First Novel Published: That First Crucial Page & Getting It Past the Reader, Editor's Panel. Illustrator's Day: Making Cracking Picture Books Using QuarkXPress, Photoshop and Freehand Drawing, Creating Winning Characters, Meet the Art Director, Writing With Pictures, Brilliant School Visits, Panel on Marketing Yourself: An editor, an art director and an artist's agent talk about How to Create Portfolios That Stand Out. Annual conference. Conference held Illustrator's Day (each spring US usually May) Writer's Day (each fall, usually in September). Registration limited to 100 people. Cost of conference: $105 for SCBWI members/$125 for nonmembers; includes tuition and lunch. "Both conferences offer the opportunity for manuscripts or portfolio critiques with editors and art directors."

SCBWI—CANADA; ANNUAL CONFERENCE, E-mail: webinfo@SCBWIcanada.org; noreen@SCBWIcanada. org. Website: www.scbwicanada.org. **Contact:** Lizann Flatt or Noreen Violetta. Writer and illustrator conference geared toward all levels. Offers spearkers forums, book sale, portfolio displays, one-on-one critiques and a silent auction. Annual conference held in May. There is also a Fall Retreat and West Events.

SCBWI—CAROLINAS; ANNUAL FALL CONFERENCE. (919)967-2549. Fax: (919)929-6643. E-mail: eld523@ea rthlink.net. **Contact:** Earl L. Davis, regional advisor. Conference will be held September 26-27 at the Sheraton Imperial Hotel, Research Triangle Park, NC. Speakers include Lin Oliver, Executive Director and founder of SCBWI, Joyce Hansen, Laurie Anderson, and Mark McVeigh, editor, HarperCollins Children's Books. Fee: $65 for SCBWI members, and $75 for nonmembers by September 1. $75 and $85 respectively after September 1. Critiques for writers, illustration portfolios displayed. Conference open to adult students.

SCBWI—DAKOTAS; WRITERS CONFERENCE IN CHILDREN'S LITERATURE, Department of English-University of North Dakota, Grand Forks ND 58202-7209. (701)777-3321. E-mail: jean@jeanpatrick.com. Website: www.u nd.edu/dept/english/childrensLitconference.htm. **SCBWI Regional Advisor:** Jean Patrick. Writer and illustrator workshops geared toward all levels. "Although the conference attendees are mostly writers, we encourage & welcome illustrators of every level." **Open to students.** "Our conference offers 3-4 children's authors, editors, publishers, illustrators or agents. Last year's conference included Kent Brown (publisher, Boyds Mills Press); Barbara Joose (picture book author); and Carol Fisher Saller (Cricket Books). Conference usually held 3rd Saturday in September. "Please call or e-mail to confirm dates. We often have a Friday evening session too. Writers and illustrators come from North Dakota, Minnesota, South Dakota, Wisconsin and Iowa." Writing facilities available: campus of University of North Dakota. Local art exhibits and/or concerts may coincide with conference. Cost of conference: $65 (less for members of SCBWI); includes Saturday's sessions and lunch; Friday night reception and speaker. A manuscript may be submitted 1 month in advance for critique (extra charge). E-mail for more information.

SCBWI DOES BOLOGNA. (33) 1 42 73 33 75 (GMT + 1). Fax: (323)782-1892. E-mail: erzsideak@scbwi.org. Website: www.kidbookprosworld.com and www.scbwi.org. **SCBWI International Coordinator:** Erzsi Deàk. Writer and illustrator conference geared toward beginner, intermediate, advanced and professional levels. **Open to students.** "A craft-based, hands-on, full day of talks and workshops and an intro to the Bologna Book Fair." Topics under consideration for writers: Slash and Burn: How to self-edit effectively; Revision; Speaking in Tongues: Working for Your Characters. For illustrators: Keep the Pages Turning: Making the Most of Your Images; Short Takes: History of Children's Book Illustration Around the World; Technical Stuff. In general: Agents; Creative Rejection: Working It into a Successful Sale. Annual conference. "New annual conference to be held each year in association with the largest international book fair in the world, the Bologna Children's Book Fair." Conference held annually in April, the day before the Bologna Book Fair. For 2004: Tuesday, April 13. Registration limited to 100. "We will have access to whatever we need for this conference; we have the entire book fair at our disposal." Cost of conference: to be determined; includes talks and hands-on workshops; portfolio critiques (may be an additional fee); group dinner (limited to 16, pre-reserved; additional cost). "The SCBWI offers this crafts-based one-day conference of talks, workshops and portfolio reviews on the site of the Bologna Book Fair the day before the Fair. 2004 will be the first year we are able to offer this one-day conference."

SCBWI—FLORIDA CONFERENCE, 2158 Portland Ave., Wellington FL 33414. (561)798-4824. E-mail: barcafer@aol .com. **Florida Regional Advisor:** Barbara Casey. Writer and illustrator workshops geared toward beginner, intermediate, advanced and professional levels. Subjects to be announced. Workshop dates and location to be announced. Write or e-mail for more information.

SCBWI—FRANCE: WRITER'S DAY WITH JACK GANTOS, International School of Paris, Paris, France. (33)1 4828 3970. E-mail: melissa@kidbookpros.com. Website: www.kidbookpros.com. **Regional Advisor-France:** Melissa Buron. Writer workshop geared toward beginner and intermediate levels. Topics emphasized: "creation of picture books and novels." One-time event, held January 31, 2004. Registration limited to 40. E-mail for more information.

SCBWI—HOFSTRA UNIVERSITY CHILDREN'S LITERATURE CONFERENCE, 250 Hofstra University, U.C.C.E., Hempstead NY 11549. (516)463-7600. Fax: (516)463-4833. E-mail: marion.flomenhaft@hofstra.edu. Website: www.hofstra.edu/writers. **Writers/Illustrators Contact:** Marion Flomenhaft, director, Liberal Arts Studies. Writer and illustrator workshops geared toward all levels. Emphasizes: fiction, nonfiction, poetry, submission procedures, picture books. Workshops will be held April 17, 2004. Length of each session: 1 hour. Cost of workshop: approximately $80;

includes 2 workshops, reception, lunch, 2 general sessions, and panel discussion with guest speakers and a critiquing of randomly selected first-manuscript pages submitted by registrants. Write for more information. Co-sponsored by Society of Children's Book Writers & Illustrators.

SCBWI—HOUSTON ANNUAL CONFERENCE, (formerly SCBWI—Houston Conference), (281)469-1133. E-mail: layne@laynejohnson.com. Website: www.scbwi-houston.org. **Regional Advisor:** Sondra Johnson. Annual conference "held November 5-7, 2004 at Wyndam Greenspoint Hotel, Houston, TX." Other Events: "Editors Open House," held February 2004; Northwest Forest Children's Writer's Retreat, April 2004; "A Day with Susan Stevens Crummel" Children's Writing Workshop June 2004. For more information on all events check our website.

SCBWI—ILLINOIS; SPRING RETREAT—THE WRITE CONNECTION: 3 ACQUIRING EDITORS, 2300 Lincoln Park W., #224, Chicago IL 60614. E-mail: esthersh@aol.com. **Regional Advisor, SCBWI-Illinois:** Esther Hershenhorn.
  ● The workshop is held in Woodstock, Illinois. Next scheduled retreat April 30-May 2, 2004. Enrollment limited to 55.
Writer workshops geared toward intermediate, advanced and professional levels. Offers teaching sessions; open mic; ms critiques; panel discussions; editor presentations. Biannual workshop.

SCBWI—IOWA CONFERENCES. E-mail: hecklit@aol.com. Website: www.schwi-iowa.org. Iowa SCBWI **Regional Advisor:** Connie Heckert. Writer workshops geared toward all levels. "Usually speakers include one to three nationally known experts in the children's literature field. Our spring annual conference is a major event over a weekend. Recent speakers include Robert Sabuda, Michael Green, Stephen Mooser and Sharelle Byars Moranville. We also offer a one-day program in the fall, or a retreat geared to a specific genre, i.e., novel revision." Annual conference. Cost of conference: $55 and up for 1-day events; under $200 for a weekend conference. Individual critiques and portfolio reviews are an extra charge. See website for more information.

SCBWI—MICHIGAN; FALL CONFERENCE, 1144 Buckingham Rd., Haslett MI 48840. E-mail: monicaharris@chartermi.net. Website: www.kidbooklink.org. **Event Chair:** Monica Harris. Co-Regional Advisors: Ann Finkelstein and Paula Payton. Speakers will include Elizabeth Law, editor (Viking) and Janell Cannon, author/illustrator. 2003 speakers included Susan Cohen, agent (Writer's House); Cammie Mannino, children's bookseller; Mark McVeigh, editor (HarperCollins); April Fritz Young, author; Lisa Wheeler, author; and Janie Bynum, illustrator. Conference held October 15-17, 2004 in Gull Lake, MI (near Battle Creek and Kalamazoo). Registration limited. Cost of retreat: TBA, but approximately $250; includes meals, lodging, and tuition. See website for details on all the upcoming events.

SCBWI—MICHIGAN; SPRING WORKSHOP, 1144 Buckingham Rd., Haslett MI 48840. Website: www.Kidsbooklink.org. **Co-Regional Advisors:** Ann Finkelstein and Paula Payton. Workshop held June 5, 2004. Location Washtenaw Community College, Ann Arbor, MI. Speakers and registration TBA. See website for details on all upcoming events.

SCBWI—MIDATLANTIC, HOLLINS UNIVERSITY CONFERENCE, P.O. Box 3215, Reston VA 20195-1215. E-mail: MidAtlanticSCBWI@TidalWave.net; marcieaf@yahoo.com. Website: www.SCBWI-MidAtlantic.org. **Conference Co-chair:** Marcie Atkins. SCBWI Regional Advisor: Ellen Braaf. Writer workshops geared toward all levels. **Open to students.** Conference held June 25-27, 2004 at Hollins University in Roanoke VA. Registration limited to 150. Cost of conference: includes all sessions and continental breakfast; and Saturday lunch. Write or e-mail for more information.

SCBWI—MIDSOUTH CONFERENCE, P.O. Box 120061, Nashville TN 37212. (615)646-4527 or (615)315-9683. E-mail: cmoonwriter@aol.com or jmamenta1@aol.com. **Conference Directors:** Candace Moonshower and Joanne Mamenta. Writer workshops geared toward all levels. Illustrator workshops geared toward all levels. **Open to Students.** Previous workshop topics have included: The Writers as Research Detective, Working the Web, Plotting Children's Fiction the Ah-ha! Way, From Slushpile to Store. There are also opportunities for ms and portfolio critiques, which may be formed at the conference. Conference held fall, 2004. Speakers include working authors, illustrators, editors, and others. Cost of conference: $65 SCBWI members; $70 nonmembers; ms critiques extra. Manuscripts for critique must be typed, double-spaced, and submitted in advance with payment. Portfolios are brought to the conference, but reservations for critique time and payment must be made in advance.

SCBWI—MISSOURI; CHILDREN'S WRITER'S CONFERENCE, St. Charles County Community College, P.O. Box 76975, 103 CEAC, St. Peters MO 63376-0975. (314)213-8000 ext. 4108. E-mail: suebe@cyberedge.net. **SCBWI MO Regional Advisor:** Sue Bradford Edwards. Writer and illustrator conference geared toward all levels. **Open to students.** Speakers include editors, writers and other professionals. Topics vary from year to year, but each conference offers sessions for both writers and illustrators as well as for newcomers and published writers. Previous topics included: "What Happens When Your Manuscript is Accepted" by Dawn Weinstock, editor; "Writing—Hobby or Vocation?" by Chris Kelleher; "Mother Time Gives Advice: Perspectives from a 25 Year Veteran" by Judith Mathews, editor; "Don't Be a Starving Writer" by Vicki Berger Erwin, author; and "Words & Pictures: History in the Making," by author-illustrator Cheryl Harness. Annual conference held in early November. For exact date, see SCBWI website: www.SCBWI.org. Registration limited to 75-90. Cost of conference includes one day workshop (8 a.m. to 5 p.m.) plus lunch. Write for more information.

SCBWI—NEW MEXICO; FALL RETREAT. Website: www.scbwi-nm.org. Weekend retreat held in early October at Hummingbird Music Camp in the Jemez Mountains of New Mexico. Workshops with directed writing/illustrating exercises, critique sessions and other time for sharing work, plus free time for illustrationg. For more information check the region's website.

SCBWI—NEW MEXICO; SPRING CONFERENCE/FALL RETREAT (Handsprings: A conference for Children's Writers and Illustrators), Albuquerque NM. Website: www.scbwi-nm.org. "Writers from around the state share their expertise in workshop sessions on such topics as business basics; voice; revision; the interplay of words and pictures; nonfiction; and inspiration. The conference includes lunch and plenty of time to network. Special guest speakers in 2003 included Susan Van Metre, Senior Editor at Abrams Books for Young Readers, Nancy Hinkle, Senior Editor at Knopf and Crown Books for Young Readers, and Sara Reynolds, Art Director of Dutton Children's Books." Conference held in April. One-day conference. Check website for more information.

SCBWI—NEW YORK; CONFERENCE FOR CHILDREN'S BOOK ILLUSTRATORS & AUTHOR/ILLUS-TRATORS, 32 Hillside Ave., Monsey NY 10952. (845)356-7273. **Conference Chair:** Frieda Gates. Held April 6, 2004 in New York, NY at the Society of Illustrators, www.societyofillustrators.org. Registration limited to 80 portfolios shown out of 125 conferees. Portfolios are not judged—first come—first served. Cost of conference: with portfolio—$100, members, $110 others; without portfolio—$70 members, $80 others; $50 additional for 30-minute portfolio evaluation; $25 additional for 15-minute book dummy evaluation. Call to receive a flier. "In addition to an exciting program of speakers, this conference provides a unique opportunity for illustrators and author/illustrators to have their portfolios reviewed by scores of art buyers and agents from the publishing and allied industries. Art buyers admitted free. Our reputation for exhibiting high-quality work of both new and established children's book illustrators, plus the ease of examining such an abundance of portfolios, has resulted in a large number of productive contacts between buyers and illustrators."

SCBWI—NORCAL (SAN FRANCISCO/SOUTH); RETREAT AT ASILOMAR. Website: www.scbwinorca.org. **Regional Advisor:** Jim Averbeck. While we welcome "not-yet-published" writers and illustrators, lectures and workshops are geared toward professionals and those striving to become professional. Program topics cover aspects of writing or illustrating picture books to young adult novels. Past speakers include editors, art directors, published authors and illustrators. Annual conference, generally held last weekend in February; Friday evening through Sunday lunch. Registration limited to 100. Most rooms shared with one other person. Additional charge for single when available. Desks available in most rooms. All rooms have private baths. Conference center is set in wooded campus on Asilomar Beach in Pacific Grove, California. Approximate cost: $295 for SCBWI members, $345 for nonmembers; includes shared room, 6 meals, ice breaker party and all conference activities. Vegetarian meals available. One full scholarship is available to SCBWI members. Registration opens at the end of September and the conference sells out very quickly. A waiting list is formed. "Coming together for shared meals and activities builds a strong feeling of community among the speakers and conferees. For more information, including exact costs and dates visit our website in September."

SCBWI—OREGON CONFERENCES. E-mail: robink@rio.com. Website: www.sparpungent.com/scbwior. **Regional Advisor:** Robin Koontz. Writer and illustrator workshops and presentations geared toward all levels. "We invite editors, art directors, agents, authors, illustrators and others in the business of writing and illustrating for children. They present lectures, workshops, and either on-site or written critiques." Annual Fall retreat and Spring conference. Two events per year: Working Writers and Illustrators Retreat: Retreat held near Portland Thursday-Sunday the 2nd weekend in October. Cost of retreat: $350 plus critique fee; includes double occupancy and all meals; Spring Conference: Held in the Portland area (1-day event in May); cost: about $60, includes continental breakfast and lunch. Registration limited to 175 for the conference and 50 for the retreat. SCBWI Oregon is a regional chapter of the SCBWI.

SCBWI—POCONO MOUNTAINS RETREAT, Website: www.scbwiepa.org. **Conference Director:** Arlette Braman. Held April 30-May 2, 2004 at Sterling Inn, Sterling PA. Faculty addresses writing, illustration, and publishing. Registration limited to 75. Cost of retreat: about $350; includes tuition, room and board. For information and registration form, visit website.

SCBWI—ROCKY MOUNTAIN; 2004 EVENTS. Website: www.rmcscbwi.org/events.php. **Co-Regional Advisors:** Denise Vega and Christine Liu Perkins. SCBWI Rocky Mountain chapter will offer these events in 2004: Spring Workshop, March 13, Golden, Colorado: "Finding Your Inner Seuss: Humor, Rhyme & Poetry in Children's Fiction and Nonfiction"; Summer Retreat, July 16-20, Colorado Springs, Colorado; Fall Conference, October (date to be determined), Golden, Colorado. For more information check website.

SCBWI—SAN DIEGO; WORKSHOPS, San Diego—SCBWI, 16048 Lofty Trail Dr., San Diego CA 92127. Chapter voice mail: (619)230-9342. E-mail: ra-sdosandiego-scbwi.org. Website: www.sandiego-scbwi.org. **Regional Advisor:** Arlene Bartle. Writer and illustrator meetings and workshops geared toward all levels. Topics vary but emphasize writing and illustrating for children. Cost $5-55 (check website). Write or e-mail for more information. "The San Diego chapter holds meetings the second Saturday of each month from September-May at the University of San Diego's Manchester Hall, from 2-4 p.m.; cost $6 (members), $8 (nonmembers)." Meeting schedule: September 13, author/illustrator Sally Warner; October 11, The Structure of Story, author Christie Ridgeway; November 8, Queries, Covers and Synopses, editor Deborah Halverson; December 13, Selling Your Book Without an Agent, author Alexis O'Neill; February 14, Self Publishing, Dan Poynter; March 13, Luann cartoonist, Greg Evans; April 10, PR, publicist Antoinette Kuritz. Workshops: January 10 and May 8. Workshops held 2-4 pm. Cost of workshops: $35 SCBWI members, $45 nonmembers. "You may also sign up through University of San Diego for an extension class, 2 units credit; class begins at 12:30 and includes the regular chapter meetings. You may sign up for class in advance or at the first class meeting. Fees are USD's fee plus Season Ticket. Season Tickets are available: discounts on regular chapter meetings, workshops, and newsletter subscription."

SCBWI—SOUTHERN BREEZE; SPRINGMINGLE '04, P.O. Box 26282, Birmingham AL 35260. E-mail: JSKittinger @bellsouth.net. Website: www.southern-breeze.org. **Regional Advisors:** Jo Kittinger and Mary Ann Taylor. Writer and illustrator workshops geared toward intermediate, advanced and professional levels. Speakers include editors Eileen Robinson (Children's Press), John Rudolph (Putnam), Melanie Cecka (Viking) and Tara Weikum (HarperCollins). **Open to college students.** Annual conference held in one of the three states comprising the Southern Breeze region, this year—Atlanta, GA. Held March 5-7, 2004. Registration limited to 100. Cost of conference: approximately $225; includes Saturday lunch and Saturday banquet. Pre-registration is necessary. Send a SASE to Southern Breeze, P.O. Box 26282, Birmingham AL 35260 for more information or visit website.

N SCBWI—SOUTHERN BREEZE; WRITING AND ILLUSTRATING FOR KIDS, P.O. Box 26282, Birmingham AL 35260. E-mail: jskittinger@bellsouth.net. Website: www.southernbreeze.org. **Regional Advisors:** Jo Kittinger and Mary Ann Taylor. Writer and illustrator workshops geared toward all levels. **Open to college students.** All sessions pertain specifically to the production and support of quality children's literature. This one-day conference offers 30 workshops on craft and the business of writing. Picture books, chapter books, novels covered. Entry and professional level topics addressed by published writers and illustrators, editors and agents. Annual conference. Fall conference is held in October. All workshops are limited to 20 or fewer people. Pre-registration is necessary. Some workshops fill quickly. This is a metropolitan area with many museums in a short driving distance. Also—universities and colleges. Cost of conference: $70 for members, $90 for nonmembers; includes program—key note and luncheon speaker, wrap-up panel, 4 workshops (selected from 30). Does not include lunch (about $6 or registrant can brown bag) or individual consultations (mss must be sent early). Registration is by mail ahead of time. Manuscript and portfolio reviews must be pre-paid and scheduled. Send a SASE to: Southern Breeze, P.O. Box 26282, Birmingham AL 35260 or visit web page. "Fall conference is always held in Birmingham, Alabama. Room block at a hotel near conference site (usually a school) is by individual reservation and offers a conference rate. Keynote speaker will be Sarah Ketcherstd, editor (Candlewick Press). Luncheon speaker will be Peter Jacob, author and educator."

N ⊕ SCBWI—TAIWAN; FALL WORKSHOP. Fax: (886)2363-5358. E-mail: scbwi_taiwan@yahoo.com. Website: scbwi.24cc.com (Chinese); www.kathleenahrens.com (English). **SCBWI Regional Advisor:** Kathleen Ahrens. Writer and illustrator workshops geared toward intermediate level. **Open to students.** Topics emphasized: "Odd numbered years are devoted to illustrator topics; even numbered years to writer topics. The 2003 workshop had Lai Ma and Chin-Lung Li, two of Taiwan's premier illustrator/authors talk about their work and critique portfolios." Conference held early September. Registration limited to 100. Cost of conference: $35; includes workshop only. "Portfolios and manuscripts may be critiqued for an additional fee. Work must be submitted in advance." E-mail for more information. Event is co-sponsored by Eslite Children's Bookstore.

SCBWI—UTAH/SOUTHERN IDAHO, E-mail: utidscbwi@aol.com. **Regional Advisor:** Kim Williams-Justensen. Writer workshops geared toward all levels. Illustrator workshops geared toward beginners and intermediate. **Open to students.** Annual conference: Forum on Children's Literature held March 18-19, 2004. Featured Guest: Richard Peck. Cost of conference: approximately $110; $120 for students. E-mail for more information.

SCBWI—VENTURA/SANTA BARBARA; FALL CONFERENCE, P.O. Box 941389, Simi Valley CA 93094-1389. (805)581-1906. E-mail: alexisinca@aol.com. Website: www.scbwisocal-org/calendar. **Regional Advisor:** Alexis O'Neill. Writers conference geared toward all levels. "We invite editors, authors and author/illustrators and agents. We have had speakers on the picture book, middle grade, YA, magazine and photo essay books. Fiction and nonfiction are covered." Conference held October 30, 2004. Scheduled at California Lutheran University in Thousand Oaks, California in cooperation with the School of Education. Cost of conference $70; includes all sessions and lunch. E-mail for more information.

N SCBWI—WASHINGTON STATE/NORTHERN IDAHO, 14816 205th Ave., SE, Renton WA 98059-8926. (425)235-0566. E-mail: scbwiwa@oz.net. Website: www.scbwi-washington.org. **Co-Regional Advisors:** Cathy Benson and Molly Blaisdell. Writer workshops geared toward all levels. **Open to students.** All aspects of writing and illustrating children's books are covered from picture books to YA novels, from contracts to promotion. Editors, an art director, an agent and published authors and illustrators serve as conference faculty. Registration limited to about 350. Cost of conference: $90-130; includes registration, morning snack and lunch. The conference is a one-day event held at Meyedenbauer Center in Bellevue, Washington. Individual critiques available for illustrators; art show.

SCBWI—WISCONSIN; FALL RETREAT FOR WORKING WRITERS, 15255 Turnberry Dr., Brookfield WI 53005. (262)783-4890. E-mail: aangel@aol.com. **Co-Regional Advisor:** Ann Angel. Writer and illustrator conference geared toward all levels. All our sessions pertain to children's writing/illustration. Faculty addresses writing/illustrating/publishing. Annual conference held October 3-5, 2003 in Racine, WI. Registration limited to 70. Bedrooms have desks/conference center has small rooms—can be used to draw/write. Program has free time scheduled in. Cost of conference: $300; includes program, meals, lodging, ms critique. Write for more information.

OTHER CONFERENCES

Many conferences and workshops included here focus on children's writing or illustrating and related business issues. Others appeal to a broader base of writers or artists, but still provide information that can be useful in creating material for children. Illustrators may be interested in painting and drawing workshops, for example, while writers can learn about techniques and meet editors and agents at general writing conferences. For more information visit the websites listed or contact conference coordinator.

AMERICAN CHRISTIAN WRITERS CONFERENCE, P.O. Box 110390, Nashville TN 37222-0390. 1(800)21-WRITE or (615)834-0450. Fax: (615)834-7736. E-mail: detroitwriters@aol.com. Website: www.ACWriters.com. **Director:** Reg Forder. Writer and illustrator workshops geared toward beginner, intermediate and advanced levels. Classes offered include: fiction, nonfiction, poetry, photography, music, etc. Workshops held in 3 dozen US cities. Call or write for a complete schedule of conferences. 75 minutes. Maximum class size: 30 (approximate). Cost of conference: $99, 1-day session; $169, 2-day session (discount given if paid 30 days in advance) includes tuition only.

N ANNUAL SPRING POETRY FESTIVAL, City College, 138th St. at Convent Ave., New York NY 10031. (212)650-6343. E-mail: barrywal23@aol.com. **Director, Poetry Outreach Center:** Barry Wallenstein. Writer workshops geared to all levels. **Open to students.** Annual poetry festival. Festival held Tuesday, May 4, 2004. Registration limited to 325. Cost of workshops and festival: free. Write for more information.

N ARKANSAS WRITERS' CONFERENCE, 6817 Gingerbread Lane, Little Rock AR 72204. (501)565-8889. Fax: (501)907-1055. **Counselor:** Peggy Vining. Writer workshops geared toward beginner, intermediate and advanced levels. **Open to students.** Annual conference. Conference always held the first full weekend in June. Cost of conference: $7.50/day; includes registration and workshops. Contest fees, lodging and food are not included. Send SASE for brochure after March 1. Offers 34 different awards for various types of writing, poetry and essay.

N ASPEN SUMMER WORDS LITERARY FESTIVAL, 110 E. Hallam St., No. 116, Aspen CO 81611. (970)925-3122. Fax: (970)920-5700. E-mail: info@aspenwriters.org. Website: www.aspenwriters.org. **Operations Manager:** Jamie Abbott. Writer workshop geared toward beginner and intermediate levels. **Open to students.** Annual children's literature workshop. Held June 19-12, 2004. Registration limited to 12. Writing facilities available: workshop space; computer, Internet, fax and copy machine at festival site; contemplative gardens. Cost of workshop: $375 (2003 tuition); includes workshop, picnic and 3 social receptions. Students are responsible for their own lodging and meals. "Applications must include: completed application, tuition payment, cover letter and manuscript of up to 10 pages. There is an April application deadline. In 2003 it was April 1. Enrollment is on a space-available basis thereafter."

AUTUMN AUTHORS' AFFAIR . . . A WRITER'S RENDEZVOUS, 1507 Burnham Ave., Calumet City IL 60409. (708)862-9797. E-mail: exchbook@aol.com. Website: www.rendezvousreviews.com. **President:** Nancy McCann. Writer workshops geared toward beginner, intermediate, advanced levels. **Open to students.** Sessions include children/teen/young adult writing, mysteries, romantic suspense, romance, nonfiction, etc. Annual workshop. Workshops held October 18-20, 2002. Cost of workshop: $75 for 1 day, $125 for weekend, includes meals, workshops, speeches, gifts. Write for more information.

BUTLER UNIVERSITY CHILDREN'S LITERATURE CONFERENCE, 4600 Sunset Drive, Indianapolis IN 46208. (317)255-2598. E-mail: kidsink@indy.net. **Contact:** Shirley Mullin. Writer and illustrator conference geared toward intermediate level. **Open to college students.** Annual conference held the last Saturday of the month of January each year featuring top writers in the field of children's literature. Includes sessions such as Nuts and Bolts for Beginning Writers. Registration limited to 350. Cost of conference: $85; includes meals, registration, 3 plenary addresses, 2 workshops, book signing, reception and conference bookstore. Write for more information. "The conference is geared toward three groups: teachers, librarians and writers/illustrators."

☑ CAPE COD WRITER'S CONFERENCE, Cape Cod Writer's Center, P.O. Box 408, Osterville MA 02655. (508)420-0200. Fax: (508)420-0212. E-mail: ccwc@capecod.net. Website: www.capecod.net/writers. Writer conference and workshops geared toward beginner, intermediate and professional levels. **Open to students.** "We hold a young writer's workshop at our annual conference each summer for writers ages 12-16. 41st annual conference held third week in August on Cape Cod. Cost of conference includes $70 to register; $90 first course. Other courses $80. Manuscript evaluations and faculty conferences available.

CELEBRATION OF CHILDREN'S LITERATURE, Montgomery College, 51 Mannakee St., Workforce Development and Continuing Education, Rockville MD 20850. (240)683-2589. Fax: (240)683-1890. E-mail: bmcleod@mc.cc.md.us. **Early Childhood Education Program Director:** Betty McLeod, Ph.D. Writer and illustrator workshops offered in conjunction with Montgomery County Public Schools, Montgomery County Public Libraries, Children's Book Guild and other local organizations is geared toward all levels. **Open to students.** New workshops and activities will be offered providing literary development strategies, elementary school readiness activities for pre-schoolers, "Babies & Books" (The Connection), hands on dictation narration and dramatic expression in pre-reading, pre-writing skill development. Annual workshop. Registration limited to 200. Art display facilities, continuing education classrooms and large auditorium. Cost of workshop: approximately $75; includes workshops, box lunch and coffee. Contact Montgomery College for more information.

CENTRAL OHIO WRITERS OF LITERATURE FOR CHILDREN: A Conference for Teachers, Parents, Writers & Illustrators, (formerly Writing for Children), 933 Hamlet St., Columbus OH 43201-3595. (614)291-8644. E-mail: cowriters@mail.com. Website: www.sjms.net/conf. **Development Director:** Jim Mengel. Writer and illustrator conference geared toward beginner, intermediate and advanced levels. **Open to full-time high school and college students.** Annual conference held Saturday, April 24, 2004. Registration limited to 160. Cost of conference: students and seniors $60; all others early-bird before January 24, 2004 $95; regular before March 24, 2004 $110; late after March 24, 2004 $120. $40 additional charge for ms or portfolio evaluations and workshops for writers and illustrators led by published authors and illustrators. Manuscript and portfolio evaluation and workshops require pre-registration (call Jim Mengel). Manuscripts and/or portfolios to be evaluated must be submitted by March 20, 2004. "Event will be at the Fawcett Center in downtown Columbus, OH and will be an all-day affair with two keynote speakers."

CHATTANOOGA CONFERENCE ON SOUTHERN LITERATURE, P.O. Box 4203, Chattanooga TN 37405-0203. (423)267-1218. Fax: (423)267-1018. E-mail: srobinson@artsedcouncil.org. Website: www.artsedcouncil.org. **Executive Director:** Susan Robinson. **Open to students.** Conference is geared toward readers. No workshops are held. Biennial conference. Conference held April 2005. Registration limited to first 1,000 people. Cost of conference: $50. Write for more information. "The Chattanooga Conference on Southern Literature is a conference that celebrates literature of the South. Panel discussions, readings, music, food and art are featured."

CHILDREN'S AUTHORS' BOOTCAMP, P.O. Box 231, Allenspark CO 80510 (303)747-1014. E-mail: CABootcamp@ aol.com. Website: www.WeMakeWriters.com. **Contact:** Linda Arms White. Writer workshops geared toward beginner and intermediate levels. "Children Authors' Bootcamp provides two full, information-packed days on the fundamentals of writing fiction for children. The workshop covers developing strong, unique characters; well-constructed plots; believable dialogue; seamless description and pacing; point of view; editing your own work; marketing your manuscripts to publishers, and more. Each day also includes in-class writing exercises and small group activities." Workshop held 6-7 times/year at various locations throughout the United States. Bootcamps are generally held in March, April, June, September, October and November. Please check our website for upcoming dates and locations. Maximum size is 55; average workshop has 40-50 participants. Cost of workshop: $239. Tuition for both Saturday and Sunday (9:00 a.m. to 4:30 p.m.); morning and afternoon snacks; lunch; handout packet.

CHILDREN'S BOOK CONFERENCE, Portland State University Haystack Program, P.O. Box 1491, Portland OR 97207 (503)725-4186. Fax: (503)725-4840. E-mail: snydere@pdx.edu. Website: www.haystack.pdx.edu. **Contact:** Elizabeth Snyder, program coordinator. Focus on the craft of writing and illustrating for children with workshops in poetry, picture books, character development, point of view, narrative techniques, setting, and dialogue. Acquire specific information on how to become a professional in the field of children's literature. Annual workshop for all levels. Conference held July 21-25, 2003. Cost of workshop: $415—noncredit; $485—3 university credits; individual ms/portfolio reviews for an additional fee. Call for more information. Linda Zuckerman, editor, coordinates conference and collects knowledgeable and engaging presenters every year. The Portland State University Haystack Program is in its 34th year on the sparkling Oregon coast.

⊠ CHRISTIAN WRITERS' CONFERENCE, P.O. Box 42429, Santa Barbara CA 93140. (805)346-1914. E-mail: h.coganptl@aol.com. **Coordinator:** Opal Dailey. Writer conference geared toward beginner, intermediate and advanced levels. **Open to students.** We always have children writing instruction. Annual conference. Conference held October 1, 2004. Registration limited to 100. Cost of conference: approximately $65; includes lunch and refreshment breaks. Write for more information.

⊠ THE COLLEGE OF NEW JERSEY WRITERS' CONFERENCE, English Dept., The College of New Jersey, P.O. Box 7718, Ewing NJ 08628-0718. (609)771-3254. Fax: (609)637-5112. E-mail: write@tcnj.edu. **Director:** Jean Hollander. Writer workshops geared toward all levels. Offers workshop in children's literature. Workshops held in April of every year. Length of each session: 2 hours. Cost of workshop: $40-70 (reduced rates for students); includes conference, workshop and ms critique. Write for more information.

THE COLUMBUS WRITERS CONFERENCE, P.O. Box 20548, Columbus OH 43220-0176. (614)451-3075. Fax: (614)451-0174. E-mail: angelapl28@aol.com. Website: www.creativevista.com. **Director:** Angela Palazzolo. Sessions geared toward all levels. "The two-day conference offers a wide variety of topics and has included writing in the following markets: children's, young adult, screenwriting, historical fiction, humor, suspense, science fiction/fantasy, travel, educational and greeting card. Other topics have included writing the novel, the short story, the nonfiction book; playwriting; finding and working with an agent; independent publishing; book reviewing; technical writing; and time management for writers. Specific sessions that have pertained to children: children's writing, children's markets, young adult and publishing children's poetry and stories. Annual conference. Conference held in August. Cost of full conference: $225 (early bird $235); Saturday only $185 (early bird $165); Friday only (does not include dinner and program) $165 (early bird $145); Friday night dinner and program $45 (early bird $38). E-mail, call or write for more information; or visit website.

⊠ CONFERENCE FOR WRITERS & ILLUSTRATORS OF CHILDREN'S BOOKS, 51 Tamal Vista Blvd., Corte Madera CA 94925. (415)927-0960, ext. 229. Fax: (415)927-3069. E-mail: conferences@bookpassage.com. Website: www.bookpassage.com. **Conference Coordinator:** Marguerita Castanera. Writer and illustrator conference geared toward beginner and intermediate levels. Sessions cover such topics as the nuts and bolts of writing and illustrating, publisher's spotlight, market trends, developing characters/finding voice in your writing. Two-day conference held each June. Registration limited to 80. Includes 3 lunches and a closing reception.

PETER DAVIDSON'S HOW TO WRITE A CHILDREN'S PICTURE BOOK SEMINAR, 982 S. Emerald Hills Dr., P.O. Box 497, Arnolds Park IA 51331-0497. E-mail: Peterdavidson@mchsi.com. **Seminar Presenter:** Peter Davidson. "This seminar is for anyone interested in writing and/or illustrating children's picture books. Beginners and experienced writers alike are welcome." **Open to students.** *How to Write a Children's Picture Book* is a one-day seminar devoted to principles and techniques of writing and illustrating children's picture books. Topics include Definition of a Picture Book, Picture Book Sizes, Developing an Idea, Plotting the Book, Writing the Book, Illustrating the Book, Typing the Manuscript, Copyrighting Your Work, Marketing Your Manuscript and Contract Terms. Seminars are presented year-round at community colleges. Even-numbered years, presents seminars in Minnesota, Iowa, Nebraska, Kansas, Colorado and Wyoming. Odd-numbered years, presents seminars in Illinois, Minnesota, Iowa, South Dakota, Missouri, Arkansas and Tennessee (write for a schedule). One day, 9 a.m.-4 p.m. Cost of workshop: varies from $40-59, depending on location; includes approximately 35 pages of handouts. Write for more information.

DUKE UNIVERSITY YOUTH PROGRAMS: CREATIVE WRITER'S WORKSHOP, Box 90702, Room 203, The Bishop's House, Durham NC 27708. (919)684-2827. Fax: (919)681-8235. E-mail: youth@duke.edu. Website: www.learnmo re.duke.edu/youth. **Director:** Sarah Collee. Writer workshops geared toward intermediate to advanced levels. **Open to students.** The Creative Writer's Workshop provides an intensive creative writing experience for advanced high school age writers who want to improve their skills in a community of writers. "The interactive format gives participants the opportunity to share their work in small groups, one-on-one with instructors, and receive feedback in a supportive environment. The review and critique process helps writers sharpen critical thinking skills and learn how to revise their work." Annual workshop. Every summer there is one 2-week residential session. Costs for 2003 were $1,475 for this 2-week residential session. Visit website or call for more information.

N: DUKE UNIVERSITY YOUTH PROGRAMS: YOUNG WRITER'S CAMP, P.O. Box 90702, Room 203, The Bishop's House, Durham NC 27708. (919)684-2827. Fax: (919)681-8235. E-mail: youth@mail.duke.edu. Website: www.lea rnmore.duke.edu/youth. **Contact:** Duke Youth Programs (919)684-6259. Writer workshops geared toward beginner and intermediate levels for middle and high school students. **Open to students** (grades 6-11). Summer Camp. The Young Writer's Camp offers courses that help participants to increase their skills in creative and expository writing. "Through a core curriculum of short fiction, poetry, journalism, and playwriting students choose two courses for study to develop creative and analytical processes of writing. Students work on assignments and projects in and out of class, such as newspaper features, short stories, character studies, and journals." Annual workshop. Every summer there are 3 2-week sessions with residential and day options. Costs for 2003 were $1,475 for residential campers and $725 for day campers. Visit website or call for more information.

N: EAST OF EDEN WRITERS CONFERENCE, California Writers Club, 1125 Miguel Ave., Los Altos CA 94024. (650)691-9802. Fax: (650)390-0234. E-mail: eastofeden@southbaywriters.com. Website: southbaywriters.com. **Conference Director:** Beth Proudfoot. Writer workshops geared toward beginner, intermediate and advanced levels. **Open to students.** "In 2002, we featured Kendra Marcus, children's literary agent, who spoke on understanding the ins and outs of writing children's books: understanding your audience and building believable characters. Summer Laurie, an editor for Tricycle Books also spoke on 'Breaking out of the Slush Pile of Children's Books.' In 2004 we'll have similar topics, plus many more, applicable to all writers." Bi-annual conference. Last held August 27-29, 2002, in Salinas, CA (at the National Steinbeck Center and the Salinas Community Center.) Registration limited to 400. Cost of conference: $225 (after May 1st—discount for CWC members and "Early Birds"); includes Friday night dinner and program; Saturday breakfast, lunch, and full day of workshops and panels; "Night Owl" sessions; Saturday dinner program and Sunday brunch at John Steinbeck's family home are available for a small additional fee. "This conference, run by the nonprofit California Writers Club, will include many top-notch seminars on the art and business of writing. We'll have panels where writers can meet literary agents and editors and an Ask-A-Pro program, where writers can sign up to speak individually with faculty members of their choice.

N: EPICON2004, P.O. Box 10371, Enid OK 73706. (580)548-5592. E-mail: tlschaefer@cox.net. Website: www.epicauth ors.com. **Conference Chair:** Terri Schaefer.

● EPIC (the Electronically Published Internet Connection) is an organization for published authors interested in learning more about and pursuing E-publishing.

"EPIC members need to be published, but we have many levels attend the conference itself, from authors seeking publishers to multi-published authors networking. We also present the anual QUASAR awards for best graphic art (i.e., cover art). Most workshops are general in nature (i.e., how to get published, how to expand your horizons as an author, etc.), but several last year were directed to target audiences . . . Writing for Children, How to Talk Like a Man, etc. A detailed schedule of this year's presentations can be found at www.epic-conference.com/schedule.html." Annual conference held March 12-14, 2004. "No registration limit of attendees, but we do cut off registration on January 31 of each year." Writing/art facilities available: business office; all guest rooms are equipped with high-speed internet connections. Cost of conference: $150; includes conference classes, continental breakfast (for at least one of the days, working on more), mixer on Friday night, and dinner banquet on Saturday night.

N: FESTIVAL OF CHILDREN'S LITERATURE, Loft Literary Center, 1011 Washington Ave. S., Suite 200, Minneapolis MN 55415. (612)215-2578. E-mail: mcummings@loft.org. Website: www.loft.org. **Education Director:** Mary Cummings. Writer workshops geared toward beginner, intermediate, advanced and professional levels. **Open to students.** Workshops include: "Nuts and Bolts of Publishing Nonfiction for Children" (by 4 writers with multi-titles published); "The Eternal Quest: Seeking the Perfect Combination of Words and Pictures" (by Melanie Kroupa, editor and publisher); "Editing Novels for Young People" (by Cecile Goyette, Sr. Editor, Dial Books for Young Readers); "Carolrhoda Books: An Overview and a Preview" (by publisher Adam Lerner and Illustrators Stephen Gammell and Cheng-Khee Chee); "School Visits and Book Tours" (by authors John Coy, Lynne Jonell, Janet Graber); "Writing (and Publishing) for Middle Graders" (by authors, Patricia Calvert, Joyce Sidman, Dianne Gray). Annual conference. Conference held April 2-3, 2004; keynote speaker: Alix Reid, senior editor, HarperCollins. Registration limited to 185 people; smaller groups for breakout sessions. Writing facilities available with a performance hall, classrooms and writers studios. Cost of conference: approximately $50 Friday; $80 Saturday; includes admission to full and break-out sessions, Saturday lunch, discount on hotel room (3 blocks from conference site at Loft Literary Center). Write for more information.

N FESTIVAL OF FAITH AND WRITING, Department of English, Calvin College, Grand Rapids MI 49546. (616)526-6770. Fax: (616)526-8508. E-mail: ffw@calvin.edu. Website: www.calvin.edu/academic/engl/festival/htm. E-mail all inquiries about attendance (for registration brochures, program information, etcetera). Geared toward all levels of readers and writers. **Open to students.** "The Festival of Faith and Writing has talks, panel discussions, and workshops by artists who compose, write, illustrate, and publish children's books and books for young adults. Each break-out session will have a session on children's books/young adult books. The following authors and illustrators are already committed to joining us in 2004: Katherine Paterson, James Ransome, Ann Turner, Ashley Bryan, Neil Waldman, Jacqueline Woodson, Miriam Bat-Ami." Conference held every other year. Held April 22-24, 2004. Registration limited to approximately 1,600 people. Cost of conference: $150/$75 for students; includes all sessions, workshops, evening speakers. Write for more information. "This conference is geared towards a variety of writers. The Festival brings together writers and readers who wonder about the intersections of faith with words on a page, lyrics in a melody, or images on a screen. Novelists, publishers, musicians, academics, poets, playwrights, editors, screenwriters, agents, journalists, preachers, students, and readers of every sort sit down together for three days of conversation and celebration."

N FIRST COAST WRITERS' FESTIVAL, 9911 Old Baymeadows Rd., Jacksonville FL 32256. (904)997-2669. Fax: (904)997-2746. E-mail: kclower@fccj.edu. Website: www.fccj.edu/wf. **Director, Media Production & Support:** Kathleen Clower. Writer workshops geared to all levels. Illustrators workshops geared to beginner level. **Open to students.** "For our 2003 Festival, children's authors and illustrators Mary and Dan Hubley presented a workshop on writing and illustrating children's books. Several workshops dealt with publishing and marketing. Annual workshop held May of each year, typically the weekend after Mothers' Day; May 15-17, 2003. Cost of workshop: 1-day festival (with lunch) $90 (early bird); 2-day festival (with lunch) $175 (early bird); Preconference workshop $40 (early bird). "Children's writing/illustration is one of many offerings at the festival. Other presentations include freelancing, writing memoirs, poetry, humouous essay, nonfiction, working with an editor, getting published and screenwriting."

FLORIDA CHRISTIAN WRITERS CONFERENCE, 2344 Armour Ct., Titusville FL 32780. (321)269-5831. Fax: (321)264-0037. E-mail: billiewilson@cfl.rr.com. Website: www.flwriters.org. **Conference Director:** Billie Wilson. Writer workshops geared toward all levels. **Open to students.** "We offer 60 one-hour workshops and 7 six-hour classes. Approximately 24 of these are for the children's genre. Annual workshop held each March. We have 30 publishers and publications represented by editors teaching workshops and reading manuscripts from the conferees. The conference is limited to 200 people. Usually workshops are limited to 25-30. Advanced or professional workshops are by invitation only via submitted application." Cost of workshop: $500; includes food, lodging, tuition and ms critiques and editor review of your ms. Write or e-mail for more information.

N GOTHAM WRITERS' WORKSHOP, New York NY 10023 (877)974-8377. Fax: (212)307-6325. E-mail: dana@write.org. Website: www.WritingClasses.com. **Director, Student Affairs:** Dana Miller. Creative writing workshops taught by professional writers are geared toward beginner, intermediate and advanced levels. **Open to students.** "Workshops cover the fundamentals of plot, structure, voice, description, characterization, and dialogue appropriate to all forms of fiction and nonfiction for pre-schoolers through young adults. Students can work on picture books or begin middle-readers or young adult novels." Annual workshops held 4 times/year (10 week and 1-day workshops). Workshops held January, April, July, September/October. Registration limited to 14 students/in-person (NYC) class; 18 students/online class; 40 students for in-person (NYC) one-day workshops. Cost of workshop: $420 for 10-week workshops; $150 for 1-day workshops; 10-week NYC classes meet once a week for 3 hours; 10-week online classes include 10 week-long, asynchronous "meetings"; 1-day workshops are 7 hours and are held 8 times/year. E-mail for more information.

N GREAT LAKES WRITER'S WORKSHOP, Alverno College, 3400 S. 43rd St., P.O. Box 343922, Milwaukee WI 53234-3922. (414)382-6176. Fax: (414)382-6332. E-mail: nancy.krase@alverno.edu. Website: www.alverno.edu. **Program Assistant:** Nancy Krase. Writing workshops geared toward beginner and intermediate levels; subjects include publishing, short story writing, novel writing, poetry, writing techniques/focus in character development, techniques for overcoming writers block. Annual workshop. Workshop held 3rd or 4th weekend in June—Friday evening and all day Saturday. Average length of each session: 2 hours. Cost of workshop: $110/entire workshop; $30/Friday only; $80/Saturday workshops. Lunch is included in Saturday program with a featured author as keynote speaker. Write for more information.

☑ THE HEIGHTS WRITER'S CONFERENCE, Sponsored by Writer's World Press, P.O. Box 284, Aurora OH 44202. (330)562-6667. E-mail: writersworld@juno.com. **Conference Director:** Lavern Hall. This conference is on hiatus, but the conference director welcomes inquiries on future events.

HIGHLAND SUMMER CONFERENCE, Box 7014, Radford University, Radford VA 24142-7014. (540)831-5366. Fax: (540)831-5004. E-mail: jasbury@radford.edu. Website: www.radford.edu/~arsc. **Director:** Grace Toney Edwards. **Assistant to the Director:** Jo Ann Asbury. **Open to students.** Writer workshops geared toward beginner, intermediate and advanced levels. Emphasizes Appalachian literature, culture and heritage. Annual workshop. Workshop held first 2 weeks in June annually. Registration limited to 20. Writing facilities available: computer center. Cost of workshop: Regular tuition (housing/meals extra). Must be registered student or special status student. E-mail, fax or call for more information. Past visiting authors include: Wilma Dykeman, Sue Ellen Bridgers, George Ella Lyon, Lou Kassem.

HIGHLIGHTS FOUNDATION WRITERS WORKSHOP AT BOYDS MILLS, Dept. CWF, 814 Court St., Honesdale PA 18431. (570)253-1192. Fax: (570)253-0179. E-mail: contact@highlightsfoundation.org. Website: www.highlightsfoundation.org. **Contact:** Kent Brown, director. Writer workshops geared toward those interested in writing for children; intermediate and advanced levels. Classes offered include: Nonfiction Research, Word Play: Poetry for Children, Writing from the Heart, Heart of the Novel. Spring/Fall workshops. Workshops held in March, April, May, 2004 at home of the Founders, Boyds Mills, PA. Workshops limited to 14. Cost of workshops range from $795 and up. Cost of workshop includes tuition, meals, conference supplies and housing. Call for availablility and pricing. Call for more information or visit the website.

HIGHLIGHTS FOUNDATION WRITERS WORKSHOP AT CHAUTAUQUA, Dept. CWL, 814 Court St., Honesdale PA 18431. (570)253-1192. Fax: (570)253-0179. E-mail: contact@highlightsfoundation.org. Website: www.highlights foundation.org. **Contact:** Kent Brown, director. Writer workshops geared toward those interested in writing for children; beginner, intermediate and advanced levels. Classes offered include: Children's Poetry; Book Promotion; Autobiographical Writing. Annual workshop. Workshops held July 17-24, 2004 at Chautauqua Institution, Chautauqua, NY. Registration limited to 100/class. Cost of workshop: $2,100; $1,685 for first-time attendees; includes tuition, meals, conference supplies. Cost does not include housing. Call for availability and pricing. Scholarships are available for first-time attendees. Call for more information or visit the website.

[N] INSPIRATIONAL WRITERS ALIVE!, 6038 Greenmont, Houston TX 77092. (713)686-7209. E-mail: martharexrog ers@aol.com. **State President:** Martha Rogers. Annual conference held 1st Saturday in August. **Open to students** and adults. Registration usually 60-75 conferees. First Baptist Church, Christian Life Center, Houston TX. Cost of conference: member $65; nonmember $75; seniors $60; at the door: members $85; nonmembers $100. Write for more information. "Annual IWA Contest presented. Manuscripts critiqued along with one-on-one 15 minute sessions with speaker(s). (Extra ms if there is room.)" For more information send for brochure or call Maxine Holder, (903)795-3986 or Pat Vance, (713)477-4968.

[N] [●] INSTITUTE FOR READERS THEATRE ANNUAL WORKSHOP, P.O. Box 17193, San Diego CA 92177. (619)276-1948. Fax: (858)576-7369. E-mail: wadams1@san.rr.com. Website: www.readerstheatre.net. **Director:** Dr. William Adams. Writer workshops geared toward beginner, intermediate and advanced levels. **Open to students.** Topics include oral interpretation; script writing (converting literary material into performable scripts); journal writing (for credit participants). Annual workshop held July 12-23, 2004. Registration limited to 50. Cost of workshop: $1,595; includes 2 weeks room and breakfast Britannia Hotel, London, England airfare and university credit (optional) are extra. Write for more information.

[N] INTERNATIONAL CREATIVE WRITING CAMP, 1725 11th St. SW, Minot ND 58701. (701)838-8472. Fax: (701)838-8472. E-mail: info@internationalmusiccamp.com. Website: internationalmusiccamp.com. **Camp Director:** Joseph T. Alme. Writer and illustrator workshops geared toward beginner, intermediate and advanced levels. **Open to students.** Sessions offered include those covering poems, plays, mystery stories, essays. Annual workshop held the last week in July of each summer. Registration limited to 20. The summer camp location at the International Peace Garden on the Border between Manitoba and North Dakota is an ideal site for generating creative thinking. Excellent food, housing and recreation facilities are available. Cost of workshop: $230. Write for more information.

[N] INTERNATIONAL WOMEN'S WRITING GUILD "REMEMBER THE MAGIC" ANNUAL SUMMER CONFERENCE, P.O. Box 810, Gracie Station, New York NY 10028. (212)737-7536. **Executive Director:** Hannelore Hahn. Writer and illustrator workshops geared toward all levels. Offers 65 different workshops—some are for children's book writers and illustrators. Also sponsors 13 other events throughout the US. Annual workshops. Workshops held 2nd or 3rd week in August. Length of each session: 1 hour-15 minutes; sessions take place for an entire week. Registration limited to 500. Cost of workshop: $375 (plus $375 room and board). Write for more information. "This workshop always takes place at Skidmore College in Saratoga Springs NY."

[N] JEWISH CHILDREN'S BOOK WRITER'S CONFERENCE, New York NY. E-mail: anna@olswanger.com. **Contact:** Anna Olswanger. "The 2003 conference featured faculty including Scott Blumenthal of Behrman House Publishers, Vice President and Publisher Beverly Horowitz of Bantam Delacorte DellYoung Readers Group, independent press founder Sallie Lowenstein, executive editor Helen Perelman of Hyperion Books, and literary agent and executive editor Ann Tobias of Handprint Books. Author Barbara Diamond Goldin, winner of the Sydney Taylor Body-of-Work Award, gave opening remarks. And the day included First Pages with the editors, a talk on the Association of Jewish Libraries' Sydney Taylor Manuscript Competition, and door prizes." Held Sunday, November 21, 2004; 9-5. Cost of workshop: includes Kosher breakfast and lunch. E-mail for more information.

[N] KIRKWOOD WRITERS' WORKSHOP: FROM PEN TO PAPER TO PUBLICATION, P.O. Box 2068, Cedar Rapids IA 52406. (319)398-1057. Fax: (319)398-5432. E-mail: heather.willard@kirkwood.edu. Website: www.kirkwood. edu/writersworkshop. **Program Director:** Heather Willard. Writer workshop geared toward all levels. "We do not have any illustrator workshops, but would be interested in making contact with illustration professionals for future workshops." **Open to students.** "We cover all facets of writing from childrens to adult, fiction to nonfiction. Some of our presenters include Katie Brogan (Writer's Digest Books), Don Harstad, Stephanie Gordon & Judy Enderle and many more. Stephanie and Judy focus primarily on children's writing. Two of their workshops are "First Pages: How to Grab an Editor" and "The Nitty Gritty of Editing." Annual event. Held in October. Writing facilities available: computer labs and atrium. Cost of workshop: $249; includes keynote and 3 days of workshops (3-4 each day, with 4-5 choices in each). Also available for extra charge: Brown Bag Lunch Panel, 1-on-1 critiques. Some workshops require a writing sample prior to the workshop. Write or e-mail for more information.

[✓] LEAGUE OF UTAH WRITERS' ROUNDUP, P.O. Box 460562, Leeds UT 84746. (435)879-8190 or (801)450-7310. Fax: (435)879-8190. E-mail: crofts@numucom.com. Website: www.luwrite.com. **Membership Chairman:** Dorothy

Crofts. Writer workshops geared toward beginner, intermediate, advanced. **Open to students**. Annual workshop. Roundup usually held 3rd weekend of September. Registration limited to approximately 400. 2004 conference location TBA. Cost of workshop: $125 for members/$160 for nonmembers; includes 4 meals, all workshops, all general sessions, a syllabus of all handout materials and a conference packet. "When requesting information, please provide an e-mail address and/or fax number."

N LIGONIER VALLEY WRITERS CONFERENCE, P.O. Box B, Ligonier PA 15658-1602. (724)537-3341. Fax: (724)537-0482. E-mail: sarshi@wpa.net. **Contact:** Sally Shirey. Writer programs geared toward all levels. **Open to students.** Annual conference features fiction, nonfiction, poetry and other genres. Annual conference. Held July 9-10, 2004. Cost of workshop: $200; includes full weekend, some meals, all social events. Write or call for more information.

N ⊕ LOS DERECHOS DE AUTOR, Mexico City, Mexico (52) 55 5291 2399. E-mail: rabkey@att.net.mx; murray@u nimedia.net.ms. Website: www.imagenypalabra.com. **Contact:** Judy Goldman, president, Imagen y Palabra, A.C., Co-Regional Advisor, SCBWI Mexico and/or Guillermo Murray, Co-Regional Advisor, SCBWI Mexico. "This will be a two day conference aimed at informing writers and illustrators about coyright (derechos de autor in Spanish). It will, most probably, be organized by several different professional associations and organizations like the SCBWI, Imagen y Palabra, A.C. (an association of writers and illustrators that work in Mexico), the CERLALC (Centro Regional del Libro para America Latina y el Caribe) and maybe the CANIEM (Cámara Nacional de la Industria Editorial Mexicana)." Imagen y Palabra/SCBWI Mexico organizes at least 2 conferences/workshops a year in Mexico. Conference held the end of May or beginning of June 2004. "Please contact Judy Goldman at rabkey@att.net.mx or Guillermo Murray at murray@unimedia.net .mx. Please check the website every once in a while because as soon as we have more information it will appear there."

MANHATTANVILLE WRITERS' WEEK, Manhattanville College, 2900 Purchase St., Purchase NY 10577-2103. (914)694-3425. Fax: (914)694-3488. E-mail: rdowd@mville.edu. Website: www.gps.mville.edu. **Dean, School of Graduate & Professional Studies:** Ruth Dowd. Writer workshops geared toward beginner, intermediate and advanced levels. **Open to students.** Writers' week offers a special workshop for writers interested in children's/young adult writing. We have featured such workshop leaders as: Patricia Gauch, Richard Peck, Elizabeth Winthrop and Janet Lisle. Annual workshop held last week in June. Length of each session: one week. Cost of workshop: $600 (non-credit); includes a full week of writing activities, 5-day workshop on children's literature, lectures, readings, sessions with editors and agents, etc. Workshop may be taken for 2 graduate credits. Write for more information.

✓ ⚅ MARITIME WRITERS' WORKSHOP, UNB College of Extended Learning, P.O. Box 4400, Fredericton, NB E3B 5A3 Canada. Phone/fax: (506)474-1144. E-mail: k4jc@unb.ca. Website: unb.ca/extend/writers/. **Coordinator:** Rhona Sawlor. Week-long workshop on writing for children, general approach, dealing with submitted material, geared to all levels and held in July. Annual workshop. 3 hours/day. Group workshop plus individual conferences, public readings, etc. Registration limited to 10/class. Cost of workshop: $395 tuition; meals and accommodations extra. Room and board on campus is approximately $320 for meals and a single room for the week. 10-20 ms pages due before conference (deadline announced). Scholarships available.

N MAUI WRITERS CONFERENCE, P.O. Box 1118, Kihei HI 96753. (888)974-8373 or (808)879-0061. Fax: (808)879-6233. E-mail: writers@maui.net. Website: www.mauiwriters.com. **Director:** Shannon Tullius. Writer workshops geared toward beginner, intermediate, advanced. **Open to students.** "We offer a small children's writing section covering picture books, middle grade and young adult. We invite one *New York Times* Bestselling Author and agents and editors, who give consultations." Annual workshop. Workshop held Labor Day weekend. Cost includes admittance to all conference sessions and classes only—no airfare, food or consultations.

MENDOCINO COAST WRITERS CONFERENCE, College of the Redwoods, 1211 Del Mar Dr., Ft. Bragg CA 95437. (707)964-7735. E-mail: mcwcreg@direcway.com. Website: www.mcwc.org. **Registrar:** Stephen Garber. Writing workshops geared toward beginner, intermediate and advanced levels. Annual conference in its 15th year. Conference takes place in June. Registration limited to 99. Conference is held on the campus of College of Redwoods ocean view Ft. Bragg campus. Cost of conference (early registration): $275-325, includes Friday and Saturday lecture sessions, 2 social events and most meals; editor/agent panels. $315 includes all of the above plus Thursday intensive workshops (choice of one) in poetry, fiction, nonfiction, screen, mystery, humor and YA/children's. After April 20, 2004 price increases to $325-375. "What we offer for children's writers varies from year to year."

MIDLAND WRITERS CONFERENCE, Grace A. Dow Memorial Library, 1710 W. St. Andrews, Midland MI 48640-2698. (517)837-3435. Fax: (517)837-3468. E-mail: ajarvis@midland-mi.org. Website: www.midland-mi.org/gracedowlibra ry. **Conference Chair:** Ann Jarvis. **Open to students.** Writer and illustrator workshops geared toward all levels. "Each year, we offer a topic of interest to writers of children's literature." Last year's workshops: Cynthia Laferle—Marketing Essays; Margo Lagattua—Dreaming of Getting Your Poetry Published?; Boyd Miller—Self-publishing; John Smolens—Perils of Publishing. Annual workshop. Workshops held usually second Saturday in June. Length of each session: concurrently, 4 1-hour sessions repeated in the afternoon. Maximum class size: 50. "We are a public library." Cost of workshop: $60; includes choice of workshops and the keynote speech given by a prominent author (last year Michael Beschloss). Write for more information.

MIDWEST WRITERS WORKSHOP, Department of Journalism, Ball State University, Muncie IN 47306. (765)282-1055. Fax: (765)285-7997. **Director:** Earl L. Conn. Writer workshops geared toward intermediate level. Topics include most genres. Past workshop presenters include Joyce Carol Oates, James Alexander Thom, Bill Brashler and Richard

Lederer. Workshop also includes ms evaluation and a writing contest. Annual workshop. Workshop will be held July 29-31, 2004. Registration tentatively limited to 125. Most meals included. Offers scholarships. Write for more information.

MONTROSE CHRISTIAN WRITER'S CONFERENCE, 5 Locust St., Montrose PA 18801-1112. (570)278-1001. Fax: (570)278-3061. E-mail: mbc@montrosebible.org. Website: www.montrosebible.org. **Executive Director:** Jim Fahringer. **Secretary-Registrar:** Donna Kosik. **Open to adults and students.** Writer workshops geared toward beginner, intermediate and advanced levels. Annual workshop. Workshop held in July. Cost of workshop: $130 tuition. Write for more information.

MOUNT HERMON CHRISTIAN WRITERS CONFERENCE, Mount Hermon Christian Conference Center, P.O. Box 413, Mount Hermon CA 95041-0413. (831)335-4466. Fax: (831)335-9413. E-mail: rachelw@mhcamps.org. Website: www.mounthermon.org/writers. **Director of Adult Ministries:** David R. Talbott. Writer workshops geared toward all levels. **Open to students over 16 years.** Emphasizes religious writing for children via books, articles; Sunday school curriculum; marketing. Classes offered include: Suitable Style for Children; Everything You Need to Know to Write and Market Your Children's Book; Take-Home Papers for Children. Workshops held annually over Palm Sunday weekend: April 6-10, 2004 and March 18-22, 2005. Length of each session: 5-day residential conferences held annually. Registration limited 45/class, but most are 20-30. Conference center with hotel-style accommodations. Cost of workshop: $650-950 variable; includes tuition, resource notebook, refreshment breaks, full room and board for 13 meals and 4 nights. Brochure available December 1, annually. Write or e-mail for more information or call toll-free to 1-888-MH-CAMPS.

THE NATIONAL WRITERS ASSOCIATION FOUNDATION CONFERENCE, 3140 S. Peoria #295, Aurora CO 80014. (303)841-0246. Website: www.nationalwriters.com. **Conference Coordinator:** Anita Whelchel. Writer workshops geared toward all levels. Classes offered include marketing, agenting, "What's Hot in the Market." Annual workshop. In 2004 the workshop will be held in Denver, Colorado, June 12-14. Write for more information or check our website.

NEW JERSEY SOCIETY OF CHRISTIAN WRITERS FALL SEMINAR, P.O. Box 405, Millville NJ 08332-0405. (856)327-1231. Fax: (856)327-0291. E-mail: daystar405@aol.com. Website: www.njscw.com. **Founder/Director:** Dr. Mary Ann Diorio. Writer workshops geared toward beginner, intermediate. **Open to students.** Annual workshop. Workshop held first Saturday in November. Cost of workshop: $75 includes lunch. Write for more information. "We have one guest speaker per conference—usually 30-50 attendees."

NORTH CAROLINA WRITERS' NETWORK FALL CONFERENCE, P.O. Box 954, Carrboro NC 27510-0954. (919)967-9540. Fax: (919)929-0535. E-mail: mail@ncwriters.org. Website: www.ncwriters.org. **Program Coordinator:** Carol Henderson. Writing workshops geared toward beginner, intermediate, advanced and professional levels. **Open to students.** "We offer workshops and critique sessions in a variety of genres: fiction, poetry, creative nonfiction, children's. Past young adult and children's writing faculty included: Louise Hawes, Jackie Ogburn, Clay Carmichael, Carol Boston Weatherford. Annual conference. Conference held November 14-16, 2003 in Wilmington, NC. Readings done by Andrei Codrescu, Haven Kimmel and others. Cost of workshop: approximately $200/NCWN members, $255/nonmembers; includes workshops, panel discussions, round table discussions, social activities and 2 meals. "Cost does not include fee for critique sessions or accommodations."

OHIO KENTUCKY INDIANA CHILDREN'S LITERATURE CONFERENCE, % Greater Cincinnati Library Consortium (GCLC), 2181 Victory Parkway, Suite 214, Cincinnati OH 45206-2855. (513)751-4422. Fax: (513)751-0463. E-mail: gclc@gclc-lib.org. Website: www.gclc-lib.org. **Staff Development Coordinator:** Judy Malone. Writer and illustrator conference geared toward all levels. **Open to students.** Annual conference. Emphasizes multicultural literature for children and young adults. Conference held annually in November. Contact GCLC for more information. Registration limited to 250. Cost of conference: $50; includes registration/attendance at all workshop sessions, Tri-state Authors and Illustrators of Childrens Books Directory, continental breakfast, lunch, author/illustrator signings. E-mail or write for more information.

OKLAHOMA WRITERS' FEDERATION, INC. ANNUAL CONFERENCE, P.O. Box 2654, Stillwater OK 74076-2654. (405)408-2141. Fax: (405)377-0992. E-mail: wileykat@cox.net. Website: www.owfi.org. **President:** Moira Wiley. Writer workshops geared toward all levels. Illustrator workshops geared toward beginner level. **Open to students.** "During 2003 event, Emily Mitchell, assistant editor with Charlesbridge Publishing, presented a session titled The Basics of Children's Book Contracts (Law Degree Not Required). Other noteworthy topics cover the basics of writing, publishing and marketing in any genre." Annual conference. Held April 30-May 1, 2004. Registration limted to 420. Writing facilities available: book room, autograph party, free information room. Cost of workshop: $100 before April 15, 2004; $125 after April 15, 2004; includes 2-day conference—all events including 2 banquets and one 10-minute appointment with an attending editor or agent of your choice (must be reserved in advance). "If writers would like to participate in the writing contest, they must become members of OWFL. You don't have to be a member to attend though." Write or e-mail for more information.

OUTDOOR WRITERS ASSOCIATION OF AMERICA ANNUAL CONFERENCE, 158 Lower Georges Valley Rd., Spring Mills PA 16875. (814)364-9557. Fax: (814)364-9558. E-mail: eking4owaa@cs.com. **Meeting Planner:** Eileen King. Writer workshops geared toward all levels. Annual workshop. Workshop held in June. Cost of workshop: $325; includes attendance at all workshops and most meals. Attendees must have prior approval from Executive Director before attendance is permitted. Write for more information.

OZARK CREATIVE WRITERS, INC. CONFERENCE, 6817 Gingerbread Lane, Little Rock AR 72204. (501)565-8889. E-mail: pvining@aristotle.net. Website: www.ozarkcreativewriters.org. **Counselor:** Peggy Vining. **Open to students.**

Writer's workshops geared to all levels. "All forms of the creative process dealing with the literary arts. We sometimes include songwriting. We invite excellent speakers who are selling authors. We also promote writing by providing competitions in all genres." Always the second full weekend in October at Inn of the Ozarks in Eureka Springs AR (a resort town). Morning sessions are given to main attraction author . . . six 1-hour satellite speakers during each of the 2 afternoons. Two banquets. "Approximately 200 attend the conference yearly . . . many others enter the creative writing competition." Cost of registration/contest entry fee approximately $60-70. Includes entrance to all sessions, contest entry fees. "This does not include banquet meals or lodging. We block off 70 rooms prior to August 15 for OCW guests." Send #10 SASE for brochure by May 1st. "Reserve early."

PACIFIC NORTHWEST WRITER ASSN. SUMMER WRITER'S CONFERENCE, P.O. Box 2016, Edmonds WA 98020 (425)673-2665. E-mail: staff@pnwa.org. Website: www.pnwa.org. **Association Executive:** Dana Murphy-Love. Writer conference geared toward beginner, intermediate, advanced and professional levels. **Open to students.** Sample sessions: Constructing a Children's Book; The Art of Promoting Your Book, Breathing Life Into Your Characters, Writing a Home-run Book for Young Readers. Annual conference. Held July 15-18, 2004. Cost of conference: $350/members (limited scholarships available to members); $400/nonmember; includes all conference materials, continental breakfasts, refreshments, awards ceremony dessert reception, keynote dinners, appointments with editors/agents. "There are approximately 30 agents/editors that attend this conference. The Literary Contest Winners are announced as well. Conference is at the Hilton Seattle Airport, Seattle, WA."

PERSPECTIVES IN CHILDREN'S LITERATURE CONFERENCE, School of Education, 226 Furcolo Hall, University of Massachusetts, Amherst MA 01003-3035. (413)545-4325 or (413)545-1116. Fax: (413)545-2879. E-mail: childlit@educ.umass.edu. Website: www.unix.oit.umass.edu/~childlit. **Coordinators of Conference:** Melissa Price and Rachel Kopke. Writer and illustrator workshops geared to all levels. Conference 2004 will feature Jerry Pinkney and Jacqueline Woodson as keynote speakers. Additional presenters include Gloria-Jean Pinkney, Leslea Newman, Ruth Sanderson, Jane Yolen and Jan Cheripko. Presenters talk about what inspires them, how they bring their stories to life and what their visions are for the future. Next conference will be held on Saturday, March 27, 2004, at the University of Massachusetts. For more information contact coordinators by phone, fax or e-mail."

GARY PROVOST'S WRITERS RETREAT WORKSHOP. (800)642-2494 (for brochure). E-mail: jssitzes@aol.com. Website: www.writersretreatworkshop.com. **Director:** Jason Sitzes. Writer workshops geared toward beginner, intermediate and advanced levels. Workshops are appropriate for writers of full length novels for children/YA. Also, for writers of all novels or narrative nonfiction. Annual workshop. Workshops held last 10 days of May. Registration limited to small groups: beginners and advanced. Writing facilities available: private rooms with desks. Cost of workshop: $1,695; includes tuition, food and lodging for nine nights, daily classes, writing space, time and assignments, consultation and instruction. Requirements: short synopsis required to determine appropriateness of novel for our nuts and bolts approach to getting the work in shape for publication. Write for more information. For complete details, call 800 number or e-mail.

ROBERT QUACKENBUSH'S CHILDREN'S BOOK WRITING AND ILLUSTRATING WORKSHOP, 460 E. 79th St., New York NY 10021-1443. Phone/fax: (212)861-2761. E-mail: rqstudios@aol.com. (E-mail inquirers please include mailing address). Website: www.rquackenbush.com. **Contact:** Robert Quackenbush. Writer and illustrator workshops geared toward all levels. **Open to students**. Four-day extensive workshop on writing and illustrating books for children, emphasizes picture books from start to finish. Also covered is writing fiction and nonfiction for middle grades and young adults, if that is the attendees' interest. Current trends in illustration are also covered. This July workshop is a full 4-day (9 a.m.-4 p.m) extensive course. Next workshop July 12-15, 2004. Registration limited to 10/class. Writing and/or art facilities available; work on the premises; art supply store nearby. Cost of workshop: $650 for instruction. Cost of workshop includes instruction in preparation of a ms and/or book dummy ready to submit to publishers. Class limited to 10 members. Attendees are responsible for arranging their own hotel and meals, although suggestions are given on request for places to stay and eat. "This unique workshop, held annually since 1982, provides the opportunity to work with Robert Quackenbush, a prolific author and illustrator of children's books with more than 170 fiction and nonfiction books for young readers to his credit, including mysteries, biographies and song-books. The workshop attracts both professional and beginning writers and artists of different ages from all over the world." Recommended by Foder's *Great American Learning Vacations*.

ROCKY MOUNTAIN RETREATS FOR WRITERS & ARTISTS, 81 Cree Court, Lyons CO 80540. (303)823-0530. E-mail: ddebord@indra.com. Website: www.expressionretreats.com. **Director:** Deborah DeBord. Writers and illustrator workshops geared to all levels. **Open to students.** Includes information on releasing creative energy, identifying strengths and interests, balancing busy lives, marketing creative works. Monthly conference. Registration limited to 4 per session. Writing studio, weaving studio, private facilities available. Cost of workshop: $1,234/week; includes room, meals, materials, instruction. "Treat yourself to a week of mountain air, sun, and personal expression. Flourish with the opportunity for sustained work punctuated by structured experiences designed to release the artist's creative energies. Relax over candlelit gourmet meals followed by fireside discussions of the day's efforts. Discover the rhythm of filling the artistic well and drawing on its abundant resources."

SAGE HILL WRITING EXPERIENCE, Writing Children's & Young Adult Fiction Workshop, Box 1731, Saskatoon, SK S7K 3S1 Canada. Phone/fax: (306)652-7395. E-mail: sage.hill@sasktel.net. Website: www.lights.com/sagehill. **Executive Director:** Steven Ross Smith. Writer conference geared toward intermediate level. This program occurs every 2 or 3 years, but the Sage Hill Conference is annual. Writing Young Adult fiction will be offered in 2004. Conference held July 25-August 5. Registration limited to 6 participants for this program, and to 37 for full program. Cost of conference: $795; includes instruction, meals, accommodation. Require ms samples prior to registration. Write or visit the website for more information.

SAN DIEGO STATE UNIVERSITY WRITERS' CONFERENCE, The College of Extended Studies, Gateway Center: Room 2503, San Diego CA 92182-1920. (619)594-2517. Fax: (619)594-8566. E-mail: extended.std@sdsu.edu. Website: www.ces.sdsu.edu. **Conference Facilitator:** Kevin Carter. Writer workshops geared toward beginner, intermediate and advanced levels. Emphasizes nonfiction, fiction, screenwriting, advanced novel writing; includes sessions specific to writing and illustrating for children. Workshops offered by children's editors, agents and writers. Workshops held third weekend in January each year. Registration limited. Cost of workshop: approximately $300. Write for more information or see our home page at the above website.

THE WILLIAM SAROYAN WRITER'S CONFERENCE, P.O. Box 5331, Fresno CA 93755-5331. Phone/fax: (559)224-2516. E-mail: law@pacbell.net. **President:** Linda West. **Conference Chair:** Stephen Mette. Writer and illustrator workshops geared toward advanced level. **Open to Students.** Past sessions have featured Barbara Kuroff, editorial director of Writer's Digest Books and Andrea Brown, agent for children's book authors and illustrators. Annual conference. Conference held March, 2004 at Piccadilly Inn-airport. Registration limited to 185. Cost of conference: $300. Friday noon to Sunday noon workshops (35 to choose from) most meals, critique groups, one-on-ones with agents, editors. Write for more information. "We try to cover a wide variety of writing. Children's books would be one topic of many."

SOCIETY OF SOUTHWESTERN AUTHORS' WRANGLING WITH WRITING, P.O. Box 30355, Tucson AZ 85751-0355. (520)546-9382. Fax: (520)296-0409. E-mail: wporter202@aol.com; apatrillo@earthlink.net. Website: www.az starnet.com/nonprofit/ssa. **Conference Director:** Penny Porter. Writer workshops geared toward all genres. "Limited scholarships available." Sessions include Writing and Publishing the Young Adult Novel, What Agents Want to See in a Children's Book, Writing Books for Young Children. "We always have several children's book editors and agents interested in meeting with children's writers." Annual workshop held January 30-31, 2004. Registration limited to 500—usually 300-400 people attend. Hotel rooms have dataports for internet access. Tucson has many art galleries. Tentative cost: $250 nonmembers, $220 for SSA members; includes 3 meals and 2 continental breakfasts, all workshop sessions—individual appointments with agents and editors are extra. Hotel accommodations are not included. "Some editors and agents like to see mss prior to the conference; information about requirements is in the brochure. If you want a portfolio of artwork critiqued, please contact us directly, and we'll try to accommodate you." Write for more information. SSA has put on this conference for over 25 years now. "It's hands-on, it's friendly, and every year writers sell their manuscripts."

SOUTH FLORIDA WRITERS' CONFERENCE, P.O. Box 570415, Miami FL 33257-0415, (786)877-0136. Fax: (305)233-8680. E-mail: greenfie@hotmail.com. **Conference Director:** Henry Greenfield. Writer conference geared toward beginner and intermediate levels. **Open to students.** Sample of sessions include Finding a Niche in the Children's Market, Riding the Boon in Young Adult Fiction, Finding Your Audience, How to Make Plots Work, Preparing a Manuscript for Submission. Annual conference. Conference held the week of Mother's Day at Barry University in Miami, FL. Writing facilities available: classrooms, dorms. Cost of conference: $200 (20% early registration by April 15th); includes all events beginning Friday afternoon through Sunday noon; banquet and continental breakfast; provides overnight accommodations: double $65/night with meals, single $75 with meals. Individual ms evaluations $35 for 15 minutes with agent, editor or author. Sponsors contest. Judges are professional writers. Prizes of $3,200 total for plays, novels, short fiction, poetry, nonfiction, juveniles. Deadline is in April. Send for Guidelines with SASE. Write for more information. "Conference focuses on short fiction, novels, poetry, juveniles, nonfiction, freelancing, playwriting, screenwriting, self-promotion, publication, e-books. Site: Barry University main campus. Tropical setting, university-type classrooms, theaters, meal service, housing. Last year's events included stage and play readings and individual manuscript evaluations by agents, editors, authors. Panelists included authors Edna Buchanan, John Dufresne, Joyce Sweeney, Marcia Preston and others. Agents included Jeff Herman, Elizabeth Pomada, Michael Larsen, James Schiavone, Janell Agyeman. Mandy Greenfield, Lois Blume, Michael Sasser, Carey Martin, Susan Cumins, Judi Welsh, and others among conference editors, packagers, publishers, poets, playwrights, etc.

SOUTHWEST WRITERS, 8200 Mountain Rd., NE, Suite 106, Albuquerque NM 87110-7835. (505)265-9485. Fax: (505)265-9483. E-mail: swriters@aol.com. Website: www.southwestwriters.org. **Open to adults and students**. Writer workshops geared toward all genres at all levels of writing. Various aspects of writing covered including children's. Examples from conferences: Preconference workshops on the juvenile/young adult/novel taught by Penny Durant; SCBWI Panel, Preconference session on generating ideas by Elsie Karr Kreischer, conference lectures on characterization by Kreischer, lecture by Kelly White of *Girl's Life* magazine. We emphasize everything from idea generating to selling to editors. There will be a few sessions on children's writing. Annual conference. Last conference was September 5-8, 2002. Length of sessions varies. Cost of workshop: started at $365, included all sessions, 4 meals, and 1 editor/agent appointment. Conference 2003 cancelled and replaced by several 1-day workshops. Regular conference (3-day) to resume 2004. Also offers critique groups (for $60/year, offers 2 monthly meetings, monthly newsletter, annual writing contest and occasional workshops). Write for more information.

SPLIT ROCK ARTS PROGRAM, University of Minnesota, 360 Coffey Hall, 1420 Eckles Ave., St. Paul MN 55108-6084. (612)625-8100. Fax: (612)624-6210. E-mail: srap@cce.umn.edu. Website: www.cce.umn.edu/splitrockarts/. Writing workshops including poetry, stories, memoirs, novels and personal essays geared toward intermediate, advanced and professional levels. Workshops begin in July for 5 weeks. Optional college credits available. Registration limited to 16/workshop.

Cost of workshop: $545 and up. On-campus housing and food services available. Printed and online catalogs available in early March.

N STEAMBOAT SPRINGS WRITERS CONFERENCE, P.O. Box 774284, Steamboat Springs CO 80477. (970)879-8079. E-mail: MsHFreiberger@cs.com. Website: www.steamboatwriters.com. **Conference Director:** Harriet Freiberger. Writers' workshops geared toward intermediate levels. **Open to students.** Some years offer topics specific to children's writing. Annual conference since 1982. Workshops will be July 17, 2004. Registration limited to 35. Cost of workshop: $45; includes 4 seminars and luncheon. Write, e-mail or see website for more information.

N SUNSHINE COAST FESTIVAL OF THE WRITTEN ARTS, P.O. Box 2299, Sechelt, BC V0N-3A0 Canada. (604)885-9631, 1-800-565-9631. Fax: (604)885-3967. E-mail: info@writersfestival.ca. Website: www.writersfestival.ca. **Festival Producer:** Gail Bull. Writer and illustrator workshops geared toward professional level. **Open to Students.** Annual literary festival held every August. Pavilion seating 500/event. Festival pass $175; individual events $12. Fee schedule available upon request.

N ⊕ SYDNEY CHILDREN'S AND ILLUSTRATORS NETWORK, The Hughenden Boutique Hotel, 14 Queen St., Woollahra NSW 2025 Australia. (61) 2 9363 4863. Fax: (61) 2 9371 9645. E-mail: gervays@bigpond.com. Website: www.hughendenhotel.com.au (writer's events). **Contact:** Susanne Gervay. Writer and illustrator workshops geared toward professionals. Topics emphasized enclude networking, information and expertise about Australian children's publishing industry. Workshop held the first Wednesday of every month, except for January, commencing at 11 a.m. Registration limited to 50. Writing facilities available: internet and conference facilities. Cost of workshop: $150 AUS; includes accomodation for one night at The Hughenden Boutique Hotel, breakfast, lunch. Must be a published children's author or illustrator to attend. Write for more information. "This is a professional meeting which aims at an interchange of ideas and information between professional children's authors and illustrators. Editors and other invited guests speak from time to time."

N TAOS INSTITUTE OF ARTS, 108 Civic Plaza Dr., Taos NM 87571. (505)758-2793. Fax: (505)737-2466. E-mail: Tia@newmex.com. Website: www.TiaTaos.com.
   • TIA has 15-20 week-long writing workshops during the summer.
Curriculum Director: Susan Mihalic. Writer workshop geared toward beginner, intermediate and advanced levels. **Open to students.** "Writing for children is one of our week-long workshops—it's a survey course. We also offer short and long fiction, mystery, science fiction, travel writing, and writing for magazines." Annual workshop. Workshop held between June and October. Registration limited to 12. Writing facilities available: "Taos is an art colony with a large population of writers." Cost of workshop: starts at $420 plus $40 regular fee. Master classes are more; includes tuition only—not food or lodging. Requirements "depend on what each instructor wants to see." Write for more information.

TAOS SUMMER WRITERS' CONFERENCE, University of New Mexico, Humanities 255, Albuquerque NM 87131. (505)277.6248. Fax: (505)277-5573. E-mail: swarner@unm.edu. Website: www.unm.edu/~taosconf. **Director:** Sharon Oard Warner. Writing workshops geared toward all levels. **Open to students.** Must be 18 years old. "Our conference offers both weekend and week-long conferences, not only in children's writing, but also adult fiction (novel, short story), creative nonfiction, poetry and screenwriting." Annual conference held July 12-18, 2003—(usually 3rd week of July). Maximum of 12 people per workshop. Usually 5 weekend workshops and 8- or 10-week-long workshops. "We provide an on-site computer room." Cost of conference: approximately $490/weeklong; $240/weekend; includes tuition, opening and closing night dinner, visit to historic D.H. Lawrence ranch. All the readings by instructors, Wednesday night entertainment. Lodging and meals extra but we offer a reduced rate at the Sagebrush Inn in Taos, Comfort Suites; breakfast included. Merit scholarships and D.H. Lawrence fellowship available. Write for more information.

N TEXAS MOUNTAIN TRAIL WRITERS' WINTER RETREAT, P.O. Box 1133, Alpine TX 79831. (432)837-2919. E-mail: rcross@brooksdata.net. **President:** Reba Cross Seals. Writer and illustrator workshops geared toward beginner, intermediate and advanced levels. **Open to students.** Topics emphasized include: inside information from editors of children's magazines; children's illustrator hints on collaboration; children's writer tips toward publication. Conference held last weekend in February. Registration limited to 30-35. Writing facilities available: large comfortable conference room, nearby dining, mountain tourist attractions. Cost of workshop: $120; includes casual, friendly entertainment, weekend conference and 4 meals, one-on-one visits with authors, illustrators, etc. Write for more information. "Nearby attractions include McDonald Observatory, Ft. Davis and Big Bend National Park."

THE 21ST CENTURY WRITER'S GET-A-WAY, 625 Schuring, Suite B, Portage MI 49024-5106. (866)888-4225. Fax: (509)694-1153. E-mail: jfriendspub@aol.com. Website: justfriendspublishing.com. **Public Relations Manager:** John Williams. Workshops geared toward new aspiring authors. Sessions offered include "Marketing Strategies For The 21st Century." **Open to students.** In this workshop our workshop facilitator brings the latest information on how to jumpstart your book including information on software for graphic arts designs. Workshop held twice a year, April 25 and August 23, 2003. Held at Wayne State University, McGregor Conference Center Room J Detroit MI 48201. Cost of workshop: $125. The fee includes: 4 workshops, a writing clinic, continental breakfast, lunch, and a notebook. Write for a full-color brochure.

M UMKC/WRITERS PLACE WRITERS WORKSHOPS, 5300 Rockhill Rd., Kansas City MO 64110-2450. (816)235-2736. Fax: (816)235-5279. E-mail: seatons@umkc.edu. **Contact:** Kathi Wittfield. Writer workshops geared toward intermediate, advanced and professional levels. Workshops open to students and community. Semi-annual workshops. Workshops held in fall and spring. Cost of workshop varies. Write for more information.

UNIVERSITY OF THE NATIONS SCHOOL OF WRITING AND WRITERS WORKSHOPS, YWAM Woodcrest, P.O. Box 1380, Lindale TX 75771-1380. (903)882-WOOD [9663]. Fax: (903)882-1161. E-mail: writingschooltx@yahoo.com. Website: www.ywamwoodcrest.com. **School Leader:** Carol Scott. Writer workshops geared toward beginner, intermediate, advanced levels. **Open to students**. Children's writing workshops include: Writing Children's Picture Books with Mona Gansberg Hodgson. Workshops held September 23-December 14, 2004. Workshops held various weeks during that time. Cost for workshop: $20 registration fee (nonrefundable) plus $175 tuition per week (the 1st week) plus $175/ week if staying on our campus. ($125 tuition each additional week.). $175 tuition/week covers lectures, critique groups, hands-on-training. Students may make own arrangements for lodging and meals. If you want college credit for the workshop or are taking the entire 12-week school of writing, you must have completed the YWAM's Discipleship Training School first. Write for more information. "Although we are associated with the Youth with A Mission missionary group, we welcome inquiries from all interested parties–not only missionaries."

N ⬛ VANCOUVER INTERNATIONAL WRITERS FESTIVAL, 1398 Cartwright St., Vancouver, BC V6H 3R8 Canada. (604)681-6330. Fax: (604)681-8400. E-mail: viwf@writersfest.bc.ca. Website: www.writersfest.bc.ca. **Artistic Director:** Alma Lee. Annual literary festival. The Vancouver International Writers Festival strives to encourage an appreciation of literature and to promote literacy by providing a forum where writers and readers can interact. This is accomplished by the production of special events and an annual Festival which feature writers from a variety of countries whose work is compelling and diverse. The Festival attracts over 11,000 people and presents approximately 50 events in six venues during six days on Granville Island, located in the heart of Vancouver. The first 4 days of the festival are programmed for elementary and secondary school students and teachers. Held in late October (6-day festival). All writers who participate are invited by the A.D. The events are open to anyone who wishes to purchase tickets. Cost of events ranges from $10-25.

✓ ⬛ THE VICTORIA SCHOOL OF WRITING, 306-620 View St., Victoria, British Columbia V8W 1J6 Canada. (250)595-3000. E-mail: vicwrite@islandnet.com. Website: www.islandnet.com/vicwrite. **Director:** John Gould. Writer conference geared toward intermediate level. In the 2004 conference there may be 1 workshop on writing for children and young adults. Annual conference. Workshop third week of July. Registration limited to 12/workshop. Conference includes close mentoring from established writers. Cost of conference: $575 (Canada); includes tuition and some meals. To attend, submit 3-10 pages of writing samples. Write for more information.

WESLEYAN WRITERS CONFERENCE, Wesleyan University, Middletown CT 06459. (860)685-3604. Fax: (860)685-2441. E-mail: agreene@wesleyan.edu. Website: www.wesleyan.edu/writers. **Director:** Anne Greene. Writer workshops geared toward all levels. "This conference is useful for writers interested in how to structure a story, poem or nonfiction piece. Although we don't always offer classes in writing for children, the advice about structuring a piece is useful for writers of any sort, no matter who their audience is." Classes in the novel, short story, fiction techniques, poetry, journalism and literary nonfiction. Guest speakers and panels offer discussion of fiction, poetry, reviewing, editing and publishing. Individual ms consultations available. Conference held annually the last week in June. Length of each session: 6 days. "Usually, there are 100 participants at the Conference." Classrooms, meals, lodging and word processing facilities available on campus. Cost of workshop: tuition—$530, room—$120, meals (required of all participants)—$190. "Anyone may register; people who want financial aid must submit their work and be selected by scholarship judges." Call for a brochure or check website.

WHIDBEY ISLAND WRITERS' CONFERENCE, P.O. Box 1289, Langley WA 98260. (360)331-6714. E-mail: writers @whidbey.com. Website: www.whidbey.com/writers. Director: Celeste Mergens. Writer and illustrator workshops geared toward beginner, intermediate and advanced levels. **Open to students**. Topics include "Writing for Children," "Writing in a Bunny Eat Bunny World," "The Art of Revision." Annual conference in March. Registration limited to 275. Cost of conference: $325; includes all workshops and events, 2 receptions, activities and daily luncheons. Those who register before September 1st get an early-bird discount rate of just $275. Volunteers who commit to work 8-10 hours either before, during, or after the conference may receive the volunteer discount rate of $180. "For writing consultations participants pay $35 for 20 minutes to submit the first five pages of a chapter book, youth novel or entire picture book idea with a written 1-page synopsis." Write, e-mail or check website for more information. "This is a uniquely personable weekend that is designed to be highly interactive." 2003 Children's Presenters were Bruce Coville, Paula Danziger, Michael Stearns and Kirby Larson.

WILLAMETTE WRITERS ANNUAL WRITERS CONFERENCE, 9045 SW Barbur Blvd., Suite 5A, Portland OR 97219. (503)452-1592. Fax: (503)452-0372. E-mail: wilwrite@willamettewriters.com. Website: www.willamettewriters.com. **Office Manager:** Bill Johnson. Writer workshops geared toward all levels. Emphasizes all areas of writing, including children's and young adult. Opportunities to meet one-on-one with leading literary agents and editors. Workshops held in August. Cost of conference: $285-350; includes membership.

N WINTER POETRY & PROSE GETAWAY IN CAPE MAY, 18 N. Richards Ave., Ventnor NJ 08406. (609)823-5076. E-mail: info@wintergetaway.com. Website: wintergetaway.com. **Director:** Peter Murphy. Writer workshops geared toward all levels. **Open to students (18 years and over).** "Writing for Children—You will learn to develop character, plot, setting, points of view. There will also be a discussion of genres in juvenile literature, of voice, of detail and of revision. Choose one of two sections: Picture books and younger readers or middle graders and teens." Annual workshop. Workshop held January 16-19, 2004. Registration limited to 7 writers in each workshop. Writing/art facilities available in hotel meeting and ballrooms. Cost of workshop: $445 double, $580 single, $275 commuter; double and single includes 3 nights at the Grand Hotel of Cape May with 3 breakfasts, lunches and snacks, most workshops and evening activities. Commuter rate includes workshop, snacks, evening activities and lunch on Saturday and Sunday. Write for more information. "The Winter Poetry & Prose Getaway is well known for its challenging and supportive atmosphere which encourages imaginative risk taking and promotes freedom and transformation in each participant's creative work."

WRITE! CANADA, (formerly God Uses Ink Conference), M.I.P. Box 487, Markham, ON L3R 3R1 Canada. (905)471-1447. Fax: (905)471-6912. E-mail: info@thewordguild.com. Website: www.thewordguild.com. Estab. 1984. Annual conference for writers who are Christian. Hosted by The Word Guild, an association of Canadian writers and editors who are Christian. The Word Guild seeks to connect, develop, and promote its members. Keynote speaker, continuing classes, workshops, panels, editor appointments, reading times, critiques, and more. For all levels of writers from beginner to professional. Held at a retreat center in Guelph ON. June 17-19, 2004. Keynote speaker is Linda Hall. Conference is open to anyone.

WRITE ON THE SOUND WRITERS CONFERENCE, 700 Main St., Edmonds WA 98020-3032. (425)771-0228. Fax: (425)771-0253. E-mail: wots@ci.edmonds.wa.us. Website: www.ci.edmonds.wa.us. **Cultural Resources Coordinator:** Frances Chapin. Writer workshops geared toward beginner, intermediate, advanced and professional levels with some sessions on writing for children. Annual conference held "in Edmonds on Puget Sound on the first weekend in October with 2 full days of a variety of lectures and workshops." 2004 conference held October 2-3. Registration limited to 200. Cost of workshop: approximately $65/day, or $99 for the weekend, includes 4 workshops daily plus one ticket to keynote lecture. Brochures are mailed in August. Attendees must preregister. Write, e-mail or call for brochure. Writing contest for conference participants.

WRITERS' LEAGUE OF TEXAS WORKSHOP SERIES, 1501 W. Fifth St., Suite E-2, Austin TX 78703. (512)499-8914. Fax: (512)499-0441. E-mail: wlt@writersleague.org. Website: www.writersleague.org. **Contact:** Beverly Horne. Writer workshops and conferences geared toward adults. Annual conferences. Classes are held during the week, and workshops are held on Saturdays during March, April, May, September, October and November. Annual Teddy Children's Book Award of $1,000 presented each fall to book published from June 1 to May 1. Write for more information.

WRITE-TO-PUBLISH CONFERENCE, 9731 N. Fox Glen Dr., #6F, Niles IL 60714-4222. (847)296-3964. Fax: (847)296-0754. E-mail: lin@writetopublish.com. Website: www.WTPublish.com. **Director:** Lin Johnson. Writer workshops geared toward all levels. **Open to students.** Conference is focused for the Christian market and includes classes on writing for children. Annual conference held June 2-5, 2004. Cost of conference: $350; includes conference and banquet. For information, call (847)299-4755 or e-mail brochure@writetopublish.com. Conference takes place at Wheaton College in the Chicago area.

WRITING CHILDREN'S FICTION, Rice University, Houston TX 77005. (713)348-4803. Fax: (713)348-5213. E-mail: scs@rice.edu. Website: www.scs.rice.edu. **Contact:** School of Continuing Studies. Weekly evening children's writing courses and workshops geared toward all levels held in most fall and spring semesters. Topics include issues in children's publishing, censorship, multiculturalism, dealing with sensitive subjects, submissions/formatting, the journal as resource, the markets—finding your niche, working with an editor, the agent/author connection, the role of research, and contract negotiation. Contact Rice Continuing Studies for current information on course offerings.

WRITING FOR CHILDREN WITH JOAN CAVANAUGH, (formerly Writing for Children and Children's Book Illustration with Joan Cavanaugh), Taos Institute of Arts, 108 Civic Plaza Dr., Taos NM 87571. (505)758-2793. E-mail: tia@taosnet.com. Website: www.tiataos.com. **Curriculum Director:** Susan Mihalic. Workshops geared toward beginner, intermediate and advanced levels. **Open to students over 18**. Workshops take place March-October 2002. Check website for dates. Registration limited to 12. All classroom needs are accommodated, but students buy/bring materials, computers, etc. Cost: $420 plus $40 registration fee.

WRITING FOR YOUNG READERS WORKSHOP, Brigham Young University, 348 Harman Bldg., Provo UT 84602-1532. (801)378-2568. Fax: (801)422-0745. E-mail susan.overstreet@byu.edu. Website: wfyr.byu.edu. **Program Administrator:** Susan Overstreet. Writer workshops geared toward all levels. **Open to students.** Offers workshops on picture books, middle grade fiction, young adult fiction, illustration, general writing for children, book-length fiction (novels) illustration, and general writing. Mornings are spent in small group workshop sessions with published author. Annual workshop held July of each year. Registration limited to 125 people. Computer lab, library, conference rooms available. Cost of workshop: $399 includes daily 4-hour workshop (limited to 12 people) with published author; afternoon break-out sessions on the craft of writing; one-on-one critiques with editors for selected participants; one-on-one meeting with writers agent for selected participants. "Workshoppers are expected to bring a manuscript-in-process." Write for more information. Editors and agents participate in conference. Previous faculty include: Claudia Mills, Eve Bunting, Lael Littke, Alane Ferguson, Tim Wynne-Jones.

Contests, Awards & Grants

Publication is not the only way to get your work recognized. Contests and awards can also be great ways to gain recognition in the industry. Grants, offered by organizations like SCBWI, offer monetary recognition to writers, giving them more financial freedom as they work on projects.

When considering contests or applying for grants, be sure to study guidelines and requirements. Regard entry deadlines as gospel and follow the rules to the letter.

Note that some contests require nominations. For published authors and illustrators, competitions provide an excellent way to promote your work. Your publisher may not be aware of local competitions such as state-sponsored awards—if your book is eligible, have the appropriate person at your publishing company nominate or enter your work for consideration.

To select potential contests and grants, read through the listings that interest you, then send for more information about the types of written or illustrated material considered and other important details. A number of contests offer information through websites given in their listings.

If you are interested in knowing who has received certain awards in the past, check your local library or bookstores or consult *Children's Books: Awards & Honors*, compiled and edited by the Children's Book Council (www.cbcbooks.org). Many bookstores have special sections for books that are Caldecott and Newbery Medal winners. Visit these websites for more information on award-winning children's books: The Caldecott—www.ala.org/alsc/caldecott.html; The Newbery—www.ala.org/alsc/newbery.html; The Coretta Scott King Award—www.ala.org/srrt/csking; The Michael L. Printz Award—www.ala.org/yalsa/printz; The Boston Globe-Horn Book Award—www.hbook.com/bghb; The Golden Kite Award—www.scbwi.org/awards.htm.

Information on contests listed in the previous edition but not included in this edition of *Children's Writer's & Illustrator's Market* **may be found in the General Index.**

N ACORN CONTESTS, Acorn, 1530 Seventh St., Rock Island IL 61201. (309)788-3980. **Contest Director:** Betty Mowery. Submit entries to Betty Mowery, editor. **Open to Students**. Annual contests. Estab. 1990. Purpose of contests: "To help young authors compete with others and to obtain discipline as to subject, word length." Unpublished submissions only. Submissions made by author. SASE for contest rules and entry forms. Entry fee is six 37¢ stamps. Awards subscription to *Acorn*. Judging by *Acorn* staff member. Open to young authors ages K-12th grade. Submissions open to all young authors. Entries without SASE will not be returned and will not receive a reply. Entries without entry fee will not be judged.

ALCUIN CITATION AWARD, The Alcuin Society, P.O. Box 3216, Vancouver, BC V6B 3X8 Canada. (604)985-2758. Fax: (604)985-1091. E-mail: jrainer@shaw.ca. Website: www.alcuinsociety.com. Annual award. Estab. 1983. Purpose of contest: Alcuin Citations are awarded annually for excellence in Canadian book design. Previously published submissions only, "in the year prior to the Awards call for entries; i.e., 2003 awards went to books published in 2002." Submissions made by the publisher, author or designer. Deadline for entries: March 15. Entry fee is $15/book; include check with book. Awards certificate. Judging by professionals and those experienced in the field of book design. Requirements for entrants: Winners are selected from books designed and published in Canada. Awards are presented annually at the Annual General Meeting of the Alcuin Society held in early June each year.

AMHA LITERARY CONTEST, American Morgan Horse Association Youth, P.O. Box 960, Shelburne VT 05482. (802)985-4944. E-mail: info@morganhorse.com. Website: www.morganhorse.com. **Open to students** under 21. Purpose of contest: "to award youth creativity." The contest includes categories for both poetry and essays. Unpublished submissions only. Submissions made by author. Deadline for entries: October 1. SASE for contest rules and entry forms. No entry fee. Awards $25 cash and ribbons to up to 5th place. "Winning entry will be published in *AMHA News and Morgan Sales Network*, a monthly publication."

AMHA MORGAN ART CONTEST, American Morgan Horse Association, Box 960, Shelburne VT 05482. (802)985-4944. Fax: (802)985-8897. E-mail: info@morganhorse.com. Website: www.morganhorse.com. **Open to students**. Annual contest. The art contest consists of two categories: Morgan art (pencil sketches, oils, water colors, paintbrush), Morgan specialty pieces (sculptures, carvings). Unpublished submissions only. Deadline for entries: October 1. Contest rules and entry forms available for SASE. Entries not returned. Entry fee is $5. Awards $50 first prize in 2 divisions (for adults) and AMHA gift certificates to top 6 places (for children). Judging by *The Morgan Horse* magazine staff. "All work submitted becomes property of The American Morgan Horse Association. Selected works may be used for promotional purposes by the AMHA." Requirements for entrants: "We consider all work submitted." Works displayed at the annual convention and the AMHA headquarters; published in *AMHA News* and *Morgan Sales Network* and in color in the *Morgan Horse Magazine* (TMHA). The contest divisions consist of Junior (to age 17), Senior (18 and over) and Professional (commercial artists). Each art piece must have its own application form and its own entry fee. Matting is optional.

AMERICA & ME ESSAY CONTEST, Farm Bureau Insurance, Box 30400, 7373 W. Saginaw, Lansing MI 48909-7900. (517)323-7000. Fax: (517)323-6615. E-mail: lfedewa@fbinsmi.com. Website: farmbureauinsurance-mi.co. **Contest Coordinator:** Lisa Fedewa. Annual contest. **Open to students only.** Estab. 1968. Purpose of the contest: to give Michigan 8th graders the opportunity to express their thoughts/feelings on America and their roles in America. Unpublished submissions only. Deadline for entries: mid-November. SASE for contest rules and entry forms. "We have a school mailing list. Any school located in Michigan is eligible to participate." Entries not returned. No entry fee. Awards savings bonds and plaques for state top ten ($500-1,000), certificates and plaques for top 3 winners from each school. Each school may submit up to 10 essays for judging. Judging by home office employee volunteers. Requirements for entrants: "Participants must work through their schools or our agents' sponsoring schools. No individual submissions will be accepted. Top ten essays and excerpts from other essays are published in booklet form following the contest. State capitol/schools receive copies."

AMERICAN ASSOCIATION OF UNIVERSITY WOMEN, NORTH CAROLINA DIVISION, AWARD IN JUVENILE LITERATURE, North Carolina Literary and Historical Association, 4610 Mail Service Center, Raleigh NC 27699-4610. (919)733-9375. Fax: (919)733-8807. E-mail: michael.hill@nemail.net. **Award Coordinator:** Mr. Michael Hill. Annual award. Purpose of award: to recognize the year's best work of juvenile literature by a North Carolina resident. Book must be published during the year ending June 30. Submissions made by author, author's agent or publisher. Deadline for entries: July 15. SASE for contest rules. Awards a cup to the winner and winner's name inscribed on a plaque displayed within the North Carolina Office of Archives and History. Judging by Board of Award selected by sponsoring organization. Requirements for entrants: Author must have maintained either legal residence or actual physical residence, or a combination of both, in the State of North Carolina for three years immediately preceding the close of the contest period. Only published work (books) eligible.

AMERICAS AWARD, Consortium of Latin American Studies Programs (CLASP), CLASP Committee on Teaching and Outreach, % Center for Latin American and Caribbean Studies, University of Wisconsin-Milwaukee, P.O. Box 413, Milwaukee WI 53201. (414)229-5986. Fax: (414)229-2879. E-mail: jkline@uwm.edu. Website: www.uwm.edu/Dept/CLACS/outreach_americas.html. **Coordinator:** Julie Kline. Annual award. Estab. 1993. Purpose of contest: "Up to two awards are given each spring in recognition of U.S. published works (from the previous year) of fiction, poetry, folklore or selected nonfiction (from picture books to works for young adults) in English or Spanish which authentically and engagingly relate to Latin America, the Caribbean, or to Latinos in the United States. By combining both and linking the "Americas," the intent is to reach beyond geographic borders, as well as multicultural-international boundaries, focusing instead upon cultural heritages within the hemisphere." Previously published submissions only. Submissions open to anyone with an interest in the theme of the award. Deadline for entries: January 15. SASE for contest rules and any committee changes. Awards $500 cash prize, plaque and a formal presentation at the Library of Congress, Washington DC. Judging by a review committee consisting of individuals in teaching, library work, outreach and children's literature specialists.

HANS CHRISTIAN ANDERSEN AWARD, IBBY International Board on Books for Young People, Nonnenweg 12, Postfach, CH-4003 Basel Switzerland. Phone: (004161)272 29 17. Fax: (004161)272 27 57. E-mail: ibby@ibby.org. Website: www.ibby.org. **Executive Director:** Kimete Basha. Award offered every two years. Purpose of award: A Hans Christian Andersen Medal shall be awarded every two years by the International Board on Books for Young People (IBBY) to an author and to an illustrator, living at the time of the nomination, who by the outstanding value of their work are judged to have made a lasting contribution to literature for children and young people. The complete works of the author and of the illustrator will be taken into consideration in awarding the medal, which will be accompanied by a diploma. Previously published titles only. Submissions are nominated by National Sections of IBBY in good standing. The National Sections select the candidates. The Hans Christian Andersen Award, named after Denmark's famous storyteller, is the highest international recognition given to an author and an illustrator of children's books. The Author's Award has been given since 1956, the Illustrator's Award since 1966. The Andersen Award is often called the "Little Nobel Prize." Her Majesty Queen Margrethe of Denmark is the Patron of the Hans Christian Andersen Awards. The Hans Christian Andersen Jury judges the books submitted for medals according to literary and artistic criteria. The awards are presented at the biennial congresses of IBBY.

ASPCA CHILDREN'S ESSAY CONTEST, American Society for the Prevention of Cruelty to Animals, 424 E. 92nd St., New York NY 10028-6804. (212)876-7700. Fax: (212)860-3435. E-mail: education@aspca.org. Website: www.aspca.org. **Contest Manager:** Miriam Ramos. Submit entries to: Miriam Ramos, manager, education programs, humane education. **Open to students.** Annual contest. Estab. 1990. An essay contest for students in grades 1-10. Unpublished submissions only. Submissions made by author, parent, teacher. Deadline for entries: December 15, 2003. SASE for contest rules and entry forms. Prizes vary, could include books, magazine subscriptions, T-shirts. Judging by ASPCA staff. Requirements for entrants: Open to all students in grades 1-10, must be student's own writing. Prizes are given for winning individuals and their classrooms. Judging in 3 categories, Grades 1-3, Grades 4-6 and Grades 7-10.

THE ASPCA HENRY BERGH CHILDREN'S BOOK AWARD, The American Society For the Prevention of Cruelty to Animals, 424 E. 92nd St., New York NY 10128-6804. (212)876-7700, ext. 4409. Fax: (212)860-3435. E-mail: education@aspca.org. Website: www.aspca.org. **Award Manager:** Miriam Ramos, manager of education programs, humane education. Competition open to adults. Annual award. Estab. 2000. Purpose of contest: To honor outstanding children's literature that fosters empathy and compassion for all living things. Awards presented to authors. Previously published submissions only. Submissions made by author or author's agent. Must be published January 2003-December 2003. Deadline for entries: October 31, 2003. SASE for contest rules and entry forms. Awards foil seals, plaque, certificate. Judging by professionals in animal welfare and children's literature. Requirements for entrants: Open to children's literature about animals and/or the environment published in 2003. Includes fiction, nonfiction and poetry in 3 categories: Companion Animals, Ecology and Environment and Humane Heroes.

■ **ATLANTIC WRITING COMPETITION**, Writer's Federation of Nova Scotia, 1113 Marginal Rd., Halifax, NS B3H 4P7 Canada. (902)423-8116. Fax: (902)422-0881. E-mail: talk@writers.ns.ca. Website: www.writers.ns.ca/competitions.html. Annual contest. Purpose is to encourage emerging writers in Atlantic Canada to explore their talents by sending unpublished work to any of five categories: novel, short story, poetry, writing for children or magazine article. Unpublished submissions only. Only open to residents of Atlantic Canada who are unpublished in category they enter. Visit website for more information.

BAKER'S PLAYS HIGH SCHOOL PLAYWRITING CONTEST, Baker's Plays, P.O. Box 6992222, Quincy MA 02269-9222. Fax: (617)745-9891. Website: www.bakersplays.com. **Contest Director:** Kurt Gombar. **Open to any high school student**. Annual contest. Estab. 1990. Purpose of the contest: to acknowledge playwrights at the high school level and to insure the future of American theater. Unpublished submissions only. Postmark deadline: January 30, 2004. Notification: May. SASE for contest rules and entry forms. No entry fee. Awards $500 to the first place playwright and Baker's Plays will publish the play; $250 to the second place playwright with an honorable mention; and $100 to the third place playwright with an honorable mention in the series. Judged anonymously. Plays must be accompanied by the signature of a sponsoring high school drama or English teacher, and it is recommended that the play receive a production or a public reading prior to the submission. "Please include a SAE with priority postage." Teachers must not submit student's work. The first place playwright will have their play published in an acting edition the September following the contest. The work will be described in the Baker's Plays Catalogue, which is distributed to 50,000 prospective producing organizations.

BAY AREA BOOK REVIEWER'S ASSOCIATION (BABRA), %*Poetry Flash*, 1450 Fourth St., #4, Berkeley CA 94710. (510)525-5476. Fax: (510)525-6752. E-mail: babra@poetryflash.org. Website: www.poetryflash.org. **Contact:** Joyce Jenkins. Annual award for outstanding book in children's literature, open to books published in the current calendar year by Northern California authors. Annual award. Estab. 1981. "BABRA presents annual awards to Bay Area (northern California) authors annually in fiction, nonfiction, poetry and children's literature. Purpose is to encourage writers and stimulate interest in books and reading." Previously published books only. Must be published the calendar year prior to spring awards ceremony. Submissions nominated by publishers; author or agent could also nominate published work. Deadline for entries: December. No entry forms. Send 3 copies of the book to attention: BABRA. No entry fee. Awards $100 honorarium and award certificate. Judging by voting members of the Bay Area Book Reviewer's Association. Books that reach the "finals" (usually 3-5 per category) displayed at annual award ceremonies (spring). Nominated books are displayed and sold at BABRA's annual awards ceremonies in the spring of each year; the winner is asked to read at the San Francisco Public Library's Main Branch.

JOHN AND PATRICIA BEATTY AWARD, California Library Association, 717 20th Street, Suite 200, Sacramento CA 95814. (916)447-8541. Fax: (916)447-8394. E-mail: info@cla-net.org. Website: www.cla-net.org. **Executive Director:** Susan Negreen. Annual award. Estab. 1987. Purpose of award: "The purpose of the John and Patricia Beatty Award is to encourage the writing of quality children's books highlighting California, its culture, heritage and/or future." Previously published submissions only. Submissions made by the author, author's agent or review copies sent by publisher. The award is given to the author of a children's book published the preceding year. Deadline for entries: Submissions may be made January-December. Contact CLA Executive Director who will liaison with Beatty Award Committee. Awards cash prize of $500 and an engraved plaque. Judging by a 5-member selection committee appointed by the president of the California Library Association. Requirements for entrants: "Any children's or young adult book set in California and published in the U.S. during the calendar year preceding the presentation of the award is eligible for consideration. This includes works of fiction as well as nonfiction for children and young people of all ages. Reprints and compilations are not eligible. The California setting must be depicted authentically and must serve as an integral focus for the book." Winning selection is announced through press release during National Library Week in April. Author is presented with award at annual California Library Association Conference in November.

THE IRMA S. AND JAMES H. BLACK BOOK AWARD, Bank Street College of Education, 610 W. 112th St., New York NY 10025-1898. (212)875-4450. Fax: (212)875-4558. E-mail: lindag@bnkst.edu. Website: http://streetcat.bnkst.edu/html/isb.html. **Contact:** Linda Greengrass. Annual award. Estab. 1972. Purpose of award: "The award is given each spring for a book for young children, published in the previous year, for excellence of both text and illustrations." Entries must have been published during the previous calendar year (between January '03 and December '03 for 2003 award). Deadline for entries: December 15th. "Publishers submit books to us by sending them here to me at the Bank Street Library. Authors may ask their publishers to submit their books. Out of these, three to five books are chosen by a committee of older children and children's literature professionals. These books are then presented to children in selected second, third and fourth grade classes here and at a few other cooperating schools on the East Coast. These children are the final judges who pick the actual award. A scroll (one each for the author and illustrator, if they're different) with the recipient's name and a gold seal designed by Maurice Sendak are awarded in May."

N WALDO M. AND GRACE C. BONDERMAN/IUPUI NATIONAL YOUTH THEATRE PLAYWRITING COMPETITION AND DEVELOPMENT WORKSHOP AND SYMPOSIUM, Indiana University-Purdue University at Indianapolis, 425 University Blvd. #309, Indianapolis IN 46202-5140. (317)274-2095. Fax: (317)278-1025. E-mail: dwebb@.iupui.edu. Website: www.liberalarts.iupui.edu/bonderman. **Director:** Dorothy Webb. **Open to students.** Entries should be submitted to Lynne Perkins, Bonderman Project Manager. Contest every two years; next competition will be 2004. Estab. 1983. Purpose of the contest: "to encourage writers to create artistic scripts for young audiences. It provides a forum through which each playwright receives constructive criticism of his/her work and, where selected, writers participate in script development with the help of professional dramaturgs, directors and actors." Unpublished submissions only. Submissions made by author. Deadline for entries: August 30, 2004. SASE for contest rules and entry forms. No entry fee. "Awards will be presented to the top ten finalists. Four cash awards of $1,000 each will be received by the top four playwrights whose scripts will be given developmental work culminating in polished readings showcased at the symposium held on the IUPUI campus and at the Indiana Repertory Theatre. The symposium is always held opposite years of the competition. Major publishers of scripts for young audiences, directors, producers, critics and teachers attend this symposium and provide useful reactions to the plays. If a winner is unable to be involved in preparation of the reading and to attend the showcase of his/her work, the prize will not be awarded. Semi-finalists will receive certificates and public readings of excerpts." Judging by professional directors, dramaturgs, publishers, university professors. Write for guidelines and entry form.

BOOK OF THE YEAR FOR CHILDREN, Canadian Library Association, 328 Frank St., Ottawa, ON K2P 0X8 Canada. (613)232-9625. Fax: (613)563-9895. Website: www.cla.ca. **Contact:** Chairperson, Canadian Association of Children's Librarians. Annual award. Estab. 1947. "The main purpose of the award is to encourage writing and publishing in Canada of good books for children up to and including age 14. If, in any year, no book is deemed to be of award calibre, the award shall not be made that year. To merit consideration, the book must have been published in Canada and its author must be a Canadian citizen or a permanent resident of Canada." Previously published submissions only; must be published between January 1 and December 1 of the previous year. Deadline for entries: January 1. SASE for award rules. Entries not returned. No entry fee. Judging by committee of members of the Canadian Association of Children's Librarians. Requirements for entrants: Contest open only to Canadian authors or residents of Canada. Winning books are on display at CLA headquarters.

THE BOSTON GLOBE-HORN BOOK AWARDS, The Boston Globe & The Horn Book, Inc., The Horn Book, 56 Roland St., Suite 200, Boston MA 02129. (617)628-0225. Fax: (617)628-0882. E-mail: info@hbook.com. Website: www.hbook.com/bghb.shtml. Annual award. Estab. 1967. Purpose of award: "to reward literary excellence in children's and young adult books. Awards are for picture books, nonfiction, fiction and poetry. Up to two honor books may be chosen for each category." Books must be published between June 1, 2003 and May 31, 2004. Deadline for entries: May 15, 2004. "Publishers usually submit books. Award winners receive $500 and silver engraved bowl, honor book winners receive a silver engraved plate." Judging by 3 judges involved in children's book field. *The Horn Book Magazine* publishes speeches given at awards ceremonies. The book must have been published in the U.S."

ANN ARLYS BOWLER POETRY CONTEST, *Read* Magazine, 200 First Stamford Place, P.O. Box 120023, Stamford CT 06912-0023. (203)705-3406. Fax: (203)705-1661. E-mail: jkroll@weeklyreader.com. Website: www.weeklyreader.com/ read.html. **Contest Director:** Jennifer Kroll. **Open to students.** Annual contest. Estab. 1988. Purpose of the contest: to reward young-adult poets (grades 6-12). Unpublished submissions only. Submissions made by the author or nominated by a person or group of people. Entry form must include signature of teacher, parent or guardian, and student verifying originality. Maximum number of submissions per student: three poems. Deadline for entries: January 15. SASE for contest rules and entry forms. No entry fee. Awards 6 winners $100 each, medal of honor and publication in *Read*. Semifinalists receive $50 each. Judging by *Read* and *Weekly Reader* editors and teachers. Requirements for entrants: the material must be original. Winning entries will be published in an issue of *Read*.

BYLINE MAGAZINE CONTESTS, P.O. Box 5240, Edmond OK 73083-5240. E-mail: mpreston@bylinemag.com. Website: www.bylinemag.com. **Contest Director:** Marcia Preston. Purpose of contest: *ByLine* runs 4 contests a month on many topics to encourage and motivate writers. Past topics include first chapter of a novel, children's fiction, children's poem, nonfiction for children, personal essay, general short stories, valentine or love poem, etc. Send SASE for contest flier with topic list and rules, or see website. Unpublished submissions only. Submissions made by the author. "We do not publish the contests' winning entries, just the names of the winners." SASE for contest rules. Entry fee is $3-4. Awards cash prizes for first, second and third place. Amounts vary. Judging by qualified writers or editors. List of winners will appear in magazine.

BYLINE MAGAZINE STUDENT PAGE, P.O. Box 5240, Edmond OK 73083-5240. (405)348-5591. Website: www.byli nemag.com. **Contest Director:** Marcia Preston, publisher. **Open to students.** Estab. 1981. "We offer writing contests for students in grades 1-12 on a monthly basis, September through May, with cash prizes and publication of top entries." Previously unpublished submissions only. "This is not a market for illustration." Deadline for entries varies. "Entry fee usually $1." Awards cash and publication. Judging by qualified editors and writers. "We publish top entries in student contests. Winners' list published in magazine dated 2 months past deadline." Send SASE for details.

RANDOLPH CALDECOTT MEDAL, Association for Library Service to Children, Division of the American Library Association, 50 E. Huron, Chicago IL 60611. (312)280-2163. E-mail: alsc@ala.org. Website: www.ala.org/alsc. **Executive**

Director: Malore I. Brown. Annual award. Estab. 1938. Purpose of the award: to honor the artist of the most outstanding picture book for children published in the US (Illustrator must be US citizen or resident.) Must be published year preceding award. Deadline for entries: December. SASE for award rules. Entries not returned. No entry fee. "Medal given at ALA Annual Conference during the Newbery/Caldecott Banquet."

CALIFORNIA YOUNG PLAYWRIGHTS CONTEST, Playwrights Project, 450 B St., Suite 1020, San Diego CA 92101. (619)239-8222. Fax: (619)239-8225. E-mail: write@playwrightsproject.com. Website: www.playwrightsproject.com. **Director:** Deborah Salzer. **Open to Californians under age 19.** Annual contest. Estab. 1985. "Our organization and the contest is designed to nurture promising young writers. We hope to develop playwrights and audiences for live theater. We also teach playwriting." Submissions required to be unpublished and not produced professionally. Submissions made by the author. Deadline for entries: April 1. SASE for contest rules and entry form. No entry fee. Award is professional productions of 3-5 short plays each year, participation of the writers in the entire production process, with a royalty awarded. Judging by professionals in the theater community, a committee of 5-7; changes somewhat each year. Works performed in San Diego at the Cassius Carter Centre Stage of the Old Globe. Writers submitting scripts of 10 or more pages receive a detailed script evaluation letter.

N **CALLIOPE FICTION CONTEST**, Writers' Specialized Interest Group (SIG) of American Mensa, Ltd., P.O. Box 466, Moraga CA 94556-0466. E-mail: cynthia@theriver.com. **Fiction Editor:** Sandy Raschke. **Open to students.** Annual contest. Estab. 1991. Purpose of contest: "To promote good writing and opportunities for getting published. To give our member/subscribers and others an entertaining and fun exercise in writing." Unpublished submissions only (all genres, no violence, profanity or extreme horror). Submissions made by author. Deadline for entries: changes annually but usually around September 15. Entry fee is $2 for non-subscribers; subscribers get first entry fee. Awards small amount of cash (up to $75 for 1st place, to $10 for 3rd), certificates, full or mini-subscriptions to *Calliope* and various premiums and books, depending on donations. All winners are published in subsequent issues of *Calliope*. Judging by fiction editor, with concurrence of other editors, if needed. Requirements for entrants: winners must retain sufficient rights to have their stories published in the January/February issue, or their entries will be disqualified; one-time rights. Open to all writers. No special considerations—other than following the guidelines. Contest theme, due dates and sometimes entry fees change annually. Always send SASE for complete rules; available after April 15 each year. Sample copies with prior winners are available for $3 and large SAE with 3 first-class stamps.

N **CANADA COUNCIL GOVERNOR GENERAL'S LITERARY AWARDS**, 350 Albert St., P.O. Box 1047, Ottawa, ON K1P 5V8 Canada. (613)566-4410, ext. 5576. Fax: (613)566-4410. E-mail: joanne.larocque-poirier@canadacouncil.ca. **Program Officer, Writing and Publishing Section:** Joanne Larocque-Poirier. Annual award. Estab. 1937. Purpose of award: given to the best English-language and the best French-language work in each of the seven categories of Fiction, Literary Nonfiction, Poetry, Drama, Children's Literature (text), Children's Literature (illustration) and Translation. Books must be first-edition trade books that have been written, translated or illustrted by Canadian citizens or permanent residents of Canada. In the case of Translation, the original work written in English or French, must also be a Canadian-authored title. English titles must be published between September 1, 2002 and September 30, 2003. Books must be submitted by publishers. Books must reach the Canada Council for the Arts no later than August 7, 2003. The deadlines are final; no bound proofs or books that miss the applicable deadlines will be given to the peer assessment committees. The awards ceremony is scheduled mid-November. Amount of award: $15,000.

CHILDREN'S WRITER WRITING CONTESTS, 93 Long Ridge Rd., West Redding CT 06896-1124. (203)792-8600. Fax: (203)792-8406. Contest offered twice per year by *Children's Writer*, the monthly newsletter of writing and publishing trends. Purpose of the award: To promote higher quality children's literature. "Each contest has its own theme. Any original unpublished piece, not accepted by any publisher at the time of submission, is eligible." Submissions made by the author. Deadline for entries: Last weekday in February and October. "We charge a $10 entry fee for nonsubscribers only, which is applicable against a subscription to *Children's Writer*." Awards 1st place—$250 or $500, a certificate and publication in *Children's Writer*; 2nd place—$100 or $250, and certificate; 3rd-5th places—$50 or $100 and certificates. To obtain the rules and theme for the current contest send a SASE to *Children's Writer* at the above address. Put "Contest Request" in the lower left of your envelope. Judging by a panel of 4 selected from the staff of the Institute of Children's Literature. "We acquire First North American Serial Rights (to print the winner in *Children's Writer*), after which all rights revert to author." Open to any writer. Entries are judged on age targeting, originality, quality of writing and, for nonfiction, how well the information is conveyed and accuracy. "Submit clear photocopies only, not originals; submission will *not* be returned. Manuscripts should be typed double-spaced. No pieces containing violence or derogatory, racist or sexist language or situations will be accepted, at the sole discretion of the judges."

CHILDREN'S WRITERS FICTION CONTEST, Stepping Stones, P.O. Box 8863, Springfield MO 65801-8863. (417)863-7369. E-mail: verwil@alumni.pace.edu. **Coordinator:** V.R. Williams. Annual contest. Estab. 1993. Purpose of contest: to promote writing for children by giving children's writers an opportunity to submit work in competition. Unpublished submissions only. Submissions made by the author. Deadline for entries: July 31. SASE for contest rules and entry forms. Entry fee is $8. Awards cash prize, certificate and publication in chapbook; certificates for Honorable Mention. Judging by Goodin, Williams and Goodwin. First rights to winning material acquired or purchased. Requirements for entrants: Work must be suitable for children and no longer than 1,500 words. "Send SASE for list of winners."

COLORADO BOOK AWARDS, Colorado Center for the Book, 2123 Downing St., Denver CO 80205. (303)839-8320. Fax: (303)839-8319. E-mail: ccftb@compuserve.com. Website: www.coloradocenterforthebook.org. **Award Director:**

Christiane Citron. Annual award. Estab. 1993. Previously published submissions only. Submissions are made by the author, author's agent, nominated by a person or group of people. Requires Colorado residency by authors. Deadline for entries: January 15, 2004. SASE for contest rules and entry forms. Entry fee is $45. Awards $250 and plaque. Judging by a panel of literary agents, booksellers and librarians. "Please note, we *also* have periodic competitions for illustrators to design a poster and associated graphics for our other book programs. The date varies. Inquiries are welcomed."

THE COMMONWEALTH CLUB'S BOOK AWARDS CONTEST, The Commonwealth Club of California, 595 Market St., San Francisco CA 94105. (415)597-4846. Fax: (415)597-6729. E-mail: blane@commonwealthclub.org. Website: www.commonwealthclub.org/bookawards. **Attn:** Barbara Lane. Chief Executive Officer: Gloria Duffy. Annual contest. Estab. 1932. Purpose of contest: the encouragement and production of literature in California. Juvenile categories included. Previously published submissions; must be published from January 1 to December 31, previous to contest year. Deadline for entries: January 31. SASE for contest rules and entry forms. No entry fee. Awards gold and silver medals. Judging by the Book Awards Jury. The contest is only open to California writers/illustrators (must have been resident of California when ms was accepted for publication). "The award winners will be honored at the Annual Book Awards Program." Winning entries are displayed at awards program and advertised in newsletter.

CRICKET LEAGUE, *Cricket* magazine, P.O. Box 300, 315 Fifth St., Peru IL 61354. (815)224-5803. Website: www.cricket mag.com. Address entries to: Cricket League. **Open to students**. Monthly contest. Estab. 1973. "The purpose of Cricket League contests is to encourage creativity and give young people an opportunity to express themselves in writing, drawing, painting or photography. There is a contest each month. Possible categories include story, poetry, or art. Each contest relates to a *specific theme* described on each *Cricket* issue's Cricket League page. Signature verifying originality, age and address of entrant and permission to publish required. Entries which do not relate to the current month's theme cannot be considered." Unpublished submissions only. Deadline for entries: the 25th of each month. Cricket League rules, contest theme, and submission deadline information can be found in the current issue of *Cricket* and via website. "We prefer that children who enter the contests subscribe to the magazine or that they read *Cricket* in their school or library." No entry fee. Awards certificate suitable for framing and children's books or art/writing supplies. Judging by *Cricket* editors. Obtains right to print prizewinning entries in magazine. Refer to contest rules in current *Cricket* issue. Winning entries are published on the Cricket League pages in the *Cricket* magazine 3 months subsequent to the issue in which the contest was announced. Current theme, rules, and prizewinning entries also posted on the website.

N MARGUERITE DE ANGELI PRIZE, Delacorte Press, Random House Books for Young Readers, 1745 Broadway, New York NY 10019. Estab. 1992. Fax: (212)782-9452 (note re: Marguerite De Angeli Prize). Website: www.randomhouse/ kids.com. Annual award. Purpose of the award: to encourage the writing of fiction for children aged 7-10, either contemporary or historical; to encourage unpublished writers in the field of middle grade fiction. Unpublished submissions only. No simultaneous submissions. Length: between 40-144 pages. Submissions made by author or author's agent. Entries should be postmarked between April 1st and June 30th. SASE for award rules. No entry fee. Awards a $1,500 cash prize plus a hardcover and paperback book contract with a $7,500 advance against a royalties to be negotiated. Judging by Delacorte Press Books for Young Readers editorial staff. Open to US and Canadian writers who have not previously published a novel for middle-grade readers (ages 7-10).

DELACORTE PRESS PRIZE FOR A FIRST YOUNG ADULT NOVEL, Delacorte Press, Books for Young Readers Department, 1540 Broadway, New York NY 10036. (212)782-9000. Fax: (212)302-7985. Website: www.randomhouse.com/ kids. Annual award. Estab. 1982. Purpose of award: to encourage the writing of contemporary young adult fiction. Previously unpublished submissions only. Manuscripts sent to Delacorte Press may not be submitted to other publishers while under consideration for the prize. "Entries must be submitted between October 1 and New Year's Day. The real deadline is a December 31 postmark. Early entries are appreciated." SASE for award rules. No entry fee. Awards a $1,500 cash prize and a $7,500 advance against royalties for world rights on a hardcover and paperback book contract. Works published in an upcoming Delacorte Press, an imprint of Random House, Inc., Books for Young Readers list. Judged by the editors of the Books for Young Readers Department of Delacorte Press. Requirements for entrants: The writer must be American or Canadian and must *not* have previously published a young adult novel but may have published anything else. Foreign-language mss and translations and mss submitted to a previous Delacorte Press are not eligible. Send SASE for new guidelines. Guidelines are also available on our website.

MARGARET A. EDWARDS AWARD, 50 East Huron St., Chicago IL 60611-2795. (312)280-4390 or (800)545-2433. Fax: (312)664-7459. E-mail: yalsa@ala.org. Website: www.ala.org/yalsa. Annual award administered by the Young Adult Library Services Association (YALSA) of the American Library Association (ALA) and sponsored by *School Library Journal* magazine. Purpose of award: "ALA's Young Adult Library Services Association (YALSA), on behalf of librarians who work with young adults in all types of libraries, will give recognition to those authors whose book or books have provided young adults with a window through which they can view their world and which will help them to grow and to understand themselves and their role in relationships, society and the world." Previously published submissions only. Submissions are nominated by young adult librarians and teenagers. Must be published five years before date of award. SASE for award rules and entry forms. No entry fee. Judging by members of the Young Adult Library Services Association. Deadline for entry: December 1. "The award will be given annually to an author whose book or books, over a period of time, have been accepted by young adults as an authentic voice that continues to illuminate their experiences and emotions, giving insight into their lives. The book or books should enable them to understand themselves, the world in which they live, and their relationship with others and with society. The book or books must be in print at the time of the nomination."

DOROTHY CANFIELD FISHER CHILDREN'S BOOK AWARD, Vermont Department of Libraries, % Northeast Regional Library, 23 Tilton Rd., St. Johnsbury VT 05819. (802)828-6954. Fax: (802)828-2199. E-mail: grace.greene@dol.st ate.vt.us. Website: www.dcfaward.org. **Chair:** Sally Margolis. Annual award. Estab. 1957. Purpose of the award: to encourage Vermont children to become enthusiastic and discriminating readers by providing them with books of good quality by living American authors published in the current year. Deadline for entries: December of year book was published. SASE for award rules and entry forms or e-mail. No entry fee. Awards a scroll presented to the winning author at an award ceremony. Judging is by the children grades 4-8. They vote for their favorite book. Requirements for entrants: "Titles must be original work, published in the United States, and be appropriate to children in grades 4 through 8. The book must be copyrighted in the current year. It must be written by an American author living in the U.S."

FLICKER TALE CHILDREN'S BOOK AWARD, Flicker Tale Award Committee, North Dakota Library Association, Bismarck Public Library, 515 N. Fifth St., Bismarck ND 58501. (701)222-6412. Fax: (701)221-6854. **Contact:** Marvia Boettcher. Estab. 1979. Purpose of award: to give children across the state of North Dakota a chance to vote for their book of choice from a nominated list of 10: 5 in the picture book category; 5 in the juvenile category. Also, to promote awareness of quality literature for children. Previously published submissions only. Submissions nominated by librarians and teachers across the state of North Dakota. Awards a plaque from North Dakota Library Association and banquet dinner. Judging by children in North Dakota. Entry deadline in June.

FLORIDA STATE WRITING COMPETITION, Florida Freelance Writers Association, P.O. Box A, North Stratford NH 03590. (603)922-8338. Fax: (603)922-8339. E-mail: contest@writers-editors.com. Website: www.writers-editors.com. **Executive Director:** Dana K. Cassell. Annual contest. Estab. 1984. Categories include children's literature (length appropriate to age category). Entry fee is $5 (members), $10 (nonmembers) or $10-20 for entries longer than 3,000 words. Awards $100 first prize, $75 second prize, $50 third prize, certificates for honorable mentions. Judging by teachers, editors and published authors. Judging criteria: interest and readability within age group, writing style and mechanics, originality, salability. Deadline: March 15. For copy of official entry form, send #10 SASE or visit website. List of 1999-2003 winners on website.

DON FREEMAN MEMORIAL GRANT-IN-AID, Society of Children's Book Writers and Illustrators, 8271 Beverly Blvd., Los Angeles CA 90048. E-mail: scbwi@scbwi.org. Website: www.scbwi.org. Estab. 1974. Purpose of award: to "enable picture book artists to further their understanding, training and work in the picture book genre." Applications and prepared materials will be accepted between January 15 and February 15. Grant awarded and announced on June 15. SASE for award rules and entry forms. SASE for return of entries. No entry fee. Annually awards one grant of $1,500 and one runner-up grant of $500. "The grant-in-aid is available to both full and associate members of the SCBWI who, as artists, seriously intend to make picture books their chief contribution to the field of children's literature."

AMELIA FRANCES HOWARD GIBBON AWARD FOR ILLUSTRATION, Canadian Library Association, 328 Frank St., Ottawa, ON K2P 0X8 Canada. (613)232-9625. Website: www.cla.ca. **Contact:** Chairperson, Canadian Association of Children's Librarians. Annual award. Estab. 1971. Purpose of the award: "to honor excellence in the illustration of children's book(s) in Canada. To merit consideration the book must have been published in Canada and its illustrator must be a Canadian citizen or a permanent resident of Canada." Previously published submissions only; must be published between January 1 and December 31 of the previous year. Deadline for entries: January 1. SASE for award rules. Entries not returned. No entry fee. Judging by selection committee of members of Canadian Association of Children's Librarians. Requirements for entrants: illustrator must be Canadian or Canadian resident. Winning books are on display at CLA Headquarters.

GOLD MEDALLION BOOK AWARDS, Evangelical Christian Publishers Association, 4816 South Ash, Suite 101, Tempe AZ 85282. (480)966-3998. Fax: (480)966-1944. E-mail: dross@ecpa.org. Website: www.ecpa.org. **President:** Doug Ross. Annual award. Estab. 1978. Categories include Preschool Children's Books, Elementary Children's Books, Youth Books. "All entries must be evangelical in nature and cannot be contrary to ECPA's Statement of Faith (stated in official rules)." Deadlines for entries: December 1. Guidelines available annually in October. SASE for award rules and entry form. "The work must be submitted by the publisher." Entry fee is $300/title for nonmembers. Awards a Gold Medallion plaque.

GOLDEN KITE AWARDS, Society of Children's Book Writers and Illustrators, 8271 Beverly Blvd., Los Angeles CA 90048. (323)782-1010. E-mail: scbwi@scbwi.org. Website: www.scbwi.org. **Coordinator:** Tanya Brown. Annual award. Estab. 1973. "The works chosen will be those that the judges feel exhibit excellence in writing, and in the case of the picture-illustrated books—in illustration, and genuinely appeal to the interests and concerns of children. For the fiction and nonfiction awards, original works and single-author collections of stories or poems of which at least half are new and never before published in book form are eligible—anthologies and translations are not. For the picture-illustration awards, the art or photographs must be original works (the texts—which may be fiction or nonfiction—may be original, public domain or previously published). Deadline for entries: December 15. SASE for award rules. No entry fee. Awards statuettes and plaques. The panel of judges will consist of professional authors, illustrators, editors or agents." Requirements for entrants: "must be a member of SCBWI." Winning books will be displayed at national conference in August. Books to be entered, as well as further inquiries, should be submitted to: The Society of Children's Book Writers and Illustrators, above address.

HIGHLIGHTS FOR CHILDREN FICTION CONTEST, 803 Church St., Honesdale PA 18431-1895. (570)253-1080. Fax: (570)251-7847. Manuscripts should be addressed to **Fiction Contest. Editor:** Christine French Clark Annual contest. Estab. 1980. Purpose of the contest: to stimulate interest in writing for children and reward and recognize excellence.

Unpublished submissions only. Deadline for entries: February 28; entries accepted after January 1 only. SASE for contest rules and return of entries. No entry fee. Awards 3 prizes of $1,000 each in cash and a pewter bowl (or, at the winner's election, attendance at the Highlights Foundation Writers Workshop at Chautauqua). Judging by *Highlights* editors. Winning pieces are purchased for the cash prize of $1,000 and published in *Highlights*; other entries are considered for purchase. Requirements for entrants: open to any writer. Winners announced in June. Length up to 800 words. Stories for beginning readers should not exceed 400 words. Stories should be consistent with *Highlights* editorial requirements. No violence, crime or derogatory humor. Send SASE for guidelines. 2003 theme: "Stories that begin with 'I have a problem.' We are seeking all types of stories: humor, world cultures, adventure, mystery."

HRC'S ANNUAL PLAYWRITING CONTEST, Hudson River Classics, Inc., P.O. Box 940, Hudson NY 12534. (518)828-0175. Fax: (518)828-1480. E-mail: jangrice2002@yahoo.com. **President:** Jan M. Grice. Annual contest. Estab. 1992. Hudson River Classics is a not-for-profit professional theater company dedicated to the advancement of performing in the Hudson River Valley area through reading of plays and providing opportunities for new playwrights. Unpublished submissions only. Submissions made by author and by the author's agent. Deadlines for entries: May 1st. SASE for contest rules and entry forms. Entry fee is $5. Awards $500 cash plus concert reading by professional actors. Judging by panel selected by Board of Directors. Requirements for entrants: Entrants must live in the northeastern US.

INSIGHT WRITING CONTEST, *Insight Magazine*, 55 W. Oak Ridge Dr., Hagerstown MD 21740-7390. E-mail: insight@rhpa.org. Website: www.insightmagazine.org. **Open to students.** Annual contest. Unpublished submissions only. Submissions made by author. Deadline for entries: June 1, 2004. SASE for contest rules and entry forms. Awards First prizes, $100-250; second prizes, $75-200; third prizes, $50-150. Winning entries will be published in *Insight*. Contest includes three catagories: Student Short Story, General Short Story and Student Poetry. You must be age 22 or under to enter the student catagories. Entries must include cover sheet form available with SASE or on website.

N INSPIRATIONAL WRITERS ALIVE! OPEN WRITERS COMPETITION, Texas Christian Writer's Forum, 6038 Greenmont, Houston TX 77092-2332. Fax: (713)686-7209. E-mail: mlrogersll@houston.rr.com; patav@aol.com. **Contact:** Contest Director. Annual contest. Estab. 1990. Purpose of contest: to help aspiring writers in the inspirational/ religion markets and to encourage writers in their efforts to write for possible future publication. Our critique sheets give valuable information to our participants. Unpublished submissions only. Submissions made by author. Deadline: May 1. SASE for contest rules. Entry fee is $10 (devotional, short story or article); $10 (3 poems). Awards certificate of merit for 1st, 2nd and 3rd place; plus a small monetary award of $25 1st, $15 2nd, $10 3rd. Requirements for entrants: Cannot enter published material. "We want to aid especially new and aspiring writers." Contest has 5 categories—to include short story (adult), short story (for children and teens) article, daily devotions, and poetry and book proposal. Request complete guidelines from M. Rogers. Entry forms and info available after January 1, 2004. "*Must* include a cover sheet with every category."

IRA CHILDREN'S BOOK AWARDS, International Reading Association, 800 Barksdale Rd., P.O. Box 8139, Newark DE 19714-8139. (302)731-1600. Fax: (302)731-1057. E-mail: exec@reading.org. Website: www.reading.org. Annual award. Awards are given for an author's first or second published book for fiction and nonfiction in three categories: primary (ages preschool-8), intermediate (ages 9-13), and young adult (ages 14-17). This award is intended for newly published authors who show unusual promise in the children's book field. Deadline for entries: November 1. Awards $500. For guidelines write or e-mail.

JOSEPH HENRY JACKSON AND JAMES D. PHELAN LITERARY AWARDS, sponsored by The San Francisco Foundation. Administered by Intersection for the Arts. 446 Valencia St., San Francisco CA 94103. (415)626-2787. Fax: (415)626-1636. E-mail: info@theintersection.org. Submit entries to Awards Coordinator. **Open to Students**. Annual award. Estab. 1937. Purpose of award: to encourage young writers for an unpublished manuscript-in-progress. Submissions must be unpublished. Submissions made by author. Deadline for entries: January 31. SASE for contest rules and entry forms. Judging by established peers. All applicants must be 20-35 years of age. Applicants for the Henry Jackson Award must be residents of northern California or Nevada for 3 consecutive years immediately prior to the January 31 deadline. Applicants for the James D. Phelan awards must have been born in California but need not be current residents.

THE EZRA JACK KEATS NEW WRITER AND NEW ILLUSTRATOR AWARDS, Ezra Jack Keats Foundation/ Administered by The Office of Children's Services, the New York Public Library, 455 Fifth Ave., New York NY 10016. (212)340-0906. Fax: (212)340-0988. E-mail: mtice@nypl.org. **Program Coordinator:** Margaret Tice. Annual awards. Purpose of the awards: "The awards will be given to a promising new writer of picture books for children and a promising new illustrator of picture books for children. Selection criteria include books for children (ages nine and under) that reflect the tradition of Ezra Jack Keats. These books portray: the universal qualities of childhood, strong and supportive family and adult relationships, the multicultural nature of our world." Submissions made by the publisher. Must be published in the preceding year. Deadline for entries: mid-December. SASE for contest rules and entry forms. No entry fee. Awards $1,000 coupled with Ezra Jack Keats Bronze Medal. Judging by a panel of experts. "The author or illustrator should have published no more than five books. Entries are judged on the outstanding features of the text, complemented by illustrations. Candidates need not be both author and illustrator. Entries should carry a 2003 copyright (for the 2004 award)." Winning books and authors to be presented at reception at The New York Public Library.

EZRA JACK KEATS/KERLAN COLLECTION MEMORIAL FELLOWSHIP, University of Minnesota, 113 Elmer L. Andersen Library, 222 21st Ave. S., Minneapolis MN 55455. (612)624-4576. Fax: (612)625-5525. E-mail: clrc@tc.umn.edu. Website: special.lib.umn.edu/clrc/. Offered annually. Deadline for entries: May 1, 2004. Send request with SASE (6×9 or

9×12 envelope), including 60¢ postage. The Ezra Jack Keats/Kerlan Collection Memorial Fellowship from the Ezra Jack Keats Foundation will provide $1,500 to a "talented writer and/or illustrator of children's books who wishes to use the Kerlan Collection for the furtherance of his or her artistic development. Special consideration will be given to someone who would find it difficult to finance the visit to the Kerlan Collection." The fellowship winner will receive transportation and per diem. Judging by the Kerlan Award Committee—3 representatives from the University of Minnesota faculty, one from the Kerlan Friends, and one from the Minnesota Library Association.

KENTUCKY BLUEGRASS AWARD, Kentucky Reading Association, % Carrie L. Cooper. Eastern Kentucky University, 521 Lancaster Ave., Richmond KY 40475. (859)622-1781. Fax: (859)622-1774. E-mail: carrie.cooper@eku.edu. Website: www.kyreading.org. **Award Director:** Carrie L. Cooper. Submit entries to: Carrie L. Cooper. Annual award. Estab. 1983. Purpose of award: to promote readership among young children and young adolescents. Also to recognize exceptional creative efforts of authors and illustrators. Previously published submissions only. Submissions made by author, made by author's agent, nominated by teachers or librarians. Must be published no more than 3 years prior to the award year. Deadline for entries: March 15. Contest rules and entry forms are available from the website. No entry fee. Awards a framed certificate and invitation to be recognized at the annual luncheon of the Kentucky Bluegrass Award. Judging by children who participate through their schools or libraries. "Books are reviewed by a panel of teachers and librarians before they are placed on a Master List for the year. These books must have been published within a three year period prior to the review. Winners are chosen from this list of pre-selected books. Books are divided into four divisions, K-2, 3-5, 6-8, 9-12 grades. Winners are chosen by children who either read the books or have the books read to them. Children from the entire state of Kentucky are involved in the selection of the annual winners for each of the divisions."

CORETTA SCOTT KING AWARD, Coretta Scott King Task Force, Social Responsibility Round Table, American Library Association, 50 E. Huron St., Chicago IL 60611. (312)280-4294. Fax: (312)280-3256. E-mail: olos@ala.org. Website: www.ala.org/srrt/csking. "The Coretta Scott King Award is an annual award for books (1 for text and 1 for illustration) that convey the spirit of brotherhood espoused by M.L. King, Jr.—and also speak to the Black experience—for young people. There is an award jury of children's librarians that judges the books—reviewing over the year—and making a decision in January. A copy of an entry must be sent to each juror by December 1st of the juried year. Call or e-mail ALA Office for Literary Services for jury list. Awards breakfast held on Tuesday morning during A.L.A. Annual Conference. See schedule at website.

ANNE SPENCER LINDBERGH PRIZE IN CHILDREN'S LITERATURE, The Charles A. and Anne Morrow Lindbergh Foundation, % Lindbergh Foundation, 2150 Third Ave., Suite 310, Anoka MN 55303. (763)576-1596. Fax: (763)576-1664. E-mail: info@lindberghfoundation.org. Website: www.lindberghfoundation.org. Contest is offered every 2 years. Estab. 1996. Purpose of contest: To recognize the children's fantasy novel judged to be the best published in the English language during the 2-year period. Prize program honors Anne Spencer Lindbergh, author of a number of acclaimed juvenile fantasies, who died in late 1993 at the age of 53. Previously published submissions only. Submissions made by author, author's agent or publishers. Must be published between January 1 of odd numbered years and December 31 of even numbered years. Deadline for entries: November 1 of even numbered years. Entry fee is $25. Awards $5,000 to author of winning book. Judging by panel drawn from writers, editors, librarians and teachers prominent in the field of children's literature. Requirements for entrants: Open to all authors of children's fantasy novels published during the 2-year period. Entries must include 4 copies of books submitted. Winner announced in winter of odd year.

LONGMEADOW JOURNAL LITERARY COMPETITION, % Rita and Robert Morton, 6750 N. Longmeadow, Lincolnwood IL 60712. (312)726-9789. Fax: (312)726-9772. **Contest Directors:** Rita and Robert Morton. Competition **open to students** (anyone age 10-19). Held annually and published every year. Estab. 1986. Purpose of contest: to encourage the young to write. Submissions are made by the author, nominated by a person or group of people, by teachers, librarians or parents. Deadline for entries: June 30. SASE. No entry fee. Awards first place, $175; second place, $100; and five prizes of $50. Judging by Rita Morton and Robert Morton. Works are published every year and are distributed to teachers and librarians and interested parties at no charge.

LOUISE LOUIS/EMILY F. BOURNE STUDENT POETRY AWARD, Poetry Society of America, 15 Gramercy Park, New York NY 10003-1705. (212)254-9628. Fax: (212)673-2352. E-mail: brett@poetrysociety.org. Website: www.poetrysociety.org. **Contact:** Award Director. **Open to students.** Annual award. Purpose of the award: award is for the best unpublished poem by a high or preparatory school student (grades 9-12) from the US and its territories. Unpublished submissions only. Deadline for entries: Oct. 1 to Dec. 22. SASE for award rules and entry forms. Entries not returned. "High schools can send an unlimited number of submissions with one entry per individual student for a flat fee of $20. (High school students may send a single entry for $5.)" Award: $250. Judging by a professional poet. Requirements for entrants: Award open to all high school and preparatory students from the US and its territories. School attended, as well as name and address, should be noted. PSA submission guidelines must be followed. These are printed in our fall calendar and are readily available if those interested send us a SASE. Line limit: none. "The award-winning poem will be included in a sheaf of poems that will be part of the program at the award ceremony and sent to all PSA members."

MAGAZINE MERIT AWARDS, Society of Children's Book Writers and Illustrators, 8271 Beverly Blvd., Los Angeles CA 90048. Fax: (323)782-1010. E-mail: scbwi@scbwi.org. Website: www.scbwi.org. **Award Coordinator:** Dorothy Leon. Annual award. Estab. 1988. Purpose of the award: "to recognize outstanding original magazine work for young people published during that year and having been written or illustrated by members of SCBWI." Previously published submissions only. Entries must be submitted between January 31 and December 15 of the year of publication. For brochure (rules) write

Award Coordinator. No entry fee. Must be a SCBWI member. Awards plaques and honor certificates for each of the 3 categories (fiction, nonfiction, illustration). Judging by a magazine editor and two "full" SCBWI members. "All magazine work for young people by an SCBWI member—writer, artist or photographer—is eligible during the year of original publication. In the case of co-authored work, both authors must be SCBWI members. Members must submit their own work." Requirements for entrants: 4 copies each of the published work and proof of publication (may be contents page) showing the name of the magazine and the date of issue. The SCBWI is a professional organization of writers and illustrators and others interested in children's literature. Membership is open to the general public at large.

MILKWEED PRIZE FOR CHILDREN'S LITERATURE, Milkweed Editions, 1011 Washington Ave. S., Suite 300, Minneapolis MN 55415-1246. (612)332-3192. Fax: (612)215-2550. E-mail: editor@milkweed.org. Website: www.milkwee d.org. **Award Director:** H. Emerson Blake, editor-in-chief. Annual award. Estab. 1993. Purpose of the award: to find an outstanding literary novel for readers ages 8-13 and encourage writers to turn their attention to readers in this age group. Unpublished submissions only "in book form." Must send SASE for award guidelines. The prize is awarded to the best work for children ages 8-13 that Milkweed agrees to publish in a calendar year by a writer not previously published by Milkweed. The Prize consists of a $10,000 advance against royalties agreed to at the time of acceptance. Submissions must follow our usual children's guidelines.

☑ **MINNESOTA BOOK AWARDS**, Minnesota Humanities Commission, 987 E. Ivy Ave., St. Paul MN 55106-2046. (651)774-0105, ext. 111. Fax: (651)774-0205. E-mail: mark@minnesotahumanities.org. Website: www.minnesotahumanitie s.org. **Award Director:** Mark Gleason. Submit entries to: Julie Haider, Minnesota Book Awards. Annual award. Estab. 1988. Purpose of contest: To recognize and honor achievement by members of Minnesota's book community. Previously published submissions only. Submissions made by author, publisher or author's agent. Fee for some categories. Work must hold 2003 copyright. Deadline for entries: December 31, 2003. Awards to winners and finalists, some cash. Judging by members of Minnesota's book community: booksellers, librarians, teachers and scholars, writers, reviewers and publishers. Requirements for entrants: Author must be a Minnesotan. The Minnesota Book Awards includes 13 awards categories for Children and young adult fiction and nonfiction titles and designs. For complete guidelines, visit website.

MYTHOPOEIC FANTASY AWARD FOR CHILDREN'S LITERATURE, The Mythopoeic Society, P.O. Box 320486. San Francisco CA 94132-0486. E-mail: emfarrell@earthlink.net. Website: www.mythsoc.org. **Award Director:** Eleanor M. Farrell. Annual award. Estab. 1992 (previous to 1992, a single Mythopoeic Fantasy Award was given to either adult or children's books). Previously published submissions only. Submissions nominated. Must be published previous calendar year. Deadline for entries: February 28. Awards statuette. Judging by committee members of Mythopoeic Society. Requirements for entrants: books only; nominations are made by Mythopoeic Society members.

NATIONAL CHILDREN'S THEATRE FESTIVAL, Actor's Playhouse at the Miracle Theatre, 280 Miracle Mile, Coral Gables FL 33134. (305)444-9293. Fax: (305)444-4181. Website: www.actorsplayhouse.org. **Director:** Earl Maulding. **Open to Students**. Annual contest. Estab. 1994. Purpose of contest: to bring together the excitement of the theater arts and the magic of young audiences through the creation of new musical works and to create a venue for playwrights/composers to showcase their artistic products. Submissions must be unpublished. Submissions are made by author or author's agent. Deadline for entries: June 1, 2004. SASE for contest rules and entry forms or online at website. Entry fee is $10. Awards: first prize of $500, full production, and transportation to Festival weekend based on availability. Final judges are of national reputation. Past judges include Joseph Robinette, Moses Goldberg and Luis Santeiro.

NATIONAL PEACE ESSAY CONTEST, United States Institute of Peace, 1200 17th St. NW, Washington DC 20036. (202)429-3854. Fax: (202)429-6063. E-mail: essay_contest@usip.org. Website: www.usip.org. **Open to students.** Annual contest. Estab. 1987. "The contest gives students the opportunity to do valuable research, writing and thinking on a topic of importance to international peace and conflict resolution. Teaching guides are available for teachers who allow the contest to be used as a classroom assignment." Deadline for entries is January 22, 2004. "Interested students, teachers and others may write or call to receive free contest kits. Please do not include SASE." Guidelines and rules on website. No entry fee. State Level Awards are $1000 college scholarships. National winners are selected from among the 1st place state winners. National winners receive scholarships in the following amounts: first place $10,000; second $5,000; third $2,500. First-place state winners invited to an expenses-paid awards program in Washington, D.C. in June. Judging is conducted by education professionals from across the country and by the Board of Directors of the United States Institute of Peace. "All submissions become property of the U.S. Institute of Peace to use at its discretion and without royalty or any limitation. Students grades 9-12 in the U.S., its territories and overseas schools may submit essays for review by completing the application process. U.S. citizenship required for students attending overseas schools. National winning essays will be published by the U.S. Institute of Peace."

NATIONAL WRITERS ASSOCIATION NONFICTION CONTEST, 3140 S. Peoria, Suite 295, Aurora CO 80014. (303)841-0246. **Executive Director:** Sandy Whelchel. Annual contest. Estab. 1971. Purpose of contest: "to encourage writers in this creative form and to recognize those who excel in nonfiction writing." Submissions made by author. Deadline for entries: December 31. SASE for contest rules and entry forms. Entry fee is $18. Awards 3 cash prizes; choice of books; Honorable Mention Certificate. "Two people read each entry; third party picks three top winners from top five." Judging sheets sent if entry accompanied by SASE. Condensed version of 1st place published in *Authorship*.

NATIONAL WRITERS ASSOCIATION SHORT STORY CONTEST, 3140 S. Peoria, Suite 295, Aurora CO 80014. (303)841-0246. **Executive Director:** Sandy Whelchel. Annual contest. Estab. 1971. Purpose of contest: "To encourage writers in this creative form and to recognize those who excel in fiction writing." Submissions made by the author.

Deadline for entries: July 1. SASE for contest rules and entry forms. Entry fee is $15. Awards 3 cash prizes, choice of books and certificates for Honorable Mentions. Judging by "two people read each entry; third person picks top three winners." Judging sheet copies available for SASE. First place published in *Authorship* Magazine.

THE NENE AWARD, Hawaii State Library, 478 S. King St., Honolulu HI 96813. (808)586-3510. Fax: (808)586-3584. E-mail: hslear@netra.lib.state.hi.us. Estab. 1964. "The Nene Award was designed to help the children of Hawaii become acquainted with the best contemporary writers of fiction, become aware of the qualities that make a good book and choose the best rather than the mediocre." Previously published submissions only. Books must have been copyrighted not more than 6 years prior to presentation of award. Work is nominated. Ballots are usually due around the beginning of March. Awards Koa plaque. Judging by the children of Hawaii in grades 4-6. Requirements for entrants: books must be fiction, written by a living author, copyrighted not more than 6 years ago and suitable for children in grades 4, 5 and 6. Current and past winners are displayed in all participating school and public libraries. The award winner is announced in April.

NEW VOICES AWARD, Lee & Low Books, 95 Madison Ave., New York NY 10016. (212)779-4400. Fax: (212)532-6035. E-mail: info@leeandlow.com. Website: www.leeandlow.com. **Executive Editor:** Louise May. **Open to students.** Annual award. Estab. 2000. Purpose of contest: Lee & Low Books is one of the few publishing companies owned by people of color. We have published over 50 first-time writers and illustrators. Titles include *In Daddy's Arms I Am Tall: African Americans Celebrating Fathers*, winner of the Coretta Scott King Illustrator Award; *Passage to Freedom: The Sugihara Story*, an American Library Association Notable Book; and *Crazy Horse's Vision*, a Bank Street College Children's Book of the Year. Submissions made by author. Deadline for entries: October 31. SASE for contest rules. No entry fee. Awards New Voices Award—$1,000 prize and a publication contract along with an advance on royalties; New Voices Honor Award—$500 prize. Judging by Lee & Low editors. Restrictions of media for illustrators: The author must be a writer of color who is a resident of the US and who has not previously published a children's picture book. For additional information, send SASE or visit Lee & Low's website, (leeandlow.com/editorial/voices3.html).

JOHN NEWBERY MEDAL AWARD, Association for Library Service to Children, Division of the American Library Association, 50 E. Huron, Chicago IL 60611. E-mail: alsc@ala.org. Website: www.ala.org/alsc. (312)280-2163. **Executive Director, ALSC:** Malore Brown. Annual award. Estab. 1922. Purpose of award: to recognize the most distinguished contribution to American children's literature published in the US. Previously published submissions only; must be published prior to year award is given. Deadline for entries: December 31. SASE for award rules. Entries not returned. No entry fee. Medal awarded at Caldecott/Newbery banquet during annual conference. Judging by Newbery Award Selection Committee.

THE NOMA AWARD FOR PUBLISHING IN AFRICA, Kodansha Ltd., P.O. Box 128, Witney, Oxon 0X8 5XU England. (44) 1993-775235. Fax: (44) 1993-709265. E-mail: maryljay@aol.com. Website: www.nomaaward.org. **Secretary to the Managing Committee:** Mary Jay. Annual award. Estab. 1979. Purpose of award: to encourage publications of works by African writers and scholars in Africa, instead of abroad, as is still too often the case at present. Books in the following categories are eligible: scholarly or academic, books for children, literature and creative writing, including fiction, drama and poetry. Previously published submissions only. 2004 award given for book published in 2003. Deadline for entries: end of March. Submissions must be made through publishers. Conditions of entry and submission forms are available from the secretariat or at website. Entries not returned. No entry fee. Awards $10,000. Judging by the Managing Committee (jury): African scholars and book experts and representatives of the international book community. Chairman: Walter Bgoya. Requirements for entrants: Author must be African, and book must be published in Africa. "Winning titles are displayed at appropriate international book events."

NORTH AMERICAN INTERNATIONAL AUTO SHOW HIGH SCHOOL POSTER CONTEST, Detroit Auto Dealers Association, 1900 W. Big Beaver Rd., Troy MI 48084-3531. (248)643-0250. Fax: (248)283-5160. E-mail: sherp@dada.org. Website: www.naias.com. **Contact:** Sandy Herp. **Open to students.** Annual contest. Submissions made by the author and illustrator. Contact DADA for contest rules and entry forms or retrieve rules from website. No entry fee. Awards in the High School Poster Contest are as follows: Chairman's Award, Best Theme, Best Use of Color, Best Use of Graphics, Most Creative, and Designer's Best of Show. A winner will be chosen in each category from grades 9, 10, 11 and 12. Each winner in each grade from each category will win $250. The winner of the Chairman's Award will receive $1,000. Entries will be judged by an independent panel of recognized representatives of the art community. Entrants must be Michigan high school students enrolled in grades 9-12. Junior high students in 9th grade are also eligible. Winners will be announced during the North American International Auto Show in January and may be published in the *Auto Show Program* at the sole discretion of the D.A.D.A. "No shared work please."

OHIOANA AWARD FOR CHILDREN'S LITERATURE: ALICE LOUISE WOOD MEMORIAL, (formerly Alice Louise Wood Ohioana Award for Children's Literature), Ohioana Library Association, 274 E. First Ave., Suite 300, Columbus OH 43201. (614)466-3831. Fax: (614)728-6974. E-mail: ohioana@sloma.state.oh.us. Website: www.oplin.lib.oh.us/OHIOANA/. **Director:** Linda R. Hengst. Annual award. Estab. 1991. Purpose of award: "to recognize an Ohio author whose body of work has made, and continues to make a significant contribution to literature for children or young adults." Deadline for entries: December 31. SASE for award rules and entry forms. Award: $1,000. Requirements for entrants: "must have been born in Ohio, or lived in Ohio for a minimum of five years; established a distinguished publishing record of books for children and young people; body of work has made, and continues to make, a significant contribution to the literature for young people; through whose work as a writer, teacher, administrator, and community service, interest in children's literature has been encouraged and children have become involved with reading."

OHIOANA BOOK AWARDS, Ohioana Library Association, 274 E. First Ave., Suite 300, Columbus OH 43201. (614)466-3831. Fax: (614)728-6974. E-mail: ohioana@sloma.state.oh.us. Website: www.oplin.lib.oh.us/OHIOANA/. **Di-**

rector: Linda R. Hengst. Annual award. "The Ohioana Book Awards are given to books of outstanding literary quality. Purpose of contest: to provide recognition and encouragement to Ohio writers and to promote the work of Ohio writers. Up to six are given each year. Awards may be given in the following categories: fiction, nonfiction, children's/juvenile, poetry and books about Ohio or an Ohioan. Books must be received by the Ohioana Library during the calendar year prior to the year the award is given and must have a copyright date within the last two calendar years." Deadline for entries: December 31. SASE for award rules and entry forms. No entry fee. Winners receive citation and glass sculpture. "Any book that has been written or edited by a person born in Ohio or who has lived in Ohio for at least five years is eligible."

OKLAHOMA BOOK AWARDS, Oklahoma Center for the Book, 200 NE 18th, Oklahoma City OK 73105. (405)521-2502. Fax: (405)525-7804. E-mail: gcarlile@oltn.odl.state.ok.us. Website: www.odl.state.ok.us/ocb. **Executive Director:** Glenda Carlile. Annual award. Estab. 1989. Purpose of award: "to honor Oklahoma writers and books about our state." Previously published submissions only. Submissions made by the author, author's agent, or entered by a person or group of people, including the publisher. Must be published during the calendar year preceding the award. Awards are presented to best books in fiction, nonfiction, children's, design and illustration, and poetry books about Oklahoma or books written by an author who was born, is living or has lived in Oklahoma. Deadline for entries: early January. SASE for award rules and entry forms. No entry fee. Awards a medal—no cash prize. Judging by a panel of 5 people for each category—a librarian, a working writer in the genre, booksellers, editors, etc. Requirements for entrants: author must be an Oklahoma native, resident, former resident or have written a book with Oklahoma theme. Winner will be announced at banquet in Oklahoma City. The Arrell Gibson Lifetime Achievement Award is also presented each year to an Oklahoma author for a body of work.

ONCE UPON A WORLD CHILDREN'S BOOK AWARD, Simon Wiesenthal Center's Museum of Tolerance Library and Archives, 1399 S. Roxbury Dr., Los Angeles CA 90035-4709. (310)772-7605. Fax: (310)772-7628. E-mail: library@wiesenthal.net or aklein@wiesenthal.net. **Award Director:** Adaire J. Klein. Submit entries to: Adaire J. Klein, Director of Library and Archival Services. Annual award. Estab. 1996. Previously published submissions only. Submissions made by publishers, author or by author's agent. Must be published January-December of previous year. Deadline for entries: March 31, 2004. SASE for contest rules and entry forms. Awards $1,000 and plaque. Judging by 3 independent judges familiar with children's literature. Award open to any writer with work in English language on subject of tolerance, diversity, and social justice for children 6-10 years old. Award is presented in October. Book Seal available from the library. 2003 winner: *Thank You Sarah: The Woman Who Saved Thanksgiving*, by Laurie Halse Anderson, illustrated by Matt Faulkner (NY:/ Simon & Schuster 2002).

ORBIS PICTUS AWARD FOR OUTSTANDING NONFICTION FOR CHILDREN, The National Council of Teachers of English, 1111 W. Kenyon Rd., Urbana IL 61801-1096. (217)328-3870. Fax: (217)328-0977. E-mail: dzagorski@ ncte.org. Website: www.ncte.org/elem/orbispictus. **Chair, NCTE Committee on the Orbis Pictus Award for Outstanding Nonfiction for Children:** Carolyn Lott, University of Montana, Missoula. Annual award. Estab. 1989. Purpose of award: To promote and recognize excellence in the writing of nonfiction for children. Previously published submissions only. Submissions made by author, author's agent, by a person or group of people. Must be published January 1-December 31 of contest year. Deadline for entries: November 30. Call for award information. No entry fee. Awards a plaque given at the NCTE Elementary Section Luncheon at the NCTE Annual Convention in November. Judging by a committee. "The name Orbis Pictus commemorates the work of Johannes Amos Comenius, 'Orbis Pictus-The World in Pictures' (1657), considered to be the first book actually planned for children."

THE ORIGINAL ART, Society of Illustrators, 128 E. 63rd St., New York NY 10021-7303. (212)838-2560. Fax: (212)838-2561. E-mail: si1901@aol.com. Website: www.societyillustrators.org. Annual contest. Estab. 1981. Purpose of contest: to celebrate the fine art of children's book illustration. Previously published submissions only. Deadline for entries: August 20. Request "call for entries" to receive contest rules and entry forms. Entry fee is $20/book. Judging by seven professional artists and editors. Works will be displayed at the Society of Illustrators Museum of American Illustration in New York City October-November annually. Medals awarded; catalog published.

HELEN KEATING OTT AWARD FOR OUTSTANDING CONTRIBUTION TO CHILDREN'S LITERATURE, Church and Synagogue Library Association, P.O. Box 19357, Portland OR 97280-0357. (503)244-6919. Fax: (503)977-3734. E-mail: csla@worldaccessnet.com. Website: www.worldaccessnet.com/~csla. **Chair of Committee:** Barbara Graham. Annual award. Estab. 1980. "This award is given to a person or organization that has made a significant contribution to promoting high moral and ethical values through children's literature." Deadline for entries: April 1. "Recipient is honored in July during the conference." Awards certificate of recognition and a conference package consisting of all meals, day of awards banquet, two nights' housing and a complimentary 1 year membership. "A nomination for an award may be made by anyone. It should include the name, address and telephone number of the nominee, plus the church or synagogue relationship where appropriate. Nominations of an organization should include the name of a contact person. A detailed description of the reasons for the nomination should be given, accompanied by documentary evidence of accomplishment. The person(s) making the nomination should give his/her name, address and telephone number and a brief explanation of his/her knowledge of the nominee's accomplishments. Elements of creativity and innovation will be given high priority by the judges."

OWL MAGAZINE CONTESTS, Writing Contest, Photo Contest, Poetry Contest and More, *OWL Magazine*, 49 Front St., E., 2nd Floor, Toronto, ON M5E 1B3 Canada. (416)340-2700. Fax: (416)340-9769. E-mail: owl@owl.on.ca. Website: www.owlkids.com. **Contact:** Kids' Page Editor. **Open to students.** Annual contests. Purpose of contests: "to encourage children to contribute and participate in the magazine." Unpublished submissions only. Deadlines change yearly. Prizes/awards "change every year. Often we give books as prizes." Winning entries published in the magazine. Judging by art and editorial staff. Entries become the property of Bayard Press. "The contests and awards are open to children up to 14 years of age. Check the Hoot section of *OWL* for information and updates. Contests have specific themes, so children should not send unsolicited poetry and fiction until they have checked contest details."

PATERSON PRIZE FOR BOOKS FOR YOUNG PEOPLE, Poetry Center at Passaic County Community College, One College Blvd., Paterson NJ 07505-1179. (973)684-6555. Fax: (973)523-6085. E-mail: mgillan@pccc.cc.nj.us. Website: www.pccc.cc.nj.us/poetry. **Director:** Maria Mazziotti Gillan. Estab. 1996. Part of the Poetry Center's mission is "to recognize excellence in books for young people." Previously published submissions only. Submissions made by author, author's agent or publisher. Must be published between January 1, 2003-December 31, 2003. Deadline for entries: March 15, 2004. SASE for contest rules and entry forms or visit website. Awards $500 for the author in either of 3 categories: PreK-Grade 3; Grades 4-6, Grades 7-12. Judging by a professional writer selected by the Poetry Center. Contest is open to any writer/illustrator.

PENNSYLVANIA YOUNG READERS' CHOICE AWARDS PROGRAM, Pennsylvania School Librarians Association, 148 S. Bethelehem Pike, Ambler PA 19002-5822. (215)643-5048. Fax: (215)628-8441. E-mail: bellavance@erols.com. **Coordinator:** Jean B. Bellavance. Annual award. Estab. 1991. Submissions nominated by a person or group. Must be published within 5 years of the award—for example, for 2003-2004 books published 1999 to present. Deadline for entries: September 1. SASE for contest rules and entry forms. No entry fee. Framed certificate to winning authors. Judging by children of Pennsylvania (they vote). Requirements for entrants: currently living in North America. Reader's Choice Award is to promote reading of quality books by young people in the Commonwealth of Pennsylvania, to promote teacher and librarian involvement in children's literature, and to honor authors whose work has been recognized by the children of Pennsylvania. Three awards are given, one for each of the following grade level divisions: K-3, 3-6, 6-8.

PEN/PHYLLIS NAYLOR WORKING WRITER FELLOWSHIP, PEN, 568 Broadway, New York NY 10012. (212)334-1660. Fax: (212)334-2181. E-mail: Peter@pen.org. Website: www.pen.org. Submit entries to: Peter Meyer. (Must have published 2 books to be eligible). Annual contest. Estab. 2001. To support writers with a financial need and recognize work of high literary caliber. Unpublished submissions only. Submissions nominated. Deadline for entries: January 14, 2004. Awards $5,000. Upon nomination by an editor or fellow writer, a panel of judges will select the winning book. Open to a writer of children's or young adult fiction in financial need, who has published at least two books, and no more than three during the past ten years.

PLEASE TOUCH MUSEUM® BOOK AWARD, Please Touch Museum, 210 N. 21st St., Philadelphia PA 19103-1001. (215)963-0667. Fax: (215)963-0424. E-mail: marketing@pleasetouchmuseum.org. Website: www.pleasetouchmuseum.org. Send submissions to Kathleen Miller. Annual award. Estab. 1985. Purpose of the award: "to recognize and encourage the publication of high-quality books for young children. The award is given to books that are imaginative, exceptionally illustrated and help foster a child's life-long love of reading. Each year we select one winner in two age categories—ages 3 and under and ages 4 to 7. These age categories reflect the age of the children Please Touch Museum serves. To be eligible for consideration a book must: (1) Be distinguished in text, illustration, and ability to explore and clarify an idea for young children (ages 7 and under). (2) Be published within the last year by an American publisher. (3) Be by an American author and/or illustrator." SASE for award rules and entry forms. No entry fee. Judging by selected jury of children's literature experts, librarians and early childhood educators. Education store purchases books for selling at Book Award Ceremony and throughout the year. Autographing sessions may be held at Please Touch Museum, and at Philadelphia's Early Childhood Education Conference.

POCKETS MAGAZINE FICTION CONTEST, *Pockets Magazine*, The Upper Room, P.O. Box 340004, Nashville TN 37203-0004. (615)340-7333. Fax: (615)340-7267. (Do not send submissions via fax.) E-mail: pockets@upperroom.org. Website: www.upperroom.org/pockets. **Contact:** Lynn W. Gilliam, associate editor. The purpose of the contest is to "find new freelance writers for the magazine." Annual competition for short stories. Award: $1,000 and publication in *Pockets*. Competition receives 600 submissions. Judged by *Pockets* editors and editors of other Upper Room publications. Guidelines available upon request and SASE or on website. No entry fee. No entry form. Note on envelope and first sheet: Fiction Contest. Submissions must be postmarked between March 1 and August 15 of the current year. Former winners may not enter. Unpublished submissions welcome. Word length: 1,000-1,600 words. Awards $1,000 and publication. Judging by *Pockets*' editors and 3 other editors of other Upper Room publications. Winner notified November 1. All other submissions returned if accompanied by SASE.

EDGAR ALLAN POE AWARD, Mystery Writers of America, Inc., 6th Floor, 17 E. 47th St., New York NY 10017. (212)888-8171. Fax: (212)888-8107. E-mail: mwa@mysterywriters.org. Website: www.mysterywriters.org. **Office Manager:** Margery Flax. Annual award. Estab. 1945. Purpose of the award: to honor authors of distinguished works in the mystery field. Previously published submissions only. Submissions made by the author, author's agent; "normally by the publisher." Work must be published/produced the year of the contest. Deadline for entries: November 30 "except for works only available in the month of December." SASE for award rules and entry forms. No entry fee. Awards ceramic bust of "Edgar" for winner; scrolls for all nominees. Judging by professional members of Mystery Writers of America (writers). Nominee press release sent after first Wednesday in February. Winner announced at the Edgar Banquet, held in late April/early May.

MICHAEL L. PRINTZ AWARD, Young Adult Library Services Association, Division of the American Library Association, 50 E. Huron, Chicago IL 60611. Fax: (312)664-7459. E-mail: yalsa@ala.org. Website: www.ala.org/yalsa/printz.

Annual award. The Michael L. Printz Award is an award for a book that exemplifies literary excellence in young adult literature. It is named for a Topeka, Kansas school librarian who was a long-time active member of the Young Adult Library Services Association. It will be selected annually by an award committee that can also name as many as 4 honor books. The award-winning book can be fiction, nonfiction, poetry or an anthology, and can be a work of joint authorship or editorship. The books must be published between January 1 and December 31 of the preceding year and be designated by its publisher as being either a young adult book or one published for the age range that YALSA defines as young adult, e.g. ages 12 through 18. The deadline for both committee and field nominations will be December 1.

PRIX ALVINE-BELISLE, Association pour l'avancement des sciences et des techniques de la documentation (AS-TED) Inc., 3414 Avenue Du Parc, Bureau 202, Montreal, QC H2X 2H5 Canada. (514)281-5012. Fax: (514)281-8219. E-mail: info@asted.org. **Award President:** Marie Hélène Parent. Award open to children's book editors. Annual award. Estab. 1974. Purpose of contest: To recognize the best children's book published in French in Canada. Previously published submissions only. Submissions made by publishing house. Must be published the year before award. Deadline for entries: June 1. Awards $1,000. Judging by librarians jury.

QUILL AND SCROLL INTERNATIONAL WRITING/PHOTO CONTEST, *Quill and Scroll*, School of Journalism, University of Iowa, Iowa City IA 52242-1528. (319)335-5795. Fax: (319)335-5210. E-mail: quill-scroll@uiowa.edu. Website: www.uiowa.edu/~quill-sc. **Contest Director:** Richard Johns. **Open to students.** Annual contest. Previously published submissions only. Submissions made by the author or school newspaper adviser. Must be published February 6, 2003 to February 4, 2004. Deadline for entries: February 5. SASE for contest rules and entry forms. Entry fee is $2/entry. Awards engraved plaque to junior high level sweepstakes winners. Judging by various judges. *Quill and Scroll* acquires the right to publish submitted material in the magazine if it is chosen as a winning entry. Requirements for entrants: must be students in grades 9-12 for high school division.

REDHOUSE CHILDREN'S BOOK AWARD, (formerly Children's Book Award), Federation of Children's Book Groups. The Old Malt House, Aldbourne Marlborough, Wiltshire SN8 2DW England. 01672 540629. Fax: 1672 541280. E-mail: marianneadey@aol.com. **Coordinator:** Marianne Adey. Purpose of the award: "The R.H.B.A. is an annual prize for the best children's book of the year judged by the children themselves." Categories: (I) books for younger children, (II) books for younger readers, (III) books for older readers. Estab. 1980. Works must be published in the United Kingdom. Deadline for entries: December 31. SASE for rules and entry forms. Entries not returned. Awards "a magnificent silver and oak trophy worth over $6,000 and a portfolio of children's work." Silver dishes to each category winner. Judging by children. Requirements for entrants: Work must be fiction and published in the UK during the current year (poetry is ineligible). Work will be published in current "Pick of the Year" publication.

TOMÁS RIVERA MEXICAN AMERICAN CHILDREN'S BOOK AWARD, Texas State University-San Marcos, EDU, 601 University Dr., San Marcos TX 78666-4613. (512)245-2357. Fax: (512)245-7911. E-mail: jb23@academia.swt.edu. **Award Director:** Dr. Jennifer Battle. Competition open to adults. Annual contest. Estab. 1995. Purpose of award: "To encourage authors, illustrators and publishers to produce books that authentically reflect the lives of Mexican American children and young adults in the United States." Previously published submissions only. Submissions made by "any interested individual or publishing company." Must be published during the year of consideration. Deadline for entries: February 1 post publication year. Contact Dr. Jennifer Battle for nomination forms, or send copy of book. No entry fee. Awards $3,000 per book. Judging of nominations by a regional committee, national committee judges finalists. Annual ceremony honoring the book and author/illustrator is held during Hispanic Heritage Month at Texas State University-San Marcos.

SASKATCHEWAN BOOK AWARDS: CHILDREN'S LITERATURE, Saskatchewan Book Awards, Box 1921, Regina, SK S4P 3E1 Canada. (306)569-1585. Fax: (306)569-4187. E-mail: director@bookawards.sk.ca. Website: www.bookawards.sk.ca. **Award Director:** Joyce Wells. Open to Saskatchewan authors only. Annual award. Estab. 1995. Purpose of contest: to celebrate Saskatchewan books and authors and to promote their work. Previously published submissions only. Submissions made by author, author's agent or publisher by September 15. SASE for contest rules and entry forms. Entry fee is $20 (Canadian). Awards $2,000 (Canadian). Judging by two children's literature authors outside of Saskatchewan. Requirements for entrants: Must be Saskatchewan resident; book must have ISBN number; book must have been published within the last year. Award-winning book will appear on TV talk shows and be pictured on bookmarks distributed to libraries, schools and bookstores in Saskatchewan.

SEVENTEEN FICTION CONTEST, 1440 Broadway, 13th Floor, New York NY 10018. Fax: (212)204-3977. Website: www.seventeen.com. **Open to students.** Annual contest. Estab. 1945. Purpose of contest: To recognize and encourage talented, young writers. Unpublished submissions only. Deadline for entries: April 30. SASE for contest rules and entry forms; contest rules also published in December issue of *Seventeen*. Entries not returned. Submissions accepted by mail only. No entry fee. Awards cash prize and possible publication in *Seventeen*. Judging by "inhouse panel of editors, external readers." If 1st, 2nd or 3rd prize, acquires first North American rights for piece to be published. Requirements for entrants: "Our annual fiction contest is open to anyone between the ages of 13 and 21 who submit on or before April 30. Submit only original fiction that has not been published in any form other than in school publications. Stories should be between 1,500 and 3,000 words in length (6-12 pages). All manuscripts must be typed double-spaced on a single side of paper. Submit as many original stories as you like, but each story must include your full name, address, birth date, e-mail address, and signature in the top right-hand corner of the first page. Your signature on submission will constitute your acceptance of the contest rules."

WRITERSMARKET.COM

If you thought there couldn't be a more valuable writer's resource than *Writer's Market*, think again. Now, get all the indispensable information of *Writer's Market* plus the power of the Internet with WritersMarket.com.

AND, GET $10 OFF THE REGULAR SUBSCRIPTION PRICE!

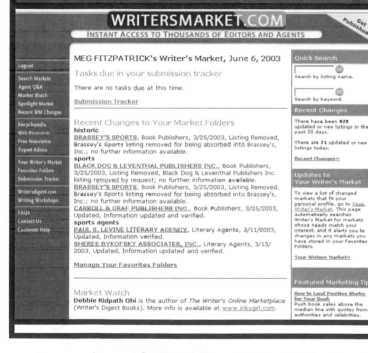

- → **5,600+ LISTINGS**
- → **SEARCHABLE DATABASE**
- → **PERSONALIZED SETTINGS**
- → **LISTINGS UPDATED DAILY**
- → **MUST-HAVE ADVICE**
- → **AND MORE!**

As a purchaser of *2004 Children's Writer's & Illustrator's Market*, get a $10 discount off the regular $29.99 subscription price for WritersMarket.com. Simply enter coupon code **WM4CW** on the subscription page at www.WritersMarket.com.

www.WritersMarket.com
—THE ULTIMATE RESEARCH TOOL FOR WRITERS

DETAILS ON BACK →

SHUBERT FENDRICH MEMORIAL PLAYWRITING CONTEST, Pioneer Drama Service, Inc., P.O. Box 4267, Englewood CO 80155-4267. Fax: (303)779-4315. E-mail: editors@pioneerdrama.com. Website: www.pioneerdrama.com. **Director:** Lori Conary. Annual contest. **Open to students.** Estab. 1990. Purpose of the contest: "to encourage the development of quality theatrical material for educational and family theater." Previously unpublished submissions only. Deadline for entries: March 1. SASE for contest rules and guidelines. No entry fee. Cover letter, SASE for return of ms, and proof of production or staged reading must accompany all submissions. Awards $1,000 royalty advance and publication. Upon receipt of signed contracts, plays will be published and made available in our next catalog. Judging by editors. All rights acquired with acceptance of contract for publication. Restrictions for entrants: Any writers currently published by Pioneer Drama Service are not eligible.

SKIPPING STONES YOUTH HONOR AWARDS, *Skipping Stones*, P.O. Box 3939, Eugene OR 97403-0939. (541)342-4956. E-mail: editor@SkippingStones.org. Website: www.SkippingStones.org. **Open to students**. Annual awards. Purpose of contest: "to recognize youth, 7 to 17, for their contributions to multicultural awareness, nature and ecology, social issues, peace and nonviolence. Also to promote creativity, self-esteem and writing skills and to recognize important work being done by youth organizations." Submissions made by the author. Deadline for entries: June 20. SASE for contest rules. Entries must include certificate of originality by a parent and/or teacher and background information on the author written by the author. Entry fee is $3. Everyone who enters the contest receives the March-April issue featuring Youth Awards. Judging by *Skipping Stones*' staff. "Up to ten awards are given in three categories: (1) Compositions—(essays, poems, short stories, songs, travelogues, etc.) should be typed (double-spaced) or neatly handwritten. Fiction or nonfiction should be limited to 750 words; poems to 30 lines. Non-English writings are also welcome. (2) Artwork—(drawings, cartoons, paintings or photo essays with captions) should have the artist's name, age and address on the back of each page. Send the originals with SASE. Black & white photos are especially welcome. Limit: 8 pieces. (3) Youth Organizations—Tell us how your club or group works to: (a) preserve the nature and ecology in your area, (b) enhance the quality of life for low-income, minority or disabled or (c) improve racial or cultural harmony in your school or community. Use the same format as for compositions." The winners are published in the September-October issue of *Skipping Stones*. The winners also receive "Honor certificates, five books and a subscription to *Skipping Stones* magazine.

KAY SNOW WRITERS' CONTEST, Williamette Writers, 9045 SW Barbur Blvd. #5A, Portland OR 97219-4027. (503)452-1592. Fax: (503)452-0372. E-mail: wilwrite@teleport.com. Website: www.willamettewriters.com. **Contest Director:** Marlene Moore. Annual contest. **Open to students.** Purpose of contest: "to encourage beginning and established writers to continue the craft." Unpublished, original submissions only. Submissions made by the author. Deadline for entries: May 15. SASE for contest rules and entry forms. Entry fee is $10, Williamette Writers' members; $15, nonmembers; free for student writers grades 1-12. Awards cash prize of $300 per category (fiction, nonfiction, juvenile, poetry, script writing), $50 for students in three divisions: 1-5, 6-8, 9-12. "Judges are anonymous."

THE STANLEY DRAMA AWARD, Stanley-Tomolat Foundation, Wagner College, One Campus Rd., Staten Island NY 10301. (718)390-3325. Fax: (718)390-3323. E-mail: froff@wagner.edu. **Award Director:** Dr. Felicia J. Ruff. **Open to students.** Annual award. Estab. 1957. Purpose of contest: to support new works and playwrights. Unpublished submissions only. Submissions made by author. Deadline for entries: October 1. SASE for contest rules and entry forms. Entry fee is $20. Awards $2,000. Judging by committee. Award is to a full-length play or musical, previously unpublished and/or produced. One-act plays must be a full evening of theater; accepts series of one-acts related to one theme. "We will consider only one submission per playwright."

GEORGE G. STONE CENTER FOR CHILDREN'S BOOKS RECOGNITION OF MERIT AWARD, George G. Stone Center for Children's Books, Claremont Graduate University, 740 N. College Ave., Claremont CA 91711-6188. (909)607-3670. **Award Director:** Doty Hale. Annual award. Estab. 1965. Purpose of the award: to recognize an author or illustrator of a children's book or a body of work exhibiting the "power to please and expand the awareness of children and teachers as they have shared the book in their classrooms." Previously published submissions only. SASE for award rules and entry forms. Entries not returned. No entry fee. Awards a scroll. Judging by a committee of teachers, professors of children's literature and librarians. Requirements for entrants: Nominations are made by students, teachers, professors and librarians. Award made at annual Claremont Reading Conference in spring (March).

SUGARMAN FAMILY AWARD FOR JEWISH CHILDREN'S LITERATURE, District of Columbia Jewish Community Center, 1529 16th St. N.W., Washington DC 20036. (202)518-9400. Fax: (202)518-9420. E-mail: brett@jcc.org. **Award Director:** Brett Rodgers. **Open to students.** Biannual award. Estab. 1994. Purpose of contest: to enrich all children's appreciation of Jewish culture and to inspire writers and illustrators for children. Newly published submissions only. Submissions are made by the author, made by the author's agent. Must be published January-December of year previous to award year. Deadline: May 30, 2004. SASE for entry deadlines, award rules and entry forms. Entry fee is $25. Award at least $750. Judging by a panel of three judges—a librarian, a children's bookstore owner and a reviewer of books. Requirements for entrants: must live in the United States. Work displayed at the D.C. Jewish Community Center Library. Presentation of awards—October 2003.

SWW ANNUAL CONTEST, SouthWest Writers, 8200 Mountain Rd. NE, Suite 106, Albuquerque NM 87110. (505)265-9485. Fax: (505)265-9483. E-mail: SWriters@aol.com. Website: www.southwestwriters.org. Submit entries to: Contest Chair. Annual contest. Estab. 1982. Purpose of contest: to encourage writers of all genres. Previously unpublished submissions only. Submissions made by author. Deadline for entries: May. SASE for contest rules and entry forms. Entry fee. Award consists of cash prizes in each of over 15 categories. Judging by national editors and agents. Official entry form is required.

N SYDNEY TAYLOR MANUSCRIPT COMPETITION, Association of Jewish Libraries, 315 Maitland Ave., Teaneck NJ 07666. Fax: (770)394-2060. E-mail: rkglasser@aol.com. Website: www.jewishlibraries.org. **Coordinator:** Rachel Glasser. **Open to students.** Annual contest. Estab. 1985. Purpose of the contest: "This competition is for unpublished writers of fiction. Material should be for readers ages 8-11, with universal appeal that will serve to deepen the understanding of Judaism for all children, revealing positive aspects of Jewish life." Unpublished submissions only. Deadline for entries: December 30, 2003. Download rules and forms from website or send SASE for contest rules and entry forms must be enclosed. No entry fee. Awards $1,000. Award will be given at the Association of Jewish Libraries annual convention. Award winner will be notified on April 15, 2004, and the award will be presented at the convention in New York in June of 2004. Judging by qualified judges from within the Association of Jewish Libraries. Requirements for entrants: must be an unpublished fiction writer; also, books must range from 64 to 200 pages in length. "AJL assumes no responsibility for publication, but hopes this cash incentive will serve to encourage new writers of children's stories with Jewish themes for all children."

THE TORONTO BOOK AWARDS, City of Toronto, 100 Queen St. W, 10th Floor, West Tower, Toronto, ON M5H 2N2 Canada. (416)392-8191. Fax: (416)392-1247. E-mail: bkurmey@toronto.ca. Submit entries to: Bev Kurmey, protocol officer. Annual award. Estab. 1974. Recognizes books of literary or artistic merit that are evocative of Toronto. Submissions made by author, author's agent or nominated by a person or group. Must be published the calendar year prior to the award year. Deadline for entries: last day of February annually. SASE for contest rules and entry forms. Awards $15,000 in prize money. Judging by committee.

TREASURE STATE AWARD, Missoula Public Library, Missoula County Schools, Montana Library Assoc., 301 E. Main, Missoula MT 59802. (406)721-2005. Fax: (406)728-5900. E-mail: bammon@missoula.lib.mt.us. Website: www.miss oula.lib.mt.us. **Award Directors:** Bette Ammon and Carole Monlux. Annual award. Estab. 1990. Purpose of the award: Children in grades K-3 read or listen to a ballot of 5 picture books and vote on their favorite. Previously published submissions only. Submissions made by author, nominated by a person or group of people—children, librarians, teachers. Must be published in previous 5 years to voting year. Deadline for entries: March 20. SASE for contest rules and entry forms. No entry fee. Awards a plaque or sculpture. Judging by popular vote by Montana children grades K-3.

VEGETARIAN ESSAY CONTEST, The Vegetarian Resource Group, P.O. Box 1463, Baltimore MD 21203. (410)366-VEGE. Fax: (410)366-8804. E-mail: vrg@vrg.org. Website: www.vrg.org. Address to Vegetarian Essay Contest. Annual contest. **Open to students.** Estab. 1985. Purpose of contest: to promote vegetarianism in young people. Unpublished submissions only. Deadline for entries: May 1 of each year. SASE for contest rules and entry forms. No entry fee. Awards $50 savings bond. Judging by awards committee. Acquires right for The Vegetarian Resource Group to reprint essays. Requirements for entrants: age 18 and under. Winning works may be published in *Vegetarian Journal*, instructional materials for students. "Submit 2-3 page essay on any aspect of vegetarianism, which is the abstinence of meat, fish and fowl. Entrants can base paper on interviewing, research or personal opinion. Need not be vegetarian to enter."

VFW VOICE OF DEMOCRACY, Veterans of Foreign Wars of the U.S., 406 W. 34th St., Kansas City MO 64111. (816)968-1117. Fax: (816)968-1149. Website: www.vfw.org. **Open to students.** Annual contest. Estab. 1960. Purpose of contest: to give high school students the opportunity to voice their opinions about their responsibility to our country and to convey those opinions via the broadcast media to all of America. Deadline for entries: November 1st. No entry fee. Winners receive awards ranging from $1,000-25,000. Requirements for entrants: "Ninth-twelfth grade students in public, parochial, private and home schools are eligible to compete. Former first place state winners are not eligible to compete again. Contact your participating high school teacher, counselor or your local VFW Post to enter."

N VIRGINIA LIBRARY ASSOCIATION/JEFFERSON CUP, Virginia Library Association, P.O. Box 8277, Norfolk VA 23503. E-mail: mwbaden@cox.net. Website: www.vla.org. **Executive Director:** Linda Hahne. **Open to students.** Award director changes year to year. Annual award. Estab. 1983. Purpose of award: "to encourage the writing of quality books for young people, to give recognition to authors who write in these disciplines, and to promote the reading of books that illustrate America's past." Previously published submissions only. Must be published in the year prior to selection. Deadline for entries: January 31. SASE for contest rules and entry forms. Judging by committee. "The book must be about U.S. history or an American person, 1492 to present, or fiction that highlights the U.S. past; author must reside in the U.S." The book must be published especially for young people.

VSA ARTS PLAYWRIGHT DISCOVERY AWARD, (formerly VSA (Very Special Arts) Playwright Discovery Program), VSA arts, 1300 Connecticut Ave., NW, Suite 700, Washington DC 20036. (202)628-2800 or 1-800-933-8721. TTY: (202)737-0645. Fax: (202)737-0725. E-mail: info@vsarts.org. Website: www.vsarts.org. **Open to students.** Annual contest. Estab. 1984. "All scripts must explore an aspect of disability." Unpublished submissions only. Deadline for entries: April 15, 2004. Write to Performing Arts Coordinator for contest rules and entry forms. No entries returned. No entry fee. Judging by Artists Selection Committee. Entrants must be students, grades 6-12. "One-act script will be selected for production at The John F. Kennedy Center for the Performing Arts, Washington DC. The winning play(s) is presented each fall."

N WASHINGTON CHILDREN'S CHOICE PICTURE BOOK AWARD, Washington Library Media Association, 4636 Camden Place, Mukilteo WA 98275. E-mail: galantek@edmonds.wednet.edu. **Award Director:** Kristin Galante. Submit entries to: Kristin Galante, chairman. Annual award. Estab. 1982. Previously published submissions only. Submissions nominated by a person or group. Must be published within 2-3 years prior to year of award. Deadline for entries: March 1. SASE for contest rules and entry forms. Awards pewter plate, recognition. Judging by WCCPBA committee.

WASHINGTON POST/CHILDREN'S BOOK GUILD AWARD FOR NONFICTION, E-mail: theguild@children sbookguild.org. Website: www.childrensbookguild.org. **President:** Betsy Kraft, 2003-2004. Annual award. Estab. 1977. Purpose of award: "to honor an author or illustrator whose total work has contributed significantly to the quality of nonfiction for children." Award includes a cash prize and an engraved crystal paperweight. Judging by a jury of Children's Book Guild librarians and authors and a *Washington Post* book critic. "One doesn't enter. One is selected. Our jury annually selects one author for the award."

WE ARE WRITERS, TOO!, Creative With Words Publications, P.O. Box 223226, Carmel CA 93922. Fax: (831)655-8627. E-mail: cwwpub@usa.net. Website: members.tripod.com/CreativeWithWords. **Contest Director:** Brigitta Geltrich. **Open to students.** Twice a year (January, August). Estab. 1975. Purpose of award: to further creative writing in children. Unpublished submissions only. Can submit year round on any topic. Deadlines for entries: year round. SASE for contest rules and entry forms. SASE for return of entries "if not accepted." No entry fee. Awards publication in an anthology. Judging by selected guest editors and educators. Contest open to children only (up to and including 19 years old). Writer should request contest rules. SASE with all correspondence. Age of child and home address must be stated and ms must be verified of its authenticity. Each story or poem must have a title. Creative with Words Publications (CWW) publishes the top 100-120 mss submitted to the contest CWW also publishes anthologies on various themes throughout the year to which young writers may submit. Request theme list, include SASE, or visit our website.

WESTERN HERITAGE AWARDS, National Cowboy and Western Heritage Museum, 1700 NE 63rd St., Oklahoma City OK 73111-7997. (405)478-2250. Fax: (405)478-4714. E-mail: editor@nationalcowboymuseum.org. Website: www.nat ionalcowboymuseum.org. **Director of Public Relations:** Lynda Haller. Annual award. Estab. 1961. Purpose of award: The WHA are presented annually to encourage the accurate and artistic telling of great stories of the West through 13 categories of western literature, television, film and music; including fiction, nonfiction, children's books and poetry. Previously published submissions only; must be published the calendar year before the awards are presented. Deadline for literary entries: November 30. Deadline for film, music and television entries: December 31. Entries not returned. Entry fee is $35/entry. Awards a Wrangler bronze sculpture designed by famed western artist, John Free. Judging by a panel of judges selected each year with distinction in various fields of western art and heritage. Requirements for entrants: The material must pertain to the development or preservation of the West, either from a historical or contemporary viewpoint. Literary entries must have been published between December 1 and November 30 of calendar year. Film, music or television entries must have been released or aired between January 1 and December 31 of calendar year of entry. Works recognized during special awards ceremonies held annually at the museum. There is an autograph party preceding the awards. Awards ceremonies are sometimes broadcast.

JACKIE WHITE MEMORIAL NATIONAL CHILDREN'S PLAY WRITING CONTEST, Columbia Entertainment Company, 309 Parkade Blvd., Columbia MO 65202-1447. (573)874-5628. Website: cec.missouri.org. **Contest Director:** Betsy Phillips. **Open to students.** Annual contest. Estab. 1988. Purpose of contest: "To promote the writing of excellent plays for family audiences and possibly to find plays for our theater school to produce." Previously unpublished submissions only. Submissions made by author. Deadline for entries: June 1. SASE for contest rules and entry forms. Entry fee is $10. Awards $500 with production possible. Judging by current and past board members of CEC and at least one theater school parent. Play may be performed during the following season. 2004 winner may be presented during CEC's 2004-05 season. We reserve the right to award 1st place and prize monies without a production. All submissions will be read by at least three readers. Author will receive a written evaluation of the script.

LAURA INGALLS WILDER AWARD, Association for Library Service to Children, Division of the American Library Association, 50 E. Huron, Chicago IL 60611. (312)280-2163. E-mail: alsc@ala.org. Website: www.ala.org/alsc. Interim **Executive Director:** Malore Brown. Award offered every 2 years. Purpose of the award: to recognize an author or illustrator whose books, published in the US, have over a period of years made a substantial and lasting contribution to children's literature. Medal presented at Newbery/Caldecott banquet during annual conference. Judging by Wilder Award Selection Committee.

PAUL A. WITTY OUTSTANDING LITERATURE AWARD, International Reading Association, Special Interest Group, Reading for Gifted and Creative Learning, School of Education, P.O. Box 297900, Fort Worth TX 76129. (817)921-7660. Fax: (817)257-7480. E-mail: c.block@tcu.edu. **Award Director:** Dr. Cathy Collins Block. **Open to students.** Annual award. Estab. 1979. Categories of entries: poetry/prose at elementary, junior high and senior high levels. Unpublished submissions only. Deadline for entries: February 1. SASE for award rules and entry forms. SASE for return of entries. No entry fee. Awards $25 and plaque, also certificates of merit. Judging by 2 committees for screening and awarding. Works will be published in International Reading Association publications. "The elementary students' entries must be legible and may not exceed 1,000 words. Secondary students' prose entries should be typed and may exceed 1,000 words if necessary. At both elementary and secondary levels, if poetry is entered, a set of five poems must be submitted. All entries and requests for applications must include a self-addressed, stamped envelope."

PAUL A. WITTY SHORT STORY AWARD, International Reading Association, P.O. Box 8139, 800 Barksdale Rd., Newark DE 19714-8139. (302)731-1600. E-mail: exec@reading.org. Website: www.reading.org. The entry must be an original short story appearing in a young children's periodical for the first time during 2003. The short story should serve as a literary standard that encourages young readers to read periodicals. Deadline for entries: The entry must have been published for the first time in the eligibility year; the short story must be submitted during the calendar year of publication. Anyone wishing to nominate a short story should send it to the designated Paul A. Witty Short Award Subcommittee Chair by December 1. Send SASE for guidelines. Award is $1,000 and recognition at the annual IRA Convention.

WOMEN IN THE ARTS ANNUAL CONTESTS, Women In The Arts, P.O. Box 2907, Decatur IL 62524-2907. (217)872-0811. Submit entries to Vice President. **Open to students.** Annual contest. Estab. 1995. Purpose of contest: to encourage beginning writers, as well as published professionals, by offering a contest for well-written material in plays, fiction, essay and poetry. Submissions made by author. Deadline for entries: November 1 annually. SASE for contest rules and entry forms. Entry fee is $2/item. Prize consists of $50 1st place; $35 2nd place; $15 3rd place. Send SASE for complete rules.

WORK-IN-PROGRESS GRANTS, Society of Children's Book Writers and Illustrators, 8271 Beverly Blvd., Los Angeles CA 90048. Fax: (323)782-1892. E-mail: scbwi@scbwi.org. Website: www.scbwi.org. Annual award. "The SCBWI Work-in-Progress Grants have been established to assist children's book writers in the completion of a specific project." Five categories: (1) General Work-in-Progress Grant. (2) Grant for a Contemporary Novel for Young People. (3) Nonfiction Research Grant. (4) Grant for a Work Whose Author Has Never Had a Book Published. (5) Grant for a Picture Book Writer. Requests for applications may be made beginning October 1. Completed applications accepted February 1-April 1 of each year. SASE for applications for grants. In any year, an applicant may apply for any of the grants except the one awarded for a work whose author has never had a book published. (The recipient of this grant will be chosen from entries in all categories.) Five grants of $1,500 will be awarded annually. Runner-up grants of $500 (one in each category) will also be awarded. "The grants are available to both full and associate members of the SCBWI. They are not available for projects on which there are already contracts." Previous recipients not eligible to apply.

WRITING CONFERENCE WRITING CONTESTS, The Writing Conference, Inc., P.O. Box 664, Ottawa KS 66067. Phone/fax: (785)242-1995. E-mail: jbushman@writingconference.com. Website: www.writingconference.com. **Contest Director:** John H. Bushman. **Open to students.** Annual contest. Estab. 1988. Purpose of contest: to further writing by students with awards for narration, exposition and poetry at the elementary, middle school and high school levels. Unpublished submissions only. Submissions made by the author or teacher. Deadline for entries: January 8. SASE for contest rules and entry form or consult website. No entry fee. Awards plaque and publication of winning entry in *The Writers' Slate*, March issue. Judging by a panel of teachers. Requirements for entrants: must be enrolled in school—K-12th grade.

▶ WRITING FOR CHILDREN COMPETITION, The Writers Union of Canada, 40 Wellington St. E, 3rd Floor, Toronto, ON M5E 1C7 Canada. (416)703-8982, ext. 223. Fax: (416)504-7656. E-mail: projects@writersunion.ca. Website: www.writersunion.ca. Submit entries to: Projects Coordinator. **Open to students.** Annual contest. Estab. 1997. Purpose of contest: to discover, encourage and promote new writers of children's literature. Unpublished submissions only. Submissions made by author. Deadline for entries: April 24, 2004. Entry fee is $15. Awards $1,500 and submission of winner and finalists to 3 publishers of children's books. Judging by members of the Writers Union of Canada (all published writers with at least one book). Requirements for entrants: Open only to writers; illustrated books do not qualify.

YEARBOOK EXCELLENCE CONTEST, *Quill and Scroll*, School of Journalism, University of Iowa, Iowa City IA 52242-1528. (319)335-5795. Fax: (319)335-5210. E-mail: quill-scroll@uiowa.edu. Website: www.uiowa.edu/~quill-sc. **Executive Director:** Richard Johns. **Open to students whose schools have *Quill and Scroll* charters.** Annual contest. Estab. 1987. Purpose of contest: to recognize and reward student journalists for their work in yearbooks and to provide student winners an opportunity to apply for a scholarship to be used freshman year in college for students planning to major in journalism. Previously published submissions only. Submissions made by the author or school yearbook adviser. Must be published between November 1, 2002 and November 1, 2003. Deadline for entries: November 1. SASE for contest rules and entry form. Entry fee is $2 per entry. Awards National Gold Key; sweepstakes winners receive plaque; seniors eligible for scholarships. Judging by various judges. Winning entries may be published in *Quill and Scroll* magazine.

▶ YOUNG ADULT CANADIAN BOOK AWARD, The Canadian Library Association, 328 Frank St., Ottawa, ON K2P 0X8 Canada. (613)232-9625. Fax: (613)563-9895. Website: www.cla.ca. **Contact:** Committee Chair. Annual award. Estab. 1981. Purpose of award: "to recognize the author of an outstanding English-language Canadian book which appeals to young adults between the ages of 13 and 18 that was published the preceding calendar year. Information is available upon request. We approach publishers, also send news releases to various journals, i.e., *Quill & Quire*." Entries are not returned. No entry fee. Awards a leather-bound book. Requirement for entrants: must be a work of fiction (novel or short stories), the title must be a Canadian publication in either hardcover or paperback, and the author must be a Canadian citizen or landed immigrant. Award given at the Canadian Library Association Conference.

Ⓝ YOUNG READER'S CHOICE AWARD, Pacific Northwest Library Association, The University of Washington, The Information School, Box 352840, Mary Gates Hall, Seattle WA 98195-2840. (206)685-9937. Fax: (406)543-5358. E-mail: monlux@montana.com. **Award Director:** Carole Monlux, chair YRCA. Annual award for published authors. Estab. 1940. Purpose of award: "to promote reading as an enjoyable activity and to provide children an opportunity to endorse a book they consider an excellent story." No unsolicited mss or published novels are accepted. Deadline for entries: February 1. SASE for award rules and entry forms. No entry fee. Awards a silver medal, struck in Idaho silver. "Children vote for their favorite books from a list of titles nominated by librarians, teachers, students and other interested persons." Contact Carole Monlux at Paxson Elementary School Library, 101 Evans, Missoula MT 59801; (406)542-4055, or fax or e-mail.

Ⓝ ZOLA LITERARY CONTEST, Pacific Northwest Writers Association, P.O.Box 2016, Edmonds WA 98020-9516. (425)673-2665. E-mail: staff@pnwa.org. Website: www.pnwa.org. **Contest/Award Director:** Dana Murphy-Love. **Open to students**. Annual contest. Purpose of contest: "Valuable tool for writers as contest submissions are critiqued (2 critiques)."

Unpublished submissions only. Submissions made by author. Deadline for entries: February 18, 2004. SASE for contest rules and entry forms. Entry fee is $35/entry for members, $45/entry for nonmembers. Awards $600-1st; $300-2nd; $150-3rd. Awards in all 10 categories.

N THE ANNA ZORNIO MEMORIAL CHILDREN'S THEATRE PLAYWRITING AWARD, University of New Hampshire, Department of Theatre and Dance, Paul Creative Arts Center, 30 College Rd., University of New Hampshire, Durham NH 03824-3538. (603)862-3038. Fax: (603)862-0298. E-mail: mike.wood@unh.edu. Website: www.unh.edu/theatre-dance. **Contact:** Michael Wood. Contest every 4 years; next contest is November 2004. Estab. 1979. Purpose of the award: "to honor the late Anna Zornio, an alumna of The University of New Hampshire, for dedication to and inspiration of playwriting for young people, K-12th grade. Open to playwrights who are residents of the U.S. and Canada. Plays or musicals should run about 45 minutes." Unpublished submissions only. Submissions made by the author. Deadline for entries: September 1, 2004. SASE for award rules and entry forms. No entry fee. Awards $1,000 plus guaranteed production. Judging by faculty committee. Acquires rights to campus production. Write for details.

Helpful Books & Publications

The editors of *Children's Writer's & Illustrator's Market* suggest the following books and periodicals to keep you informed on writing and illustrating techniques, trends in the field, business issues, industry news and changes, and additional markets.

BOOKS

AN AUTHOR'S GUIDE TO CHILDREN'S BOOK PROMOTION, by Susan Salzman Raab, 345 Millwood Rd., Chappaqua NY 10514. (914)241-2117. E-mail: info@raabassociates.com. Website: www.raabassociates.com/authors .htm.

THE BUSINESS OF WRITING FOR CHILDREN, by Aaron Shepard, Shepard Publications. Website: www.aaronshep.com/kidwriter/Business.html. Available on www.amazon.com.

CHILDREN'S WRITER GUIDE, (annual), The Institute of Children's Literature, 93 Long Ridge Rd., West Redding CT 06896-0811. (800)443-6078. Website: www.writersbookstore.com.

CHILDREN'S WRITER'S REFERENCE, by Berthe Amoss and Eric Suben, Writer's Digest Books, 4700 E. Galbraith Rd., Cincinnati OH 45236. (800)448-0915. Website: www.writersdigest.com.

CHILDREN'S WRITER'S WORD BOOK, by Alijandra Mogilner, Writer's Digest Books, 4700 E. Galbraith Rd., Cincinnati OH 45236. (800)448-0915. Website: www.writersdigest.com.

THE COMPLETE IDIOT'S GUIDE® TO PUBLISHING CHILDREN'S BOOKS, by Harold D. Underdown and Lynne Rominger, Alpha Books, 201 W. 103rd St., Indianapolis IN 46290. Website: www.idiotsguides.com.

CREATING CHARACTERS KIDS WILL LOVE, by Elaine Marie Alphin, Writer's Digest Books, 4700 E. Galbraith Rd., Cincinnati OH 45236. (800)448-0915. Website: www.writersdigest.com.

FORMATTING & SUBMITTING YOUR MANUSCRIPT, by Jack and Glenda Neff, Don Prues and the editors of *Writer's Market*, Writer's Digest Books, 4700 E. Galbraith Rd., Cincinnati OH 45236. (800)448-0915. Website: www.writersdigest.com.

HOW TO PROMOTE YOUR CHILDREN'S BOOK: A SURVIVAL GUIDE, by Evelyn Gallardo, Primate Production, P.O. Box 3038, Manhattan Beach CA 90266, Website: www.evegallardo.com/promote.html.

✔ **HOW TO WRITE A CHILDREN'S BOOK & GET IT PUBLISHED**, by Barbara Seuling, John Wiley & Sons, 111 River St., Hoboken NJ 07030. (201)748-6000. Website: www.wiley.com.

HOW TO WRITE AND ILLUSTRATE CHILDREN'S BOOKS AND GET THEM PUBLISHED, edited by Treld Pelkey Bicknell and Felicity Trottman, Writer's Digest Books, 4700 E. Galbraith Rd., Cincinnati OH 45236. (800)448-0915. Website: www.writersdigest.com.

HOW TO WRITE ATTENTION-GRABBING QUERY & COVER LETTERS, by John Wood, Writer's Digest Books, 4700 E. Galbraith Rd., Cincinnati OH 45236. (800)448-0915. Website: www.writersdigest.com.

IT'S A BUNNY-EAT-BUNNY WORLD: A Writer's Guide to Surviving and Thriving in Today's Competitive Children's Book Market, by Olga Litowinsky, 435 Hudson St., New York NY 10014. (212)727-8300. Website: www.walkerbooks.com.

PICTURE WRITING: A New Approach to Writing for Kids and Teens, by Anastasia Suen, Writer's Digest Books, 4700 E. Galbraith Rd., Cincinnati OH 45236. (800)448-0915. Website: www.writersdigest.com.

STORY SPARKERS: A Creativity Guide for Children's Writers, by Marcia Thornton Jones and Debbie Dadey, Writer's Digest Books, 4700 E. Galbraith Rd., Cincinnati OH 45236. (800)448-0915. Website: www.writersdigest.com.

A TEEN'S GUIDE TO GETTING PUBLISHED, by Danielle Dunn & Jessica Dunn, Prufrock Press, P.O. Box 8813, Waco TX 76714-8813. (800)998-2208.

THE WRITER'S ESSENTIAL DESK REFERENCE, Second Edition, Writer's Digest Books, 4700 E. Galbraith Rd., Cincinnati OH 45236. (800)448-0915. Website: www.writersdigest.com.

THE WRITER'S GUIDE TO CRAFTING STORIES FOR CHILDREN, by Nancy Lamb, Writer's Digest Books, 4700 E. Galbraith Rd., Cincinnati OH 45236. (800)448-0915. Website: www.writersdigest.com.

WRITING AND ILLUSTRATING CHILDREN'S BOOKS FOR PUBLICATION: Two Perspectives, by Berthe Amoss and Eric Suben, Writer's Digest Books, 4700 E. Galbraith Rd., Cincinnati OH 45236. (800)448-0915. Website: www.writersdigest.com.

☑ **WRITING BOOKS FOR YOUNG PEOPLE**, Second Edition, by James Cross Giblin, The Writer, Inc., P.O. Box 600160, Newton MA 02460. (617)423-3157.

WRITING FOR CHILDREN & TEENAGERS, Third Edition, by Lee Wyndham and Arnold Madison, Writer's Digest Books, 4700 E. Galbraith Rd., Cincinnati OH 45236. (800)448-0915. Website: www.writersdigest.com.

☑ **WRITING WITH PICTURES: How to Write and Illustrate Children's Books**, by Uri Shulevitz, Watson-Guptill Publications, 770 Broadway, New York NY 10003. (800)278-8477.

YOU CAN WRITE CHILDREN'S BOOKS, by Tracey E. Dils, Writer's Digest Books, 4700 E. Galbraith Rd., Cincinnati OH 45236. (800)448-0915. Website: www.writersdigest.com.

THE YOUNG WRITER'S GUIDE TO GETTING PUBLISHED, by Kathy Henderson, Writer's Digest Books, 4700 E. Galbraith Rd., Cincinnati OH 45236. (800)448-0915. Website: www.writersdigest.com.

PUBLICATIONS

BOOK LINKS: Connecting Books, Libraries and Classrooms, editor Laura Tillotson, American Library Association, 50 E. Huron St., Chicago IL 60611. (800)545-2433. Website: www.ala.org/BookLinks. *Magazine published 6 times a year (September-July) for the purpose of connecting books, libraries and classrooms. Features articles on specific topics followed by bibliographies recommending books for further information. Subscription: $25.95/year.*

CHILDREN'S BOOK INSIDER, editor Laura Backes, 901 Columbia Rd., Ft. Collins CO 80525-1838. (970)495-0056 or (800)807-1916. E-mail: mail@write4kids.com. Website: www.write4kids.com. *Monthly newsletter covering markets, techniques and trends in children's publishing. Subscription: $29.95/year. Official update source for* Children's Writer's & Illustrator's Market, *featuring quarterly lists of changes and updates to listings in the book.*

☑ **CHILDREN'S WRITER**, editor Susan Tierney, The Institute of Children's Literature, 93 Long Ridge Rd., West Redding CT 06896-0811. (800)443-6078. Website: www.childrenswriter.com. *Monthly newsletter of writing and publishing trends in the children's field. Subscription: $26/year; special introductory rate: $15.*

☑ **THE FIVE OWLS**, editor Dr. Mark West, 2000 Aldrich Ave. S., Minneapolis MN 55405. (612)890-0404. Website: www.fiveowls.com. *Bimonthly newsletter for readers personally and professionally involved in children's literature. Subscription: $35/year.*

THE HORN BOOK MAGAZINE, editor-in-chief Roger Sutton, The Horn Book Inc., 56 Roland St., Suite 200, Boston MA 02129. (800)325-1170. E-mail: info@hbook.com. E-mail: jlorder@jhu.edu. Website: www.hbook.com. *Bimonthly guide to the children's book world including views on the industry and reviews of the latest books. Subscription: special introductory rate: $29.95.*

THE LION AND THE UNICORN: A Critical Journal of Children's Literature, editors Jack Zipes and Louisa Smith, The Johns Hopkins University Press, P.O. Box 19966, Baltimore MD 21211-0966. (800)548-1784 or (410)516-6987. E-mail: jlorder@jhu.edu. Website: www.press.jhu.edu/press/journals/uni/uni.html. *Magazine published 3 times a year serving as a forum for discussion of children's literature featuring interviews with authors, editors and experts in the field. Subscription: $26.50/year.*

ONCE UPON A TIME, editor Audrey Baird, 553 Winston Court, St. Paul MN 55118. (651)457-6223. Fax: (651)457-9565. Website: http://members.aol.com/OUATMAG/. *Quarterly support magazine for children's writers and illustrators and those interested in children's literature. Subscription: $25/year.*

PUBLISHERS WEEKLY, editor-in-chief Nora Rawlinson, Reed Business Information, a division of Reed Elsevier Inc., 360 Park Ave. S., New York NY 10010. (800)278-2991. Website: www.publishersweekly.com. *Weekly trade publication covering all aspects of the publishing industry; includes coverage of the children's field and spring and fall issues devoted solely to children's books. Subscription: $189/year. Available on newsstands for $4/issue. (Special issues are higher in price.)*

RIVERBANK REVIEW of books for young readers, editor Martha Davis Beck, 1624 Harmon Place, Suite 305, Minneapolis MN 55403. (613)486-5690. E-mail: mail@riverbankreview.com. Website: www.riverbankrevie w.com. *Quarterly publication exploring the world of children's literature including book reviews, articles and essays. Subscription: $22.95/year.*

SOCIETY OF CHILDREN'S BOOK WRITERS AND ILLUSTRATORS BULLETIN, editors Stephen Mooser and Lin Oliver, SCBWI, 8271 Beverly Blvd., Los Angeles CA 90048. (323)782-1010. Website: www.scb wi.org/pubs.htm. *Bimonthly newsletter of SCBWI covering news of interest to members. Subscription with $60/ year membership.*

Useful Online Resources

The editors of *Children's Writer's & Illustrator's Market* suggest the following websites to keep you informed on writing and illustrating techniques, trends in the field, business issues, industry news and changes, and additional markets.

AMAZON.COM: www.amazon.com
Calling itself "A bookstore too big for the physical world," Amazon.com has more than 3 million books available on their website at discounted prices, plus a personal notification service of new releases, reader reviews, bestseller and suggested book information.

AMERICA WRITES FOR KIDS: usawrites4kids.drury.edu/
Lists book authors by state along with interviews, profiles and writing tips.

ARTLEX ART DICTIONARY: www.artlex.com
Art dictionary with more than 3,200 terms

ASSOCIATION FOR LIBRARY SERVICE TO CHILDREN: www.ala.org/alsc/awards.html
This site provides links to information about Newbery, Caldecott, Coretta Scott King and Michael L. Printz Awards as well as a host of other awards for notable children's books.

N 🌐 ASSOCIATION OF ILLUSTRATORS: www.theaoi.com
This U.K.-based organization has been working since 1973 to promote illustration, illustrators' rights and standards. The website has discussion boards, artists' directories, events, links to agents and much more.

AUTHORS AND ILLUSTRATORS FOR CHILDREN WEBRING: www.webring.org/cgi-bin/webring?ring = aicwebring;list
Here you'll find a list of link of sites of interest to children's writers and illustrators or created by them.

THE AUTHORS GUILD ONLINE: www.authorsguild.org/
The website of The Authors Guild offers articles and columns dealing with contract issues, copyright, electronic rights and other legal issues of concern to writers.

BARNES & NOBLE ONLINE: www.bn.com
The world's largest bookstore chain's website contains 600,000 in-stock titles at discount prices as well as personalized recommendations, online events with authors and book forum access for members.

N THE BOOK REPORT NETWORK: *includes* www.bookreporter.com; www.readinggroupguides.com; www.authorsontheweb.com; www.teenreads.com *and* www.kidsreads.com
All the sites feature giveaways, book reviews, author and editor interviews, and recommended reads. A great way to stay connected.

BOOKWIRE: www.bookwire.com
A gateway to finding information about publishers, booksellers, libraries, authors, reviews and awards. Also offers frequently asked publishing questions and answers, a calendar of events, a mailing list and other helpful resources.

CANADIAN CHILDREN'S BOOK CENTRE: www.bookcentre.ca
The site for the CCBC includes profiles of illustrators and authors, information on recent books, a calendar of upcoming events, information on CCBC publications, and tips from Canadian children's authors.

▪ CANADIAN SOCIETY OF CHILDREN'S AUTHORS, ILLUSTRATORS AND PERFORMERS: www.canscaip.org
This organization promotes all aspects of children's writing, illustration and performance.

THE CHILDREN'S BOOK COUNCIL: www.cbcbooks.org
This site includes a complete list of CBC members with addresses, names and descriptions of what each publishes,

and links to publishers' websites. Also offers previews of upcoming titles from members; articles from CBC Features, *the Council's newsletter; and their catalog.*

CHILDREN'S LITERATURE: www.childrenslit.com
Offers book reviews, lists of conferences, searchable database, links to over 1,000 author/illustrator websites and much more.

CHILDREN'S LITERATURE WEB GUIDE: www.ucalgary.ca/~dkbrown/index.html
This site includes stories, poetry, resource lists, lists of conferences, links to book reviews, lists of awards (international), and information on books from classic to contemporary.

CHILDREN'S WRITING SUPERSITE: www.write4kids.com
This site (formerly Children's Writers Resource Center) includes highlights from the newsletter Children's Book Insider; *definitions of publishing terms; answers to frequently asked questions; information on trends; information on small presses; a research center for Web information; and a catalog of material available from* CBI.

THE COLOSSAL DIRECTORY OF CHILDREN'S PUBLISHERS ONLINE: (formerly Children's Publishers' Submission Guidelines) www.signaleader.com/childrens-writers/
This site features links to websites of children's publishers and magazines and includes information on which publishers offer submission guidelines online.

DATABASE OF AWARD-WINNING CHILDREN'S LITERATURE: www.dawcl.com
A compilation of over 4,000 records of award-winning books throughout the U.S., Canada, Australia, New Zealand and the U.K. You can search by age level, format, genre, setting, historical period, ethnicity or nationality of the protagonist, gender of protagonist, publication year, award name, or even by keyword. Begin here to compile your reading list of award-winners.

THE DRAWING BOARD: members.aol.com/thedrawing
This site for illustrators features articles, interviews, links and resources for illustrators from all fields.

EDITOR & PUBLISHER: www.mediainfo.com
The Internet source for Editor & Publisher, *this site provides up-to-date industry news, with other opportunities such as a research area and bookstore, a calendar of events and classifieds.*

IMAGINARY LANDS: www.imaginarylands.org
A fun site with links to websites about picture books, learning tools and children's literature.

INTERNATIONAL BOARD ON BOOKS FOR YOUNG PEOPLE: www.ibby.org
Founded in Switzerland in 1953, IBBY is a nonprofit that seeks to encourage the creation and distribution of quality children's literature. They cooperate with children's organizations and children's book institutions around the world.

INTERNATIONAL READING ASSOCIATION: www.reading.org
This website includes articles; book lists; event, conference and convention information; and an online bookstore.

NATIONAL ASSOCIATION FOR THE EDUCATION OF YOUNG CHILDREN: www.naeyc.org.
This organization is comprised of over 100,000 early childhood educators and others interested in the development and education of young children. Their website makes a great introduction and research resource for authors and illustrators of picture books.

NATIONAL WRITERS UNION: www.nwu.org
The union for freelance writers in U.S. Markets. The NWU offers contract advice, greviance assistance, health and liability insurance and much more.

ONCE UPON A TIME: members.aol.com/OUATMAG
This companion site to Once Upon A Time *magazine offers excerpts from recent articles, notes for prospective contributors, and information about OUAT's 11 regular columnists.*

PICTUREBOOK: www.picture-book.com
This site brought to you by Picturebook *sourcebook offers tons of links for illustrators, portfolio searching, and news, and offers a listserv, bulletin board and chatroom.*

PUBLISHERS' CATALOGUES HOME PAGE: www.lights.com/publisher/index.html
A mammoth link collection of more than 6,000 publishers around the world arranged geographically. This site is one of the most comprehensive directories of publishers on the Internet.

PUBLISHERS WEEKLY CHILDREN'S FEATURES: www.publishersweekly.com/childrensindex.asp
This is a direct link to Publishers Weekly *articles relating to children's publishing and authors.*

THE PURPLE CRAYON: www.underdown.org
Editor Harold Underdown's site includes articles on trends, business, and cover letters and queries as well as interviews with editors and answers to frequently asked questions. He also includes links to a number of other sites helpful to writers and excerpts from his book The Complete Idiot's Guide to Publishing Children's Books.

SLANTVILLE: www.slantville.com
An online artists community, this site includes a yellow pages for artists, frequently asked questions and a library offering information on a number of issues of interest to illustrators. This is a great site to visit to view artists' portfolios.

ⓝ SMARTWRITERS.COM: www.smartwriters.com
Writer, novelist, photographer, graphic designer, and co-founder of 2-Tier Software, Inc., Roxyanne Young, runs this online magazine, which is absolutely stuffed with resources for children's writers, teachers and young writers. It's also got contests, interviews, free books, advice and well—you just have to go there.

SOCIETY OF CHILDREN'S BOOK WRITERS AND ILLUSTRATORS: www.scbwi.org
This site includes information on awards and grants available to SCBWI members, a calendar of events listed by date and region, a list of publications available to members, and a site map for easy navigation. Follow the Regional Chapters link to find the SCBWI chapter in your area.

THE SOCIETY OF ILLUSTRATORS: www.societyillustrators.org
Since 1901, this organization has been working to promote the interest of professional illustrators. Information on exhibitions, career advice, and many other links provided.

ⓝ ⊕ U.K. CHILDREN'S BOOKS: www.ukchildrensbooks.co.uk
Filled with links to author sites, illustrator sites, publishers, booksellers, and organizations—not to mention help with website design and other technicalities—visit this site no matter which side of the Atlantic you rest your head.

UNITED STATES POSTAL SERVICE: www.usps.gov/welcome.htm
Offers domestic and International postage rate calculator, stamp ordering, zip code look up, express mail tracking and more.

VERLA KAY'S WEBSITE: www.verlakay.com
Author Verla Kay's website features writer's tips, articles, a schedules of online workshops (with transcripts of past workshops), a good news board and helpful links.

WRITERSDIGEST.COM: www.writersdigest.com
Brought to you by Writer's Digest *magazine, this site features articles, resources, links, writing prompts, a bookstore, and more.*

WRITERSMARKET.COM: www.writersmarket.com
This gateway to the Writer's Market *online edition offers market news, FAQs, tips, featured markets and web resources, a free newsletter, and more.*

WRITING-WORLD.COM: www.writing-world.com/children
Site features reams of advice, links and offers a free bi-weekly newsletter.

Glossary

AAR. Association of Authors' Representatives.

ABA. American Booksellers Association.

ABC. Association of Booksellers for Children.

Advance. A sum of money a publisher pays a writer or illustrator prior to the publication of a book. It is usually paid in installments, such as one half on signing the contract; one half on delivery of a complete and satisfactory manuscript. The advance is paid against the royalty money that will be earned by the book.

ALA. American Library Association.

All rights. The rights contracted to a publisher permitting the use of material anywhere and in any form, including movie and book club sales, without additional payment to the creator.

Anthology. A collection of selected writings by various authors or gatherings of works by one author.

Anthropomorphization. The act of attributing human form and personality to things not human (such as animals).

ASAP. As soon as possible.

Assignment. An editor or art director asks a writer, illustrator or photographer to produce a specific piece for an agreed-upon fee.

B&W. Black & white.

Backlist. A publisher's list of books not published during the current season but still in print.

Biennially. Occurring once every 2 years.

Bimonthly. Occurring once every 2 months.

Biweekly. Occurring once every 2 weeks.

Book packager. A company that draws all elements of a book together, from the initial concept to writing and marketing strategies, then sells the book package to a book publisher and/or movie producer. Also known as book producer or book developer.

Book proposal. Package submitted to a publisher for consideration usually consisting of a synopsis, outline and sample chapters. (See Before Your First Sale, page 8.)

Business-size envelope. Also known as a #10 envelope. The standard size used in sending business correspondence.

Camera-ready. Refers to art that is completely prepared for copy camera platemaking.

Caption. A description of the subject matter of an illustration or photograph; photo captions include persons' names where appropriate. Also called cutline.

Clean-copy. A manuscript free of errors and needing no editing; it is ready for typesetting.

Clips. Samples, usually from newspapers or magazines, of a writer's published work.

Concept books. Books that deal with ideas, concepts and large-scale problems, promoting an understanding of what's happening in a child's world. Most prevalent are alphabet and counting books, but also includes books dealing with specific concerns facing young people (such as divorce, birth of a sibling, friendship or moving).

Contract. A written agreement stating the rights to be purchased by an editor, art director or producer and the amount of payment the writer, illustrator or photographer will receive for that sale. (See The Business of Writing & Illustrating, page 13.)

Contributor's copies. The magazine issues sent to an author, illustrator or photographer in which her work appears.

Co-op publisher. A publisher that shares production costs with an author, but, unlike subsidy publishers, handles all marketing and distribution. An author receives a high percentage of royalties until her initial investment is recouped, then standard royalties. (*Children's Writer's & Illustrator's Market* does not include co-op publishers.)

Copy. The actual written material of a manuscript.

Copyediting. Editing a manuscript for grammar usage, spelling, punctuation and general style.

Copyright. A means to legally protect an author's/illustrator's/photographer's work. This can be shown by writing ©, the creator's name, and year of work's creation. (See The Business of Writing & Illustrating, page 13.)

Cover letter. A brief letter, accompanying a complete manuscript, especially useful if responding to an editor's request for a manuscript. May also accompany a book proposal. (See Before Your First Sale, page 8.)

Cutline. See caption.

Disk. A round, flat magnetic plate on which computer data may be stored.

Division. An unincorporated branch of a company.

Dummy. A loose mock-up of a book showing placement of text and artwork.

Electronic submission. A submission of material by modem or on computer disk.

E-mail. Electronic mail. Messages sent from one computer to another via a modem or computer network.

Final draft. The last version of a polished manuscript ready for submission to an editor.

First North American serial rights. The right to publish material in a periodical for the first time, in the United States or Canada. (See The Business of Writing & Illustrating, page 13.)

F&G's. Folded and gathered sheets. An early, not-yet-bound copy of a picture book.

Flat fee. A one-time payment.

Galleys. The first typeset version of a manuscript that has not yet been divided into pages.

Genre. A formulaic type of fiction, such as horror, mystery, romance, science fiction or western.

Glossy. A photograph with a shiny surface as opposed to one with a non-shiny matte finish.

Gouache. Opaque watercolor with an appreciable film thickness and an actual paint layer.

Halftone. Reproduction of a continuous tone illustration with the image formed by dots produced by a camera lens screen.

Hard copy. The printed copy of a computer's output.

Hardware. All the mechanically-integrated components of a computer that are not software—circuit boards, transistors and the machines that are the actual computer.

Hi-Lo. High interest, low reading level.

Home page. The first page of a website.

IBBY. International Board on Books for Young People.

Imprint. Name applied to a publisher's specific line of books.

Internet. A worldwide network of computers that offers access to a wide variety of electronic resources.

IRA. International Reading Association.

IRC. International Reply Coupon. Sold at the post office to enclose with text or artwork sent to a recipient outside your own country to cover postage costs when replying or returning work.

Keyline. Identification of the positions of illustrations and copy for the printer.

Layout. Arrangement of illustrations, photographs, text and headlines for printed material.

Line drawing. Illustration done with pencil or ink using no wash or other shading.

Mass market books. Paperback books directed toward an extremely large audience sold in supermarkets, drugstores, airports, newsstands, online retailers, and bookstores.

Mechanicals. Paste-up or preparation of work for printing.

Middle grade or mid-grade. See middle reader.

Middle reader. The general classification of books written for readers approximately ages 9-11. Also called middle grade.

Ms (mss). Manuscript(s).

Multiple submissions. See simultaneous submissions.

NCTE. National Council of Teachers of English.

One-time rights. Permission to publish a story in periodical or book form one time only. (See The Business of Writing & Illustrating, page 13.)

Outline. A summary of a book's contents; often in the form of chapter headings with a descriptive sentence or two under each heading to show the scope of the book.

Package sale. The sale of a manuscript and illustrations/photos as a "package" paid for with one check.

Payment on acceptance. The writer, artist or photographer is paid for her work at the time the editor or art director decides to buy it.

Payment on publication. The writer, artist or photographer is paid for her work when it is published.

Picture book. A type of book aimed at preschoolers to 8-year-olds that tells a story using a combination of text and artwork, or artwork only.

Print. An impression pulled from an original plate, stone, block, screen or negative; also a positive made from a photographic negative.

Proofreading. Reading text to correct typographical errors.

Query. A letter to an editor or agent designed to capture interest in an article or book you have written or propose to write. (See Before Your First Sale, page 8.)

Reading fee. Money charged by some agents and publishers to read a submitted manuscript. (*Children's Writer's & Illustrator's Market* does not include operations that charge reading fees.)

Reprint rights. Permission to print an already published work whose first rights have been sold to another magazine or book publisher. (See The Business of Writing & Illustrating, page 13.)

Response time. The average length of time it takes an editor or art director to accept or reject a query or submission and inform the creator of the decision.

Rights. The bundle of permissions offered to an editor or art director in exchange for printing a manuscript, artwork or photographs. (See The Business of Writing & Illustrating, page 13.)

Rough draft. A manuscript that has not been checked for errors in grammar, punctuation, spelling or content.

Roughs. Preliminary sketches or drawings.

Royalty. An agreed percentage paid by a publisher to a writer, illustrator or photographer for each copy of her work sold.

SAE. Self-addressed envelope.

SASE. Self-addressed, stamped envelope.

SCBWI. The Society of Children's Book Writers and Illustrators. (See listing in Clubs & Organizations section.)

Second serial rights. Permission for the reprinting of a work in another periodical after its first publication in book or magazine form. (See The Business of Writing & Illustrating, page 13.)

Semiannual. Occurring every 6 months or twice a year.

Semimonthly. Occurring twice a month.

Semiweekly. Occurring twice a week.

Serial rights. The rights given by an author to a publisher to print a piece in one or more periodicals. (See The Business of Writing & Illustrating, page 13.)

Simultaneous submissions. Queries or proposals sent to several publishers at the same time. Also called multiple submissions. (See Before Your First Sale, page 8.)

Slant. The approach to a story or piece of artwork that will appeal to readers of a particular publication.

Slush pile. Editors' term for their collections of unsolicited manuscripts.

Software. Programs and related documentation for use with a computer.

Solicited manuscript. Material that an editor has asked for or agreed to consider before being sent by a writer.

SPAR. Society of Photographers and Artists Representatives.

Speculation (spec). Creating a piece with no assurance from an editor or art director that it will be purchased or any reimbursements for material or labor paid.

Subsidiary rights. All rights other than book publishing rights included in a book contract, such as paperback, book club and movie rights. (See The Business of Writing & Illustrating, page 13.)

Subsidy publisher. A book publisher that charges the author for the cost of typesetting, printing and promoting a book. Also called a vanity publisher. (*Children's Writer's & Illustrator's Market* does not include subsidy publishers.)

Synopsis. A brief summary of a story or novel. Usually a page to a page and a half, single-spaced, if part of a book proposal.

Tabloid. Publication printed on an ordinary newspaper page turned sideways and folded in half.

Tearsheet. Page from a magazine or newspaper containing your printed art, story, article, poem or photo.

Thumbnail. A rough layout in miniature.

Trade books. Books sold in bookstores and through online retailers, aimed at a smaller audience than mass market books, and printed in smaller quantities by publishers.

Transparencies. Positive color slides; not color prints.

Unsolicited manuscript. Material sent without an editor's or art director's request.

Vanity publisher. See subsidy publisher.

World Wide Web. An Internet resource that utilizes hypertext to access information. It also supports formatted text, illustrations and sounds, depending on the user's computer capabilities.

Work-for-hire. An arrangement between a writer, illustrator or photographer and a company under which the company retains complete control of the work's copyright. (See The Business of Writing & Illustrating, page 13.)

YA. See young adult.

Young adult. The general classification of books written for readers approximately ages 12-18. Often referred to as YA.

Young reader. The general classification of books written for readers approximately ages 5-8.

Age-Level Index

This index lists book and magazine publishers by the age-groups for which they publish. Use it to locate appropriate markets for your work, then carefully read the listings and follow the guidelines of each publisher. Use this index in conjunction with the Subject Index to further narrow your list of markets. **Picture Books** and **Picture-Oriented Material** are for preschoolers to 8-year-olds; **Young Readers** are for 5- to 8-year-olds; **Middle Readers** are for 9- to 11-year-olds; and **Young Adults** are for ages 12 and up.

BOOK PUBLISHERS

Young Readers

MAGAZINES

Subject Index

This index lists book and magazine publishers by the fiction and nonfiction subject area in which they publish. Use it to locate appropriate markets for your work, then carefully read the listings and follow the guidelines of each publisher. Use this index in conjunction with Age-Level Index to further narrow your list of markets.

BOOK PUBLISHERS: FICTION

BOOK PUBLISHERS: NONFICTION

SUBJECT INDEX

MAGAZINES: FICTION

SUBJECT INDEX

MAGAZINES: NONFICTION

Poetry Index

This index lists markets that are open to poetry submissions, and is divided into book publishers and magazines. It's important to carefully read the listings and follow the guidelines of each publisher to which you submit.

Photography Index

This index lists markets that buy photos from freelancers, and is divided into book publishers, magazines and greeting cards. It's important to carefully read the listings and follow the guidelines of each publisher to which you submit.

General Index

Market listings that appeared in the 2003 edition of *Children's Writer's & Illustrator's Market* but do not appear in this edition are identified with a two-letter code explaining why the listing was omitted: (**ED**)—Editorial Decision; (**NR**)—No (or late) Response to Listing Request; (**NS**)—Not Currently Accepting Submissions; (**OB**)—Out of Business; (**RP**)—Business Restructured or Purchased; (**RR**)—Removed by Request; (**UF**)—Uncertain Future.